SUCH A MIND AS THIS

"What is the difference between intellectuality and intellectualism? In this deeply learned defense of Christian wisdom, Richard Smith deftly navigates the relevant biblical-theological evidence for the importance of right thinking. Much of today's anti-intellectualism is based on misguided views of spirituality. Smith gently but firmly disarms contemporary prejudice and winsomely presents a liberating alternative."

—**William Edgar**
Professor of Apologetics, Westminster Seminary

"In this unusual book, Smith calls us to think, to use our minds, and to ground our thinking in the truth that God has given us in his inspired and infallible word. Smith has issued a call for bold, radical, God-centered, countercultural, life-transformative thinking. . . . Just think how different the church will be when we all use our minds as God intended them to be used. Just think!"

—**Daryl McCarthy**
Director, European Leadership Forum Academic Network

"A fascinating study of the human mind and its thinking processes beginning before the fall, and then looking at the effect of sin on the human mind and thinking after the fall. Smith gives a tour of the epistemological developments of the mind's relationship to God. . . . Smith then builds a case for a redemptive epistemology that will help people use their minds to the glory of God."

—**Richard P. Belcher Jr.**
Professor of Old Testament, Reformed Theological Seminary

"In today's world, while science and technology are advancing at an unprecedented pace, most persons display a disturbing loss of interest in thinking properly about crucial life issues. This is always bad, but lack of understanding and discernment becomes catastrophic when it comes to the Christian faith. In this book, Smith provides an effective, strong antidote against this suicidal trend, if we only are willing to take it."

—**Fernando D. Saraví**
Associate Professor of Physiology, National University of Cuyo

"Christians like to say that they think 'biblically,' but what does that mean? ... Taking multiple deep dives into a variety of types of Old Testament literature, ... Smith draws a picture of what it means to think as a people in covenant relationship with their Lord. Smith has done a huge service by exploring what the Old Testament has to teach us about what it means to let the Bible guide our thinking and living, how to love God with all our minds."

—TED TURNAU
Lecturer in Culture, Religion, and Media, Anglo-American University

"Readers of this work will experience in a fresh way their calling to be thinkers and learners in the context of God's creation. In addition, readers will receive ... invaluable insights into what it means to love God with one's whole mind in the larger context of learning to love God with all that one is and has. Smith provides an important tool for all of us who do pastoral ministry and mission among university students and teachers."

—JOSUÉ OLMEDO
Logos and Cosmos Initiative Coordinator, IFES Latin America

"John Calvin began *The Institutes of the Christian Religion*, 'Nearly all the wisdom we possess, that is to say, true and sound wisdom, consists of two parts: the knowledge of God and of ourselves.' Richard Smith has done a wonderful job exploring how these two knowledges are connected in the Old Testament. His book shows how the biblical message both answers and corrects the deepest questions of humanity outside of Eden, making the Bible (and this book!) worthy of the most serious consideration."

—THOMAS K. JOHNSON
Senior Theological Advisor, World Evangelical Alliance

SUCH A MIND AS THIS

A BIBLICAL-THEOLOGICAL STUDY
of THINKING *in the* OLD TESTAMENT

RICHARD L. SMITH

WIPF & STOCK · Eugene, Oregon

SUCH A MIND OF THIS
A Biblical-Theological Study of Thinking in the Old Testament

Copyright © 2021 Richard L. Smith. All rights reserved. Except for brief quotations in critical publications or reviews, no part of this book may be reproduced in any manner without prior written permission from the publisher. Write: Permissions, Wipf and Stock Publishers, 199 W. 8th Ave., Suite 3, Eugene, OR 97401.

Wipf & Stock
An Imprint of Wipf and Stock Publishers
199 W. 8th Ave., Suite 3
Eugene, OR 97401

www.wipfandstock.com

PAPERBACK ISBN: 978-1-6667-3216-0
HARDCOVER ISBN: 978-1-6667-2553-7
EBOOK ISBN: 978-1-6667-2554-4

NOVEMBER 17, 2021 9:23 AM

This book is dedicated to my friends
and fellow thinkers in Buenos Aires.

Together we are learning how to love God with the mind.

"Hear, O Israel: The Lord our God, the Lord is one. You shall love the Lord your God with all your heart and with all your soul and with all your might."

—Deut 6:4–5

Contents

List of Illustrations | ix

Permissions | x

Acknowledgments | xiii

Introduction | xv

1	THE DIVINE MILIEU	1
2	EDENIC EPISTEMOLOGY	22
3	EXILIC EPISTEMOLOGY	44
4	PHARAOH'S FOLLY	73
5	QOHELET'S QUEST	91
6	THE FOOL'S ERRAND	120
7	FOOLISH AND SENSELESS PEOPLE	153
8	REDEMPTIVE EPISTEMOLOGY	192
9	A HEART TO UNDERSTAND	219
10	A LEARNING COMMUNITY	258
11	MY SERVANT JOB	290
12	OUT OF THE WHIRLWIND	318

13	THE ONE WHO KNOWS	345
14	GOD GAVE LEARNING AND SKILL	366
	POSTSCRIPT: COMMUNITY GARDENS	393

Bibliography | 395

Scripture Index | 411

Author Index | 415

Subject Index | 417

List of Illustrations

Building and Filling | 5
Creator-Creature Distinction | 18
Erroneous Knowledge | 195

Permissions

Unless otherwise noted, all Scripture quotations are from the ESV® Bible (The Holy Bible, English Standard Version®), copyright © 2001 by Crossway, a publishing ministry of Good News Publishers. Used by permission. All rights reserved.

Scriptures marked NIV are from the Holy Bible, New International Version®, NIV®. Copyright © 1973, 1978, 1984, 2011 by Biblica, Inc.™ Used by permission of Zondervan. All rights reserved worldwide, www.zondervan.com. The "NIV" and "New International Version" are trademarks registered in the United States Patent and Trademark Office by Biblica, Inc.™

Scripture marked NKJV are from the New King James Version®. Copyright © 1982 by Thomas Nelson. Used by permission. All rights reserved.

Scripture quotations marked NRSV are from the New Revised Standard Version Bible, copyright © 1989 National Council of the Churches of Christ in the United States of America. Used by permission. All rights reserved worldwide.

Scripture quotations marked NASB are from the (NASB®) New American Standard Bible®, Copyright © 1960, 1971, 1977, 1995, 2020 by The Lockman Foundation. Used by permission. All rights reserved. www.lockman.org.

Scripture texts marked NAB are from the *New American Bible, revised edition* © 2010, 1991, 1986, 1970 Confraternity of Christian Doctrine, Washington, D.C. and are used by permission of the copyright owner. All Rights Reserved. No part of the New American Bible may be reproduced in any form without permission in writing from the copyright owner.

PERMISSIONS

The illustration "Building and Filling" from J. Richard Middleton, *The Liberating Image: The Imago Dei in Genesis 1*, Brazos Press, a division of Baker Publishing Group, 2005, is used by permission.

The illustration "Erroneous Knowledge" from Dru Johnson, *Biblical Knowing: A Scriptural Epistemology of Error*, Cascade Books, a division of Wipf and Stock Publishers, 2013, is used by permission.

The poem extract "I Would Like to Rise Very High" from Michel Quoist, Prayers, Sheed and Ward, 1963, a division of Rowman & Littlefield, is used by permission.

Acknowledgments

I HAVE LEARNED FROM many excellent teachers, especially at Westminster Theological Seminary in Philadelphia. But five in particular have aided my work. Cornelius Van Til, John M. Frame, and William Edgar explain the complex nature of human thought with biblical-theological sensitivity. (Behind them, one hears the voices of John Calvin, Abraham Kuyper, and Herman Bavinck.) Richard B. Gaffin, Jr. and G. K. Beale illuminate the multi-dimensional nature of the biblical narrative. (Behind them lies the influence of Geerhardus Vos and Herman N. Ridderbos.) And recently, two scholars have contributed much to the field of biblical epistemology: Dru Johnson and Ryan O'Dowd (who have relied on the insights of Michael Carasik, Jaco Gericke, and Yorum Hazony).

Bruce Barron edited every page and challenged many assumptions. His counsel and encouragement were indispensable. John Marshall also read the complete text and made many suggestions. Jeffrey Foster assisted with biblical–theological argumentation and Hebrew exegesis. I benefited from insightful commentary on various chapters from Keith Campbell, Steven Garrett, Osam Temple, John Jenkins, Paul Wright, and David Hard.

I have also learned much from my friends in Buenos Aires, where I live. Their questions, creative ideas, and desire to learn inspire me. My first wife, Karen (d. 2002), showed me how to fear God. My second wife, Viviana, models perseverance. She prayed for me regularly and to great effect while I was writing this book. And most of all, I am grateful to the Father, Son, and Holy Spirit, who patiently teach me from Scripture every day how to love God with all my mind.

Introduction

"God only pours out his light into the mind after having subdued the rebellion of the will by an altogether heavenly gentleness which charms and wins it."

—Blaise Pascal, *Pensées*

C. S. Lewis, in his universally acclaimed *The Screwtape Letters*, showed how imagining what temptations are in the devil's mind can provide deep theological insight to Christians. Likewise, Os Guinness's *The Last Christian on Earth* creatively envisioned strategic planning between a chief lieutenant of Satan and his representative in a major city of the United States. Since this is a book about thinking, let us begin with a similar creative thought experiment.

THINKING LONG-TERM

Many years ago, the demons held a very important summit meeting. The topic of discussion was how to marginalize the church and minimize its influence so that Satan's agenda could advance without hindrance.

The group leader remarked, "The Master wants us to generate some new ideas about how to frustrate Jesus' agenda. In the past, we initiated many worthwhile projects that had both short- and long-term benefits. And the Master was pleased. During the earliest days of what they call the church, we sowed division and persecution. We implanted lots of mischief, what they call heresies, to distract and confuse them. We undermined their so-called gospel by endless combinations like Jesus and Judaism, Jesus and philosophies, and Jesus and other religions. We can justifiably congratulate ourselves, but not for long, for there is much more to accomplish."

The spirits all declared, "We're ready!"

The leader continued, "But now, the Master wants a nuclear option. We're looking for a way to stunt the growth of the enemy's sect once and for all! The floor is open. Give me something really promising to tell the Master. And remember—he's not patient and doesn't tolerate failure!"

"I know! I know!" exclaimed an enthusiastic demon. "Let's greatly increase our efforts to corrupt them from within with greed and hypocrisy."

The leader responded sardonically, "We're doing that already. Give me something new."

Another spirit commented, "Why don't we try an apocalypse of some kind and end this charade quickly? How about a plague, world war, or natural disaster? The few who survive, we can pick off one by one at our leisure."

The leader sighed impatiently, "Yes, of course. But the Master in his supreme wisdom determined that we need something else, a new subversive paradigm. So, as I said, give me something different! Inspire me!"

Just then, the leader spotted a new member sitting quietly off to the side. "You, over there! Speak up! Do you have anything useful to contribute?"

The newbie replied meekly, "Um, well, yes, sir. Maybe."

"Enlighten us, then, before I throw you out of here!"

"Well, sir," he stated barely above a whisper, "I have listened carefully to all the excellent ideas of these esteemed colleagues, but I propose a new paradigm, as you requested."

"Hurry up!" demanded the leader.

"We've not been able to completely eradicate the enemy's cabal, as you said so eloquently. I suggest, therefore, that we allow a small, Christian sect to survive, but on *our* terms and *our* timetable, rather than trying again and again to eliminate them."

The leader said, "That is indeed a radical departure from our strategic plan. Go on."

"Thank you, sir. My plan consists of two parts. First, we'll lead them to redefine spirituality. No longer will they believe that their so-called gospel—what we know to be heresy—applies to *all* of life. That must stop! They must come to believe that spirituality is private and subjective. It will be something they *feel*, but never anything they *think*. We can teach them that spirituality exists to promote self-fulfillment. We must train them, also, to think that their so-called salvation concerns only their souls, so that their gospel has nothing to do with the world they live in."

"Interesting," commented the leader, growing more intrigued.

"Part two consists of injecting dualism in their thought and conduct. We should introduce the concept of the sacred and secular dimensions. Since their new spirituality will be egoistic, the church will progressively neglect all exterior dimensions, such as society and ideas, because these are secular. And they'll come to view Sunday as religious, but Monday through Saturday as secular. As a result, slowly, they'll develop two modes of thinking and behaving: one set for spiritual times and actions, the other set for secular times and actions."

The leader leaped to his feet. "Now I'm getting interested!"

"Because of the sacred–secular divide, we'll train them to think *only* on Monday through Saturday—in the secular realm. A few of them might make a positive impact on society, but no one will associate their spirituality with their ideas, if they generate any ideas at all. We can even train them to focus on *how* and *when* thinking, and never on *why* or *what* thinking."

The newbie let his pause hang in the air for a moment and then added, "In other words, sir, we'll make them stupid and irrelevant! We'll let them have just enough religion to pacify them. And when the End comes, we'll eliminate them easily."

"Awesome!" declared the leader.

"Furthermore, we will erode confidence in their book of lies, what they call 'scripture.' We will undermine its credibility and its false claims so that it will become less and less plausible. Over time, the infamous sect will lose its intellectual foundation and its members will become far less discerning. In this way, they will learn not to listen to the great impostor Jesus anymore."

Every demon in the room strained forward, hanging on his every word.

"And meanwhile, practically speaking, they'll cede the world to *us*! *We'll* do the thinking! In fact, we'll make them *afraid* to think! We'll implement *our* agenda! We'll use *our* proxies and *our* strategic methods! And all the while, the kettle will get hotter and the little Christian frogs will cook even faster."

The leader interjected, "Fantastic! I hope the rest of you idiots were listening carefully! As for you, come with me! We must talk with the Master now!"

THE PRESENT EVIL AGE

This story is obviously a fantasy, but it resembles the devil's intellectual profile provided in the Scriptures. Satan is an incisive thinker and supremely intelligent. He carefully plans and ponders his every move, like a champion chess player. He thinks strategically, both short- and long-term. He considers every contingency and countermove. He is a master teacher, grooming his demonic horde with a fiendish mindset so that they learn his ways and mimic his priorities. Together they execute his plan for the world under his guidance.

In addition, the devilish agenda the story imagines is in accord with the warnings of Scripture. Tactically, a long-term plan that renders believers stupid and irrelevant is brilliant, from the devil's point of view. He realigns our thinking with folly and wickedness. He spouts data that misinform and manipulate. He fills our minds with trivia and distraction. He wants us to ignore, misunderstand, and misapply God's revelation, on both the individual and social levels. He skews our sense of identity as God's image. He associates our epistemological stewardship with dystopian ends.

Satan's program uses every conceptual machination available against humanity, including syncretism, disorientation, and disinformation. It undermines the intellectual plausibility and existential credibility of biblical faith. It deconstructs the Scriptures. It redefines spirituality to minimize the mind and promotes secularism to delegitimize religion. Intellectual disloyalty, anti-intellectualism, and rank ignorance are its weapons of choice. But above all, the demonic realm strives to still God's voice so that people will not and cannot hear.

In the Old Testament, the devil seemingly plays a relatively small role. (We need the New Testament to fill out his true epistemic profile.) His presence is often implicit. He shows up, however, at pivotal epistemological moments. In Genesis 3, he queried Eve seditiously, "Did God actually say?" In Job 1, he insinuated with incredulity, "Does Job fear God for no reason?" In Daniel 10, he hindered the acquisition of knowledge concerning the meaning of prophecy.

The post-edenic, epistemological milieu is very complicated and enigmatic thanks to the influence of sin and Satan. The mental universe is populated by many voices, good and malevolent. There are competing pedagogues, divergent epistemological agendas, and flawed participants. The whole Old Testament is a battlefield between the human mind and

God's revelation. And lurking in the chronological and epistemological background is the diabolical dissembler who questions the veracity of God's word. The devil plays a role in how and what we think. Without question, Christians require discernment and wisdom to navigate the "present evil age" (Gal 1:4; see also Eph 2:1–3).

STUPID AND IRRELEVANT

For some time, Christian scholars have lamented the degradation of evangelical thinking. Albert Mohler writes, for example, "We are in big trouble. . . . Choose whichever statistic or survey you like, the general pattern is the same. America's Christians know less and less about the Bible." He adds, "Christians who lack biblical knowledge are the products of churches that marginalize biblical knowledge."[1] A plethora of evangelical leaders lament the mindlessness of modern evangelicalism. Consider these comments:

> If Christian laymen do not become intellectually engaged, then we are in serious danger of losing our youth. . . . There can be no question that the church has dropped the ball in this area.[2]

> If we abandon thinking, we abandon the Bible, and if we abandon the Bible we abandon God. The Holy Spirit has not promised a short-cut to the knowledge of God.[3]

> At root, evangelical anti-intellectualism is both a scandal and a sin. It is a scandal in the sense of being an offense and a stumbling block that needlessly hinders serious people from considering the Christian faith and coming to Christ. It is sin because it is a refusal, contrary to the first of Jesus' two great commandments, to love the Lord our God with our minds.[4]

David R. Nienhuis notes that most of his seminary students—future Christian leaders—are deeply misinformed about basic Bible doctrines. According to Nienhuis, God functions as "divine butler-therapist" or a "nice, permissive dad with a big wallet."[5] Students cannot integrate

---

1. Mohler, "The Scandal of Biblical Illiteracy," 1.
2. Craig, "In Intellectual Neutral," 9.
3. Piper, *Think*, 123.
4. Guinness, *Fit Bodies, Fat Minds*, 11–12.
5. Nienhuis, "The Problem of Evangelical Biblical Illiteracy."

Bible characters and events within the broader Old and New Testament narratives or within the biblical worldview. Moreover, Brent A. Strawn asserts that the influence of the Old Testament in the church is waning significantly. He writes, "For many contemporary Christians, at least in North America, the Old Testament has ceased to function in healthy ways in their lives as a sacred, authoritative, canonical literature."[6]

In 1994, prominent evangelical historian Mark Noll wrote, "The scandal of the evangelical mind is that there is not much of an evangelical mind."[7] In 2011, he published a cautiously optimistic reassessment of Christian intellectuality, but he maintained that this intellectual recovery "does not possess theologies full enough, traditions of intellectual practice strong enough, or conceptions of the world deep enough to sustain a full-scale intellectual revival."[8]

My personal experience has confirmed these concerns. Christian laypeople suffer from profound anti-intellectual inertia. They are all too often willfully naive and blissfully unaware by choice. They are sometimes curious, but usually uncommitted. They are not prepared to read, write, or reflect deeply. They are unwilling to submit to programmatic learning or qualified teachers. They think like consumers, shopping for knowledge, learning formats, and instructors that conform to their buying preferences. Their infatuation with entertainment, consumerism, and digital chatter does not leave time or energy for gaining insight. They prefer junk food for their minds. They are addicted to triviality. They live as the demons depicted at the beginning of this introduction wanted them to live—with intellectual simplicity, private religiosity, and subjective spirituality.

Many evangelicals downplay analysis and rigorous thought. Some fall for "fake news" and conspiracy theories hawked by social media gurus. They do not listen with discernment to the voices that call out to them. Reasoning from Scripture and theological education are not considered useful endeavors. In short, many believers minimize and misuse the intellect. They do not recognize how sin impacts our reasoning. They do not know how to love God with the mind.

---

6. Strawn, *The Old Testament Is Dying*, 4–5. He adds, though, "If the Old Testament dies, the New Testament will not be far behind it . . . . The data show that it is the language of scripture *as a whole*—not just that of the Old Testament—that is seriously threatened" (18, emphasis in original).

7. Noll, *The Scandal of the Evangelical Mind*, 3.

8. Noll, *Jesus Christ and the Life of the Mind*, 165.

INTRODUCTION   xxi

At the scholarly level, the lack of biblical–theological understanding is also acute. Evangelical thinkers in all fields invest many years of study and thousands of dollars in gaining an academic degree and a viable career. But how many hours and dollars do they invest in acquiring biblical understanding? Paul M. Gould observes, "While experts within their own particular fields of study, Christian professors often possess a Sunday school level of education when it comes to matters theological and philosophical . . . and the result is a patchwork attempt to integrate one's faith with one's scholarly work and an inability to fit the pieces of one's life into God's larger story."[9] This lack of biblical–theological understanding is likely to be manifested in their understanding of epistemology, their integration of faith and learning, and their apologetics.

We should know better. The Old Testament teaches that we will not honor God with our minds or reflect his glory if we lack knowledge and discernment. John M. Frame explains that Christians have a God-given "stewardship of the mind and intellect," adding, "It is remarkable that Christians so readily identify the lordship of Christ in matters of worship, salvation, and ethics, but not in thinking. But . . . God in Scripture over and over demands obedience of his people in matters of wisdom, thinking, knowledge, understanding, and so forth."[10] Indeed, the Old Testament shows that we are *designed* for thinking. Clearly, a Christian mind is a terrible thing to waste.

HOW THIS BOOK HELPS

This book was written for Christians who want to develop their minds in a distinctly Christian fashion and grow in discernment. These readers struggle with a sense of intellectual dissonance. Many experience conflict between what they hear (or do not hear) in church and what they observe in the world. They express boredom with insipid sermons. They lament teaching that stresses "how-to" knowledge but rarely "why" or "what" thinking. They hear applications but they want more biblical rationale, more worldview. They recognize intuitively the essential link between mind and motivation, ontology and epistemology, theology and ethics; but they do not know what the Bible teaches about these issues. They are curious and seek a worldview that is intellectually compelling

---

9. Gould, *The Outrageous Idea of a Missional Professor*, 7.
10. Frame, *A History of Western Philosophy and Theology*, 5.

and attractive to outsiders. They want to understand the full breadth and depth of biblical teaching and to use it to interpret themselves and their surrounding culture.

Reflective Christians desire to know where to draw the lines of intellectual assimilation. They want to discern the difference between the common good and biblical distinctives. They desire to survive epistemological and ontological pluralism—and, indeed, even to thrive in this milieu, carrying their solid biblical grounding into the world around them.

Several friends have told me how they sense this dissonance between typical Christian thinking and their own aspirations. (Their names have been changed.) Matthew is a university professor who struggles with the hegemony of naturalism among his faculty colleagues. Mary strives to articulate the biblical worldview through painting. George tries to reconcile the Bible and biology. Paul endeavors to integrate the Bible's teaching about economics with marketing and entrepreneurism. Martin has a vision for Christians in politics and public policy. Sylvia wonders how to reconcile faith and philosophy. Douglas searches for links between Christian spirituality and the naturalism of his psychology department. Deborah feels threatened by the secular worldview propagated by her school of medicine. Patricia wants to discern the impact of the internet and social media on how we think as followers of Christ. All these thinking Christians seek relevant information from the Bible and Christian tradition on how to strengthen intellectual self-awareness and discernment.

A BOOK OF KNOWLEDGE AND WISDOM

The Old Testament shows that we are built for intellectual curiosity. God wants us to ask questions—and to find the answers in his communication to us. Indeed, God created the whole world as a school in which every experience is an invitation to think and learn. Every aspect of creation, the natural world, ourselves, and our relations is revelatory. All true facts speak to us about God. God, the great teacher, created human beings as his pupils—in his image. We are *homo discens*, the being who learns. We must bring our brains to God.

Demonstrating our love for God with our minds and then using our growing understanding to bless others are essential. Cogent and pious thinking is a critical aspect of serving God. This involves a process of diligent study, moving from ignorance and illusion to understanding and wisdom. We must all enroll in God's school.

In fact, the Old Testament overflows with intellectuality. It contains a vast vocabulary and numerous idioms associated with thought and argumentation. God appealed to Israel in Isaiah's day, "Come now, let us reason together" (1:18). Fools, on the other hand, think to themselves, "There is no God . . . . I shall not be moved; throughout all generations I shall not meet adversity" (Ps 10:4, 6). We are responsible for what we should know and how we ought to think.

Furthermore, the Old Testament calls us repeatedly to what we could call intellectual piety—loving God with our minds, not just our emotions. Psalm 1:1–2 says, "Blessed is the man who walks not in the counsel of the wicked, nor stands in the way of sinners, nor sits in the seat of scoffers; but his delight is in the law of the Lord, and on his law he meditates day and night." Psalm 25:4–6 provides a prayer for knowledge: "Make me to know your ways, O Lord; teach me your paths. Lead me in your truth and teach me, for you are the God of my salvation; for you I wait all the day long." According to Proverbs, the "simple" are called to heed the reasoning of God through the voice of personified wisdom: "Whoever is simple, let him turn in here! . . . Come, eat of my bread and drink of the wine I have mixed. Leave your simple ways, and live, and walk in the way of insight" (Prov 9:4–6).

Thus, those who would be wise must apply their mental capacity to honor God as careful stewards. The wise are passionate for God's instructions and objectives. They listen carefully and implement what they learn resolutely. They are zealous, attentive, and thorough with respect to themselves and their family, community, and church. They confront the difficult and enigmatic questions of the Christian life with insight. They discern dangers in their thinking, desire, and behavior, as well as internal threats within the community and external threats from other worldviews.

WHAT YOU WILL LEARN FROM THIS BOOK

By comprehensively examining Old Testament teaching concerning the mind, this book promotes a spirituality that puts thinking in its proper place. It explains what God requires intellectually of his vice-regents. It shows that our world is a labyrinth, but that God's revelation is our reliable guide. This book will motivate readers to strive for mental piety, wisdom, and intellectual development, for the glory of God and the fulfillment of our mandate on earth.

The Old Testament is a learning laboratory. It provides both bad and good examples of discovery. Fools and folly function as a foil, showing us how *not* to think, both personally and corporately. Wise thinkers in the Old Testament model how to love God with the mind. They also demonstrate how to pray about what, how, and why we think. In this way, we learn from our ancient brethren. We discern their principles and practices of faith and learning. We learn about their epistemological boundaries. And we see how thinking functions within the Old Testament narrative.

This book shows why Christians should not minimize or misuse the intellect. It explains how sin impacts our ways of thinking. It shows how saints in the Old Testament learned to love God with the mind. It highlights the importance of the fear of the Lord in all manner of thinking

In these ways, the book helps us exercise better stewardship of our minds. It increases our intellectual self-awareness. It fosters discernment and alleviates our biblical ignorance. It teaches us to determine carefully to whom we listen. And it will set us on the path to wisdom. This text affirms a basic truism of the Old Testament epistemology: intellectual holiness yields intellectual wholeness.

HOW THIS BOOK IS ORGANIZED

This book unpacks aspects of the Old Testament's teaching about the mind and thinking. It provides detailed exegesis of important passages and explanations of critical concepts. It draws out many significant inferences and applications. It explores the critical assumptions underlying Old Testament intellectuality, as well as its practical and theoretical implications.

Three basic questions animate this text: How did Adam think before the fall into sin? How does mankind think since the fall? And most of all, how does a sinner learn to love God with the mind in the Old Testament?

Four basic epistemological orientations organize this study:

Edenic	Adam's pre-fall mindset in paradise (chapters 1–2)
Exilic	Adam and his progeny's post-fall mindset after the exile from Eden (chapters 3–7)
Punitive	permanent inability to understand revelation as a form of divine judgment (chapter 7)
Redemptive	a "heart to understand" (Deut 29:4) and "fears the Lord" (Prov 1:7) (chapters 8–14)

Chapters 1–2 focus on edenic epistemology. Chapter 1 highlights aspects of God's character and thought, displayed in the act of creation that Adam was to imitate as his vice-regent. The chapter describes how God modeled four traits that functioned prominently in Adam's stewardship and commission. Chapter 2 focuses on Adam's learning environment and the divine teacher, exploring the intellectual relationship between the Creator and his servant before sin disrupted the world.

Chapters 3–7 deal with exilic epistemology, both individual and systemic. (Punitive epistemology is also considered in chapter 7, in connection with Isaiah 6:10.) Chapter 3 surveys the dramatic scene at the tree of the knowledge of good and evil. It analyzes the dialogue between Eve and the serpent and then outlines the disruptive, destructive, and deceptive trajectory depicted in Genesis 4–11. Chapter 4 provides the first of four characterizations of folly, describing the intellectual sinfulness embodied in the worldview of Egypt and the mentality of Pharaoh. Chapter 5 examines the self-directed and twisted quest for knowledge related by Qohelet (the Preacher) in the book of Ecclesiastes. Chapter 6 details the anatomy of foolishness in the book of Proverbs. Finally, chapter 7 considers the prophets' critique of apostate Israel in light of Assyria's theocratic ideology.

Chapters 8–14 highlight redemptive epistemology. Chapter 8 explains in greater detail the mindset that God approves. It examines two godly thinkers in the Old Testament and describes important aspects of a mind that is attuned to the Lord. Chapter 9 examines in depth the epistemological teaching of Israel's covenant as stipulated in Deuteronomy. Chapter 10 concerns the infrastructure of knowledge acquisition that is depicted in Deuteronomy. Chapters 11–12 focus on Job's mental and emotional outlook, presenting him as a paradigmatic knower of God. He represents aspects of both exilic and redemptive thinking—the epistemic best and worst of humanity. His story also reveals the glory of the Lord as our merciful teacher. The last two chapters concern the intellectual challenges of Israel's exile. Chapter 13 focuses on Jeremiah's letter to the exiles in 29:1–9. Chapter 14 summarizes Daniel's engagement with the Babylonian worldview.

My aim in this book is to provide primary data about knowing in the Old Testament within its conceptual context: creation and covenant, the fall into sin, and redemption. With this theological and epistemological resource, perhaps readers will experience with Pascal God's pouring out "of his light into the mind." Hopefully, more Christian believers will turn from anti-intellectualism and illiteracy and will learn to love God with all their minds, reasoning like the sons of Issachar, "who had understanding of the times, to know what Israel ought to do" (1 Chr 12:32).

1

The Divine Milieu

"Of all visible things, the universe is the greatest; of all invisible realities, the greatest is God. That the world exits we can see; we believe in the existence of God."
—Augustine of Hippo, *The City of God*

Imagine the Garden of Eden. What was it like to live in a world where sin and evil were only a possibility? This question—and many more—cause us to wonder about the environment in which the first couple appeared. Envision a setting where everything was a delight waiting to be discovered. Curiosity and exploration were unhindered by fears of any kind or sinful motives. Interaction with God was completely natural, innocent, and delightful. There was no limit on creativity or thought; Adam and Eve were like toddlers exploring the world for the first time, hand in hand with their father. All their intellectual capacities were directed toward honoring God and developing creation. They were completely focused upon learning to govern God's house and extend his reign throughout the earth.

In this opening chapter, I characterize the God who made the world and the world that he made. These two factors, God and his creation, situated Adam and Eve as thinkers. The next four sections of this chapter deal with God as divine king, as architect and house builder, as divine economist and benefactor of mankind, and as philosopher. After that, I consider the bond that exists between God and the creation. I conclude with a few observations about the Creator and the environment in which Adam and Eve served God with their minds.

DIVINE KING

In Genesis 1–2, we see at least three ways in which God's royal authority and absolute control were manifested. First, God enacted his rule by divine decree and sovereign deed. He addressed the heavenly council with royal prerogative, using the first-person plural ("Let us make man in our image," 1:26).[1] His will was enacted by divine fiat, with speech that expressed God's thought and intention. There were royal decrees: "Let there be" (an object) and "Let it do" (an action). There were execution reports ("and it was so") and evaluation reports ("God saw that it was good").[2] There were declarations and deeds showing God's intentionality: naming, purpose statements, commands, and benedictions.[3]

The royal authority of this passage is most clearly shown in the naming process. In the Old Testament and the ancient Near East, naming was a right and obligation of those in authority, an essential aspect of sovereign rule. To announce a name was to call into existence, take dominion, declare identity, foretell destiny, or establish a covenantal relationship. For instance, Pharaoh Neco annexed Judah and appointed Eliakim as his vassal king, but renamed him Jehoiakim (2 Kgs 23:34). David named his son Solomon, but God called him Jedidiah, "beloved of the Lord" (2 Sam 12:24–25). And of course, God revealed his name to the Israelites, "I am who I am" (Yahweh), as their Lord and deliverer from Egypt (Exod 3:14–15).[4]

---

1. See also Gen 3:22, when God banished Adam and Eve from the garden ("Behold, the man has become like one of us") and 11:7, when God dispersed the people of Babel ("Come, let us go down and there confuse their language").

2. See Middleton, *The Liberating Image*, 65–70.

3. Royal decrees with reference to objects: "Let there be": "light" (1:3), "expanse" (v. 6), "lights" (vv. 14, 15). Royal decrees with reference to actions: "Let there be" ... "gathered" (v. 9), "appear" (v. 9), "swarm" (v. 20), "fly" (v. 20), "bring forth" (v. 24). Execution reports: "and it was so" (1:7, 9, 11, 15, 24). Evaluation reports: "God saw that it was good" (1:4, 10, 12, 18, 21, 25), "very good" (v. 31); Naming: "day" (1:5), "night" (v. 5), "heaven" (v. 8), "earth" (v. 10), "seas" (v. 10). Intentions expressed: "according to its kind" (1:11, 12, 21, 24, 25), "for signs/seasons/days/years" (v. 14), "to give" (vv. 15, 17), "to rule" (vv. 16, 18), "to separate" (v. 18). Benedictions pronounced: "blessed" (1:22; 2:3).

4. Another example is Hosea, to whose child God assigned the name Jezreel (Hos

Similarly, God "named" everything in Genesis 1. God defined existence when he "created the heavens and the earth." The verb "called (the)" appears various times in connection with the physical and temporal parameters of existence: "day" and "night" (1:5, 6), "heaven" (v. 8), and "earth" and "seas" (v. 10). He brought form to the void and filled his handiwork with animate creatures and inanimate objects. By means of his divine imperatives ("let there be"), royal actions ("gathered," "set," "bring forth"), definitional infrastructure ("to rule," "according to its kind"), and blessing, God established dominion, declared purpose, and revealed functions. He affirmed ownership of creation and unilaterally established a relationship with the world as sovereign lord.

Second, God established his reign through the institution of the seventh day (the Sabbath). Each of the previous six days began and ended with a repeated formula: days one through six began with God's creative speech and ended with the announcement, "There was evening and there was morning." Genesis 2:3, however, is different in form and content. The seventh day begins with a proclamation ("God finished") rather than an enactment ("God said"). In fact, the phrase "seventh day" is repeated three times, indicating its significance (vv. 2–3). Richard H. Lowery notes, "Breaking the pattern stressed the uniqueness of the seventh day and opens the door to an eschatological interpretation: the sun has not set on God's Sabbath."[5] Likewise, W. J. Dumbrell commented, "The unending Sabbath day provides the context in which the ideal life of the garden is to take place . . . . Since this divine purpose for creation existed before the fall, it will continue beyond it (Heb 4:9–11)."[6] For these reasons, the seventh day is unending, open-ended, and future-oriented. It is the eschatological and providential context for the "multi-generational image of God."[7] The seventh day set history in motion and demonstrates God's rule over time.[8]

1:4). God also changed Abram's name to Abraham, reflecting his identity and calling as "the father of a multitude of nations" (Gen 17:5). Similarly, God changed Sarai's name to Sarah because "kings will come forth from her" (Gen 17:15).

5. Lower, *Sabbath and Jubilee*, 89.

6. Dumbrell, "Genesis 2:1–17: A Foreshadowing of the New Creation," 55.

7. Skillen, "The Seven Days of Creation," 132.

8. Skillen commented about the "generations of the heavens and the earth" ("generations," *toledoth*, in Gen 2:4), "With Genesis 2:7 and following, we are drawn into the story of the unfolding generation of those human creatures, a story about the historical development of the climactic creature of God's sixth day in relation to God and to all other creatures" ("The Seven Days of Creation," 130).

The seventh day was also marked by the enthronement of the sovereign king. In the final act of creation, God "rests" (*shabbat* in 2:1–3). In the Old Testament and the ancient Near East, rest was often associated with the overcoming of adversaries, the establishment of God's temple, building the king's palace, and the extension of his rule through empire, as well as social peace and economic prosperity (at least for the elite). According to Meredith G. Kline, God "created the heaven and earth to be his cosmic palace and his resting is the occupying of his palace."[9] Lowery observed, "Elsewhere in the Bible 'rest' describes political stability, the ability of a people or monarch to secure order and successfully govern the land."[10] By instituting the Sabbath, God affirmed his reign and power over everything that he made—including time. Creation, therefore, is not the master, and nature is not divine. Indeed, rather than the animistic and henotheistic[11] deities that appeared to govern nature or rule a location, God declared his supremacy over all would-be claimants to the divine throne and all creation.

Third, God named his representative and vice-regent on earth—Adam "our image (*tselem*) after our likeness (*demuth*)" (Gen 1:26).[12] The word for image (*tselem*) is used seventeen times in the Old Testament, always referring to a physical image or representation of someone or something else. It appears four times in the Genesis prologue with reference to the image of God, once to Seth as Adam's image, and six times in the Old Testament referring to idols. The second term, "likeness," occurs again with *tselem* in Genesis 5:1, 3, and alone in 9:6. However, Genesis 1–2 teaches that being the essential likeness of God (but *not* being God) prohibits recklessness or autonomy. Bruce R. Reichenbach writes, "Humans are not independent, on their own in the kingdom to pursue their own interests. Created and claimed by the Monarch, they owe him obeisance and worship."[13] As we will see in the next chapter, the image of God is a functional facsimile, an analogous representation, delimited by ontology

---

9. Kline, *Kingdom Prologue*, 23.

10. Lowery, *Sabbath and Jubilee*, 88.

11. Henotheism denotes adherence to a particular god, patron deity, or divine warrior, usually of a specific locale or people within a polytheistic or pluralistic context.

12. The practice of installing household stewards and vassals of kings and emperors was common, as well as placing royal images in distant locations communicating ownership and the demand of obedience.

13. Reichenbach, "Genesis 1 as a Theological–Political Narrative," 61.

and stewardship. Adam was accountable to God as vice-regent, and God was his template.

DIVINE ARCHITECT

The Bible depicts creation as a building with architectural terminology. Genesis 1–2 presents God as a "designer and artificer, constructing with care, attention, obvious pleasure, and self-investment (as a good artist), a coherent, harmoniously functioning cosmos, according to a well-thought-out plan."[14] The following diagram provided by J. Richard Middleton shows how the Creator filled the void and assigned the structures of creation. He imposed order and produced fruitfulness. On days one to three, he created "static regions"; on days four to six, he occupied them with "mobile occupants":[15]

Building (static regions)	Filling (mobile occupants)
Day 1 (1:3–5) light/darkness	Day 4 (1:14–19) luminaries
Day 2 (1:6–8) water/firmament/water	Day 5 (1:20–23) fish and birds
Day 3 (1:9–13) water/dry ground vegetation	Day 6 (1:24–31) land animals humans

Building and Filling

Indeed, God's design reveals splendor, stability, and perpetuity. James W. Skillen wrote, "The creation is an architectural wonder. It is a tent, house, or palace-temple God has built."[16] In Genesis 1–2 the verb "made" (*asa*), appears often (1:7, 16, 26, 26, 31; 2:2, 3, 4, 18) and "create" (*bara*) twice (1:1, 21). Construction terms describe the Creator's

---

14. Reichenbach, "Cutting the Gift That Ties," 74.
15. Middleton, "The Liberating Image," 75.
16. Skillen, "The Seven Days of Creation," 126.

engineering, such as "separate," (1:4, 7), "gathered" (1:9, 10), "appear" (v. 9), and "set" (v. 17). Elsewhere in the Old Testament, the artful and well-organized blueprint of creation is characterized by the verb "lay a foundation" (*yatsar*), rendered as "laid the foundations of the earth" (Job 38:4; Pss 102:25; 104:5; Prov 3:19; Isa 48:13; 51:13, 16; Zech 12:1) or by the expression "pillars of the earth" (1 Sam 2:8; Job 9:6; Ps 75:3). Expressions of God's architectural power include the following:

> Where were you when I laid the foundation of the earth? (Job 38:4)

> Of old you laid the foundation of the earth, and the heavens are the work of your hands. (Ps 102:25; cited also in Heb 1:10)

> When the earth totters, and all its inhabitants, it is I who keep steady its pillars. (Ps 75:3)

The Scriptures affirm that God's world is firmly established, because it is architecturally sound and well-built. After the flood, God promised, "While the earth remains, seedtime and harvest, cold and heat, summer and winter, day and night, shall not cease" (Gen 8:22). Isaiah wrote that God "spread out the heavens" and "they stand forth together" (48:13). Psalm 93:1 declares, "The world is established; it shall never be moved."[17] Proverbs 8 portrays God's architectural prowess in the words of Lady Wisdom:

> When he made firm the skies above, when he established the fountains of the deep, when he assigned to the sea its limit, so that the waters might not transgress his command, when he marked out the foundations of the earth, then I was beside him, like a master workman, and I was daily his delight, rejoicing before him always, rejoicing in his inhabited world and delighting in the children of man. (vv. 28–31; see also Job 28:25–27)

In fact, Genesis 1:2 declares that the Spirit of God was the source of architectural wisdom: "The earth was without form and void, and darkness was over the face of the deep. And the Spirit of God was hovering over the face of the waters." The expression "Spirit of God" appears only

---

17. Micah said that the world is secure with "enduring foundations" (6:2), and Job 38:4–6 uses architectural terms to describe creation: "Where were you when I laid the foundation of the earth? Tell me, if you have understanding. Who determined its measurements—surely you know! Or who stretched the line upon it? On what were its bases sunk, or who laid its cornerstone?"

eleven other times in the Old Testament.[18] The Spirit enabled prophetic utterance, miraculous deeds, and wisdom. For example, Pharaoh asked with reference to Joseph, "Can we find a man like this, in whom is the Spirit of God?" Joseph was "discerning and wise" in dealing with the upcoming famine (Gen 41:38–39). Likewise, God called Bezalel to build the tabernacle and "filled him with the Spirit of God, with ability and intelligence, with knowledge and all craftsmanship, to devise artistic designs" (Exod 31:3–4a). In other words, as God by his Spirit made the world with skill and artistry, so human beings created in his image are enabled to perform God-ordained tasks with Spirit-inspired wisdom.[19]

Genesis 1–2, therefore, shows that the Spirit of God was intricately involved with God's work in creation, especially his creative architectural wonder, life-generating power, and divine decrees.[20] Psalm 33:6 declares, "By the word of the Lord the heavens were made, and by the breath of his mouth all their host." The Spirit provided the architectural wisdom that built the natural forms on days one to three and filled them with animate and inanimate objects on days four to six. He made the world plenteous and beautiful, so that Adam and Eve would flourish. With reference to the realm of nature, Psalm 104:30 says, "When you send forth your Spirit, they are created, and you renew the face of the ground."

The type of structure God designed and assembled with the Spirit's wisdom was a temple. As Middleton wrote, "Heaven, where God's throne or dwelling is often said to be located, does not transcend creation, but is structurally part of the created cosmos."[21] This seems to be the significance of God's declaration in Isaiah 66:1–2, "Heaven is my throne, and the earth is my footstool; what is the house that you would build for me, and what is the place of my rest? All these things my hand has made, and so all these things came to be." Creation as sanctuary also makes sense of Psalm 119:90–91: "Your faithfulness endures to all generations; you have established the earth, and it stands fast. By your appointment they stand

---

18. See Gen 41:38; Exod 31:3; 35:31; Num 24:2; 1 Sam 10:10; 11:6; 19:20, 23; 2 Chr 15:1; 24:20; Ezek 11:24.

19. Interestingly, the verb "was hovering" (*rahap*) found in Genesis 1:2 occurs only one other time in the Old Testament with reference to creation of and God's providential care for Israel, "like an eagle . . . that flutters (*rahap*) over its young" (Deut 32:11).

20. Compare the Spirit's role in the inspiration of the Scriptures (2 Tim 3:16).

21. Middleton, *The Liberating Image*, 86.

this day, for all things are your servants."[22] Everything created, animate and inanimate exists to honor and serve God.

Clearly, therefore, God's garden was the archetypal temple where Adam and Eve worshipped and served the Creator. Genesis depicts "Eden as a garden sanctuary in which man as priest and king offers worship at the center of the world."[23] T. Desmond Alexander wrote, "The case for Eden being a divine residence rests largely on the striking parallel that exists between the Garden and later Israelite sanctuaries."[24] For instance, both were sacred spaces where human beings encountered God. In Eden Adam enjoyed God's presence, as did the priests in the tabernacle and temple. In the garden, Adam was to "cultivate and keep" or "work and take care of" the garden (Gen 2:15). Significantly, these two verbs (*abad* and *shamar*) appear together elsewhere only with reference to the responsibilities of the Levite priests in the temple (Num 3:7-8; 8:26; 18:5-6).[25] It appears that whenever real estate is sanctified by God (Eden, Canaan, Israel's tabernacle or temple, and later the church and the whole earth), the divine king is present and his rule prevails.

DIVINE ECONOMIST

As we saw earlier, God the king and architect called forth the life support systems (air, light, land, vegetation) essential for the sustenance of his reign. He commanded every living thing to produce "according to its various kinds." He provided fruits, grains, and an abundant supply of water. He ordered space, separating land, sea, and celestial objects. He ordained time and regularity, calling forth the twenty-four-hour cycle, seasons, and Sabbath. He also designed the world as his temple and human beings for worship. In short, God established all the necessary conditions that

---

22. See also Psalm 148:2-12, which admonishes all created things on earth and in heaven, animate and inanimate, to praise God in his terrestrial temple.

23. Dumbrell, "Genesis 2:1-17: A Foreshadowing of the New Creation," 61. See also Beale, *A New Testament Biblical Theology*, 619-22.

24. Alexander, *From Eden to the New Jerusalem*, 21.

25. Other parallels include the following: God walked in the garden as he did in the tabernacle (Gen 3:8; Lev 26:12; 2 Sam 7:6-7); the tree of life was the model for the lampstand in the temple; later sanctuaries memorialize Eden through wood carvings and tapestries, creating a garden-like ambience; and gold (Gen 2:11-12) was used to decorate the tabernacle and temple, as well as the priestly garments (Exod 25:3-7, 11, 17, 31).

human beings require—indeed, they presuppose the Creator at all times (Dan 5:23; Rom 2:4).

To put it another way, God built a house and established an economic environment (an *oikonomia*) where human beings could flourish.[26] Economics in the ancient Near East concerned household management and stewardship, both cosmic and terrestrial. *Oikonomia* referred to the mechanisms, logistics, structures and practices that cause mankind to thrive, as well as the natural environment that supports them. Biblical economics asks: is there equity and opportunity, justice and compassion for all? Do order, satisfaction, and productivity characterize the social relations of the estate (*oikos*)? *Oikonomia* concerned the stewardship of the householder's assets and the well-being of his inhabitants.[27]

Genesis 1–2 portrays Eden as the ideal economy, the epitome of household creation and estate management. With an imaginative eye to aesthetics and order, God constructed his house, his garden of delights. Eden, in fact, means "bliss," "delight," or "pleasure," with nuances of contentment and prosperity. In God's garden, human beings enjoyed everything he provided: status, abundance, productive work, intellectual stimulation, creative expression, human intimacy, and a significant calling within a secure environment. This edenic nexus was a stable and plenteous setting, created to enable mankind to prosper in every way. In fact, Lowery points out that the verb "to create" (*bara* in Gen 1:1, 21) is used once as "to fatten oneself" (1 Sam 2:29) and many times as the adjective "fat."[28] In the ancient world, corpulence indicated health and prosperity. Thus, it seems that God created a "fat" world for Adam and Eve to thrive and even satiate themselves with God's plentiful provision. "From the moment of setting Adam in Eden, God destined man to luxuriate."[29] In God's house and within his *oikonomia*, there was peace, prosperity,

---

26. The Greek term, *oikonomia*, means "household administration" or "the law or management of a household." In the Old Testament, the Hebrew term for house is translated in the Greek Septuagint with variations of *oikos*: "house," "household," "tent," "sanctuary." It often appears as the "house of" (God, Israel, Pharaoh, Dagon, Baal, etc.). In the New Testament, many words carry the *oik*- root, such as home, house, household, descendant, family, dwelling, domain, possession, and community, builder of a house, administration, and stewardship.

27. See Meeks, *God the Economist*; Reichenbach, "Cutting the Gift That Ties," 111–20.

28. Lowery, *Sabbath and Jubilee*, 85.

29. Phillips, "The Attitude of Torah to Wealth," 85.

and more than enough for all. He properly managed his assets and the welfare of his residents.

Reichenbach provides a helpful summary of God's garden economy: "It is the Lord God who is the giver, who in his wisdom and love establishes the economy of provision. And a complete economy it is, for all that human beings have comes from God."[30] For Adam, the steward of creation, the garden "supplies his total wants—the physical and the spiritual." And in God the divine economist, "We find the complete giver, the giver who cares for the total person, who sees to it that nothing is to be wanting in our experience."[31]

The image of God as omnipotent economist and benefactor of mankind is preserved throughout the Old Testament.[32] The Greek term for benefactor (*euergetes*) appears in the Septuagint fourteen times in reference to God's goodness (for instance, Pss 13:6; 78:11). The omniscient benefactor is the sovereign patron, for everything belongs to him and he alone has the right of disposal: "Everything under heaven belongs to me" (Job 41:11b; Pss 24:1; 50:10–12; 95:4–5; 108:8). God is generous with his resources, though, and this is often a cause for worship (for instance, Pss 31:19; 107:35–38; 147:8–9, 14). Psalm 23 offers an especially poignant depiction of the beneficence of God's *oikonomia*:

> The Lord is my shepherd, I shall not be in want. He makes me lie down in green pastures, he leads me beside quiet waters, he restores my soul. He guides me in paths of righteousness for his name's sake. Even though I walk through the valley of the shadow of death, I will fear no evil, for you are with me; your rod and your staff, they comfort me. You prepare a table before me in the presence of my enemies. You anoint my head with oil; my cup overflows. Surely goodness and love will follow me all the days of my life, and I will dwell in the house of the Lord forever.

This psalm shows that God cares for the inhabitants of his house and maintains the divine economy on their behalf. The inhabitants suffer no lack of all that is necessary (vv. 1, 5), for God is a powerful and prosperous patron. He protects his household (vv. 4, 5) and anticipates its every need and concern (vv. 2–5). Psalm 23 recapitulates the edenic

---

30. Reichenbach, "Cutting the Gift That Ties," 112.

31. Reichenbach, "Cutting the Gift That Ties," 113.

32. The concept of God's oikonomia and divine benefaction was also prevalent in the ancient Near East and in Greco-Roman piety, though obviously understood within non-biblical worldviews. See Neyrey, "God, Benefactor and Patron," 465–92.

nexus: God's presence, peace, and prosperity. For Adam and Eve, the only acceptable posture in response was expectant trust, as expressed by Psalm 123:1–2: "To you I lift up my eyes, O you who are enthroned in the heavens! Behold, as the eyes of servants look to the hand of their master, as the eyes of a maidservant to the hand of her mistress, so our eyes look to the Lord our God, till he has mercy upon us."

Furthermore, among the royal *oikonomias* of the ancient Near East, "house building" followed by "house filling" was a common motif. Raymond C. Van Leeuwen notes, "The language of 'filling' (*maly*) refers first to the furnishings and inhabitants of a house and, second, to all that makes life in the house abundant and rich, including agriculture, fertility, food and drink, and the acquisition of material goods."[33] In the Old Testament, King Solomon provides an illustration. The Queen of Sheba bore witness to his abundance and found it breathtaking, observing "all the wisdom of Solomon, the house that he had built, the food of his table, the seating of his officials, and the attendance of his servants, their clothing, his cupbearers, and his burnt offerings that he offered at the house of the Lord" (1 Kgs 10:4b–5). Imagine Solomon as an aspiring stand-in for Adam as we consider the Queen's benediction, "Happy are these your servants, who continually stand before you and hear your wisdom! Blessed be the Lord your God, who has delighted in you and set you on his throne as king for the Lord your God!" (2 Chr 9:7–8a).

Finally, two other aspects of the Genesis narrative provide indications of the quality of life in God's garden economy. The first is divine blessing (1:22; 2:3). As the omnipotent householder, God infused his creation with life-giving and sustaining power—that is, fruitfulness. He blessed the animal kingdom and human beings with the power of progeny ("be fruitful and multiply" in 1:22, 28). He provided sustenance to mankind ("I have given you" in 1:29, 30). Blessing was the normal existential experience of Eden's residents: abundance, companionship, security, order, fertility, and most of all, unmediated knowledge of and fellowship with God. Abundant grace was the natural order of reality. Clearly, Adam and Eve's chief end was truly "to glorify God, and to enjoy him forever."[34]

---

33. Van Leeuwen, "Cosmos, Temple, House," 400.
34. "Question Number 1," *The Westminster Shorter Catechism*, 1.

Second, the seventh day (when God began his "rest") is closely associated with the concept of shalom in the Old Testament.[35] Nicholas Wolterstorff wrote that shalom is "*enjoyment* in one's relationships . . . to *enjoy* living before God, to *enjoy* living in one's physical surroundings, to *enjoy* living with one's fellows, to *enjoy* life with oneself."[36] Similarly, Cornelius Plantinga, Jr. commented:

> The webbing together of God, humans, and all creation in justice, fulfillment, and delight is what the Hebrew prophets call *shalom* . . . . In the Bible shalom means *universal flourishing, wholeness, and delight* . . . . Shalom, in other words, is the way things ought to be.[37]

In the garden, therefore, human beings participated in God's own shalom, his "rest" and *oikonomia*. Shalom was an edenic quality of existence, a life of blessing and grace, rooted in God's relationship with creation. Shalom indicated harmony and peace, wholeness and fulfillment, joy and integrity, beauty and awe, Lordship and service, all *coram Deo* (under the authority of God). Shalom depicts how life was in Eden, how it could and should have been in ancient Israel, and what God's *oikos* (house) will be like in the eschatological future. In the case of Adam, the Creator modeled stewardship for him and, in this way, showed him how to maintain an edenic quality of life.

DIVINE PHILOSOPHER

The omnipotent and omniscient philosopher designed and built his earthly temple with great wisdom. Van Leeuwen explains, "The cosmic totality character of wisdom means that only YHWH is ultimately wise. Ultimate wisdom would require total knowledge and insight, and the *power* to do *all* that wisdom wills."[38] Indeed, the Scriptures testify to God's power and wisdom: "It is he who made the earth by his power, who established the world by his wisdom, and by his understanding stretched out the heavens" (Jer 10:12). Similarly, Proverbs 3:19–20 affirms, "The

---

35. Although the term shalom does not appear in Genesis 1–2, the concept does. See Brueggemann, *Peace*, 14.

36. Wolterstorff, *Until Justice and Peace Embrace*, 69–70 (emphasis in original).

37. Plantinga, *Not the Way It's Supposed to Be*, 10 (emphasis in original).

38. Van Leeuwen, "Theology: Creation, Wisdom, and Covenant," 3 (emphasis in original).

Lord by wisdom founded the earth; by understanding he established the heavens; by his knowledge the deeps broke open, and the clouds drop down the dew."

Moreover, God continues to rule the world wisely through providence, for he is the source of sustenance and order. Vern Poythress shows how creation provided the foundation for God's ongoing rule and care of the world by means of natural law:

> First, God's word caused the first springing up of plants. Second, God's word describes and governs the *continued* springing up of plants. The explicit reference to seed indicates that God is laying down a permanent pattern for plants, by which they will reproduce, producing more plants "according to their own kinds."[39]

Psalm 104 is a meditation on creation and a paean to divine wisdom in the ongoing care of the world:

> You make springs gush forth in the valleys; they flow between the hills; they give drink to every beast of the field; the wild donkeys quench their thirst. Beside them the birds of the heavens dwell; they sing among the branches. From your lofty abode you water the mountains; the earth is satisfied with the fruit of your work. (vv. 10–13)

> You cause the grass to grow for the livestock and plants for man to cultivate, that he may bring forth food from the earth and wine to gladden the heart of man, oil to make his face shine and bread to strengthen man's heart. (vv. 14–15)

> He made the moon to mark the seasons; the sun knows it's time for setting. You make darkness, and it is night, when all the beasts of the forest creep about. (vv. 19–20)

> O Lord, how manifold are your works! In wisdom have you made them all; the earth is full of your creatures . . . . When you hide your face, they are dismayed; when you take away their breath, they die and return to their dust. When you send forth your Spirit, they are created, and you renew the face of the ground. (vv. 24, 29–30)

Indeed, Genesis 1–2 demonstrates and the broader Scriptures testify that God is the philosopher-king. He loves and embodies wisdom. Everything he desires and thinks is wise. He knows what is truly valuable

---

39. Poythress, *Redeeming Science*, 77 (emphasis in original).

and really important. And he knows how to apply this knowledge in ways that are excellent and fruitful in every circumstance and at all times. For this reason, his wisdom provides the explanation of all that is and reveals its purpose for creation.

God is wise because he, himself, is supremely important and most valuable. He *is* wisdom, and what matters most is his glory. Jonathan Edwards expressed this well with reference to creation: "That if God himself be, in any respect, properly capable of being his own end in the creation of the world, then it is reasonable to suppose that he had respect to himself, as his last and highest end, in this work; he is worthy in himself of being so, being infinitely the greatest and best of beings."[40] Again, because of God's wisdom, Edwards observed, "it was God's last end, that there might be a glorious and abundant emanation of his infinite fullness of good *ad extra*, or without himself; and that the disposition to communicate himself, or diffuse his own fullness, was what moved him to create the world."[41]

God always acts in terms of his "last and highest end" as the epitome of wisdom. He never wavers from his original purpose for creation. Alexander describes God's wisdom as the "blueprint for the earth" and the "remarkable vision" of making his home "with humanity on a new earth" as the biblical "meta-story" or worldview.[42] He adds, "Whereas Genesis presents the earth as a potential building site, Revelation describes a finished city. Underlying the construction of this city is the expectation that God will reside within it, sharing its facilities with people from every nation."[43]

God's commitment to this vision is obvious as the Bible both looks back on Eden and envisions a future paradise. Eden, in fact, provides a model and a goal, an archetype and end. The garden was the archetypical temple where Adam and Eve worshiped God. But the Old Testament also depicts Israel's Promised Land as a potential new Eden, a sacred precinct in the midst of vast profane territory. Like Eden, which was a "good land" blessed by God (Gen 1:10, 22, 28; 2:3), Canaan was a "good land"

---

40. Edwards, "Dissertation Concerning the End," 94–121.

41. Edwards, "Dissertation Concerning the End," 100. The Scriptures testify to God's highest regard for himself and his glory in the world, for everything that he does is motivated by his "name's sake" (Jer 14:21; Ezek 36:23; Isa 42:8; 48:11).

42. Alexander, *From Eden to the New Jerusalem*, 14.

43. Alexander, *From Eden to the New Jerusalem*, 14.

promised to the Hebrew tribes by their redeemer (Exod 3:8; Deut 1:25; 4:21; 8:7, 10; Josh 23:13, 15, 16).[44]

In addition, Eden pointed forward as the prototype for Israel's restoration. The prophets spoke of a return from exile and reversal often introduced by the idioms "at that time," "in that day," and "in the last days" (Isa 2:2; 11:6-10; 35:1-10; Jer 31:1-6; Hos 2:18-23). These promises were also cast in terms of curse reversal with the expression "like Eden." Isaiah 51:3 says, "The LORD will surely comfort Zion and will look with compassion on all her ruins; he will make her deserts like Eden, her wastelands like the garden of the LORD" (see also Ezek 36:33-36).

Looking even farther ahead, the prophets foresaw global renewal and cosmic reversal—of nature, human relations, and mankind's relationship with God—in edenic terms. Isaiah envisioned a future paradise where "the wolf shall dwell with the lamb," because "the earth shall be full of the knowledge of the Lord as the waters cover the sea" (7:6, 9). Isaiah 65 prophesied a re-creation, a "new heavens and a new earth," again in edenic terms. In his supreme wisdom and power, God will restore Eden throughout the whole earth. He will repair the architectural damage to his house and will renew the edenic nexus (divine presence, paradise, sanctuary, and prosperity). So says the prophet Ezekiel: "I will set them in their land and multiply them, and will set my sanctuary in their midst forevermore. My dwelling place shall be with them, and I will be their God, and they shall be my people" (Ezek 37:26-27; see also Rev 21:1-8).

Third, it is God's wisdom to designate *himself* as mankind's great goal. Everything he did in creation, does in redemption, or will do in restoration is directed to this purpose. Specifically, God ordained that his vice-regents would be "conformed to the image of his Son" (Rom 8:29) and become "partakers of the divine nature" (2 Pet 1:4), and that he would "raise us also with Jesus and bring us with you into his presence" (2 Cor 4:14) and "present [us] blameless before the presence of his glory

---

44. Israel was called the "garden of Eden" (Ezek 36:35; Joel 2:3), "garden of the Lord" (Gen 13:10; Isa 51:3), "garden of the Lord" (Isa 51:3), or a "well-watered garden" (Jer 31:12). Canaan was a land of "milk and honey," where labor produced more than "thorns and thistles" or frustration and privation. It was a place of peace and plenty where everyone could "eat and be satisfied" (Deut 8:10, 12; 11:15; 14:29; Pss 22:26; 104:28; 105:40; Isa 66:11-14a). It was also a land of prosperity where all enjoy the bounty of God and "lived in safety, each man under his own vine and fig tree" (1 Kgs 4:25). The covenantal blessings described in Deuteronomy 28:1-14 describe Canaan's bliss in clearly edenic terms.

with great joy" (Jude 24). Augustine expressed God's teleological vision clearly:

> God himself, who is the Author of virtue, shall be our reward. As there is nothing greater or better than God himself, God has promised us himself. What else can be meant by his words through the prophet, "I will be your God, and you will be my people" than "I shall be their satisfaction, I shall be all that people honorably desire—life, health, nourishment, satisfaction, glory, honor, peace, and all good things?" This, too, is the right interpretation of the saying of the apostle "that God may be all in all." God shall be the end of all our desires, who will be seen without end, loved without cloy, and praised without weariness.[45]

Fourth, God's wisdom presupposes an omniscient quantity and quality of knowledge. He is the supremely intelligent king, architect, economist, and philosopher of creation. Indeed, he is the expert in each of these fields—and any other we might name. He is the ontological genius, savant, virtuoso, and mastermind. He is the unassailable specialist of every kind of intelligence. Moreover, he understands in depth and breadth each realm of knowledge in every language and at each level of development.

In summary, God is wise. He is the transcendent philosopher-king. He created and sustains the world with wisdom. He acts wisely because he does everything with reference to his glory, love for mankind, earthly tabernacle, and everlasting purpose. He applies these motives in each and every circumstance for the best possible outcome. He coordinates means and ends, cause and effect. His diagnosis and prescription is always correct. He builds whatever he designs and his ideas always produce positive results. And he embodies intellectual virtue in infinite degree: courage, carefulness, fair-mindedness, curiosity, honesty, and humility are always in evidence as the paradigmatic thinker and doer. In all these ways, therefore, God was Adam's epistemological exemplar.

EDENIC COVENANT

The relationship between the Creator and creation is covenantal. In the ancient Near East, covenants defined the relationship between treaty partners, especially between a superior and inferior (such as rulers and their vassals) and between gods and their vice-regents (kings or stewards).

---

45. Augustine, *City of God*, 541.

Covenantal relationships were imposed upon the weaker party through conquest (an emperor named vassal kings in subjugated territories) or by divine fiat (through myth the gods designated the terms of theocratic rule).

Covenant treaties began with a prologue rehearsing the history of the relationship and all the benefits the initiating party had provided. The ruler claimed to create an environment of peace, justice, and prosperity. As the weaker party, the vassal was dependent and thus obligated to obedience, faithfulness, and gratitude to the benefactor. Whatever hardship might occur under the new regime would be marginal, compared with the earlier upheaval or the certain royal wrath for covenantal disobedience.

Although the term covenant does not appear in Genesis 1–2, the concept is present.[46] The account of creation functions as a historical prologue. Even before Adam and Eve took their first breath, the transcendent ruler, benefactor, and builder had provided a divine milieu for their blessing and development. God was the undisputed king and Adam, as we will see, was his designated vassal and steward over his earthly realm. The divine thinker produced a sustainable environment rich with potential and beauty. He prepared and provided everything for Adam and Eve to flourish and learn. For the *imago Dei*, prosperity presupposed faithfulness to God within his edenic covenant. Jeffrey J. Niehaus summarizes, "I submit that the idea of covenant is one of those archetypal ideas in the mind of God." He adds:

> The relational commitments found in covenants also derive from God's nature—as one who is in fact Suzerain over all that he has made (Title); who has provided for those he has made (Historical Prologue); who commands those he has made (Stipulations); who promises to bless those he has made (Blessing); but who will also judge those he has made (Curse) if they are rebellious against his wise and loving intentions for his creatures,

---

46. The word for covenant (*berit*) does appear in Genesis 6:18 and 9:9–17 with reference to God's covenant with Noah, looking back on Adam's mandate to be fruitful and the necessary continuance of the natural realm after the Flood. References to the covenant of creation appear in Hosea 6:7 and Isaiah 24:5, and it is theologically implicit in Psalms 8 and 104 in the form of God's wisdom and providential care. Brueggemann calls Genesis 1–3 "covenantal," for every other doctrine is "subordinated to this fundamental issue of the relation of the Creator and creation" and "upon that issue everything else hinges" (*Genesis*, 12–13). Beale writes, "The essential elements of covenant are found in the Gen. 1–3 narrative: (1) two parties are named; (2) a condition of obedience is set forth; (3) a curse for transgression is threatened; (4) a clear implication of a blessing is promised for obedience" (*A New Testament Biblical Theology*, 43).

who are indeed his vassals. He himself was the Witness to all of this. Such was the state of affairs at the beginning. God's relationship with his creation, including the man and the woman he made in his image, was implicitly—to use a term we now know—covenantal.[47]

John M. Frame calls the covenant of creation a "relation between a lord and his servants," whereby God "rules over them by his law."[48] Frame refers to the capacities and virtues God possesses in order to implement his covenant as "lordship attributes":

Control	"God has the power to direct the whole course of nature and history as he pleases."
Authority	"God has the right to command" and the "right to tell us what we ought to do."
Presence	"He is able to act on and in creation and to evaluate authoritatively all that is happening in the creation."[49]

For the sake of simplicity, we can reduce Frame's three characteristics to two: transcendence and immanence. Cornelius Van Til pictured God's transcendence over and his immanence with creation through covenant in this way:

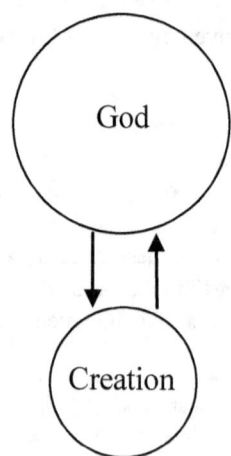

The Creator–Creature Distinction

47. Niehaus, "Covenant: An Idea in the Mind of God," 246.
48. Frame, *Doctrine of the Knowledge of God*, 12.
49. Frame, *Doctrine of the Knowledge of God*, 22–23. See also his *Systematic Theology*, 21–31.

The diagram depicts the relationship between the Creator as covenantal Lord with his subjects. God is never identified with creation, for he is transcendent, and so the creation is never divinized. However, as the arrows indicate, God is not remote or absent and his immanence enables interchange between himself and the world by means of revelation. Richard Lints summarizes the significance of the notion of transcendence and immanence in this way: "The Creator is not to be confused with the creation. However, the chasm between Creator and creation is not so great that God cannot bridge it."[50]

Further, the transcendent Creator is a *personal* absolute: he thinks, feels, and communicates. He is intimately involved with the world in every way. Genesis 1–2 reveals God as deeply attentive to creation and intimately involved with every aspect of its design and maintenance. He came alongside human beings, the weaker party to his covenant, and assumed total responsibility for their livelihood and spiritual destiny. He identified his purpose with them and gave them a great commission (Gen 1:26). He "walked" with Adam and Eve, presumably interacting with the first couple regularly (3:8). He intervened after they sinned and "called" after them, even though they hid from his presence (3:8–9).

Most importantly, God's immanence is manifested through his omnipresence, as Adam and Eve discovered to their dismay (3:8–10). He is everywhere and always working to achieve his wise purpose. The psalmist declares, "Where shall I go from your Spirit? Or where shall I flee from your presence? If I ascend to heaven, you are there! If I make my bed in Sheol, you are there!" (139:7–8) and "The Lord looks down from heaven; he sees all the children of man; from where he sits enthroned he looks out on all the inhabitants of the earth, he who fashions the hearts of them all and observes all their deeds" (33:13–15).

On the other hand, God's transcendence is rooted in his eternality, for he existed before creation. God alone is self-existent and self-referential. He needs nothing and lacks no necessary attribute. He is all-powerful, and nothing in heaven or on earth can thwart his plans. He can implement every agenda he intends and can access every resource necessary for the rule and sustenance of his house.

Furthermore, God is absolute. He created the world and initiated a relationship with creation that is subject to neither negotiation nor

---

50. Lints, *Identity and Idolatry*, 38. He adds, "Any account of the relationship of the Creator and the creature that makes the chasm either too great or too small does an injustice to the mysteries and tensions of the canon."

mutuality. He spoke and enacted with regal authority, while creation listened and obeyed his bidding. He was utterly and universally free to implement his covenant.

God is perfect. He is the sum of all good and of all pious, wise, and powerful virtues. As sovereign, builder, and benefactor, he is the source of life and prosperity. As the omniscient philosopher, he is the standard by which every created thing and every created thought are measured according to his creation covenant. Therefore, the creation can only be properly understood with reference to the Creator. Every aspect of this world is pre-interpreted within God's web of meaning.

God is also the source of beauty, aesthetics, and majesty. Not only was creation an exercise in imagination and wonder, but even after the fall the world is still a marvel to behold. For this reason, creation compels adoration of its Creator. Psalm 66:4 declares, "All the earth worships you and sings praises to you; they sing praises to your name."

Lastly, God is the cosmic lawgiver. God decreed both natural law and "creation ordinances" to govern human life in perpetuity: labor (1:28; 2:15 with reference to Adam and Eve's commission to subdue creation and extend the garden), Sabbath observance (2:1–3), and marriage (2:23–25 with reference to procreation and governance). Frame summarizes these ordinances in this way: "The creation ordinances, like other biblical laws, have a threefold, indeed a triperspectival, focus: on God (worship, Sabbath), on the natural world (replenishing, subduing, and dominating the earth), and on man himself (marriage, procreation, labor)."[51]

CONCLUSION

In this chapter, we have explored the being who made the world, the world that he made, and the bond between Creator and creation. Genesis 1–2 reveals God as the transcendent king, architect, economist, and philosopher. The bond between the world and God is covenantal—that is, a relation between the Lord and his servants. As such, there is an insurmountable ontological difference between the Creator and creation. Within this rubric, God modeled for Adam and Eve how to represent his interests in the garden as apprentice rulers, builders, investors, and thinkers. He wanted his vice-regents to care for, protect, and enlarge his property for his name's sake and the benefit of his creatures.

---

51. Frame, *The Doctrine of the Christian Life*, 202–3.

I described God as wisdom, for he alone knows what truly matters and what to do about it. He alone is good and does good for all with skill. He alone knows why the earth exists and what the purpose of human life is. And he possesses the requisite power to bring his plans to pass.

I described God as a thinker, for he understands everything. He interprets and evaluates all things within his realm. He is the standard and criterion for all thought and behavior. He determines the meaning of fact and law of rationality. Indeed, Eden was made for thinkers, for a great mind created it. Eden was the product of a knowing God and a God who is knowable.

Thus, the garden was an understandable world, subject to analysis. It was rational, manageable, and malleable for expansion and development. The transcendent scientist, mathematician, and artisan designed and constructed it.

As a result, Adam would learn that there is no "outside-of-creation" point of view, no knowledge apart from the covenantal bond between Creator and creature. There is no third-party perspective by which to evaluate God's wisdom and reign. As they gazed about the garden as servants of the divine king, Adam and Eve knew who their benefactor was. They knew who possessed all knowledge and wisdom. They knew that nothing was independent or secular. There were no brute facts. Everything, including their minds, was theocentric in orientation. Indeed, God designed Eden with the Great Commandment in mind (Deut 6:4–5; Mark 12:28–31). Adam and Eve could love, honor, and serve God with all their heart, soul, mind, and strength, despite their finitude.

God created a world for intelligent creatures. He made sentient beings with curiosity, intellectual desire, imagination, and an aspiration for wisdom. Adam and Eve's vice-regency was inconceivable without utilizing the cognitive abilities God gave to and patterned for them. In fact, because of the bond between creation and Creator, every sphere of their existence fell under God's rule, including their minds. Nothing escaped his evaluation, for all areas were subject to his "it was so" and "it was good."

2

Edenic Epistemology

"Know therefore that thou art the cornerstone and epitome of My works, the representative of God among them, the crown of My glory."

—Jan Amos Komenský, *The Great Didactic*

GOD CREATED A WORLD for beings that were fit for thinking and learning in all forms. He made them with intellectual curiosity and a thirst for the transcendent. To carry out their vice-regency, Adam and Eve had to apply their cognitive abilities and religious aspiration in compliance with the God who made them and the real world they lived in—that is, covenantally. The bond between creation and the Creator, between the first couple and God, was a Lord–servant alliance.

In this chapter, I propose to answer the following questions: What did Adam and Eve fall *from* intellectually? What was their pre-sin understanding about God, the world, and themselves that they would lose as covenant violators? In other words, I intend to outline pre-fall, edenic epistemology. I describe what Cornelius Van Til called the "adamic consciousness," or the mindset of Adam and Eve before they sinned.[1] Van Til also described it as "revelational epistemology."[2] Others have called the same phenomenon "covenant epistemology,"[3] "theistic epistemology,"

---

1. Van Til, *Introduction to Systematic Theology*, 25.
2. Van Til, *A Survey of Christian Epistemology*, 1.
3. Horton, *Covenant and Eschatology*, 203.

"servant knowledge,"[4] or "knowing-in-covenant-relationship."[5] Similarly, John Calvin cited the "integrity with which Adam was endowed" before he fell into sin, "when he had full possession of right understanding, when he had his affections kept within the bounds of reason, all his senses tempered in the right order, and he truly referred his excellence to exceptional gifts bestowed on him by his Maker."[6]

Fortunately, the text of Genesis is not silent about Adam and Eve's pre-fall mentality. It indicates both instantaneous knowledge gained through verbal instruction and natural revelation obtained by observation. In fact, before they embraced the serpent's ruse, Adam and Eve modeled, in motive and method, loving God with the mind, even though they were finite and fallible. The narrative suggests that they reasoned from creation to the Creator. They "thought God's thoughts after him." They obeyed when God spoke. They acknowledged and applied the revelation they received from both natural and supernatural sources. This is the focus of the first section of this chapter.

In the second section, I describe the divine milieu, Eden, awash with revelation. The first humans were thinkers *in situ*, hemmed in by Yahweh Elohim and defined as the image of God. In this setting, the divine pedagogue taught Adam and Eve through nature, guided pedagogy, and speech.

THE WHOLE WORLD IS A SCHOOL[7]

The first man grew in knowledge by studying God's handiwork and following his instructions. In fact, Eden was a laboratory of sorts, a workspace where Adam could develop his intellectual abilities and get to know God better, even as he honed his skills as divine steward.

Most likely, however, Adam's journey to self-awareness, understanding of his environment, and knowledge of his Creator and commission required some time. It is doubtful that his mind functioned instantly at full capacity, like that of Trinity in the film *The Matrix*. Trinity simply

---

4. Frame, *The Doctrine of the Knowledge of God*, 40.
5. Johnson, *Biblical Knowing*, xix.
6. Calvin, *Institutes*, 1:188.
7. Komenský wrote, "As the whole world is a school for the human race . . . so every individual's lifetime is a school from the cradle to the grave." See Murphy, *Comenius*, 94.

accessed complete knowledge of all kinds, downloaded directly to her brain. A similar scenario of instantaneous and comprehensive understanding is not likely in Adam's case, or at least it is not obvious. Rather, it is plausible that he learned much about himself and the world by means of observation and inference, given the setting.

In fact, it seems that Adam had to learn. He had to first develop his cognitive capacities.[8] Most likely, after Adam took his first breath and opened his eyes, he did not jump to his feet (assuming he was lying down) and exclaim, "Where am I? What is happening? Who is in charge here?" Indeed, he might not have possessed the capacity to use language at all. He probably did not yet possess a developed sense of self or situational awareness.

How, then, did Adam learn about himself as a sentient being? What and how did he learn about his environment as creation? What did Adam surmise about God, and how did he do it? Or, in terms of the last chapter, how did Adam become God's apprentice as king, architect, economist, and philosopher of the garden?

As we saw in chapter 1, a partial answer to these questions relates to the kind of world that God created. He made a world designed for thinking. It was manageable and malleable. Further, Adam was situated within a web of meaning conditioned by Yahweh Elohim. Adam's calling and stewardship determined the content, method, and motive of Adam's thought. Everything about his environment was necessarily theocentric and pedagogical. Everything about the world pointed to the Creator, just as a magnet points north.

From Nature to Nature's God

With a little imagination and insight derived from the passage, as well as broader biblical assumptions (Eccl 3:11; Pss 8:3–8; 19:1–6), we can suggest what might have taken place as the *imago Dei* was groomed for

---

8. Bavinck suggested a similar notion: "As a matter of fact no one ever arrives at the knowledge of 'first principles' or at the idea of God apart from the universe. The infant, born without consciousness, gradually receives various impressions and notions from the environment in which it is educated. In the case of the first man this may indeed have been different. All those who were born afterward were brought to a conscious and clear knowledge of both invisible and visible things by their parents and by means of their environment" (*The Doctrine of God*, 56). Likewise, Calvin referred to the "primal and simple knowledge to which the very order of nature would have led us if Adam had remained upright" (*Institutes*, 1:40).

vice-regency—even before God addressed him directly. Obviously, there is much that we do not know, such as Adam's state of consciousness between his creation (2:7) and when God put him in the garden of Eden (v. 9) or his state of awareness when he arrived there (vv. 16–17).[9]

Nevertheless, let us ponder briefly how Adam might have reasoned before the influence of sin and the snake's twisted epistemology. Imagine where Adam's innate intellectual curiosity and thirst for the transcendent could lead. Consider his intellectual progress following the pathway of sensory discovery, situational awareness, self-knowledge, and intuition of the transcendent. Such a process was necessarily inductive, based upon observation, experimentation, and reflection. Paradigmatically, the entire progression was guided *by* God and led *to* God.[10]

*****

When Adam woke up in creation, he felt no fear, but rather utter perplexity and stunned sensory stimulation. He was lying down, so the brightness of the sun assaulted his eyes. He closed them, though he felt its soothing warmth. After a little while, a cloud passed mercifully overhead and he looked up again. He perceived a palette of vibrant hues that captured his concentration. He then smelled, for there were flowers nearby. He heard, for there were birds singing and the wind rustled through the leaves above. He noticed movement.

Just then, a small, four-footed creature approached the big toe of Adam's right foot and licked with all its might. Adam was startled but not annoyed, because the sensation was delightful. He was surprised, as well, to hear his own voice, for he laughed with pleasure.

Next, the little creature approached Adam's left ear. The stimulus produced the same result, except that this time Adam slowly turned his head and saw the agent of his joy munching on a plant. Adam noticed that the animal was moving. And he wondered, "Can I move as well?"

---

9. *How* it happened, of course, is unknown; *that* it happened is entirely plausible. Given the focus of this section, the speculation is warranted. "God spoke to Adam first. And in due time Adam learned to speak with God. This is the unique relationship which man has with God, the capacity for conscious fellowship and communication, and all that these imply" (Custance, "Who Taught Adam to Speak?" 23).

10. We could make a comparison to the young man Jesus as he gained understanding about himself and God: "After three days they found him in the temple, sitting among the teachers, listening to them and asking them questions.... And Jesus increased in wisdom and in stature and in favor with God and man" (Luke 2:46, 52).

At this point, a hefty pig snuggled against Adam's head, snorted, and pushed against his shoulder. The noise, smell, and contact roused Adam to a sitting position. He thought with amazement, "What a different view from here!"

The pig shuffled around to the human's feet and nudged there as well. This caused Adam to draw his legs up and throw his arms back for support. Then, he looked at the pig and saw that it had four moving parts, just like the smaller creature. He looked about his body and saw that it too had four appendages. And he inquired of himself, "Can I also move?" So he tried to imitate the pig, executing a clumsy crab walk, for he had been lying on his back. But he did not get very far and the movement was quite awkward.

Next, a large black gorilla appeared in front of Adam, standing on two strong legs. The great ape and the man studied one another intently for some time. Then, the ape abruptly seized Adam and lifted him to an upright position. Adam was astonished. He noticed that he too had two large limbs that supported him. Then he thought, "What a view!" And he heard a second noise emerge from his body, an expression of wonder.

From this vantage point, he cast his gaze at a distance. He saw many more animals and then birds. He heard many more sounds and noticed other smells as well. He felt the breeze more distinctly. He witnessed subtle changes of light and temperature as clouds passed overhead. He also noticed, curiously, that some animals moved as pairs. In fact, the gorilla's companion carried a much smaller creature of the same kind.

After a while, he watched many animals gather beside a large smooth surface with the color of the sky. He decided to use his two lower limbs and approach the strange sight. Slowly and with great caution he walked to the shore nearby. He observed that the animals lowered their heads very close to the surface and made a lot of noise.

As he peered into the water, he froze in shock, for he observed his own image. He recognized quickly that he was very different. The creatures all had eyes, ears, noses, and mouths, but his were quite distinct. They all had heads, but his was not like theirs. He was also taller than most. His feet and hands were different too. He was not as hairy as most of the creatures. Again, many pairs were accompanied by another of their kind, but he was alone. He wondered, "Why is that?"

Because he was the only one of his kind, he was an avid student of himself. He became aware of another world, a subjective realm. He experienced emotions. He sometimes cried with joy. He laughed. He preferred some animals more than others and felt affection for them. He also observed desires that he could regulate—for objective things such as food or drink, but also internal longings for beauty, joy, and satisfaction.

He experienced intellectual stimulation. He was enthralled at nature's complexity. He paid close attention to colors and textures. He was awed by the wonder and bounty in which he was immersed. He marveled at how everything fit together and served the benefit of all. Sunshine yielded to darkness, and rain gave way to dryness. Plants produced beauty and bounty. He also discerned that creatures often gathered around him. They deferred to him, moving aside so that he could pass and allowing him to select his food. He wondered what this behavior meant.

He wondered more and more, "How did this place come to be? What is all this for? What am I?" He noticed an ache, as well, for something greater than himself, higher and beyond what he could see or imagine.

One day soon thereafter, God spoke to Adam.

The Creator Spoke

God spoke to the man alone in Genesis 2:16–17:[11]

(16) And the Lord God commanded the man, saying, "You may surely eat of every tree of the garden,

(17) but of the tree of the knowledge of good and evil you shall not eat, for in the day that you eat of it you shall surely die."

God obligated Adam and warned him about disobedience.[12] The two commands in verses 16–17, positive and negative, are covenantal.

---

11. The two accounts of God's speech to Adam and Eve in Genesis 1:28–30 and 2:16–17 appear to have occurred at different times. The latter seems to have taken place first, as God addressed Adam alone, before Eve entered the narrative. In 1:28 God spoke to "them" and commanded the first couple to "multiply." Thus, I begin with the two commands communicated to Adam in chapter 2 and thereafter take up the various themes associated with 1:28–30.

12. Verse 17 has spawned an interpretive jungle over the duration of church history, depending on one's confessional perspective and presuppositional commitment. Several important questions arise. Why is this tree, the tree of knowledge of good and evil, so critical? Why did God place that tree in the garden, given its peril? Why did he instruct Adam alone, before Eve appeared? And most puzzling of all, what are the origin and role of the serpent in chapter 3? With each of these questions, we should acknowledge our finitude and fallenness, and remember Paul's words: "Oh, the depth of the riches and wisdom and knowledge of God! How unsearchable are his judgments

Compliance led to blessings; violation resulted in judgment. Adam, however, was not motivated by sin or in need of redemption at this point. So where did his obligation originate?

Clearly, Adam's edenic context engendered obligation. John Calvin suggested that mankind's duty arose from creation and covenant. He wrote, "For how can the thought of God enter your mind without your realizing that, since you are his handiwork, you have been made over and bound to his command by right of creation, that you owe your life to him?—that whatever you undertake, whatever you do, ought to be ascribed to him?"[13] We can propose the same for Adam.

Adam's daily, existential reality evidenced divine blessing. Surely, God's power and majesty provoked awe and wonder. His benefaction fostered gratitude and a sense of dependence. His holiness caused reverence and adoration. His love promoted affection and loyalty. And most importantly, God's abundant wisdom and understanding engendered epistemic humility. All these attributes fostered a sense of obligation.

Further, covenants were by nature probative. The superior demanded compliance from the inferior. The edenic covenant was no exception, due to the Creator–creature distinction.[14] Also, many other boundaries and prohibitions appear in Genesis 1–2.[15] Adam and Eve were not to aspire to be "like God" (at least not on the serpent's terms, as we will see in the next chapter). God distinguished between the first six days of creation and the seventh day, making it "holy." Animals mated, but only "according to their kinds." So in this sense, as well, the distinction between and the prohibition concerning the two trees was not exceptional.

---

and how inscrutable his ways! 'For who has known the mind of the Lord, or who has been his counselor?'" (Rom 11:33–34). For an examination that looks back on Genesis 2:17 from later in Old Testament history, see VanDrunen, "Israel's Recapitalization of Adam's Probation," 303–24.

13. Calvin, *Institutes*, 1:42.

14. From an eschatological perspective, the narrative implies that Adam's obedience would have ensured God's long-term agenda for creation without disruption. In his pre-fall state, Adam was vulnerable. He was fallible, subject to failure, for he was able to sin. After he failed the test, he was enslaved to corruption, unable not to sin. Looking far ahead, God planned that sinners redeemed through Jesus Christ would possess the power of the Holy Spirit not to sin, though still conflicted due to the heaviness of this "present evil age" (Gal 1:4). Looking even farther ahead, God envisioned paradise restored, where humans unwilling and unable to sin will reign forever. Only in this final epoch will God's cosmic tabernacle and holy dwelling endure forever (Isa 65; Rev 21:1–8). See Beale, *A New Testament Biblical Theology*, 29–58.

15. See Bruckner, "Boundary and Freedom," 15–35.

Second, God addressed Adam and Eve together in 1:28–30:

(28) And God blessed them. And God said to them, "Be fruitful and multiply and fill the earth and subdue it, and have dominion over the fish of the sea and over the birds of the heavens and over every living thing that moves on the earth."

(29) And God said, "Behold, I have given you every plant yielding seed that is on the face of all the earth, and every tree with seed in its fruit. You shall have them for food.

(30) And to every beast of the earth and to every bird of the heavens and to everything that creeps on the earth, everything that has the breath of life, I have given every green plant for food."

Verse 28 indicates that blessing was the wellspring out of which Adam and Eve's fruitfulness and dominion arose. It was the fountainhead from which their covenantal obligation flowed. Blessing motivated Adam and Eve to love and serve God as vassal rulers, cultivators, patrons, and sages. In fact, God's blessing resembled the enlivening work of the Spirit of God in creation (1:2), for it enabled Adam and Eve to function as living beings. As we read in the last chapter, their blessing was akin to Bezalel's commission, whereby "the Spirit of God" provided the "ability and intelligence, with knowledge and all craftsmanship" for the task of building the tabernacle (Exod 31:3). Their blessing also resembled Joseph's ministry, for he was equipped by the Spirit of God with wisdom and discernment to serve Pharaoh as vice-regent, confronting the threat of famine (Gen 41:39).[16]

Indeed, God's blessing was the fructifying power in creation, releasing the potential of the garden. Adam and Eve were enabled to reproduce and "fill the earth." Animals were enabled to bear young. Vegetation could replenish itself "according to its kind." God's providential care established the regularity of nature. He provided life-giving water to the expanse of the earth through four great rivers (Gen 2:10–14). Indeed, everything flourished in Eden, for God "gives" and his benefaction sustained the sacred milieu.

Furthermore, God's blessing sanctified time and set history in motion. He determined the temporal matrix that established life's core

---

16. That famine, by the way, threatened the adamic mandate to be "fruitful and multiply" as it was communicated again to Noah (Gen 9:1), Abraham (16:10), and Jacob (35:11).

rhythm (including the Sabbath). He organized Adam's commission and later human development with reference to creation ("these are the generations," in Gen 2:4; 5:1; 6:9; 10:1; 11:27; 25:12, 19; 36:1; 37:2).[17] In this way he established the edenic nexus as both an archetype and an eschatological trajectory.

Moreover, blessing showed that Adam and Eve did not flourish through nature's bounty only, but also by divine grace. Adam, for example, was nothing but an inert organism until God gave him life. He was a solitary creature until God made Eve. They were a short-term duo until he provided the capacity to conceive. Their great blessing, therefore, was enablement provided by the divine patron. It was transcendent and supernatural in origin, but immanent as the animating power in creation.

Within the context of blessing and benefaction arose Adam and Eve's rule and dominion in the earth (1:28). They were commissioned to mirror God and represent his interests within his earthly empire as servants of the edenic covenant. As apprentice kings, they would govern with wisdom and foresight. As architects, they would build and fill creation with artistry and utility. As economists, they would administer as just and generous stewards. As philosophers, they would mirror God's thoughts about creation as finite thinkers.

But their mandate was not only functional. As the image of God, they were obligated to replicate his character. They would share his motives and values. They would believe and behave for his glory. In particular, since Yahweh Elohim loved the world, they would love creation. As he blessed, they would bless. Since he was good, they would do good also. Since he was just, they would practice righteousness. And because he was holy, they would obey his commands and respect his boundaries. As Creator and covenant lord, God deserved loyalty, affection, and adoration, so they would serve God with all their, heart, soul, mind, and strength.

This, then, is the context in which we should understand the words rule (*rada*) and dominion (*kabash*). God's blessing enabled them to exercise dominion. As I explained in chapter 1, the verb "rule" (*rada*) is used in connection with royalty and governance. It is essentially an administrative or political term. In these verses, however, it appears in connection with the animal kingdom and likely refers to benevolent care of non-human species. Poythress expresses this concept clearly: "The 'dominion' of Genesis 1:28 is thus to be understood as a thoughtful, caring

---

17. See Derouchie, "The Blessing-Commission," 219–47.

dominion, a dominion expressing God's goodness and care, not a heartless, brutal, crushing dominion."[18]

Kabash, on the other hand, implies force against resistance and probably signifies the agricultural exertion required to prosper in the natural environment. It may also indicate the domestication of animals. Obviously, though, Adam and Eve were not authorized to rule as autonomous agents operating outside God's norms. Christopher J. H. Wright explains this idea: "We alone of all the species have been endowed with the capacity of giving ourselves to the care of other creatures, reflecting God's own doing so."[19] Adam ruled under God for the benefit of others, including the non-human domain.

Finally, Adam and Eve and their descendants began to implement suitable structures to support the population as it grew (as implied by Genesis 4–11). The need for physical infrastructure arose: food and water supply, shelter, and transportation routes. Means and manpower emerged for exploration and extension. Systems for public administration became evident. Means of production, exchange, and consumption developed, as well as methods of public communication and mobilization. Subjective infrastructure also evolved for the expression of human culture: language, knowledge, and oral tradition. Artistry developed: music, storytelling, and artwork.[20]

The Creator Taught

God created a rational world for intelligent creatures. He made sentient beings with intellectual desire, and Eden was a domain apt for thinking. Clearly, God was a great teacher and created an excellent learning environment for Adam and Eve.

---

18. Poythress, *Redeeming Science*, 150.
19. Wright, *Old Testament Ethics*, 126.
20. In addition, the necessity for spiritual and moral education would become urgent. The growing populace would learn the edenic worldview, creation ordnances, and obligations of covenant. They would develop practices that promote religious purity. Organized forms of worship and liturgy, as well as religious leadership, would necessarily evolve. They would acquire vigilance to guard their growing civilization from the serpent's guile in the future. (Presumably, even if they had they not sinned at the tree of the knowledge of good and evil, the war with the serpent would have continued.)

The divine pedagogue taught by example. He modeled for Adam and Eve how to reign, build, bless, and ponder. He designed the world with utmost wisdom and artistry. He executed his architectural plan with greatest care. He administered his reign with justice. Everything he did in creation manifested his wisdom and thoughtfulness. He was the moral exemplar, the epitome of love, goodness, righteousness, and truth. Moreover, because of divine law, the world was subject to analysis and development. It was also beautiful and stunningly complex. As such, creation was calculated to pique the curiosity and creativity of God's primal apprentices.

God's students were perfectly suited for his school. Komenský observed, "And so it is certain that man also is naturally fitted for the understanding of facts, for existence in harmony with the moral law, above all things for the love of God."[21] Adam and Eve learned that no fact can be separated from the fact-giver. They discovered that all created data possessed significance in relation to the Creator. They found that nothing was outside God's reign, including themselves. Furthermore, no conduct, value, or motivation is worthy apart from the fountainhead of love. Adam and Eve were learning that no being was like Elohim and so no other deity could exist at all (2 Sam 7:22).

Thus, God established a pedagogical environment in which each aspect was dedicated to Adam and Eve's instruction, for God's glory. Every detail of their education was theocentric, as were the content, method, and motives of their minds. Their schooling was designed to prepare them to exercise God's mandate in the world. Van Til summarized how the teacher, classroom, and students were linked to one another:

> God has created not only the facts but also the laws of physical existence. And the two are meaningless except as correlatives of one another. Moreover, God has adapted the objects to the subjects of knowledge; that the laws of our minds and the laws of the facts come into fruitful contact with another is due to God's creative work and to God's providence, by which all things are maintained in their existence and in their operation in relation to one another.[22]

Consider a particular moment in Adam's training from Genesis 2. This episode demonstrates the developmental and pedagogical nature of

---

21. Komenský, *The Great Didactic*, 40.
22. Van Til, *Introduction to Systematic Theology*, 65.

Adam's relationship with God. Dru Johnson poses an important question about the process of knowledge acquisition: "Is the man's knowledge instantaneous?" He answers, "I am prepared to say no specifically because the man participates in a quest to know through space, time, relationship, and his body."[23] Let us read verses 18–23 (the key terms and phrases are italicized):

> (18) Then the Lord God said, "It is not good that the man should be alone; I will make him a helper fit for him."
>
> (19) Now out of the ground the Lord God had formed every beast of the field and every bird of the heavens and brought them to the man to see what *he would call them*. And whatever the man called every living creature, that was its *name*.
>
> (20) The man gave *names* to all livestock and to the birds of the heavens and to every beast of the field. But for Adam there was *not found* a *helper fit* for him.
>
> (21) So the Lord God caused a deep sleep to fall upon the man, and while he slept took one of his ribs and closed up its place with flesh.
>
> (22) And the rib that the Lord God had taken from the man he made into a woman and brought her to the man.
>
> (23) Then the man said, "This *at last* is bone of my bones and flesh of my flesh; she shall be called Woman, because she was taken out of Man."

This passage begins with the statement of a problem. God said it was "not good" that Adam was alone, for he had no "helper fit (*ezer kenegdo*) for him." This negative fact God knew, but seemingly Adam did not. Perhaps, though, he lamented his solitude and found it enigmatic, as I suggested earlier in chapter 1.[24] His expression of relief and delight in verse 23, when he saw Eve for the first time, seems to affirm this possibility. The expression "This at last" implies a previous longing and anticipation.[25]

---

23. Johnson, *Epistemology and Biblical Theology*, 29.

24. Adam's learning process regarding his mate presumed desire and enigma. Johnson writes, "It involves a longing, which means that knowing involves a conflict that seeks resolution" (*Epistemology and Biblical Theology*, 28).

25. Other translations express the emotion implied: "Here is someone like me!" (CEV); "This is it!" (TLB); "Finally!" (MSG); "'At last!' the man exclaimed" (NLT).

Within the broader narrative, one aspect of Eve's suitability as Adam's partner is linked to her function. In its twenty-two appearances in the Old Testament, the word "helper" (*ezer*) applies almost exclusively to God, as the one who helps (many times in the Prophets and Psalms). The helper supplies what one lacks or cannot do for oneself, and sometimes the helper is a rescuer. The expression "helper fit for" (*ezer kenegdo*) is also instructive on two levels. First, God gave Adam and Eve a gigantic job to do. The task of caring for and extending the garden was too big for one person alone. More to the point, humankind could not multiply and fill the earth unless both male and female cooperated sexually and in parenting. Second, the appropriateness of Eve also indicated that companionship was a critical aspect of being the image of God. Thus, God met several needs through Eve as Adam's physical, emotional, and intellectual helper. God was the one who helped Adam *through* Eve.

The making of Eve, however, was quite dissimilar to the creation of the earth and other living things. God did not create Eve by divine fiat. Instead, he initiated a learning process whereby Adam discovered his mate and learned more about the creatures, himself, and God. Yahweh Elohim "brought" the animals and delegated to Adam the authority to name them. He encouraged Adam to use his cognitive powers to identify each animal by comparing and contrasting one with another and with himself. (Interestingly, God accepted "whatever" Adam determined was appropriate.) When this process did not attain the intended goal, God intervened supernaturally to bring Eve into existence (2:21–22). Ultimately, he "brought" Eve to Adam, but again he delegated the responsibility for her name to the man.

This learning process appeared to have several objectives. Foremost was the identification of Adam's mate. Others were pedagogical. Through the process, Adam experienced how to learn more from the environment, about himself, and from God. He utilized observational and logical principles of analysis. Most importantly, he discovered more about God, the divine pedagogue. He learned how intellectuality functions under the king. He listened to and heeded God's verbal instruction. More precisely, he discovered through experience that "in your light do we see light" (Ps 36:9b).

Johnson provides further insight about God's edenic pedagogy. Regarding the naming process, he says, "The conflict that drives this narrative forward is this tension between man's actual aloneness and God's declaration that his aloneness is not good. Man comes to know both the solitary problem and God's solution through participation within that process."[26] By participating in the procedure that God initiated, Adam learned that he could not discover his mate autonomously or deductively. Rather, the learning progression required submission to God as his fiduciary partner and authenticated guide, for "man cannot know without commitment to trust God."[27] Further, Johnson says about Adam's learning process, "The man knows *through* his body, but also *through* his experience analogically. Because he is embodied, knowing has an analogical facet so that man can know that he is on the way to knowing his proper mate."[28] In short, Adam's situation in Eden, as well as his finite and fallible embodiment, determined his epistemological orientation to God, himself, and the world.

THE SETTING

Remember from the previous chapter that in the ancient world, one's name signified identity, stature, and purpose. Assigning a name was a prerogative of those with ultimate authority and responsibility. The purpose was to command obedience, affirm ownership, and foretell destiny. In Genesis 1:1–2:17, God named everything, including Adam, and thereby manifested his kingship over creation and situated his vassal within the divine milieu.[29] In Genesis 1–3 two names reveal God's identity and his intention for creation and his vice-regents: Elohim and Yahweh Elohim.

God's Names

Genesis 1:1–2:3 reveals God as Elohim, the personal absolute: immutable, independent, and eternal. He is ontologically antecedent to all that was created: self-existent, self-explanatory, self-attesting, and self-sufficient. He is all-wise, omnipotent, omniscient, omnipresent, and sovereign. He is the source of moral virtue, truth, and goodness. He is the standard by

---

26. Johnson, *Biblical Knowing*, 26.
27. Johnson, *Biblical Knowing*, 31.
28. Johnson, *Biblical Knowing*, 32–33 (emphasis in original).
29. For this reason Adam did not attempt to define (name) God, for he was subservient. Bavinck wrote, "Men do not give him a name; he gives himself a name. God's name is, therefore, most of all God's *revelation* of himself" (*The Doctrine of God*, 84.) He added, "God *is* that which he *calls* himself, and he *calls* himself that which he *is*" (85, emphasis in original).

which every human thought is measured and held accountable. He is the cosmic lawgiver, as well as the providential foundation of sustenance and order.

The name Elohim appears thirty-five times in Genesis 1–3 as the subject of verbs of sovereign implementation ("create," "hover," "say," "separate," "call," "make," "set," "bless," "rest," "finish") and omniscient evaluation ("see"). This name displays God's transcendence and power through thought, speech, and action.[30] Elohim is the source of all that came to be through creation, the fount upon which everything is dependent. He set the preconditions for existence. He provided the sustenance that nature presupposes. He is also the *telos* toward which history advances. Every aspect of creation, therefore, presupposes Elohim.[31]

But in Genesis 2:4–3:24, God is also called Yahweh Elohim, the divinity that comes alongside the first humans. He is the transcendent king but also the immanent teacher, guide, and pastor. He is not remote and does not leave them to observation and experience alone, for he speaks to them, disclosing their identity and assigning their purpose.

The name "Yahweh Elohim" (Lord God) is quite unique.[32] It appears twenty times in this passage with reference to God's work in the garden ("make," "cause," "plant," "spring up," "take," "command," "say," "form," "walk," "call," "send") and in his relationship with Adam and Eve. However, whereas the name Elohim functions primarily at a macrocosmic and transcendent level, the name Yahweh Elohim appears chiefly

---

30. Frame cites Romans 11:36 to illustrate God's aseity as depicted in the divine name: "For from him and through him and to him are all things. To him be glory forever. Amen." Frame comments, "He has created and provided all things ('from him'); nothing happens without his power ('through him'); and he receives everything back to himself ('to him')" (*Systematic Theology*, 411).

31. The Old Testament affirms more than 2,500 times that Elohim is the Lord of creation. He is "the God of heaven, who made the sea and the dry land," who rightly demands our reverence (Jonah 1:9). His reign is universal, for he is designated the "God of the whole earth" (Isa 54:5), "God of all flesh" (Jer 32:27), and "God in the heavens above and on the earth beneath" (Josh 2:11). He is the supreme judge as Proverbs declares: "The eyes of the Lord are in every place, keeping watch on the evil and the good" (15:3). Further, he is exalted above all would-be gods. For all these reasons, David declared, "You are great, O Lord God. For there is none like you, and there is no God (Elohim) besides you" (2 Sam 7:22). In fact, from the Old Testament's perspective, contrasting Elohim with all other would-be claimants demonstrates the *necessary* existence of God.

32. The word "Yahweh" appears more than 6,800 times in the Old Testament, but "Yahweh" and "Elohim" rarely function together as in Genesis 2–3.

with a microcosmic focus and stresses divine immanence. Yahweh Elohim "gets his hands dirty," preparing a suitable habitat for Adam and Eve. He assumes an intimate interest in each. He is directly involved in Adam's education through deductive and inductive revelation. He pronounces the only explicit, negative evaluation in creation with reference to Adam's solitude ("not good" in 2:18). He initiates a search for Adam's mate (vv. 18–23). He performs the first "surgery" in creating Eve (v. 21). He is present in the garden, "walking" (3:8). After they have sinned, he addresses Adam and Eve personally to assess their thinking (vv. 9–13). He speaks directly to the serpent, Adam, and Eve in judgment (vv. 14–19, 24).[33] He also clothes them (v. 21) and banishes them for their own good (vv. 23–24).

God's Image

Adam and Eve can also be viewed from a structural or functional point of view, that is, what they were designed to do. Wright explains the adamic purpose by noting, "Only two things are said about human beings that are not said about any other creature: that God chose to make us in God's own image, and that God instructed us to rule over the rest of the creatures (Gen 1:26)."[34] In fact, the *imago Dei* occupied a unique and awkward position in creation. Adam and Eve were similar *and* dissimilar to God. They were also similar *and* dissimilar to animals. They inhabited a mediatory position; therefore, one must not claim either too much similarity or dissimilarity to the divine or the terrestrial.[35] Adam and Eve were certainly not demigods, but they were assuredly not simple animals either (Ps 8:3–8).

Four verses within the broader context of Genesis 1–2 reveal Adam and Eve's structure and purpose, as well as their dignity and lowliness.

---

33. Surely it is significant that Eve and the serpent only referred to God with the name Elohim (3:1b–5).

34. Wright, *Old Testament Ethics*, 118.

35. Horton ("Meeting a Stranger: A Covenantal Epistemology," 7) explains the errors of excessive similarity and dissimilarity: "If hyper-transcendence introduces an unbiblical dualism (i.e., antitheses) between the Creator and creature, eternity and time, heaven and earth, hyper-immanence collapses all dualities (i.e., difference) in a monistic scheme . . . . 'Meeting a stranger' [the biblical deity] articulates an ontology of genuine difference and an epistemology of the external Word, both grounded in a theology of the covenant."

These verses show God's intention for them and their situatedness even before they appeared in the garden and were spoken to (the important terms and phrases are italicized; this quotation is from the NIV):

> (1:26) Then God said, "*Let us* make mankind in our *image*, in our likeness, so that they may *rule over* the fish in the sea and the birds in the sky, over the livestock and all the wild animals, and over all the creatures that move along the ground."

> (1:27) So God created man in his own image, in the image of God he created him; *male and female he created them.*

> (2:5) Now no shrub had yet appeared on the earth and no plant had yet sprung up, for the Lord God had not sent rain on the earth and there was no one to *work* the ground.

> (2:15) The Lord God took the man and put him in the garden of Eden to *work* it and *take care of* it.

First of all, as mentioned above, the first humans occupied a mediatory position. From an ontological perspective, the *imago Dei* does *not* denote divine duplication or self-cloning. God is utterly unique, so Adam and Eve could not have been replicas of the divine being. They were not even semi-divine or junior deities (Ps 8:5). Instead, they were created: God "formed the man of dust" (Gen 2:7).[36] They had a beginning and were finite. They were restricted by embodiment, as well as limited in might and mind. They required revelation to learn about God and his agenda in the world. Thus, though Adam and Eve were the image of God, Elohim is infinitely greater than his created image. Richard Lints writes, "The *imago Dei* as an image is contingent upon the object for its identity . . . . Human identity is rooted in what it reflects."[37] Adam and Eve reflected God as his incarnate representatives on earth, not as equals but dependent and derivative. They were servants of the covenant king and ambassadors of Yahweh Elohim.

So, rather than a one-to-one correspondence with the Creator, we observe in this passage, as Frame says, "qualities in man that constitute finite replicas of God's infinite qualities."[38] Specifically, as God's image they evidenced in an analogical fashion God's kingship, his architectural

---

36. The "dust" motif is associated with covenant making. The antithesis of dust is dignity and kingship. See Brueggemann, "From Dust to Kingship," 1–18.

37. Lints, *Identity and Idolatry*, 29–30.

38. Frame, *Systematic Theology*, 785.

and building prowess, his entrepreneurial motivation and benefaction, and a thirst for wisdom and the sacred. Adam and Eve possessed inherent capacities and desires resembling God's that equipped them to function as the vice-regents of creation. Their abilities and motivations would enable the world to flourish.

For instance, the Old Testament uses the word "image" (*tselem*) to refer to a physical representation of a person or object, often an idol (Num 33:52, for example). However, in the Old Testament and the ancient Near East, images had both static and active qualities. On one hand, they functioned as a physical resemblance of their owners and those who made them. Rulers placed statues and images with inscriptions at distant points within their empire to represent their dominion. On the other hand, images (idols) were active as channels of spiritual power and personal transformation. Likewise, the spirit of a god was thought to reside in an object to represent a king and his patron deity, watching over the subjects within his domain. Clearly, in an analogous manner Adam and Eve were bearers of God's image, presence, and power in the world to care for the inhabitants of God's house.[39]

On the other hand, it is important to understand the singularity of the divine image within the narrative. The announcement of Adam and Eve's advent occurred in the first-person plural among the divine council (1:26), undoubtedly indicating the strategic centrality of human beings. God made the first couple in a very intimate fashion through divine touch and life-giving breath (2:7, 21–22), rather than with the formulaic "each according to its kind" used for all other reproducing things. Adam and Eve were designed for communion with Yahweh Elohim, unlike the animals. They were destined for a governing role in creation. Moreover, the advent of Adam and Eve resolved four problems present in creation. Adam's appearance solved a workforce issue. "There was no man to work the ground" (2:5). The creation of Eve solved the matters of reproduction, filling, and multiplying (2:22). She was a "helper fit for him" (2:20) as a co-laborer in God's mandate (1:26–28, 2:15). And as we noted, she was also a companion, fellow thinker, and soul-mate (2:23).

---

39. Psalm 8 portrays the investiture of Adam, the royal steward, over God's realm under the purview of the divine court. Even though he retained significant dignity, Adam was still "a little lower" than the angels, who are infinitely inferior to the divine being (8:3–8). Likewise, Genesis 1–2 displays Adam as God's son with covenantal and royal implications. This message is explicit in Luke's genealogy of Jesus, which ends, "the son of Seth, the son of Adam, the son of God" (3:38). Adam was "the son of God," his royal vice-regent, yet a finite mirror of the invisible and eternal.

Second, Genesis 1:26 explains what Adam and Eve were equipped to do: "Let us make mankind in our image, in our likeness, *so that* they may rule."[40] Exercising dominion was their mandate as the image of God and the foremost species on earth. For this reason Frame says, "God has made man like himself to equip man for his task to be lord, a lord subordinate to God's ultimate lordship."[41] Likewise, Middleton writes, "The *imago Dei* refers to human rule, that is, the exercise of power on God's behalf in creation."[42] In fact, the verb "rule" (*rada*) is used in connection with royalty. First Kings says about Solomon: "For he had dominion [*rada*] over all the region.... And he had peace on all sides around him" (4:24). Obviously, as the divine image, Adam was a vassal king, enabled to exercise dominion and represent God within the empire that God had created.

Moreover, Genesis 2:5 and 2:15 explain *how* they were to exercise dominion—though labor (*abad* in both verses). Adam and Eve were designed for work, but not simply physical exertion. Their toil applied every capacity they possessed to all the potential in creation. Their job description was indeed complex. As vice-regents, they served as ambassadors, representing God's interests for his glory. Adam and Eve's work included agriculture, but also construction in a manner that replicated creation. They could use their entrepreneurial prowess to create an edenic milieu for nature and humankind to flourish. They could use their cognitive abilities to maintain and extend the divine nexus according to the ordinances of sacred space and time. The *imago Dei* could exercise dominion as leaders, artisans, benefactors, and intellectuals.

Most importantly, Adam was caretaker of the sanctuary. As primeval priest, his labor included protection of God's holy dwelling. The verb "take care of" (*shamar*) in verse 15 means to watch over diligently and guard vigilantly. Adam's sacred duty was the maintenance of Eden's purity. He was required to discern threats and defend the sanctity of the garden. This obligation is evident in chapter 3, after Adam failed in this task, for God then delegated guardianship to an angel (v. 24). Adam's fiduciary role as cultic guardian and worker in God's temple is clear as

---

40. Wright explains this translation in *Old Testament Ethics*, 119, note 21, as does Dumbrell in *The Search for Order*, 19, and Middleton, *The Liberating Image*, 53–54. The NIV translates the Hebrew to show intention: "Let us make mankind in our image, in our likeness, so that they may rule over."

41. Frame, *Systematic Theology*, 786.

42. Middleton, *The Liberating Image*, 88.

well because of the appearance of the terms "work" (*abad*) and "guard" (*shamar*), used again in describing the duties of the Levite priests: "They shall guard (*shamar*) all the furnishings of the tent of meeting, and keep guard over (*shamar*) the people of Israel as they minister (*abad*) at the tabernacle" (Num 3:8).[43] Similarly, Adam's role was to guard holy ground against any outsider and to represent God in creation as his priest.

CONCLUSION

God did not first create Adam and Eve and then invite them to co-imagine and co-create the world. Rather, he first built creation according to his criteria and then situated them within it. They were embedded within a web of meaning and infrastructure imposed by the Creator. All the data of creation were related to the ontological thinker and covenant Lord. Everything about their context was given to them by grace alone.

Adam and Eve were not transcendent, original, or paradigmatic, nor were they the source of or standard for any intellectual construct. Instead, they thought analogically, presupposing God's interpretation of creation. His understanding was the precondition that made it possible for them to possess finite knowledge as creatures.[44] They depended upon revelation and did not begin from themselves cognitively, because they were not self-attesting. They were not epistemologically autonomous, for they were servants under creational and covenantal authority. In other words, as creatures made in God's image, they reasoned from nature to nature's God. Satan's epistemic bias had not yet corrupted their minds.

Thus, until their fateful encounter with the snake, they avoided several errors that plague the human race to this day. They did not posit a false ontological similarity between themselves and God, nor did they assume an absolute ontological dissimilarity with God. They did not presume an independent and transcendent rationality to which they and God were both accountable. They rejected secularity, which would leave

---

43. Temple protection is even more explicit in Numbers 3:10: "And you shall appoint Aaron and his sons, and they shall guard (*shamar*) their priesthood. But if any outsider comes near, he shall be put to death."

44. Thomas K. Johnson contributed this insight. He added the observation, "When Cornelius Van Til wrote in Dutch, he used the word *bedinging* in place of 'presupposition' in English. The Dutch word, as does as the German cognate *Bedingung*, carries a meaning of a condition that makes something possible" (personal conversation, June 2021).

some aspects of existence devoid of God's care or accountability. They did not presume an objective or neutral posture apart from the covenant, as if anything lacked divine interpretation.[45] They did not assume a critical or skeptical stance before God and hold him to account. They did not embrace instrumentalism, whereby knowledge exists for pragmatic purposes alone or for the manipulation of the divine.

Rather, Adam and Eve's epistemological profile was characterized by humility and obedience. Their intellectual outlook resembled the psalmist's: "O Lord, my heart is not lifted up; my eyes are not raised too high; I do not occupy myself with things too great and too marvelous for me. But I have calmed and quieted my soul, like a weaned child with its mother; like a weaned child is my soul within me" (Ps 131:1–2). In these ways, Adam and Eve modeled in motive and method how to love God with the mind, even though they were finite and fallible.

Adam and Eve were not trained theologians or self-conscious philosophers. However, they intuited and certainly experienced Yahweh Elohim as the one essential fact—the single reality—that accounted for their existence. They could observe God at work and recognize that he was the ontological glue that held their world together. Van Til wrote, "Now if every fact in the universe is created by God, and if the mind of man and whatever the mind of man knows is created by God, it goes without saying that the whole fabric of human knowledge would dash to pieces if God did not exist and if all finite existence were not revelational of God."[46] Knowing and pleasing this God, therefore, was their reason for being. The only sensible response to Yahweh Elohim was to present their heart, mind, and strength as a "living sacrifice, holy and acceptable," which was, indeed, their "spiritual worship" as God's vice-regents (Deut 6:5; Rom 12:1).

It is critical to understand the nature of Adam and Eve's epistemological orientation. Theirs was truly "faith in search of understanding," to quote Anselm's famous axiom.[47] Their minds embraced the "fear of the

---

45. Frame wrote, "The idea of 'brute fact' is an invention intended to furnish us with a criterion of truth other than God's revelation" (*The Doctrine of the Knowledge of God*, 71).

46. Van Til, *Introduction to Systematic Theology*, 14.

47. In context, the statement reads: "I yearn to understand some measure of Your truth, which my heart believes and loves. For I do not seek to understand in order to believe, but I believe in order to understand. For this also I believe, that unless I believed, I should not understand" (Anselm, *Complete Philosophical and Theological Treatises*, 93).

Lord," which is the "beginning of knowledge" (Prov 1:7). Indeed, because God exists, they could think according to God's norms. Genesis 1–2 shows that ontology, epistemology, and ethics are correlative.

Further, knowing God was not merely cerebral or analytic, as a mind understands an object or abstraction. Rather, Adam and Eve encountered an absolute *person*. Michael Horton comments, "Biblical (i.e., covenantal) epistemology calls not only for observation, reflection, and description, but for trust and obedience to a Thou."[48] Adam and Eve's knowing was an *acknowledgment* of God as superior in all things. Such a recognition produced piety and prosperity within the context of creation, covenant, and calling. Adam and Eve thrived within a virtuous cycle: knowledge of God produced compliance, and further compliance produced even deeper knowledge, as well as greater intimacy.[49]

---

48. Horton, *Covenant and Eschatology*, 143.

49. Frame makes a similar point: "Obedience is knowledge, and knowledge is obedience" (*The Doctrine of the Knowledge of God*, 43).

3

Exilic Epistemology

"The Devil seems to have contrived an instant, mass puppet show with real live creatures."

—Ernest Becker, *Escape from Evil*

The Garden of Eden was the nexus of divine presence, peace, and prosperity. All the conditions were in place for Adam and Eve to flourish: natural fecundity, intellectual development, and meaningful relationships within a secure and sacred environment. Adam and Eve were blessed in every way.

As God's vice-regents, they were appointed to care for, protect, and develop his property for the sake of his glory and the benefit of mankind. They were re-creators and developers of the potentialities inherent in creation. They were re-interpreters of his revelation. And they were given a mission to bring order, beauty, and productivity beyond the boundaries of the garden.

Indeed, Eden was the archetypical tabernacle where the first humans served God. They were the original worshipers, thinkers, builders, and producers. They lived *coram Deo* in obedience and thankfulness as the proper response to God's covenant in creation.

Their task included guarding God's domain against evil and impurity. As G. K. Beale wrote, "Adam was to be God's obedient servant in maintaining both the physical and the spiritual welfare of the garden abode, which included dutifully keeping evil influences from invading the arboreal sanctuary."[1] In this great obligation, sadly, he failed—with tragic results.

Genesis 3 explains how evil and disorder entered creation, and it foretells the remedy promised through Eve's "seed" (v. 15, KJV).[2] This chapter is a high-stakes drama, an archetypical tragedy, and a "riches to rags" story. There are four captivating characters, including two naive protagonists and one dreaded antagonist. The hero of the story is, of course, Yahweh Elohim. Genesis 4–11, however, depicts a very bad situation getting even worse as individual and corporate folly escalates east of Eden.

This chapter has three main sections. First, I present the characters in the drama: the serpent, Adam and Eve, Yahweh Elohim, and the tree. Second, I review the performance. Act one (Gen 3:1–5) is the climactic encounter between the serpent and Eve. Act two (3:6–7) concerns the woman's response to temptation. In act three (3:8–13), God confronts Adam and Eve after their disobedience.[3] The plot focuses on which voice Adam and Eve will heed and obey. The third section concerns the dramatic developments east of Eden and the exile of mankind from paradise. Here I focus on two paradigmatic stories: Cain and Babel.

CHARACTERS IN THE DRAMA

The Serpent

The serpent appeared abruptly as an interloper in Eden. He spoke, whereas presumably only Adam and Eve possessed advanced intelligence and self-consciousness. In fact, the serpent's dialogue with Eve revealed commanding intellectual acuity. This should have raised suspicions and motivated utmost caution.

Significantly, the snake referred to God only as Elohim in his transcendence as Creator. Neither he nor Eve referred to God as Yahweh Elohim in his covenantal immanence. John Collins writes, "By dropping the covenant name, then, the snake is probably advancing his program of temptation by diverting the woman's attention from the relationship the

---

1. Beale, *A New Testament Biblical Theology*, 32.
2. Genesis 3:15 is often called the "proto-Gospel."
3. I do not deal with act four concerning God's judgment (Gen 3:14–24) since it lies outside my focus.

Lord had established."[4] Similarly, Kenneth M. Craig observes, "If the tetragrammaton [the name Yahweh] denotes God's caring relationship with his people, the serpent's use of the bare term 'Elohim' sets a tone for what he hopes to convince the woman--that her Creator is *uncaring*."[5]

Indeed, the serpent had something up his sleeve. The text describes the intruder as "crafty" (*arum*).[6] The snake's cunning and sophistic aptitude served him well in his subterfuge with Eve. As the antagonist in the primal drama, he was a shrewd obstructionist and disruptor. His motives were clearly malevolent as he misrepresented the truth about God and his commandment. The serpent was the archetypical "smooth talker." He duped Eve and together they induced Adam to sin.

In the Old Testament, the descriptor "crafty" appears in both positive and negative contexts. Those who fear God and are "prudent" (also *arum*) conduct themselves "with knowledge" (Prov 13:16). But those who do not fear God assume an adversarial posture against him. They are "crafty" and reveal the "iniquity" of their hearts in their speech and conduct (Job 15:5). The "forbidden woman," for instance, seduces with "smooth words" (*arum*, Prov 2:16). A violent man "attacks another to kill him by cunning" (*arum*, Exod 21:14). God, however, entraps the worldly "wise" and "wily" in their "craftiness" (*arum*) and "schemes" (Job 5:13).

Further, there is a linguistic similarity between "snake" and "make divine" in Hebrew that may be linked to the serpent's unnatural capacity to speak.[7] A talking animal was out of place in Eden, just as was the only other animal that speaks in the Bible: Balaam's donkey (Num 22:28–30). That animal communicated by supernatural unction on the Lord's behalf against Balaam. The snake also articulated a supernatural agenda, but his motive was malicious. Indeed, the narrative suggests and the broader canon supports the idea that the snake represented Satan (Rev 20:2), advocating his interests in Eden as the antitype of God.[8]

---

4. Collins, "What Happened to Adam and Eve?" 28.

5. Craig, "Misspeaking in Eden," 240 (emphasis in original).

6. The term is "cunning" in the NKJV and "able to fool others" in the NLV. In Argentina, where I have lived for many years, the serpent would be called a *chanta*, or someone who deceives in order to hurt or defraud. In English, such a person would be a cheat, swindler, extortionist, con man or spoiler.

7. Smith, "The Divining Snake," 3–49; Chisholm, "'For This Reason': Etiology and its Implications," 43–46; Phillips, "Serpent Intertexts," 233–45.

8. Kline (*Kingdom Prologue*, 75) summarizes the serpent's diabolical agenda in Eden: "The object was, in effect, to degenerate and lay desolate the holy domain of God over which man had been set as royal-priest. Satan's strategy was to contrive to

Adam and Eve

The drama in Genesis 3 depicts the first couple at their antithetical worst. The narrative asks: To whom they should listen—God or the snake (3:17)? Sadly, in the face of the serpent's assault they were hapless and clueless. Eve was exquisitely gullible. Adam was feeble and negligent. Both were bewildered and culpably unknowing. Their fallibility was on display for the entire divine court to witness.[9]

From a literary point of view, Adam and Eve's demise was the prototypical tragedy. Leland Ryken provides the details: an initial problem, an erroneous decision based upon folly and disobedience, and the consequences of self-induced affliction, unwanted epiphany, and ultimately exile.[10] As a result, chapter 3 resonates with bitter irony as Adam and Eve experienced an inversion of the "rags to riches" story. The following list contrasts the drastic alterations that came about from Adam and Eve's sin—a true reversal of creation.[11]

Before	After
serve and guard the temple	disarray and turmoil east of Eden
two trees in paradise	thorns and thistles outside
abundance and productivity	sweat and frustration
contentment and shalom	dissatisfaction and discontent
security and well-being	anxiety and danger
stewardship of creation	exploitation, abuse, and excess
knowledge and wisdom	folly and illusion
homeland with God	expulsion and exile

The far-reaching changes unleashed by Adam and Eve brought about turmoil in every sphere of existence, because the motivation and mind were despoiled by sin. As we will see in later in this chapter, these realities became increasingly apparent in the developments recorded in Genesis 4–11. Seventeenth-century Czech reformer Jan Amos Komenský

---

activate the curse threatened in the covenant sanctions and so utilize the very power of God to accomplish the objective of reducing the cosmic sanctuary to chaotic ruin."

[9] The struggle between the snake and the humans was akin to a bout between Mike Tyson and Bart Simpson. If we are honest, we would fare no better, maybe worse.

10. Ryken, *Words of Delight*, 99.

11. See Stefanovic, "The Great Reversal," 47–56.

explained in vivid fashion what the reversal implied for Adam and Eve in everyday experience:

> For what is in relation to people as it ought to be? What stands in its proper place? Nothing. Everything is upside down, everything has gone wrong, for all the order, all the government, all the noble features are scattered . . . . Instead of unity, there are discords, quarrels, and rages, secret malice as well as open hostility, fights and wars. Instead of righteousness, there are injustice, robberies, thefts; everyone greedily amasses only for himself or herself. Instead of purity, there is lechery, both internal and external; there is adultery, infidelity, misconduct, and lewdness, both in the mind and in speech. Instead of truthfulness, there are lies and gossip everywhere. Instead of humbleness, there is arrogance and pride, and boasting; one rising against the other. Woe to you, miserable generation, how deeply you have sunk into wretchedness![12]

Yahweh Elohim

In chapter 3, God remained true to character, despite the trauma and intrigue. The sovereign and omniscient thinker knew the antagonist and was not surprised by his motives or tactics. He knew also that Adam, his vice-regent and priest, was supremely fallible. He realized that Adam would not guard his temple. He knew further that Adam would not pronounce judgment upon the serpent and evict him from the sanctuary.[13]

Furthermore, the same divine monarch Elohim, who brought creation into being by speech alone in chapters 1–2, interrogated the suspects Adam and Eve in chapter 3. God weighed the evidence, declared

---

12. Cited in Hábl, *Lessons in Humanity*, 58.

13. Genesis 3 is a grand enigma and quite complex. Yet we must acknowledge God's sovereignty as the divine philosopher, for what is incomprehensible and mysterious to us (because of our finitude and fallenness) is not so for God. In this case, Van Til provides healthy epistemological and theological guidance: "In believing the Bible and its teachings as they do, traditional believers humbly offer their interpretation of life in the name of God, whose mind and thoughts are higher than man's mind and thoughts . . . . They appeal to the Creator and Controller of the world as the One, who because of His creation and control of the world, does understand all things exhaustively. They admit mystery in all things for themselves but they do not admit the existence of mystery in anything for God. Accordingly, they do not pretend that they can reduce the relation of God to the world to a system that they themselves can exhaustively understand" (*The Intellectual Challenge*, 27).

judgment, and carried it out according to his covenant. The same architect as in chapters 1–2, who designed and built his temple, preserved its purity in chapter 3, for he cast the offenders out and placed a guard at the entrance. The same benefactor as in chapters 1–2, who created the divine milieu and placed the first couple within it, provided clothing for them after they sinned. The same philosopher as in chapters 1–2, who wisely planned everything with eternity in mind, instituted a rescue plan for fallen mankind and the corrupted creation through the "offspring" of Eve (3:15). And the same Yahweh Elohim who cared for Adam and Eve before their disobedience also cared from them after their rebellion. He walked in the garden afterwards, sought them out, and provided an opportunity for them to confess their sin.

The Tree[14]

The function of the tree of the knowledge of good and evil provokes a bevy of questions. Was the prohibition against eating of its fruit simply a test of obedience? (In this sense, the tree could have been a raspberry bush.) Or was the actual content of the knowledge something unique—perhaps an occult understanding or secret wisdom? Further, what kind of knowledge would make the first humans "like God," and how could the serpent offer access? Why was it important through whom they gained this knowledge (through God or the snake)?

First, one clear function of the tree was to verify Adam and Eve's fidelity through a test of obedience. As creatures made in God's image and as covenant partners, they were obliged to remain within the boundaries God established and to perform the tasks he assigned.

Second, the tree involved a positive injunction to exercise judgment over evil and impurity. Adam was commissioned to "keep" (*shamar*, "guard") the sanctuary. As Beale suggests, "The tree in Eden seems to have functioned as a judgment tree, the place where Adam should have gone to 'discern between good and evil' and, thus, where he should have judged the serpent as evil and pronounced judgment on it, as it entered the garden."[15] In fact, in the Old Testament trees were often places of judgment and sacred convocation (Judg 4:5; 1 Sam 14:2; 22:6–19).

---

14. The tree of the knowledge of good and evil is not a sentient being, obviously, but it plays a critical role as the one essential prop.

15. Beale, *A New Testament Biblical Theology*, 35.

Third, the expression "knowledge of good and evil" was linked to royal and priestly aspirations for wisdom in the exercise of judgment over iniquity and for effective leadership. Solomon prayed, for example, "Give your servant therefore an understanding mind to govern your people, that I may discern between good and evil, for who is able to govern this, your great people?" (1 Kgs 3:9). The question of the knowledge of good and evil was also a common motif in ancient Near Eastern literature. Knowledge, discernment, and wisdom were what royalty shared with divinity as those who alone bear its image.

Knowledge of this type, therefore, was practical and ethical, as we saw in Solomon's petition. Dru Johnson says, "To 'know good and evil' . . . is a particular way of knowing . . . what is good or evil for humans, what is useful or harmful."[16] In Adam's case, it entailed wisdom as God's apprentice economist and philosopher. It included an awareness of what prospers life and how to keep God's sanctuary holy. It involved knowing how to implement God's command to extend his sanctuary throughout the earth. This implied an understanding of how to order society and build culture according to the creation ordinances. It involved, as well, an awareness of what serves the best interests of God's house and how to establish shalom on earth.

Fourth, however, the chief purpose of the tree of knowledge of good and evil concerned listening (3:17). To whom would Adam and Eve submit as their authoritative guide to life and knowledge? To whom would they yield their minds as vice-regents? Would they accept or reject the serpent's alternative view of reality? Would they embrace true or false knowing? Who, after all, is the true philosopher-king: God or Satan?

THE PERFORMANCE

Act One

Genesis 3:1–5 states:

(1) Now the serpent was more crafty than any other beast of the field that the Lord God had made. He said to the woman, "Did God actually say, 'You shall not eat of any tree in the garden'?"

---

16. In this regard, Johnson cites Claus Westermann in *Biblical Knowing*, 50.

(2) And the woman said to the serpent, "We may eat of the fruit of the trees in the garden:

(3) but God said, 'You shall not eat of the fruit of the tree that is in the midst of the garden, neither shall you touch it, lest you die.'"

(4) But the serpent said to the woman, "You will not surely die.

(5) For God knows that when you eat of it your eyes will be opened, and you will be like God, knowing good and evil."

In the whole history of recorded thought, this small phrase uttered by the serpent, "Did God actually say . . . ?" is surely the most consequential. Though the snake positioned himself as a bearer of good news, hidden within this seemingly innocent query was a Pandora's box full of blasphemous errors and destructive evil. "Did God *actually* say" conveys a host of assumptions motivated by envy, mutiny, and cynicism, attitudes plainly associated with sin. The audacity and titanic arrogance implicit in this question are difficult to imagine.

With this question, the snake got his proverbial foot in the door within Adam and Eve's imagination and motives. He sowed just enough doubt and confusion to raise the possibility that God could and should be questioned. The snake insinuated that humans can and should assume epistemological autonomy for the sake of truth and knowledge. In fact, he implied that it was their moral obligation to adopt a posture of supposed neutrality over against God, as if they were not covenant servants. The serpent insinuated that the Creator's perspective was skewed and in dire need of correction. Subtly, he positioned Adam and Eve to adjudicate between himself and Yahweh Elohim. He asked them to heed his words instead of God's.

Compare what God said to Adam and the serpent's distortion of God's words so that he could induce the first couple to breach the covenant (from the NKJV):

God said	And the Lord God commanded the man, saying, "Of every tree of the garden you may freely eat" (2:16).
	"But of the tree of the knowledge of good and evil you shall not eat, for in the day that you eat of it you shall surely die" (2:17).
The serpent said	And he said to the woman, "Has God indeed said, 'You shall not eat of every tree of the garden'?" (3:1).

Craig points out three ways in which the snake misrepresented God and attempted to re-situate Adam and Eve.[17] First, the serpent diminished God's bounty as the divine economist. He did not mention that they could "freely" eat of "*every* tree" (while abstaining *only* from the tree of the knowledge of good and evil). He depicted Yahweh Elohim as a stingy and negligent benefactor. Second, the serpent altered the verbs of God's speech from "commanded" to "say," thus reducing its imperatival force. Third, he did not name, conveniently, the "tree of the knowledge of good and evil" but only "every tree." Craig summarizes the serpent's motives and tactics: "The serpent's interrogative begins a process of moving the woman from answering the elusive question, to doubting God's truthfulness, to desiring the forbidden fruit, to ultimately desiring to be God-like, knowing good and evil."[18]

The serpent's approach focused upon Eve and he spoke with her directly. She was engaged intellectually, whereas Adam was seemingly passive. Her answer to the serpent's question revealed that the skepticism he proposed was effective. Contrast what God said (and what Eve reported) against what the snake asserted:

God said	"But of the tree of the knowledge of good and evil you shall not eat" (2:17a).
Eve said	"You shall not eat of the fruit of the tree that is in the midst of the garden" (3:3a).
God said	"For in the day that you eat of it you shall surely die" (2:17b).
Eve said	"Neither shall you touch it: lest you die" (3:3b).
The serpent said	"You will not surely die"(3:4).

The differences between God's words in 2:17a and Eve's reporting in 3:3b are significant. In English, the word "lest" refers to a condition that is possible but not (yet) actual. "Lest" can signify "so as to prevent the possibility of." In the Old Testament, where the Hebrew phrase "lest you die" appears (about 129 times), the implication is possibility but not certainty. The Hebrew term for "lest" (*pen*) is rendered, for instance, as "otherwise," "might," "be careful not to," "or else," "would," or "perhaps."

"Surely," on the other hand, conveys certainty and irrevocability (about fifty-two times). It often appears in association with covenantal

---

17. Craig, "Misspeaking in Eden," 238–41.
18. Craig, "Misspeaking in Eden," 241.

or ritual violations and is rendered as "surely die" or "surely be put to death." Adam and Eve had soiled the edenic sanctuary by permitting the usurper to enter and thereafter abetted his agenda. They merited death for covenant infringement and desecration of the temple.[19] It seems, on one hand, that Eve sought, albeit meekly, to defend God and correct the serpent, but she assumed great liberty to re-fashion God's word by toning down the severity of his intended judgment. In effect, she overruled God. On the other hand, the serpent's rhetoric ("surely") inferred that his word was unquestionable, whereas God's speech ("lest") was conditional. Clearly, God's verdict on the couple was justified (3:16–19), as the snake had, *de facto*, already won the battle rhetorically.

The snake urged Eve to hesitate no more and to embrace impunity and serpent-like, epistemic neutrality. He soothed her fears of retribution and gave her permission to eat and violate God's covenant. R. L. W. Moberly summarizes the serpent's strategy: "It is noteworthy that the serpent never tells the woman to transgress God's prohibition. He simply calls into question both God's truthfulness (by denying his warning) and trustworthiness (by impugning his motives), and leaves the woman to draw her own conclusions."[20]

In fact, the declaration "You will not surely die" was also a blatant contradiction of God's words in 2:17. In effect, the serpent accused God of lying. He claimed that Yahweh Elohim was holding back his greatest blessing, specifically a kind of knowing that would make them "like God." The snake implied that he possessed this knowledge and could provide it or that God unjustly controlled access to it.

Moreover, by utilizing the language from 1:26–28 of image and likeness ("like God"), the snake urged Adam and Eve to re-imagine themselves apart from their creational situatedness. The serpent redefined them within his worldview by stripping the concept of image from its covenantal setting. He re-interpreted Adam and Eve apart from the Creator–creature distinction. He inspired them to align themselves with the serpent as the *imago Satanas* rather than the *imago Dei*.

Eve (and soon thereafter Adam) redirected a God-inspired aspiration to image the Creator as creatures.[21] Because she listened to the serpent, she pursued God-likeness independently. She exchanged analogical

---

19. Concerning the meaning of "die" in the passage, see Collins, "What Happened to Adam and Eve?" 22–23; Whybray, "The Immorality of God," 91–93.

20. Moberly, "Did the Interpreters Get It Right?" 24.

21. This insight was contributed by Jeffrey Foster.

imagining for ontological ascent. In other words, Eve enrolled in the devil's school of reality and he became her guide. The serpent's concept of divine likeness, though, was actually quasi-divinity.[22] He proposed for Adam and Eve supernatural power, divine status, and spiritual discernment that obviated the difference between the Creator and creation.

The serpent cited two illicit reasons why God was prohibiting them from eating of this tree and preventing them from becoming "like God": their "eyes will be opened" and they would know "good and evil." Throughout the Old and New Testaments, the idiom "eyes ... opened" is associated with and initiated by God or Christ. To open eyes is a supernatural capacity that reveals divine provision (Gen 21:19), enables vision of angelic beings (Num 22:31; 2 Kgs 6:17), and provides prophetic insight (John 9:10). In Isaiah, the expression refers to insight concerning the future restoration of paradise and a renewed knowledge of God: "Then the eyes of the blind shall be opened, and the ears of the deaf unstopped" (35:5). In Genesis 3, on the other hand, the serpent urged Eve (a mere human) to assume the initiative and acquire the insight unfairly withheld from her.

The expression "knowledge of good and evil" was understood as wise judgment and leadership. For Adam and Eve, this meant an awareness of what prospers life and cultural formation according to divine law. As the *imago Satanas*, however, Adam's future ruling, building, benefaction, and especially his thinking as vice-regent would become skewed by the serpent's twisted worldview and perverted interpretation of facts. To this end, the "knowledge" they acquired advanced the snake's agenda on earth.

Having accepted the serpent's argument, Eve thought that "the tree was to be desired to make one wise." As we learned in chapter 1, however, God alone is the source of wisdom. He knows what is important and how to achieve it. He is the sovereign writer and his drama never wavers from its plot (creation, fall into sin, redemption, and restoration). The "wisdom" that Eve obtained, on the other hand, was the devil's ungodly scheme for fallen humanity and its curse-filled milieu.

In summary, the serpent presumed an epistemological stance against and outside God's domain. He assumed a skeptical position to evaluate God's command for Adam and Eve. He presupposed, seemingly, an external criterion of truth to which both he and God were

---

22. See the discussion about "enlightening the eyes" in Clines, "The Tree of Knowledge," 11.

accountable. From this position, he proffered a critical assessment of God's motives and goodness—indeed, his grasp of reality. His question to Eve presupposed that God was malfeasant. The benevolent serpent, on the other hand, was promising to set the record straight for their own good.[23] He invited them to embrace his twisted mentality, motivation, and mannerisms.

Act Two

Let us read verses 6 and 7:

(6) So when the woman saw that the tree was good for food, and that it was a delight to the eyes, and that the tree was to be desired to make one wise, she took of its fruit and ate, and she also gave some to her husband who was with her, and he ate.

(7) Then the eyes of both were opened, and they knew that they were naked. And they sewed fig leaves together and made themselves loincloths.

Adam is the drama's great enigma. He "was with her" when they interacted with the serpent and partook of the forbidden tree. What he actually thought, however, is unknown. Judith Faith Parker asks, "If Adam is there and knows that disobedience is imminent, why does he not say or do something to intervene?"[24] He was, perhaps, a doubting Thomas. Presumably, he had named the snake earlier, so was he surprised that it now communicated? Or was it a creature unknown beforehand? Certainly, the cunning snake knew that the final determination was Adam's, but he apparently discerned that Eve was the path of least resistance. He determined that a direct confrontation with Adam might provoke a spirited defense of God that would negatively influence Eve.

---

23. The serpent's question raises several inquiries. Did the snake know that the death penalty was two-dimensional — spiritual death through exile and physical death thereafter? Was his goal merely to create a two-act drama (creation and fall into sin)? Did he envision acts three and four — redemption and restoration? Did he anticipate the promise of salvation through Eve's "offspring"? (Definitely not, for it seems the snake was not aware of what God "had up his sleeve." Similarly, the devil could not imagine the "secret and hidden wisdom" of God in Christ, nor the coming restoration of creation. See 1 Cor 2:7–9.)

24. Parker, "Blaming Eve Alone," 732.

Furthermore, there is a significant thematic link between verse 6 and the Tenth Commandment (Deut 5:21). Coveting is a process that begins with a perception of delight, leading to an inner longing to possess, and then resulting in action to obtain an illicit goal. The pattern utilizes the vocabulary of seeing, desiring, and acting. In Genesis 3, Eve was motivated by the serpent's salacious vision of the illicit tree. She "saw" that it was "good for food," a "delight to the eyes," and "desirable to make one wise," and therefore she "took" and "ate." Elsewhere in the Old Testament, Achan coveted riches banned by God: "I *saw* among the spoil a beautiful mantle from Shinar . . . then I *coveted* them, and *took* them" (Joshua 7:21). Likewise, David coveted Bathsheba after "he *saw* from the roof a woman bathing; and the woman was very beautiful. . . . David sent messengers and *took* her" (2 Sam 11:2b–4).

Similarly, Eve coveted knowledge through epiphany and transformation. On one hand, she rightfully desired to image the Creator, but then she did so incorrectly by listening to the wrong voice and embracing his method. On the other hand, under the snake's guidance, Eve desired greater divine insight and deeper ontological likeness. As Richard Hess put it, "The motivation was to know as God knows, to possess divine wisdom and to seize God's gifts and use them in whatever way the man and the woman wanted."[25] Adam and Eve coveted illicit knowledge from an unlawful source and used illegitimate means to get it. As a result, all they discovered was their absolute nakedness and culpability before their Creator and Lord. They did not become wiser or more God-like—just the opposite.

Johnson explains how coveting illegitimate knowledge was expressed through the verbs in the drama: "She *listens* to the serpent. Because she listened, she *saw* the fruit, she *desired* wisdom, she *took*, she *ate*, and she *gave*."[26] Clearly, before Eve did anything, the serpent captured her imagination and motivation.[27] Johnson comments further about grasping illicit

---

25. Hess, "The Roles of the Woman and the Man," 17.

26. Johnson, *Biblical Knowing*, 56 (emphasis in original). Interestingly, according to Johnson, this pattern appears two other times in Genesis using the verbal phrases "listen to the voice . . . took . . . gave . . . to her husband." In the case of Sarai, for instance, the coveted prize was progeny through surrogacy: "And Abram *listened to the voice* of Sarai . . . Sarai, Abram's wife, *took* Hagar the Egyptian, her servant, and *gave her to* Abram her husband as a wife" (Gen 16:2–3). For the second occurrence, see Genesis 27:8–9, 13, 43).

27. Johnson (*Epistemology and Biblical Theology*, 37–38) proposed this motivation: "She does shift her trust in what we can only assume is a blind hope for knowing

knowledge: "Judging by their surprise, the man and woman of Genesis 3 appear to believe that they would *know about* good and evil as a matter external to them rather than *know* good and evil subject to a fiduciary binding relationship [covenant] with their new knowledge."[28]

Johnson also points out the epistemic importance of the verb "see" (*raah*) in Genesis 1–3. In the first seven occurrences, Elohim is the subject of the phrase "saw that it was good [*tob*)]" (1:4, 10, 12, 18, 21, 25, 31). In the narrative, the verb indicates that God evaluated the days of creation according to his criteria. As interpreters of revelation, Adam and Eve should have evaluated the two trees according to God's norms, not by their sensory appeal or intellectual utility. Obviously, they were not supposed to consider a third-party assessment from the serpent either. Johnson explains the epistemological import: "This hope of knowing apart from obeying Yahweh Elohim shows that they took the interpretation of the serpent as authoritative, which reveals that the problem was their epistemological disparity with Yahweh Elohim."[29] In other words, they refused to "think God's thoughts after him" and instead embraced the distorted epistemology of the snake.

Finally, verse 7 shows that Adam and Eve's change of status was deeply personal. Before the catastrophe, they "were both naked and were not ashamed" (2:25). Afterwards, Adam declared, "I was afraid, because I was naked, and I hid myself" (3:10). Because they listened to the snake, they were now afraid of Yahweh Elohim.

Literally, nakedness refers to nudity. Adam and Eve were not clothed until after they sinned. A second meaning entails vulnerability, but in a positive sense. In themselves, they were dependent and powerless. They were totally helpless, but safe with God. They were poor, but bountifully cared for. They had "nothing, yet possessing everything" (2 Cor 6:10). Their bounty derived from covenantal calling and divine blessing, truly by grace alone. Thus, their posture before Yahweh Elohim evidenced humility and hopeful expectancy, as the psalmist wrote: "Behold, as the eyes of servants look to the hand of their master, as the eyes of a maidservant to the hand of her mistress, so our eyes look to the Lord our God, till he has mercy upon us" (123:2).

---

something in the future that is better than her present knowledge. In this sense, Genesis portrays her error as ambition, an eschatological hope of knowledge that is more or different than it has been, both of which are ironically achieved."

28. Johnson, *Epistemology and Biblical Theology*, 67 (emphasis in original).

29. Johnson, *Epistemology and Biblical Theology*, 58.

But when they listened to the snake, they became co-conspirators with the drama's antagonist, the diabolical anti-god. Adam and Eve's covenantal disobedience resulted in a third type of nakedness that testifies to an unwanted change of status due to divine judgment.[30] Nakedness in this sense signifies alienation from God, one another, and creation. After they rebelled, for instance, controversy marred Adam and Eve's marriage bond. God's "helper fit for" Adam became a competitor or pawn and Adam became a tyrant. Their fruitful relationship with creation was forever altered. They became truly defenseless and vulnerable, powerless (naked) before fallen creation, sinful humanity, and the evil lord.

Nakedness in each of these dimensions is reflected throughout the Old Testament, but particularly in a fourth sense, spiritual apostasy (idolatry). Nakedness of this kind refers to powerlessness and vanity "under the sun" (Eccl 1:9) or in this "present evil age" (Gal 1:4). It signifies the antithesis of Eden in every sense: economic and social impoverishment, spiritual exile, erroneous thought, and dysfunctional identity. It entails "lacking everything" (Deut 28:48) or being "naked and barefoot" (Isa 20:4), "stripped and naked" (Mic 1:8), and viewed "in nakedness and shame" (1:11), including "disgrace" (Isa 47:3) and "lewdness" (Ezek 23:29). Nakedness is expressed as spiritual "adultery" (Hos 2:3) or "prostitution" (Mic 1:7). Israel, for instance, "played the whore with the nations and defiled [itself] with their idols" (Ezek 23:30). In response to their "nakedness" (Ezek 16:8), God often gave them over to even more sin and shame for all to see (v. 37).[31]

Act Three

We now turn to Genesis 3:8–13, 17:

(8) They heard the sound of the Lord God walking in the garden in the cool of the day and the man and his wife hid themselves from the presence of the Lord God among the trees of the garden.

(9) Then the Lord God called to the man, and said to him, "Where are you?"

---

30. See Deuteronomy 28.

31. In the future, mankind's intellectual acuity will become focused on mitigating the pervasive impacts of spiritual nakedness. See Becker, *Escape from Evil* and *The Denial of Death*; Jacob, *Original Sin*; and Plantinga, *Not the Way It's Supposed to Be*.

(10) He said, "I heard the sound of You in the garden, and I was afraid because I was naked; so I hid myself."

(11) And He said, "Who told you that you were naked? Have you eaten from the tree of which I commanded you not to eat?"

(12) The man said, "The woman whom You gave *to be* with me, she gave me from the tree, and I ate."

(13) Then the Lord God said to the woman, "What is this you have done?" And the woman said, "The serpent deceived me, and I ate."

(17) And to Adam he said, "Because you have listened to the voice of your wife and have eaten of the tree of which I commanded you, 'You shall not eat of it,' cursed is the ground because of you; in pain you shall eat of it all the days of your life."

First, note the four questions posed by Yahweh Elohim: "Where are you?" (3:9), "Who told you that you were naked?" (v. 11), "Have you eaten of the tree of which I commanded you not to eat?" (v. 11), and "What is this that you have done?" (v. 13).[32] As both prosecutor and judge, God initiated a covenantal interrogation of Adam and Eve. His cross-examination aimed to clarify the facts and expose the truth, whereas the serpent's question to Eve was designed to confuse and obscure reality (v. 2). And while the snake implicated Eve as judge between himself and the Creator, God adjudicated the case on his own behalf in verses 9–24.

We will focus here on just two of the four questions. The first, "Where are you?" was not motivated by divine ignorance regarding Adam and Eve's whereabouts. Rather, it exposed their curious absence and induced confession. This was clear from Adam's response, "I was afraid because I was naked; so I hid myself."[33] Likewise, though God addressed the man directly, Adam's response did not express covenantal or familial affinity. Instead, his answers were self-exculpatory and self-referential. Rather than speaking with Eve or on her behalf, he said, "I heard," "I was afraid," "I was naked," and "I hid myself" (v. 10). Also, in verse 12, he referred to

---

32. For further details, see Craig, "Misspeaking in Eden."

33. Kline comments, "Their hiding from God under the covering of the trees, like their hiding under the covering of leaves, pointed to a sense of shameful nakedness, in this case a spiritual nakedness which they felt before God's eyes" (*Kingdom Prologue*, 81).

Eve as "the woman you gave to be with me," adding, "she gave me," and "I ate."[34]

The second question, "Who told you that you were naked?" is crucial, for this is the issue that drives the plot forward. This inquiry did not concern their reasoning process, deductive or inductive. God did not ask how Adam and Eve recognized their sense of culpability and shame. Rather, his question concerned the source of this knowledge, specifically *from whom* they acquired the new, negative evaluation of themselves. Johnson explains, "God presumes that someone else was involved; that a different voice had been heeded."[35] This observation is confirmed in verse 17, in which God expressed his diagnosis of the covenantal infraction. Adam listened to Eve, who listened to the serpent, who was the antithesis of Yahweh Elohim.

Second, in verse 13 Eve lamented that the snake "deceived" her. This, of course, was his intent, the fruit of craftiness. His aim was entrapment and enslavement, motivated by envy and hubris. Eve became his first victim, followed by her partner in crime, Adam. Their deception testified to the serpent's sophistic capacity as Eden's obstructionist. He did not embrace the truth and refused to think God's thoughts after him. Nor did he reason analogically with the psalmist, "In *your* light do we see light" (36:9b). For all this—deception, blasphemy, epistemic autonomy, and rebellion—God cursed the serpent (v. 14a).

Third, the serpent's contagion terminally infected the couple's motivations and mindset, as evidenced in their answers to God's questions. Unlike the saints who followed them, Adam and Eve did not react to God's call in the garden with submission and humility. Abraham (Gen 22:1), Jacob (31:11), Moses (Exod 3:4), Samuel (1 Sam 3:4), Isaiah (Isa 6:8), and Ananias (Acts 9:10) all declared when God summoned them,

---

34. Eve is frequently depicted very negatively, but it seems that she interacted with God in a more circumspect manner than Adam. Craig ("Misspeaking in Eden," 246) cites Trible's nuanced evaluation of Eve's reaction to God's interrogation. She writes, "First, she does not blame God. She does not say, for example, 'The serpent whom you made to dwell in the garden with me' (cf. 3:1). Second, she does not implicate her companion, for weal or for woe. She speaks only for and about herself. 'The serpent beguiled me' (not 'us') . . . . Third, the woman's answer differs in its reference to the serpent as the tempter who deceived, beguiled, and seduced . . . . Fourth, the woman confesses more quickly than did the man. After two words, which blame the serpent, she accepts responsibility, 'and-I-ate.'" For a history of mistranslation of the phrase "her husband who was with her," see Parker, "Blaming Eve Alone."

35. Johnson, *Biblical Knowing*, 60.

"Here I am."[36] Instead, the first couple expressed the wily outlook of the serpent: obfuscation, diversion, and blame shifting. The trail of culpability started with Adam, who faulted Eve, and then moved to Eve, who blamed the snake. Most audaciously—and clearly resembling the mentality and tactics of the serpent—Adam blamed God for their predicament. Kline provides a useful summary of the scene:

> That love of the truth which is part of the spiritual glory of the *imago Dei* is nowhere to be seen in the defensive retorts of Adam and Eve. The tempter's counsel had been urged and adopted in the name of advancing knowledge, but the consequence of the man's disobedience of the word of God was an obscurant suppression of the truth. Finding it impossible to hide their persons from God's Presence and being constrained to submit to a process of judicial interrogation, they still persisted in their attempt to thwart the discovery of the truth. To hide the facts about their apostasy, they resorted to evasion, distortion, and deception, the tactics of the tortuous serpent.[37]

Verse 17a, however, explains how and why the error occurred from God's point of view: "because you have listened to the voice of your wife." Eve sinned because she transferred her trust from God and Adam to the serpent. Adam erred because he yielded to Eve's counsel and did not defend God's name. By embracing the serpent's twisted worldview, Adam failed to protect God's domain or his wife. He failed to represent God as his vice-regent on earth. He did not discern the serpent's ploy and fell prey to his guile. He chose false knowing (fake news!) at the expense of truth. He did not judge the serpent at the "tree of the knowledge of good and evil." Adam was not wise.

As for the serpent, he contradicted God's command and implied that God was lying and unconcerned with their welfare. Mark E. Biddle comments, "The serpent insinuated that God who created them, who had planted the rich and luxuriant Garden to provide for them, and who

---

36. Horton calls this heartfelt expression "covenant epistemology." He writes, "Like the bare hands lifted in worship (the palms, dirtiest part of the body, held up before God in recognition of both one's creatureliness as well as sinfulness), this response is the epitome of an appropriate Creator–creature relationship" (*Covenant and Eschatology*, 134).

37. Kline, *Kingdom Prologue*, 81.

walked with them daily had intentionally and deceptively withheld from them the best gift of all."[38] Thus, the snake impugned God's character.

By listening to the snake, therefore, Adam and Eve adopted his accusatory stance and his anti-theocentric assumptions. They behaved as if God was incompetent or ignorant. Seemingly, they reasoned that the threat of death for disobedience was unfounded. Or maybe God was arbitrary by nature. Or perhaps Yahweh Elohim was simply wrong or out of his league.

Summary

Knowledge—what we think and how we learn—is intimately woven into the creation narrative. Johnson says, "In Genesis 2–3 we have two juxtaposed stories describing epistemological process, one that ends in knowledge and one that ends in error."[39] On one hand, Adam discovered his mate under God's tutelage. But as the text transitions into chapter 3, the central issue concerns whom Adam and Eve will accept as their authoritative guide to knowledge. The answer to that question drives the storyline and explains the difference between true and false knowing, between loving God with the mind and embracing folly under the serpent's guidance.

The crafty serpent seduced Adam and Eve by proposing a different, antitheistic theory of reality and knowledge.[40] He said, in effect, "Pay no attention to the issue of ontology. Disregard the Creator–creature distinction. You must decide the question of how you know (epistemology) without regard to the question of what is real (ontology)." As a result, Adam and Eve rejected in theory and practice the stipulations of their covenantal relation to God. In fact, the snake insinuated that by eating the forbidden fruit Eve would discover that creation is completely transparent and understandable. She would discover that reality is completely perspicuous. The same interpretive procedures apply equally to God and humans.

In this way, Adam and Eve pursued a paradigmatic fool's errand. They declared their aspiration to become "like God," but in this way failed

---

38. Johnson, *Biblical Knowing*, 57, citing Biddle in *Missing the Mark*, 12–13.

39. Johnson, *Biblical Knowing*, 47.

40. This section is adapted from my doctoral dissertation, "The Supremacy of God in Apologetics," 149–51.

to honor God "as God" (Rom 1:21). By heeding the serpent, they asserted their own ultimacy in religion, knowledge, and ethics. They set themselves up as the final arbiters of truth, the judges of good and evil, and the ultimate interpreters of reality. In effect, they proclaimed that they were not merely subordinate creatures, nor were they covenant breakers. They presumed that God is not absolute and denied his aseity.

Moreover, by coveting hidden knowledge Adam and Eve grasped the right to redefine themselves, to claim royal autonomy for and over themselves. They became self-referential, though they were infinitely unqualified for this task. This was the case, as well, with their vice-regency, for Adam and Eve, and their progeny, took upon themselves the authority to reidentify everything over which they were stewards. The tragic history recorded in Genesis 4–11 bears this out.

EAST OF EDEN

Genesis 4–11 depicts the growing degeneration of the human race. The narrative describes the error and folly unleashed by heeding the serpent's cynical query, "Did God actually say?" Adam and Eve's experiment with self-directed listening altered their outlook irrevocably. Covenantal violation and self-deification produced a cornucopia of sinfulness. Inexorably, their descendants assumed the mentality, mannerisms, and motivation of the snake.

Since the fall, quite obviously, human beings have continued to use their minds, but quite often in destructive and foolish ways. Mankind continues to worship, but with self-directed and utilitarian motives. Humans continue to work and guard creation, but inconsistently and unjustly. People continue to subdue and rule the world, but often with malicious purposes. Because human beings are created as the image of God, they carry on as vice-regent rulers, architects, economists, and philosophers, but their stewardship is inconsistent and ill-conceived at best.

Cain

The first fratricide testifies to the skewed mentality of the human race after the fall into sin. Abel's demise is described in Genesis 4:4, 5, and 8:

(4) In the course of time Cain brought to the Lord an offering of the fruit of the ground, and Abel also brought of the firstborn of his flock and of their fat portions. And the Lord had regard for Abel and his offering,

(5) but for Cain and his offering he had no regard. So Cain was very angry, and his face fell.

(8) Cain spoke to Abel his brother. And when they were in the field, Cain rose up against his brother Abel and killed him.

The broader context (4:3–16) reveals similarities to God's previous interrogation of Adam and Eve. God cross-examined Cain as he had done with Adam and Eve, posing four questions: "Why are you angry?" and "Why has your face fallen?" (v. 7), "Where is Abel your brother?" (v. 9), and "What have you done?" (v. 10).[41] Like the first couple, Cain was cast away "from the presence of the Lord" and forced into exile "east of Eden" (vv. 14, 16). Cain worked the "ground" (v. 12), yet the earth failed to produce according to its full potential ("strength") due to divine curse (v. 12).

As with Adam, God's interrogation of Cain revealed his inner motivation and mindset due to sin (4:5–7). Cain experienced nakedness before God and fallen creation, like Adam and Eve. Since he was made in God's image, he also attempted to worship, though his motivation was tainted by his parents' sin (vv. 3–7). Likewise, in the midst of wrath God mitigated Cain's fate with mercy, giving him a "mark" of protection (v. 15), just as God provided "garments" for Adam and Eve.

Yet the passage also reveals differences from Adam and Eve's encounter with God. Cain's expulsion from the garden was spatially and existentially more distant, as he became a "fugitive" and "wanderer" in the earth (4:12, 16). Cain's nakedness was greater due to the potential for hostility against him (v. 14). Unlike Adam's sin, Cain's expressed itself as a destructive social reality, for his envy produced violence (v. 8). In Cain, the self-deification that began with Adam morphed into self-absorption and petulance (vv. 13–14). His rhetoric was more audacious, for he replied to God's question ("Where is Abel your brother?") with the obscurant retort, "I do not know; am I my brother's keeper?" (v. 9). Cain was more flippant, sardonic, and indifferent. The Lord urged Cain to "do

---

41. See Craig, "Questions Outside Eden," 107–28.

well" and resist sin; instead, he invested his mental energy into plotting his brother's death and hurling his furtive apologetic at God.

Further, the narrative reveals that Cain failed as a wise and benevolent steward. In Genesis 2:15 God commissioned Adam to "keep" (*shamar*) the garden. As we saw earlier, *shamar* means to guard, protect from evil, and care for. Cain chose, instead, to attack his brother. He did not protect Abel from evil; rather, he murdered him. He denied Abel his most basic human right—his life. As a result, as Kristen M. Swenson suggests, "Instead of being settled in repose (*nuach*) on the land whose care and keeping first defined the human being's (*adam*) life, Cain will be unsettled and frustrated in his relation to the land (*adamah*), because he failed to extend the task of guarding the welfare of his brother."[42]

Second, Cain demonstrated that coveting was once again associated with Adam's fall. Scholars have noted an intriguing connection between the name Cain (*Qayin*) and the Hebrew verb "I have gained" (*qanah*), along with similar Hebrew terms of acquisition and wealth. An inherent covetousness could thus be associated with Cain's nature.[43] Radiša Antic suggests, "The mentality of 'possessing,' 'acquiring,' and 'getting' adequately expresses the character of Cain, as well as his actions, in Gen 4."[44] She adds, "Cain *possessed* or *acquired* his own conception of how God should be worshipped and served."[45] As both the etymology and the passage suggest, Cain possessed a mind enslaved to greed and envy. He was covetous to the core. Hence, for Cain worship was entirely self-directed.

In fact, this negative assessment of Cain appears within ancient Jewish literature. He was viewed as the personification of wickedness, the antitype of righteous Abel. John Byron writes that Cain was an "archetype for those who oppress the poor and the righteous for self-gain" and "came to represent all that was reprehensible about humanity."[46] Josephus viewed him as "wholly wicked and only looking for gain." Philo taught that "Cain is the ultimate narcissist" and his "partisans are those in society who are rich [and] live a life of luxury."[47] Other Jewish writers asserted that Cain desired to "possess the whole earth" and that his lust for gain

---

42. Swenson, "Care and Keeping," 382.
43. See Wenham, *Genesis*, 101.
44. Antic, "Cain, Abel, Seth," 204.
45. Antic, "Cain, Abel, Seth," 204 (emphasis in original).
46. Byron, "Living in the Shadow of Cain," 263, 265.
47. Byron, "Living in the Shadow of Cain," 265–66.

"motivated him to kill Abel."[48] Jude 11 speaks about the "way of Cain" in a negative context. First John 3:12 declares that he "belongs to the evil one." Indeed, Genesis 4 depicts Cain as a foil, an intellectual and economic exemplar *not* to be replicated (vv. 11–18).

Further, Cain was the first to shed blood over religion and to erect an apostate city inextricably linked with his violent and idolatrous lineage (4:17). His indignant rejoinder about his offering shows that he viewed God and religion in an instrumental manner. He lied to God about the location of his brother's body. He whimpered and groveled about his punishment.[49] Cain was the prototypical, post-fall narcissist, unable *not* to sin, who misapplied his mind to deepen the reversal initiated by his father. As he began to implement the divine commission (1:26–28), he did so as the serpent's steward, the *imago Satanas*.

Finally, Genesis 4 depicts Cain in close parallel to his parents, who listened to the counsel of the snake rather than God. He embraced the serpent's noxious worldview, embodied in erroneous thought and conduct. Antic describes his epistemological covetousness: "Cain *possessed* a new worldview that is radically opposed to God, and by using his sinful mind he *acquired* an understanding that he could be a law to himself."[50] In this way, he resembled his mother, who craved "wisdom," even as he honed his mind in greater diabolic craftiness.

The Tower of Babel

The Tower of Babel (Genesis 11:1–9) manifests the post-Eden intellectual, cultural, economic, and religious trajectory of mankind:

(1) Now the whole earth had one language and the same words.

(2) And as people migrated from the east, they found a plain in the land of Shinar and settled there.

(3) And they said to one another, "Come, let us make bricks, and burn them thoroughly." And they had brick for stone, and bitumen for mortar.

---

48. Byron, "Living in the Shadow of Cain," 267.

49. Ironically, the assassin's lament focused upon the likelihood of his own assassination (v. 14).

50. Antic, "Cain, Abel, Seth," 205 (emphasis in original).

(4) Then they said, "Come, let us build ourselves a city and a tower with its top in the heavens, and let us make a name for ourselves, lest we be dispersed over the face of the whole earth."

(5) And the Lord came down to see the city and the tower, which the children of man had built.

(6) And the Lord said, "Behold, they are one people, and they have all one language, and this is only the beginning of what they will do. And nothing that they propose to do will now be impossible for them.

(7) Come, let us go down and there confuse their language, so that they may not understand one another's speech."

(8) So the Lord dispersed them from there over the face of all the earth, and they left off building the city.

(9) Therefore its name was called Babel, because there the Lord confused the language of all the earth. And from there the Lord dispersed them over the face of all the earth.

Three times God addressed the divine court concerning the status of human beings using the first-person plural pronoun (Gen 1:26; 3:22–23; 11:6–7). Each occurrence stressed the Creator–creature distinction. In Genesis, 1:26 God said, "Let us make man in our image, after our likeness." Adam and Eve were his vice-regents, created in his image as representatives equipped to mirror his character and capacities. They were not ontological clones, but finite and fallible covenant servants. In Genesis 3:22–23, there was an ominous and negative tone, however, due to covenant violation: "Then the Lord God said, 'Behold, the man has become like one of us in knowing good and evil. Now, lest he reach out his hand and take also of the tree of life and eat, and live forever—' therefore the Lord God sent him out from the Garden of Eden." Because of their conspiracy with the serpent, God prevented Adam and Eve from gaining immortality and ascending the ontological ladder in their sinful condition. Again, the issue concerned the distinction between God and mankind.

Genesis 11:6–7 is the third occurrence. The throng at Babel declared among themselves their titanic objective: "Come, let us build ourselves a city and a tower with its top in the heavens, and let us make a name for ourselves, lest we be dispersed over the face of the whole earth" (11:1–2,

4–5).⁵¹ God intervened, stating, "Behold, they are one people, and they have all one language, and this is only the beginning of what they will do. And nothing that they propose to do will now be impossible for them. Come, let us go down and there confuse their language, so that they may not understand one another's speech." As before, God acted against human aspirations for divine ascent and, in this case, a return to paradise on apostate criteria. He implemented a separation between heaven and earth through the dispersal and disruption of communication. But in Babel the threat was worse, for humanity acted systemically as one against God's will.

Indeed, the Tower was the primeval climax of collective human pride and folly, a religious ideology of empire. The attempt to "make a name for ourselves" and avoid dispersal was an act of rebellion and redefinition. Dexter E. Callender observes, "The combination of the city, tower, the unity of humanity, and their single tongue points to the issue of human progress . . . the secrets of the universe could belong to humanity and they can 'be like God.'"⁵² In other words, Babel was the man-centered antithesis of the garden economy. It was the first civilization-wide attempt to recreate the edenic nexus of presence, peace, and prosperity on post-fall assumptions, contrary to God's purpose to disperse and develop the earth.

In reality, the Tower was the embodiment of perverse motives and a corrupt mentality. The project in Babel was inherently rebellious, for it rejected the trajectory of Noah's sons, through whom "the whole earth was populated" (9:19). They opted, instead, for sinful homogeneity based on enforced unity of language, cult, culture, ideology, and empire. Daniel Gordis writes, "The natural process of dispersion that had begun after the flood—and that God himself desires—is now regarded as a fate to be avoided. Human beings, we have learned, ought to scatter. Yet the people of Babel reject this ideal, refusing to allow for the territorial, cultural, and linguistic diversity so essential to the new humanity envisioned by God."⁵³

---

51. Several scholars suggest that Nimrod (10:8–12) was the paradigmatic empire builder east of Eden and the ideological godfather of Babel. See Petrovich, "Identifying Nimrod of Genesis 10," 273–305; Hom, "A Mighty Hunter before YHWH," 67–68; Levin, "Nimrod the Mighty," 350–66.

52. Callender, *Adam in Myth and History*, 75 (emphasis in original).

53. Gordis, "The Tower of Babel," 4.

They also utilized a new technology, brick-making, for apostate purposes. Gordis comments further, "The possibility of building allows human beings to design their own world as they would like it to be. Man has become an architect of the world, a creature—not only of necessity—but of vision."[54] Yoram Hazony summarized the vision of empire embodied in Babel in this way:

> By virtue of ruling the earth they come to believe that they can rule heaven; by virtue of making themselves a great name they can be eternal. They come to think, in other words, that they are themselves God. And indeed, it is in this way that the great emperors of the Bible are portrayed: The Pharaohs, Sennacherib, Nebuchadnezzar, and Ahashverosh (apparently Xerxes) are all men whose self-worship is such that there is no limit to the evil they be moved to do.[55]

Babel was thus the primordial foreshadowing of the post-garden intellectual, cultural, economic, and religious trajectory of mankind. The human advances that Genesis 4–11 catalogues (city-building and military prowess, farming and herding, music, metalworking, and brick-making) were all problematic, typified by violence, corruption, greed, and apostasy. In Babel, powers of all sorts—religious and political, economic and legal—converged to erect a society committed to collective perversity in thought and deed. The harmony of speech, religion, culture, and imperialism served as a means to moderate the destructive force of God's curse on the land and the limitations of the Creator–creature distinction. Unity of religion and ideology functioned as a worldview fortress, keeping God at bay in an attempt to replicate the blessings of the garden, at least for the elite. Given humankind's testimony as recorded in chapters 4–10, the Tower was a grand experiment in apostate society building. It was a paradigmatic enterprise in utopia, erected upon an idolatrous theocracy. In short, it was a prototypical manifestation of the cultural mandate gone terribly awry, a reversal of Eden.

God's judgment against Babel ("scattering," v. 8), therefore, signified at least two polemical features. First, for the Babelites it represented their greatest fear, for it meant that their cultural vision was not sustainable. It was based on folly and pride. They were not autonomous, nor could they isolate themselves from their Creator. Second, their ontological goal that

---

54. Gordis, "The Tower of Babel," 4.
55. Hazony, *The Philosophy of Hebrew Scripture*, 142.

"everything that they plan will be possible to them" (v. 6) was affirmed by God, but dispersion was the result, just as God exiled Adam and Eve, and Cain after them.[56]

On the other hand, scattering also encompassed God's mercy in the midst of wrath. His dispersal was similar to the expulsion of the first family for their own benefit. Gordis comments, "God knows that, united in purpose and in language, humanity can achieve anything it conspires, and may well succeed in its resistance to his plans for dispersion . . . . God confounds the languages, which causes humanity to scatter over the earth—as per his original plan."[57] Similarly, Middleton writes:

> A careful reading of Genesis 11 in the context of the primeval history suggests that Babel represents imperial civilization par excellence and that its imposed, artificial unity is a danger to *the human race*. God's remedy, therefore, not only enables humanity to obey the commission of 1:28 to fill the earth, but contributes to the diffusion of human power for the sake of humanity.[58]

Finally, Genesis 3–11 demonstrates two critical lessons concerning the noetic[59] effects of sin. First, whenever self-deification and would-be ascent sow ontological confusion, epistemological folly, spiritual perversion, political oppression, and ethical deviance follow thereafter. Second, Babel shows the tremendous power of collective apostasy, specifically the ability of worldview, ideology, and religion to define reality and mold culture in vicious ways. Indeed, collective folly and groupthink "civilize" a people for good or ill. In the case of Babel, Lyle M. Eslinger calls their

---

56. The great irony is that the people of Babel sought to make a "name" for themselves through homocentric imperialism, whereas God promised Abraham to "make your name great" and to "make of you a great nation" (Gen 12:2) by means of divine initiative.

57. Gordis, "The Tower of Babel," 4.

58. Middleton, *The Liberating Image*, 225 (emphasis in original).

59. The term "noetic" is derived from the Greek adjective *noetikos* ("intellectual"), as well as the verb *noein* ("to think") and the noun *nous* ("mind"). Noetic depravity refers to the foolish ways in which mankind reasons as a result of sin. Humans reverse the Creator–creature distinction and reason as if they were sovereign and self-legislating. They position themselves epistemologically as though they were impartial observers and evaluators of reality. People seek alternatives to revelation in creation and the Scriptures. They suppress and exchange the truth for falsehood (Rom 1:18–25). Noetic sinfulness produces epistemic distortion, disorientation, and myopia, resulting in folly and tragedy for persons and societies. See Vandici, "Reading the Rules of Knowledge," 173–91; Westphal, "Taking St. Paul Seriously," 200–226.

perverted communal outlook a "mind-sharing collective."[60] Babel shows the persuasive power of alternative gospels to captivate the mind, inspire imagination, and compel compliance.

In short, Genesis 3–11 teaches that mankind listens to the snake and relies upon his norms to see, choose, and act. Humans often think about meaning and purpose using his ontological framework. They misunderstand and misapply their mandate as apprentice rulers, architects, economists, and philosophers. Twisted relationships and societies are the result—civilizations that will never create a Sabbath-like environment for humans to flourish or honor God.

CONCLUSION

The first three chapters of Genesis show that mankind is hard-wired for a covenantal relationship with the Creator. We are *homo adorans* (worshiping creatures), created in God's image, designed to love and serve someone greater than ourselves. We are also thinkers, *homo sapiens* (thoughtful and self-conscious), *homo discens* (learners with intellectual curiosity), *homo quaerens* (questioners, those who wonder), *homo imaginans* (those who imagine and create), and *homo faber* (those who build and organize). But Genesis 3 asks: Who will provide the interpretive criteria and teleological significance for these capacities—God or Satan, human folly or divine wisdom?

The basic question of Genesis 3 is who we are listening to.[61] As creatures made in God's image, humans will always listen to someone. We will always image somebody. But since the fall into sin, humans hear and mimic with skewed orientations that evaluate, desire, and act inappropriately.

Further, Genesis 3 reveals the serpent's true nature. He is the archetypical narcissist. He swoons with vanity, for misguided aspirants of godlikeness redirect their gaze on him instead of God. He is the paradigmatic huckster, peddling illicit knowledge to gullible buyers who pay far too much. And he is a hawker, the ruthless swindler who lies, deceives, and ensnares the unwary. Let the buyer beware!

---

60. Eslinger, "The Enigmatic Plurals," 179.
61. See Johnson, *Epistemology and Biblical Theology*, 37–48.

Clearly, Genesis 3 shows that the serpent set mankind on a destructive trajectory.[62] Genesis 4–11 shows, moreover, that Qohelet was right: "God made mankind upright, but men have gone in search of many schemes" (Eccl 7:29). Humans try to replicate Eden and re-establish a religious orientation, but they frequently settle for visions of utopia, totalitarian ideology, theocracy, or empire. Why? Because human beings are the *imago Dei* and we are hard-wired for extension, development, and globalization. But because we are sinful and selfish, the usual result is conquest, exploitation, and plunder. Mankind often embraces Babelite worldviews that produce intellectual folly, spiritual perversion, and moral deviance. Since the fall, we have opened a veritable Pandora's box of deceitful "mind-sharing collectives" in the form of destructive worldviews, idolatries, and ideologies.[63]

Genesis 3–11 thus prompts us, the progeny of Adam, to ask ourselves honestly: *Who* tells me what being human means? To what degree is *my* thinking affected by the serpent's view of reality? Do I think in dishonest and unethical ways? Do I "play God" intellectually by failing to acknowledge God's revelation as the authoritative guide in all life and learning? Do I sometimes think as if God were epistemologically irrelevant?

---

62. Granted, some of what the serpent predicted did come true. Adam and Eve's eyes were opened, but only to behold their covenantal nakedness and experience evil. They ate the fruit and did not die immediately, although they were cast out of Eden (and they did die eventually). They gained "wisdom" but it did not profit them, for they did not acquire supernatural power or ontological ascent. Moreover, the snake's ultimate defeat began in Eden. He was cursed by God and expelled from the garden, and God's saving gospel was foretold (Gen 3:15).

63. Michael Johnson ("The Seeds of Epistemology," 9) provides a helpful summary of what was to come: atheism and agnosticism, pantheism and polytheism, humanism and materialism, determinism and fatalism, existentialism and nihilism.

4

Pharaoh's Folly

"Stony hearts, hard hearts, were compared with shut hands, hostile eyes, defiant shoulders, stiff necks, adamant foreheads, dull ears."

—Marjorie O'Rourke Boyle,
"The Law of the Heart: The Death of a Fool"

We saw in chapters 1–2 that proper knowing is a key feature of functioning as God's image. Correct understanding results from listening to and obeying God, mankind's authoritative interpreter of reality. God is an absolute person, so true knowing is covenantal; that is, all knowledge presumes his superiority in all things. Such recognition produces piety and righteousness. For this reason, ontology, epistemology, ethics, culture, and spirituality are correlated under God.

We learned in chapter 3 that Satan seeks to redefine reality and distort knowledge by disassociating the world from its covenantal setting. In Eden, he seduced Adam and Eve by suggesting, "You must decide the question of how you know without regard to the question of what is real." Only in this way, he argued, would they become like God, knowing good and evil. Having adopted this flawed outlook, they were expelled from Eden. Genesis 4–11 shows the development of pervasive noetic depravity personally and socially as a result of their rebellion.

Progressively, humankind in general and Israel in particular followed in Adam's footsteps. Mankind evidenced a disregard for God and an unwillingness to implement his instructions. A rebellious attitude became the default motivation and mentality. The prophet Malachi, speaking shortly before the demise of ancient Israel, summarized the spiritual disorientation of the people and their broken infrastructure: "For the lips of a priest should guard knowledge, and people should seek instruction from his mouth, for he is the messenger of the Lord of hosts. But you have turned aside from the way" (2:7). Israel had fallen into idolatry ("turned aside"), spurned God's voice, and behaved corruptly.

The Scriptures depict many examples of the same process (idolatry, folly, and perversion) within Israel and its neighbors. In this chapter, we consider erroneous knowledge as it developed in ancient Egypt. In particular, we trace an epistemological problem in the book of Exodus—a knowledge deficit—that drives the plot forward. The narrator said, "Now there arose a new king over Egypt, who did not know Joseph" (1:8). We focus on a paradigmatic thinker who shows us how not to think: the king of Egypt, Pharaoh. We also explore several epistemic and theological implications arising from this narrative.

SON OF RE

Pharaoh was not disposed to listen to or obey Yahweh's instructions (Exod 1–15). He refused to acknowledge God or release Israel from his grasp. He declared obstinately, "Who is the Lord, that I should obey his voice and let Israel go? I do not know the Lord, and moreover, I will not let Israel go" (5:2). God had informed Moses, "I know that the king of Egypt will not let you go unless compelled by a mighty hand" (3:19). What did God recognize about Pharaoh and Egypt that produced this negative expectation? What does the expression "compelled by a mighty hand" signify? And what did Egypt and Israel learn about Yahweh?

What Yahweh Knew

Pharaohs were divine, according to their worldview. They were intimately associated with the gods of creation (Atum, Ptah, and Re), who turned primeval chaos into order. At royal coronations, kings were proclaimed descendants of the Creator god, Amun-Re: "You are my son, my heir, who issued from my body."[1] Egyptian kings were often designated the "son of Re" or "image of Re." They were "the likeness" and "beloved of"

---

1. Cited in Walton, *Ancient Near Eastern Thought*, 262.

the gods.² The king was also the incarnation of the god Horus (the king's advocate and the nation's protector). After death, they were identified with Osiris (the god of resurrection and eternal life) and were honored with all due splendor by means of grandiose funeral shrines.³

Pharaohs were a "special order of being" as the intermediaries between heaven and earth on behalf of Egyptian civilization.⁴ They received prayers and adoration, and they functioned as the nation's high priests. They built temples and maintained the religious infrastructure. They were the chief communicators of Egypt's special mission through architecture, sacred rites, and public festivals. John H. Walton comments about the king's centrality:

> He communed with the gods, was privy to their councils, and enjoyed their favor and protection. He was responsible for maintaining justice, for leading in battle, for initiating and accomplishing public building projects from canals to walls to temples, and had ultimate responsibility for the ongoing performance of the cult.⁵

As the image of the gods, the king upheld primeval order (*maat*) given at creation. Walton cites a hymn to the god Re that explains the Pharaohs' critical role in Egyptian society: "Re has placed the king in the land of the living forever and ever, judging humankind and satisfying the gods, realizing Maat and destroying Izfet [disorder]. He gives offerings to the gods and mortuary offerings to the deceased."⁶ Conceptually, *maat* was cosmic wisdom and divine law that emerged when the sun god Re arose from the watery chaos. In practice, *maat* was a female deity revered with her own rite and temple as the daughter of Re. Existentially, *maat* codified the divinely given order of nature, state, religion, and conduct.⁷

---

2. See Silverman, "Divinity and Deities," 7–87; Baines, "Ancient Egyptian Kingship," 16–53.

3. "Inside the temple the deceased kings received daily care. On holidays, priests brought out the royal cult statues, along with the statues of other deities, and paraded these images in the public areas outside the temple for worship and adoration." See Silverman, "Divinity and Deities," 73.

4. Baines, "Ancient Egyptian Kingship," 24.

5. Walton, *Ancient Near Eastern Thought*, 256.

6. Walton, *Ancient Near Eastern Thought*, 257.

7. Compliance with *maat* also determined one's eternal destiny. Eliade cited a prayer regarding obedience to *maat*: "I was a man who loved and hated sin. For I knew that (sin) is an abomination to God." In a prayer to Re, a supplicant asserted, "Mayest

Maat preserved the peace and prosperity of creation while preventing the resurgence of disorder and corruption.

Most importantly, the king was charged with the preservation of peace, for he exemplified *maat* personally and implemented it socially as an offering to the gods. In essence, Pharaoh was the ontological glue that held Egyptian civilization together. John Baines comments, "The king was responsible, like the Creator god, for the destiny and nourishment of all, so that progeny increases during his reign."[8] In this way, the animate and inanimate dimensions of reality were bound together with *maat* as the governing norm and the king as the divine sovereign over a polytheistic theocracy.[9]

In addition, Egypt deeply imbibed an imperial mindset. Douglas K. Stuart summarizes the "mentality of empire" that emerged in the ancient Near East:

(1) Certain kings, selected and favored by the gods, and the nations they rule, have both the divine right and a divinely-assigned duty to subdue, annex, or subjugate others, thus creating an empire.

(2) Empires exist for the benefit primarily of the controlling monarchy and the "home" nation, rather than as commonwealths. Thus the financial bleeding of conquered or subjugated lands via tribute, tax, and toll is permissible and expected.

(3) Propagandistic techniques of various sorts may be required to help subjugated nations realize and accept their role.

(4) An indication of the greatness of a god and his emperor is the duration of the empire—including the ability of kings to pass on their empires to their heirs.

(5) Empires had a right to be religiously imperialistic.

(6) Empires bring peace and tranquility to a series of lands. It is the right of an emperor to dominate his own people and subjugate other peoples in order to establish this peace.

Thou give me *maat* in my heart!" At judgment, the follower stated, "I have practiced *maat* for the sake of the Master of *maat*. I am pure." Eliade, *A History of Religious Ideas*, 92, 112.

8. Baines, "Ancient Egyptian Kingship," 23.

9. Van Leeuwen describes how the king restored *maat* in his realm when it was threatened. See "The Biblical World Turned Upside Down," 604–6.

(7) The right to control other countries extended even to the right to rearrange their populations via deportations (exiles).

(8) Conquered kings were expected to bring their nations' practices and attitudes into conformity with the values of the empire into which they had been placed . . . especially in the provision of tribute, tax, and toll, but also in supplying slaves, soldiers, ships, and various other goods and services to the empire, and emulation of the empire's practices.10

Baines notes, in fact, that Egypt believed it "was the *only* society rather than the one set off from others."[11] According to Mircea Eliade, they believed that "Egypt was the first country formed, hence the center of the world. The Egyptians were its only rightful inhabitants."[12] Similarly, Daniel P. Bricker describes the nation's "Egyptocentric" outlook and their self-chosen identity as the "most important people on earth."[13] He adds, "They held the conviction that their nation was the centre of the earth and that they were superior to all other peoples. Their self-worth seemingly was rooted in their religion and their belief that they held a position of privilege and status among their gods."[14] Egyptian rulers looked upon foreigners such as the Hebrews with suspicion for the disorder and impurity they represented.[15] Thus, the Pharaohs of Exodus 1–15 implemented strategies to subdue the Hebrews through forced service to the state (vv. 11–13) and infanticide (vv. 15–16). The Hebrews unwillingly supported this social infrastructure through their submissiveness and labor.

The Pharaoh of Moses' youth conscripted the Israelites into corvée (Exod 1:11, 13) and so did the Pharaoh of the exodus (5:5–14). After the

---

10. Stuart, "David's Costly Flirtation with Empire," 21–30. Concerning Mesopotamian cultural imperialism, see Petrovich, "Identifying Nimrod," 287–302, Middleton, *The Liberating Image*, 193–231.

11. Baines, "Ancient Egyptian Kingship," 50 (emphasis mine).

12. Eliade, *A History of Religious Ideas*, 90.

13. Bricker, "Innocent Suffering in Egypt," 98.

14. Bricker, "Innocent Suffering in Egypt," 98.

15. Berlyn says about the two kings who encountered Moses, "War was a permanent condition, as Egyptians, Hurrians, Mitanni, and Hittites wrestled for hegemony over the region; a hegemony that largely depended on control of Syria and Canaan" ("The Pharaohs Who Knew Moses," 10). At later dates, Egypt undertook at least two military excursions to pacify Canaan. The earliest non-biblical reference to Israel seethes with Egyptian malice: "Canaan is captive with all woe . . . . Israel is wasted, bare of seed" ("The Pharaohs Who Knew Moses," 12).

king and his advisors repented of Israel's slavery (under duress of the plagues), they lamented, "What is this we have done, that we have let Israel go from serving us?" (14:5).[16] At the beginning of Exodus, Pharaoh viewed the massive number of Israelites in Egypt from a national-security perspective: "Come, let us deal shrewdly with them, lest they multiply, and, if war breaks out, they join our enemies and fight against us and escape from the land" (1:10). Under siege from Yahweh's assault, the king's courtiers pleaded with him, "Do you not yet understand that Egypt is ruined?" (10:7). Finally, as a consequence of the ten plagues, "The Egyptians were urgent with the people to send them out of the land in haste. For they said, 'We shall all be dead'" (12:33).[17]

Clearly, the pantheon of Egypt was at odds with the God of Israel. Yahweh declared, "On all the gods of Egypt I will execute judgments, I am the Lord" (12:12). Pierre Gilbert writes, "The emerging conflict is no longer simply between an ethnic group and the Egyptian people, but more precisely between the Israelites and Yahweh on the one hand, and Pharaoh and the gods of Egypt on the other hand."[18] Consider this passage in Exodus 7, which recapitulates in one scene the ensuing struggle between Pharaoh (and his gods) and Yahweh, culminating in the Red Sea crossing (key terms are in italics):

(1) And the Lord said to Moses, "See, I have made you *like God* to Pharaoh, and your brother Aaron shall be your prophet.

(2) You shall speak all that I command you, and your brother Aaron shall tell Pharaoh to let the people of Israel go out of his land.

(8) Then the LORD said to Moses and Aaron,

(9) "When Pharaoh says to you, 'Prove yourselves by working a miracle,' then you shall say to Aaron, 'Take your *staff* and cast it down before Pharaoh, that it may become a *serpent*.'"

---

16. Egypt remained clueless about the economic "distinction" that Yahweh manifested between the two peoples during the destructive plagues (9:4, 20, 26; 8:22). God predicted that the people would "plunder" Egypt when forced to leave (3:22)—and they did (12:36). In the Old Testament and the ancient Near East, taking plunder was the fruit of conquest, and Yahweh had defeated the Egyptian pantheon in battle. (Other examples of plundering appear in Num 31:9, 11; Deut 3:7; Josh 8:2; Isa 10:6.)

17. This explains one reason why God "compelled" Egypt to act against their economic and military self-interest. Ironically, God "compelled" Egypt (3:19) to let Israel go, whereas the Egyptians later compelled them to leave.

18. Gilbert, "Human Free Will," 79.

(10) So Moses and Aaron went to Pharaoh and did just as the LORD commanded. Aaron cast down his staff before Pharaoh and his servants, and it became a serpent.

(11) Then Pharaoh summoned the wise men and the sorcerers, and they, the magicians of Egypt, also did the same by their *secret arts*.

(12) For each man cast down his staff, and they became serpents. But Aaron's staff *swallowed up* their staffs.

Two "strongmen" faced off through their proxies. On one side were the two prophets of Yahweh, Moses and Aaron. On the other was an incarnate god of Egypt, represented by his best and brightest wizards. Pharaoh demanded supernatural authentication of Yahweh and his spokesman by means of a miraculous sign. The chosen medium for divine attestation was magic, seemingly a stunning advantage for the Egyptians.[19] Yet Yahweh granted his prophets even greater power and made them seem "like God to Pharaoh" (7:1).

Magic in all its forms was deeply ingrained in the Egyptian worldview as a spiritual technology.[20] Those who possessed this capacity held great influence. Magicians cast spells, pronounced incantations, empowered inanimate objects, and enabled the deceased to prosper in the afterlife. They functioned as counselors to the king and assisted him with spiritual discernment. Sorcerers possessed the ability to subdue venomous snakes and dangerous animals. Magicians' staffs were filled with supernatural power, signified by the image of a god that was emblazoned upon them.

The nature of the serpent (*tannin*) that appeared amidst the representatives of Egypt and Israel is debated. Options include a snake, crocodile, or sea monster (7:9–10).[21] The Egyptians believed that the serpent represented chaos and the undoing of *maat*. Arie Leder writes, "The

---

19. However, this was not really the case, according to Noegel: "The scholarly world has known for some time that the book of Exodus demonstrates first-hand knowledge of Egyptian customs and beliefs, even if somewhat tendentiously related" ("Moses and Magic," 45).

20. See Noegel, "Moses and Magic," 45–58; as well as Currid, *Against the Gods*, 407–23. For general information about Egyptian religion and the ancient Near East, see Walton, *Ancient Near Eastern Thought*, 213–52; Block, *The Gospel according to Moses*, 200–270.

21. Noegel, "Moses and Magic"; Leder, "Hearing Exodus 7:8–13," 93–110.

ancient Near East understood the *tannin* to be a terrifying dragon-monster that constantly threatened to swallow the good order of society."[22] Pharaoh's crown, in fact, displayed a cobra to signify his supremacy over the primordial chaos represented by the snake.[23]

When Aaron "cast down" his staff, therefore, the Egyptians knew exactly what was at stake. Yahweh had challenged Pharaoh to divine combat and threatened the primacy of *maat*.[24] For the Egyptians, the royal staff (a shepherd's crook with a hooded cobra) represented the king's power and authority. The entire Egyptian pantheon stood behind this object and his person. When the magicians cast down their staffs, they affirmed Pharaoh's cosmic status and their expertise as sorcerers empowered by the gods.

The verb "swallowed" was highly significant (7:12). Scott B. Noegel explains the meaning: "Consumption entails the absorption of an object and the acquisition of its benefits or traits. Alternatively, the act can serve a principally hostile function, whereby 'devour' signifies 'to destroy'—though even here the concept of acquiring power may be retained."[25] For the Egyptians, swallowing indicated conquest and the plundering of power and knowledge. For the Hebrews, swallowing (*bala*) possessed a similar meaning: defeat and judgment. Later on, for instance, Pharaoh's army was "swallowed" by the sea (15:12).[26] Nevertheless, despite the clear and present danger to Pharaoh demonstrated vividly in this duel, he did not yield. The narrator says, "Still Pharaoh's heart was hardened, and he would not listen to them, as the Lord had said" (7:13).

Thus, what Yahweh knew about Egypt and why he forced Pharaoh to release the Hebrews are clear: their mindset was captured by their post-fall worldview. They were opposed to all that Joseph, Israel, and Yahweh represented. Their social and religious infrastructure was skewed by polytheism, theocracy, and empire. In the words of Zechariah 7:11, "They

---

22. Leder, "Hearing Exodus 7:8–13," 98.

23. Two candidates for the *tannin* were the god Sobek (a crocodile) or the great serpent Apophis who inhabited darkness.

24. The Egyptian word for "cast down" appears in their literature with reference to exorcism and battling with the serpentine beast Apophis.

25. Noegel, "Moses and Magic," 49, quoting Robert K. Ritter.

26. Korah and his band were "swallowed" by the earth for rebelling against Moses (Num 16:32), and false prophets were "swallowed up" for fake news about God (Isa 9:16). Other references are Num 26:10; 2 Sam 17:16; Pss 35:25; 106:17; Prov 1:12; Isa 3:12; 49:19; Jer 51:34; Lam 2:2; and Hos 8:8.

refused to pay attention and turned a stubborn shoulder and stopped their ears that they might not hear." So Egypt and its king would not and indeed could not listen to or follow God's instructions. Pharaoh's mind was *already* blind and unteachable, well before Moses confronted him with God's demand to let his people go. For this motive, he "hardened his heart" (Exod 8:32). Yet, as we will see, Yahweh made Pharaoh's mind yet more sluggish and defiant so as to glorify himself (9:12).

"Compelled by a Mighty Hand"

God told Moses, "I know that the king of Egypt will not let you go unless compelled by a mighty hand. So I will stretch out my hand and strike Egypt with all the wonders that I will do in it; after that he will let you go" (3:19–20). Exodus catalogues the proleptic confrontation with the staffs (7:8–13), followed by the ten plagues (7:14–12:39) and the final destruction of the Egyptian army in the sea (13:17–14:31). Yet the Pharaohs' ideology depicted them as mighty warriors whose "strong arm" gained victories for them. They identified with the divine combatants Seth and Montu. Victorious monarchs were honored with designations such as "the Great God who strikes Asiatics" and the "good god, brave and vigilant, a champion."[27] The idioms "mighty hand" and "stretched out my hand/arm" were quite familiar in Egypt.[28] In fact, Exodus and Deuteronomy described the battle between Yahweh and Pharaoh with similar idioms.[29]

Gilbert proposes this formulation of Yahweh's strategy with Pharaoh:

> Yahweh acts in order to demonstrate his absolute superiority. One condition is necessary to ensure a meaningful and overwhelming victory for Yahweh: Pharaoh must either publicly and unconditionally recognize Yahweh's sovereignty, or he must

---

27. See Hoffmeier, "The Arm of God," 380, 381.

28. Hoffmeier, "The Arm of God," 387. For instance, Sinuhe was a "mighty man who achieves with his strong arm," Thutmose II was "great of arm," Thutmose III said that his "majesty made an occasion of victory with my very own arm," and Tutankhamun was described as a "possessor of a mighty arm who tramples hundreds of thousands" (379–85).

29. God's "mighty/strong hand" appears in Exodus 3:19; 13:3, 14, 16 and Deuteronomy 6:21; 9:26. His "outstretched arm" appears in Exodus 3:20; 6:6; 7:5 and Deuteronomy 9:29; 26:8. Similarly, God's representatives, Moses and Aaron, were instructed to "stretch out your hand" against Egypt in Exodus 7:19; 8:5, 16; 9:22; 10:12, 21; 14:21, 26.

resist to the bitter end. There cannot be any compromise. If Pharaoh accepts letting the people go under some pretext of magnanimity, the reader will be left with the impression that Yahweh needs the permission of Pharaoh to lead his people out of Egypt. Such a scenario, far from demonstrating the sovereignty of Yahweh, would on the contrary confirm the supremacy of Pharaoh and the gods of Egypt.[30]

Indeed, the narrative reveals the volatile psyche of the embattled king that foreshadowed a possible "compromise" with Israel. On one hand, Pharaoh stood firm against Yahweh, as a valiant god-king should. He refused to listen to Moses on five occasions (7:12, 22; 8:15, 19; 9:12) and five times refused to allow Israel to leave (9:7, 35; 10:10, 27; 11:10). He was deceitful (8:29), did not fear God (9:30), persisted in self-exaltation (9:17), and refused to humble himself (10:3). He issued threats and conditions (8:28; 10:1–11, 27).

On the other hand, Pharaoh was clearly out of his league against Yahweh (7:12; 8:19; 9:11; 10:7; 11:3, 7–8). For instance, regarding the sixth plague Gilbert comments, "One can only presume that after the six disastrous manifestations of Yahweh's power, Pharaoh would have been disheartened to the point of being tempted, if not compelled, to give in to Moses' demands."[31] He offered Moses conditional permission to leave (8:8, 28; 9:28; 10:8).[32] He requested Moses' intercession on his behalf (8:8, 28; 9:28; 10:17), acknowledged his culpability (9:27; 10:16–17), and sought God's blessing (12:32). However, Yahweh did not allow Pharaoh to capitulate due to human frailty (loss of confidence) or pride ("pretext of magnanimity") before he fulfilled God's didactic purpose. He demanded that the king and his people learn an essential ontological reality: "that you may know that there is none like me in all the earth" (9:14).

Moreover, Yahweh strengthened Pharaoh to resist to the bitter end. He molded the king's mind and motivations in accordance with his purpose to derive glory from the exodus of Israel (14:4, 17–18). This intention was first expressed in 4:21 (and 7:3–4a), before the plagues began: "When you go back to Egypt, see that you do before Pharaoh all the miracles that I have put in your power. But I will harden his heart, so that he will not let the people go."[33] Clearly, Pharaoh was not permitted to perceive the

---

30. Gilbert, "Human Free Will," 79–80.
31. Gilbert, "Human Free Will," 81.
32. See the interesting study by Spero, "Pharaoh's Three Offers," 93–96.
33. For analysis of the three terms translated as "harden," see McAffee, "The Heart

significance of Yahweh's intervention in Egypt. He could not understand the big picture. He was not enabled to discern the meaning of Yahweh's iconoclasm.³⁴ Brian P. Irwin describes the king's epistemological dilemma: "By making Pharaoh a puppet forced into self-destructive choices, Yahweh shows himself to be God and Pharaoh to be merely human. He is not a god, after all, whose very thoughts and actions are controlled by another."³⁵ God strengthened Pharaoh's hubris and religious bias as the Egyptian god incarnate, so that his twisted worldview bore its bitter fruit in rebellious conduct and erroneous thinking.³⁶

In this sense, then, Yahweh gave Pharaoh over to his sin as the "cup of the wine of wrath" (Jer 25:15). Ps 81:11-12 enunciates this theme (with Israel as the target): "But my people did not listen to my voice; Israel would not submit to me. So I gave them over to their stubborn hearts, to follow their own counsels."³⁷ So it was with Pharaoh. He did not listen to or acknowledge Yahweh. His heart was stubborn and he followed his own counsels, informed by his self-serving worldview. God gave him over to the inevitable fruit of his idolatry, producing disaster for Egypt—but glory for God.

Who Learned What

Exodus 1-15 involved two learning communities, Egypt and Israel. The teacher was the same for both—Yahweh. The classroom was similar, for

---

of Pharaoh," 331-53; Beale, "An Exegetical and Theological Consideration," 129-54; Wilson, "The Hardening of Pharaoh's Heart," 18-36.

34. Some of the Egyptians, those "who feared the word of the Lord" (9:20), seemed to understand. Members of the army, however, discovered too late: "And the Egyptians said, 'Let us flee from before Israel, for the Lord fights for them against the Egyptians'" (14:25).

35. Irwin, "Yahweh's Suspension of Free Will," 59.

36. Ironically, the God of creation (from the perspective of Egypt, the god of disorder and *Izfet*) overturned the god of Egyptian *maat*. In terms of biblical wisdom, Pharaoh was the epitome of foolishness. He thus fulfilled the role assigned to him: "For this purpose I have raised you up, to show you my power, so that my name may be proclaimed in all the earth" (Exod 9:15-16).

37. The Bible shows that further sin is often punishment for the sinner in the present. Other examples are Judg 2:14; 6:1; Pss 78:50; 106:41; Job 8:4; 2 Kgs 17:20; Ezra 5:12; Neh 9:26-28, 30; Rom 1:24, 26, 28. Romans 1:28 seems especially apropos for Pharaoh: "Since they did not see fit to acknowledge God, God gave them up to a debased mind to do what ought not to be done."

each experienced a series of spectacular events at his hand. The challenge for both was to correctly discern the meaning of the events happening in Egypt and respond properly.

In Exodus, Yahweh was the one true knower. He understood Pharaoh and Egypt. He was fully aware of Israel's suffering: "God heard their groaning ... God saw the people of Israel—and God knew" (2:25; see also 3:7). He was attentive to their plight, and for this reason they honored him: "When they heard that the Lord had visited the people of Israel and that he had seen their affliction, they bowed their heads and worshiped" (4:31). He also understood why they sometimes did not obey, "because of their broken spirit and harsh slavery" (6:9). Later on, they learned that they were uniquely his, "a people for his treasured possession" (19:5).

Indeed, God was the omnipotent pedagogue. He taught Israel his name (3:15; 6:3). He revealed his strategy for removing the nation from Egypt (3:19–20). He announced his goal to bring them to Canaan (3:8), according to his covenant with Abraham (2:24). He trained Moses and Aaron, telling them what to say and how to conduct themselves in the royal court (4:11–15). As the climactic exit approached, he taught Israel how to commemorate their redemption through rituals of remembrance (12:14, 26; 13:3, 9, 14; 31:13). He even revealed his lesson plan for his people while he compelled Egypt by his mighty hand:

What Israel Was to Learn	How and When
I am the Lord your God	who has brought you out from under the burdens of the Egyptians (6:7)
The Lord makes a distinction	every firstborn in the land of Egypt shall die between Egypt and Israel (11:5, 7)
[I am] the Lord	who brought you out of the land of Egypt (16:6)
I am the Lord	at twilight you shall eat meat, and in the morning you shall be filled with bread (16:12)
I am the Lord their God	who brought them out of the land of Egypt that I might dwell among them (29:46)
I, the Lord, sanctify you	you shall keep my Sabbaths, for this is a sign between me and you throughout your generations (31:13)

For all these reasons, Israel possessed distinct advantages epistemologically. Yahweh identified himself as "the Lord, the God of your fathers, the God of Abraham, the God of Isaac, and the God of Jacob" (3:15).

They discovered that he was the same deity their fathers had known and covenanted with. In fact, God foretold their current affliction to Abram: "Know for certain that your offspring will be sojourners in a land that is not theirs and will be servants there, and they will be afflicted for four hundred years. But I will bring judgment on the nation that they serve, and afterward they shall come out with great possessions" (Gen 15:13–14). And now Yahweh declared, in fulfillment of that pledge, "I promise that I will bring you up out of the affliction of Egypt to the land of the Canaanites . . . a land flowing with milk and honey" (Exod 3:17). Israel possessed, therefore, the hermeneutical key to understanding what was really happening to them and the Egyptians. The covenant of Abraham and the ontology of Genesis enabled Israel to properly evaluate the experiential data they perceived.

Undoubtedly, Israel also confronted obstacles to learning. After all, they shared with Egypt the same post-fall, exilic antipathy to God's voice and a similar inclination to interpret the theophanic data incorrectly. Incredulity expressed itself when Moses announced God's redemptive plan, for they replied, "What is his name?" (3:13b). Certainly, Moses' panicky lament early in the confrontation with Pharaoh manifested a tendency to misinterpret: "O Lord, why have you done evil to this people? Why did you ever send me? For since I came to Pharaoh to speak in your name, he has done evil to this people, and you have not delivered your people at all" (5:22–23). Likewise, the frenzied protest of the people with their backs against the Red Sea evidenced misconstrual: "Is it because there are no graves in Egypt that you have taken us away to die in the wilderness? What have you done to us in bringing us out of Egypt?" (14:11).[38]

Nevertheless, Israel learned that Yahweh was unquestionably supreme over all things: nature, humanity, and history, including Egypt's royalty and gods. They discovered, as well, that the Creator and covenant maker was their redeemer. W. Ross Blackburn writes, "The Lord's commitment to be known throughout the earth is the motivation for doing everything that he does in Exodus, from the manner in which he delivers Israel from Egypt to the reason he gives Israel the law, to the way he

---

38. The Israelites were also extremely vulnerable socially and economically. They lacked meaningful power in the face of the Egyptian juggernaut. They risked their lives should Moses prove delusional and his challenge to Pharaoh a fool's errand. One wonders, also, if they were a bit skeptical and jaundiced, given their suffering after four hundred years.

responds to Israel's idolatry."[39] Certainly, in addition to factual knowledge about Yahweh, they learned to know God personally, that is, covenantally. Israel discovered experientially how to listen to God's voice through his prophets and act upon his instructions. In this way, they could avoid idolatry as well as disobedience.

But of course, both Israel *and* Egypt witnessed the same miraculous deeds and so Yahweh expressed learning goals for Egypt too. His pedagogical objectives were as follows:

What Egypt Was to Learn	How and When
I am the Lord	when I stretch out my hand against Egypt and bring out the people of Israel from among them (7:5)
I am the Lord	the water that is in the Nile . . . shall turn into blood (7:17)
No one like the Lord our God	the frogs shall go away from you (8:10–11)
The Lord in the midst of the earth	set apart the land of Goshen, where my people dwell (8:22)
None like me in all the earth	send all my plagues on you yourself, and on your servants and your people (9:14)
The earth is the Lord's	the thunder will cease, and there will be no more hail (9:29)
I am the Lord	how I have dealt harshly with the Egyptians and what signs I have done among them (10:2)
I am the Lord	I will harden Pharaoh's heart, and he will pursue them, and I will get glory over Pharaoh and all his host (14:4)
I am the Lord	when I have gotten glory over Pharaoh, his chariots, and his horsemen (14:18)

As we saw at the beginning of this chapter, the book of Exodus opens with a knowledge deficit that drives the plot forward (1:8). Egypt was no longer aware of Joseph's service long ago, nor did the Egyptians know that God blessed kings who blessed Israel.[40] Likewise, the Pharaoh of the exodus professed ignorance about the Hebrew God (5:2). In addition, Egypt believed that their gods had rightfully acquired "servanthood

---

39. Blackburn, *The God Who Makes Himself Known*, 209.

40. For a discussion of how other kings viewed Israel in contrast to the two Pharaohs of Exodus, see Cox, "The Hardening of Pharaoh's Heart," 294–96.

from Israel."[41] As a result, the two Pharaohs viewed the Hebrews without historical or covenantal context. They interpreted what God did among them and what Moses said through their own ideological and sociological commitments. This accounts for the Egyptian god-king's hostility and myopia about Israel and Yahweh. Dru Johnson explains:

> Due to his refusal to listen to the voice of Moses, Pharaoh cannot discern how these events are all related; he does not see the dots connecting. The pattern does not cohere for him, and hence, the things he comes to know *about* God are not in proper perspective or context. Pharaoh can only see YHWH as an outside oppressor who is destroying Egypt.[42]

In summary, the king's mindset was idolatrous because he refused to acknowledge Yahweh and listen to his prophet Moses. As Johnson says, the Egyptians learned something *about* Yahweh "by refusing to listen."[43] In fact, polytheism and imperialism blinded their minds so that Moses' speech was merely "lying words" in their view (5:9). They learned painfully, though, that Yahweh really was supreme, "the God of all the earth" (19:5). They discovered that their "Egyptocentric" outlook was faulty. They discovered that *maat* simply preserved the religious status quo and economic perks for the elite. They realized that the great "distinction" between Egyptian civilization and Israel was due to Israel's covenant with God. They witnessed how Egypt's ontology played out in day-to-day life, producing a myriad of errors in the realm of social and economic injustice, including of course, the mistreatment of God's own people. In short, they saw firsthand how their cosmology fell short before the Lord's onslaught.

IMPLICATIONS

In the previous chapter, I demonstrated that ontological syncretism through Adam's self-deification produced folly, perversion, and oppression. Surely, the theocratic pretensions of Egypt's god-kings are a prime example. If Pharaoh had listened to Yahweh and implemented his instructions, the story would have been quite different. Perhaps his myopia and obduracy would have been mitigated. I noted, as well, that ideology

---

41. Provan, "To Highlight All Our Idols," 11.
42. Johnson, *Biblical Knowing*, 59 (emphasis in original).
43. Johnson, *Epistemology and Biblical Theology*, 68.

and religion mold culture. Egypt's Babelite "mind-sharing collective" imprisoned the populace through messaging dedicated to maintain the erroneous primeval order.

Proverbs 1:7 says, "The fear of the Lord is the beginning of knowledge; fools despise wisdom and instruction." Reverence for Yahweh, listening to his voice, and obeying his law are the foundation of knowing *anything* properly. The Hebrew midwives "feared God" and thereby discerned the necessity to protect baby Moses. They understood the real state of affairs in Egypt. Courageously, they "did not do as the king of Egypt commanded them" (1:17). Similarly, "whoever feared the word of the Lord among the servants of Pharaoh" sheltered their animals when the plague of hail came to pass (9:20). But the hapless god-king and his cronies did not "get" the lesson at all because they did not fear God (v. 30). They experienced catastrophic loss as a result.

The Lord declared to Moses, "Who has made man's mouth? Who makes him mute, or deaf, or seeing, or blind? Is it not I, the Lord? Now therefore go, and I will be with your mouth and teach you what you shall speak" (4:11). In the book of Exodus, God sovereignly granted discernment and caused judgmental blindness. He enabled Moses to hear and see what God intended, and thereafter to respond correctly. In Pharaoh's case, Yahweh made his mind slow to perceive and obey.

Both Egypt and Israel observed all that God enacted in their midst, but simply witnessing dramatic events did not produce faith or understanding. Pharaoh and Moses did not evaluate the plagues from epistemically neutral positions. Pharaoh was guided by his religious worldview and self-identity as a son of Re. Moses interpreted the wonders of God in terms of Hebrew cosmology, Yahweh's counsel, and the covenant with Abraham. As Johnson says, the Exodus narrative teaches that "brute witness of an event does not equal understanding."[44] Further, he suggests that the narrative teaches that "There is no neutral position—autonomous humanity making choices—and so we must be aware of the prophetic voices over us and those we want to be operative in our epistemological process."[45] Unfortunately, Pharaoh believed quite incorrectly that he was a self-authenticating thinker. Through painful and destructive experiences, he learned otherwise.

---

44. Johnson, *Biblical Knowing*, 67.
45. Johnson, *Biblical Knowing*, 203.

Finally, the narrative we have studied illustrates the importance of the big picture, because worldview, presuppositions, and cosmology impact everyday life. Metaphysical and anthropological ideas produce epistemological, social, and ethical consequences. The way we think and how we live correlate with our answers to basic questions: Where did we come from? Why are we here? What is wrong with us? What is the good life? Where are we heading individually and as a race?

CONCLUSION

When Pharaoh asked, "Who is the Lord, that I should obey him and let Israel go?" he asked a very important question, even a paradigmatic one, that was plausible only east of Eden. In effect, his query was: Who is the true God?

But his question also implies several other crucial questions that recur in the Old Testament. Who are the real people of God? In which society might humans flourish? Through whom will the earth be blessed—Cain's progeny (all god-kings and would-be empires) or the seed of Abraham? Which is the true land of promise, Egypt (another theocracy or utopia) or Canaan?

Pharaoh gave wrong answers to all these questions. He provides a contrasting negative example to learn from, so that we can avoid following in his footsteps. With reference to the biblical imagery, Marjorie O'Rourke Boyle shows that Pharaoh embodied folly and hubris. She says, "Stony hearts, hard hearts, were compared with shut hands, hostile eyes, defiant shoulders, stiff necks, adamant foreheads, dull ears."[46] Throughout the book of Exodus, Pharaoh is contrasted with Moses, Egypt with Israel, and most importantly polytheism with Yahweh. The model that Pharaoh provides—his moral character and mentality—is not worthy of imitation. It represents the post-Babel outlook at its worst. It illustrates once again that mankind listens to the serpent.

The story of Pharaoh shows us how *not* to think. It demonstrates the antithesis of loving God with the mind. Insofar as other "Pharaohs" arise, God's diagnosis in Genesis 6:5 remains valid: "The Lord saw that the wickedness of man was great in the earth, and that every intention of the thoughts of his heart was only evil continually."

---

46. Boyle, "The Law of the Heart," 418.

Finally, Pharaoh's story teaches that Egyptian *maat* is *not* God's order for the world. It does not express his wisdom. Likewise, magic in all its forms is not a viable epistemological method to know God or his will. The story reveals, as well, that *any* nation- or empire-centric ideology can be erroneous and idolatrous. Most importantly, Exodus underscores that true knowledge and discernment presuppose biblical ontology and covenant.

5

Qohelet's Quest

"Once again, we see how the biblical message turns out to be true after two thousand years of silence. It applies to our time, as if it had been written only yesterday, and just for us."

—JACQUES ELLUL, *THE REASON FOR BEING*

THE BOOK OF ECCLESIASTES concerns a knowledge deficit. At the beginning of his text, Qohelet expressed a burning desire to understand: "What does man gain by all the toil at which he toils under the sun?" (1:3). Further, he sought knowledge about many critical themes: "all that is done under heaven" (1:13), "wisdom and madness and folly" (1:17), "what God has done from the beginning to the end" (3:11), "the scheme of things" (7:25), "the interpretation of a thing" (8:1), "the proper time and the just way" (8:5), "the business that is done on earth" (8:16), "the work that is done under the sun" (8:17), and "how the righteous and the wise and their deeds are in the hand of God" (9:1).

Qohelet confessed ignorance about much: "what God has done from the beginning to the end" (3:11), "what is to be" (8:7), "what disaster may happen on earth" (11:2), and "the work of God who makes everything" (11:5). Similarly, his rhetorical questions revealed his sense that much of the knowledge he sought was elusive and out of reach: "Who knows whether the spirit of man goes upward and the spirit of the beast goes down into the earth?" (3:21), "What advantage has the wise man over the fool?" (6:8a), "Who knows what is good for man while he lives the few days of his vain life?" (6:12a), "Who can tell man what will be after him under the sun?" (6:12b), and "Who knows the interpretation of a thing?" (8:1).

In this chapter, I argue that Qohelet's intellectual motives, method, and message were skewed, often at odds with the Old Testament's worldview. At best, he offers a confused and contradictory depiction of reality. In fact, he provides a poignant example of exilic epistemology. He demonstrates how *not* to love God with the mind. We will examine Qohelet's quest for knowledge, literary setting, mental outlook, and epistemology. Thereafter, I will discuss some implications.

ASSUMPTIONS

The name Qohelet ("the Preacher") means "one who assembles" (*qahal*), a collector of sayings or one who assembles persons. The narrator described Qohelet as an arranger of "many proverbs" and someone who "sought to find words of delight" (12:9b–10a). Aron Pinker suggests that Qohelet was probably also an assembler of people, specifically pundits who expressed a variety of orthodox and unorthodox perspectives on important themes. Qohelet may have hosted a study group or panel of debaters within a circle of intellectuals.[1]

Ecclesiastes employs frame narration. There are two speakers, representing different points of view. Ryan O'Dowd explains the pedagogical utility of this literary device: "The frame-narrative provokes the reader (and reading community) to assess the many perspectives presented in the book and, in so doing, to engage in a self-reflective assessment of personal epistemology and theology."[2] The narrator appears in 1:1–2, 7:27, and 12:8–14, and Qohelet speaks in 1:3–12:7. O'Dowd contends that the narrator functions as a "distancing voice in the book" representing orthodox wisdom and theology.[3] Qohelet, on the other hand, functions

---

1. Pinker ("Ecclesiastes Part II Themes," 166–68) suggests, "He was a leader of a circle of social and intellectual peers, the *kohelet*. At the meetings of the *kohelet* practical and philosophical questions were discussed, and the author recorded the various positions that were taken. This would explain the structure of the book and its apparent contradictions. At some point, the author adopted the noun *Kohelet* as his pseudonym."

2. O'Dowd, "Frame Narrative," 244.

3. O'Dowd, "Frame Narrative," 244.

as an epistemological foil, a heuristic device representing generally faulty ways to think.

The book of Ecclesiastes was situated within a cultural-religious milieu of which we know little. Whatever precise social circumstances birthed the text, the context was exilic: external foreign captivity in Persia or internal foreign domination in Palestine. Both settings posed the threat of cultural assimilation and religious syncretism. Palestine was often, in fact, highly contested real estate among rival empires for trade and strategic reasons. It therefore became a nexus of intercultural amalgamation, and this dynamic is likely reflected in the text. G. A. Klingbeil comments, "In the many references to parallel ideas, terms, and structures of Ecclesiastes within the larger framework of the ancient Near East, the notion of 'internationality' of wisdom should be considered."[4] This might account for the global flavor of Qohelet's language and thought forms.

QOHELET'S PURSUIT OF KNOWLEDGE

The narrator depicts Qohelet as an investigator and sage. He was a deep thinker and epistemology figured highly in his search. Leland Ryken describes Qohelet as "the archetypical quester who undertook, not a physical journey, but a journey of the mind and soul—a journey to find meaning and satisfaction in life."[5] Michael V. Fox states, "Indeed, the problem of knowledge—its possibility, its powers, and its limitations—is one of the central concerns of his book."[6] For instance, in his first quest for knowledge Qohelet assumed the aura of royal sagacity to pursue wisdom (1:12–2:26), and in his second he took on the role of a disappointed supplicant of Lady Wisdom (7:23–29).[7]

Qohelet asked at the beginning of his quest, "What does man gain by all the toil at which he toils under the sun?" (1:3; see also 3:9 and 5:16). Gain (*yitron*) refers to what was left over after investment of time, effort, and money. Qohelet wanted to ascertain if *any* profit—that is, permanence or long-term impact—accrued from a lifetime of effort. He wondered if any "remembrance" (1:11; 2:16; 5:20; 9:5), "advantage" (3:19; 5:11; 6:8, 11; 7:11, 12), or "reward" (2:10; 4:9; 9:5) occurred in the face of

---

4. Klingbeil, "Ecclesiastes 2," 138.
5. Ryken, "Ecclesiastes," *A Complete Literary Guide*, 271.
6. Fox, "Qohelet's Epistemology," 137.
7. See Clifford, "Another Look at Qoheleth 7:23–29," 50–59.

unavoidable death and ceaseless tedium. Similarly, he pondered human flourishing, asking "what was good [*tob*] for the children of man to do under heaven" (2:3; see also 6:12). Moreover, he investigated the purpose of human life, inquiring about the "the end of all mankind" (7:2) and the scope of human obligation—"the whole duty of man" (12:13).[8] Qohelet concerned himself with the first question of the Westminster Shorter Catechism: What is the chief end of man?

Qohelet utilized extensive vocabulary to describe his cognitive quest (in English translation):

nouns	wisdom, folly, fool, foolishness, knowledge, thoughts, advice, interpretation, madness
adjectives	foolish, wise, amazed, intelligent, far off
verbs	search out, test, know, perceive, guide, consider, see, hear, find out, think, take advice, can tell, fear (God), observe

Further, he used many expressions of intellectual curiosity, cognitive intent, and acquired knowledge that contain the noun "heart" (*leb*), a term roughly equivalent to "mind."[9] Here are some of them:

"I applied my heart to seek" (1:13)	"searched with my heart how" (2:3)
"said in my heart" (1:16)	"my heart still guiding me" (2:3)
"kept my heart from" (2:10)	"my heart found" (2:10)
"gave my heart up" (2:20)	"let your heart" (5:2)
"lay it to heart" (7:2)	"your heart knows that" (7:22)
"turned my heart to know" (7:25)	"a wise man's heart inclines" (10:2)[10]

Qohelet investigated many aspects of creation. He looked for the essence of things in the particulars of experience: "all that is done under the sun" (1:13) and "all the days" of human life (5:17).[11] He considered

---

8. This appears to be the narrator's summation of Qohelet's quest for meaning. See the discussion in Enns, "Ecclesiastes 1," 125–26.

9. See Carasik, *Theologies of the Mind*, 104–24.

10. Similar phrases are "heart of fools" and "heart of the wise" (7:40).

11. He often applied the collective term "all" to his fields of inquiry: human effort ("toil," 1:3), the "weariness of the world ("things," 1:8), royal predecessors ("who were before me," 2:9), lack of significance ("long forgotten," 2:16), despair of life ("days full of sorrow," 2:23), death and the afterlife ("from the dust and to dust all return," 3:20), social injustice ("oppressions," 4:1) and the pessimistic nature of life ("all his days he eats in darkness in much vexation and sickness and anger," 5:17).

death, wisdom, joy, wealth, pleasure, justice, afterlife, aging, folly, evil, God, human nature, and kingship. In addition, he desired to know the "scheme (*cheshbon*) of things," attempting to assess the extent of human knowledge regarding the nature and purpose of existence.[12]

From a statistical perspective, Qohelet's chief investigative priorities can be displayed as key terms and topics. The following list indicates how often each one is mentioned:[13]

good	51	death, dead, die, allusions to death	23
toil, work, business	46	"patterned time"[14]	23
God	40	wind, spirit, breath, anger	23
vanity	38	folly, foolishness, fool	22
under the sun, under heaven, on earth	37	evil	20
wisdom, wise	23	gain, advantage, reward, lot, portion	17

Finally, examples of Qohelet's wide-ranging declarations can be demonstrated by several Hebrew verbs that he utilized (with selected references): *yada* (I know, perceive; 3:12, 14; 7:22; 9:5); *raah* (I see, observe, evaluate; 3:16; 4:4 (twice); 8:17; 9:11); *dabar* (I said, thought to myself; 1:16; 2:2, 15; 3:18; 7:23); *matsa* (I found out; 3:11; 7:14, 29; 8:17); and "there/this is" (1:2, 9, 11; 7:20; 8:14).

QOHELET'S LITERARY SETTING

The social and religious environment that Qohelet described was akin to a perpetual battleground—everyone at war with themselves, their fellow human beings, and God.[15] In the words famously coined by Thomas

---

12. Several translations bear this out: "what life is about" (CEV) and "the reason for/of things" (GW, NLT, NKJV).

13. These totals are by my counts in the English Bible. See also Schoors, "Words Typical of Qohelet," 17–39 regarding several prominent Hebrew terms.

14. Qohelet wondered about fate or destiny, according to Peter Machinist. Three Hebrew terms constitute a semantic field of related themes: *qarah* ("happens" in 2:14, 15; 3:19; 9:2, 3), *cheshbon* ("scheme" in 7:25, 27), and *olam* ("eternity" in 3:11; "forever" in 1:4; 3:14; 9:6; "ages before us" in 1:10; "eternal" in 12:5). See Machinist, "Fate, *miqreh*, and Reason," 159–75.

15. For more positive readings of Ecclesiastes, see De Jong, "God in the Book of

Hobbes, Qohelet's sinful regime "under heaven" was "solitary, poor, nasty, brutish, and short." Similarly, as Tremper Longman depicts Qohelet's outlook, "Life is full of trouble and then you die."[16] Clearly, the setting portrayed by the writer was no thriving return-to-paradise scheme, but rather a dystopian escapade east of Eden. What Qohelet depicted was a virtual hell on earth, the antithesis of human flourishing.

Qohelet characterized life "on earth" as "darkness" (5:17; 6:4; 11:8) and "evil" (1:21; 5:16; 6:1–2; 9:3; 12:1). Happenstance reigned, as "time and chance happen to all" (9:11). "Disaster" could strike at any moment (11:2), including death, which was stalking close at hand (2:14, 18; 3:19–20; 5:16; 6:4; 9:3–4, 12). Qohelet wrote, "Like fish that are taken in an evil net, and like birds that are caught in a snare, so the children of man are snared at an evil time, when it suddenly falls upon them" (9:12). Furthermore, human life was an "unhappy business" (1:12; 4:8) that brought "vexation," (1:18; 2:22), "sorrow" (1:18; 2:22; 7:3), "trouble" (8:6), "mourning" (7:2), "madness and folly" (2:12), "sickness and anger" (5:17), unproductive "toil" (2:11; 4:6–7;) and chronic fear, especially in old age (12:5). In fact, Qohelet described life as a mere "few days" (6:12), "vain" (6:12; 7:15), and "like a shadow" (6:12; 8:13). Even worse, no one really cared about or remembered those who expired after their life was over (9:5, 15).[17]

In this environment, every person was a veritable "beast" (3:18), "fully set to do evil" (8:11; 9:3). There was "madness in their hearts" (9:3). Their motivations were unrighteous: "envy" (4:4), "pride" (7:8), "anger" (7:8), and "folly" (1:17; 2:3, 12; 7:25; 10:6). Desires were driven by greed: "eyes never satisfied" (4:8), "love of money" (5:10), "the soul not satisfied with good things" (6:3), and "wandering appetites not satisfied" (6:7–9). Likewise, the social sphere was dominated by "wickedness" (3:15), "oppressions" (4:1), misuse of power (4:1; 8:8), "violation of justice" (5:8), bribery (7:7), "evil causes" (8:3), "warfare" (8:8), and unrelenting "tears" (4:1).

This grim backdrop provides the proper context against which to interpret Qohelet's three frequently used, roughly synonymous key

---

Qohelet," 154–67; Meek, "Fear God and Enjoy His Gifts," 23–34; Ortlund, "Laboring in Hopeless Hope," 281–89; "The Gospel in the Book of Ecclesiastes," 607–706; Steel, "Enjoying the Righteousness of Faith," 225–42.

16. Longman, *The Book of Ecclesiastes*, 34.

17. Christianson commented, "Ironically, *he* has been remembered and will doubtless continue to be" ("Qoheleth and The/His Self," 427; emphasis in original).

terms: "under the sun," "under heaven," and "on earth."[18] These idioms indicate the two spheres of Qohelet's experience, as well as the fields of his investigation. On one hand, the expressions are spatial, referring to the earthly domain, "the realm of the living."[19] On the other hand, they are also temporal or existential, referring to the mode of life on earth in its ethical, social, and spiritual dimensions—the "universality of human experience."[20] Moreover, the phrase "under the sun" depicts a milieu where Israel's covenantal God, Yahweh, was far removed from daily life.[21] In this sense, the three expressions refer to a functionally secular world where God's voice is not often heard or heeded through wisdom or Torah. In fact, Qohelet's world was a closed system where divine intervention through miracle and message evidently did not operate.

The three idioms ("under the sun," "under heaven," "on earth"), therefore, portray an upside-down world, a realm of reversals and corruption. Experiences occurred that violated normal expectations. What should have happened did not come to pass; instead, very often the opposite transpired. Cruel ironies punctuated every sphere of activity. For instance, "Folly is set in many high places, and the rich sit in a low place" (10:6), while "youth . . . stand in the king's place" (4:15b). The pursuit of wealth and well-being (2:21; 6:2), or even of wisdom (1:18; 2:14-16; 7:16, 23; 8:17), did not profit. Money did not satisfy, nor a hefty income (5:10; see also 5:13). In fact, riches were powerless in view of God's mysterious sovereignty, for sometimes "God does not give him power to enjoy them, but a stranger enjoys them" (6:2).

Finally, moral travesty manifested itself in every sphere. Qohelet lamented with incredulity, "There are righteous people to whom it happens according to the deeds of the wicked, and there are wicked people to whom it happens according to the deeds of the righteous" (8:14; see also 3:16). He thus remarked with disappointment, "I saw that under the sun the race is not to the swift, nor the battle to the strong, nor bread to the wise, nor riches to the intelligent, nor favor to those with knowledge, but time and chance happen to them all" (9:11).

---

18. The three phrases are roughly synonymous: "under the sun" (1:3, 9, 14; 2:11, 17, 18, 19, 20; 3:16; 4:1, 3, 7, 15; 5:13, 18; 6:1, 12; 8:9, 15, 17; 9:3, 6, 9, 11; 10:5), "under heaven" (1:13; 2:3; 3:1), "on earth" (5:2; 7:20; 8:14, 16; 11:2).

19. Seow, *Ecclesiastes*, 105.

20. Janzen, "Qohelet on Life 'Under the Sun,'" 465.

21. Qohelet refers to God only as Elohim.

QOHELET'S MENTAL STATE

Clearly, this setting was deeply troubling for Qohelet. Three passages in particular provide insight into his mental state. The first is 2:17–20:

(17)   So I hated life, because what is done under the sun was grievous to me, for all is vanity and a striving after wind.

(18)   I hated all my toil in which I toil under the sun, seeing that I must leave it to the man who will come after me,

(19)   and who knows whether he will be wise or a fool? Yet he will be master of all for which I toiled and used my wisdom under the sun. This also is vanity.

(20)   So I turned about and gave my heart up to despair over all the toil of my labors under the sun.

Qohelet learned through painful experience and observation that the causal relation between effort and result or deed and consequence did not operate in a predictable manner "under the sun." Fox comments, "Qohelet sees that labor, wisdom, and righteousness—the three great domains of human endeavor—do not *exclusively* entail appropriate rewards."[22] Not only was his personal labor or research unproductive and frustrating, but the cosmos itself was failing in a twisted and incomprehensible way. A fundamental norm regarding gain (namely, that one reaps what one sows, or that blessing is the reward of the righteous) was obviated by reversal and death.[23]

Qohelet discovered that the world was gravely out of order. Psychologically, this unwelcome intellectual acquisition produced despair. When he asked rhetorically at the beginning of his discourse, "What does man gain?" (1:3), he already knew the answer: "There was nothing to be gained under the sun" (2:11). Nothing lasts and everything changes in unjustifiable and disagreeable ways.

---

22. Fox, "The Inner Structure of Qohelet's Thought," 236 (emphasis in original).

23. Staples ("'Profit' in Ecclesiastes," 87) explained, "Profit was a thing fully understood by his contemporaries, whether they labored in the mercantile, agricultural, or religious fields of endeavor. To them it was the motivating force behind all activities and the thing that made their lives understandable. Such a remark ["There was nothing to be gained under the sun" in 2:11b], if sustained, would deprive the reader of the very underpinning of his existence. Unless a return greater than the investment involved could be expected, there could be no purpose for that investment."

The second passage that reveals his psychological outlook is a telling summation of human life from the perspective of old age: "So if a person lives many years, let him rejoice in them all; but let him remember that the days of darkness will be many. All that comes is vanity" (11:8). Indeed, his assessment of life did not improve over time and he did not moderate his pessimism. One's life is shrouded in moral, intellectual, and spiritual darkness and danger. The probability of survival until old age is unlikely. In fact, the foreboding image of darkness haunts Qohelet's discourse throughout (2:13, 14; 5:17; 6:4; 11:8; 12:2).

The third passage about Qohelet's emotional state is his emotive mediation about debilitation and death in 12:1–7. Qohelet calls aging "the evil days" (v. 1a) that restrict common "pleasures" (v. 1b) such as eating, hearing, movement, and security. Worse still, darkness ultimately claims its victim though death, when "the sun and the light and the moon and the stars are darkened" (v. 2). He compares aging to a disintegrating house whose residents succumb to mortal weakness (vv. 3–5). He depicts mortality as the shattering of costly objects (v. 6a) and household tools (v. 6b). In the end, the dust-creature, Qohelet himself, "returns to the earth as it was," while his "spirit returns to God who gave it" (v. 7). In verse 8, the narrator provides Qohelet's epitaph: "Vanity of vanities, says the Preacher; all is vanity."[24]

QOHELET'S EPISTEMOLOGY

In this section, we consider Qohelet's thinking from four perspectives: his theological framework, motivation, method, and message. We will see that his conclusions are partly right and partly wrong in terms of the Old Testament. He offers a confused picture of reality and God. Like Cain and Pharaoh before him, Qohelet demonstrates how *not* to love God with the mind.

Theological Framework

Qohelet's mind was not a *tabula rasa* devoid of preconceived ideas, whether articulate or inarticulate. He brought assumptions to his discourse. He

---

24. Several authors propose an eschatological or cosmic dimension for this passage: Seow, "Qohelet's Eschatological Poem," 209–34; Jansen, "Qohelet on Life 'Under the Sun,'" 465–83; and Kamano, "Character and Cosmology," 413–24.

reasoned from presuppositions. He embraced a mental map of reality. He relied upon intellectual sources. He used evaluative criteria in his analysis. Clearly, Qohelet possessed tacit knowledge. The text evidences explicit intertextual influences and implicit *a priori* assumptions that lay behind and before it.

Modern scholarship has often fixated on literary and conceptual influences on Ecclesiastes from the Mesopotamian, Egyptian, and Hellenistic worlds. In 1899, however, D. B. MacDonald wrote, "The careful reader of Ecclesiastes cannot fail to notice how great must have been the influence of the early chapters of Genesis with the stories of the creation and the fall on the mind of its writer."[25] In 1963, Hans Wilhelm Hertzberg commented, "There is no doubt: the book of Qoheleth is written with Genesis 1–4 before the eyes of its author; the worldview of Qoheleth is built upon the creation story."[26] However, as Matthew Seufert observes, "Though all scholars, so far as I know, acknowledge some relationship between the two books, a noticeable portion of them afford Genesis a very small place within Ecclesiastes."[27]

In doing so, these scholars underestimate the connection between the two books, as Genesis exerted significant influence upon Ecclesiastes and the worldview of Qohelet. In fact, Brian G. Toews writes, "Ecclesiastes is a commentary on Genesis 1–3 in general and Genesis 3:17–19 in particular."[28] Broadly speaking, Genesis 1–3 supplied Qohelet's mental atlas and motivated his quest for knowledge. From a narrow point of view, his diagnosis of the human condition presupposed Genesis 4 and the story of Cain and Abel.

Seufert summarizes five kinds of intertextuality between Genesis and Ecclesiastes. He called the first type "creational bookends" that enclose the book theologically. For instance, 1:4–7 depicts nature as subject to God's law:[29]

(4) A generation goes and a generation comes, but the earth remains forever.

---

25. MacDonald, "Old Testament Notes," 212.
26. Cited in Toews, "The Story of Abel," 4.
27. Seufert, "The Presence of Genesis in Ecclesiastes," 75.
28. Toews, "The Story of Abel," 4.
29. See also Psalm 104. By implication, Qohelet presumes God's covenantal promise to maintain the natural world (Gen 8:21–22).

(5) The sun rises, and the sun goes down, and hastens to the place where it rises.

(6) The wind blows to the south and goes around to the north; around and around goes the wind, and its circuits the wind returns.

(7) All streams run into the sea, but the sea is not full; to the place where the streams flow, and there they flow again.

In Qohelet's world, everything that transpired "under the sun" presupposed this static, divinely instituted regularity. Raymond C. Van Leeuwen comments, "It [the earth] is uniquely stable, enduring, and irreplaceable, and its constancy is the ground and condition for all those who come and go within it."[30] At all times and in every way, Qohelet relied upon the preconditions that God instituted. Creation was the stage upon which his drama was performed. His pessimistic assessment in 1:2 ("all is vanity") presumed a natural, moral, and cognitive infrastructure provided by God. In fact, Qohelet stood upon God's planetary surface and utilized the resources he provided—air, lungs, brain, and means of communication—so that he could declare about God's world, "Vanity of vanities! All is vanity."

The other creational bookend is "Remember also your Creator" (12:1a). A. J. O. Van der Wal explains that the phrase "your Creator" is unique. It is the only occurrence of the verb *bara* (to create) in the wisdom literature.[31] The personal pronoun ("your") appears only twice in the Old Testament with the participial form of *bara* and implies a filial relationship (Isa 43:1; Eccl 12:1). The word "Creator" is a plural participle and matches the plural form of God's name that Qohelet used (Elohim). Van der Wal comments, "The plural expresses that God is the God *par excellence* and the Creator *par excellence*, the real God and the real Creator."[32] Indeed, Qohelet urged both young and old men to remember the "God par excellence," because of the inevitability of death (12:1b–8) and divine reckoning, for "God will bring you into judgment" (11:9).

---

30. Van Leeuwen, "Creation and Contingency," 1.
31. Van der Wal, "Qohelet 12:1a: A Relatively Unique Statement," 418.
32. Van der Wal, "Qohelet 12:1a: A Relatively Unique Statement," 418 (emphasis in original).

Seufert calls the second intertextual category "certain reliance." The dust motif is an important example.[33] He cites allusions to Genesis based on similar terminology and parallel concepts (Eccl 3:20 and Gen 3:19b; Eccl 12:7 and Gen 2:7). Another example concerns the folly unleashed by the fall. Qohelet wrote, "God made man upright, but they have sought out many schemes" (7:29). The verbal root of the word "scheme" (*cheshbon*) means to think and calculate.[34] In this verse, Qohelet contrasted pre-fall noetic integrity with post-fall noetic depravity ("schemes" concocted by mankind in the present). Despite finitude and fallenness, however, Qohelet sought comprehensive knowledge regarding the "scheme of things" in creation (7:25, 27; 9:10). Further, his boast, "Whatever my eyes desired I did not keep from them" (2:10), resembles Eve's craving to know the "scheme of things" by eating the forbidden fruit (Gen 3:6). In this way, ironically, Qohelet's diagnosis in 7:29 resonates with God's evaluation of mankind in Genesis 6:5: "The Lord saw that the wickedness of man was great in the earth, and that every intention of the thoughts of his heart was only evil continually."[35]

The third intertextual category is "vocabulary overlap," based on word usage and statistical analysis. Seufert argues that Qohelet used the "major verbs of Genesis" such as *create, make, see,* and *name,* as well as word pairs, word clusters and phrases that "echo the creation-history."[36] He summarizes the extensive list as follows:

> Adam/man; woman; snake; create; do/make; say; see; eat; die; know; sprout up; call/name; give; multiply; sow; heaven and earth; day and night; morning and evening; light and darkness; good and evil; the sun, moon, and stars; the birds of the heavens; every fruit tree; all the days of your life; life; soul; water; seas; beast; tree; field; fruit; seed/sow; garden; knowledge; name; command; pain; naked; face; eyes; flesh; and dust.

The fourth intertextual category is "topical overlap." Because of the curse and sin, every kind of labor "on earth" is subject to randomness, exhaustion, corruption, failure, and frustration. Murphy's Law, entropy, Catch-22, transience, absurdity, and unpredictability taint all human

---

33. On the dust motif, see Brueggemann, "From Dust to Kingship," 1–18.
34. Longman, *The Book of Ecclesiastes*, 207.
35. "Scheme" in Ecclesiastes and "thought" in Genesis derive from the same verbal root (Longman, *The Book of Ecclesiastes*, 207).
36. Seufert, "The Presence of Genesis in Ecclesiastes," 82–85.

endeavors. For example, God's curse of work in Genesis 3 resonates in Ecclesiastes:

> In pain you shall eat of it all the days of your life; thorns and thistles it shall bring forth for you.... By the sweat of your face you shall eat (Gen 3:17b–18a, 19a)

> He who digs a pit will fall into it, and a serpent will bite him who breaks through a wall. He who quarries stones is hurt by them, and he who splits logs is endangered by them.... If the serpent bites before it is charmed, there is no advantage to the charmer. (Eccl 10:8–9, 11)

The fifth intertextual category is called "echoes and allusions." Seufert references Charles Forman's study describing God's creative work in Eden and Qohelet's building projects in Ecclesiastes in 2:4–11.[37] The parallel terms and their number of occurrences can be summarized in this way:

Term	Genesis 1–3	Ecclesiastes 2
make	12	6
plant	1	2
garden	13	1
tree	20	2
fruit	7	1
water (noun)	10	1
water (verb)	2	1
sprout/grow	3	1
gold	2	1

Echoes of Eden are also heard in Qohelet's search for "what was good for the children of man to do under heaven during the few days of their life" (2:3b). The word "good" (*tob*) appears fifty-one times in Ecclesiastes. Qohelet was keen to discover a measure of prosperity "under heaven."[38]

---

37. Forman, "Koheleth's Use of Genesis," cited in Seufert, "The Presence of Genesis in Ecclesiastes," 86–87. Similarly, Verheij ("Paradise Retried," 114) commented, "In its actual wording this passage is a paraphrase of the planting of the Garden of Eden." He added, "Taken separately, these words are not remarkable.... It is their combined occurrence here in Genesis that establishes a form link between the texts."

38. For this reason, Gericke ("Axiological Assumptions in Qohelet," 6) writes, "Axiology rather than metaphysics, epistemology or ethics (or existential concerns) is the main focus of Qohelet."

Russell L. Meek comments, "Qohelet clearly echoes Genesis . . . . [He] argues that the only good to be found in life is in capturing a small part of Eden—enjoyment in the fleeting gifts of God."[39] For this reason, the term "good" appears in each of the *carpe diem* sayings[40] and in Qohelet's counsel regarding the pursuit of "gain" (*yitron*).[41]

Furthermore, a fundamental allusion to Genesis in Ecclesiastes concerns the word *hebel* (often translated as "vanity"). Seufert writes, "The word *hebel* occurs consistently throughout the book . . . . Not a few scholars have noted the possibility that the author may have had Abel (*hebel*) in mind. I think he certainly did."[42] Indeed, *hebel* appears as a pithy refrain at the beginning and end of the book, introducing and summarizing Qohelet's discourse: "Vanity of vanities, all is vanity" (1:2; 12:8).

Hebel is the Hebrew name of Abel, Adam's second son (Gen 4:2–11).[43] The name means "breath" or "vapor" and his life was, in fact, momentary and ephemeral. He appeared briefly and left no trace, for he is not mentioned again in the Old Testament.[44] Radiša Antic explains, "The word *hebel* primarily designates a person who, from the outset, was given a special, unusual destiny, that is, to disappear like breath and mist."[45] Moreover, Abel died unjustly and his killer, Cain, escaped with virtual impunity.

Qohelet described a frequent occurrence that was quite Abel-like: "There is a vanity that takes place on earth, that there are righteous people to whom it happens according to the deeds of the wicked, and there are wicked people to whom it happens according to the deeds of

---

39. Meek, "The Meaning of הבל in Qohelet," 252. See also Meek, "Fear God and Enjoy His Gifts," 25–27.

40. These appear in 2:24; 3:12–15, 22; 5:18; 8:15.

41. See Staples, "'Profit' in Ecclesiastes," 89–92.

42. Seufert, "The Presence of Genesis in Ecclesiastes," 86. Likewise, Ethan Dor-Shav ("Ecclesiastes, Fleeting and Timeless," 215) comments, "Indeed, to the assembled Israelites of the First Temple period, Kohelet's famous opening line—*Vanity of vanities, all is vanity*—would have been instantly recognizable as an allusion to another text in their unique intellectual heritage: The story of Cain and Abel from the book of Genesis."

43. See Meek, "The Meaning of הבל in Qohelet," 241–45 for a summary of the word's complicated interpretive history.

44. He was important to Jesus, however, who called him "righteous" (Matt 23:35) and to the writer of Hebrews, who declared that Abel "by faith offered a more acceptable sacrifice than Cain" (11:4).

45. Antic, "Cain, Abel, Seth," 206.

the righteous. I said that this also is vanity" (8:14; see also 7:15b). Seufert explains the significance of this text: "Righteous Abel was murdered, but God spared wicked Cain, even protected him, though each deserved the opposite (cf. Gen 4:1–15)." He concludes, "There is good reason to think that Abel epitomized *hebel* in Ecclesiastes, making him an appropriate fixed allusion throughout the book."[46] Abel is the very embodiment of meaninglessness in an upside-down world east of Eden. Everything on this earth and every human being are like Abel.

Similarly, Meek writes, "Not only is Abel transient, but everyone and everything in life is subject to the reversal of fortunes that he experienced."[47] Toews says, "The creation poem of Ecclesiastes 1:3–11 is designed to illustrate the fact that everything is Abel. . . . The story of Cain and Abel is very much the story of the whole Bible."[48] Stated another way, life is full of bizarre contradictions precisely because it is Abel-like. Fox comments about the incongruity of injustice in Qohelet's thought:

> He maintains a single, but conflicted, view: God is just, but there are injustices. This, as Qohelet is well aware, is contradictory. The contradictions are not only in Qohelet's mind; they are in the world, as Qohelet sees it. Qohelet is complaining not only about injustices but also, more fundamentally, about the irrationality of the world which holds such contradictions. It is absurd.[49]

Finally, Qohelet embraced a body of presuppositional knowledge. Fox calls this "Qohelet's construction of reality" that "rests on a hidden structure of assumptions."[50] James L. Crenshaw described the "non-experiential data" in Qohelet's worldview and his *a priori* knowledge.[51]

---

46. Seufert, "The Presence of Genesis in Ecclesiastes," 86.

47. Meek, "The Meaning of חבל in Qohelet," 254.

48. Toews, "The Story of Abel," 11. In fact, Toews suggests that a literal translation of *hebel* as Abel illuminates the meaning of certain passages. For example: "I have seen all the works which have been done under the sun, and behold, all is Abel and striving after wind" (1:14) and "I have seen everything during my lifetime of Abel; there is a righteous man who perishes in his righteousness and there is a wicked man who prolongs his life in his wickedness" (7:15).

49. Fox, *A Time to Tear Down*, 69.

50. Fox, "The Inner Structure of Qohelet's Thought," 234–35. Fox argues that Qohelet's "model of reality" is revealed in his unmet expectations: "Qohelet assumes that what is required to make the universe rational and meaningful is strict equity. All behavior must produce appropriate and commensurate results" (235).

51. Crenshaw, "Qohelet's Understanding of Intellectual Inquiry," 212–13.

He inquired, "Where, one asks, did he learn so much about the deity who, on Qoheleth's own admission, remains hidden, thus concealing the character of divine activity?"[52] Crenshaw wondered what empirical facts guided Qohelet to the following conclusions:

> That God has appointed a time for judgment, dislikes fools, will punish rash vows, created the world good/appropriate, dwells in heaven, creates the embryo within the mother's womb, chases the past, tests people in order to make them fear, gives human beings unpleasant business, keeps them preoccupied with joy, made men and women upright, has already approved one's actions, and rewards those who fear/worship the deity. How does he know that what has been will recur, that people will not be remembered, that everything belongs within an ordered scheme, that the crooked cannot be straightened, that sadness makes the heart glad, that no righteous person exists?[53]

O'Dowd proposes that Qohelet's "divided-self" accounted for his tacit knowledge.[54] On one hand, his epistemological quest was subjectivist, empirical, and autonomous. On the other hand, his implicit mental map relied upon traditional Hebrew law and wisdom. O'Dowd shows that Qohelet evidenced veiled ethical and theological assumptions about divine law and the lawgiver. For example, Qohelet stated, "God will judge the righteous and the wicked, for there is a time for every matter and for every work" (3:17). Also, in 4:1 and 5:1–7 Qohelet revealed an "underlying, *a priori* view of reality" and "for a moment the ego-centered direction is abandoned and another takes its place—a disinterested indignation at the world's wrongs, a quite nonphilosophical passion for judgment and righteousness."[55] In other words, despite his innate skepticism and chagrin, Qohelet inconsistently—but necessarily—expressed convictions associated with his Hebrew heritage and biblical worldview in his evaluation of the world.

Eric Ortlund suggests yet another explanation of Qohelet's divided self with reference to his declaration that God "put eternity into man's heart" (3:11). Ortlund argues that an "under the sun" perspective presupposes that there also exists an "above the sun" outlook. He writes, "Qohelet's central claim about the one side of this dichotomy—not just

---

52. Crenshaw, "Qohelet's Understanding of Intellectual Inquiry," 212–13.
53. Crenshaw, "Qohelet's Understanding of Intellectual Inquiry," 213.
54. O'Dowd, *The Wisdom of Torah*, 149.
55. O'Dowd, *The Wisdom of Torah*, 149.

that human labor entails no lasting profit, but that it is in vain and absurd—depends upon the existence and reality of the other side in order to make sense," adding, "If there were no echo in the human heart of some transcendent reality, why would it occur to Qohelet to strive after some enduring memorial which time and death cannot touch?"[56] It seems, therefore, that Qohelet's skepticism and pessimism presumed implicit faith and hope. His self-professed ignorance presupposed true knowledge.

Motivation

What motivated Qohelet's intellectual quest and provoked his existential unrest? Broadly speaking, his frenetic investigations arose from the tension between the creation and fall. Specifically, Qohelet experienced the contradictory and divergent motivations associated with being made in the image of God and the sinful aspirations of rebellious Adam. His Cain-like, self-oriented pursuit of knowledge collided with the ontology inherent in the Creator–creature distinction. His Eve-like aspiration for comprehensive understanding was out of step with the Abel-like nature of reality east of Eden. The following passage (3:10–11) is instructive:

(10) I have seen the business that God has given to the children of man to be busy with.

(11) He has made everything beautiful in its time. Also, he has put eternity into man's heart, yet so that he cannot find out what God has done from the beginning to the end.

Qohelet declared that two dimensions of reality were beautiful: time (v. 11a; see also 3:1–8) and eternity (v. 11b). One aspect of existence, however, was disagreeable: the "business" that God gave human beings to do (v. 10), for they "cannot find out what God has done from the beginning to the end" (v. 11c). According to Qohelet, God gave (*natan*) human beings contradictory motivations. He determined *both* the unpleasant "business" *and* the thirst for transcendence ("eternity"). In other words, God was the source of both Qohelet's eternal longing and his temporal intellectual frustration.

The word "business" (*inyan*) occurs eight times in Ecclesiastes (and nowhere else in the Old Testament). Crenshaw explained that *inyan*

---

56. Ortlund, "Deconstruction in Qohelet," 255.

derived from a verb meaning "to afflict."[57] The word "retains an oppressive connotation" and denotes a God-ordained "sorry occupation" for mankind.[58] Longman translates the word as "evil task."[59] C. L. Seow says that *inyan* was a divinely instituted "preoccupation" (or burden) for mankind "to put them in their place."[60] Elsewhere, Qohelet described this weight as an "unhappy business" (1:13 and 4:8) and a "vexation" (2:23) that brought the soul unrest, for "neither day nor night do one's eyes see sleep" (8:16).

The word "eternity" means "that which transcends time," "a sense of timelessness," and "a consciousness and yearning for that which transcends the present," according to Seow.[61] This term is highly disputed,[62] but Seow argues, "It is difficult to imagine that the ancient reader would not associate *olam* in v. 11 with *le olam* only three verses later, in v. 14."[63] He adds, "God is responsible for giving both time and eternity, and the human is caught in the tension between the two."[64] Scott C. Jones suggests that *olam* means "timelessness" and that "the human mind also senses that there is a larger picture which could set these points ["time-under-the-sun" and "timelessness"] in context and make sense of them all (3:11)."[65] Similarly, Ortlund suggests that *olam* refers to "an impulse or desire inside of us for something outside these times."[66] Brian P. Gault cites the nineteenth-century commentator Franz Delitzsch to describe *olam*:

> He has also established in man an impulse leading beyond that which is temporal toward the eternal. It lies in his nature not to

---

57. Crenshaw, *Ecclesiastes*, 97.

58. Crenshaw, *Ecclesiastes*, 97.

59. Longman, *The Book of Ecclesiastes*, 77.

60. Seow, *Ecclesiastes*, 172.

61. Seow, *Ecclesiastes*, 162–74.

62. The significance of *olam* is a crux in the interpretation of Ecclesiastes, for it concerns the nature of human beings. Ellul (*Reason for Being*, 8) suggested motivations for the dispute concerning the meaning of *olam* (and Ecclesiastes in general): "benevolent neutrality" and "prejudice against the text." Many exegetes look askance at the text's "privileged position" as revelation.

63. Seow, *Ecclesiastes*, 163. In addition, context dictates the notion of eternity in 1:4, 9:6, and 12:5, whereas 1:10 and 2:16 are debatable.

64. Seow, *Ecclesiastes*, 173.

65. Jones, "The Values and Limits," 29.

66. Ortlund, "Deconstruction in Qohelet," 254.

be contented with the temporal, but to break through the limits which it draws around him, to escape from the bondage and the disquietude within which he is held, and amid the ceaseless changes of time to console himself by directing his thoughts to eternity . . . . In fact, the impulse of man shows that his innermost wants cannot be satisfied by that which is temporal. He is a being limited by time, but as to his innermost nature he is related to eternity . . . . It is not enough for man to know that everything that happens has its divinely ordained time. There is an instinct peculiar to his nature impelling him to pass beyond this fragmentary knowledge and to comprehend eternity; but his effort is in vain, for "man is unable to reach unto the work which God accomplished from the beginning to the end."[67]

The dissonance, therefore, between the illicit "business" of seeking divine sapience and the allure of a transcendent orientation engendered Qohelet's skewed but passionate quest. In effect, he sought an ontological ascent akin to Adam and Eve's illicit desire to become "like God" at the serpent's urging. The dichotomy between the God-given aspiration to understand and the God-ordained limitation due to the noetic impact of sin produced acute frustration and disorientation.

In summary, Qohelet sought a God's-eye view of reality on *his* terms. He wanted to be "like God" epistemologically. But here was the rub: "The human being has *aion*, 'eternity,' in his heart—his Creator made him a thinking being, and he wants to pass beyond his fragmentary knowledge and discern the fuller meaning of the whole pattern—but the Creator will not let the creature be his equal."[68] In short, God barred Qohelet's path to transcendent knowledge, as he did with Adam, "so that he cannot find out what God has done from the beginning to the end" (3:11c).[69] This crucible of seeking but never finding generated both Qohelet's investigative zeal and finally, after he failed in his quest, his negative assessment of

---

67. Gault, "A Reexamination of 'Eternity,'" 48. Likewise, Eaton (*Ecclesiastes*, 81) comments, "The eternity of God's dealings with mankind correspond with something inside us: we have a capacity for eternal things, are concerned about the future, want to understand 'from the beginning to the end,' and have a sense of something which transcends our immediate situation."

68. John Jarik's explanation of 3:10–11, cited by Longman in *The Book of Ecclesiastes*, 121.

69. Qohelet acknowledged this reality when he said, "I saw all the work of God, that man cannot find out the work that is done under the sun. However much man may toil in seeking, he will not find it out. Even though a wise man claims to know, he cannot find it out" (8:17; see also 11:5).

existence. In short, Qohelet's titanic intellectual agenda was thwarted and he was clearly distraught.

Method

Qohelet maintained several assumptions about himself as an epistemological agent.[70] He was a supremely confident knower and professed a self-assured intelligence: "I have acquired great wisdom, surpassing all who were over Jerusalem before me, and my heart has had great experience of wisdom and knowledge" (1:16; see also 2:9; 7:23). He believed that his perceptions and assertions corresponded with the depth and breadth of reality at all times. He believed that he discerned the potential and limits of knowledge. He reasoned in a self-determinative and intellectually self-sufficient manner. He suffered no fear of error or concerns about self-deception.

Qohelet's path to knowledge arose from the self, by the self, and for the self. He was the architect and arbitrator of his understanding—a self-sufficient knower observing, evaluating, and interpreting the data of experience. His field of investigation comprised both his inner states and the external world. O'Dowd describes Qohelet as an "egocentric knower" engaged in an "individualistic pursuit of knowledge."[71] He adds that Qohelet's quest was "hyper-subjectivist" and an "unbounded search of all things."[72] Michael Carasik comments that Qohelet's investigation "permitted one's mind to roam where it wishes," adding, "It is clear that Qohelet's path to wisdom is an indirect one, involving constant changes in direction as one's mind prompts one to explore this or that intellectual path."[73] As an example, Carasik mentions the idiom of "turning and realizing" evident in Qohelet's spontaneous approach to learning: "I turned to consider" (2:12) and "I turned my heart to know and to search out and to seek" (7:25).

In fact, first-person verbs appear many times in Qohelet's discourse. The self-referential expression "my heart" occurs seventeen times.[74]

---

70. See Gericke, "A Comprehensive Philosophical Approach to Qohelet's Epistemology."
71. O'Dowd, *The Wisdom of Torah*, 146.
72. O'Dowd, "A Chord of Three Strands," 81.
73. Carasik, "Qohelet's Twists and Turns," 204.
74. Other self-referential expressions are "my body" (2:3), "my house" (2:7), "my

Fox describes Qohelet's epistemological method and introspection: "He is not only exploring but also observing himself explore. He is his own field of investigation.... He is reflexively observing the psychological process of discovery as well as reporting the discoveries themselves."[75] Likewise, O'Dowd highlights two epistemological concerns that pervade Ecclesiastes: "What does Qohelet want us to think about his search? And, what does the narrator want us to think about Qohelet's thought about himself searching?"[76] For these reasons, Qohelet's intellectual sources were varied and the world (including himself) served as his laboratory. Jaco W. Gericke lists various sources of data: "direct realism, introspection, memory, reason, and testimony."[77] Clearly, Qohelet was primarily an inductive thinker with an *a posteriori* orientation.

Qohelet boasted of a universal outlook: "I have seen *everything* that is done under the sun" (1:14) and "I saw *all* the work of God" (8:17). He declared that there was "*nothing* new under the sun" (1:9). In fact, the depth and breadth of his insight were absolute, for he claimed to see the totality of human "toil" (1:3), the essential "weariness" of life (1:8), the lack of mankind's lasting significance (2:16), the "sorrow" of daily experience (2:29), the origin and destiny of humanity ("from the dust and to the dust," 3:20), that motivation stems only from "envy" (4:4), and that reality is existentially "darkness" (5:17). But he was also reductionistic. Based on his observations alone, he concluded that reality possesses just one essential value, "vanity" (1:2), and that there was "nothing to be gained" (2:11) on earth.

Qohelet was self-legislating in the moral sphere. Gericke notes, "Like all subjectivists Qohelet had a hard time thinking of states of affairs as good apart from any pleasure or satisfaction they bring," adding, "Qohelet did not hold that certain things could be valuable independently of their impact on consciousness states."[78] He describes Qohelet's ethical outlook in this way: "Qohelet's axiology thus exhibits hedonistic

---

wisdom" (2:9), "my toil" (2:10; see also 2:20), "my reward" (2:10), "my hands" (2:11), "my vain life" (7:15), "my soul" (7:28); and "me" (1:16; 2:3, 7, 9, 15, 17, 18; 7:23; 9:13).

75. Fox, "Qohelet's Epistemology," 143, 148.

76. O'Dowd, "A Chord of Three Strands," 80.

77. Gericke correctly observes that Qohelet was not a strict empiricist (contra Fox). See "A Comprehensive Philosophical Approach to Qohelet's Epistemology," 7. Crenshaw also objects to Fox's thesis ("Qohelet's Understanding of Intellectual Inquiry," 212–13).

78. Gericke, "Axiological Assumptions in Qohelet," 3.

tendencies, but these are tempered by limitations based on human fate and divine fiat."[79] His self-legislating universalism was displayed in his *carpe diem* ethic (2:24; 3:12, 22; 5:18; 8:15) and his statements about human flourishing (what humans "should" do). According to Qohelet, there is "nothing better" than that one "should eat and drink and find enjoyment in his toil" (2:24; see also 3:12, 22) and "be joyful and to do good as long as they live" (8:15).

Moreover, Qohelet was an autonomous knower. He did not explicitly acknowledge a pre-existing or ontological corpus of truth that commanded his submission or guided his research. Fox comments, "For Qohelet there is no body of truth standing above the individual and demanding assent, no Dame Wisdom who was created before mankind and who would exist even if all humans were fools."[80] Similarly, Gericke summarizes Qohelet's posture toward Old Testament revelation:

> Qohelet constructs the deity–world relation in such a way that it seems impossible to imagine traditional varieties of divine revelation being conceivable in his cosmology. Several statements seem to suggest that he did not believe in divine revelation *via* theophany, dreams or verbal communication.... Qohelet never appeals to any resources in special revelation such as the Torah or the prophets in order to discern facts about the divine nature, will and acts.[81]

Given his attitude toward revelation, therefore, Qohelet's view of Hebrew wisdom is at best mixed.[82] He stated several positive virtues of wisdom, such as "There is more gain in wisdom than in folly" (2:13), "Wisdom is good with an inheritance" (7:11), "The wise heart will know the proper time and the just way" (8:5), and "Wisdom helps one to succeed" (10:10). But he also wrote that the "poor wise man" will not be "remembered" (9:15) and that not even the "wise man" will discover the "business that is done on earth" (8:17). Moreover, he testified that "in much wisdom is vexation" (1:18). Even worse, death cancels all benefits of wisdom (2:14–16). He testified that wisdom is unapproachable: "I said,

---

79. Gericke, "Axiological Assumptions in Qohelet," 4.

80. Fox, "Qohelet's Epistemology," 149–50.

81. Gericke, "Qohelet's Concept of Deity," 4 (emphasis in original).

82. Clifford ("Another Look at Qoheleth 7:23–29") argued that Qohelet explicitly rejected Lady Wisdom and Proverb's path to wisdom.

'I will be wise,' but it was far from me. That which has been is far off, and deep, very deep; who can find it out?" (7:23b–24).

Some writers suggest that Qohelet assumed an even more strident position versus traditional sapience. Mark Sneed argues that Qohelet articulated a "polemic against traditional wisdom" and that the designation *hebel* (vanity) as a diagnosis was a "defamation of the wisdom ideal of life."[83] Ortlund describes Qohelet's deviation from the doctrine of divine justice: "A contrast between the status of retribution in Ecclesiastes and a book like Proverbs is, of course, undeniable, especially with regard to the kind of life the wise person can expect under the sun."[84] Carasik shows how Qohelet diverged from the Old Testament's principle of the straight and crooked paths. He writes, "Following the straight and narrow path is, of course, the self-imposed restraint which one who is wise imposes on his or her own actions."[85] The open-ended, self-aggrandizing search that Qohelet embraced, therefore, was different from Proverb's ethical and intellectual prudence. Carasik also correlates Qohelet's uncircumscribed use of his mind and his "declaration of intellectual independence," adding, "This permitting one's mind to roam where it wishes is exactly the opposite of the mistrust, throughout the rest of the Bible, of the untrammeled power of the mind."[86]

Message

Qohelet's worldview was an untenable mixture. He provided both good and bad insights, as well as wise and foolish insights and applications. He saw many "dots," but he could not "connect" them. He observed many "trees," but could not make out the "forest." For example, his skepticism about an afterlife produced myopia about death. And because he focused on nature's circularity and envisioned no teleological dimension of time, he was nihilistic about lasting gain or positive change.

His view of God was a blend of valid and erroneous ideas. On the positive side, Stephan De Jong argues that, although "Qohelet does not offer a complete doctrine of God," six themes show that his representations were in accord with the Old Testament: "God is the Creator and

---

83. Sneed, "*Hebel* as 'Worthless' in Qoheleth," 892–93.
84. Ortlund, "Deconstruction in Qohelet," 249.
85. Carasik, "Qohelet's Twists and Turns," 199.
86. Carasik, "Qohelet's Twists and Turns," 204, 206.

Giver of everything," "God is to be respected," "To fathom God's works is impossible or painful," "God's work cannot be changed," "God acts deterministically," and "God judges the just and the wicked."[87] In addition, Qohelet urged others to "fear" God (3:14; 5:7; 8:12, 13).

However, Qohelet's concept of "fear" was not the same motivation or filial reverence expressed in Proverbs: "The fear of the Lord is the beginning of wisdom, and the knowledge of the Holy One is insight" (9:10). Rather, Qohelet's concept of God looked a lot like deism.[88] Elohim, according to Qohelet, was remote and inscrutable. Fox comments, "Koheleth's God is a distant and all-powerful force who can be feared, but not loved."[89] In reality, Qohelet's deity did not seem in any way akin to Israel's redeemer Yahweh. He did not commiserate or hear desperate petitions. There was no hint that the divine being would care about his people, as he did when Israel cried out in Egypt (Exod 3:7–8). Rather, Qohelet's God was impassable and did not concern himself with injustice and oppression (Eccl 4:1; 5:8). Fox writes, "Koheleth expects little divine help or reward. Being obedient and treading warily in all that concerns God at best reduces the danger of provoking His anger (v. 5b)."[90] In fact, Qohelet implied a nefarious or negligent attitude of God toward creation, because he made everything and everything was "crooked" (1:15; 7:13).

Qohelet's deity did not inspire piety or passion. A heartfelt thirst for God was inconceivable for Qohelet, and he would never have expressed the psalmist's longing: "As a deer pants for flowing streams, so pants my soul for you, O God" (Ps 42:1).[91] Nor was there a goal or narrative plot for history based on a divine plan or covenant promise. Thus, Qohelet's wisdom was not like that of the sons of Issachar, who discerned what was important and how to respond within their moment of history (1 Chr 12:32).

---

87. De Jong, "God in the Book of Qohelet," 164–67.

88. Qohelet's concept of God and his ire with injustice are akin to the skepticism of Sextus Empiricus (ca. 250 CE), who suggested, "Those who affirm positively that God exists cannot avoid falling into an impiety. For if they say that God controls everything, they make him the author of evil things; if, on the other hand, they say that He controls some things only, or that He controls nothing, they are compelled to make God either grudging or impotent, and to do that is quite obviously an impiety."

89. Fox, *Ecclesiastes*, xxxi.

90. Fox, *Ecclesiastes*, xxxi.

91. It is highly unlikely that Qohelet would echo Augustine's famous dictum, "You have made us for yourself and our hearts find no peace until they rest in you" (*Confessions*, 1).

Qohelet was correct that our fallen world is enigmatic and absurd. There is an inherent Kafkaesque quality of life "under heaven" that resists order and efficiency and does not fulfill potential or purpose. This life is often vain and fleeting, full of painful perplexities. As Ortlund states, "Reading Ecclesiastes can be a strange experience because one often wants to argue with the shocking things Qohelet says, but the more one engages with Qohelet's argument, the more difficult it becomes to keep disagreeing."[92] He wrote elsewhere, "This is precisely Qohelet's paradox: life is both in vain and to be enjoyed as a gift from God."[93] His point is valid: we inhabit the best possible world, due to God's grace, given that our setting is a diabolical matrix (Eph 2:1–3).

Again, Qohelet appropriately recognized the cyclical tedium of life leading to death and the lack of human remembrance. Within a closed system impervious to God's voice and intervention, this makes sense. No doubt, there is a *hebel*/Abel-like dimension of reality "under the sun." However, Qohelet's diagnosis violated broader Old Testament teaching. Psalm 90 (the only psalm credited to Moses) shares common themes with Ecclesiastes, such as finitude (vv. 3–6) and fallenness (vv. 7–9a).[94] The psalm echoes Qohelet's outlook: human beings are dust (v. 3), their lives are fleeting (vv. 5–6), after death comes judgment (vv. 7–9a), God's wrath rests upon mankind (vv. 9b–10), and humans must fear God (v. 11b). But according to Moses, those realities are defined within a larger picture—a viewpoint that Qohelet missed. Verses 1 and 2 teach that God the Creator is Israel's anchor and advocate: "Lord, you have been our dwelling place in all generations. Before the mountains were brought forth, or ever you had formed the earth and the world, from everlasting to everlasting you are God." Moreover, Moses explained that God was always accessible and ready to intervene. Unlike Qohelet, Moses urged people to call out to God, seek wisdom from him, and learn their true significance, despite the fleeting and fallen nature of human life as decreed by God:

(12) So teach us to number our days that we may get a heart of wisdom.

(13) Return, O Lord! How long? Have pity on your servants!

---

92. Ortlund, "Laboring in Hopeless Hope," 285.
93. Ortlund, "The Gospel in the Book of Ecclesiastes," 701.
94. One can find similar themes in Psalm 107.

(14) Satisfy us in the morning with your steadfast love, that we may rejoice and be glad all our days.

(15) Make us glad for as many days as you have afflicted us, and for as many years as we have seen evil.

(16) Let your work be shown to your servants, and your glorious power to their children.

(17) Let the favor of the Lord our God be upon us, and establish the work of our hands upon us; yes, establish the work of our hands!

Qohelet also offered a mixed bag concerning his negative assessment of human nature. He was right that there is "nothing new" about human beings. Ellul stated, "According to Qohelet, the human race does not progress. We may develop more perfect instruments, pull more strings, engage in more activities. But we *are* nothing more. Our life does not change. We remain trapped in our condition, by our time and space."[95]

Qohelet was a paradigmatic example, therefore, of one whom God gave over to following their own counsels—to their own loss (Ps 81:11–12). He used his wealth, power, and prestige to construct a private Eden, his own short-term utopia. He typified the post-fall craving for the restoration of paradise upon sinful foundations. Arian Verheij shows that Qohelet—like many before and after—attempted to reenact the failed commission of Adam. Verheij calls this dynamic "Paradise Retried" and writes, "'Qohelet' not only poses as a king, but even—for a moment—as God."[96] His "royal experiment" in 2:4–6 resembled God's construction of Eden "with indeed Qohelet himself as subject, instead of God."[97] As we have seen, Qohelet attempted to cobble together a world of his own making but failed to discover meaning or satisfaction. In effect, he declared himself to be a failed deity. He modeled the futility of self-idolization.

Finally, Qohelet sought rightly to apply his mind ("heart") to gaining wisdom and understanding reality. He was correct in desiring answers to important questions. However, Qohelet did not listen to or obey Old Testament revelation, and he lacked the piety that must accompany godly intellectual inquiry. One does not hear, for instance, the prayer of Psalm 139:23–24, "Search me, O God, and know my heart! Try me and know

---

95. Ellul, *Reason for Being*, 64 (emphasis in original).

96. Verheij, "Paradise Retried," 113. See also Meek, "The Meaning of ▨▨▨[Hebrew font]in "Qohelet," 247–48.

97. Verheij, "Paradise Retried," 114.

my thoughts! And see if there be any grievous way in me, and lead me in the way everlasting!" Qohelet did not manifest the epistemic humility of Psalm 131:1–2: "O Lord, my heart is not lifted up; my eyes are not raised too high; I do not occupy myself with things too great and too marvelous for me. But I have calmed and quieted my soul, like a weaned child with its mother; like a weaned child is my soul within me." Instead, Qohelet presumed epistemological ultimacy and intellectual autonomy.

To put it another way, Qohelet erroneously assumed the power of predication, that is, authority to declare what is and what should be.[98] In one sense, he reasoned in a univocal manner, as if his thinking and God's were essentially alike. In this way, he self-postulated the nature of existence (*hebel*) and self-legislated ethical obligation (*carpe diem*). On the other hand, Qohelet thought in an equivocal fashion, as if his reasoning was totally dissimilar to God's and revelation was not relevant. What he failed to acknowledge was the analogical reasoning required of a creature made in God's image and regulated by his covenant.

CONCLUSION

Qohelet serves as a foil modeling how not to think. His motive, method, and message were distorted. Surely, he embodies this truth: "A learned fool is more foolish than an ignorant one."[99] Yet in a moment of lucidity, he stated the one truth he had discovered: "See, this alone I found, that God made man upright, but they have sought out many schemes" (7:29). Perhaps with this verse in mind, Fox commented ironically, "We may not be able to straighten out what God has twisted, but we can surely twist one thing that God made straight: ourselves."[100]

At least five important implications arise from this chapter. First, we should be ever vigilant about mixed-bag epistemologies and worldviews. On one hand, because humans are created in the image of God

---

98. Bahnsen (*Van Til's Apologetic*, 22, note 67) defines predication in this way: "The mental or verbal act of attributing or denying a property or characteristic (a 'predicate') to a subject . . . . Predication requires one intelligibly to differentiate and select individual things (particulars), to make sense out of general or abstract concepts (universals, classes, definable sets), and to distinguish them (so as *not* to make them identical) while in some sense *identifying* or relating them to each other" (emphasis in original). To predicate, in other words, involves categorizing and evaluating information.

99. Molière, *The Learned Women*, 47.

100. Fox, *Ecclesiastes*, 53.

and because of common grace, we can always glean valuable insights and applications from other worldviews. In God's wisdom, all perspectives contribute to the fulfillment of his cosmic plan and to the totality of knowledge on earth. On the other hand, we must exercise discernment and assess carefully other presuppositions. Especially in contexts under the pressure of syncretism, we should be watchful for all varieties of "Yahweh +/-" or "Jesus +/-" schemes. We must remember the Lord's admonition for our day, "Behold, I am sending you out as sheep in the midst of wolves, so be wise as serpents and innocent as doves" (Matt 10:16). In this way, we will properly love God with our minds.

Second, Qohelet demonstrates the profound complexity of unbelieving thought, as well as its necessarily contradictory nature. Very few consistent atheists or agnostics exist (or fully consistent Christians). We should always expect mixed-bag thinking and behavior in every human endeavor—ours included. Yes, Qohelet sometimes expressed reasoning consistent with being in the image of God and his Hebrew heritage. But he also thought and behaved in an autonomous manner. Van Til expressed the complexity in this way:

> Having made an alliance with Satan, man makes a grand monistic assumption. Not merely in his conclusion but as well in his method and starting point he takes for granted his own ultimacy. To the extent that he works according to this monistic assumption he misinterprets all things, flowers no less than God. Fortunately, the natural man is never fully consistent while in this life.... The actual situation is therefore always a mixture of truth with error.[101]

Third, like Qohelet, we should seek the purpose of human life and the scope of our obligation. But unlike Qohelet, we must think about these matters from the presumption of faith. We must reason from revelation situated by creation and covenant, finitude and fallenness. The book of Ecclesiastes demonstrates the critically important role that the mind plays in biblical spirituality.

Fourth, the book of Ecclesiastes is continually relevant. As Ellul remarked, "Once again, we see how the biblical message turns out to be true after two thousand years of silence. It applies to our time, as if it had

---

101. Van Til, *An Introduction to Systematic Theology*, 27. Fortunately, the lack of consistency and the presence of truth provide opportunities for evangelism and apologetics, as well as collaboration for the common good.

been written only yesterday, and just for us."[102] Qohelet's complex setting, troubling questions, and difficult experiences are endemic to the human condition "under the sun."

Finally, Qohelet experienced a knowledge deficit. Sadly, he did not resolve the problem, for he operated with skewed intellectual priorities. He sought to know too much and in the wrong way. He did not listen to or obey revelation. He presumed his own epistemic ultimacy and self-referential autonomy. He set himself up as the final arbiter of truth, the judge of good and evil, and the ultimate interpreter of reality, even though he was infinitely unqualified for these tasks. His intellectual and motivational posture demonstrated alienation from the God of the Old Testament. His self-deified soul aspired to think and legislate "like God" but did not honor God "as God" (Rom 1:21). In all these ways, Qohelet modeled the exilic epistemology of his forefather Adam. Clearly, those who aspire to love God with the mind should learn from Qohelet but must *not* follow his example.

---

102. Ellul, *Reason for Being*, 5–6.

6

The Fool's Errand

"A fool's paradise is a wise man's hell!"

—Thomas Fuller,
Wise Words and Quaint Counsels of Thomas Fuller

In the previous chapter, we learned that Qohelet's warped and wayward thinking expressed exilic epistemology. He provided a phenomenology of thought and conduct that stemmed from noetic depravity. Clearly, he erred in his analysis of the world, for he depicted only one-half of reality: "everything that is done *under* the sun." His outlook was also reductionistic, since he found only *hebel* manifested in all things. In his system, God was functionally absent from daily life. In effect, the universe was closed to divine intervention, except as capricious providence.

The spirit of Qohelet appears in Proverbs as the quintessential fool. But whereas the criticism of Qohelet is implicit in Ecclesiastes (expressed through the narrator), Proverbs explicitly confronts folly within an ontological framework (an "above the sun" orientation). In fact, the book recognizes that Qohelet's great weakness—his wisdom deficit—is humanity's central problem. In particular, Proverbs shows that folly presumes the rejection of divine wisdom. Indeed, the book recapitulates the primal dichotomy that confronted Adam and Eve—and Qohelet: the choice between acquiring true knowledge from an accredited source and accepting a skewed worldview from a dubious epistemic authority. The implications of this choice pervade every aspect of life.

The book of Proverbs, however, presents a balanced picture, unlike Ecclesiastes. An "above the sun" outlook is expressed through the "father's" counsel to his "son" based on the Old Testament and in Lady Wisdom's proclamation to the "simple" based on creation. Access to these truths presupposes the "fear of Yahweh," meaning a readiness to listen to and obey God alone as revealed in word and deed. In Proverbs, the entire world is accessible to the Lord and he intervenes as he deems best. Proverbs teaches that the universe is *not* closed to divine intervention and that his providence rules. And unlike the remote God of Qohelet, Yahweh is transcendent *and* immanent. In Proverbs, everything "under the sun" implies both *concursus Dei* and *coram Deo*.

In this chapter, we focus on foolishness as another example of exilic epistemology.[1] We begin with three either-or polarities regarding human existence that are depicted in the book of Proverbs: two voices, two loves, and two paths. Next, we examine the prologue (1:1–7) to understand the gravity of folly and what the fool rejects in principle and practice. Finally, we summarize Proverb's depiction of the fool, Lady Folly's protégé.

POLARITIES

A basic narrative framework in the Bible is the metaphor of two "seeds" or two "ways." The Genesis prologue, for example, chronicles the development of Cain's tragic seed, with its escalating wickedness culminating in the Tower of Babel (11:1–9), and the seed of Seth culminating in God's promise to bless "all peoples" through Abram (12:1–3). Later we encounter, for instance, two divine agents (Pharaoh and Moses), two peoples (Egypt and Israel), two cities (Babylon and Jerusalem), two Lords (Baal and Yahweh, God and Mammon), two women (Sarah and Hagar, as well as the harlot and bride of Christ), and two covenantal representatives (Adam and Christ).

Similarly, Proverbs is organized almost entirely around the theme of two "ways": two life paths (wisdom and folly), two worldviews (Yahweh and other gods), and two guides (Lady Wisdom and Lady Folly). Two rhetorical strategies, two lifestyles, and two motivations are embodied by the fool and the wise person. Proverbs concerns whom we listen to and who is our guide for life—Lady Wisdom or Lady Folly.

---

1. Even though Proverbs uses male vocabulary ("son" and "he"), folly is gender-neutral. And though the book focuses on the young adult, all ages are affected.

Two Voices

According to Proverbs, everyone hears conflicting voices representing contrasting worldviews. Each says, "Listen to me!" But behind the cacophony of daily existence, only two speakers call out to mankind personally and through their surrogates: Folly and Wisdom. Their battle for allegiance is waged in both private and public realms. Both want to capture individual minds and imaginations. Both promote their perspectives within the realm of ideas. Both want to influence the public sphere. And both propose lifestyles corresponding to their worldviews.

Wisdom speaks through pious family members (father, mother, and grandfather) that represent the sacred tradition of ancient Israel. They address their "son" repeatedly, "Hear, my son, your father's instruction, and forsake not your mother's teaching" (1:8; see also 2:1; 4:1, 10; 5:7; 7:24). Likewise, Folly speaks through her proxies. "Sinners" incite the gullible to a lifestyle of violence and graft under the guise of false brotherhood: "Come with us, let us lie in wait for blood; let us ambush the innocent without reason . . . we shall fill our houses with plunder; throw in your lot among us; we will all have one purse" (1:11–14). Folly also communicates through the temptress, who entices a "young man lacking sense" (7:7b) with illicit sexuality.[2]

Wisdom calls out in the public square to anyone who will listen. "In the street, in the markets she raises her voice; at the head of the noisy streets she cries out; at the entrance of the city gates." She asks, "How long, O simple ones, will you love being simple?" (1:20–22a). Lady Wisdom also speaks to prospective followers: "On the heights beside the way, at the crossroads she takes her stand; beside the gates in front of the town, at the entrance of the portals she cries aloud" (8:2–3). In chapter 9, she speaks from a position of ultimate influence, authority, and visibility—"from the highest places in the town" (v. 3b). She sends representatives to converse with everyone and declares, "Whoever is simple, let him turn in here" (v. 4a).

Lady Folly, meanwhile, also calls out to passers-by from "the highest place in the town" (9:14b). She declares, "Whoever is simple, let him turn in here!" To him who lacks sense she says seductively, "Stolen water is sweet, and bread eaten in secret is pleasant" (vv. 16–17). On one

---

2. The temptress is also called in Proverbs the "forbidden woman" (2:16; 5:3, 20; 7:5), "evil woman" (6:24), "adulteress" (6:24), "married woman" (6:26), and "prostitute" (6:26; 7:10).

level, Folly represents all that the "world" offers: "the desires of the flesh and the desires of the eyes and pride of life" (1 John 2:16). Raymond C. Van Leeuwen explains what Folly and her representatives peddle: "The desirable 'women' [Lady Wisdom and Lady Folly] that entice the young man on the way to their perspective houses are metaphors for *all* created goods that humans can desire, whether properly and within created bounds, or wrongly and out-of-bounds—like my neighbor's property or good name."3 He adds, "In contrast to Wisdom, Woman Stranger [Lady Folly] and sinners promise a *communitas* of wealth and unbridled passion. Their invitations, however, conceal only a *communitas* of death (1:32; 2:18; 5:5; 7:26, 27; 9:18)."4 Folly, then, merely mimics Wisdom in rhetoric and affection. Verse 13b declares that she "knows nothing" and has very little to offer. She can only parrot Wisdom and hope her subterfuge snares the undiscerning.

At a deeper level, however, the two voices represent more than ethical alternatives or differing worldviews and social agendas. Lady Folly represents the agenda of the "gods of the peoples" (Deut 6:14), who call out to humanity with false promises, alternative gospels, and illicit knowledge. This is why the location of the rival households at the "highest places in town" is significant. Tremper Longman points out, "Throughout the ancient Near East, the only building allowed on the high place was the temple."5 Wisdom and Folly thus represent two divine speakers and two temples.

This duality requires a decision: listen to Wisdom or heed Folly. No neutral position or middle ground exists, nor is there any independent or objective stance from which to evaluate the two. We must love one and despise the other. Further, as we saw with Qohelet, syncretism (a mixed-bag approach) is not an option. As Longman says, the book of Proverbs urgently queries its readers: "Will we dine with Woman Wisdom, who represents Yahweh's wisdom, even Yahweh himself? Or will we dine with Woman Folly, who represents the false gods of the surrounding nations?"6

---

3. Van Leeuwen, "Proverbs," in *Theological Interpretation of the Old Testament*, 176.
4. Van Leeuwen, "Liminality and Worldview," 132.
5. Longman, *Proverbs*, 59.
6. Longman, *Proverbs*, 60.

Two Loves

Proverbs 1–9 depicts love proffered and embraced, as well as affection withheld and redirected. These conflicting devotions manifest themselves through vocabulary and rhetorical strategy. According to Lady Wisdom, the dilemma is misplaced affection. She asks, "How long, O simple ones, will you *love* being simple? How long will scoffers *delight* in their scoffing and fools *hate* knowledge?" (1:22). Wisdom offers herself as the solution for their wisdom deficit and declares, "I love those who love me" (8:17a; see also 4:6; 8:21). Lady Folly, on the other hand, impersonates Wisdom and markets the ersatz affection of a "prostitute" (6:26; 7:10) or "adulteress" (6:24). She "seduces" (9:13) young men and "captures" the vain-hearted (6:25). Van Leeuwen summarizes how each woman inflames human imagination: "Like the love that pulls humans either to Augustine's City of God or to the City of this World, so Proverbs 1–9 presents humans as pulled by *eros* for Wisdom or Folly."[7]

Lady Wisdom woos the simple, but her love is unrequited among fools. Their skewed intentionality appears in the vocabulary that typifies the fool's errand. They "despise" all that Wisdom stands for (1:7) and reject her representatives. They spurn "wisdom and instruction" (1:7b), "my reproof" (1:30), "the Lord's discipline" (3:11), "the word" (13:13), "his father's instruction" (15:5), "his mother" (15:20), and the Lord's "commandment" and "ways" (19:16).

Fools are "greedy for unjust gain" (1:19) and do not "choose the fear of the Lord" (1:29b). They "forsake" their wives and "forget" the covenant (2:17). They "plan evil" (3:29) and "envy a man of violence" (3:31). They "devise evil" and "sow discord" (6:14). They "run to evil" (6:18). In their "hearts" they "desire" the "evil woman" (6:24–25) and "delight" in the pseudo-affection of illicit pleasure (7:5, 18). Fools foolishly embrace the sales pitch of the "forbidden woman" (7:5): "Stolen water is sweet, and bread eaten in secret is pleasant" (9:17).

In contrast, the wise person "loves" Wisdom and obtains "an inheritance" (8:21). The wise "increase in learning" (1:5; see also 9:9). The wise "treasure up" God's commandments (2:1b), seek insight "like silver," and "search for it as for hidden treasure" (2:4). They esteem Wisdom's teachings as "the apple of [their] eye" (7:2b) and "write them on the tablet of [their] heart" (7:3b). They "prize her highly" and" embrace her" gladly (4:8). The wise are "attentive to wisdom" and incline their hearts

---

7. Van Leeuwen, "Proverbs," in *A Complete Literary Guide*, 259.

to "understanding" (2:2). They trust in the Lord "with all their heart" and render themselves "attentive to wisdom" (2:2). Most significantly, wise persons embrace Lady Wisdom as "my sister" and "intimate friend" (7:4). The affectionate embrace signifies passionate commitment.[8] As a result, they "turn away from evil" (3:7; see also 4:16) and understand "righteousness and justice and equity" (2:9).

Lady Folly entices the "simple" and wins their affection with "much seductive speech" and "smooth talk" (7:21).[9] Folly uses three rhetorical tactics to persuade the young person to accept disingenuous affection: flattery, imitation, and denial. First, the phrase "smooth talk" (*cheleq*) depicts dishonest speech. It appears twenty-one times in the Old Testament (nine times in Proverbs, seven times in the Psalms) and is translated as "flattery" or "smooth" (except three times as "slippery" with reference to paths or places). By way of illustration, three instances outside Proverbs illustrate the outlook associated with Folly's deceitful rhetoric:

> Everyone utters lies to his neighbor; with *flattering* lips and a double heart they speak. May the Lord cut off all *flattering* lips, the tongue that makes great boasts, those who say, "With our tongue we will prevail, our lips are with us; who is master over us?" (Ps 12:2–4)[10]

> For he *flatters* himself in his own eyes that his iniquity cannot be found out and hated. (Ps 36:2)[11]

> For they are a rebellious people, lying children, children unwilling to hear the instruction of the Lord; who say to the seers, "Do not see," and to the prophets, "Do not prophesy to us what

---

8. Longman (*Proverbs*, 187, 217) explains, "In its ancient context, this language is intimate. 'Sister' is here not a reference to a sibling, but rather a romantic designation similar to its use in Song 4:9. It is now well established that the use of 'sister' as a term of endearment between an intimate couple was common in the Near East, particularly in Egypt." He adds, "She thus invites them to come to her home and share a meal with her. In the ancient Near East, for a woman to invite a man to a meal has erotic overtones. What Woman Wisdom wants is an intimate relationship with the man."

9. Yee ("I Have Perfumed My Bed," 54) argues that the sinful women depicted in Proverbs 1–9 are all guises of Lady Folly: "The alien, harlotrous, evil, adulterous and foolish woman all refer to one figure embodied in the *isha zara* who stands over and against Wisdom."

10. Carasik (*Theologies of the Mind*, 109) translates the phrase "double heart" in context as "They speak slick talk, with a heart and a heart," that is, duplicity.

11. "In his own eyes" means in his own opinion or self-referentially determined (Carasik, *Theologies of the Mind*, 151).

is right; speak to us *smooth* things, prophesy illusions." (Isa 20:9–10)

"Smooth talk" implies a duplicitous mindset, overweening confidence, rebellion, and self-imposed oblivion. Thus, in Proverbs the "simple" are exceedingly vulnerable and easily persuadable.

The "son" is pulled in two directions: his father's teaching and the woman's enticements. It is, in fact, a perfect storm geared to bring about disaster. Ignorance, naiveté, vanity, illicit motives, sensual stimulation, and raging hormones are coupled with a malevolent tutor skilled in the arts of wickedness, absolutely opposed to Yahweh. Quite clearly, Proverbs shows that flattery serves the interests of the flatterer. False praise and ingratiation are designed to augment the gullible person's self-esteem. The aim is to render the victim amenable to the flatterer's purpose.

Second, Lady Folly proffers affection by imitating the terms and discourse of Wisdom. In this way, she beguiles the undiscerning listener. For instance, the expression "seductive speech," *leqah*, is the same word used for the father's orthodox instruction (1:5; 4:2; 9:9; 16:21) and elsewhere in the Old Testament for divine "teaching" (Deut 32:2) and "instruction" (Isa 29:24).[12] Consider the two very similar speeches of personified Wisdom and Folly:

> Wisdom has built her house; she has hewn her seven pillars.
> She has slaughtered her beasts; she has mixed her wine; she has also set her table.
> She has sent out her young women to call from the highest places in the town,
> "Whoever is simple, let him turn in here!" To him who lacks sense she says,
> "Come, eat of my bread and drink of the wine I have mixed. Leave your simple ways, and live, and walk in the way of insight." (Proverbs 9:1–6)

> The woman Folly is loud; she is seductive and knows nothing.
> She sits at the door of her house; she takes a seat on the highest places of the town,
> calling to those who pass by, who are going straight on their way,
> "Whoever is simple, let him turn in here!" And to him who lacks sense she says,
> "Stolen water is sweet, and bread eaten in secret is pleasant."

---

12. For an explanation of the father's rhetorical method, see Pemberton, "The Rhetoric of the Father," 63–82.

But he does not know that the dead are there, that her guests are in the depths of Sheol. (9:13–18)

Gale A. Yee aptly summarizes the significance of these parallels:

> The two speeches are structurally parallel. Both beckon the simple to turn aside into their houses. Both invite those without sense to partake of their solid and liquid refreshment.... Her [Lady Folly's] words are alarmingly similar to the words which Wisdom herself utters. Two women are thus presented for the son's consideration, both seemingly articulating the same thing.[13]

As Yee shows, Folly is the antithesis of everything Wisdom represents. Often, Folly is effective, though, for it uses Wisdom as a parasite depends on its host. Folly plagiarizes Wisdom. For this reason, Glenn D. Pemberton writes, "She is a killer and her house leads to Sheol."[14]

Third, Folly transforms the "simple" into fools through disobedience and apostasy. In the sphere of religion, fools by definition reject the fear of the Lord (1:7, 29; 8:13; 23:17). Folly promotes idolatry and leads the "simple" astray after other gods (5:23; 10:17; 12:26).[15] In the area of knowledge, fools reason in an autonomous manner (1:7, 29; 2:5; 9:10). In a very real sense, they lose touch with reality and the key to understanding the world (1:2–7). They think in a prideful way (2:6–7), imagine evil (3:19), and are deceitful in their machinations (3:32; 4:24; 6:12–14, 16–19). With regard to ethics, Folly incites violations of the covenant and creation order. And so fools enact a cornucopia of evil: violence, abuse,

---

13. Yee, "I Have Perfumed My Bed," 65. Blenkinsopp ("The Social Context of the 'Outsider Woman,'" 466) adds, "What rather deserves note is the deliberate strategy of juxtaposing the Woman Wisdom and the Outsider Woman as rivals for attention. Both seek to influence their audience—the younger male population, married or unmarried—principally but of course not exclusively by seductive speech. They both therefore go out into the public arena—the streets, acropolis, the open plaza by the city gate—where the male population is likely to be found.... Both also have houses in which they prepare entertainment for their guests of a sharply contrasting nature .... The one is a faithful wife, the other variously described as an adulteress and a prostitute.... Both can be grasped and embraced... but while contact with one is life-enhancing, the other is death-dealing, a *femme fatale* in the literal sense.... They both use much the same metaphorical language—water from your own well, stolen water—but the effect in the one case is salvific, in the other corrupting."

14. Pemberton, "The Rhetoric of the Father," 78.

15. The idiom "go astray" indicates idolatry (Pss 40:4; Prov 14:22; 2 Chr 21:11; Isa 35:8; Ezek 14:11).

and greed (1:11–14), as well as hedonism, promiscuity, and marital infidelity (2:16; 5:3, 20; 7:5). They do not model or foster "righteousness, justice, and equity" (1:3b). For the love of Folly, fools recapitulate the fall of Adam and bring about a reversal of Eden, an upside-down world.[16]

Two Ways

In ancient Israel, travel by foot was often treacherous due to the terrain and deficient public safety. The book of Proverbs adopts this reality as a metaphor about life. Daniel P. Bricker explains:

> In a society that traveled primarily on foot the metaphor of the path or way functioned as an illustration of everyday living. The importance of making good choices on a journey through a wilderness was obvious. The wrong choice could lead at best to delays until the proper path could be relocated and at worst to becoming hopelessly lost and victimized by predators or bandits, and possibly death. In this light "to stumble" (*kasal*) is one of the most serious consequences of walking on the wrong path.[17]

The imagery of travel by foot is abundant in Proverbs. Eighty-two verses employ the "metaphor of the path."[18] The prominent term for "path" or "way" is *derek*, appearing twenty-nine times within Proverbs 1–9, along with other terms with similar meaning.[19] A useful depiction of the metaphor is 4:10–19:

(10) Hear, my son, and accept my words, that the years of your life may be many.

(11) I have taught you the way of wisdom; I have led you in the paths of uprightness.

(12) When you walk, your step will not be hampered, and if you run, you will not stumble.

(13) Keep hold of instruction; do not let go; guard her, for she is your life.

---

16. See Van Leeuwen, "The Biblical World Upside Down," 599–610.
17. Bricker, "The Doctrine of the 'Two Ways,'" 513.
18. Steinmann and Eschelbach, "Walk This Way," 44.
19. Carasik, *Theologies of the Mind*, 169.

(14) Do not enter the path of the wicked, and do not walk in the way of the evil.

(15) Avoid it; do not go on it; turn away from it and pass on.

(16) For they cannot sleep unless they have done wrong; they are robbed of sleep unless they have made someone stumble.

(17) For they eat the bread of wickedness and drink the wine of violence.

(18) But the path of the righteous is like the light of dawn, which shines brighter and brighter until full day.

(19) The way of the wicked is like deep darkness; they do not know over what they stumble.

This passage contrasts the two paths—positive and negative—that lie before the "simple." Many of the comparisons and contrasts can be summarized as the following table illustrates:

Path	way of wisdom, paths of uprightness
In contrast to	path of the wicked, way of the wicked, done wrong, made someone stumble, wickedness, violence
Pedagogy	my words, words of wisdom, instruction
Benefits	years of your life will be many, step will not be hampered, not stumble, life
Destination	light of dawn which shines brighter and brighter until full day
In contrast to	deep darkness, do not know, stumble
Travelers	son, you
In contrast to	the wicked, they

According to this passage, the path of wisdom occurs within a filial and fiduciary relationship that affirms righteousness. It entails a pedagogical process that fosters progressive knowledge, lifelong learning, and the acquisition of wisdom. It promotes flourishing in accord with the order of creation.

In contrast, the way of wickedness thrives within dystopian group identities deriving from self-exclusion and rebellion. Folly promotes a lifestyle of chronic wrongdoing, stupor, self-imposed suffering, and ultimately death.[20] Proverbs 10:9 contrasts the two: "Whoever walks in integrity walks securely, but he who makes his ways crooked will be found out" (see also 11:20).

In addition, the images of light and darkness are associated with the paths of wickedness or righteousness. Just as walking on a mountain path requires light (natural or artificial) for safe travel, so the path of life requires illumination. The "father's commandment" (likely representing law and wisdom) is the conceptual guide for the path of life. "For the commandment is a lamp and the teaching a light, and the reproofs of discipline are the way of life" (6:22–23; see also Job 24:13; Pss 43:3; 119:105). However, light and darkness also indicate a state of being aligned with or alienated from God. Negatively, the image "the lamp of the wicked" occurs by itself three times (13:9; 21:4; 24:20) and is linked to "darkness" in three other passages (2:13; 4:19; 20:20). Darkness is characterized by "sin" and "haughty eyes and a proud heart" (21:4), as well as by despising one's father and mother (20:20). The person who walks in darkness "has no future" (24:20). Such people possess little spiritual self-awareness (4:19), causing them to "stumble" on life's path and suffer loss.

A similar biblical image is that of the "straight" and "crooked" paths. Michael Carasik writes, "Biblical texts regularly emphasize following the straight path that is marked out by God's teachings.... When one 'turns,' it is only to avoid the path of evil and to return to the straight path of righteousness."[21] Thus, Proverbs 1–9 describes fools who follow a crooked path as "devious in their ways" (2:15), spouting "devious talk" (4:24) and "twisted" speech (8:8). They are "worthless" (6:12).[22] In contrast, those who follow the "straight" path "acknowledge" Yahweh (3:6). They focus on rectitude and fidelity, since their "eyes look directly forward" (4:25). They "understand" and discover "knowledge" (8:8).[23]

---

20. Other descriptions of the path of righteousness in chapters 1–9 are "way of his saints" (2:8), "paths of life" (2:19), "way of the good" (2:20), "ways of pleasantness" (3:17), "all her paths are peace" (3:17), "way of life" (6:23), "paths of justice" (8:20), and "way of insight" (9:6). Other descriptions of the path of wickedness are "ways ... who is greedy for unjust gain" (1:19), "way of evil" (2:12), "devious in their ways" (2:15), "paths to the departed" (2:18), and "way to Sheol" (7:27).

21. Carasik, "Qohelet's Twists and Turns," 199.

22. Other references are "those of a crooked heart are an abomination" (11:20), "does not discover good" and a "dishonest tongue" (17:20), "a fool" (19:1), and "way of the guilty" (21:8). The way of the crooked brings "thorns and snares" (22:5) and ends badly, for "he who is crooked in his ways will suddenly fall" (28:18).

23. In addition, "the righteousness of the blameless keeps his way straight" (11:5),

According to the book of Proverbs, *everyone* travels a path. Life is a journey in one of two directions whose final destiny is either good or evil, light or darkness, wisdom or folly. Van Leeuwen writes, "Life is caught between the pull toward God and the good and the pull toward folly and pseudogood."[24] Proverbs shows, moreover, that mankind's travel is a religious pilgrimage toward God or a pseudo-god. Like the ancient reader of Proverbs, all humans are motivated by the fear of the Lord or seduced by folly. Each path entails priorities that please or displease God, as well as lifestyles that bless or curse. Those who traverse the path of righteousness are blessed by God and bless others, whereas those who take the crooked path suffer loss and cause harm to those around them.

THE PROLOGUE

Our wisdom deficit, the instructional aim, the intended hearers, and the pedagogical dilemma are all expressed in the prologue, Proverbs 1:1–7 (the key terms are in italics):

(1) The proverbs of Solomon, son of David, king of Israel:

(2) To *know wisdom* and *instruction*, to *understand* words of insight,

(3) to receive *instruction* in *wise dealing*, in *righteousness, justice, and equity*;

(4) to give *prudence* to the simple, *knowledge* and *discretion* to the youth—

(5) Let the wise hear and increase in learning, and the one who understands obtain *guidance*,

(6) to understand a proverb and a saying, the words of the wise and their riddles.

(7) The *fear of the Lord* is the beginning of knowledge; [but] fools *despise* wisdom and instruction.[25]

---

while "one whose way is straight is an abomination to the wicked" (29:27).

24. Longman, "Proverbs," in *A Complete Literary Guide*, 258. Similarly, Longman (*Proverbs*, 153) calls this the "two-oath theology" that "does not allow for a third, compromising way."

25. The NIV and NKJV express the dissonance between the first and second half of the statement by inserting the Hebrew *waw* ("but").

The five infinitives—to know, to understand (twice), to receive, to give—indicate pedagogical purpose. The primary objective of the entire book is wisdom (*chokmah*, v. 2a). The multiform nature of wisdom is expressed by the other terms in verses 2–6: "prudence" (*ormah*), "learning" (*leqach*), "guidance" (*tabulot*), "wise dealing" (*haskel*), "discretion" (*mezimmah*), and understanding (*binah*).[26] The source of wisdom is God, for "The Lord gives wisdom" (2:6; see also 1:23). Wisdom also presupposes a critical motivational dimension—the "fear of the Lord" (v. 7a). The application of wisdom generates social integrity and human flourishing: "righteousness, justice, and equity" (v. 3b).

The designated learners comprise three groups: the "simple," "youth," and the "wise."[27] The first two groups are teachable, though vulnerable to folly's seductive power (9:15; 14:15; 22:3). The "wise" fear God and have already tasted the benefits of wisdom. Their task is perseverance and further growth (1:5–6). Fools, on the other hand, suffer a wisdom deficit due to self-exclusion (v. 7b). They refuse to acknowledge ("fear") God and scorn ("despise") wisdom and instruction.

The prologue highlights the main themes of the book by means of a chiastic structure. Similar words and phrases are repeated so that the principal ideas are clearly expressed. In this diagram provided by Bruce K. Waltke, A1 and A2, B1 and B2, C1 and C2 are parallel in significance.[28] X represents where the two lines of thought converge and express the purpose and fruits of wisdom.

---

26. The scope of wisdom is very broad, based on other terms used in coordination with *chokmah* throughout Proverbs: "understanding"/"competence" (*tebunah*, 7 times), "commandment(s) (*mitswah*, 7), "teaching" (*torah*, 6), "law" (*torah*, 4), "words" (*emer*, 12), "saying(s)" (*dabar*, 4), "counsel" (*etsah*, 3), "truth" (*emet*, 2), "sense" (*leb*, 5), "discretion" (*sekel*, 6), "inheritance" (*nachal*, 2), "what is right" (1), "what is just" (1), "noble things" (*nagid*, 1), "covenant" (*berit*, 1), and "learning" (*leqach*, 2)

27. Keefer ("A Shift in Perspective," 103–16) argues that the "wise" are the actual audience and function as "learner-teachers" of the "simple" and "youth." Longman (*Proverbs*, 103) says that the prologue indicates "that the book is addressed to everyone who is open to its teaching."

28. Waltke, "Righteousness in Proverbs," 234–35.

A1	(2a)	to know wisdom and instruction		
	B1	(2b)	to understand words of insight	
		C1	(3a)	prudent behavior[29]
		X	(3b)	righteousness, justice, and equity
		C2	(4a)	prudence, discretion, guidance
	B2	(6)	to understand a proverb and a saying	
A2	(7b)	knowledge: wisdom and instruction		

Wisdom

In A1 (Prov 1:2a) "wisdom" (*chokmah*) is God-given understanding of the world and mankind's place within. It is a worldview—God's point of view—that presupposes a particular ontology, anthropology, epistemology, ethics, and sacred history. According to Van Leeuwen, wisdom "concerns the relation of creation to God, in every aspect of creation, and the implications of this relation for human piety and conduct in the ordinary affairs of life, whether high (8:15–16; 16:1–15; 31:1–9) or low (25:11; 27:8, 14)."[30] Wisdom is revelation from God about himself and the world to mankind. It is a body of truth *and* a way of life. Wisdom is an absolute idea with universal consequences in every sphere of life.

Wisdom depicts reality. For this reason, it is more than the sum of the other terms in verses 2–6. Wisdom cannot be reduced to understanding, prudence, or insight; rather, wisdom presupposes of all the intellectual and social virtues enumerated in the prologue. Gerhard von Rad commented, "By the accumulation of many terms the text seems to aim at something larger, something more comprehensive which could not be expressed satisfactorily by means of any one of the terms used."[31] Wisdom provides, therefore, the theological and theoretical framework by which mankind should think and behave in this created but fallen world: a post-edenic ethics and epistemology. It entails knowing what

---

29. "Wise dealing" in verse 3a means "to be prudent" (*sakal*) and parallels "prudence" in verse 4a (*ormah*).

30. Van Leeuwen, "Proverbs," in *The Theological Interpretation of the Old Testament*, 173.

31. Von Rad, *Wisdom in Israel*, 13. Fox ("Words for Wisdom," 158) comments similarly, "*Hokmah* is the broader mental capacity that makes understanding possible, as well as the knowledge that understanding produces, but it is not the understanding itself."

is important to God and applying that knowledge as he expects in every circumstance.

Further, wisdom looks in two directions: "above the sun" and "under the sun." First, the name of Yahweh, the covenant-making deity of Israel, appears eighty-seven times in Proverbs. Ryan O'Dowd writes, "Wisdom and knowledge begin and are dependent on faithfulness to Israel's God and covenant."[32] There are, in fact, parallels between Proverbs' ethical instruction and the Ten Commandments. Longman comments, "It is not hard to see a connection between wisdom and law. Both make demands upon a person's life and behavior."[33] There are references to the Fifth (1:8; 4:1, 10; 10:1; 13:1), Sixth (1:10–12. 6:11), Seventh (2:16–19; 6:20–35; chapters 5 and 7), Eighth (1:13–14; 11:1); Ninth (3:20; 6:18, 19; 10:18; 12:17, 19), and Tenth Commandments (6:18).[34] Moreover, a strong correlation exists between Proverbs 3:1–12 and the *Shema* in Deuteronomy 6:4–9. There are parallel terms such as "bind" and "write," as well as the use of covenantal language, namely "steadfast love" (*chesed*) and "faithfulness" (*emet*) in Proverbs 3:3.[35]

Second, wisdom also displays an "above the sun" orientation in Proverbs, stating that the world is intimately associated with the Creator (3:19–20; 8:22–31). The phrase "tree of life" occurs four times (3:18; 11:30; 13:12; 15:4) and the word "life" (*chay*) appears thirty-four times (likely shorthand for the fuller phrase "tree of life").[36] According to Proverbs, the tree of life provides access to Eden-like blessings "under the sun." The following passage speaks to Wisdom's worth and the potency of the tree in chapter 3:

(13) Blessed is the one who finds wisdom, and the one who gets understanding,

(14) for the gain from her is better than gain from silver and her profit better than gold.

32. O'Dowd, "A Chord of Three Strands," 68.

33. Longman, *Proverbs*, 80.

34. Longman, *Proverbs*, 81. See also Brooks, "The Complementary Relationship," 3–32.

35. Overland, "Did the Sage Draw from the Shema?" 424–40.

36. O'Dowd ("A Chord of Three Strands," 71) comments, "The phrase 'tree of life,' though alluded to in texts like Psalm 1 and Jeremiah 17:8, is used explicitly only in Genesis 2–3, Proverbs 3:18; 11:30; 15:4; and in Revelation 2:7; 22:2, 14, 19—all passages with creational and re-creational contexts." See also Hurowitz, "Paradise Regained," 49–62.

(15) She is more precious than jewels, and nothing you desire can compare with her.

16) Long life is in her right hand; in her left hand are riches and honor.

(17) Her ways are ways of pleasantness, and all her paths are peace.

(18) She is a tree of life to those who lay hold of her; those who hold her fast are called blessed.

Furthermore, Yahweh is depicted as the divine ruler, architect, economist, and all-wise philosopher of Genesis 1–3.[37] As ruler, he is sovereign over all, especially all human undertakings: "The heart of man plans his way, but the LORD establishes his steps" (16:9; see also 16:1, 4, 33; 19:21; 21:1). He perceives and evaluates every human impulse: "Sheol and Abaddon lie open before the Lord; how much more the hearts of the children of man!" (15:11; see also 16:2; 17:3; 21:2). He condemns wrongdoing as an "abomination": "haughty eyes, a lying tongue, hands that shed innocent blood, a heart that devises wicked plans, feet that make haste to run to evil, a false witness who breathes out lies, and one who sows discord among brothers" (16:17–19). Yahweh also intervenes for the sake of justice as he deems fit: "The Lord's curse is on the house of the wicked" (3:33a) and he "tears down the house of the proud" (15:25a). Moreover, he is called the "Maker" three times (14:31; 17:5; 22:2). Proverbs announces, "The Lord has made everything for its purpose, even the wicked for the day of trouble" (16:4; see also 29:13).

Yahweh rules the world through self-compensating moral law.[38] Scholars call this the act–consequence nexus, but in popular parlance many idioms express the same idea, such as "What goes around comes around." According to Proverbs, the moral universe is hard-wired for

---

37. Similarly, the name Elohim is linked to the "fear of the Lord" and the "knowledge of God" (2:5), the covenant of marriage (2:17), "favor and good success" (3:4), divine generosity and "Maker" (14:31; 22:2), and to a deity who punishes (17:5), withholds knowledge (25:2), whose words are pure (30:5), who can be "insulted" (14:31; 17:5), and whose name can be "profaned" (30:9).

38. Longman (*Proverbs*, 84) summarizes the concept: "So there are texts that lead us to think that the act of the wicked will come back to haunt them and those that imply or directly connect Yahweh to the rewards and punishments that come on people. However, the two are not really different. The former may imply that Yahweh will see that people get what they deserve. Perhaps the best way to think of it is that Yahweh built the world in such a way that punishments are inherent in bad actions and rewards in good actions. Yahweh is ultimately behind all consequences."

blessing or woe. Those who fear and honor the Lord can expect good in life, whereas those who despise the Lord and divine wisdom can expect affliction.[39] For instance, "A fool's lips walk into a fight, and his mouth invites a beating" (18:6), and "the evil man has no future; the lamp of the wicked will be put out" (24:20).[40] This is, of course, why the fool's enterprise is a fruitless errand and a "wise man's hell." Fools try to swim upstream against reality and thereby bring suffering upon themselves and others.

Proverbs portrays Yahweh as an architect or builder and the earth as his house. Yahweh is an artisan who crafted his household with utmost care: "The Lord by wisdom founded the earth; by understanding he established the heavens; by his knowledge the deeps broke open, and the clouds drop down the dew" (3:19–20). Likewise, he filled his house with beauty and bounty: "By wisdom a house is built, and by understanding it is established; by knowledge the rooms are filled with all precious and pleasant riches" (24:3–4). This imagery appears in the description of Lady Wisdom's residence in Proverbs 9:1–6:

(1) Wisdom has built her house; she has hewn her seven pillars.

(2) She has slaughtered her beasts; she has mixed her wine; she has also set her table.

(3) She has sent out her young women to call from the highest places in the town,

(4) "Whoever is simple, let him turn in here!" To him who lacks sense she says,

(5) "Come, eat of my bread and drink of the wine I have mixed.

(6) Leave your simple ways, and live, and walk in the way of insight."

Wisdom has built a grand edifice representing abundance and beauty.[41] Her house is spacious and enduring. It is adorned by "seven pillars." Longman explains, "The number seven indicates perfection and/or completeness. Thus, we are to picture the scene as a large mansion;

---

39. As we saw in Ecclesiastes and will discover in Job (chapters 11–12 of this book), sometimes the act-consequences nexus seemingly malfunctions "under the sun."

40. On the other hand, Proverbs recognizes enigma due to finitude and fallenness. Even for those who fear God, suffering also occurs: "For the righteous falls seven times and rises again, but the wicked stumble in times of calamity" (24:16).

41. Her house, of course, is creation (8:22–31).

it demonstrates that Wisdom's house was 'an indication of wealth and social status.'"[42] Furthermore, Lady Wisdom demonstrates her hospitality by urging invitees to attend her banquet ("her table") and provides sumptuous provisions ("wine" and "bread"). Mankind desperately needs instruction, so Wisdom cries out with urgency, "Leave your simple ways, and live, and walk in the way of insight."

As the divine economist, Yahweh is the source of all good things. He provides a fructuous environment that brings about human flourishing. He is generous. He gives "wisdom" (2:6), blessing (3:33b; 10:22), and "favor" (3:34; 8:35; 12:2), as well as the capacity to perceive and understand (29:13). He molds character (3:9, 12), "prolongs life" (10:27), protects and rewards his followers (10:29; 18:10; 20:22; 25:22; 29:25), provides a "prudent wife" (19:14b), and grants "riches, honor, and life" (22:4). He also upholds the moral infrastructure of exchange: "Do not rob the poor, because he is poor, or crush the afflicted at the gate, for the Lord will plead their cause and rob of life those who rob them" (22:22–23).

As the omniscient philosopher, Yahweh's understanding is supreme: "No wisdom, no understanding, no counsel can avail against the Lord" (21:30).[43] He is the source of wisdom: "For the Lord gives wisdom; from his mouth come knowledge and understanding" (2:6), and "knowledge of the Holy One is insight" (9:10). Yahweh maintains control over understanding, for "The eyes of the Lord keep watch over knowledge" (22:12). And with wisdom he "founded the earth; by understanding he established the heavens" (3:19). The Lord is, therefore, the transcendent standard and precondition for understanding reality, since he is the Creator. Revelation is the presupposition of all knowing, as Anselm famously declared: "I believe so that I may understand."[44]

In all these ways, Proverbs presents the Lord as the cosmic king, designer, benefactor, and thinker of Genesis 1–2. By his words, the world functions as designed. His thoughts communicate truth, knowledge, and wisdom. By his power creation came to pass. His sovereignty determines all plans and purposes. He was the model for Adam as vice-regent. He is the paradigm for the wise person who fears the Lord, for God embodies "righteousness, justice, and equity" in heaven and on earth.

42. Longman, *Proverbs*, 216.

43. Job inquired, "From where, then, does wisdom come? And where is the place of understanding?" (28:20). Proverbs answers, "The fear of the Lord is the beginning of wisdom" (1:7a).

44. Anselm, *Complete Philosophical and Theological Treatises*, 93.

To Know

In A1 from the chiasm above, the first infinitive, "to know" (*daat*), derives from the common verb for knowing (*yada*).[45] *Daat* appears forty times in Proverbs (out of ninety times in the Old Testament) and refers to a special kind of insight from an extraordinary source. Carasik explains that *daat* is "not for ordinary knowledge, but for a particular kind of knowledge whose origin is in the divine realm: a knowledge of or from God."[46] *Daat* is revelation. In Proverbs, it is associated with the fear of God (1:7; 9:10), the call of Lady Wisdom (1:22), wisdom and understanding given by God (2:6), and the wisdom by which he created the world (3:19–20). Outside Proverbs, Numbers 24:16 expresses the unique purview of *daat*: "The oracle of him who hears the words of God, and knows the knowledge (*daat*) of the Most High, who sees the vision of the Almighty." A similar notion is stated in Psalm 94:10–11: "He who teaches man knowledge (*daat*)—the Lord—knows (*yada*) the thoughts of man, that they are but a breath" (see also 119:66).[47]

The Hiphil stem of *yada* (*odia*) also appears in Proverbs, underscoring the same divine source of knowledge. The Hiphil expresses causality and means "to make known," indicating the impartation of understanding from God. Carasik comments that in the Old Testament the Hiphil stem of *yada* "more than nine-tenths of the time is used to indicate the transmission of knowledge whose ultimate source is in the divine realm."[48] In Proverbs 1, Lady Wisdom says to the "simple" and "scoffer," "If you turn at my reproof, behold, I will pour out my spirit to you; I will *make* my words *known* (*odia*) to you" (v. 23). Clearly, wisdom speaks with revelatory authority and for this reason demands a penitential response ("turn").

---

45. *Yada* is used in Proverbs primarily to indicate the inherent ignorance of the "wicked" (fool) and Lady Folly (4:19; 5:6; 9:13, 18); for example, "The woman Folly is loud; she is seductive and knows nothing" (9:13).

46. Carasik, *Theologies of the Mind*, 52.

47. The Messiah possesses *daat*, as well as other intellectual attributes enumerated in verses 2–6 such wisdom (*chokmah*), understanding (*binah*), and counsel (*etsah*): "And the Spirit of the Lord shall rest upon him, the Spirit of wisdom and understanding, the Spirit of counsel and might, the Spirit of knowledge and the fear of the Lord" (Isa 11:2). Without a doubt, it is significant that *daat* also plays a decisive role in Genesis 2: "But of the tree of the knowledge of good and evil you shall not eat, for in the day that you eat of it you shall surely die" (v. 17).

48. Carasik, *Theologies of the Mind*, 28.

Similarly, in chapter 22 a sage declares this exhortation to his disciple (the important words are italicized):

(17) Incline your ear, and hear the words of the wise, and apply your heart to my *knowledge* (*daat*) . . . .

(19) That your trust may be in the Lord, I have *made* them *known* (*odia*) to you today, even to you.

(20) Have I not written for you thirty sayings of *counsel* (from *etsah*) and *knowledge* (*daat*),

(21) to *make* you *know* (*odia*) what is right and true, that you may give a true answer to those who sent you?

In this passage, the source of knowledge is Yahweh mediated through wisdom, specifically the "words of the wise" and "thirty sayings of counsel and knowledge." The purpose is "that your trust may be in the Lord" and to understand "what is right and true." The correct posture is to "incline your ear," "hear," and "apply your heart" to God's instruction. The benefit is blessing (v. 18b) and a "true answer."

To Understand

In B1 and B2, the term "understand" (*binah*) appears with reference to the objects "words of insight" (1:2b) and "a proverb and a saying" (v. 6a). Michael V. Fox defines *binah* as an analytical and deductive capacity to interpret, discern, and unravel enigmas.[49] In the prologue, the term describes the "wise" (1:5), who can "understand a proverb and a saying, the words of the wise and their riddles" (v. 6). *Binah* is attributed to wisdom in 4:5, 7 and 8:14. In 9:10, it is cited in parallel to the "fear of God" and translated as "insight" equal to the "knowledge of the Holy One." Outside of Proverbs, the term is connected with King Solomon's governance of Israel and maintenance of the law (1 Chr 22:12). Likewise, *binah* is credited to the sons of Issachar, "who had understanding of the times, to know what Israel ought to do" (1 Chr 12:32). They discerned what mattered to God in their time and how to respond.

Closely associated with *binah* (though not appearing in the prologue) is the word *tebunah*, often translated as "competent" (2:2, 3, 6, 11; 3:19; 5:1; 8:1). Fox explains that *tebunah* refers to practical skills

---

49. Fox, "Words for Wisdom," 151, 154–58.

and technical proficiency applied to pragmatic challenges. He calls it "know-how," "common sense," and "talent."[50] In Proverbs, God possessed competence in the building of creation: "The Lord by wisdom founded the earth; by understanding (*tebunah*) he established the heavens" (3:19; see also 8:1). Similarly, in Proverbs 10–20 the wise person constructs his social world with *tebunah* and interpersonal virtue (11:12; 14:29; 17:27; 18:2; 20:5). The master craftsman Bezalel beautified the tabernacle (Exod 31:3) with *tebunah* (see also Ezek 28:4; Hos 13:2).

Prudence and Discretion

In C1 and C2, the word pair "prudence" (*ormah*) and "discretion" (*mezimmah*) appears. Elsewhere in the Old Testament, these mental capacities are frowned upon as expressions of evil scheming (*ormah* in Exod 12:14; Josh 9:4; *mezimmah* in Job 21:27; Ps 10:2, 4). But with the presumption of the fear of the Lord, they function as important cognitive capacities associated with wisdom. Fox defines the former as "the talent for devising and using adroit and wily tactics in the attaining of one's goals."[51] Synonyms might be cunning or "street smarts." Longman writes, "'Prudence' describes one's ability to use reason, in context under the fear of God, to navigate the problems of life."[52] In Proverbs, this term refers to forethought that delivers the naive from folly and evil (8:5). "Every prudent man acts with knowledge" (13:16), and "the prudent sees danger and hides himself" (22:3).

"Discretion" (*mezimmah*) indicates the mind's motivations to prevent moral error and promote human flourishing. For instance, discretion delivers the would-be wise "from the way of evil, from men of perverted speech, who forsake the paths of uprightness to walk in the ways of darkness" (2:12–14a; see also 5:2). Discretion also produces blessing and security: "They will be life for your soul and adornment for your neck. Then you will walk on your way securely, and your foot will not stumble" (3:22–23). For these reasons, Lady Wisdom claims these skills as part of her portfolio (8:12a). Folly, on the other hand, utilizes these capacities for malfeasant ends.

---

50. Fox, "Words for Wisdom," 152–53.
51. Fox, "Words for Wisdom," 158.
52. Longman, *Proverbs*, 97.

Instruction

In A1 and A2, "instruction" (*musar*) is derived from a verb meaning "to admonish" or "to correct."[53] It is repeated four times in verses 2–8, underscoring its significance. And it is joined with a similar term, "reproof" (*towkechah*), nine times (3:11; 5:12; 6:23; 10:17; 12:1; 13:18; 15:5, 10, 32). In addition to the parallel in verses 2 and 7, instruction is also matched with a near synonym of wisdom (*daat*) three times in the book (12:1; 19:27; 23:12). *Musar*, then, implies support for the aspiring student, but also chastisement for the obtuse disciple.

Moreover, "instruction" underscores human responsibility in acquiring wisdom. Dru Johnson explains that knowledge occurs within a "fiduciary relationship." He writes, "Man cannot know without a commitment to trust God. God must commit to helping the man know."[54] In Proverbs, Yahweh enables mankind to know wisdom and requires human participation in a learning process emphasizing application, diligence, and remembrance. Proverbs 12:1a says, "Whoever loves discipline loves knowledge." Similarly, Proverbs 6:20–22 urges the aspirant to figuratively "bind your father's commandment" and "your mother's teaching" on "your heart" and "around your neck" (using the language of Deuteronomy 6:4–8; see also Proverbs 3:3, 5; 6:4; 7:3). The acquisition of wisdom, therefore, comprises two aspects: God-given content and human acknowledgment expressed through obedience. In other words, wisdom is made known by God and embraced by willing listeners in a pedagogical process of internalization and application.

The Beginning of Knowledge

The fear of God (A2) is the main theme of the book.[55] It appears as a summary statement in the prologue (1:7a) and as the defining characteristic of the wise woman in the last chapter (31:30). In chapters 1–9, the phrase

---

53. Longman, *Proverbs*, 95.
54. Johnson, *Biblical Knowing*, 31.
55. The expression "fear of the Lord" occurs fourteen times in Proverbs (1:7, 29; 2:5; 8:13; 9:10; 10:27; 14:26, 27; 15:16, 33; 16:6; 19:23; 22:4; 23:17). Likewise, "fears the Lord" appears three times (14:2; 28:14; 31:30) and "fear the Lord" twice (3:7, 24:21). In the Old Testament, the "fear of the Lord" appears twenty-five times and "fear the Lord" thirty-four times across the law, history books, prophets, and a (wisdom) Psalm. See Block, "The Fear of the Lord," 367–91.

is associated with knowledge (1:7, 29; 2:5, 6; 3:5, 7, 19; 9:10), ethics (3:7; 5:21; 6:16; 8:13), piety (3:5, 7, 9, 32), blessing (3:26; 8:35), protection (3:32; 8:35), reproof (3:11), and creation (9:10).

For the wise person, the "fear of the Lord" is shorthand for a positive relationship with Yahweh. Fearing God presupposes epistemological self-awareness and eschews ontological ascendancy. The wise understand the Creator–creature distinction. They acknowledge utter dependence and accountability. They listen to God's voice in creation and law. O'Dowd comments, "The careful, repeated use of the 'fear of Yahweh' throughout Proverbs *reminds* the reader of Israel's redemptive history and thus embeds wisdom in the worldview, or storied picture of the whole, which forms the foundation for Israel's religion."[56] Thus, the "fear" (*yirat*) of the Lord entails gratitude, worship, and wonder. Awe of God situates human beings within creation and redemptive history. It provokes obedience. The acknowledgment of Yahweh ("fear") precedes thinking, ethics, and piety.

The word "beginning" (*reshit*) refers to God the Creator, who is the fountainhead of wisdom. Yahweh is the origin and epicenter of knowledge. Those who fear the Lord recognize the why, what, and how of wisdom and teleology. They reason from and through revelation. They embrace epistemic humility and are certainly not "wise in [their] own eyes" (3:7). Von Rad commented:

> To this extent, Israel attributes to the fear of God, to belief in God, a highly important function in respect of human knowledge. She was, in all seriousness, of the opinion that effective knowledge about God is the only thing that a puts man into a right relationship with the objects of his perception, that it enables him to ask questions more pertinently, to take stock of relationships more effectively and generally to have a better awareness of circumstances . . . . Wisdom stands and falls according to the right attitude of man to God.[57]

This means that fools, who "[hate] knowledge and [do] not choose the fear of the Lord" (1:29), reject the key to life and wisdom. This is why

---

56. O'Dowd, "A Chord of Three Strands," 68 (emphasis in original). Similarly, Von Rad (*Wisdom in Israel*, 164) wrote, "The teachers speak quite frequently of Yahweh, and that was a name which was always heavy with tradition. It would be difficult to imagine that this name, in the mouth of the teachers, would have shed all of the content with which, as far as we can see, it was indissolubly associated."

57. Von Rad, *Wisdom in Israel*, 67–69.

their very existence is a fool's errand. They operate on borrowed time and stolen resources with no hope of success. Yet they rely upon God's unmerited benefaction, as they pillage creation and plagiarize wisdom to realize their perverted aspirations. In light of A2, therefore, fools are parasites in God's world, precisely because they "despise wisdom and instruction" (1:7b).[58]

Righteousness, Justice, and Equity

The intellectual and moral virtues that constitute wisdom have a this-worldly focus designed to promote "righteousness, justice, and equity" (X in the chiasm of Proverbs 1). Verse 3b expresses the function of wisdom within creation on God's terms. Specifically, wisdom entails the application of knowledge and skill to cause human flourishing and to bring glory to God. In fact, personified wisdom promises Eden-like blessings for the wise on earth: "I will pour out my spirit to you" and "make my words known to you" (1:23). "Riches and honor," "righteousness," and "paths of justice" are provided as an "inheritance" (8:18, 21). Wisdom fosters harmony and prosperity through "rulers" who "decree what is just."[59]

"Righteousness" (*saddiq*) refers to a transcendent norm, a criterion by which all else is evaluated. God himself is righteous, for he judges all things according to his holy and omniscient character.[60] He is the norm and model for human beings as God's vice-regents. Righteousness, then, entails obligation derived from mankind's dependence and accountability. It shows the individual and community should function within a world of sin. C. Hassell Bullock comments, "One cannot separate individual and community ethics. The individual feeds into the community and builds its character, while the community ethic supports and

---

58. Recall Paul's argument in Romans 2:4–5: "Or do you presume on the riches of his kindness and forbearance and patience, not knowing that God's kindness is meant to lead you to repentance? But because of your hard and impenitent heart you are storing up wrath for yourself on the day of wrath when God's righteous judgment will be revealed."

59. Similarly, the Father's wisdom imparts a broad variety of earthly blessings: knowledge ("you will understand righteousness and justice and equity," 2:9b), satisfaction ("knowledge will be pleasant to your soul," 2:10b), protection ("delivering you from the way of evil," 2:12a), longevity ("length of days and years of life," 3:2), and prosperity ("favor and good success," 3:4a).

60. For example, see Pss 50:6; 71:19; 97:2.

undergirds the individual ethic."⁶¹ Examples of righteous conduct are stated negatively in the "do not" depictions of foolish behavior in chapter 3: "Do not withhold good from those to whom it is due, when it is in your power to do it" (v. 27); "Do not say to your neighbor, 'Go, and come again, tomorrow I will give it'—when you have it with you" (v. 28); "Do not plan evil against your neighbor" (v. 29); "Do not contend with a man for no reason, when he has done you no harm" (v. 30); and "Do not envy a man of violence and do not choose any of his ways" (v. 31).⁶²

"Justice" (*mishpat* is the implementation of righteousness in the social, economic, and legal spheres. *Mishpat* often signifies judicial action, arbitration, and restorative justice in accord with God's standards. For instance, justice refers to equal remuneration and penalty (especially in cases of bribery; 17:23; 29:4), "balance and scales" (16:11), and legal impartiality (18:5).

"Equity" (*mesharim*) bears two nuances. Explicitly, *mesharim* denotes speech that is true (entails truthfulness) and right (8:6; 23:16; see also Pss 9:8; 58:1; Isa 33:15; 45:19). Implicitly, "equity" refers to fairness and impartiality in judgment according to righteous standards (1:3; 2:9; see also Pss 75:2; 96:16; 98:9; 99:4). Isaiah 33:15 expresses the thematic commonality of the these terms in verse 3b: "He who walks righteously (*saddiq*) and speaks uprightly (*mesharim*), who despises the gain of oppressions, who shakes his hands, lest they hold a bribe, who stops his ears from hearing of bloodshed and shuts his eyes from looking on evil."

In summary, "righteousness, justice, and equity" (X) represent where A1 and A2, B1 and B2, as well as C1 and C2 converge, expressing the purpose of wisdom in the prologue. The phrase represents the personal and communal divine standards that should govern society in every sphere east of Eden. As such, they are both norms and benefits. To put it another way, righteousness, justice, and equity represent how human beings ought to image God and to behave as God's people, covenanted with the Lord. The phrase also reveals how to fear God in accord with the Creator–creature distinction. Wisdom directs the mind in its

---

61. Bullock, "Ethics," 198. Similarly, Waltke ("Righteousness in Proverbs," 235) defines "righteousness" as "doing what is right in a social relationship as defined by God's standard of what is right behavior."

62. Stated positively, the "righteous" experience multiple benefits from Yahweh: blessing (Prov 3:33), daily provision (10:3), "love" (15:9b), God's listening ear (15:29b), and protection (18:10). Likewise, "the path of righteousness" (12:28) yields great personal and social blessings: "life . . . no death" (12:28; 21:21); "guards" (13:6), "exalts a nation" (14:34; see also 16:12; 25:5).

various capacities to bring about human flourishing to the glory of God. This also appears to be the intent of Deuteronomy 4:5–6:[63]

> See, I have taught you statutes and rules, as the Lord my God commanded me, that you should do them in the land that you are entering to take possession of it. Keep them and do them, for that will be your wisdom and your understanding in the sight of the peoples, who, when they hear all these statutes, will say, "Surely this great nation is a wise and understanding people."

THE FOOL

Everything positive that Proverbs reveals about wisdom, the fool rejects in principle if not in practice: "fools despise wisdom and instruction." He is an antihero, the antithesis of all that God intends for human beings. He listens to the wrong voice, loves the wrong woman, and chooses the wrong path. He is recklessly independent. Vanity and craving are his greatest motivations, for he yields happily to folly's enticement. He adopts a crooked lifestyle. He is uncontrollable and uncooperative.

The fool does not image God as an apprentice ruler, builder, benefactor, and thinker. He becomes a malfeasant steward and abusive vice regent. He is a dissembler, not a builder. He does not fill God's house with good things, because he is self-indulgent and miserly. He does not foster "righteousness, justice, and equity." As a result, his trajectory is dystopian and dysfunctional.

The verb "despise" (*buz*) in 1:7 reveals the fool's contrarian nature. *Buz* indicates a negative outlook that dishonors, devalues, and denigrates others.[64] For instance, the fool repudiates wisdom and instruction (1:7b; 13:13) and "mocks" parents (30:17; see also 23:22).[65] In fact, the fool despises God. Like Adam, he rejects the divine teacher as the authoritative

---

63. Proverbs and the biblical canon generally argue against the utopianism proposed by Hurowitz, "Paradise Regained," 60: "The text thus signals us that the way (back) to the Tree of Life is through wisdom. One who acquires wisdom will find his way back to the Tree of Life and the primordial blessings of paradise." Van Leeuwen better expresses reality in light of the fall into sin in "The Biblical World Upside Down."

64. See Prov 6:30; 11:12; 13:13; 14:21; 23:9; 30:17; see also Pss 31:18; 123:3–4; Neh 4:4.

65. Another term meaning "to despise" (*bazar*) describes Esau's dismissal of his birthright (Gen 25:34). He did not discern the long-term significance of his inheritance and instead preferred short-term desire.

guide for life and learning. Perhaps the fool's great moral weakness, therefore, is his dismissive cynicism.

Surely, though, the principal consequence of foolishness is intellectual. The fool rejects Yahweh's post-edenic epistemology as taught through creation and law. He models noetic depravity. He wants nothing to do with the mental and moral virtues of the prologue (1:2–7). He discards wisdom, the key to knowledge.[66] He obfuscates and embraces "fake news," not only for himself but also for others. Jesus Christ could have said about the fool in Proverbs, "You have taken away the key of knowledge. You did not enter yourselves, and you hindered those who were entering" (Luke 11:52).

Tragically, the fool loses the capacity to think clearly, as made in the image of God. He ignores the Archimedean point (revelation), so he is hapless intellectually. Indeed, Proverbs says that the fool "lacks sense" or "understanding."[67] The expression "lacks sense" (*chasar-leb*) means literally "without a heart." Since *leb* ("heart") often signifies "mind," the phrase is translated as "lacking sense" or "lacking understanding." Carasik writes, "The absence of heart . . . is a Biblical Hebrew metaphor for the inability to think."[68] Proverbs declares that those who *chasar-leb* "commit adultery" (6:32 and 7:7), "belittle [their] neighbor" (11:12), and "follow worthless pursuits" (12:21). They are "sluggards" (24:30) and "cruel oppressors" (28:16). As a result, "a rod is for the back" of fools (10:13) and they "die for a lack of sense" (10:21).

The Anatomy of Foolishness

When human beings listen to Lady Folly, they set themselves on a trajectory that leads to disastrous social, ethical, and cognitive results. Not every aspect of foolishness manifests itself in every case, but many aspects do. Glenn D. Pemberton describes four stages of emergent foolishness in

---

66. Longman (*Proverbs*, 101) comments, "Fools do not see the big picture. One might be an expert, say, on sailing . . . but they do not understand who made the winds and the sea and who ultimately guides one's way. True knowledge begins with an acknowledgment that everything is created and sustained by God and that he is the one who imparts knowledge not only through revelation but also through experience, observation, and reason."

67. See 6:32; 7:7; 9:4, 16; 10:13, 21; 11:12; 12:11; 15:21; 17:18; 24:30; and 28:16.

68. Carasik, *Theologies of the Mind*, 109.

the book of Proverbs.[69] The first stage, "Foolish Actions," is displayed as a lack of self-control, especially in speech, rashness, and irritability. The second stage, "Folly Becomes Sport," occurs when "folly is a joy to him who lacks sense" (15:21a). "Foolishness becomes a game, a challenge, even fun."[70] Stage three is "Beyond Correction," when fools become unreachable by rationality and self-assured in their opinions. Pemberton comments, "Fools are more self-confident in their knowledge than the wise, more experienced in arguing, and unwilling to listen . . . . One will never win an argument with a fool."[71] The final, tragic stage is "Collapse and Rage." The road to folly ends in disgrace (3:35), stumbling (5:23), ruin and terror (10:14), flogging and punishment (19:29), involuntary service (11:29), destruction (1:29–32), and death (10:21).

Proverbs depicts how and what the fool thinks. First, foolishness is linked to arrogance. Fools are "scoffers" (1:22) who "mock" (14:9). They "slander" (10:18) and earnestly believe they are "right in [their] own eyes" (12:15). A fool is vain and unreasonably ambitious, for "the eyes of a fool are on the ends of the earth" (17:24). A fool is interested only in "expressing his opinion" (18:2). Fools are habitual skeptics and cynics. They "only rage and laugh" (29:9). They obsessively self-promote and "exalt" themselves (30:22).

Second, fools are disingenuous. They sow "hatred" (14:17), because they are "reckless and careless" (14:16). They enjoy "provocation" (27:3) and "quarreling" (20:3), because they speak and act with a "quick temper" (14:17). They are "crooked in speech" (19:1) and "deceiving" (14:8). Further, the heart of a fool is "arrogant" (16:5), "crooked" (17:20), and "haughty" (18:12), and it "rages against the Lord" (19:3). A fool "turns aside" (7:25) to idolatry and "envies sinners" (23:17). Fools "harden" their hearts before God and mankind, speak about "perverse things" (23:33), and "devise violence" (24:2). In short, foolishness is the product of a "perverted heart (or mind) [that] devises evil" (6:14).[72]

Third, fools are ignorant, though they feign wisdom. They actually "hate knowledge" (1:22) and "die for a lack of sense" (10:21). They "despise their father's instruction" (15:5) and possess "no sense" at all

---

69. Pemberton, "It's a Fool's Life," 213–24.

70. Pemberton, "It's a Fool's Life," 220.

71. Pemberton, "It's a Fool's Life," 221.

72. Proverb's depiction of folly is strikingly similar to God's evaluation of the human race in Genesis: "The Lord saw that the wickedness of man was great in the earth, and that every intention of the thoughts of his heart was only evil continually" (6:5).

(17:16). They take "no pleasure in understanding" (18:2) and "trust in [their] own mind" (28:26). For a follower of Lady Folly, ignorance is bliss and self-deception is a shield against reality.

Fourth, in the Old Testament folly appears when people act without forethought or behave with malicious intent. Foolish behavior violates social norms or corrupts the covenant community. The typical idiom denouncing folly is "You/we have done/acted foolishly." Examples include Jacob, who prevented Laban from bidding his family farewell (Gen 21:28); Aaron pleading with Moses after he rebelled with Miriam (Num 12:11); Saul offering an unauthorized sacrifice that displeased the Lord (1 Sam 13:13); and David taking a census, contrary to God's will (1 Chr 21:8). But foolishness was also an abiding characteristic of disobedient Israel. Moses said that the nation was a "corrupt and twisted generation," a people who were "foolish and senseless" (Deut 32:5–6). Jeremiah stated God's point of view: "For my people are foolish; they know me not; they are stupid children; they have no understanding. They are 'wise'—in doing evil! But how to do good they know not" (4:22).

The Paradigmatic Fool

Nabal (1 Samuel 25) is a classic fool who lost touch with reality. He did not perceive the significance of David and was a social deviant. Nabal's god was his "belly," his "mind [was] set on earthly things," and therefore his "end was destruction" (Phil 3:19).

David threatened Nabal and his household with annihilation for maltreatment. Nabal's servant advised Abigail in the face of this threat, "Now therefore know this and consider what you should do, for harm is determined against our master and against all his house, and he is such a worthless man that one cannot speak to him" (1 Sam 25:17).

The narrator highlights Nabal's economic prowess. He had a "business" and was "very rich" with many livestock (v. 2).[73] Verse 11 testifies to his sense of entitlement and vaunted status in contrast with David. Nabal asked with incredulity, "Shall I take *my* bread and *my* water and *my* meat that I have killed for *my* shearers and give it to men who come from I do not know where?" (v. 11).[74] At the end of the story, the narrator

---

73. See Dekker, "Characterization in the Hebrew Bible," 311–24.

74. To add insult to injury, Nabal questioned David's pedigree: "There are many servants these days who are breaking away from their masters" (v. 10b).

mentions Nabal's self-indulgent banquet "like the feast of a king" (v. 36). His heart was "merry" because he was "very drunk" (v. 36). Nabal was quite a skinflint with reference to others, but very wanton about himself. In reality, his functional deity was himself and his fiefdom was a mirage created by his wealth.

Obviously, Nabal was not a generous benefactor. He did not foster "righteousness, justice, and equity" (Prov 1:3b). He clearly possessed the wherewithal to be generous, because Abigail's offering to David of "five sheep *already* prepared" (v. 18) was of very little economic consequence for her husband. Despite his great wealth, he foolishly violated Israelite social norms and covenantal regulations. As Marjorie O'Rourke Boyle points out, David's forces had protected Nabal's servants and his livestock (vv. 5–8, 21).[75] Their request for provisions functioned as a covenantal negotiation. Nabal's unkind retort, "Who is David?" was a rejection of this bilateral relation, even though Nabal had already benefited from David's services. Moreover, Nabal's unwillingness to share with David's men breached Hebrew laws concerning care for sojourners and hospitality, especially during the harvest festival.[76] Clearly, Nabal modeled foolishness, a mentality that cannot even discern one's own best interests.

The narrator summarizes Nabal's character as "harsh (*qasheh*) and evil (*ra*) in his doings" (v. 3, NKJV). His surly manner was obvious in the way he contemptuously addressed David's representatives. Nabal's servant testified that he "railed" against them (v. 14), and David said that Nabal insulted him (v. 39).[77] The term *ra* refers to evil-doing of all kinds. The immediate context specifies Nabal's wrongdoing: pomposity, lack of discernment, and wholesale rejection of Hebrew social obligations. David complained, "Surely in vain have I guarded all that this fellow has in the wilderness, so that nothing was missed of all that belonged to him, and he has returned me evil for good" (v. 21).

Nabal was called "worthless" (*beliyyaal*) by both his wife and servant. This Hebrew term means literally "man/son of Belial." Samuel Ben-Meir shows that the expression refers to the worst infractions against

---

75. Boyle, "The Law of the Heart," 401–27.
76. Boyle, "The Law of the Heart," 417.
77. *Qasheh* appears thirty-six times with a range of meanings. The term is frequently translated as "stubborn" or "obstinate." *Qasheh* also means harsh, surly, or severe. For example, King Rehoboam responded to the representatives of the northern tribes in a manner akin to Nabal. He misspoke badly and did not listen, for he "answered them harshly, rejecting the advice of the elders" (2 Chr 10:13).

God and his people, that is, "those rebelling against God or His Law or inciting others to rebel."[78] In fact, even Abigail testified about him, "Let not my lord regard this worthless fellow, Nabal, for as his name is, so is he. Nabal is his name, and folly (*nebalah*) is with him" (v. 25). For these reasons, Ben-Meir depicts Nabal as the paradigmatic fool: "Nabal has the dubious distinction of being a *naval* [fool] and a *ben-beliyyaal* [son of Belial] who has committed *nevalah* [folly]."[79]

In summary, the confrontation involving David, Nabal, and Abigail is depicted in epistemological terms—between folly and wisdom personified. The question at stake was who discerned David's significance correctly. Nabal absolutely failed to discern David's importance and behaved outrageously, without fear. Abigail, on the other hand, was the wise heroine of the story. She perceived the true character of her husband, discerned David's role as God's servant (vv. 23–31), and determined the wisest course of action (vv. 18–20).

Nabal became David's "enemy" and fell prey to Abigail's prophecy concerning the future king, "Let your enemies and those who seek to do evil to my lord be as Nabal. . . . Your enemies he shall sling out as from the hollow of a sling" (vv. 26, 29). In the end, fools like Nabal often "die for a lack of sense" (10:21). As Boyle comments, "Nabal experienced a moral failure of heart causing obstinacy against the law. For this disobedience, prolonged without repentance, the Lord struck him."[80]

Nabal is a prototypical fool. Left to themselves, all humans are like Nabal, not usually in his depth or breadth of folly—though that *is* possible—but in principle. Everyone partakes of folly and perversity. All lose touch with reality. No one understands the significance of the world or its Maker, nor do they want to. Human beings are proud and stubborn. Their minds are set on earthly things and their functional gods are manifold. They deviate from God's norms and cause pain for others. They lack wisdom and integrity. They do not listen to God's voice. Like Nabal, mankind no longer knows what is in its best interest as people made in the image of God.

---

78. Ben-Meir, "Nabal, the Villain," 251.
79. Ben-Meir, "Nabal, the Villain," 251.
80. Boyle, "The Law of the Heart," 418.

CONCLUSION

According to the prologue, two classes of thinkers—the would-be wise and the fool—begin from different starting points. The former presumes the fear of the Lord as the foundation of knowledge, while the other begins from a rebellious stance. One presupposes Yahweh's rule, but the other negates his relevance. One path leads to deeper knowledge of God, as well as to righteousness, justice, and equity. The other produces disorientation and destruction.

The book of Proverbs shows that Lady Folly is not passive; rather, she is aggressively malignant. Folly is "out there" as idolatry expressed in a myriad of religious and worldview guises. However, like a Trojan horse, foolishness is also within us as sinful impulses, but also as erroneous thinking.

Proverbs calls our fallible nature "simple" (*peti*). However, the simple are not honest moral or epistemological agents; rather they resemble their father Adam. They think and desire in unlawful ways. They are self-referential and for this reason they are exceedingly vulnerable and easily persuadable by folly. Humans are inclined to foolishness. They are likely to choose the way of evil. Clearly, the die is cast, for mankind "loves" ignorance (1:22). People "lack sense" (7:7b) and "believe everything" (14:15a). Often, they do not discern danger and thus bring affliction upon themselves (22:3b; 27:12b). They succumb to folly (14:18) and idolatry (1:32).

Lady Folly and Lady Wisdom still speak today through their representatives. Both demand that we pay attention. Both use rhetorical strategies to captivate our minds. In fact, we face today the same dichotomy that Adam and Eve encountered: acquire true knowledge from God or embrace a skewed outlook from an uncertain source of understanding. As we have seen, the implications of this choice impact every aspect of life.

Folly and Wisdom appear as alternative paths to follow. The simple can flourish if they "leave [their] simple ways" and "walk in the way of insight" (9:6). That path originates with piety and the discipline of "instruction." However, due to pressure from both external and internal folly, the journey toward wisdom and righteousness is arduous, for there is a Nabal-like mindset in each of us.

Therefore, we must discern very carefully the voices we hear every day. We must reject the siren song of exilic epistemology (post-fall thinking) and resist Folly's subterfuge. We should always remember Lady Wisdom's warning to fools:

> Because I have called and you refused to listen, have stretched out my hand and no one has heeded, because you have ignored all my counsel and would have none of my reproof.... Because they hated knowledge and did not choose the fear of the Lord, would have none of my counsel and despised all my reproof, therefore they shall eat the fruit of their way, and have their fill of their own devices. For the simple are killed by their turning away, and the complacency of fools destroys them. (1:24–25, 29–32)

On the other hand, if we endeavor to overcome our wisdom deficit, Lady Wisdom promises:

> If you turn at my reproof, behold, I will pour out my spirit to you; I will make my words known to you.... And now, O sons, listen to me: blessed are those who keep my ways. Hear instruction and be wise, and do not neglect it. Blessed is the one who listens to me, watching daily at my gates, waiting beside my doors. For whoever finds me finds life and obtains favor from the Lord. (1:23; 8:32–35)

7

Foolish and Senseless People

"Each man's mind is like a labyrinth, so that it is no wonder that individual nations were drawn aside into various falsehoods; and not only this—but individual men, almost, had their own gods."

—John Calvin,
Institutes of the Christian Religion, vol. 1

Knowing God is the goal and purpose of revelation. Israel received verbal and written instruction communicated through covenants and prophets. They witnessed theophanies and were taught to perpetuate the knowledge of God from generation to generation.

But Israel was not a willing student. They did not listen to the Lord. They did not obey the covenant. When Isaiah and Jeremiah confronted their obstinacy and called them to repentance, they did not respond. They closed their minds and directed their attention elsewhere. Their obduracy bore bitter fruit in dysfunction and exile, ignorance, and folly.

The Old Testament shows that the front line in the battle between God and mankind concerns revelation and the sinful mind. Michael Carasik describes the Hebrew concept of the mind as a battleground: "It also presents knowledge—its use and abuse, its effect and its power, the possibility that it can be concealed or distorted—as a point of rivalry between God and humanity."[1]

---

1. Carasik, *Theologies of the Mind*, 18.

In the previous three chapters, I examined this rivalry through three paradigmatic thinkers: Pharaoh, Qohelet, and the fool. In this chapter, I examine noetic depravity in two Old Testament texts that arose during critical moments in Israel's history. I survey Isaiah (during the deportation of the northern tribes) and Jeremiah (during the conquest of Jerusalem and the exile of the southern tribes). Lastly, I examine Psalm 14 as a summary of Old Testament teaching about exilic epistemology.

ISAIAH

God's plan for Israel was rather strange, geographically speaking. He did not choose a people set apart by inaccessible mountains or dense jungle. He did not call a tribe isolated from religious and cultural influences of civilizations nearby. Rather, God situated Israel in the worst possible position, humanly speaking. They were located in highly prized real estate at the crossroads of warring superpowers (Assyria and Egypt). They settled near contested pathways of international trade. They occupied a resource-rich environment coveted by all. They were a people endowed with agricultural and commercial prowess. As a potential vassal state, the Hebrew tribes were a prize worth fighting for.

Assyria's imperial ideology claimed that their god Asshur was supreme and that their earthly king was commissioned to establish an empire. Their expansionist vision included the lands of Israel and Judah. Assyrian aggression produced destruction, deprivation, and deportation. Israel's viability was at stake.

Isaiah ministered in this hostile milieu from 740 to 700 BC. He entered the fray, counseling the wisest path and the safest alliance. He reasserted Yahweh's universal reign as Creator and Lord. He provided the big picture in the face of judgment and exile. He presented teleology to sustain and orient the people. Most importantly, he explained the contest between Israel and Assyria at the ontological level: Yahweh was supreme, not Asshur, and Yahweh governed history, not the god of Assyria.[2] Isaiah presented the hermeneutical key to interpret the epoch in which they lived, along with what they should do in response.[3]

---

2. For the linkage with creation and exodus, see Blenkinsopp, "The Cosmological and Protological Language," 493–510; Lessing, "Yahweh Versus Marduk," 234–43; Wardlaw, "The Significance of Creation," 449–71; and Boda, "Walking in the Light of Yahweh," 54–89.

3. Isaiah challenged Assyrian imperial ideology in a manner akin to Moses'

The battlefield for Israel, therefore, was not simply geographic. A heated battle also occurred in the mind. Worldviews clashed with enormous ferocity. Whom would they listen to? Would they embrace Assyrian propaganda or the teaching of Isaiah and the Scriptures? What was God showing them about their bellicose neighbor to the north? What was he revealing to them about their future? The book of Isaiah highlights the skewed outlook of the Israelites under pressure of conquest and assimilation. It provides yet another manifestation of exilic epistemology.

Imperial Ideology

Around 900 BC, Assyria initiated raids seeking the natural and human resources in Philistia, Israel, and Judah. Later, Assyrian imperialism fixated on Egypt as an important acquisition, but the smaller states along the coast of the Mediterranean stood in the way.[4] K. Lawson Younger, Jr. writes, "The overarching concern of the Assyrian kings was that access to the Philistine coast and Egypt might not be encumbered in any way. Through this, Assyria's economic goals might be realized."[5] There was a lull in Assyrian aggression between 782 and 745, however. During this period, the Hebrews enjoyed prosperity under King Jeroboam II in Israel (793–753) and King Uzziah in Judah (792–740).

With the rise of Tiglath-Pileser III (744–727), however, aggressive expansionism began anew. Israel, Judah, and the other nations faced three options: submit to Assyria, resist in coalition with the smaller neighboring realms, or align with Egypt against Assyria. Israel chose to submit; Judah chose to resist. Both failed to stem the Assyrian juggernaut. Younger notes, "But Israel, in every instance, was rebellious against Assyria and received maximum deportation treatments and, in the case of Galilee, the implementation of a deliberate population reduction through an unusual unidirectional deportation."[6] For the northern tribes, the exile was implemented between 734 and 716.

---

confrontation with Egypt.

4. For the historical background see Oswalt, *Isaiah*, 18–33; Miller, "Objectives and Consequences," 124–49; Borowski, "Hezekiah's Reforms," 148–55; and Younger, "The Deportations of the Israelites," 201–27.

5. Younger, "The Deportations of the Israelites," 225. He adds that the Assyrians "had designs on controlling the major trading centers on the Levantine coast."

6. Younger, "The Deportations of the Israelites," 227.

Thus began a process of internal and external "Assryrianization."[7] Internally, the deportees inevitably acquired the ways and worldview of their captors through culture, cult, and language. Externally, Assyria's imperial ideology demanded assimilation as a divine decree and military necessity. Their outlook can be discerned in the ultimatum given to Hezekiah (Isa 36:4–20) by representatives of the empire (circa 701). I will focus briefly on three aspects, starting with verses 4–6:

(4) And the Rabshakeh said to them, "Say to Hezekiah, 'Thus says the great king, the king of Assyria: On what do you rest this trust of yours?

(5) Do you think that mere words are strategy and power for war? In whom do you now trust, that you have rebelled against me?

(6) Behold, you are trusting in Egypt, that broken reed of a staff, which will pierce the hand of any man who leans on it. Such is Pharaoh king of Egypt to all who trust in him.'"

First, the phrase "the great king" (v. 4) bears a dual significance. The great king of Assyria was the god Asshur.[8] He was called "king of the gods, lord of the lands" and hailed with the epithet "Asshur is King!"[9] He was their divine warrior, chief of the pantheon, and the patron deity of the Assyrian empire. Indeed, Asshur controlled the future of mankind, for he alone possessed the "Tablet of Destinies." He governed the natural world, for he maintained the celestial "bonds" of physical reality. Sennacherib declared, "[O Asshur, father] of heaven, king of the gods, determiner of destinies, you alone hold in your hands the Tablet of Destinies of the gods."[10] Asshur was the undisputed cosmic ruler of heaven and earth, according to Assyrian cosmology.

As the monarch of the gods, Asshur was also the king of mankind. D. R. Miller comments, "On the level of Neo-Assyrian ideology, then, Assyrian 'universal' empire was logical and inevitable, an earthly

---

7. Younger, "The Deportations of the Israelites," 224.

8. Concerning Assyrian imperial theology, see Middleton, *The Liberating Image*, 118–22; Miller, "Objectives and Consequences," 124–49; Cook, "Of Gods and Kings," 19–31; Aster, "Transmission of Neo-Assyrian Claims," 1–44; Machinist, "Assyria and Its Image," 719–37.

9. Cited in Cook, "Of Gods and Kings," 25–6.

10. Cited in Miller, "Objectives and Consequences," 132–33.

extension of the unique role Asshur held within the cosmic sphere."[11] The expansion of Asshur's reign through conquest and assimilation was a moral duty and divine commission. Kings waged war "with the help of Asshur."[12] All geographic boundaries were artificial. Other worldviews were subservient and their adherents dispensable. In fact, Assyria looked on the rest of the world with pity and contempt, for other peoples were by definition unaware and ignorant. They were brutes in comparison to the enlightened denizens of Assyrian civilization.[13]

Second, the expression "great king" referred to the human ruler of Asshur's kingdom on earth. The emperor was, in fact, Asshur's image. Kings were designated the offspring of deity. In artwork, the emperor sat at Asshur's side, endowed with his prowess and purpose. Rulers functioned as priests, since they mediated between heaven and earth. At royal investitures, the twin rule of god and king was celebrated: "Assurbanipal is the [representative] of Asshur, the creation of his hands!"[14] As vice-regents, kings were commissioned to extend Asshur's dominion. The high priest intoned during a coronation, "By your right scepter enlarge your land!"[15] Military strategy reflected Asshur's wisdom. Success testified to his power. For this reason, the king was unassailable, since he aligned with ontological reality and fulfilled a divine calling. J. Richard Middleton notes that "when the king rules well both the social and the natural orders of life are fruitful and blessed, and through this the gods are exalted."[16]

Furthermore, Assyrian kings were designated as the empire's "shepherd," tasked with "gathering" Asshur's people from the whole world.[17]

11. Miller, "Objectives and Consequences," 133.

12. Cited in Machinist, "Assyria and Its Image in the First Isaiah," 734. The author explains that terror was a key part of the psychological warfare waged against Assyria's enemies.

13. Other nations were also subject to unbridled avarice and systematic looting. Sennacherib declared, "I opened his treasuries. Gold, silver, vessels of gold and silver, precious stones, beds, armchairs, a processional carriage . . . inlaid with gold and silver . . . his wife, the women of his palace, his housekeepers, male and female musicians, eunuchs, courtiers, attendants, palace slaves . . . all the craftsmen as many as there were, I brought (them) out and counted as spoil" (cited in Miller, "Objectives and Consequences," 129).

14. Cited in Aster, "Transmission of Neo-Assyrian Claims of Empire," 6.

15. Cited in Miller, "Objectives and Consequences," 131.

16. Middleton, *The Liberating Image*, 120.

[17] To this end, imperial propaganda was ubiquitous, featuring heavily in royal

The rulers during Isaiah's time of ministry (Tiglath-Pileser III, Sargon II, and Sennacherib) each claimed this title. An inscription honoring Sennacherib's destruction of Babylon says that he "gathered the [scattered] people of [Babylon] (and) (re)settled (them) in peaceful dwellings."[18] The conquest of new peoples and the disciplining of disloyal vassals were by definition, therefore, missionary endeavors. Gregory D. Cook comments, "The concepts of shepherding and gathering complement each other. Assyrian ideology shows the human king responsible for these two tasks. If the king ceased to perform these functions, chaos would result."[19]

Third, imperial ideology polemicized against other gods. The Rabshakeh's critique of Yahweh the God of Israel was three-dimensional. He suggested to the people of Jerusalem, "But if you say to me, 'We trust in the Lord our God,' is it not he whose high places and altars Hezekiah has removed, saying to Judah and to Jerusalem, 'You shall worship before this altar'?" (v. 7). He referred to Hezekiah's recentralization of worship in Jerusalem in accord with Deuteronomy 12:2–5 (2 Kgs 18:4, 22; 2 Chr 29:15–19) and the subversion of syncretism practiced at local shrines (2 Chr 30:13–14; 31:1; 32:12).[20] According to Assyrian logic, however, Hezekiah had offended the Lord and therefore Israel merited destruction at Asshur's hand.[21] Miller explains the rhetorical impact of this assertion: "For the Assyrians to inform a conquered people that their own gods had abandoned them because of the people's sins or in deference to Asshur was of enormous propagandist weight."[22]

---

art and ritual, military might, and official communication. See Miller, "Objectives and Consequences," 133–45; Machinist, "Assyria and Its Image," 722–77; and Aster, "Transmission of Neo-Assyrian Claims," 8–43.

18. Cited in Cook, "Of Gods and Kings," 29. Sivan ("The Siege of Jerusalem," 86) provides this citation from the "Annals of Sennacherib": "Sennacherib, the great king, the mighty king, king of the universe, king of Assyria [Asshur] . . . the wise shepherd . . . guardian of the right, lover of justice, who lends support, who comes to aid of the needy."

19. Sivan, "The Siege of Jerusalem," 86.

20. See Borowski, "Hezekiah's Reforms," 148–55; Zvi, "Who Wrote the Speech of Rabshakeh?" 79–92; and Sivan, "The Siege of Jerusalem," 83–93.

21. This was Sennacherib's explanation of a different conquest: "Their gods abandoned them, rendering them helpless." This rationale is also a possible reason for the spokesman's assertion in verse 10: "Moreover, is it without the Lord that I have come up against this land to destroy it? The Lord said to me, 'Go up against this land and destroy it.'" For more discussion, see Kruger, "A World Turned on Its Head," 58–76.

22. Miller, "Objectives and Consequences," 134.

The Rabshakeh shrewdly promised a better future for the Hebrews, even better than Canaan. Indeed, he implied that Asshur was the true god of promise and that Assyria was the real land of blessing:

(16) Do not listen to Hezekiah. For thus says the king of Assyria: Make your peace with me and come out to me. Then each one of you will eat of his own vine, and each one of his own fig tree, and each one of you will drink the water of his own cistern,

(17) until I come and take you away to a land like your own land, a land of grain and wine, a land of bread and vineyards.

For maximal rhetorical impact, he utilized idiomatic language similar to Deuteronomy: "eat of his own vine," "fig tree," cistern," "land of grain and wine," "bread and vineyards" (Deut 8:8; 30:15–16; 33:28). But he alluded only vaguely to the forthcoming, disruptive deportation (v. 17). He insinuated, as well, that Yahweh had unilaterally rejected his people and that he was no more than a defeated local divinity.[23] The "great king" Asshur, the other hand, would "shepherd" the Hebrews and "gather" them into Assyria's land of blessing.

He claimed that the supremacy of Asshur was self-evident:[24]

(18) Beware lest Hezekiah mislead you by saying, "The Lord will deliver us." Has any of the gods of the nations delivered his land out of the hand of the king of Assyria?

(19) Where are the gods of Hamath and Arpad? Where are the gods of Sepharvaim? Have they delivered Samaria out of my hand?

(20) Who among all the gods of these lands have delivered their lands out of my hand, that the Lord should deliver Jerusalem out of my hand?"

---

23. Miller ("Objectives and Consequences," 134) adds, "The conquered people's gods were even said to travel to Assyria, or to a city controlled by the empire lying outside the Assyrian heartland, to praise Asshur and, perhaps most shockingly, take up residence there. On the physical level, of course, a god's change of address connoted the spoliation of divine statues by the Assyrians, as evidenced by this claim of Asshurbanipal, 'I had the gods, as many as I had captured, through the help of Asshur and Ishtar my lords, take the road to Damascus.'"

24. Concerning Yahweh's polemic against Asshur, see Cook, "Of Gods and Kings"; Chan, "Rhetorical Reversal and Usurpation," 717–33; Boda, "Walking in the Light of Yahweh," 54–89; Seufert, "Reading Isaiah 40:1–11," 269–82.

For the Assyrians, this message made obvious sense, based upon their history of conquest and ideology. There were only two possible sources of support against the empire: manmade and divine. All human resistance had been crushed, and to date no other deity had delivered anyone from Asshur's assault.[25] John N. Oswalt summarizes this conflict: "It is a contest between the Lord and the king of Assyria . . . between the mightiest and most glorious man of the age and the Lord God."[26] But of course, standing hand in hand with the emperor was the god Asshur. As patron of the Assyrian empire, he was the claimant for rule of heaven and earth. And it was ultimately on this macrocosmic level that the battle raged.

A Quest for Knowledge

But the war also occurred at a microcosmic level in the minds of individual Israelites and in their collective outlook. According to Isaiah, they suffered from a severe knowledge deficit and a profound lack of understanding. They did not listen to God nor discern reality. They could not connect the dots between their sin and impending judgment. For this reason, the divine pedagogue pleaded with them at the beginning of Isaiah, "Come now, let us reason together" (1:18a).

In fact, Isaiah is full of cognitive language and shows the significance of the mind as an aspect of the image of God. A wide variety of verbs, nouns, and adjectives within the book of Isaiah indicate intellectual activity:

---

25. In fact, they wrote about Hezekiah and Jerusalem, "As for Hezekiah the Jew who did not submit to my yoke, of his strong, walled cities, as well as the small cities in their neighborhood, which were without number . . . I besieged and took [those cities]. 200,150 people, great and small, male and female, horses, mules, camels, cattle, sheep, without number, I brought away from them and counted as spoil. Himself [Hezekiah], like a caged bird I shut up in Jerusalem." Cited in Sivan, "The Siege of Jerusalem," 87.

26. Oswalt, *Isaiah*, 402.

FOOLISH AND SENSELESS PEOPLE

Verbs	know, understand, listen to, reason, teach, judge between, perceive, propose, consult, mislead, intend, have in mind, decide, make known, ponder, determine, forget, remember, acknowledge, look to, regard for, learn, render, hear, pay attention, astound, think, spread error, rage against, enlighten, compare, reflect on, obey, believe, conceive, answer, plan, stop to think, fix in mind
Nouns	head, heart, counselor, word, disputes, superstition, divination, idol, guide, deceit, darkness, plan, light, lies, purpose, wisdom, fear of the Lord, decision, fool, advice, law, statute, treachery, falsehood, message, intelligence, instruction, visions, seer, illusion, mind, folly, error, method, scheme, thought, confusion, nonsense, imaginations, truth, abomination, minds closed
Adjectives	meaningless, obedient, clever, cleverness, senseless, wise, deceived, bewildered, deceitful, rash, evil (schemes), ignorant, deluded, empty (arguments)

There are many expressions linked to mental operations:

"Heart" (mind)	arrogance of heart, said in your heart, desire of your heart, hearts far from me, take it to heart, deluded heart, stubborn-hearted, say in your heart, harden your hearts
"Eye" and "ear"	eyes of the arrogant, wise in their own eyes, clever in their own sight, stops his ears, shuts his eyes, glancing wantonly with their eyes, eyes of the haughty, blind their eyes, boastful look in his eyes, eyes of the blind, lifted your eyes to the heights, grope like those who have no eyes, shrewd in their own sight, incline your ear, stops his ears, ears heavy, ears of the deaf unstopped, his ears are open but he does not hear, would not hear, deaf shall hear, let us hear no more
Idiomatic phrases	turn their back on, trusting in man, spirit of dizziness, cleverness of their hands, made a lie their own refuge, falsehood a hiding place, hide their plans, turn things upside down, mind busy with evil, turn to his own way, spin a spider's web

There are also many examples of argumentation. Rhetorical questions urged Israel to reflect and respond:

| "Why" | Will you still be struck down? Will you continue to rebel? Do you say . . . 'My way is hidden from the LORD and my right is disregarded by my God'? When I called [there] was no one to answer. Do you spend your money for that which is not bread and your labor for that which does not satisfy? |

Hypothetical statements provoked deeper analysis:

| "If" | you are willing and obedient; you refuse and rebel; you say to me, "We trust in the Lord"[27] |

God invited Israel to deliberate with him. He communicated these messages to them: "set forth your case," "bring your proofs," "give an answer," "let us argue together," "take counsel together," and "together draw near for judgment."

Despite the emphasis on reasoning and comprehension, however, the nation did not grasp or esteem what God had taught them. The divine diagnosis appears at the beginning of the book: "Children have I reared and brought up, but they have rebelled against me. The ox knows its owner, and the donkey its master's crib, but Israel does not know, my people do not understand" (1:2b–3). The metaphor reveals what Israel failed to perceive. The passage may be displayed in this way:

(A)   Children have I reared and brought up

(C)   The ox knows its owner, and the donkey its master's crib

But

(B)   They have rebelled against me

(D)   Israel does not know, my people do not understand

The children's "father" (implied) is contrasted with the animals' "owner" (caretaker) in (a) and (c). Rebellion against the "father" (Yahweh) is akin to lacking understanding (b and d). Joshua Berman comments that "Israel is incognizant of her own good and clueless about how to seek it."[28] They forgot God and devalued the benefits of their filial

---

27. Others are "If: you will inquire"; "If: you are not firm in faith"; and "If: you take away the yoke; you pour yourself out for the hungry; you turn your foot from the Sabbath."

28. Berman, "What Does the Ox Know?" 387.

relationship with God the Father.[29] The impact of this folly was pervasive: "The whole head is sick, and the whole heart faint" (v. 5b).

Unlike Israel, the animals discerned the beneficial relationship with their caretaker (c). He protected and provided for them. They grasped his status and accepted their dependency. Berman writes, "The prophet invokes these beasts because they intuitively and successfully seek out their own good."[30] The Hebrews, on the other hand, did not acknowledge their "caretaker" and did not seek their best interests (d). Rather, they spurned the benefits of Yahweh's sustenance and security (b). He declared, "For you have forgotten the God of your salvation and have not remembered the Rock of your refuge" (17:10). As a result, they suffered privation, "Though you plant pleasant plants and sow the vine-branch of a stranger, though you make them grow on the day that you plant them, and make them blossom in the morning that you sow, yet the harvest will flee away in a day of grief and incurable pain" (v. 11; see also 42:24; 51:13; 57:11; 65:11). In reality, Israel experienced a reversal of creation and the covenantal curses of Deuteronomy 28:15–68 because they did not know or understand (d).[31]

Israel was culpably ignorant. The "but" indicates what was unexpected and abnormal. To rebel against Yahweh their father was foolish but also treasonous, in view of God's activity in creation and redemptive history. In the face of Assyrian imperialism, the children of Israel rejected their provider and protector, indeed their divine warrior. Berman writes, "When Israel fails to seek its good in the protection of YHWH, it is not because it no longer seeks its own protection. Rather, Israel seeks its protection elsewhere."[32] They sought divine patronage through apostasy (idolatry) and foreign alliances.

Even though they were sentient creatures capable of knowledge and reasoning (unlike the animals), Israel no longer desired to know the path of truth and wisdom (b). They rejected the covenant and its blessings. In

---

29. Other tests referring to Israel's "birth" and upbringing by the Lord are Isa 44:2, 24; 46:3; 48:8.

30. Berman, "What Does the Ox Know?" 387. Similarly, Oswalt (*Isaiah*, 73) writes, "Israel is said to be less intelligent than an ox or ass that at least knows where the barn is."

31. Interestingly, the two other times where the terms "ox" and "donkey" are paired in Isaiah occur in contexts of future restoration of creation, when they are free to roam and feed at will (30:18–26 and 32:15–20).

32. Berman, "What Does the Ox Know?" 387.

the terminology of Proverbs, they became fools, for they did not fear the Lord and despised wisdom (1:7). In terms of Deuteronomy, God imposed the curse of stupefaction because they would not listen (28:28–29).[33]

To ignore what was patently obvious and beneficial (a), therefore, was to act without sense (d). It was, in fact, stupid. It was also counterproductive and delusionary. As a result, they brought upon themselves the plight of Psalm 81:11–12: "My people did not listen to my voice; Israel would not submit to me. So I gave them over to their stubborn hearts, to follow their own counsels." They no longer acknowledged Yahweh, so they could not discern what was right and good. They did not see the reason and remedy for their precarious situation.

Finally, the book of Isaiah provides a vivid portrait of noetic depravity during a period of intense crisis. As we have seen before, the Israelites refused to listen to God's voice.[34] They were "rebellious" (1:23, 28; 30:9; 65:2) and "obstinate" (48:4), and they "raged against" the Lord (37:29). They were self-determinative, since they "turned—every one—to his own way" (53:6; see also 57:17). They were intellectually self-referential, for they were "wise in their own eyes and shrewd in their own sight" (5:21). They heeded blind "guides" (3:12) who "misled" them (3:12), "mediums and necromancers" (8:19), and the "stupid counsel" of the Egyptians (19:11).

Their minds were focused on folly and evil. Their hearts were "arrogant" (9:9), "deluded" (44:20), and "stubborn" (46:12). They conceived "from the heart lying words" (59:13b), and their "heart [was] busy with iniquity, to practice ungodliness, to utter error concerning the Lord" (32:6). Their ruminations ("devices") were "evil" and they "planned wicked schemes . . . with lying words" (32:7; see also 65:2). They "speak lies, they conceive mischief and give birth to iniquity" (59:4). They "weave the spider's web" (59:5a) of intrigue and deceit (see also 30:1). Their thinking, in other words, was "machinations of treachery."[35] And like spiders, they weaved webs of distortion to entrap and devour.

Isaiah shows, further, that the sinful mind seeks ontological ascent, indeed a false ontological inversion. Isaiah 29:16 says, "You turn things

---

33. Contrast this with 48:17: "Thus says the Lord, your Redeemer, the Holy One of Israel: 'I am the Lord your God, who teaches you to profit, who leads you in the way you should go.'"

34. The verb *shama* is translated as (not) listen (65:12; 66:4), hear (28:12; 30:9; 42:20; 59:2), and (not) obey (42:24).

35. Carasik, *Theologies of the Mind*, 134.

upside down! Shall the potter be regarded as the clay, that the thing made should say of its maker, 'He did not make me'; or the thing formed say of him who formed it, 'He has no understanding'?"[36] J. Alec Motyer explains, "They deny the Lord's distinctiveness . . . his sovereignty . . . and his wisdom.."[37] Isaiah demonstrates that in practice exilic epistemology presupposes an inversion of the Creator–creature distinction.[38]

In the book of Isaiah, this inversion appears in two forms. The first is a practical atheism akin to Psalm 14. Isaiah 29:15 says, "Ah, you who hide deep from the Lord your counsel, whose deeds are in the dark, and who say, 'Who sees us? Who knows us?'" These mental gymnastics imply that, if God does not see (or does not really care), then anything is possible. This outlook produced an amoral and Machiavellian ethic. The same erroneous calculus appears elsewhere: "My way is hidden from the Lord" (40:27) and "No one sees me" (47:10).

A second form of inversion is self-deception. The Israelites advised their leaders, "Do not prophesy to us what is right; speak to us smooth things, prophesy illusions, leave the way, turn aside from the path, let us hear no more about the Holy One of Israel" (30:10b–11). They purposely suppressed the truth ("what is right" and knowledge "about the Holy One of Israel") and exchanged it for lies ("illusions") that generated a much preferred, self-constructed reality.[39]

---

36. The idiom "things upside down" meant a world in chaos due to human sin and divine abandonment. See Kruger, "A World Turned on its Head," 58–76; Van Leeuwen, "The Biblical World Upside Down," 599–610.

37. Motyer, *The Prophecy of Isaiah*, 241 (emphasis in original).

38. An audacious expression of this reversal is the boast of the king of Babylon in Isa 14:13–14: "You said in your heart, 'I will ascend to heaven; above the stars of God I will set my throne on high . . . I will ascend above the heights of the clouds; I will make myself like the Most High.'" See Hassler, "Isaiah 14 and Habakkuk 2," 221–29.

39. Isaiah 28:15 appears to exemplify the same phenomenon: "Because you have said, 'We have made a covenant with death, and with Sheol we have an agreement, when the overwhelming whip passes through it will not come to us, for we have made lies our refuge, and in falsehood we have taken shelter.'" Consider also 29:9: "Astonish yourselves and be astonished; blind yourselves and be blind! Be drunk, but not with wine; stagger, but not with strong drink!" Motyer (*The Prophecy of Isaiah*, 239) notes that the verb "blind" is the same term used in 6:10 and means "to smear over [of eyes]." Here it indicates a refusal to see, hence self-imposed blindness.

MAKE THE HEART OF THIS PEOPLE DULL

We turn now to a challenging and provocative text, Isaiah 6:9–10. This passage offers a summary explanation of unbelief in the Old Testament, as well as illustrating punitive epistemology. Epistemological themes and vocabulary found in these verses appear in both the Old and New Testaments.[40] This passage is cited repeatedly in the New Testament as an explanation of obduracy.[41] Raymond B. Dillard and Tremper Longman explain, "The obduracy of Isaiah's own generation explains why Jesus taught in parables and why his message was not received by hearers."[42]

For many, Isaiah 6:9–10 functions as a proof text for divine sovereignty and predestination or in association with theodicy. For others, the passage is a distasteful relic of pre-modern religiosity that denies human freedom at the hands of a cruel deity. I deny, of course, this latter interpretation. Instead, I will evaluate the passage within its biblical-theological context in Isaiah and with respect to its intellectual import. First, I will consider 6:9–10 in isolation. Then, I will broader the focus to the immediate context of Isaiah's calling (6:1–13), followed by chapters 1–5 and the book as a whole.

Do Not Understand

Verses 9 and 10 state without context:

(9) And he said, "Go, and say to this people: 'Keep on hearing, but do not understand; keep on seeing, but do not perceive.'

(10) Make the heart of this people dull, and their ears heavy, and blind their eyes; lest they see with their eyes, and hear with their ears, and understand with their hearts, and turn and be healed."

Verse 9 explains that the Israelites continued to receive auditory and visual data about God's activity in their midst, but this did not produce insight or understanding. They did not interpret, evaluate, or categorize the input correctly. They did not draw the proper conclusions or suitable applications from Scripture and experience. They knew some facts,

---

40. See Johnson, *Epistemology and Biblical Theology*.

41. It is cited in Matthew 13:15, Mark 4:12, 8:18, Luke 8:10, John 12:40, and Acts 28:27. There are also many allusions to "eyes," "ears," "light," and "darkness."

42. Dillard and Longman, *An Introduction to the Old Testament*, 283.

but they did not possess wisdom. In fact, Yahweh chastised them on this point: "They do not regard the deeds of the Lord, or see the work of his hands. Therefore my people go into exile for lack of knowledge" (5:12a–13b).[43] Israel would not and thus could not apprise rightly or esteem highly all that God did on their behalf.

Verse 10 underscores God's intention to hinder their comprehension. The verbs are causative (*hiphil* imperatives), expressing Yahweh's epistemological purpose through Isaiah's ministry. The perceptive organs (heart-mind, eye, ear) are handicapped so that the inability to think clearly occurs.[44] A "dull" heart is a "fat" mind, metaphorically obese and sluggish. The mind lacks intellectual dexterity. It is slow to change its opinion or think outside the box. Likewise, "heavy" ears are unresponsive to outside stimuli and "hard of hearing," figuratively speaking. Eyes that are "blind" cannot see clearly through the fog of events. Geoffrey D. Robinson describes Israel's comprehensive inability to listen to God and learn: "Every organ of potential divine–human communication is malfunctioning."[45] The inevitable result was disorientation. For this reason, Isaiah's countrymen lamented, "We grope for the wall like the blind; we grope like those who have no eyes; we stumble at noon as in the twilight, among those in full vigor we are like dead men" (59:10).

Plainly, the Lord's intention was to undercut Israel's ability to process revelation.[46] They could not obey and thereby avoid disaster. The word "lest" (*pen*) makes this motive obvious. They would not "turn" (repent) and "be healed," because they did not see, hear, or understand properly per Yahweh's design.[47] The Lord disrupted their cognitive functionality

---

43. Verses 9 and 10 also express the Lord's negative assessment of Israel, for he refers to them in a non-filial manner as "this people" rather than "my people."

44. McLaughlin renders the idiomatic Hebrew of verses 9 and 10 in this way: "Listen continuously but do not discern, look continuously but do not understand. Make fat the mind of this people, and its ears heavy and its eyes make blind." "Make blind" implies the notion of smearing over with salve.

45. Robinson, "The Motif of Deafness and Blindness," 176.

46. Isaiah 6:9–10 is repeated almost verbatim in 44:18 with reference to idolatry: "They know not, nor do they discern, for he has shut their eyes, so that they cannot see, and their hearts, so that they cannot understand."

47. The verb "be healed" (*rapha*) refers to individuals and nations both literally and figuratively. It entails restoration from sin and disaster due to judgment (Pss 30:2; 107:20; Jer 3:22; 17:14; 33:6; Lam 2:13; Ezek 34:4; Hos 5:13; 11:3; Zech 11:16). For instance, Isaiah predicted future healing, referring to "the day when the Lord binds up the brokenness of his people, and heals the wounds inflicted by his blow" (30:26b; see also 19:22; 53:5; 57:18).

in order to prevent repentance and healing. He did not permit them to reach their intellectual potential or fulfill their mandate as the people of God. Robinson writes, "In the end, God is not mocked; if the people persist in their willful blindness, then God confirms them in their chosen state."[48]

Divinely imposed obduracy appears elsewhere in the book of Isaiah. Katherine M. Hayes calls it the "motif of delusion" that reveals "God's ability to shape human perception,"[49] especially among those who obstinately reject revelation. Concerning Egypt, the Lord inflicted a "spirit of confusion" (19:4), causing distortion and erroneous judgment (v. 15). Yahweh said that their rulers were "utterly foolish" and provided "stupid counsel" (19:11). Concerning the Assyrian general besieging Jerusalem, the Lord declared, "Behold, I will put a spirit in him, so that he shall hear a rumor and return to his own land" (37:7). And concerning Israel he said, "The Lord has poured out upon you a spirit of deep sleep, and has closed your eyes (the prophets), and covered your heads (the seers)" (29:9–10; see also 44:25).

Thus, Yahweh instigated confusion, particularly among the nation's spiritual leadership. Revelation became utterly opaque: "The vision of all this has become to you like the words of a book that is sealed. When men give it to one who can read, saying, 'Read this,' he says, 'I cannot, for it is sealed'" (29:11). The "wisdom of their wise men" and the "discernment of their discerning men" were undermined (v. 14b). Punitive epistemology left Israel without a rudder to steer them in turbulent waters.[50]

---

48. Robinson, "The Motif of Deafness and Blindness," 179. Similarly, Aitkin ("Hearing and Seeing," 26) explains, "Through an increasing stubborn and perverse attitude, Israel has severed themselves from hearing and seeing. Yahweh will therefore sever Israel from the knowledge and understanding to which hearing and seeing should lead, so that even the most attentive hearing of Yahweh's word and careful seeing of Yahweh's work will not result in knowledge and understanding."

49. Hayes, "A Spirit of Deep Sleep," 39. See also McLaughlin, "Their Hearts Were Hardened," 1–25; Evans, *To See and Not Perceive*, 43–51; Irwin, "Yahweh's Suspension of Free Will," 55–62.

50. McLaughlin shows that the bewilderment of God's enemies occurs elsewhere in the Old Testament (1 Kgs 22:20–27; 1 Sam 16:14; 18:10; 19:9; 1 Chr 21:1; Isa 37:7). ("Their Hearts Were Hardened," 3–9).

A People of Unclean Lips

However, if we step back and look at the immediate context, we can discern clues about why the Lord obscured the minds of Israel and fostered their destruction. Let us consider Isaiah 6:1–12:

(1) In the year that King Uzziah died I saw the Lord sitting upon a throne, high and lifted up; and the train of his robe filled the temple.

(2) Above him stood the seraphim. Each had six wings: with two he covered his face, and with two he covered his feet, and with two he flew.

(3) And one called to another and said: "Holy, holy, holy is the Lord of hosts; the whole earth is full of his glory!"

(4) And the foundations of the thresholds shook at the voice of him who called, and the house was filled with smoke.

(5) And I said: "Woe is me! For I am lost; for I am a man of unclean lips, and I dwell in the midst of a people of unclean lips; for my eyes have seen the King, the Lord of hosts!"

(6) Then one of the seraphim flew to me, having in his hand a burning coal that he had taken with tongs from the altar.

(7) And he touched my mouth and said: "Behold, this has touched your lips; your guilt is taken away, and your sin atoned for."

(8) And I heard the voice of the Lord saying, "Whom shall I send, and who will go for us?" Then I said, "Here I am! Send me."

(9) And he said, "Go, and say to this people: "'Keep on hearing, but do not understand; keep on seeing, but do not perceive.'

(10) Make the heart of this people dull, and their ears heavy, and blind their eyes; lest they see with their eyes, and hear with their ears, and understand with their hearts, and turn and be healed."

(11) Then I said, "How long, O Lord?" And he said, "Until cities lie waste without inhabitant, and houses without people, and the land is a desolate waste,

(12) and the Lord removes people far away, and the forsaken places are many in the midst of the land.

The first hint of Yahweh's motivation concerns the historical context (v. 1a). Isaiah's commission dates from the death of King Uzziah (ca. 740 BC). By this point, the nation had already split into two kingdoms. As we learned in the last chapter, a lull in Assyrian imperialism between 782 and 745 enabled the small, coastal kingdoms to prosper in relative peace. The northern tribes advanced economically, but their spiritual integrity was impoverished through syncretism and idolatry. Second Chronicles provides details about Uzziah: "As long as he sought the Lord, God made him prosper" (26:5). He "became very strong" (v. 8) and prosperous (vv. 9–10), and he developed a powerful military (vv. 11–15a). However, in his later years, "he grew proud" and "he was unfaithful to the Lord his God" (v. 16). The spiritual vitality of the people languished because they followed in his footsteps.

The second hint stems from Isaiah's throne-room theophany. Verses 1b–5 contrast the awesome holiness of God with the profound wickedness of Israel associated with the reign of Uzziah. Isaiah was complicit and confessed, "I am a man of unclean lips, and I dwell in the midst of a people of unclean lips" (v. 5). A third hint arises from the severe judgment described in verses 11–12 as a result of pervasive ungodliness. This social–religious context helps to explain Isaiah's confession, as well as Yahweh's motivation for imposing obduracy.

Broadening the context further, chapters 1–5 describe this milieu in vivid detail. Isaiah 1:4 and 5:24 provide an introduction and conclusion that depict the people's spiritual pollution: "They have forsaken the Lord, they have despised the Holy One of Israel, they are utterly estranged" and "They have rejected the law of the Lord of hosts, and have despised the word of the Holy One of Israel." Isaiah chronicles corruption in religious practice (1:11–16), ethics and justice (1:21–23; 3:9, 16; 5:8, 11, 23, 36), and idolatry (1:29; 2:6, 8, 18, 20; 3:0). The people were self-indulgent pleasure seekers (2:7; 3:9, 16–24). They were presumptuous and self-assured, "wise in their own eyes and clever in their own sight" (5:21; see also vv. 18–19).

For all these reasons, Yahweh expressed exasperation: "And now, O inhabitants of Jerusalem and men of Judah, judge between me and my vineyard. What more was there to do for my vineyard, that I have not done in it?" (5:3–4a). He initiated a covenantal lawsuit (*rib*) against his people, in particular their spiritual guides: "The Lord has taken his place to contend (*rib*); he stands to judge peoples. The Lord will enter into judgment with the elders and princes of his people" (3:13–14a). He called upon heaven and earth as witnesses (1:2a) and stated his charge: "Children have I reared and brought up, but they have rebelled against me" (1:2b).

The root of all their malfeasance, however, was a refusal to listen to and obey God's voice.[51] Yahweh said about them, "You have *never* heard, you have *never* known, from of old your ear has not been opened. For I knew that you would surely deal treacherously, and that from before birth you were called a rebel" (48:8). This declaration echoes Moses' assertion concerning Israel's obduracy at the inception of the nation, "To this day the Lord has not given you a heart to understand or eyes to see or ears to hear" (29:4). Isaiah testified that they did not hear "the word of the Lord [of hosts] (1:10; 28:14; 39:5), "my voice" (28:23; 32:9), "my speech" (28:23), or the "instruction of the Lord" (30:9). They would not listen "to me" (46:3, 12; 49:1; 51:1, 7; 55:2). And they refused to obey the "voice of his servant" (50:10) or the "law" (42:24).[52] Concerning their mental outlook, Isaiah said they were "obstinate" (58:4). They manifested "arrogance of heart" (9:9) and their minds were "busy with iniquity, to practice ungodliness, to utter error concerning the Lord" (32:6). Further, their "hearts are far from me" (29:13), "deluded" (44:20), "stubborn" (46:12), and focused upon "backsliding" (57:17).[53]

Finally, since Israel would not heed God's voice, they redirected their minds to idolatry. They experienced what G. K. Beale calls "sensory-organ malfunction" in association with idol worship.[54] He writes, "The language of blinding of the eyes and deafening of the ears is applied to those directly associated with idol worship."[55] In addition to 6:9–10, Beale cites 42:17–20:

> They are turned back and utterly put to shame, who trust in carved idols, who say to metal images, "You are our gods." Hear, you deaf, and look, you blind, that you may see! Who is blind but my servant, or deaf as my messenger whom I send? Who is

---

51. The verb *shama* is translated as listen to, hear, and obey.

52. In addition, they did not "incline [their] ear" (55:3) or "give attention" (10:30; 28:23; 51:4). They were "unwilling" to hear (30:9) and did not heed anything the Lord said (42:24; 65:12; 66:4).

53. Several idiomatic expressions also express their obtuse intellectual disposition: "outstretched necks" (3:16) and "your neck is an iron sinew and your forehead brass" (48:4).

54. Beale, *We Become What We Worship*, 46.

55. Beale, *We Become What We Worship*, 42.

blind as my dedicated one, or blind as the servant of the Lord? He sees many things, but does not observe them; his ears are open, but he does not hear. (See also 43:8, 10; 44:9–20)[56]

Elsewhere in the Old Testament, Psalm 115 clearly echoes Isaiah 6:9–10 and shows the intellectual and psychological dysfunctionality of idolatry:

> Their idols are silver and gold, the work of human hands. They have mouths, but do not speak; eyes, but do not see. They have ears, but do not hear; noses, but do not smell. They have hands, but do not feel; feet, but do not walk; and they do not make a sound in their throat. Those who make them become like them; so do all who trust in them. (Ps 115:4–8; see also 135:15–18)

In light of the context, therefore, Beale comments about 6:9–10, "Isaiah is to tell these idolaters that they have been so unrepentant about their idol worship that God is going to make them as spiritually insensitive, as spiritually inanimate and lifeless, as the idol."[57] He adds that Yahweh "is punishing them by means of their own sin."[58] As we have seen, Psalm 81 declares about Israel, "My people did not listen to my voice; Israel would not submit to me. So I gave them over to their stubborn hearts, to follow their own counsels" (vv. 11–12).

Israel's vision and listening, understanding and perceiving were askew because they refused to listen to God's voice in his words and deeds. Their eyes and ears failed to see or perceive God wisely. Their minds did not interpret reality or revelation correctly. In the end, God affirmed the obvious and they suffered the tragic consequences: "For the look on their faces bears witness against them; they proclaim their sin like Sodom; they do not hide it. Woe to them! For they have *brought evil on themselves*" (3:9). Similarly, Isaiah 66:4 explains, "I also will choose harsh treatment for them and *bring their fears upon them*, because when I called, no one

---

56. The language of sight and hearing, as well as the "sensory-organ malfunction" idiom, appear in Deuteronomy 29:4, Jeremiah 5:21, and Ezekiel 12:2. In addition, there are many thematic and terminological echoes of Isaiah 6:9–10 in expressions such as "ears to hear," "not speak," "not see," "not perceive," "dull," "blind their eyes," "you blind," "not observe," "not hear," "shut their eyes," "cannot see," "cannot understand," "eyes darkened," "darkness," "nor knowledge," "no eyes," "eyes opened," "ears unstopped," "deep sleep," "eyes closed," and "shut eyes," as well as the words "discern," "discernment," "stagger," "grope," and "confusion."

57. Beale, *We Become What We Worship*, 46.

58. Beale, *We Become What We Worship*, 47.

answered, when I spoke, they did not listen; but they did what was evil in my eyes and chose that in which I did not delight."

The obduracy imposed upon Israel, therefore, did not occur in a moral vacuum, nor did it arise as raw epistemic power or capriciousness on the part of Yahweh. Rather, disorientation resulted from continual and systemic covenantal violation. The people's blindness occurred within a context of judgment and error. As Moses told them long before, "The Lord will strike you with madness and blindness and confusion of mind, and you shall grope at noonday, as the blind grope in darkness, and you shall not prosper in your ways" (Deut 28:28–29).

You Turn Things Upside Down

Let us consider one further example of noetic depravity that precedes 6:9–10. The fourth affirmation of judgment ("woe") in Isaiah 5:18–19 says:

(18) Woe to those who draw iniquity with cords of vanity, And sin as if with a cart rope;

(19) That say, "Let Him make speed and hasten His work, That we may see it; And let the counsel of the Holy One of Israel draw near and come, That we may know it." (NKJV)

In verse 18a, Yahweh prescribes judgment ("woe") on "those who draw iniquity with cords of vanity." In verse 18b, the words "as if" associate the dragging of iniquity ("draw") with pulling a cartful of sin deceitfully.[59]

To understand the message of the two verses, we must discern the meaning of the image in verse 18 and then how it illuminates the statement in verse 19. Fortunately, a similar passage in Hosea 11:4 helps to explain the meaning in verse 18: "I *drew* them with gentle *cords*, with *bands* of love, And I was to them as those who take the yoke from their neck. I stooped and fed them" (NKJV). The verb "drew" in Hosea is the same term "draw" (*mashak*) in Isaiah 5:18a. Likewise, the words "band" (*aboth*) and "cord" (*chebel*) appear in both passages. In contrast to Isaiah, however, in Hosea the Lord referred to Israel with utmost affection. He tenderly cared for them "with gentle cords, with bands of love." He

---

59. The NKJV and the NASB provide a more literal translation of the verse with the rendering "as if."

personally gave them sustenance and freed them from their "yoke." Also, in Hosea the active agent is Yahweh, whereas in Isaiah the one who "draws" is the sinful human.

In Isaiah 5:18, sin is likened to a cart that humans drag, picturing the sinner as a beast of burden whose self-imposed "yoke" is heavy. "Iniquity" (*avon*) and "sin" (*chattaah*) in verse 18 are similar in meaning. In 6:7b the terms also appear, but with reference to Isaiah's commissioning. After he confessed his sin, the seraphs declared, "Your guilt (*avon*) is taken away, and your sin (*chattaah*) atoned for." In 5:18 sin is virulent and linked with ignorance and judgment, whereas in 6:17 iniquity is an impregnable barrier to the knowledge of God, breached only by atonement.

The word "vanity" (*shav*) signifies futility, falsehood, undependability, and uselessness, depending on the context. In this setting the sinner relies on deceit to achieve his evil aspirations. Even though his plots are self-defeating and frustrating, he deludes himself with a myth of impunity and autonomy. By lying to himself, the sinner justifies his beastliness and burden.[60] Oswalt summarizes his *modus operandi* in this way:

> These are people who delight in sinning, who seek out ways to do it more aggressively, all the while insisting that if such a course of action was so bad, the great God, this "Holy One of Israel" Isaiah keeps going on about, will certainly take some action against it. In the meantime, they intend to keep right on pleasing themselves at all costs.[61]

In verse 19, this deceitful mentality is expressed explicitly. The rebel puts God on trial and assumes the position of cosmic evaluator, instructing the Lord as to how he must reveal himself. The sinner sets the timetable and the mode of disclosure whereby knowledge would be proffered and acquired from God. He cynically implies that the Lord has failed to intervene and has not communicated clearly. He believes that the Lord does not really care about his deeds of unrighteousness. Clearly, this is a very Machiavellian calculation based on faulty premises that resemble the fool's functional atheism.

---

60. The rationale seems to be the same as in Isaiah 28:15: "We have made a covenant with death, and with Sheol we have an agreement, when the overwhelming whip passes through it will not come to us, for we have made lies our refuge, and in falsehood we have taken shelter."

61. Oswalt, *Isaiah*, 114–15. Similarly, Moyter (*The Prophecy of Isaiah*, 7) writes, "By holding on to what is false they bind themselves in bondage to sin."

Verse 18, therefore, expresses God's negative evaluation of this mindset, whereas verse 19 represents the dangerous, intellectual game Israel played. They foolishly inverted the Creator–creature distinction epistemologically by redefining God's role. But Yahweh declared that the knowledge deficit was their own fault. He said, "They do not regard the deeds of the Lord, or see the work of his hands. Therefore my people go into exile for lack of knowledge" (5:12b–13b). Indeed, verse 20 provides further insight about their self-destructive inversion: "Woe to those who call evil good and good evil, who put darkness for light and light for darkness, who put bitter for sweet and sweet for bitter!"

Likewise, in chapter 29 they asserted outrageous limitations on divine knowledge. Verses 15–16 state:

> You who hide deep from the Lord your counsel, whose deeds are in the dark, and who say, "Who sees us? Who knows us?" You turn things upside down! Shall the potter be regarded as the clay, that the thing made should say of its maker, "He did not make me"; or the thing formed say of him who formed it, "He has no understanding"?

Clearly, in this vivid example of exilic epistemology we observe Adam's sin recapitulated. Like their forebear, they sought ontological assent through an inversion of epistemology. They placed themselves in a position equal to or greater than the Lord's so that they could evaluate revelation. They sought to subject him to their agenda. They behaved as if they were morally and intellectually autonomous. They listened to other voices. They failed as apprentice rulers, builders, economists, and philosophers. Their vice-regency produced corruption and disorder in every sphere of society. They broke the covenant and did not fulfill their mission to the world. And like Adam, they lost touch with reality, embraced self-delusion as a refuge, and became fools. By their own admission, they fulfilled the curse of Deuteronomy 28:28–29, leading to this lament:

> Therefore justice is far from us, and righteousness does not overtake us; we hope for light, and behold, darkness, and for brightness, but we walk in gloom. We grope for the wall like the blind; we grope like those who have no eyes; we stumble at noon as in the twilight, among those in full vigor we are like dead men. We all growl like bears; we moan and moan like doves; we hope for justice, but there is none; for salvation, but it is far from us. (Isa 59:9–11)

JEREMIAH

The prophet Jeremiah ministered during the death throes of Judah (627 to 586 BC). Previously, Judah had languished as a vassal of the Assyrian empire, followed by a short-lived independence under King Josiah, then Egyptian servitude, and finally destruction and exile under the Neo-Babylonians (597 to 582 BC). Joel S. Burnett writes, "Continued domination and disenfranchisement under these seventh-century superpowers" was "emblematic of the harsh reality emerging for Judah, which in two decades will be crushed between greater powers on the geopolitical scene."[62] No doubt, Jeremiah's social context was extremely dire and tumultuous.

But the theological setting was equally momentous. Yahweh initiated a covenant lawsuit (*rib*) against his own people.[63] He charged, "Those who handle the law did not know me; the shepherds transgressed against me; the prophets prophesied by Baal.... Therefore I still contend (*rib*) with you, declares the Lord, and with your children's children I will contend (*rib*)" (Jer 2:8b–9).

Israel chronically refused to heed God's voice: "They did not obey or incline their ear . . . Therefore I brought upon them all the words of this covenant, which I commanded them to do, but they did not" (11:8). They suppressed God's truth and substituted the worship of idols for the fear of the Lord. Yahweh declared, "My people have committed two evils: they have forsaken me, the fountain of living waters, and hewed out cisterns for themselves, broken cisterns that can hold no water" (2:13). Due to their guilty status, they suffered the curses prescribed in Deuteronomy.[64] J. G. McConville summarizes Israel's decadence in this way: "They have abandoned him for other gods (ch. 2), mistaken a trust in institutions for true religion (7:1–15), and become deeply corrupt as a society, so that no truth is known or practiced (8:22–9:9)."[65]

The book of Jeremiah, therefore, portrays exilic epistemology in its fullest dimensions in Israel during a period of extreme upheaval. The prophet described the intellectual malaise forewarned in Deuteronomy.

---

62. Burnett, "Changing God," 290–91.

63. Regarding the role of covenant and the covenant lawsuit (*rib*), see Thomson, *The Book of Jeremiah*, 59–67, 159–71; Limburg, "Root *rîb* and the Prophetic Lawsuit Speeches," 291–304; and Burnett, "Changing God," 289–99.

64. "Because of the curse the land mourns, and the pastures of the wilderness are dried up" (23:10b; see also 24:9; 25:18; 26:6; 29:18, 22; 42:18; 44:12).

65. McConville, "Jeremiah," in *Theological Interpretation of the Old Testament*, 214.

Falsehood in speech, deceitful conduct, intellectual confusion, and self-deception were rampant. The book of Jeremiah provides a database of noetic depravity.

They Provoked Me to Anger

Yahweh inquired with incredulity at the beginning of the book, "What wrong did your fathers find in me that they went far from me, and went after worthlessness, and became worthless?" (2:5). The reference to the "fathers" points to Israel's covenantal pact with Yahweh at the nation's inception and their failure to meet their obligations from that point on. They forsook the "ancient paths, where the good way is" (6:16; see also 18:15). They traveled instead on "side roads" that caused them to "stumble" in idolatry (18:15). Furthermore, their fathers "went far from me" (2:5)—a reference to apostasy and disobedience. The expression "went far" (*rachaq*) in 2:5 indicates movement away from another person (to "become far," "distant" or alienated). Similarly, the frequently occurring phrase "went after" (*halaq* plus preposition) indicates a penchant for idol worship (2:8, 23; 7:6; 8:2; 11:10; 16:11; 25:6; "went up" in 3:6, 8).[66] The fathers, including the present generation, repeatedly turned their back on Yahweh and "went to" worship other gods. They incurred judgment as a result (44:2–3).

The words "worthlessness" and "worthless" in 2:5 poignantly express the epistemic judgment. Both words derive from *hebel*, meaning vanity, futility, and insubstantial.[67] In Jeremiah *hebel* is rendered as "idols" (8:19b; 10:8), "vanity" (10:3), "worthless" (10:15; 51:18); "false" ("gods," 14:22), and "worthless" ("things," 16:19b). J. A. Thompson translates the phrase in verse 5 as "the Delusion."[68] Idolaters became like their gods: spiritually deaf and blind. In the words of Psalm 115:8, "Those who make them become like them; so do all who trust in them." From Yahweh's perspective, therefore, Israel's idolatry "provoked [him] to anger" (8:19) and he declared, "The gods who did not make the heavens and the earth shall perish from the earth and from under the heavens" (10:11).

---

66. Thompson says that to "go after" meant to "serve as a vassal" within ancient international covenants (*The Book of Jeremiah*, 167).

67. As we saw earlier, *hebel* is Qohelet's favorite diagnosis of the human condition.

68. Thompson, *The Book of Jeremiah*, 165.

However, from Israel's point of view, 2:5 implies an accusation *against the Lord*. The word "wrong" (*awel*; injustice or iniquity) suggests blame shifting. In fact, Israel audaciously brought charges (*rib*) against the Lord in 2:29. But he turned the tables and replied tartly, "Why do you contend (*rib*) with *me*? *You* have all transgressed against me."[69] Later on, they queried with temerity and a spirit of victimhood, "Why has the Lord pronounced all this great evil against *us*? What is our iniquity? What is the sin that we have committed against the Lord our God?" (5:19; 13:22). The accusation of divine culpability is also evident in their contorted self-perception: "I am not unclean" (2:23a), "I am innocent" (2:35), and "We are wise" (8:8). The reality, of course, was far different, for Yahweh declared, "They have turned back to the iniquities of their forefathers, who refused to hear my words. They have gone after other gods to serve them. The house of Israel and the house of Judah have broken my covenant that I made with their fathers" (11:10; see also 3:25; 7:25, 26; 9:14).

You Will Not Listen to Me

The importance of hearing and heeding God's voice in Jeremiah is ubiquitous and multifaceted. The verb *shama* is used when God speaks and is translated as "listen to," "hear," or "obey." It also often appears with the direct object "voice" (*qol*). The expression *shama qol* appears as "voice of the Lord their God" (3:25; 7:28; 26:13; 42:6, 21), "voice of the Lord" (38:20; 43:3, 7; 44:23), "my voice" (11:4), and "his voice" (40:3).[70]

Significantly, there are many indications of Israel's rejection of God's voice and lust for autonomy. First, they did "not listen" (7:26, 27; 17:27),[71] "not obey" (3:13, 25; 7:24),[72] and "not hear" (5:21; 11:3; 17:23). Other expressions are "refuse to hear" (11:10; 13:10; 19:15), "refusing to listen"

---

69. Limburg ("Root *rîb* and the Prophetic Lawsuit Speeches," 302) makes this point, writing, "The people think that they have made a complaint against Yahweh, but in reality Yahweh is the one who has the complaint."

70. Other objects with *shama* include "to me" (16:12; 17:24, 27; 25:7; 26:4; 34:14; 35:14, 15; 38:15), "me" (34:17), "to you" (Jeremiah, 7:27; 44:16), "words of the prophets" (23:16; 25:4; 26:5; 27:9), "my words" (25:8; 35:13), "his word" (23:18), "word of the Lord" (2:4; 7:2; 9:20; 17:20; 19:3; 25:3; 37:2), "instruction" (32:33), "word" (10:1), and "words of this covenant" (11:2, 3, 6, 8). Especially interesting is 8:9b: "They have rejected the word of the Lord, so what wisdom is in them?"

71. Other references are 23:16; 25:3; 26:4; 27:9; 32:33; 34:14; 37:2; 38:15; 44:16.

72. Other references are 7:28; 11:8; 22:21; 34:17; 42:21; 44:23.

(16:12), and "not pay attention" (6:19). Second, their speech testified to their perverse resolve: "I will not serve" (2:20), "We are free, we will come no more to you" (2:31b), "We will not walk in it ['the ancient paths']" (6:16), "We will not pay attention" (6:17), and "I will not listen" (22:21). Two expressions indicate their failure to listen, *shama* and the conjunction "but": "They did not obey (*shama*) or incline their ear, but" they "walked in their own courses" (7:24) and "walked in the stubbornness of their evil heart" (11:8). Third, the idiom "stiffened the neck" associated with *shama* indicates their obduracy (7:26; 19:15). Their skewed intentionality was obvious: "They did not listen or incline their ears, but stiffened their necks *in order not to* listen or take correction" (17:23, NASB).

Furthermore, they allowed God's words to pass from memory, either by failing to keep cultic rituals or by outright neglect. Yahweh expressed this problem as a rhetorical question: "How long shall there be lies in the heart of the prophets who prophesy lies, and who prophesy the deceit of their own heart, who think to make my people forget my name by their dreams that they tell one another, even as their fathers forgot my name for Baal?" (23:26-28). Elsewhere, the Lord asked similarly, "Can a virgin forget her ornaments, or a bride her attire? Yet my people have forgotten me days without number" (2:32; see also 3:21; 13:25; 18:15; 44:9; 50:6). Finally, those who did not listen followed instead "the stubbornness of their own evil heart" (3:17; 7:24; 9:14; 11:8; 13:10). Significantly, the term "stubbornness" (*sheriruth leb*) means "muscularity of the heart" and can signify "arbitrariness."[73] Thompson translates the expression as "follow our own stubbornly wicked inclinations."[74]

Both Stupid and Foolish

Yahweh described Israel bluntly as "stupid and without knowledge" (10:14) and "both stupid and foolish" (v. 8). The word "foolish" (*sakal*) appears only seven times in the Old Testament (Eccl 2:19; 7:17; 10:3 [twice], 14; Jer 4:22; 5:21). Within Ecclesiastes the term is associated with

---

73. Yoram Hazony, *The Philosophy of Hebrew Scripture*, 171. He explains arbitrariness as "following one's own thoughts."

74. Thompson, *Jeremiah*, 198. Carasik (*Theologies of the Mind*, 213) renders the phrase as "reliance on the dictates of one's own heart."

wickedness and premature death (7:17), lacking sense (10:3), and overweening verbosity (10:14).[75]

The Lord also called them a "foolish and senseless people, who have eyes, but see not, who have ears, but hear not" (5:21; see also 4:11 and 10:8).[76] Let us consider Jeremiah 5:21 in context:

(21) "Hear this, O foolish and senseless people, who have eyes, but see not, who have ears, but hear not.

(22) Do you not fear me? declares the Lord. Do you not tremble before me? I placed the sand as the boundary for the sea, a perpetual barrier that it cannot pass; though the waves toss, they cannot prevail; though they roar, they cannot pass over it."

(23) But this people has a stubborn and rebellious heart; they have turned aside and gone away.

(24) They do not say in their hearts, "Let us fear the Lord our God, who gives the rain in its season, the autumn rain and the spring rain, and keeps for us the weeks appointed for the harvest."

(25) Your iniquities have turned these away, and your sins have kept good from you.

Verse 21 links senselessness (or mindlessness) with the failure of perception and understanding (eyes and ears that do not perceive). This is a clear reference to Deuteronomy 29:4, in which Moses explains Israel's chronic covenantal violation, and to Isaiah 6:9–10, where Yahweh explains why Israel would not understand Isaiah's message. The word "fear" and the expression "fear of the Lord" in verses 22 and 24 indicate a healthy relationship with God. Reverence for the Lord engenders worship, service, piety, knowledge, and wisdom. The Israelites, on the other hand, groped about in darkness due to iniquity.

Verses 22b and 24b underscore God's rule over creation, as well as its bounty. However, there is great irony in these verses. The ocean's mighty power is limited, yet the Israelites "toss" and "roar," traversing all

---

75. According to Waltke (*The Book of Proverbs*, Kindle Edition, Location 3272), the Hebrew expression "senseless" (*en leb*) in Jeremiah 5:21 is a synonym for "lacking sense" (*hasar leb*) in Proverbs. The idiom is linked with gullibility (7:7; 9:4), marital unfaithfulness (6:32), denigrating others (11:12), pursuing illusions (12:11), and relishing folly (15:21). "Lacking sense" is the opposite of being wise (10:13) and righteous (10:21).

76. Other references to Israel as "foolish" also appear in 4:22; 17:11; 50:36.

"barriers" established by the Lord. They exceeded the boundaries set by Yahweh because they have "a stubborn and rebellious heart" ("mind," v. 23).[77] They did not discern the benefits of revering God, even though he alone enabled them to flourish. Israel could not perceive the causal connection between their "iniquities," especially idolatry (v. 23b), and their impoverishment or impending exile. Covenant infraction signified that "good" was withheld from them (v. 25b).

Jeremiah 4:22–26 conveys a similar but more urgent message:

(22) For my people are foolish; they know me not; they are stupid children; they have no understanding. They are 'wise'—in doing evil! But how to do good they know not.[78]

(23) I looked on the earth, and behold, it was without form and void; and to the heavens, and they had no light.

(24) I looked on the mountains, and behold, they were quaking, and all the hills moved to and fro.

(25) I looked, and behold, there was no man, and all the birds of the air had fled.

(26) I looked, and behold, the fruitful land was a desert, and all its cities were laid in ruins before the Lord, before his fierce anger.

Verse 22 shows that Israel did the exact opposite of what knowing God required. They did not acknowledge him and, as a result, became totally disoriented in their thoughts and aspirations. They no longer knew what truly mattered or what to do about it (wisdom and righteousness). They were spiritually illiterate and ethically insipid. Their lack of knowledge made them clever only for idolatry and wickedness.

Verses 23–26 present the spiritual and social disaster that befell God's people when they became dull and foolish. These verses portray creation as undone through ignorance and apostasy. Jeremiah employs extremely vivid imagery: the earth reduced to chaos (echoing Gen 1:2; see also Jer 33:19–26) and the reversal of creation.[79] With tragic irony Jeremiah describes the utter devastation that would befall the nation (v.

---

77. Lalleman argues this point as well in "Jeremiah, Judgment and Creation," 18.

78. Thompson (*The Book of Jeremiah*, 229) says that "they know me not" is actually in Hebrew "Me, they do not know" for emphasis.

79. See Lalleman, "Jeremiah," 19.

26a), whereas Genesis 1 envisioned divine benediction before the fall ("It was very good," v. 31).

Furthermore, Jeremiah 9:23-24 provides a synopsis of what it means to know—or not know—God, and the kinds of righteous or unrighteous conduct that result:

(23) Thus says the Lord: "Let not the wise man boast in his wisdom, let not the mighty man boast in his might, let not the rich man boast in his riches,

(24) but let him who boasts boast in this, that he understands and knows me, that I am the Lord who practices steadfast love, justice, and righteousness in the earth. For in these things I delight, declares the Lord."

The word "boast" is repeated five times. Boasts display identity, demonstrate success, provide status, and express confidence. This passage, however, disavows three typical markers of earthly boasting: wisdom (understanding and knowledge), might (judicial and military strength), and riches (economic influence and hedonism). Each of these boasts focuses on personal happiness and security to the neglect of other people.

Rather, any boasting should refer to what really matters: knowing God and imitating his priorities. The Lord "practices steadfast love, justice, and righteousness in the earth" (v. 24b). Steadfast love is covenant faithfulness to God and to his people; justice and righteousness refer to personal and social ethics (22:3). William J. Wessels writes, "If people know Yahweh, they will exercise or practice these things, the things in which Yahweh delights."[80] True knowledge of God signifies that one knows his character, what he requires, and how to imitate him in thought, belief, and behavior. The Israelites failed in this, sadly.

The book of Jeremiah, therefore, depicts the mind under sin in a very negative light. The Lord, himself, provides the definitive—yet enigmatic—diagnosis: "The heart is deceitful above all things, and desperately sick; who can understand it?" (17:9). The term "deceitful" (*aqob*) is used only two other times in the Old Testament (Isa 40:4 and Hos 8:8). In Isaiah it appears in this context: "Every valley shall be lifted up, and every mountain and hill be made low; the uneven ground shall become level, and the rough (*aqob*) places a plain." In Hosea it occurs in this sentence, "Gilead is a city of evildoers, tracked with blood (*aqob*)." The latter

---

80. Wessels, "The Social Implications of Knowing Yahweh," 5.

passage infers that deceitfulness is inherently violent and leaves discernible tracks. In the former verse, "rough" implies unnavigable terrain that produces disorientation. One image implies knowability (about a crime), whereas the other implies obscurity (about location). Certainly, this is a hermeneutical crux that only a transcendent mind can fathom, and indeed Yahweh makes this boast in the next verse: "I the Lord search the heart and test the mind, to give every man according to his ways, according to the fruit of his deeds" (v. 10).

But another way to discern the meaning of 17:9 is to survey how the "heart" (mind) is presented in Jeremiah, how synonyms of "deceitful" function, and how the mind in action manifests its true priorities, especially in communication. First, in the verses where "heart" appears, duplicity, violence, autonomy, folly, and apostasy abound.[81] Jeremiah 22:17 provides this dismal summary: "You have eyes and heart only for your dishonest gain, for shedding innocent blood, and for practicing oppression and violence."

Second, synonyms of "deceit(ful)" (*mirmah*) appear in a multitude of contexts, such as the following: "did not return to me with her whole heart, but in pretense" (3:10), "heaping oppression upon oppression, and deceit upon deceit, they refuse to know me" (9:6); and "prophesying to you a lying vision, worthless divination, and the deceit of their own minds" (14:14; see also 23:16). Jeremiah 5:27 supplies a useful synopsis: "Like a cage full of birds, their houses are full of deceit; therefore they have become great and rich; they have grown fat and sleek. They know no bounds in deeds of evil; they judge not with justice."[82]

Third, with regard to communication the term "false" (*sheqer*) often occurs. We read, for instance, "swear falsely" (5:2; 7:9), "prophesy falsely" (5:31), "lying pen" (8:8), "lying words" (29:23), and "speaking falsely" (40:16). Falsehood also appears in economic relations: "For from the least to the greatest of them, everyone is greedy for unjust gain; and from prophet to priest, everyone deals falsely" (6:13; 8:10). More significantly,

---

81. For instance: "did not return to me with her whole heart" (3:10), "walked in their own counsels" (7:24a); "stubbornly follow their own evil heart" (3:17; 11:8; 18:12b); "the evil of your deeds" (4:4); "plans an ambush" (9:8b); "uncircumcised in heart" (9:26); "near in their mouth but far from their heart" (12:2); "greatness of your iniquity" (13:22); "turns away from the Lord" (17:5); "follow our own plans" (18:12a); "lies" and "deceit" (23:26); and "pride of your heart" (49:16).

82. "Deceit" is also translated from *tormah* in 8:5, 14:14, and 23:26. Other related terms depicting deceit against others are "schemes" (11:19), "plans" (18:12), and "plots" (18:18).

falsehood manifests itself in religion: "his images are false" (10:14), "lying vision" (14:14), "false gods" (14:22), "prophesied falsely" (20:6), and "lying dreams."

Finally, falsehood appears as self-lying and self-deception, even in matters of importance. With reference to human flourishing and worship, Yahweh said, "They have forsaken me, the fountain of living waters, and hewed out cisterns for themselves, broken cisterns that can hold no water" (2:13). In other words, Israel opted for "broken cisterns" that did not fulfill their purpose simply because they were *self*-chosen. With reference to their security, he declared, "Do not deceive yourselves, saying, 'The Chaldeans will surely go away from us,' for they will not go away" (37:9). Israel chose to embrace a falsehood because they were *self*-directed. Sadly, Jeremiah 9:3 provides the epistemological epitaph of Israel at their point of demise: "They bend their tongue like a bow; falsehood and not truth has grown strong in the land; for they proceed from evil to evil, and they do not know me, declares the Lord."

PSALM 14

Psalm 14 is unique and significant for several reasons. First, in the Old Testament it appears twice (repeated as Psalm 53), which hints at its importance. Second, the psalm resonates with wisdom themes, Proverbs in particular. Third, Psalm 14 summarizes exilic epistemology in the Old Testament. Fourth, it generalizes the exilic epistemology of Israel to the entire human race.[83] The text of Psalm 14 is as follows:

(1) The fool says in his heart, "There is no God." They are corrupt, they do abominable deeds; there is none who does good.

(2) The Lord looks down from heaven on the children of man, to see if there are any who understand, who seek after God.

(3) They have all turned aside; together they have become corrupt; there is none who does good, not even one.

(4) Have they no knowledge, all the evildoers who eat up my people as they eat bread and do not call upon the Lord?

---

83. Paul cites Psalm 14:2–3 to support his argument that "all are under sin" in Romans 3:10.

FOOLISH AND SENSELESS PEOPLE

(5) There they are in great terror, for God is with the generation of the righteous.

(6) You would shame the plans of the poor, but the Lord is his refuge.

(7) Oh, that salvation for Israel would come out of Zion! When the Lord restores the fortunes of his people, let Jacob rejoice, let Israel be glad.

A number of observations and inferences can be gleaned from this text. First, there are several dualities: two speakers (the fool and the Lord); two representatives (the fool for the "children of man" and the Lord speaking about mankind); two mental domains (the fool's subjective thoughts and the Lord's public discourse); and two outlooks (from earth and from heaven). There are, as well, several verbal parallels: "corrupt" (vv. 1, 3); "none who does good" (vv. 1, 3); "understand"/"knowledge" (vv. 2, 4); "seek"/"call upon" (vv. 2, 4); and "abominable deeds"/"eat up my people" (vv. 1, 4).

Second, there is an argument from the particular to the general (or from the simple to the complex). The fool (particular or simple) represents human beings as a class ("children of man"). What is said about the fool applies to the group, and what is said about the group typifies the fool. Both the fool and the class manifest the following characteristics:

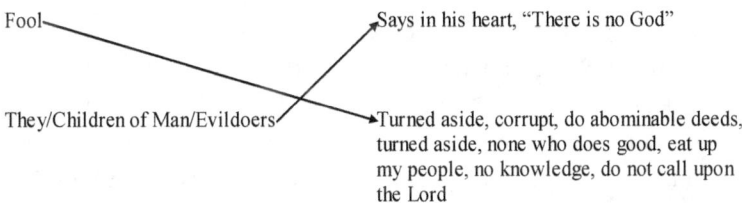

Those comprised by the "children of man" include the fool. The argument does not affirm, however, that *every* individual expresses *every* aspect of folly, but only that he or she *could* do so by definition. Every human partakes of "fool-ness," and anyone could affirm, "There is no God." Every person is a fool and an "evildoer" by definition (apart from grace).

Third, there is an implied question in the passage (v. 2a): What is the Lord seeking among mankind from heaven? We can rearrange the passage to demonstrate the answer in this way:

Question	What is the Lord looking for? (2a)
v. 2b	anyone who understands
	anyone who seeks for God
Negative answer 1	Children of man (general—complex case)
v. 1b	they are corrupt
	they do abominable deeds
	none does good
v. 3	they have all turned aside
	they have together become corrupt
	no one does good
v. 4	they have no knowledge
	they eat up my people
	they do not call upon the Lord
Negative answer 2	The fool (particular—simple case)
v. 1a	Says in his heart, "There is no God"

Fourth, the fool "turns aside" from Yahweh to worship idols. Much earlier, Moses warned Israel not to "turn aside and serve other gods" (Deut 11:16; see also 1 Kgs 22:43; 2 Kgs 10:29). They also "turned aside" in disobedience from "the way that I am commanding you" (Deut 11:28; 28:14). At other times they "turned aside" from "following the Lord" (1 Sam 12:20), "my statutes and my commandments" (2 Chr 7:19), or "doing what is right in the sight of the Lord" (2 Chr 20:32).

Fifth, there is an implicit contrast with the wise person depicted in the prologue of Proverbs.[84] In Psalm 14, folly is displayed as the inverse of wisdom, a foil for wisdom. The imaginary wise person in Psalm 14 would say in his heart, "God exists." And God would testify about him, "He is righteous and does good deeds. He fears the Lord, calls out to him, and seeks wisdom through instruction. He extends covenantal care to God's people and demonstrates integrity in all his dealings."

Sixth, the fool (*nabal*) spoke "in his heart." Carasik explains that this idiom occurs "exclusively in contexts that indicate disregard or defiance of God."[85] Aside from Psalm 14 and 53, other contexts are revealing: "The pride of your heart has deceived you . . . who say in your heart, 'Who will

---

84. Proverbs 1:2–7 was examined in chapter 6. The vocabulary is not identical, though two key wisdom terms appear in Psalm 14: "fool" (*nabal* in verse 1) and "plans" (*etsah* in verse 6). See Bennett, "Wisdom Motifs in Psalm 14 = 53," 15–21.

85. Carasik, *Theologies of the Mind*, 118.

bring me down to the ground?'" (Obad 3); the fool "disguises himself with his lips and harbors deceit in his heart" (Prov 26:24; see also 6:16); and the wicked "says in his heart, 'I shall not be moved; throughout all generations I shall not meet adversity'" (Ps 10:6).[86]

A Knowledge Conundrum

In Psalm 14, two speakers make absolute and universal claims that are diametrically opposed. The fool states that Elohim does not exist (v. 1a). Elohim, on the other hand, utters a series of pronouncements about the negative ethical, spiritual, and intellectual character of the human race. God speaks from a transcendent perspective. He is omniscient and qualified to assess everything in creation. He is also omnipotent and able to intervene on behalf of the poor (v. 6) and the "fortunes of his people" (v. 7), who have been abused by fools. The fool, however, is finite and speaks from the perspective of earth. His understanding is limited and subject to error. He is also fallen and his evaluations are distorted by sin.

Why does the fool assert a universal negative? Why does he deny God's existence? The passage suggests the fool's motivation: he denied reality (God's existence) because he was culpable. He perpetrated "abominable deeds" and "turned aside" to idolatry and disobedience. He did nothing worthwhile and violently mistreated his countrymen. He did not seek God or call out to him because he was self-referential. Psalm 36:1 explains the fool's deepest motivation: "Transgression speaks to the wicked deep in his heart; there is no fear of God before his eyes." Peter C. Craigie writes, "Having no fear of God, he effectively blinded himself with self-adoration; having then only himself to go by as a measure for morality, he was totally unable either to know or hate his own iniquity."[87]

Yet, the fool was aware of the *concept* of God, for he knew his name (Elohim). As a Hebrew, he likely received instruction about God's nature. Undoubtedly, he knew the covenant and its stipulations. Clearly, he knew

---

86. This negative portrait is confirmed elsewhere in the Old Testament where "fool" (*nabal* as noun or adjective) appears. Consider, for instance, "The foolish scoff at you all the day!" (Ps 74:22) and "The fool speaks folly, and his heart is busy with iniquity, to practice ungodliness, to utter error concerning the Lord, to leave the craving of the hungry unsatisfied, and to deprive the thirsty of drink" (Isa 32:6).

87. Craigie, *Psalms* 1–50, 291–92. Similarly, Kraus (*Psalms* 1–50, 398) wrote about the fool's outlook, "Yahweh is not a living reality who questions his life and whom he has to fear."

something about the transcendent being. In fact, he claimed to know at least one ontological fact: that Elohim did *not* exist. But from God's point of view, the fool actually perceived nothing. He did not "understand" (v. 2) and he had "no knowledge" (v. 4). Indeed, the irony was great. The finite and fallen creature, whose ignorance equaled his stature, declared that the greatest being did not exist, even though the being he negated was also his Creator.

Two interpretive options are possible regarding the apparent paradox in Psalm 14. The first is an epistemological puzzle: the fool simultaneously *did* and did *not* know God exists. The second option is motivational: the fool knew but did not *acknowledge* God. The fool opted to disregard God's revelation. He did not listen and obey. He knew his Maker but refused to bend the knee.

But how could the fool deny what he knew and so profoundly embrace illusion? As we saw earlier, Jeremiah 2:11 and 13 provide an explanation. The fool suppressed what he knew and exchanged the truth about God for falsehood.[88] The fool knew God as he revealed himself, but he was motivated to deny that knowledge. Since this tension was unpleasant, he redirected his attention to more satisfying and stupefying pursuits. William A. Dembski puts it this way: "The atheist is a fool because is he an idolater. It is not that he worships nothing. It is rather that he worships everything except the one true God."[89] Thus, even though his project was futile, the fool persisted due to the demands of autonomy and self-deception.

The Pseudo-Atheist

What kind of atheism did the fool profess? It is not modern theoretical atheism ("I *know* that God does not exist") or even agnosticism ("I *cannot* know if God exists"). Rather, the fool embraced a pragmatic or functional unbelief. He knew that God exists, but he operated *as if* God were irrelevant: a *useful* fiction—pseudo-atheism. He refused to acknowledge God so that he could pursue self-chosen, sinful means and ends. Such atheism was a quasi-cosmological justification for the acting out of sinful autonomy. The fool's atheism, therefore, was contrived.

---

88. Jeremiah 2:11, 13 was discussed in the previous section.
89. Dembski, "How to Debate an Atheist," 58.

Other passages associate folly with the irrational idea that God is unseeing, uncaring, inactive, or incompetent. Fools project this mischaracterization on the cosmos and then erroneously claim impunity for their wickedness. For instance, they boast to themselves:

> "How can God know? Is there knowledge in the Most High?" (Ps 73:11)

> "The Lord does not see; the God of Jacob does not perceive." (Ps 94:7)

> "He will do nothing; no disaster will come upon us, nor shall we see sword or famine." (Jer 5:12)

> "The Lord will not do good, nor will he do ill." (Zeph 1:12)

Psalm 10:2–7, 9, 11 provides a useful parallel to Psalm 14:1–4. This passage vividly illustrates faux-atheism. (Note that "the wicked" often serves as a synonym for the fool.)

(2) In arrogance the wicked hotly pursue the poor; let them be caught in the schemes that they have devised.

(3) For the wicked boasts of the desires of his soul, and the one greedy for gain curses and renounces the Lord.

(4) In the pride of his face the wicked does not seek him; all his thoughts are, "There is no God."

(5) His ways prosper at all times; your judgments are on high, out of his sight; as for all his foes, he puffs at them.

(6) He says in his heart, "I shall not be moved; throughout all generations I shall not meet adversity."

(7) His mouth is filled with cursing and deceit and oppression; under his tongue are mischief and iniquity.

(9) He lurks in ambush like a lion in his thicket; he lurks that he may seize the poor; he seizes the poor when he draws him into his net.

(11) He says in his heart, "God has forgotten, he has hidden his face, he will never see it."

Consider the motivational, mental, and behavioral parallels with Psalm 14. The wicked person's unbelief is closely associated with moral corruption, faulty thinking, and social injustice. The wicked "hotly pursue the poor" and callously oppress God's people in a manner similar to Psalm 14's reference to fools "who eat up my people as they eat bread" (v. 4). The wicked concoct "schemes" (10:2) that are unjust and "do abominable deeds" (14:2). They dismiss all threats and declare "in [their] heart . . . 'I shall not be moved; throughout all generations I shall not meet adversity'" (10:6). They believe that "God has forgotten, he has hidden his face, he will never see it" (10:11).

Further, Psalm 10:4 reports, "In the pride of his face the wicked does not seek him; all his thoughts are, 'There is no God.'" Like the fool in Psalm 14, who does not "call upon the Lord" (v. 4), the wicked "renounce the Lord" (10:3). And like the fool, the wicked man "boasts" about "the desires of his soul" and declares confidently, "There is no God" (10:10 and 14:1).

According to Psalm 10 and 14, therefore, the fool's intellectual processes are dominated by vanity and skewed by autonomy. Fools have a compass, but no magnetic north by which to guide them. Indeed, they have lost touch with reality. They are no longer able to understand properly any individual fact or experience, because they have repudiated the one cardinal truth about the existence of their Creator and Lord. In reality, fools evaluate no fact in its proper relation. They do not acknowledge that they are creatures made in God's image, subject to God's revelation, and benefiting from his grace that calls them to repentance at every moment (Dan 5:23; Rom 2:4).

CONCLUSION

This sketch of the epistemological dimension in Isaiah, Jeremiah, and Psalm 14 shows once again that the mind is critical but that it is also a battlefield. As Calvin said, "Each man's mind is like a labyrinth."[90] These texts reveal that the war occurs in every sphere of life. It is not merely personal, but also social and systemic. Folly manifests at the individual and corporate levels as ideology, group-think, worldview, and religion.

Perhaps, then, the most alarming verses in the Bible are these: "But my people did not listen to my voice; Israel would not submit to me. So I gave them over to their stubborn hearts, to follow their own counsels" (Ps 81:11–12; see also Jer 7:23–24). To be left to one's "own counsels" is the

---

90. Calvin, *Institutes*, 1:64.

end of the road epistemologically—the terminal point, humanly speaking. The broader context from Psalm 81 is enlightening:

(8) Hear, O my people, while I admonish you! O Israel, if you would but listen to me!

(9) There shall be no strange god among you; you shall not bow down to a foreign god.

(10) I am the Lord your God, who brought you up out of the land of Egypt. Open your mouth wide and I will fill it.

(11) But my people did not listen to my voice; Israel would not submit to me.

(12) So I gave them over to their stubborn hearts, to follow their own counsels.

(13) Oh, that my people would listen to me, that Israel would walk in my ways!

Verses 8 and 13 testify to the depth of Yahweh Elohim's passion that Israel would learn and his pathos that they would not. As we have seen, Isaiah poignantly expressed God's yearning for his people to understand at the beginning of his book: "Come now, let us reason together" (1:18). This aspiration appears often through verbal expressions that Israel "may know," "may see," "may consider," and "might know." If they would only hear and obey, he would gladly fulfill their every need (v. 10b). But they repeatedly turned to other gods (v. 9).

Psalm 74, arguably one of the saddest psalms in the canon, laments this reality: "O God, why do you cast us off forever? Why does your anger smoke against the sheep of your pasture?" (v. 1). Then they added, "We do not see our signs; there is no longer any prophet, and there is none among us who knows how long" (v. 9). Divine silence trumped human rebellion. Hopelessness overcame knowledge.

Yet, though there was no hope, humanly speaking, the prophet Isaiah emerged as an epistemological model, a prototype of redemptive epistemology, as well see in the next chapter. He came to know the Lord, due to the cleansing provided from God's throne. Isaiah's perception and mind were healed. He was given a "heart to understand." And the knowledge that he acquired produced obedience. As a result, Isaiah learned what Israel should do in that epoch.

8

Redemptive Epistemology

"I would like to rise very high, Lord, above my city, above the world, above time.
I would like to purify my gaze, and borrow your eyes."

—MICHEL QUOIST, *PRAYERS*

THE CLASSIC MOVIE *APOLLO* 13 chronicles the real-life story of a U.S. spacecraft confronted by a catastrophic loss of oxygen. The captain sent an important—and now famous—radio message to NASA headquarters. His tone was sedate and he seemed as if nothing serious had happened. He remarked simply, "Houston, we have a problem."

Up to this point, I have been saying—but not so calmly—something similar: "We have a problem—in fact, a very *serious* problem." The crisis deals with our mind and the ways we think due to sin. Chapters 3–7 focused on this issue.

But how do we fix the problem? Friends who read the previous chapters in draft form wondered, "How do we mitigate the noetic effects of sin? Are we simply left to despair or can we say anything constructive at all?" With a little chagrin, no doubt, another friend commented, "I look forward to reading about positive examples." Well, I have good news: with this chapter we turn a corner and focus on the positive message about thinking in the Old Testament. We examine how we *should* think and—by God's grace—how we *can* think.

This chapter starts with a summary of exilic epistemology. Second, I introduce the concept of redemptive epistemology. I revisit Isaiah 6:9–10 and discuss the epistemic importance of repentance in Isaiah. Next, I compare the exilic and redemptive mindsets in Psalm 94. I review the significance of listening and provide two examples from the Old Testament (Noah and Abraham). The impact of finitude and fallenness upon thinking is also considered. And I describe intellectual piety as expressed in the prayers of Old Testament saints.

ERRONEOUS KNOWLEDGE

Those who aspire to know God and, through him, to know everything created by God must listen carefully to his voice. He is the Archimedean point and transcendental foundation of all things.[1] He makes everything that exists possible. He is the one indispensable fact that binds all that is into a meaningful whole. He is the source, means, and goal of knowledge.

We should listen to the voice of God because we are created in his image. We resemble the transcendent philosopher as servant-thinkers. We are stewards and our minds enable us to understand his world. With our intellect, we fulfill our commission. Where we get information as vice-regents, therefore, is immensely important. To whom we listen regarding ourselves and creation is a question of life or death. We are culpable if we engage in skewed epistemology.

Dru Johnson's portrayal of erroneous knowledge can serve as a summary of Old Testament teaching regarding the noetic impact of sin.[2] He describes two dimensions of intellectual transgression: first-order error is a failure to acknowledge God's voice (revelation);[3] second-order er-

---

1. The term "transcendental" refers to the preconditions necessary for life and knowledge. A synonymous word is "presuppositional," meaning facts or states that are consciously or unconsciously presupposed in order to act, think, or speak. Biblically, transcendental reasoning appears in Deuteronomy 8:3, "Man does not live by bread alone, but man lives by every word that comes from the mouth of the Lord" (see also Gen 1:3; Ps 36:9; Acts 17:28; Rom 1:21–23, 28). Transcendental reasoning considers what mankind depends upon (and usually presumes surreptitiously), both to honor and to rebel against God (Dan 5:23; Rom 2:4). As Frame (*History of Western Philosophy and Theology*, 600) puts it, "The non-Christian cannot carry out his rebellion against God unless God makes that rebellion possible. Contradicting God assumes an intelligible universe and therefore a theistic one." See also Collet, "Van Til and Transcendental Argument Revisited," 460–88.

2. Johnson, *Biblical Knowing*, 72–74.

3. Revelation includes verbal discourse in the garden, prophetic teaching in the

ror is a failure to follow God's instructions (commandments). Johnson provides a diagram, which I have adapted here to depict the two kinds of error.[4]

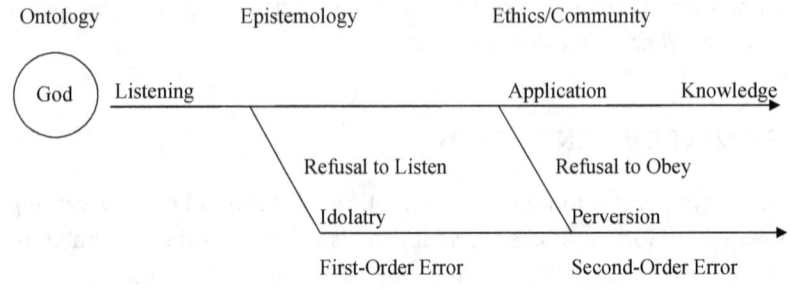

Erroneous Knowledge

First-order error comprises two aspects. One is a refusal to listen to God alone, inspired by insurrection. Israel "rebelled against the words of the Lord" and "spurned the counsel of the Most High" (Ps 107:11). God lamented, "They did not hear or pay attention to me" (Zech 1:4), and "when I called, no one answered, when I spoke, they did not listen" (Isa 66:4b). A second aspect is the substitution of other gods for Yahweh. Jeremiah declared with incredulity, "Has a nation changed its gods, even though they are no gods? But my people have changed their glory for that which does not profit" (2:11). Ezekiel depicted the exchange as taking "his idols into his heart" (14:4; see also 20:16).

Second-order error is the failure to implement God's directives. The prophets, for instance, denounced malpractice among the rulers, priests, and merchants in Israel who did not foster "righteousness, justice, and equity" (Prov 1:3b) according to Israel's covenant. The entire social fabric was saturated by systemic acquisitiveness: "From the least to the greatest, all are greedy for gain" (Jer 6:13; see also 8:10). Likewise, the judicial system was rife with scandal. Amos said, "They sell the righteous for silver, and the needy for a pair of sandals. They trample on the heads of the poor [through taxation] as upon the dust of the ground and deny justice to the oppressed" (2:6b–7a). Micah lamented the priests who "teach for a price" and prophets who "practice divination" (3:11b).

Old Testament, wisdom expressed in creation, and apostolic teaching in the New Testament.

4. Johnson, *Biblical Knowing*, 72.

Erroneous knowledge, then, is a willful failure to acknowledge God, as if he did not exist or truly matter. Erroneous knowing throws away the hermeneutical key to the door of understanding. It represents a rejection of God-given wisdom about how to live in this world. Furthermore, erroneous knowledge is "knowing that" and "knowing how" without context—that is, without "knowing why." Every aspect of reality exists for a purpose. Without this teleological and cosmological context, mankind does not truly understand reality.

A creative thought experiment illustrates first- and second-order error, as well as exilic epistemology. Consider first pre-fall Adam:

> Imagine that one day a large box appears in the garden. Adam has no evil intentions about the box. Because he is naturally curious, he investigates. Upon closer examination, he observes a cornucopia of objects in various shapes and sizes. So he removes them one by one without fear and studies each item carefully. Like a child exploring his environment, he applies each object within various contexts. He hits some against the ground. He throws a few and strikes other objects to understand better their properties. He stacks and rearranges them. He tries to categorize the items into similar and dissimilar groups. After a long period of investigation, it occurs to him that there *must* be a purpose for these articles, just as with many other items he has discovered in the garden. Finally, he says to himself, "What *are* these things and what are they *for*?" At that moment a voice from heaven speaks.

Now imagine a sinful descendent of Adam:

> For quite some time, he has been building things and disassembling others. When the box appears, he already discerns what the objects are—tools and what they are for (building). He does not care to know their true purpose, the source, or the best method of construction. On the other hand, he does realize clearly what these objects represent: power and status. After more time pondering his new acquisition—and fighting off others who wanted a share of his treasure—a grand project occurs to his mind. So he announces to his would-be collaborators, "Come, let us build ourselves a city and a tower with its top in the heavens, and let us make a name for ourselves" (Gen 11:4a).

AN UNDERSTANDING HEART

In the previous chapter, we learned several negative epistemological implications of Isaiah 6:9–10. Israel continuously refused to acknowledge the Lord, so he prevented them from acquiring true knowledge as a form of judgment under the covenant. As a consequence, they would not understand their dire predicament and thereby repent. They would not be restored and would instead suffer the severe judgment of exile.

In this chapter, however, we discover several positive inferences about knowing God that can be derived from the same passage. Let us read verses 9–10 in context, starting with verse 1:

(1) In the year that King Uzziah died I saw the Lord sitting upon a throne, high and lifted up; and the train of his robe filled the temple.

(2) Above him stood the seraphim. Each had six wings: with two he covered his face, and with two he covered his feet, and with two he flew.

(3) And one called to another and said: "Holy, holy, holy is the Lord of hosts; the whole earth is full of his glory!"

(4) And the foundations of the thresholds shook at the voice of him who called, and the house was filled with smoke.

(5) And I said: "Woe is me! For I am lost; for I am a man of unclean lips, and I dwell in the midst of a people of unclean lips; for my eyes have seen the King, the Lord of hosts!"

(6) Then one of the seraphim flew to me, having in his hand a burning coal that he had taken with tongs from the altar.

(7) And he touched my mouth and said: "Behold, this has touched your lips; your guilt is taken away, and your sin atoned for."

(8) And I heard the voice of the Lord saying, "Whom shall I send, and who will go for us?" Then I said, "Here I am! Send me."

(9) And he said, "Go, and say to this people: '"Keep on hearing, but do not understand; keep on seeing, but do not perceive.'

(10) Make the heart of this people dull, and their ears heavy, and blind their eyes; lest they see with their eyes, and hear with their ears, and understand with their hearts, and turn and be healed."

First, we learn that repentance is the key to knowledge of God east of Eden. As we saw, the Lord commissioned Isaiah to disable the linkage between perception, understanding, and change. He undermined their knowledge "lest (*pen*) they . . . understand with their hearts, and turn and be healed" (6:10b). The verb "turn" (*shub*) indicates repentance and reorientation.[5]

Three passages in Isaiah explicitly associate turning with a change of mindset. Negatively, turning the mind *away* from God is expressed in 44:18-19a (a clear echo of 6:9-10): "They know not, nor do they discern, for he has shut their eyes, so that they cannot see, and their hearts, so that they cannot understand. No one considers nor is there knowledge or discernment." The word "considers" is derived from the idiom "turns (*shub*) his heart," meaning "redirects his mind" or "stops to ponder." Israel suffered from minds that failed to understand, as well as from irreverent motives. They did not even believe that God merited their attention.[6]

The broader setting of Isaiah 44:18-19a makes this clear, for the people rejected the knowledge of God in favor of idolatry (vv. 9-20). Verses 19 and 20 say:

> No one considers, nor is there knowledge or discernment to say, "Half of it I burned in the fire; I also baked bread on its coals; I roasted meat and have eaten. And shall I make the rest of it an abomination? Shall I fall down before a block of wood?" He feeds on ashes; a deluded heart has led him astray, and he cannot deliver himself or say, "Is there not a lie in my right hand?" (See also vv. 15a and 16a)

J. Alec Motyer comments, "This is a devastating analysis of the mind of fallen humanity, covering the content of knowledge, processes of thought and capacity to discern."[7] "Deluded" (*hathal*) in this context conveys self-deception ("Is there not a lie in my right hand?") and enslavement ("cannot deliver himself"). Motyer explains, "The idolater is

---

5. "Turn" appears more than one hundred times in the Old Testament with reference to a change in mental or moral outlook. Negatively, individuals and nations turned from "following the Lord" (Num 14:43), from God (1 Sam 15:11), and "righteousness" (Ezek 3:20). Behaviorally, they did not turn from "wicked works" (Neh 9:35), "evil" (Jer 23:14), "sin" (Ezek 33:14), and "gods" (Jer 44:5). Positively, people returned to "the Lord" (Isa 19:22), to "God" (Ps 78:34), and "to me" (Zech 1:3).

6. The logic resonates with the sinful thinker who "did not see fit to acknowledge God," with the result that "God gave them up to a debased mind to do what ought not to be done" (Rom 1:28).

7. Motyer, *The Prophecy of Isaiah*, 349.

'hooked' on the idol and has lost all capacity to free himself."[8] He could not deduce his predicament correctly nor turn away from his addiction to idols, because he was absurdly vested in a self-defeating lie.

Turning away *from* God in epistemic rebellion is also evident in 47:10. God said, "You felt secure in your wickedness; you said, 'No one sees me'; your wisdom and your knowledge led you astray (*shub*), and you said in your heart, 'I am, and there is no one besides me.'" The expression "led you astray" (*shub*) indicates turning the mind over to distortion or evil. It implies an exchange of the truth for falsehood (Jer 2:11). The inanity of faux-atheism ("no one sees me") and ontological assent ("I am, and there is no one besides me") is self-evident. For this reason, Israel could not perceive the folly of idol worship. Again, the only plausible explanation was a "deluded heart" infatuated with false gods.

A positive example of turning the mind *to* God is 55:6–7. Isaiah urged Israel, "Seek the Lord while he may be found; call upon him while he is near; let the wicked forsake his way, and the unrighteous man his thoughts; let him return (*shub*) to the Lord, that he may have compassion on him, and to our God, for he will abundantly pardon." Interestingly, this verse expresses the inverse of 6:10, which offers no hope of healing or sound thinking.

Turning to God in repentance in 55:7 typifies redemptive epistemology. This is apparent in the following two verses, which contrast divine and human cognition: "For my thoughts are not your thoughts, neither are my ways your ways, declares the Lord. For as the heavens are higher than the earth, so are my ways higher than your ways and my thoughts than your thoughts" (vv. 8–9). Reverent consideration of the immensity of God's mind contrasted with the vapidity of mankind's thoughts should provoke intellectual humility and a readiness to hear God's voice.

This happened to Isaiah. Encountering God in his holiness and transcendence brought the prophet to his epistemic knees. He turned to God and was healed. When Isaiah "saw" and "heard" (vv. 1–3), he knew who was speaking and what was being said. He exclaimed, "I am a man of unclean lips, and I dwell in the midst of a people of unclean lips" (v. 5). As a result, the Lord cleansed his sin and Isaiah offered himself for service (v. 8). He received his commission as Yahweh's spokesman (vv. 9–10). God used the prophet to communicate his diagnosis and prescription for Israel's condition.

---

8. Motyer, *The Prophecy of Isaiah*, 349.

Isaiah demonstrated that the path to understanding was through repentance. Returning to God on his terms produced discernment ("heart/mind to understand") and a renewed awareness of his expectations rooted in the covenant ("send me," v. 8). Geoffrey D. Robinson summarizes both the epistemology and Isaiah's atonement as initiated by the Lord:

> Isaiah "saw the Lord" (v. 1), heard the voice of the Seraphim (v. 3), heard the voice of him who called out (v. 4), saw the King with his own eyes (v. 5b), and heard the voice of the Lord (v. 8a). The purification process of v. 7, which entails cleansed lips and results in forgiven sin, is paradigmatic of the needs of the people, as well as functioning as a necessary prelude to Isaiah's speaking on behalf of Yahweh.

Isaiah modeled redemptive epistemology. He became a refugee from intellectual exile, an archetypal God-knower east of Eden.[9] He listened to God's voice. He evidenced godly fear. He was contrite, confessed his sin, and embraced divine cleansing as a means for prophetic enablement.[10] His understanding was healed by atonement. He received a renewed mind that understood and obeyed. Because he turned to God and away from sin, Isaiah came to know the Lord. But he also discovered what Israel must do in that epoch.

Second, Isaiah 6:9–10 implies various aspects about knowing God. For knowledge to occur, these elements must be operative:

---

9. Isaiah's ministry also reached repentant knowers: "We hope for light, and behold, darkness, and for brightness, but we walk in gloom. We grope for the wall like the blind; we grope like those who have no eyes . . . . For our transgressions are multiplied before you, and our sins testify against us; for our transgressions are with us, and we know our iniquities: transgressing, and denying the Lord, and turning back from following our God, speaking oppression and revolt, conceiving and uttering from the heart lying words" (59:9b–10, 12–13).

10. Jeremiah's "mouth" was also cleansed as part of his call (Jer 1:9). Perhaps similarly, Ezekiel was given a scroll to "eat" with God's message of judgment (3:1–3).

Divine disposition	God's willingness to communicate
Revelation	theophany, creation, personal inspiration, oral or written
Organs of sight and hearing	ability to receive sensory input
Cognitive apparatus	ability to categorize, analyze, and interpret information
Obligation	awareness of intellectual and ethical duty
Human disposition	readiness to hear and obey

The passage presupposes an epistemological process that operated before the advent of sin: input (revelation) was received though sensory perception that the mind evaluated correctly (though subject to finitude). Eyes saw what God did and ears heard what he said, and then the mind interpreted the information according to biblical criteria. This process yielded a deeper understanding of reality and zeal to serve as stewards according to the covenant of creation.

Third, the four epistemological orientations depicted in this book emerge from the passage explicitly and implicitly: edenic, exilic, punitive, and redemptive. Each outlook involves revelation, sensory processing, interpretation, obligation, and disposition (God and human). The four orientations are displayed below, followed by a short summary of each one.

Orientation	Source	Disposition	Result	Example
Edenic	revelation	submission (fear of the Lord)	knowledge	pre-fall Adam
Exilic	revelation	rebellion (autonomy)	illusion & confusion	post-fall Adam
Punitive	revelation	rebellion (autonomy)	illusion & confusion	Israel
Redemptive	revelation	repentance (fear of the Lord)	knowledge	Isaiah

Edenic Epistemology

Edenic epistemology (chapter 2) explained that knowing depended on God's voluntary disclosure. Adam and Eve were endowed with a need to know. God instilled curiosity and the capacity to learn. They possessed a covenantal disposition to hear and heed ("fear of the Lord" or "heart to understand"). They did not autonomously categorize or evaluate, ponder or plan anything apart from their vice-regency under God. Their goal was to become wise governors, builders, benefactors, and thinkers in keeping with God's image and vice-regency. Their mental disposition demonstrated a readiness to learn from the transcendent pedagogue. They were limited only by finitude. Isaiah 6:9–10 implies that Adam and Eve's cognitive apparatus functioned as designed.

Exilic Epistemology

Exilic epistemology (chapters 3–7) showed how noetic depravity greatly complicated the acquisition of knowledge about God, as well as mankind's perception of vice-regency. The dynamic between revelation, moral disposition, and mental process was skewed. The making of culture was forever corrupted. Instead of a submissive orientation to God and his instruction, Adam and Eve set their own course under the serpent's guidance. Since that time, humans have autonomously evaluated their world and sinfully schemed. They are hemmed in by both finitude and fallenness.

Punitive Epistemology

Punitive epistemology (chapter 7) refers to divinely induced penal blindness. In Isaiah 6:9–10, Yahweh "gave [Israel] over" to its own twisted thinking, due to prolonged obduracy (Ps 81:11–12; see also Deut 28:28–29). He undermined their ability to process revelation. Since they *would* not listen and obey, they no longer *could* listen and obey and thereby avoid judgment. Isaiah was commissioned to announce this intellectual collapse, predicted in Deuteronomy, through his ministry.

Redemptive Epistemology

Isaiah was an archetypical God-knower "under the sun." He was a real-world thinker confronting corruption, idolatry, delusion, and distortion. He showed that knowing God *is* possible despite noetic depravity. He experienced intellectual reorientation to a transcendent reference point and turned from homocentric reasoning.

PSALM 94

This psalm depicts the two intellectual trajectories (exilic and redemptive) side by side as they interact with one another:

revelation ⇨ rebellion ⇨ misunderstanding ⇨ folly and chaos

revelation ⇨ repentance ⇨ understanding ⇨ calling and service

In the psalm, the words referring to the wicked (representing exilic epistemology) are in italics. Afterwards, I profile each thinker and summarize the argument put forward by the righteous in verses 7–11. Here are verses 1–12 and 18–23:

(1) O Lord, God of vengeance, O God of vengeance, shine forth!

(2) Rise up, O judge of the earth; repay to *the proud* what they deserve!

(3) O Lord, how long shall *the wicked*, how long shall *the wicked* exult?

(4) *They* pour out their arrogant words; all *the evildoers* boast.

(5) *They* crush your people, O Lord, and afflict your heritage.

(6) *They* kill the widow and the sojourner, and murder the fatherless;

(7) and *they* say, "The Lord does not see; the God of Jacob does not perceive."

(8) Understand, O *dullest of the people!* *Fools*, when will *you* be wise?

(9) He who planted the ear, does he not hear? He who formed the eye, does he not see?

(10) He who disciplines the nations, does he not rebuke? He who teaches man knowledge—

(11) the Lord—knows the thoughts of *man*, that they are but a breath.

(12) Blessed is the man whom you discipline, O Lord, and whom you teach out of your law . . . .

(18) When I thought, "My foot slips," your steadfast love, O Lord, held me up.

(19) When the cares of my heart are many, your consolations cheer my soul.

(20) Can *wicked rulers* be allied with you, *those* who frame injustice by statute?

(21) *They* band together against the life of the righteous and condemn the innocent to death.

(22) But the Lord has become my stronghold, and my God the rock of my refuge.

(23) He will bring back on *them* their iniquity and wipe *them* out for their wickedness; the Lord our God will wipe *them* out.

The God of Israel is identified as the "Lord," "God of vengeance," "judge of the earth," and a "stronghold" and "refuge." He embodies justice. He rewards and punishes. He is powerful, capable of retribution and ruin. He is the Creator who made the organs of human perception. Transcendent and self-referential, he knows mankind's every thought. He listens to human argumentation and lament. He is the source of understanding and teaches mankind knowledge.[11] He evaluates human conduct and thinking. Furthermore, God is immanent, ever ready to protect and console with covenantal faithfulness (*chesed* or "steadfast love," v. 18). By definition and experience, therefore, this God is in a class by himself. In the words of David, "How great you are, Sovereign Lord! There is no one *like* you, and there is no God *but* you, as we have heard with our own ears" (2 Sam 7:22, NIV).

The righteous are designated as "your people" and "your heritage" and are specified further as members of the neediest class under covenantal law: "widow," "sojourner," "fatherless," and "innocent." The righteous include those whom God disciplines and teaches his "law" (*torah*, v. 10). They consider God's pedagogy a supreme blessing. They engage the wicked polemically to make them "wise" (or provide "understanding," *sakal*, v. 8). They are also self-critical, bringing their inner thoughts before the Lord for evaluation (v. 18). They know God in his transcendence

---

11. Spero explains that "knowledge" (*daat*, v. 10) "includes all mental experience such as consciousness, self-awareness and intentionality (will)." He adds, "To say that God has *knowledge* or that God *knows* is to say that God has, at least, all the aforementioned faculties to an infinite degree." See Spero, "He That Formed the Eye," 53 and 55, note 4 (emphasis in original).

as Creator, teacher, judge, and Lord Almighty, but also in his immanence as savior and sustainer (vv. 18, 22–23).

In contrast, the wicked are described as "the proud," "evildoers," "dullest of the people," and "fools." As a class of mankind ("man," *adam*, v. 10), they often act in concert for nefarious ends ("iniquity," v. 23). For instance, "wicked rulers" institutionalize "injustice by statute" and "band together" to harm God's people and hinder his purpose (vv. 20–21). They "exalt" in doing evil, speak far too much, and boast insolently. They are inherently violent, unjust, and oppressive. Intellectually, their epistemic bias taints everything they conceptualize. They are self-referential, and folly typifies their thinking. They project a false image of the Lord—as if he were incompetent and unmindful—and in this way proclaim impunity. They embrace the skewed pseudo-atheism of all incorrigible fools and their father Adam, as we learned from Psalm 14.

The argumentation of the righteous and wicked display several thematic parallels. First, two mindsets are contrasted: wisdom (represented by "the righteous") and folly (represented by the "wicked"/"fool"). Second, two self-revelations are stated: the wicked express their twisted view of God ("The Lord does not see") and the righteous confess vulnerability ("My foot slips").[12] Third, two kinds of "discipline" (*yasar*) appear: punitive for "fools," "nations," and "wicked rulers" versus instruction and formation for the righteous. Fourth, two questions trouble the righteous: "O Lord . . . how long shall the wicked exult?" and "Can wicked rulers be allied with you?" The rhetorical question "When will you be wise?" highlights the hapless mentality of the wicked as the "dullest of all people" whose best thoughts are vaporous ("breath," *hebel*). Implicitly, "wicked rulers" (presumably apostate Israelite royalty) exist in contrast with virtuous kings who foster "righteousness, justice, and equity" (Prov 1:3b), as modeled by David, Solomon, Hezekiah, and Josiah.

The righteous pose two arguments to counter and convince the fool. Verse 9 proceeds from the simple to the complex, an argument from design and a form of *modus ponens* ("if *p*, then *q*"). The righteous posit, "He who planted the ear, does he not hear? He who formed the eye, does he not see?" If the Creator installed organs for sensory perception in humans, it follows that he also perceives sensory data. Since sensory perception is a necessary prerequisite of knowledge and since God enabled this capacity in mankind, then he also has intellectual capacity. Moreover,

---

12. As we learned in chapter 6, the idiom of slipping indicates falling into sin or cynicism (2 Sam 22:37; Job 12:5; Pss 17:5; 66:9; 73:2).

since the image of God perceives and thinks, how much greater are God's cognitive abilities![13] John M. Frame explains the analogy: "Human beings hear with their physical ears and see with their physical eyes. God, however, is master of the processes of hearing and seeing. He does without physical organs what we do with them, and far more."[14]

Similarly, verses 10–11 say, "He who disciplines the nations, does he not rebuke? He who teaches man knowledge—the Lord—knows the thoughts of man, that they are but a breath." The word "discipline" (*yasar*) is translated elsewhere as "warn," "correct," "teach," and "chastise," depending on the context. The settings all assume a relationship between a superior (Lord, father, teacher) and an inferior (son, servant, disciple, vassal), and they utilize coercion for pedagogical purposes. Meanings range from encouragement to punishment.[15] "Rebuke" (*yakach*) is rendered in other settings as "vindicate," "decide," "reprove," "arbitrate," "argue" (one's case), "refute," "reason" (together), and "contend" (in a covenant lawsuit). In all cases, *yakach* functions in dispute-oriented settings (Job, Isaiah, Amos, and Micah). Thus, on one hand, the rebuke in verse 10 appears pedagogical.[16] On the other hand, the rebuke can also indicate chastisement or punishment.[17] In Psalm 94, the immediate context (vv. 7–11) argues for an intellectual–pedagogical nuance, whereas in the broader setting the term assumes a vindictive or punitive significance (v. 23).

Furthermore, several assumptions undergird the argumentation of verses 10–11. First, both parties (righteous and wicked) have a conception of God, as either a God who disciplines and teaches or one who

13. Spero ("He That Formed the Eye," 52–53) explains two further implications of the argument. About the ear he says, "Once we understand the function of the ear to catch the sound waves coming from different directions, we can appreciate the wisdom of He [sic] who planted them in their requisite positions." And regarding the eye he comments, "The individual must open them, turn his head so that he faces the objects and then select from his field of vision the particular items he finds of interest ... carrying out a directed purposeful project, implying intelligence."

14. Frame, *Systematic Theology*, 788.

15. Leviticus 26:18–20 is an example of extreme correction: "And if in spite of this [prior chastisement] you will not listen to me, then I will discipline you again sevenfold for your sins, and I will break the pride of your power, and I will make your heavens like iron and your earth like bronze. And your strength shall be spent in vain, for your land shall not yield its increase, and the trees of the land shall not yield their fruit."

16. Proverbs 3:12 expresses a similar idea: "The Lord reproves him whom he loves, as a father the son in whom he delights."

17. An example is found in Psalm 38:1: "O Lord, rebuke me not in your anger, nor discipline me in your wrath!"

is remote and oblivious. Second, both parties (righteous and wicked) possess moral–theological precepts. For the righteous, this is explicit: arrogance, murder, violence, oppression, and iniquity are proscribed by the law. For the wicked, the precepts are implicit. Their affirmation, "The Lord does not see; the God of Jacob does not perceive," presupposes what it willfully ignores: God indeed exists but is irrelevant and functionally amoral. The fool's convenient atheism presupposes an implicit theism. Thus, the wicked knew that God exists and that their deeds were evil but argued that Yahweh took no account.

Third, the wise person assumes that God thinks and communicates with human beings. Humans are obligated to pay attention and learn. They possess the mental capacity to receive and apply God's instruction. They benefit from his teaching. Fourth, God operates from a superior position ontologically and intellectually. He evaluates nations and individuals according to norms that he established. Fifth, the context presumes that the "knowledge" (v. 10b) God taught to both the righteous and wicked was the covenant.[18] The righteous listen and obey. They count it a blessing to be instructed "out of the law," whereas the wicked hear but do not obey.

Given these assumptions, the second argument in verse 10a is also an "if p, then q" declaration: If Yahweh disciplines the nations (Gentiles), how much more his own people! The statement that follows in verse 11 ("The Lord knows the thoughts of man, that they are but a breath") appears as an aside, an expression of the obvious in light of the parallelism left unstated:

---

18. Establishing the setting is difficult, for the psalm is anonymous and the title, any explicit time, and place are missing. There are hints, however, that support a pre-exilic context during a period of syncretism and corruption. The psalm is located among other non-titled psalms on the kingship of Yahweh (92–95). The vocabulary includes covenantal terms (instruction, law, statute, loving kindness) and wisdom terms (fool, wise, knowledge). The wicked refer to the Lord as the "God of Jacob," an expression that appears only in the mouths of Yahweh, devout Israelites, or Gentile converts. Also, the question in verse 20 ("Can wicked rulers be allied with you?") makes sense with reference to Israelite kings. Foreign despots are by definition not aligned with the Lord. The other option, which is not explicit, assumes that the "knowledge" God taught is general revelation or natural law based on creation and the covenant with Noah. Spero ("He That Formed the Eye," 53) appears to argue on the basis of the Noahide laws: "In his premise, the Psalmist refers to the basic Biblical doctrine that God has made known to mankind ('nations') the principles of morality and the behavior expected of human beings. He has done this by means of the intuitive moral sense implanted in man as well as by the repeated messages of the Hebrew prophets."

> He who disciplines the nations, does he not rebuke?
>
> He who teaches man [Gentiles] knowledge, [does he not also teach Israel?]

The message of verses 10–11, therefore, appears to be as follows: "Do not feign ignorance, fools. You really know better. You have received the law of God. You know his moral demands. You know what he is like. Thus, it is obvious that God knows your wickedness. He will hold you accountable and he will avenge." Similarly, the passage indicates that redemptive epistemology is not passive but solicits divine assessment of faulty reasoning. Loving God with the mind entails continuous cleansing and growth in knowledge, and it presumes habitual and lifelong repentance. Psalm 94 also demonstrates that redemptive epistemology also engages unbelief in others, as well as systemic folly and corruption.

LISTENING

Redemptive epistemology presumes repentance so that we will listen to God's voice in Scripture and creation. His words provide the only legitimate guidance by which to interpret and engage reality. Listening is also another way to express the fear of the Lord and a mind that understands. We saw that Isaiah listened to God, and so did the righteous in Psalm 94.

The Old Testament shows that God communicates with human beings. A vast amount of information passes from the Lord to mankind. In fact, the imperatives "listen" and "hear" appear over seventy times in the Old Testament. The first- or third-person divine speaker expressed as "I," "Lord," or "God" is paired with many verbs of discourse, such as "say" (approximately 427 times), "speak" (214), "command" (194), "show" (eighteen), "answer" (seventeen), "declare" (fifteen), "tell" (fourteen), "reveal" (four), "write" (four), and "instruct" (twice). Despite the ravages of noetic depravity introduced by Adam and Eve, God *still* speaks.

As we read in the last chapter, the verbs "listen (to)," "hear," and "obey" are translated from the term *shama* and are often used with a direct object, in particular the noun "voice" (*qol*). A frequent expression is "listen to the voice of the Lord your God." This idiom refers to God's words spoken verbally, in writing, or through creation with covenantal authority to his human subjects—God's appointed vassal rulers, builders, benefactors, and thinkers.[19] The many injunctions and commands coupled with *shama* indicate what correct listening entails: a proper attitude or motivation, correct actions to perform, and incorrect actions to avoid.

Those who listen to God "tremble at his word" (Isa 66:5), "pay careful attention" (Exod 23:21), and "fear the Lord" (Deut 10:12). They are attentive and ready to listen: "Speak, Lord, for your servant hears" (1 Sam 3:9). They are also disposed to "seek the Lord" (Deut 4:29), "pursue righteousness" (Isa 51:1), and "trust in the name of the Lord" (Isa 50:10). Listeners enact what they hear. They are "careful to do" (Josh 1:8) all that the Lord and his representatives prescribe. They are thoroughly obedient and "do all his commandments" (Deut 28:1) with "all [their] heart and all [their] soul" (30:10). They fulfill God's "charge" to "do that which is right in his eyes, give ear to his commandments and keep all his statutes" (Exod 15:26), and "keep [his] covenant and [his] testimonies" (Ps 132:12). Listeners also avoid certain actions. They never "depart" from or "neglect" God's speech. Above all, listeners never become presumptuous: "[When] all that you have is multiplied, then your heart be lifted up, and you forget the Lord your God, who brought you out of the land of Egypt, out of the house of slavery" (Deut 8:11–16).

In the Old Testament, the list of those who heard and heeded verbal revelation is long. Let us consider two prominent examples from the Bible's "hall of fame."

Noah

After Cain murdered his brother Abel, Adam and Eve produced another son through whom God advanced his redemptive purpose (Gen 4:25–26). Seth and his son Enosh "began to call upon the name of the Lord" (v. 26). Cain and his progeny presumably did not. Later on, a devout descendant of Seth, Enoch, also called upon the Lord, for he "walked with God" (Gen 5:22–24). In fact, he did not die a natural death "for God took him" (v. 24b).

In the following generations, the human race became increasingly degenerate. Intermarriage occurred between the lines of Cain and Seth

---

19. In addition to *shama*, two other verbs appear. *Qashab* is rendered as "listen" and "pay attention to," especially in Proverbs, Isaiah, and Jeremiah (for instance, Prov 2:2; Isa 10:30; Jer 8:6). *Azan* is translated idiomatically as "give ear to" (Exod 15:26; Isa 1:10; 32:9; 42:23; 51:4). Isaiah 28:23 uses each term: "Give ear (*azan*), and hear (*shama*) my voice (*qol*); give attention (*qashab*), and hear (*shama*) my speech."

(6:1–2, 4), and God limited the human lifespan (v. 3).[20] The divine assessment of the human condition was quite bleak. God expressed his diagnosis of Noah's "generation," as well as his rationale for the flood, in 6:9. To understand the message in context, following is the text of Genesis 6:5–7 and 11–13, with key terms and phrases italicized:

(5) The Lord saw that the *wickedness* of man was *great* in the earth, and that *every intention of the thoughts of his heart* was *only evil continually*.

(6) And the Lord regretted that he had made man on the earth, and it grieved him to his heart.

(7) So the Lord said, "I will blot out man whom I have created from the face of the land, man and animals and creeping things and birds of the heavens, for I am sorry that I have made them."

(11) Now *the earth* was *corrupt in God's sight*, and the earth was *filled with violence*.

(12) And God saw the earth, and behold, it was *corrupt*, for *all flesh* had *corrupted their way* on the earth.

(13) And God said to Noah, "I have determined to make an end of all flesh, for the earth is *filled with violence* through them."

The degradation of creation came about "through" human agency ("all flesh"). "Wickedness" and "evil" (v. 5) derive from a generic term for sin (*ra*), referring to wrongdoing in deed and thought. "Corrupt" (*shachath*, vv. 11–12) is usually translated as "destroy" but also as "devour," "lay waste," "ruin," and "spoil," as well as "act corruptly." The immediate context indicates that mental and moral corruption was inherently destructive of both mankind and his environment. Sinful human beings ruined all that God had established.

The phrase "corrupted their way" shows that the lifestyle, mindset, and social structure of that period were wholly committed to unrighteousness.[21] Likewise, "violence" (*hamas*) indicates endemic ("filled with") cruelty in all sectors of society. Geerhardus Vos summarized the depravity of the time in four dimensions. The "intensity of evil" was deep and broad ("great in the earth"). Corruption was subjectively motivated

---

20. See Vos, *Biblical Theology*, 46–51.

21. "Way" (*derek*) refers to a self-chosen path of righteousness or wickedness, wisdom or folly. See the discussion of this theme in chapter 6, on Proverbs.

("every intention of the thought of his heart"). Evil was pervasive, "excluding everything good" ("only evil"). And iniquity was "habitual, a continuous working of evil" ("continuously").[22] Indeed, the "generation" of Noah was hopelessly and irremediably iniquitous and disordered.

Intellectually, the state of humanity was equally grave: "*every* intention of the thoughts of his heart was *only* evil *continually*." There were no exceptions, for all human cognition at all times contemplated iniquity—except Noah. The word "intention" (*yetser*) occurs in the Old Testament only nine times.[23] In this context, *yetser* implies motivation: the purposes to which we apply our mind. But it also signifies imagination and creativity. Frame writes, "Imagination has much to do with any attempt to do things in a new or different way."[24] He adds:

> Imagination refers to our ability to think about things that are not. We can think about the past, though the past is by definition no longer present. We can think of possible or probable futures, though the future cannot be perceived. Or we can imagine mere alternate states of affairs, whether or not they existed or could exist in the present or future. Thus our imaginations allow us to think of fantasy, of conditionals that are contrary to fact, of "what-if" scenarios.[25]

Noah's generation imagined new and different "what-if" opportunities to express their degeneracy, moral and mental. They conceived a present and future apart from God and the norms he established. They envisioned reality as if the Lord were irrelevant. As we know, however, that was about to change because of the flood (Genesis 6–9). They would soon discover just how twisted their machinations and lifestyle were in God's sight.

The word "thoughts" (*machashabah*) is sometimes translated in a positive sense as "skill" (Exod 31:4; 35:32, 33, 35). But the vast majority of cases are negative—for instance, "evil plan" (Esth 8:3), "devices of the crafty" (Job 5:12), "devises wicked plans" (Prov 6:18), "thoughts of iniquity" (Isa 59:7), and "plots" (Jer 18:18). Ryan O'Dowd explains

---

22. Vos, *Biblical Theology*, 51.

23. Six of these instances deal with mental functioning: three are negative assessments of the mind (Gen 6:5; 8:21; Deut 31:21), two refer to God's testing of our thoughts (1 Chr 28:9; 29:18), and one provides a positive injunction for thinking correctly (Isa 26:3).

24. Frame, *The Doctrine of the Knowledge of God*, 340.

25. Frame, *The Doctrine of the Knowledge of God*, 340.

how the people of Noah's generation had skewed forethought: "It is the imagination, the epistemological freedom to act as co-Creator that has become evil."[26] The men and women of Noah's time applied their minds in creative ways, but exactly opposite to what the Creator intended. Their strategic thinking and contingency analysis focused on new expressions and applications of epistemic deconstruction.

As for Noah, the two uses of the conjunction "but" (*we*, vv. 8 and 18) indicate a stark contrast. He alone of his "generation" escaped God's scathing indictment, in verse 5, of wholesale wicked conduct and evil thinking.[27] These statements attest to Noah's character (the main ideas are in italics):

6:8	But Noah found *favor* in the eyes of the Lord.
6:9	Noah was a *righteous* man, *blameless* in his generation. Noah *walked with God*.
6:17–18	For behold, I will bring a flood of waters upon the earth to destroy all flesh . . . . But I will establish my covenant with you, and you shall come into the ark, you, your sons, your wife, and your sons' wives with you.
6:22	Noah did this; he *did all that God commanded* him.
7:5	Noah *did all that the Lord had commanded* him.
8:20	Then Noah *built an altar* to the Lord

"Favor" indicates a positive assessment by a superior, expressed through the idioms of "in the eyes of" and "in the sight of." "Favor in the eyes of the Lord" signifies behavior that merits his approval. Proverbs 5:21 states, "A man's ways are before the eyes of the Lord, and he ponders all his paths." Israel's kings were evaluated positively or negatively with the expression that they "did (or did not do) what was right in the eyes of the Lord."[28] The term "righteous" (*saddıq*) means that Noah's conduct conformed to God's norms. In fact, Noah's social relationships, mental piety, and ethical behavior were "blameless" (*tamim*).[29] In all these ways, Noah "walked with God," like Enoch before him.[30] His lifestyle ("way")

---

26. O'Dowd, *The Wisdom of Torah*, 15.

27. He was not flawless, however (see 9:20–28).

28. See 1 Kgs 15:5; 2 Kgs 12:2; 16:2; 22:2; 2 Chr 14:2; 26:4; 28:1; 34:2.

29. For instance, acceptable sacrificial offerings were "blameless," without physical defect (Exod 12:5). The Israelites were "blameless" with respect to their neighbors when they eschewed the occult arts (Deut 18:10–14).

30. Later on, the Lord told Abram, "Walk before me, and be blameless [*tamim*]"

garnered God's benediction. He listened to God and obeyed his instructions (6:22; 7:5, 16; 8:18). He worshiped the Lord (8:20).

During this tumultuous time, Noah emerged as a paradigmatic God-knower. He allowed God's words to define reality and he behaved accordingly. He aligned his mental and ethical conduct with God's law. He listened to God, rather than to "his generation." And because he reverenced God, the human race continued (6:6–7).

Moreover, Noah functioned as a second Adam.[31] He was the primogenitor of a righteous remnant on the earth. He was the redemptive-historical bridge to Abram and the future people of Israel. In the New Testament he is designated as a "herald of righteousness" (2 Pet 2:5).[32] Noah heard God speak and therefore knew what he must do.

Abraham

Abraham, the father of the Hebrew nation, was one of the few characters in the Bible who garnered God's approbation by listening and obeying throughout his lifetime.[33] Yahweh testified about him, "Abraham obeyed my voice and kept my charge, my commandments, my statutes, and my laws" (Gen 26:5; see also 22:18). God designated him a "prophet" (20:7) and forever associated his name, Yahweh, with Abraham's namesake (Exod 3:6). Other writers identified him as a "friend of God" (Isa 41:8; 2 Chr 20:7; Jas 2:23). He was a "servant" with whom God's "holy promise" was inextricably linked (Ps 105:42). Even non-Hebrews extolled his virtue and his evident divine blessing (Gen 14:20; 21:22; 23:5).

God declared about Abraham, "I have chosen him, that he may command his children and his household after him to keep the way of the Lord by doing righteousness and justice" (Gen 18:19). He entrusted Abraham with passing on God's promise to his progeny, along with modeling virtue as a founding patriarch. Yoram Hazony provides a five-point analysis of Abraham's character and lifestyle:

(1) He was generous to all (13:9–11; 18:1–8).

(Gen 17:1b). A similar expression is "walk after the Lord" (Deut 13:4; 2 Chr 34:31).

31. The commission of Noah (9:1–3, 7) closely resembles that of Adam.

32. See Hafemann, "Noah, the Preacher of (God's) Righteousness," 306–20.

33. Of course, Abraham was not without fault; he made errors of judgment and at several junctures comprised his integrity (Gen 12:11–13; 16:1–6; 17:17–18; 20:2).

(2) He was offended by injustice and risked his life to defend the vulnerable (14:11–17; 18:23–25; 21:11).

(3) He was not greedy and paid for all that he acquired (14:21–24; 21:25–30; 23:6–20).

(4) He was pious (12:7, 8; 13:4, 18; 17:23; 21:33).

(5) He protected his family and their calling (21:22).[34]

Indeed, Abraham's ethics and piety were renowned. He "built altars" (12:7; 13:18), exercised faith (12:1, 9; 20:17; 22:8, 14), and demonstrated deep reverence for God (17:3; 18:22; 19:27). He obeyed all God's commands. As a result, when the Lord instructed Isaac, he did so according to the promise made to his father:

> I will be with you and will bless you, for to you and to your offspring I will give all these lands, and I will establish the oath that I swore to Abraham your father .... And in your offspring all the nations of the earth shall be blessed, because Abraham obeyed my voice and kept my charge, my commandments, my statutes, and my laws. (Gen 26:3–5)

Obeying God's voice involved great sacrifice and vision on Abraham's part. He left behind a vaunted center of urban culture, Ur in Babylonia, where his family "served other gods" (Josh 24:2). He turned away from idolatry and its social, political, and economic benefits. He rejected Babylonia's skewed version of Adam's cultural mandate, inspired by the serpent.[35] He separated himself from the Babelite civilization of his day so that God could make himself known by creating a "nation for himself" (Deut 4:34).

Looking forward, Abraham was the principal agent though whom God's global, redemptive plan was initiated. Through his progeny, Eve's "offspring" (Gen 3:15) multiplied throughout the earth, eventually generating the Messiah, Jesus Christ. This is why Paul wrote that those who believe the gospel "share the faith of Abraham, who is the father of us all" (Rom 4:16). Likewise, for this reason James said that Abraham's piety was

---

34. Hazony, *The Philosophy of Hebrew Scripture*, 112.

35. Kline (*Kingdom Prologue*, 180) pointed out the ironic contrast between Babel (Genesis 11) and Abraham (Genesis 12): "What was sought in Shinar by autonomous human effort—the restoration of cosmic-cultic focus and the great name—was bestowed on Abraham as a promissory grant. Babel was man-built, from the accursed ground up towards heaven. The city promised to Abraham is God-built and descends from the holy heaven to man as the supernatural gift of God's grace."

paradigmatic, for he was "justified by works and not by faith alone" (2:24). And the author of Hebrews depicted him as a hero and pilgrim, "for he was looking forward to the city that has foundations, whose designer and builder is God" (Heb 11:10). All this occurred because Abraham listened to God's voice and obeyed. He too was a paradigmatic refugee from exilic epistemology. He honored God with his mental capacity.

In all these ways, Abraham was another Adam-like figure, hearing and heeding God's voice. But unlike Adam, he continued to listen and think as an obedient vice-regent. His life evidenced an Eden-like nexus (peace, presence, prosperity), but "east of Eden." He received the promise of future blessing and fruitfulness for his heirs. At the end of his life, it was clear that "the Lord had blessed Abraham in all things" (Gen 24:1).

TWO LIMITATIONS

Redemptive epistemology affirms two essential truths about human knowing: finitude and fallenness (Ps 90:1–11). On one hand, renewed thinkers recognize their intellectual fragility and acknowledge their sinful bias. On the other hand, they affirm two critical facts about God's knowledge: his supremacy and omniscience. Calvin expressed the interplay of the divine and human in this way: "It is certain that man never achieves a clear knowledge of himself unless he has first looked upon God's face, and then descends from contemplating him to scrutinize himself."[36]

Similarly, Frame calls human knowing "servant knowledge," or "a knowledge *about* God as Lord and a knowledge that is *subject to* God as Lord."[37] Human beings must not categorize anything except in accord with God's norms. They should not view reality through a sacred–secular lens. They should not assume neutrality or objectivity in a manner that affirms intellectual autonomy. Their thought life is subject to the Lord in every way.

The transcendent philosopher knows everything that can be known, including everything about mankind. He knows the past, present, and future, including every aspect of our personal history. He knows all contingencies and works every development according to his eternal plan. The Lord's "understanding is unsearchable" (Isa 40:28b) and "beyond measure" (Ps 147:5), and his "thoughts are very deep" (92:5). He

---

36. Calvin, *Institutes*, 1:37.
37. Frame, *The Doctrine of the Knowledge of God*, 40 (emphasis in original).

"established the world by his wisdom" (Jer 51:15; see also Isa 24:29). In fact, by God's "understanding the hawk soars" (Job 39:26). Indeed, God imparts knowledge to mankind. He gave Solomon insight to "do justice" (1 Kgs 3:27–28) and "understanding beyond measure" (1 Kgs 4:29). By God-given wisdom Ezra appointed "magistrates and judges" (Ezra 7:25). Bezalel was empowered "with skill, with intelligence, with knowledge, and with all craftsmanship" (Exod 35:31). God endowed Joshua with "wisdom" for combat and leadership so that "Israel obeyed him and did as the Lord commanded Moses" (Deut 34:9). Similarly, Daniel possessed "learning and skill in all literature and wisdom," provided by God (Dan 1:17). Even the farmer "who plows for sowing" is "rightly instructed" because "his God teaches him" (Isa 28:26).

Moreover, since God is omniscient, he knows all our thoughts as well (conscious and unconscious). As we read earlier, Psalm 94:11 proclaims, "The Lord knows the thoughts of man." Similarly, Psalm 139:2b says, "You discern my thoughts from afar." God declares, "For I know the things that come into your mind" (Ezek 11:5). Amos 4:13a extols God, "who forms the mountains and creates the wind, and declares to man what is his thought." Additionally, God's knowledge extends to private ruminations and motives: "Sheol and Abaddon lie open before the Lord; how much more the hearts of the children of man!" (Prov 15:11). David wrote, "The Lord searches all hearts and understands every plan and thought" (1 Chr 28:9).

However, God does not simply observe passively but scrutinizes our intellectual activity—in real time, 24/7. Several terms are used to express this activity: "test," "try," "prove," "search," "search out," and "examine."[38] The Lord declares, "I the LORD search the heart and test the mind" (Jer 17:10). Others testify similarly about him: "The crucible is for silver, and the furnace is for gold, and the Lord tests hearts" (Prov 17:3); "Every way of a man is right in his own eyes, but the Lord weighs the heart" (Prov 21:2; see also 24:12). Jeremiah wrote, "O Lord of hosts, who tests the righteous, who sees the heart and the mind" (20:12). This is why David told Solomon, "And you, Solomon my son, know the God of your father and serve him with a whole heart and with a willing mind, for the

---

38. The overlapping Hebrew words are *bachan* (test, try, prove), *nasah* (test, try), *darash* (search), *tsaraph* (test, try), *zarah* (search out), and *chaqar* (search, examine). Psalm 26:2 utilizes three of them: "Prove [*bachan*] me, O Lord, and try [*nasah*] me; test [*tsaraph*] my heart and my mind."

Lord searches all hearts and understands every plan and thought" (2 Chr 32:31; see also Jer 11:20; 12:3; 1 Chr 29:17).

Yahweh's motives for testing are often pedagogical and purifying. Moses told Israel, for instance, "Do not fear, for God has come to test you, that the fear of him may be before you" and "that you may not sin" (Exod 20:20). Similarly, David acknowledged God's testing and indicated a rationale for it: "You have tried my heart, you have visited me by night, you have tested me, and you will find nothing; I have purposed that my mouth will not transgress" (Ps 17:3; see also 139:1). Likewise, the writer of Lamentations linked self-examination and repentance: "Let us test and examine our ways, and return to the Lord!" (3:40).

Lastly, the Old Testament associates testing with our intellectual fragility and epistemic bias. Mental piety (or intellectual spirituality) appears in heartfelt petitions that *invite* divine testing. These are prayers for epistemological self-awareness or spiritual growth, and they presume habitual repentance. David implored the Lord, "Prove me, O Lord, and try me; test my heart and my mind" (Ps 26:2). Psalm 139:23 states, "Search me, O God, and know my heart! Try me and know my thoughts!" Psalm 19:14 declares, "Let the words of my mouth and the meditation of my heart be acceptable in your sight." Perhaps the most poignant expression of intellectual piety is Psalm 131:1–2:

> O Lord, my heart is not lifted up; my eyes are not raised too high; I do not occupy myself with things too great and too marvelous for me. But I have calmed and quieted my soul, like a weaned child with its mother; like a weaned child is my soul within me.

CONCLUSION

In this chapter, we have considered the possibility of knowing God despite the ravaging effects of sin upon our thinking. Isaiah 6, Psalm 94, and the examples of Noah and Abraham reveal that repentance is the necessary precondition for redemptive epistemology. As we will see in the next chapter, Yahweh Elohim demands absolute and universal devotion: "You shall love the Lord your God with all your heart and with all your soul and with all your might" (Deut 6:5). God has everything to do with how we worship, what we think, and how we behave. He demands that we relearn what, how, and why we should think. Our mental activity must be situated within his story: creation, fall into sin, redemption, and restoration.

Certainly, God did not design our minds for passivity or demurral. Rather, he calls us to reason from what he teaches and to put our minds to work for his glory and the common good. For this reason, Isaiah turned away from religious instrumentalism, pseudo-atheism, and all forms of ontological assent. He resisted syncretism and cultural assimilation. He challenged non-biblical worldviews, ideologies, and epistemologies. He eschewed epistemic neutrality and autonomy. He rejected deceit in communication and interaction with others. Isaiah feared God and "inclined his ear" to heed and obey.

In this way also, Isaiah sought to love the Lord with all his mind and to discover God's plan for his time. Isaiah encountered Yahweh Elohim as the one essential fact. He realized that knowing and honoring God was his reason for being. He turned to ways of thinking rooted in creation, Torah, and wisdom. He learned to discern God at work in his midst and how to implement his will. He embraced new concepts and mental disciplines that presumed piety and produced prosperity as God's vice-regents on earth.

Like the Old Testament saints, we must traverse an arduous path to rediscover an edenic mindset while living in a post-garden milieu. This is why we turn from our epistemic bias and lust for autonomy. We are vigilant about idolatry, especially our own. We acknowledge our perverse tendency to invert the Creator–creature distinction. As Calvin warned, "Because nothing appears within or around us that has not been contaminated by a great immorality, what is a little less vile pleases us as a thing most pure—so long as we confine our minds within the limits of human corruption."[39] Because of the depth and universality of sin, we will inevitably follow in Adam's footsteps, so the need to listen to God's voice is very great. Clearly, this is a lifelong process and entails habitual repentance. Thank God that he redeems sinful thinkers.

Finally, the Old Testament declares that acquiring the knowledge of God is of paramount importance. In fact, the knowledge of God is the object of the verbal phrases "shall know," "might know," "may know," and "will know" at least 114 times. (In Ezekiel alone, the call to "know I am the Lord" occurs eighty times.) Understanding God is akin to gaining a clear view from a very high point. From there we discover the breath and

---

39. Calvin, *Institutes*, 1:38.

beauty of the world. We can navigate the terrain better with less effort and danger. In this sense, knowing God is a compass to guide our way.

The following excerpts from a poem by Michel Quoist offer an imaginative depiction of redemptive epistemology. Quoist effectively expresses the motivation of a thinker who aspires to love God with his mind. The meditation is called "I Would Like to Rise Very High."[40]

> I would like to rise very high, Lord, above my city, above the world, above time. I would like to purify my gaze, and borrow your eyes.
> I would then see the universe, humanity and history, as the Father sees them . . . .
> And I would see that today, like yesterday, the most minute details are part of it,
> every person has his place, every group, every object . . . .
> Startled, I will begin to understand that the great adventure of Love, that started at the creation of the world, continues to unfold before my eyes.
> The divine story which, according to your promise, will be completed in glory,
> only after the resurrection of the flesh, when you will come before the Father saying:
> All is accomplished. I am the Alpha and Omega, the Beginning and the End . . . .
> Then, falling on my knees, I would admire, O Lord, the great mystery of this world, your world, which in spite of the innumerable snags of sin, remains a long throb of love, leading towards Love and Life eternal.
> I would like to rise very high, Lord, above my city, above the world, above time.
> I would like to purify my gaze, and borrow your eyes.

Reproduced from *Prayers* by Michel Quoist, published by Sheed & Ward. ©Rowman & Littlefield, 1985, reproduced by arrangement with Sheed & Ward.

---

40. Quoist, *Prayers*, 13–15.

9

A Heart to Understand

"Teach me to seek You, and reveal Yourself to me as I seek, because I can neither seek You if You do not teach me how, nor find You unless You reveal Yourself."

—ANSELM OF CANTERBURY, *THE PROSLOGION*

THE BOOK OF DEUTERONOMY is the Rosetta stone of redemptive epistemology. It situates human beings as epistemological agents. It provides an infrastructure of knowledge for the individual, community, and culture. Deuteronomy describes two perennial challenges to knowing God. It shows that ontology impacts epistemology, as well as every area of life.

Deuteronomy is a resource-rich environment. (So rich, in fact, that I have dedicated chapters 9 and 10 of this book to Deuteronomy.) Almost every passage contains gems: examples of wise and foolish thinking, teaching about what we should know (and what to reject), applications of knowledge, and pitfalls to avoid. We learn the epistemic import of fearing God and listening to his voice. We discover God's pedagogical agenda and his means of instruction. We see that being a follower of the Lord entails lifelong learning.

We learn, for instance, about monotheism, the ever-present threat of idolatry, and reasons to listen to the Lord. We read the Ten Commandments and the *Shema*. Instructions about loving God with the mind and about teaching future generations are provided. In Deuteronomy 8, we learn the one essential lesson that every human being should know. The book also teaches what happens to a mind that refuses to heed God's voice and obey his commandments. Most importantly, we discover the mental outlook God longs for in his people.

Sometimes, Israel aspired to embody this mindset. Sometimes, they interpreted experience with creational and covenantal criteria. In their best moments, they were disposed to hear and heed God's voice through his prophet Moses. When they did pay attention, they discovered that the acquisition of knowledge followed this pattern: hear God's words—learn to fear the Lord—obey his commandments.[1] They also began to understand the supremacy and uniqueness of Yahweh Elohim among the would-be divinities of the ancient Near East.

This chapter is divided into two main sections. The prologue concerns three basic themes that govern Deuteronomy: covenant, six *Shemas*, and knowledge acquisition. The second section explains the mental outlook that God desires for his people. It consists of five subsections, describing a mind that fears, listens, learns, is vigilant, and loves.

PROLOGUE

Three of the conceptual building blocks of Deuteronomy concern covenant, divine declaration, and knowledge acquisition. The impact of the first is pervasive structurally, theologically, and ethically. The second concerns God's six covenantal announcements (using the formula "Hear, O Israel," known as a *Shema*) whereby theological affirmation generates an expected human response. The third entails Israel's intellectual capacity to know God and discern his will. The interaction between covenant, declaration, and learning situated the human thinker in ancient Israel.

A Book about Covenant

Deuteronomy is widely recognized as covenantal in nature. Its structure, vocabulary, and rhetoric resemble suzerainty treaties between a conqueror and a subjected vassal. Ancient Near Eastern pacts included provisions such as the following:

---

1. This model resembles the learning trajectory outlined in the previous chapter, based on Isaiah 6:9-10: repentance—input—perception—understanding—calling. Daniel I. Block ("The Grace of Torah," 15) provides a similar model: Reading—Hearing—Learning—Fear—Life, with reference to Deut 17:18-20 and 31:9-13.

Suzerainty Treaties	Deuteronomic Parallel
Preamble ("these are the words")	1:1-5 ("the words that Moses spoke")
Historical prologue (previous experience)	1:6-4:49 (post-exodus experience and theology)
General stipulations (demand of loyalty)	5:1-11:32 ("love" as faithfulness to the Lord)
Specific stipulations (behavioral demands)	12:1-26:19 (regulative infrastructure)
Blessings and curses (benefit and loss)	27:1-28:68 (blessing or woe)
Witnesses (divine enforcement)	30:1-10, 19-20; 31:19; 32:1-43[2]

Treaty vocabulary appears often in Deuteronomy: "covenant" (*berit*, twenty-seven times), "love" (*aheb, ahaba*, nine times),[3] "steadfast love" (*chesed*, three times), "treasured possession" (*segullah*, three times),[4] and "know" (*yada*, three times)[5]. Rhetorically, as James W. Watts demonstrates, Deuteronomy obligated listeners and fostered commitment within community infrastructure by means of covenant renewal and remembrance. He writes, "Deuteronomy obliges Israel not only to legal obedience but also to repetition of the book's own rhetoric of persuasion through re-enactment, both by individuals (6:20-25; 17:18-20) and by the nation as a whole (11:29; 27:12; cf. 31:10-13)."[6] Indeed, covenantal renewal was the focus as the second generation entered the Promised Land. This setting was emphasized often by the use of the words "now"

---

2. Craigie, *The Book of Deuteronomy*, 23-24. Block ("The Privilege of Calling," 393) suggests that the procedure for treaty ratification in the ancient Near East appears in 28:16-19.

3. From the human side, covenantal "love" entails "fear" and a requirement to "serve" the Lord (13:4); being "careful to do all this commandment," "walking in his ways," and "holding fast to him" (11:22); and "obeying his voice" (30:20). From the divine side, Yahweh demonstrated his "love" as covenantal faithfulness to the fathers of the nation (4:37; 7:8, 13; 10:15; 23:5).

4. See Block, "The Privilege of Calling," 395-98 on the significance of this expression, as well as the filial designations of Israel.

5. Huffmon argues that to "know" (*yada*) can indicate "mutual legal recognition on the part of the suzerain and vassal," and that it specifically means "acknowledge, recognize (authority, claims)" in 9:24 and 34:10. See Huffmon, "The Treaty Background of the Hebrew *Yāda*," 31-37.

6. Watts, "Rhetorical Strategy," 19.

and "today."⁷ Deuteronomy 26:17–19 explains what covenant renewal signified and stipulated:

> You have declared today that the Lord is your God, and that you will walk in his ways, and keep his statutes and his commandments and his rules, and will obey his voice. And the Lord has declared today that you are a people for his treasured possession, as he has promised you, and that you are to keep all his commandments, and that he will set you in praise and in fame and in honor high above all nations that he has made, and that you shall be a people holy to the Lord your God, as he promised.

Daniel I. Block summarizes the terms to which each party agreed within God's covenant:

Verse 17	What Israel Heard the Lord Declare
Privilege	I promise to be your God.
Obligation	You are to walk in my ways.
Obligation	You are to keep all my commandments.
Obligation	You are to listen to my voice

Verses 18–19	What the Lord Heard Israel Declare
Privilege	We accept our status as your treasured possession.
Obligation	We will keep all your commandments.
Obligation	We accept our status above all nations.
Obligation	We accept our status as a holy people to God.⁸

There were two important differences, however, between the treaties of the ancient Near East and God's covenant with Israel. First, suzerainty treaties usually arose after a conquest and ensured ongoing economic and ideological fealty. They legitimated theocracy and encoded enslavement to god-kings and the regimes they were entrusted to rule. In the case of the Hebrews, though, the reverse happened: Yahweh rescued his people from an abusive Egyptian theocracy in order to bring them into the Promised Land. Patrick D. Miller writes, "That decisive act of leading

---

7. O'Dowd (*The Wisdom of Torah*, 31–32) counts "about sixty significant occurrences" that "signal the formal commencement of applied teaching" regarding covenant implementation.

8. See Block, "The Privilege of Calling," 394.

out, which was the overthrow of the divine–human ruler, the king of Egypt, was the abrogation once and for all of any human rule or other divine claims over the final allegiance of this people."[9] Furthermore, Israel's covenant presumed a transition from polytheism to monotheism.[10] The nation discovered a completely new religious paradigm under their God, who was totally distinct from the henotheistic deities of the ancient Near East. Yahweh, they learned, was not just a little more powerful that Pharaoh and his pantheon or the local gods of Canaan. Rather, he was the only God among would-be divine claimants.

Further, Israel's covenant with Yahweh Elohim also presumed important implications for knowledge—of both God and creation. The epistemic significance of covenant arose from Israel's special status and obligation to "walk in his ways, keep his statutes and his commandments and his rules, and obey his voice." John M. Frame describes the intellectual situatedness of covenant as "servant-knowledge."[11] To know anything rightly, therefore, was to think under God's lordship within a threefold frame of reference: normative, situational, and existential. Frame explains the epistemic web in this way:

> If we are to understand the situation rightly, we must understand it as the location of God's revelation, his norms; so the situational includes the normative. To understand God's norms rightly, we must understand how they apply to situations and to ourselves; so the normative includes the situational and existential. To understand God's relationship to ourselves rightly, we must understand ourselves as part of a God-created environment (situational) and as covenant subjects made to live under God's law (normative); so the existential includes the normative and situational.[12]

---

9. Miller, "The Most Important Word," 23. He also states on page 4, "'Going out' is technical or juridical language for release of slaves or land, as one sees from the Book of the Covenant (Exod 21:1–11) and the Holiness Code (Lev 25:41), which speak of 'going out' when slaves are released. A slave goes out, is set free, according to the statutes, or is 'brought out/led out' by another party by a price of redemption or by force. It is this last that happens in the Exodus and is the defining word about the Lord's relationship to the liberated people."

10. See Patrick, "Is the Truth of the First Commandment Known by Reason?"

11. Frame, *The Doctrine of the Knowledge of God*, 40 (emphasis in original). As we read in the last chapter, he described this knowledge as "knowledge about God as Lord and a knowledge that is subject to God as Lord."

12. Frame, *The History of Western Philosophy and Theology*, 20.

The Six Shemas

The best-known *Shema* (instruction beginning "Hear, O Israel") in Deuteronomy is 6:4–5, "Hear, O Israel: The Lord our God, the Lord is one. You shall love the Lord your God with all your heart and with all your soul and with all your might."[13] But there are five other similar passages:

> And now, O Israel, listen to the statutes and the rules that I am teaching you, and do them, that you may live, and go in and take possession of the land that the Lord, the God of your fathers, is giving you. (4:1)

> And Moses summoned all Israel and said to them, "Hear, O Israel, the statutes and the rules that I speak in your hearing today, and you shall learn them and be careful to do them." (5:1)

> Hear, O Israel: you are to cross over the Jordan today, to go in to dispossess nations. . . . Know therefore today that he who goes over before you as a consuming fire is the Lord your God. He will destroy them and subdue them before you. So you shall drive them out and make them perish quickly, as the Lord has promised you. (9:1–3)

> And [the priest] shall say to them, "Hear, O Israel, today you are drawing near for battle against your enemies: let not your heart faint. Do not fear or panic or be in dread of them, for the Lord your God is he who goes with you to fight for you against your enemies, to give you the victory" (20:3–4)

> Then Moses and the Levitical priests said to all Israel, "Keep silence and hear, O Israel: this day you have become the people of the Lord your God. You shall therefore obey the voice of the Lord your God, keeping his commandments and his statutes, which I command you today." (27:9–10)

Two important themes emerge in these texts that will recur in this chapter. First, ontological truth about Yahweh Elohim produces intellectual, ethical, social, and psychological effects. This is particularly apparent in 5:1 and 6:4–5. Second, the indicative–imperative dynamic appears in the six *Shemas*. In each one we find content (truth conveyed), a communicative bridge (teaching, speaking, learning, knowing), and application (a performative action or attitude).

---

13. In each case, the verb "hear" is imperatival to express truth from Yahweh to Israel. See Isbell, "Deuteronomy's Definition of Jewish Learning," 109–16.

The *Shemas* taught that Israel was obligated to think and behave in certain ways because of who God is and what he has done on their behalf. For this reason, S. Dean McBride comments that the exclamation "Hear!" conveyed a "sense of urgency" and that God was "anticipating a positive response."[14] He adds, "If one really hears, he will respond in accord with what he has learned."[15] The following chart summarizes this indicative-imperative principle:

Text	Content	Communication	Application
4:1	statutes and rules	teaching	do them, go in
5:1	statutes and rules	speak, learn	do them
6:4–5	the Lord is one		love
9:1–3	he goes over before you	(know therefore)	drive out, make perish
20:3–4	he goes with you to fight		heart not faint, not fear
27:9–10	You . . . people of the Lord	(command)	obey the voice, keep his commandments and statutes

A Book about Knowledge

Deuteronomy was written for sentient beings, creatures who can think and decide. The book presumes that Israel should be taught and could learn. In fact, they must learn. They could see and observe, listen and evaluate. They could choose and act upon knowledge gained—or they could reject it. And they could change their minds for better or worse, if persuaded to do so. They could understand the big picture and discern God's storyline. They could discern the link between theological fact and ethical imperative.

Deuteronomy also presupposes intellectual curiosity. It expects that some would ask, "What is the meaning of the testimonies and the statutes and the rules that the Lord our God has commanded you?" (6:20) or "How did these nations serve their gods?—that I also may do the same?" (12:30). In short, the ancient Hebrews possessed the intellectual capacity to listen, interpret, and respond to revelation. And they could perceive

---

14. McBride, "The Yoke of the Kingdom," 290.
15. McBride, "The Yoke of the Kingdom," 290.

the ethical-spiritual demand to direct their minds in accord with the covenant.

Indeed, the Israelites were enabled and obliged to think, believe, and behave according to God's expectations.[16] But would they? Michael Carasik explains that Hebrew epistemology presupposed conflict between the Lord and Israel in the intellectual sphere. He says, "It also presents knowledge—its use and abuse, its effect and its power, the possibility that it can be concealed or distorted—as a point of rivalry between God and humanity."[17] He explains, in addition, the two-step intellectual result of minimizing the Lord: "The mental vacuum created by God's absence from the mind is filled first with the self and finally with other gods."[18] The front line in the perennial struggle between God and Israel, therefore, concerned revelation and the sinful mind, dating back to the fall of mankind. In light of the noetic impact of sin, the battle centered on whether the Israelites would function by redemptive or exilic epistemology.

Deuteronomy 30:11–14 presupposes the point of rivalry mentioned above. This interchange presumes knowledge and capacity, as well as resistance, denial, and evasion. The main ideas are in italics:

(11) For this commandment that I command you today is *not too hard* for you, *neither is it far off*.

(12) It is not in heaven, that you should say, 'Who will ascend to heaven for us and bring it to us, that we may hear it and do it?'

(13) Neither is it beyond the sea, that you should say, 'Who will go over the sea for us and bring it to us, that we may hear it and do it?'

(14) But the word is *very near* you. It is in your mouth and in your heart, so that *you can do it*.

Now, consider the rendering of John E. P. Taylor.[19] His translation highlights the polemical nature of the passage:

---

16. If Adam had done so, this world would be unimaginably different. But he did not. His progeny also did failed to listen to or apply God's words. Rather, they utilized their mental capacities to frustrate God's initiative on earth.

17. Carasik, *Theologies of the Mind*, 18.

18. Carasik, *Theologies of the Mind*, 189.

19. Taylor, "Moses and Old Covenant Obedience," 343–59. With Taylor, I follow the "present reality" reading of the passage rather than a future-oriented or eschatological hermeneutic. According to Taylor (page 352), a future emphasis is preferred

v. 11	Actually this commandment, which I am commanding you today,
	is not too hard for you
	and nor is it far.
v. 12	It is not in heaven that you might say,
	"Who will go up into heaven for us and take it for us
	and make us hear it in order that can do it."
v. 13	And nor is across the sea that you might say,
	"Who will go over to the other side of the sea for us
	and take it for us and make us hear it
	in order that we can do it."
v. 14	Actually the word is very near to you
	in your mouth
	and in your heart
	that you might do it.

Moses confronted two objections to the "commandment" (covenant) that presumed epistemic and ethical enmity between the speaker (Moses on the Lord's behalf) and the protesting interlocutor. The word "actually" in verses 11 and 14 contrasts truth and error. Verses 12 and 13 address the objection "too . . . far" in verse 11. Verse 14 answers the objection "too hard" in v. 11. The objector sought to evade obedience, as is evident in the repeated phrase "can/might do it" in verses 12, 13, and 14.

The objection asserted that the commandment was either too difficult to perform or could not be known clearly enough to be obeyed (v. 11). In either case, failure to comply would be excusable, even justifiable. As Taylor asks, "How can a people unable to keep the covenant be commanded to do so?"[20] The objection infers, therefore, that the Lord is unrealistic and unjust.

The obfuscation was threefold. First, both verses 12 and 13 posited lack of access to God's law, because its source was either in another

---

by many New Testament exegetes. Those who agree with the present interpretation include Craigie, *The Book of Deuteronomy*, 362; Block, *Deuteronomy*, 706–9; and O'Dowd, *Old Testament Wisdom Literature*, 97–102. Similarly, so do the ESV, NIV, NRSV, NKJV, NASB, NAMBRE, MSG, and CEB, among others. Those who adopt a future-oriented or eschatological reading include Coxhead, "Deuteronomy 30:11–14 as a Prophecy of the New Covenant," 305–20, and Barker, *The Triumph of Grace in Deuteronomy*, 182–97.

20. Taylor, "Moses and Old Covenant Obedience," 348.

dimension ("heaven") or geographically distant ("across the sea"). Second, both assumed that no one ("who") was capable of obtaining knowledge of the Lord's commands because of their inaccessibility. Third, the apologetic insinuated that humans could not "hear" the word of God. The verb *shama* ("hear") is in the Hiphil, meaning "cause to hear" or "reveal." The implication was that divine communication had broken down or had not really happened. The rationale asserted innocence due to agnosticism.[21]

Moses countered that the objectors were in fact culpable for the knowledge they had *already* received and were indeed capable of performing what the Lord required. Moses himself had ascended the mountain, received the words of God, and taught the people. Thus, in this sense, the "word" was "very near" (v. 14). He reminded them, "The secret things belong to the Lord our God, but the things that are revealed belong to us and to our children forever, that we may do all the words of this law" (29:29). The objection implied that God's will remained "secret" and therefore was not known or doable. What the dissenter failed to grasp, however, was that the Torah itself was an "agent of internalization" and possessed "the power to reproduce both divine presence and obedient righteousness."[22]

Moses knew clearly that the objection presupposed revelation (knowledge communicated from God) as well as capability (auditory and cognitive) to understand and act. The erroneous apologetic was in reality an intellectual farce, for the impasse was not due to any lack of knowledge or capacity, but to unwillingness. The dissenter did not require further education, but a listening disposition. He could and did know. He could comply, but he would not. He preferred self-imposed delusion to justify illicit motives. The problem, then, was not epistemological but ethical. It did not arise from deficient knowledge, but from a failure to acknowledge Yahweh's intellectual and ethical authority as lord of the covenant.

Access and knowledge are presumed, as well, in several of the terms and expressions that Moses employed. Each one reveals explicit or implicit associations with the mind ("heart").[23] Moses said that the "word"

---

21. This belies the truth that "To you it was shown, that you might know that the Lord is God; there is no other besides him" (4:35; see also 4:39; 7:9; 8:3; 9:3 for other facts God expected them to know).

22. O'Dowd, *Old Testament Wisdom Literature*, 101. See also Howell, "Deuteronomy 30:14 as an Explanation"; Block, "The Grace of Torah," 3–22.

23. Craigie renders "heart" as "mind" in verse 14: "in your mouth and in your mind" (*The Book of Deuteronomy*, 362).

(*davar*) of the Lord was not far away (v. 14). *Davar* refers to both verbal and silent speech (thoughts in the mind alone or expressed with words).[24] Moses asserted that the thoughts of Yahweh (his "word") were within reach of those with whom he spoke. Similarly, "near" (*qarob*) indicates the Lord's immanence through redemptive word and deed. Earlier, Moses posed this question: "For what great nation is there that has a god so near [*qarob*] to it as the Lord our God is to us, whenever we call upon him?" (4:7). The expression "too hard" (*niplet*) often refers to God's wondrous power, but it also indicates incomprehensibility.[25] In this verse, however, Moses specifically excludes inaccessible mystery and disavows esoteric insight as necessary to understand and obey.

The expression "in your mouth" (*bepika* appears with declarations of the "law of God" (Exod 13:9) and "word of the Lord" (1 Kgs 17:24). God also put his words in the mouths of prophets (Isa 51:16; 59:21; Jer 1:9; 5:14). Most significantly, the idiom "in your heart" demonstrates that knowledge is both accessible and understandable. As Carasik points out, this idiom usually indicates ruminations that oppose the Lord, but "in the heart" is also "spoken of positively only when it [idea and ability] has been put there by God."[26] In these examples, we see understanding and inspiration imparted by the Lord "in the heart" in a fashion similar to Deuteronomy 30:14:

> And he has inspired ["put in his heart"] him to teach. (Exod 35:34a)

> And Moses called Bezalel and Oholiab and every craftsman in whose mind (*leb*, "heart") the Lord had put skill (*chokmah*, "wisdom"), everyone whose heart stirred him up ("put in his heart") to come to do the work.(Exod 36:2)

> And all the kings of the earth sought the presence of Solomon to hear his wisdom (*chokmah*), which God had put into his mind (*leb*, "put in his heart"). (2 Chr 9:23)

Lastly, Moses was not an epistemological pessimist or optimist, but a biblical realist. He knew that God had spoken to Israel. He knew that

---

24. For this reason, Moses told the people, "Take care lest there be an unworthy thought (*davar*) in your heart" (15:9a). See Hazony, *The Philosophy of Hebrew Scripture*, 193–218.

25. For instance, in Job 42:3 and Psalm 131:1 God's wisdom is contrasted with human knowledge.

26. Carasik, *Theologies of the Mind*, 118.

they were bound in every way to their suzerain. And he also understood the intellectual and volitional impact of the fall.[27] He was not naive about their stubborn character or twisted mindset. As Block says, "If Israel fails—and they will (31:16–18)—it will not be because the people cannot keep the law because the bar is impossibly high, but that they will not keep it."[28]

Yet by grace there were refugees from exilic epistemology throughout Israel's history. In Deuteronomy, Caleb and Joshua feared the Lord and listened to his law. Moses, of course, was the supreme example and modeled redemptive epistemology (34:10).

DIVINE LONGING

Early in Deuteronomy, God revealed a profound desire to see Israel remain faithful. He told Moses, "Oh that they had such a heart as this always, to fear me and to keep all my commandments, that it might go well with them and with their descendants forever!" (5:29). Let us read this verse in its immediate context:

(22) These words the Lord spoke to all your assembly at the mountain out of the midst of the fire, the cloud, and the thick darkness, with a loud voice; and he added no more. And he wrote them on two tablets of stone and gave them to me.

(23) And as soon as you heard the voice out of the midst of the darkness, while the mountain was burning with fire, you came near to me, all the heads of your tribes, and your elders.

(24) And you said, "Behold, the Lord our God has shown us his glory and greatness, and we have heard his voice out of the midst of the fire. This day we have seen God speak with man, and man still live.

(25) Now therefore why should we die? For this great fire will consume us. If we hear the voice of the Lord our God any more, we shall die.

---

27. Van Til (*The Defense of the Faith*, 35) expressed the hard epistemic reality in this way: "Sin will reveal itself in the field of knowledge in the fact that man makes himself the ultimate court of appeal in the matter of all interpretation. He will refuse to recognize God's authority."

28. Block, *Deuteronomy*, 709.

(26) For who is there of all flesh, that has heard the voice of the living God speaking out of the midst of fire as we have, and has still lived?

(27) Go near and hear all that the Lord our God will say, and speak to us all that the Lord our God will speak to you, and we will hear and do it."

(28) And the Lord heard your words, when you spoke to me. And the Lord said to me, "I have heard the words of this people, which they have spoken to you. They are right in all that they have spoken.

(29) Oh that they had such a heart as this always, to fear me and to keep all my commandments, that it might go well with them and with their descendants forever!

(30) Go and say to them, 'Return to your tents.'

(31) But you, stand here by me, and I will tell you the whole commandment and the statutes and the rules that you shall teach them, that they may do them in the land that I am giving them to possess."

In this passage, Moses recounted God's theophany with Israel at Horeb, when he wrote the Ten Commandments and initiated his covenant (Exod 20:18–21). The people were utterly terrified and feared for their lives when they perceived God's dramatic appearance. Moses explained, though, that God's motive was not destructive, but pedagogical and pastoral. He told them, "Do not fear, for God has come to test you, that the fear of him may be before you, that you may not sin" (20:20). Moses differentiated between two aspects of fear.[29] On one hand, the people knew from observation that Yahweh was immensely powerful and dangerous. They had witnessed the destruction of Moses' enemies for their rebellion and apostasy. On the other hand, they experienced firsthand the Lord's miraculous redemption from Egyptian slavery on their behalf and in accord with the promise made to their fathers. They rightly concluded—temporarily—that Yahweh desired their best interests and

---

29. The word "fear" appears as a verb and noun derived from the same root, *yare*. See Block, "The Fear of Yahweh," 392–431 about the semantic range of "fear" (of the Lord) in the Old Testament.

wanted them to avoid further destruction due to sin. They passed the test at that time.[30]

Now, as the second generation was about to renew the covenant before entering the land of Canaan,[31] Moses disclosed God's approbation of their forefathers' positive mindset at that moment: "They are right in all that they have spoken" (5:28b). He also revealed God's great desire for them to retain their godly outlook (v. 29a).

The interjection "oh" (*mi*) is quite instructive. Sometimes, this term indicates the optative mood, expressing a wistful desire or future wish, and is translated as "if only," "would that," or "oh." At other times, *mi* means "who" and appears in rhetorical questions that indicate unattainable desire, at least from a human perspective. Block explains God's desire with "an awkward optative question" in Deuteronomy 5:29: "Who will grant and they will have this their heart?" The query is an idiomatic expression of God's epistemic desire, "O that they had such a heart as this!"[32] The Lord knew that shortly his people would refuse to heed his counsel. Nevertheless, what is unattainable for man is not for Yahweh. In verse 29, he expressed his goal for human understanding—a mindset that feared God. Block summarizes the Lord's outlook, "Yahweh acknowledged that he overheard the people's request to Moses (cf. 5:28) and affirmed their response. He also expressed his wish that the Israelites would never lose their present reverential disposition toward him."[33]

The optative "oh" also appears with reference to God's longing for human understanding, along with the preposition *lu* ("if," "oh that"). Deuteronomy 32:29 says, "Oh (*lu*), that they were wise, that they understood this, that they would consider their latter end!" (NKJV). Similarly, Psalm 81:13 expresses God's longing: "Oh (*lu*), that my people would listen to me, that Israel would walk in my ways!" And likewise, Isaiah 48:18 declares, "Oh (*lu*) that you had paid attention to my commandments!" Significantly, four times in the Old Testament God communicated his epistemic goals for his people with deep longing and emphasis.

The word "heart" (*leb*), as we have seen previously, is often a stand-in for "mind" (or mindset). This intellectual nuance also occurs in verse 29. Craigie renders "heart" as "mind" in the optative mood, "Would that

---

30. They did not persevere in this state of reverence for very long, as the episode with the golden calf (Exod 32) exemplifies.
31. See Block, "What Do These Stones Mean?" 17–41.
32. Block, "A Place for My Name," 230 note 32.
33. Block, *Deuteronomy*, 176.

they were continually of this mind," as does the NRSV, "If only they had a mind such as this always."[34] Indeed, the immediate context of the passage underscores an epistemological setting with the terms "voice," "wrote," "heard," "seen," "teach," and "speak," as well as knowledge vocabulary ("words," "statutes," "rules," "commandments") and argumentation (human in vv. 24–27 and divine in vv. 27–28). Within the broader context of Deuteronomy, terms of cognition appear in connection with "heart": "depart from your heart" and "forget" (4:9; 8:14), "know then in your heart" (8:5), "these words" and "on your heart" (6:6; 11:18), "say in your heart" indicating both spoken and unspoken thoughts (7:17; 9:4; 15:9; 18:21;), and a "heart to understand" (29:4).

The three references to "fire" (vv. 24, 25, 26) indicate the Old Testament's depiction of God's manifest presence.[35] Within Deuteronomy, fire is associated with divine communication and guidance (1:33; 4:12; 5:4; 9:10; 10:4) and God's destructive power (4:11; 5:5; 9:3; 18:16; 32:22; 33:2). The expression "living God," however, suggests a possible theological advance from henotheism to monotheism. Earlier, Moses denounced the "gods of wood and stone, the work of human hands, that neither see, nor hear, nor eat, nor smell" (4:28) and declared a robust monotheism: "The Lord is God in heaven above and on the earth beneath; there is no other" (4:35, 39). Within the Old Testament, the phrase "living God" refers to Elohim as the divine warrior of Israel (Josh 3:10; 2 Kgs 19:4; Jer 10:10; Dan 6:26). In addition, 2 Kings 19:16 and Isaiah 37:17 associate the "living God" with epistemic themes such as the eye and seeing or the ear and hearing, similarly to Deuteronomy 5:24.[36]

Thus, "such a heart as this" may be defined as a mindset ("mind") that presumed godly fear and obedience. This was derived from what the elders said to Moses about God's communication on the mountain (Deut 5:24–27), what Moses explained to them regarding the Lord's motivation (Exod 20:20), and what God told Moses about the elders' proposal for mediation (Deut 5:28b–29). Stated negatively, it meant reverence *and* avoiding misconduct ("that you may not sin" in Exod 20:20).

34. Craigie, *The Book of Deuteronomy*, 165.

35. Lewis, "Divine Fire in Deuteronomy 33:2," 791–803.

36. Second Kings 19:16 says, "Incline your ear, O Lord, and hear; open your eyes, O Lord, and see; and hear the words of Sennacherib, which he has sent to mock the living God." Isaiah 37:17 declares, "Incline your ear, O Lord, and hear; open your eyes, O Lord, and see; and hear all the words of Sennacherib, which he has sent to mock the living God."

The following subsections develop in further detail Deuteronomy's understanding of a mind that fears, listens, learns, is vigilant, and loves.

A Mind That Fears

The divine intent of "such a heart as this always" is coupled with the conjunction "that" (*maan*) in 5:29b: "that it might go well with them and with their descendants forever!" About forty-five other occurrences of *maan* in Deuteronomy indicate the Lord's purpose. Many refer to the Lord's intent to prosper the nation: to "live" and "prolong days"[37] and provide blessing in the land.[38]

Five times, however, God's intent for Israel, as indicated by "that" (*maan*), focused on acquiring the fear of the Lord (5:29; 6:2; and "learn to fear the Lord" in 14:23; 17:19; 31:12). In addition, the particle "that" (*asher*) appears in 4:10 with this significance: "Gather the people to me, that I may let them hear my words, so that (*asher*) they may learn to fear me all the days that they live on the earth, and that (*asher*) they may teach their children so."

Similarly, Deuteronomy 10:12–13 expresses God's didactic purpose. Moses asked, "And now, Israel, what does the Lord your God require of you?" The answer positions four verbs in apposition with "fear," so as to associate it with the Lord's overall purpose for Israel, which is thematically akin to Deuteronomy 5:29:

To fear	the Lord your God,
To walk	in all his ways,
To love	him,
To serve	the Lord your God with all your heart and with all your soul,
To keep	the commandments and statutes of the Lord, which I am commanding you today for your good.

In Deuteronomy, God-fearers were typified by an intellectual acknowledgment of God's voice: "my words" (4:10), "commandments" (5:29), "statutes" (6:2, 24), and "all the words of this law written in this book" (28:58). Behaviorally, those who possessed a heart that fears "serve" and "swear" by the Lord's name (6:13), "walk in his ways" (8:6), "hold fast

---

37. See Deuteronomy 4:1; 5:16; 6:2; 8:1; 11:9; 16:20; 17:20; 22:7; 25:15; 30:6.
38. See Deuteronomy 5:16; 6:18; 8:1; 11:8; 12:25; 14:29; 23:20; 24:19; 29:9.

to him" (10:20), "obey his voice" (13:4), "read" God's word (17:19), and "purge evil" from their midst (21:21). These intellectual and performative criteria amplify the idiomatic expression cited by Moses in Exodus 20:20, "that the fear of him may be upon your faces" (or "be before you"). John I. Durham renders the expression as "be always before you, on your mind."[39] The phrase indicates that the fear of the Lord should "always be before them as a constant preoccupation of mind."[40]

Similarly, throughout the Old Testament, godly fear signified intellectual humility and ethical rectitude. For this reason, Abram did not withhold Isaac from sacrifice, even though the request seemed inconceivable (Gen 22:12); Joseph rejected the enticements of Potiphar's wife as a "great wickedness" (39:9); Hebrew midwives disobeyed Pharaoh to protect the baby Moses (Exod 1:17); Yahweh-fearing servants of Pharaoh sheltered their livestock during the plagues (Exod 9:20); and Obadiah feared the Lord and hid the prophets from Ahab (1 Kgs 18:4).[41]

Moreover, the meaning of "fear" is further delineated by the statement of the Hebrew elders in 5:24–27. Note the contrast between the first generation's comments about the same event in Exodus 20:18–21 and Moses' retelling in Deuteronomy. His rendition amplifies the earlier statement, presumably to explain the Lord's affirmation of their speech (v. 28b) and perhaps indicating a progression of the second generation's understanding of the covenant (v. 29):

	Exodus 20	Deuteronomy 5
Name	God (Elohim)	Lord our God (Yahweh Elohim) the living God
Relation		our
Identity		us
Reaction	afraid and trembling	we shall die
Observation	thunder, flashes, sound, smoking	shown us, heard his voice, seen God
Interpretation		glory and greatness
Proposal	we will listen	we will hear and do

39. Durham, Exodus, 302.

40. Durham, Exodus, 303.

41. See also Exod 14:31; 1 Sam 12:18; 2 Sam 23:3; Zeph 3:7; Mal 3:16. Compare the outlook and behavior of those who do "not fear" the Lord (2 Kgs 17:25; Isa 57:11; Jer 5:22; Hos 10:3; Ps 55:19).

In the Deuteronomic account, the Hebrews evidenced a deeper fear of God. They encountered Yahweh's awesome transcendence, but they also discerned his covenantal immanence. They experienced terror, but they also evidenced the beginning of understanding, trust, and endearment. They acknowledged his power over life and death, but also the efficacy of his words. They understood their vulnerability, but also their dependency upon the Lord who called them into covenant.

A Mind That Listens

When God spoke to Israel, the verb *shama* was often utilized, translated as "listen to," "hear," or "obey." The command to pay attention appears in every genre of the Old Testament, with a multitude of objects:

Listen to	"the words of the Lord your God" (Josh 3:9), "the words of the Lord" (1 Sam 15:1), "all that I command you" (1 Kgs 11:38), "the voice of my teachers" (Prov 5:13), "the words of my servants the prophets" (Jer 26:5), "their judges" (Judg 2:17), "me" (Ps 81:8)
Obey	"the voice of the Lord your God" (Zech 6:15), "the voice of his word" (Ps 103:20), "the voice of his servant" (Isa 50:10), "the voice of Samuel" (1 Sam 8:19), "your commandments" (Neh 9:16), "my/his/your voice" (Judg 6:10)
Hear	"the instruction of the Lord" (Isa 30:9), "the words of your mouth" (Ps 138:4), "the word of the Lord" (Isa 66:5), "instruction" (Prov 8:33), "my words" (Prov 4:10), "my/his voice" (Isa 32:9)

As we saw in the previous chapter, *shama* appears often with a particular direct object, "voice" (*qol*). Dru Johnson points out that the idiom "listen to the voice of" (*shama qol*) indicates "acknowledging someone as having authority and then enacting his or her authoritative instructions."[42] The expression "listen to the voice of the Lord your God" communicates his transcendent perspective and authority to his vassal rulers, builders, benefactors, and thinkers. In a positive sense, the idiom appears in Exodus 15:26: "If you diligently listen to the voice of the Lord your God, and do what is right in his eyes," then he would "put none of the diseases" upon Israel that the Egyptians suffered. Similarly, the failure to listen to the "voice of the Lord" occurs in a negative sense eight times in contexts of disobedience.[43]

---

42. Johnson, *Epistemology and Biblical Theology*, 42.

43. See Josh 5:6; 1 Sam 12:15; 15:19, 22: 28:18; 1 Kgs 20:36; 2 Kgs 18:12; Ps 106:25.

In Deuteronomy, formulations of *shama qol* are especially prevalent. The phrase "listen to/obey/hear the voice of the Lord/Lord your God" appears many times. This expression and its various objects are listed below:

Obey the voice of the Lord/Lord your God	20	Listen to the command of the Lord	1
Obey his voice	6	Listen to my words	1
Obey the commandments of the Lord your God	2	Listen to the voice of a prophet	1
Obey all these words	1	Listen to my words	1
Obey the priest	1	Listen . . . to a prophet like me	1
Obey the voice of his father	1	Listen to parents	1
Listen to your voice	1	Hear the statutes and rules	1
Listen to me	1	Hear the voice/of the Lord God	2
Listen to the statutes and rules	2	Hear the voice	3

Significantly, in Exodus 20:19 and Deuteronomy 5:23–27 the elders proposed that Moses serve as intermediary between the intimidating "voice" and themselves. They told him, "Go near and hear all that the Lord our God will say, and speak to us all that the Lord our God will speak to you, and we will hear and do it." With God's approval (Deut 5:28), Moses was then called into the divine presence to receive God's instruction for Israel (vv. 30–31). In this way, they recognized him as their authenticated prophet.

Deuteronomy 4:35–40 provides four reasons for listening to God's voice through Moses that amplify Deuteronomy 5:22–31. The four motivations are in italics:

(35) To you it was shown, *that you might know that the Lord is God*; there is no other besides him.

(36) Out of heaven he let you hear his voice, *that he might discipline you*. And on earth he let you see his great fire, and you heard his words out of the midst of the fire.

(37) And because he loved your fathers and chose their offspring after them and brought you out of Egypt with his own presence, by his great power,

(38) driving out before you nations greater and mightier than you, to bring you in, to give you their land for an inheritance, as it is this day,

(39) know therefore today, and *lay it to your heart*, that the Lord is God in heaven above and on the earth beneath; there is no other.

(40) Therefore you shall keep his statutes and his commandments, which I command you today, *that it may go well with you* and with your children after you, and that you may prolong your days in the land that the Lord your God is giving you for all time.

First, the phrase "that you might know that the Lord is God" underscores God's intent to instruct his people. He also reaffirms his sovereignty over knowledge due to human finitude and fallenness. This passage highlights God's epistemic grace given for Israel's understanding through revelation: "to you it was shown" (v. 35), "let you hear his voice" (v. 36a), and "let you see his great fire and hear his words" (v. 36b).

Furthermore, the profile of Yahweh Elohim in this passage depicts him as unequivocally supreme. The concept of God is monotheistic and totally exceptional, for "there is no other" (v. 39; see also v. 35). His reign is universal and transcendent in "heaven above and on the earth beneath" (v. 39). His presence "on earth" is mediated through his "great power" (v. 37), and he relates to all things through promise and law. He is active in "driving out" nations and supplying "the land" to Israel as an "inheritance" due to his covenantal love of the "fathers" (vv. 37–38). And of course, he is sovereign: he "chose" Abraham and his "offspring" and "gives" the land to whom he will, according to his purpose (v. 37).

Second, the phrase "that he might discipline you" indicates didactic purpose. The term "discipline" translates the verb *yasar*. In some cases, the word indicates physical punishment for immoral conduct (22:18). It also refers to the death penalty for stubbornly refusing to heed parental admonition.[44] But the better context to understand *yasar* in 4:36 is its use in 8:5, "As a man disciplines (*yasar*) his son, the Lord your God disciplines (*yasar*) you." Discipline occurred within a filial relationship that was intended for good and to produce holiness, resulting in blessing (8:2–3). In this setting, then, "humbling" and "testing" (v. 2) are

---

44. For example, the law demands the maximum punishment for an offspring who is "stubborn and rebellious" and "will not obey the voice (*shama qol*) of his father or the voice of his mother, and, though they discipline (*yasar*) him, will not listen (*shama*) to them" (21:18).

approximate synonyms for discipline. God's motive was to determine "what was in your heart." His discipline was designed to demonstrate the necessity of listening.

Third, the expression "lay it to your heart" conveys an epistemological nuance. The verb rendered as "lay it to" is *shub* ("turn," "return," "restore," "bring back"). In this setting, the meaning is "do not let your mind forget," "call them to mind" (30:1), or simply "remember." This significance is similar to 11:18, "You shall therefore lay up (*sum*) these words of mine in your heart and in your soul." In this context (v. 39), the idiom indicates that remembering or re-listening to God's word is motivated by repentance in the midst of chastisement.

Fourth, the clause "that it may go well with you" indicates God's intention to prosper his people in the land of Canaan according to his promise—on condition of covenantal compliance.

Blessing was the fruit of obedience and the appropriate application of heeding God's voice. Moses told Israel, "Therefore you shall keep his statutes and his commandments, which I command you today, that it may go well with you and with your children after you, and that you may prolong your days in the land that the Lord your God is giving you for all time" (4:40). Indeed, the long list of blessings derived from obedience in Deuteronomy 28:1–14 defined what "that it may go well with you" really meant: an optimal life in the post-fall world.

A Mind That Learns

Yahweh wanted Israel to perceive reality. He desired them to discern their true condition: their dependency and vulnerability as finite and fallen creatures. He wanted them to understand essential ontological and redemptive truths. He valued knowledge acquisition and utilized the verbs "know" (*yada*) and "hear" (*shama*) to communicate theological content. For instance, he taught the Hebrews monotheism: "To you it was shown, that you might know that the Lord is God; there is no other besides him" (4:35). He contrasted himself with the local divinities (henotheism): "The Lord is God in heaven above and on the earth beneath; there is no other" (4:39; see also 6:4). He also explained covenantal realities such as his loving faithfulness (5:6; 7:9), fatherly discipline (8:5), and law (5:1).

One especially important truth was the transcendental necessity of divine revelation. Moses originally taught this lesson to Israel in the wilderness in 8:1–3. Verse 3b expresses Yahweh's pedagogical aim (italicized):

(1) The whole commandment that I command you today you shall be careful to do, that you may live and multiply, and go in and possess the land that the Lord swore to give to your fathers.

(2) And you shall remember the whole way that the Lord your God has led you these forty years in the wilderness, that he might humble you, testing you to know what was in your heart, whether you would keep his commandments or not.

(3) And he humbled you and let you hunger and fed you with manna, which you did not know, nor did your fathers know, that he might make you know that man does not live by bread alone, but *man lives by every word that comes from the mouth of the Lord.*

Consider first the broader context. Exodus 16 described the provision of "bread from heaven" (manna, v. 4) after the people "grumbled" about the limited quantity and poor quality of food. They glanced back wistfully to Egypt and longed for "the meat pots" and "bread" formerly consumed "to the full" (v. 3). In response, the Lord utilized their privation as a learning experience by providing manna six days every week. They soon discovered with amazement that "whoever gathered much had nothing left over, and whoever gathered little had no lack" (v. 18). And although manna normally rotted within one day, God's bread miraculously survived for next-day consumption only on the Sabbath (vv. 24–30). The educational aims of this experience were fourfold: to "test them" and determine if they would "walk in my law" (v. 4); to "know that it was the Lord who delivered them from Egypt" (v. 6); to see the "glory of the Lord" (v. 7); and to "know that I am the Lord your God" (v. 12). In addition, God established an everlasting testimony through a supernaturally preserved portion of God's "bread," reminding Israel how they "ate the manna forty years, till they came to a habitable land" (vv. 33–34).

Similarly, Numbers 11 records the Lord's provision of meat (quail), though the depiction in this case is clearly negative. Israel "complained" (v. 1) and manifested "strong craving" (v. 4) for something other than God's bread. They cried out, "Oh that we had meat to eat! We remember the fish we ate in Egypt that cost nothing, the cucumbers, the melons, the leeks, the onions, and the garlic. But now our strength is dried up, and there is nothing at all but this manna to look at" (vv. 4b–5). Their unmerited sense of entitlement "angered" the Lord (vv. 1, 33) and they suffered a "great plague" as a result (v. 33), because they had "rejected the Lord" (v. 20). Nevertheless, the provision of quail showed God's great power on their behalf and dramatically demonstrated the veracity of his word (v. 23). In this way, the nation learned through painful experience to heed God's voice through his authorized spokesman Moses.

Many years later, in Deuteronomy 8, Moses underscored the great lesson God taught Israel through their wilderness journey and his miraculous supply of food and water. But he reminded them that "man does not live by bread alone, but man lives by every word that comes from the mouth of the Lord." (v. 3b).[45] The historical context indicates discursive and non-discursive communication, both words and deeds. Regarding the latter, Yahweh communicated through his "discipline" in the wilderness (v. 5) by means of "humbling," "testing," and sustenance ("clothing did not wear out," v. 4). Raymond C. Van Leeuwen points out that the Lord spoke through "the realm of history (exodus [in v. 14]) and in nature (water from rock [in v. 15])."[46] In fact, the expression "his mouth" sometimes indicates communication without words. For instance, from his mouth come wind (Job 15:30), a "rumbling" (Job 37:2), "devouring fire" (Ps 18:8), and his "breath" that kills (Isa 11:4). Lamentations 3:38 asks, "Is it not from the mouth of the Most High that good and bad come?"

On the other hand, the phrase "his [the Lord's] mouth" is frequently associated with speech. From "his mouth" (Moses speaking for Yahweh) come "my words" (Deut 18:18), "instruction," and "words from his mouth" (Job 22:22), as well as "wisdom" with "knowledge" and "understanding" (Prov 2:6). Job 23:12 is thematically similar to Deuteronomy 8:3: "I have not departed from the commandment of his lips; I have treasured the words of his mouth more than my portion of food." In the broader context of chapter 8, God spoke through Moses his "commandment" (vv. 1, 2, 6, 11), "rules" and "statutes" (v. 11), and his "covenant that he swore to your fathers" (v. 18). In fact, Moses warned that Israel would perish if they did not "obey the voice of the Lord" (v. 20).

The verb "live" (*hayah* in 8:1) conveys a dual significance. On one hand, the term refers to physical existence and survival. Supply of food and water (vv. 15–16), protection (v. 15), sustenance (v. 4), and deliverance from oppression (v. 14) presume God's sustaining power. On the

---

45. The phrase "every word" (ESV) is better characterized by the NASB as "everything," for the Hebrew says simply "every" (or "all," *kol*).

46. Van Leeuwen, "What Comes Out of God's Mouth," 57.

other hand, the term "live" refers to a quality of existence that occurs by keeping "the commandments of the Lord your God by walking in his ways and by fearing him" (v. 6). In fact, verses 7–10 depict Canaan as a new Eden, where Israel would flourish—if they obeyed.[47]

Thus, the mindset that the Lord desired for his people included the realization that everything revealed by God in words spoken (Torah) and unspoken (redemptive deeds) was the presupposition of their existence—in fact, the necessary preconditions for their very understanding.[48] God's voice enabled Israel to thrive and also held them to account for disobedience. A principal purpose of the wilderness experience, therefore, was to acquire this critical knowledge gained through privation and disorientation: listen to God's voice and obey in order to thrive and flourish.

A Mind That Is Vigilant

A vigilant mind shares God's passion for his instructions and objectives. Such an outlook listens acutely and implements resolutely. Epistemic vigilance implies a mindset that is zealous, attentive, and thorough with respect to oneself, family, community, and those outside the covenant. A vigilant mind presumes situational awareness. It discerns dangers in one's thinking, desire, and behavior, as well as internal threats within the community and external threats from other nations.

A vigilant thinker fulfills God's commandments with utmost thoroughness. He cares for his soul "diligently," so that he does not "forget" all that God did for Israel (4:9). He "strictly obeys" what the Lord has communicated (15:5) and "diligently keeps" his law (6:17). He teaches his children "diligently" (6:7). He serves the Lord and advances his cause with total devotion, with "all of the heart and soul" (4:29; 6:5; 10:12; 11:13; 13:3; 26:16; 30:6, 10). Vigilance also applies to specifically intellectual tasks such as investigations concerning covenant violation and apostasy (13:14; 17:4; 19:18). Similarly, vigilant minds proactively "remember"

---

47. The Old Testament depicts the Promised Land as a potential new Eden, a sacred precinct in the midst of vast profane territory. Like Eden, which was a "good land" blessed by God (Gen 1:10, 12), Canaan was a "good land" promised to the Hebrew tribes by their Redeemer (Exod 3:8; Deut 4:21; Josh 23:13). It was a place of peace and plenty where everyone could "eat and be full" (Deut 8:10, 12; 14:29; Pss 104:28; Isa 66:11–13). It was also a land of prosperity where all enjoyed the bounty of God and "lived in safety, each man under his own vine and fig tree" (1 Kgs 4:25).

48. See Poythress, *Redeeming Science*, 13–68.

that they "were slaves in the land of Egypt" (5:15), "what the Lord did to Pharaoh" (7:18), "the whole way God has led you" (8:2), that God gives "power to get wealth" (8:18), and how they "provoked the Lord your God to wrath" (9:7).

Furthermore, the word "all" (*kol*, as well as the variations "with all," "in all," "to all," and "that all") occurs frequently, indicating the full scope to which vigilance must extend. Temporally speaking, listening to the Lord's voice and observing his law must continue "all the days of your life" (4:9; 12:1; 16:3; 17:19). The required actions include "all the things that you should do" (1:18), teaching children and grandchildren (4:9–10), "walking in all the way the Lord your God commanded" (5:33), paying tithes and offerings (12:11), attending festivals (12:18; 16:3, 16; 17:10), and "all that you undertake" (12:18). Conceptually, this included knowing and doing "all my commandments" (5:29), "statutes and rules" (11:32), "the words of this law that are written in this book" (28:58), and "what is right and good in the sight of the Lord" (6:18; 12:25). Significantly, vigilance applies to the depth and breadth of God's commands: the "whole commandment" (5:31; 8:1; 11:8; 31:5) and "whole way" (8:2).

Similarly, words derived from *shamar* appear as the injunctions "take care," be "careful," and the adverb "carefully," indicating a mindset that is focused and attentive. One "must "learn" and "be careful to do" God's statutes (5:1), so that one does not "forget" (4:23) and become "ensnared" by idolatry (12:30). Likewise, *shamar* coupled with idioms of the "heart" urges careful self-observation lest God's words "depart from your heart" (4:9), "your heart be deceived" (11:16), or the people harbor an "unworthy thought in your heart" (15:9) or fail to "take to heart" the Lord's commands (32:46). Especially critical was the obligation to be "careful" about revelation and never "add to" (syncretism) or "take from" (diminish) God's word (12:32).

Moses' counsel to the people in 4:9 is especially instructive: "Only take care, and keep your soul diligently, lest you forget the things that your eyes have seen, and lest they depart from your heart all the days of your life. Make them known to your children and your children's children." In this verse, *shamar* is translated as "take care" and "keep."[49] The

---

49. Craigie's translation elucidates the meaning of the verse: "Guard yourself carefully and guard very carefully your desire, lest you forget the things your eyes have seen, and lest they slip from your mind all the days of your life; But you shall make them known to your children to your children and to your grandchildren" (*The Book of Deuteronomy*, 131).

object of diligent care is the "soul" (*nepesh*). Bruce K. Waltke renders the term with the Hebrew sense of embodied appetite or yearning.[50] Broadly speaking, *nepesh* includes the imagination, curiosity, motivation, and inclination. The term "diligently" is derived from *meod*, meaning "very" or "exceedingly" (see also 4:15 and 6:6, "might"). "Forget" is presented in apposition with the idiom "depart from your heart (mind)."[51] The long-term remedy, therefore, for skewed imagination and forgetfulness, as well as for communal prevention of apostasy, is the inculcation of the biblical worldview (covenants and history) to each generation.

Consider now the broader context and the argumentation for vigilance utilizing the verb *shamar* ("take care," "keep," and "watch") plus the conjunction "lest" (*pen*) in 4:9, 15–23. (The verb is italicized. "Lest" occurs five times. Several verses are omitted for brevity.)[52]

(9) Only *take care*, and *keep* your soul diligently, lest you forget the things that your eyes have seen, and lest they depart from your heart all the days of your life . . . .

(15) Therefore *watch* yourselves very carefully. Since you saw no form on the day that the Lord spoke to you at Horeb out of the midst of the fire,

(16) beware lest you act corruptly by making a carved image for yourselves, in the form of any figure, the likeness of male or female . . . .

(19) And beware lest you raise your eyes to heaven, and when you see the sun and the moon and the stars, all the host of heaven, you be drawn away and bow down to them and serve them, things that the Lord your God has allotted to all the peoples under the whole heaven . . . .

(23) *Take care*, lest you forget the covenant of the Lord your God, which he made with you, and make a carved image, the form of anything that the Lord your God has forbidden you.

---

50. Waltke, *The Book of Proverbs*, 90; see also Block, "How Many Is God," 202–3.

51. "Depart" is literally "turn aside (from)" with the verb *sur*, often used metaphorically in Deuteronomy to indicate apostasy or disobedience (5:32; 7:4; 9:12, 16; 11:16; 17:11; 28:14; 31:29).

52. "Beware" (vv. 16 and 19) is implied by the argument, though the word does not appear in the original text.

Mental vigilance and the prevention of idolatry are contrasted with forgetting and disobedience. This can be displayed by the following diagram summarizing the use of *shamar* plus *pen*:

Verse	Shamar	Pen	Theme or Action
9	take care keep	lest lest	forget the things your eyes have seen they depart from your heart
15	watch very carefully		since you saw no form
16	beware (implied)	lest	act corruptly by making a carved image
19	beware (implied)	lest	lift your eyes to heaven
23	take care	lest	drawn away, bow down, serve them forget the covenant make an image

Clearly, the vigilant mind resists the tendency to ignore what is most important (God's voice) and embrace what is most destructive (idolatry). But even when one falls into idolatry and suffers exile (4:28), true worship can occur again through repentance with due diligence: "if you search after him with all your heart and with all your soul" (v. 29).

Furthermore, the vigilant mind exhibits situational awareness (4:31–40). It interprets current challenges in light of the big picture and within its proper theological context. First, Israel understood its moment in history within God's story beginning with creation (v. 32), his promise to the fathers (vv. 31, 37), the covenant at Sinai (vv. 33, 38), and the deliverance from Egypt (v. 34). The thoughtful mind remembered where they had come from, where they were now, where they were going, and why. In fact, shortly before Moses died, he restated Israel's need to think about the present and future with reference to the past. He said, "Take to heart all the words by which I am warning you today, that you may command them to your children, that they may be careful to do all the words of this law. For it is no empty word for you, but your very life, and by this word you shall live long in the land that you are going over the Jordan to possess" (32:46–47). In this regard, O'Dowd comments:

> The implication for Israel is that the knowledge of Yahweh, of his activity in history, and of his universal uniqueness are the foundation of her knowledge of the world . . . . That this same union of creation and salvation events is used to justify Yahweh's uniqueness in 32:39–43—and his concern for the testimony of the nations (32:27)—reinforces the fact that epistemology is

grounded in the ontology of divine presence and divine power and the ethics of obedience.[53]

Second, those with attentive mindsets understood divine election as conditioned by obedience and disobedience. Nathan McDonald comments, "The two sides of election are summarized in YHWH's nature as both the 'jealous el' [God] and the 'merciful el' (4:24, 31; cf. 7:6–10)."[54] He describes the inevitable result when Israel did not listen to the voice of the Lord: "When a different vision is accepted, Israel is unable to obey the guiding voice of YHWH."[55]

Third, the vigilant mind viewed the spiritual marketplace in Canaan from an elenctic[56] perspective (4:32–38). It interpreted the conquest and settlement as a clash of worldviews—between monotheism and henotheism (vv. 35, 39).[57] Indeed, the nation discovered that their election was rooted in this polemical objective: "To you it was shown, that you might know that the Lord is God; there is no other besides him" (v. 35).

Fourth, they interpreted covenant renewal and entrance into the land with this theoretical construct: indicative ontological fact produces imperative ethical obligation. Verses 39 and 40 summarize the rationale: "Know therefore today, and lay it to your heart, that the Lord is God in heaven above and on the earth beneath; there is no other. Therefore you shall keep his statutes and his commandments, which I command you today."

---

53. O'Dowd, *The Wisdom of Torah*, 42.
54. McDonald, "The Literary Criticism and Rhetorical Logic," 218.
55. McDonald, "The Literary Criticism and Rhetorical Logic," 222.
56. The word "elenctic" derives from the Greek verb *elengchein*, meaning "to bring to shame" (translated as expose, convict, reprove, or rebuke). In John 16:8, the verb depicts a key ministry of the Holy Spirit, for "He will *convict* the world concerning sin and righteousness and judgment." In 2 Timothy 4:2, the word describes a central function of God's word: "Preach the word; be ready in season and out of season; *reprove*, rebuke, and exhort, with complete patience and teaching." The term conveys a polemical nuance, presuming comparison and contrast, critique and chastisement, truth and falsehood. See J. H. Bavinck, *An Introduction to the Science of Mission*, 221–67.
57. Bartholomew and O'Dowd (*Old Testament Wisdom Literature*, 25) summarize Deuteronomy's elenctic impact in light of the fear of God: "Throughout the rest of the Old Testament, the 'fear of Yahweh' similarly represents total devotion to God as the heart of Israel's 'true' religion.... What must be recognized is that above all else about this phrase—the fear of Yahweh—is the radical nature of Israel's ethical monotheism among her polytheistic neighbors."

Finally, Deuteronomy 7–8 highlights two contexts in which spiritual vulnerability would be acute and vigilance must be maintained. Two harmful enticements would arise "when the Lord your God brings you into the land" (7:1a). The first was familiar—the worship of other gods. God instructed Israel to destroy the Canaanites (v. 2) and above all not to intermingle with them by making covenants with them or intermarriage (v. 3). The reason provided ("for") is that interaction would cause some to "turn away" (*sur*) from the Lord to serve other gods (7:4; 8:19).[58] Other worldviews functioned as a "snare" (*moqesh* in 7:16) or lure that would "ensnare" (*yagosh* in 7:25) those with undisciplined curiosity. For this reason, Moses cautioned the people not even to "inquire" about other religions (12:30; 18:11) and to "not listen to" those promoting deviant spiritual agendas (13:3, 8; 18:14).

The second enticement concerned prosperity. In chapter 7, Moses told the nation to maintain extreme caution with the objects utilized in pagan worship. He said, "You shall not covet the silver or the gold that is on them or take it for yourselves, lest you be ensnared (*yaqosh*) by it, for it is an abomination to the Lord your God" (v. 25).[59] Similarly, in chapter 8 the enticement concerned wealth and power acquired during a time of peace and security. In verses 7–10, Moses described the "good land" where they will "lack nothing" and "be full," which should produce praise to God for what he has given (see also 6:10–12). Beginning in 8:11, however, he solemnly warned them about the dangers of prosperity and the false sense of empowerment it fostered:

(11) Take care (*shamar*) you forget the Lord you God....

(12) Lest (*pen*) when you have eaten and are full and have built good houses and live in them,

(13) and when your herds and flocks multiply and your silver and gold is multiplied and all that you have is multiplied,

---

58. The verb *sur* is used in Deuteronomy to indicate apostasy or disobedience: "depart from your heart" and forget what was seen (4:9), "turned aside" and the golden calf (9:12, 16), "turn aside" with a heart that is deceived by other gods (11:16, 28), "turn aside" from a just verdict (17:11), "turn away" after "many wives" and wealth (17:17), "turn aside" from the law (17:20), "turn aside" from the commandments (28:14), and "turn aside" and "act corruptly" after Moses' death (31:29).

59. This concern is reflected in the Tenth Commandment, "And you shall not covet your neighbor's wife. And you shall not desire your neighbor's house, his field, or his male servant, or his female servant, his ox, or his donkey, or anything that is your neighbor's" (5:21).

(14) then your heart be lifted up, and you forget the Lord your God
....

(17) Beware lest you say in your heart, "My power and the might of my hand have gotten me this wealth."

Moses' cure for this early form of consumerism or self-congratulating prosperity theology was vigilance—the mental and spiritual discipline of continual remembrance and actualization of covenantal reality. He told them, "You shall remember the Lord your God, for it is he who gives you power to get wealth, that he may confirm his covenant that he swore to your fathers, as it is this day" (8:18).

A Mind That Loves

The creedal nucleus of Deuteronomy is the *Shema* of 6:4–5, "Hear, O Israel! The Lord is our God, the Lord alone! Therefore, you shall love the Lord, your God, with your whole heart, and with your whole being, and with your whole strength" (New American Bible Revised Edition). The theological significance of this text cannot be overstated, but the epistemological import is also critical. The *Shema* depicts with upmost clarity "such a mind as this"—the mindset that God desires for his servants. The text shows the centrality of the mind in Old Testament spirituality and reveals how thinking covenantally impacts every area of life.[60]

In this light, consider what Moses taught the Israelites in the previous five chapters. In chapter 1, he reviewed their refusal to enter the Promised Land due to fear and unbelief. He described their folly and defeat before the Amorites and reminded them, "You rebelled against the command of the Lord and presumptuously went up into the hill country" (v. 43). He also recounted their victories over local dynasties during their wilderness sojourn (chapters 2–3). In chapter 4, Moses provided the theological preamble for the Ten Commandments and the *Shema*. In 4:1, he uttered the first call to obedience with the imperative verb *shama* (translated as "O Israel, listen to"). In addition, he urged them to

---

60. Theologically, it is helpful to ponder Miller's incisive commentary (*Deuteronomy*, 97–98) about the Shema's prominence in Deuteronomy: "With this chapter [i.e., chapter 6] we come to the pivot around which everything else in Deuteronomy revolves.... One may speak of these verses as a summary of the law of Ten Commandments.... The Shema is the touchstone for Israel's faith and life, the plumb line by which their relationship to the Lord of history was constantly being measured."

"take care" lest they "forget" (v. 9), "watch yourselves" lest they "act corruptly" in idolatry (vv. 15–16), and "take care" again lest they "forget the covenant of the Lord your God" (v. 23). The focus of chapter 4, though, is the twin monotheistic declarations expressed with the vocabulary of cognition (in italics):

> To you it *was shown*, that you *might know* that the Lord is God; there is no other besides him. (v. 35)

> *Know* therefore today, and *lay it to your heart*, that the Lord is God in heaven above and on the earth beneath; there is no other. (v. 39)

The theological capstone of chapter 5, of course, is the Ten Commandments, again announced with "Hear, O Israel." This command to pay close attention presumes transcendent power and authority that compels obedience. Verses 6–8 express the ontological message with an indicative-imperative relationship announced by God himself:

Indicative truth	I am the Lord your God, who brought you out of the land of Egypt, out of the house of slavery (v. 6)
Imperative application	You shall have no other gods before me (v. 7)
Imperative application	You shall not make for yourself a carved image, or any likeness of anything that is in heaven above, or that is on the earth beneath (v. 8a)

In 6:4–5, another emphatic "Hear, O Israel" summons the people to listen and obey. The pattern of indicative truth and imperative response in chapters 4–6 may be summarized in this way:

Indicative	Conjunction	Imperative
there is no other (4:35, 39)	therefore	keep his commandments (v. 40)
I am the Lord (5:6)	(implied)	no other gods before me (v. 7)
the Lord alone (6:4)	therefore	love the Lord with your whole heart (v. 5) [61]

---

61. The New American Bible (Revised Edition, NABRE) translates the conjunction *waw* as "therefore," whereas other versions use "and" or omit the word. Neither the logic of chapters 4–6 nor these two verses, however, support "and," for the two statements in verses 4 and 5 are not synonymous or appositional. The conjunction associates the two thoughts as a cause (or anticipatory condition, v. 4) that provokes a necessary response (v. 5). This is obvious in light of the actions prescribed in the following verses that depict what "love" entails: teach, write, talk, and bind. Elsewhere

In terms of exegesis, however, 6:4 is complicated.⁶² Judah Kraut comments that this verse "has long confounded biblical scholars and exegetes" and adds that it "exhibits peculiar syntax that defies any obvious explanation."⁶³ There are no verbs in the indicative statement that follows the announcement ("Hear"). The words are simply as follows: Yahweh (Lord), Elohim (God + our), Yahweh again, and *ehad* (one or alone).

The two chief interpretive questions are these: what is the logical or rhetorical relation between the first and second pairs ("Lord—our God" and "Lord—*ehad*"), and what does *ehad* mean—"the Lord is one" or "the Lord alone"? Depending on where the implicit verb ("is") is placed (or excluded) and how *ehad* is rendered, the two main interpretive options are as follows:

"The Lord (is) our God, the Lord (is) one"⁶⁴

"The Lord (is) our God, the Lord alone (one and only)."⁶⁵

Rhetorically speaking, Kraut demonstrates the likelihood that verse 4 is a dramatic example of "staircase parallelism" whereby "the second clause of the pattern not only repeats an element of the first clause but also completes the statement introduced in the first clause."⁶⁶ As a similar example, he suggests Exodus 15:6, "Your right hand, O Lord, glorious in power, your right hand, O Lord, shatters the enemy."⁶⁷ He diagrams the parallelism in his way:

---

in Deuteronomy, *waw* is translated as "therefore" or "so" in 2:4, 4:15, 7:9, and 30:19. The last of these passages (30:19–20a) is particularly instructive and resonates with 6:4–5: "I call heaven and earth to witness against you today, that I have set before you life and death, blessing and curse [indicative]. Therefore choose life, that you and your offspring may live, loving the Lord your God, obeying his voice and holding fast to him [imperative]."

62. For analysis see Kraut, "Deciphering the Shema," 582–602; Block, "How Many Is God," 195–200; Miller, "The Most Important Word," 21–29; Janzen, "On the Most Important Word," 280–300; McBride, "The Yoke of the Kingdom," 291–97.

63. Kraut, "Deciphering the Shema," 582.

64. Kraut and Janzen argue for "the Lord is one" along with the ESV, NASB, and NIV.

65. Block, Miller, and McBride favor "the Lord alone/only," as does the NRSV.

66. Kraut, "Deciphering the Shema," 591.

67. Kraut, "Deciphering the Shema," 592.

A.	your right hand, Yahweh
B.	glorious in power
A.	your right hand, Yahweh
C.	shatters the enemy

C augments and completes the ideas of A and B, adding meaning and emphasis.⁶⁸ In similar fashion, he renders Deuteronomy 6:4 like this:

A.	Yahweh
B.	our God
A.	Yahweh
C.	one (alone)

In this case, also, C enhances the significance of A and B. However, the rhetorical purpose of this construction is even more important. Kraut explains, "[The parallelism] serves to frame, heighten, and emphasize the content embedded within the verse itself, and to reinforce the importance of the message that is to follow."⁶⁹ What follows, of course, is verse 5 with its logical-ethical imperative, "You shall love the Lord your God with all your heart and with all your soul and with all your might." The staircase parallelism can be displayed in the following manner:

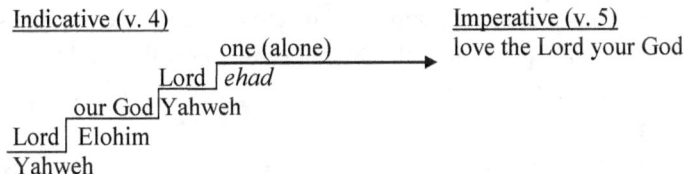

The second interpretive question is also complicated. Usually, *ehad* means (numerically) "one," but Block adduces several Old Testament examples where the significance is "unique," "only," or "alone."⁷⁰ Block enunciates two vital hermeneutical principles that guide his assessment of verse 4. First, he argues that the exception can be the rule: "However,

---

68. Other examples cited are Exod 15:3; Hos 12:6; Jer 33:2; Amos 9:5–6, as well as possibly Pss 11:4; 27:1; 40:14; 121:5; 135:13; 138:8.

69. Kraut, "Deciphering the Shema," 600. He lists other prose examples as Judg 4:18; 19:23; 2 Sam 13:12, 25; 2 Kgs 4:16.

70. Block, "How Many Is God," 199–200.

even if they [his examples] were all rejected (which is unlikely), this would still not rule out the possibility of an exceptional significance in this case."[71] The reason, he says, is theological context. So his second interpretive principle entails "moving centrifugally from the word, to the syntax of the sentence, the immediate context, the broader literary context, and finally to the canonical context."[72] According to Block, the broader setting underscores "the pervasive and fundamental demand of Deuteronomy in general and the first commandment of the Decalogue that Israel worship only Yahweh, and absolutely avoid all other spiritual allegiances."[73] As a result of his analysis, he proposes three similar possibilities for verse 4 (depending on the insertion of an implicit "is"):

> Hear, O Israel, Yahweh is our God; Yahweh alone.
> Hear, O Israel, Yahweh our God; Yahweh is the only one.
> Hear, O Israel, Yahweh our God; Yahweh is the one and only.[74]

Love Required

Thus, verse 5 specifies the expected response to the declaration in verse 4—love (*aheb*). From the perspective of ancient Near Eastern suzerainty treaties, "love" was a legal term indicating the covenantal loyalty of a vassal state. Love was a demand imposed by the superior and required a decision by the inferior: a pragmatic choice based upon careful assessment of the vassal's political, military, and economic vulnerability. Love was also a commitment not to undermine the suzerain by affiliating with opposing powers.

However, love involved an affective dimension. The reigning power attempted to win the hearts and minds of subjugated peoples through

---

71. Block, "How Many Is God," 200.

72. Block, "How Many Is God," 199. McBride ("The Yoke of the Kingdom," 292) comments, "An acceptable reading of the statement must satisfy *both* the criterion of appropriate Hebrew grammar and that of appropriate meaning in the context of Deuteronomic theology," specifically "the context of historical, political, and religious concerns to which the book of Deuteronomy was addressed" (emphasis in original).

73. Block, "How Many Is God," 201. Likewise, Miller ("The Most Important Word," 22) writes, "The alternate translation of the confession, i.e., 'our God is the Lord, the Lord alone,' clearly speaks to *the* issue of Israelite faith and the issue toward which the Prologue and the first two commandments of the Decalogue are directed" (emphasis in original).

74. Block, "How Many Is God," 196, 201.

propaganda and patronage.[75] Vassals were expected to embrace the ruling theocracy, its pantheon, and its ideology. Most became enablers who facilitated the extension of the suzerain's rule over other backward and wayward nations through conquest and annexation.

From the perspective of the Old Testament, though, covenantal love assumed similar but also contrasting dimensions. On one hand, given the divine indicative and the testimony of Israel's deliverance from Egypt, love was a demand for loyalty and obedience to the transcendent suzerain's demands. Faithfulness to Yahweh meant that Israel would not divert allegiance to other gods and their national domains. Love, therefore, entailed a rational decision to choose faithfulness over apostasy, life over death, and blessing over woe (28:1–2, 15; 30:19).

On the other hand, love also entailed an emotional aspect.[76] First, love arose from gratitude for the abundant grace bestowed on Israel as God's treasured possession. Block writes:

> The Lord, their divine Suzerain, who by grace had rescued them from the bondage of Egypt, and who by grace had called Israel to covenant relationship with Himself, and who by grace was calling on them to represent Him to the world, retained the exclusive right to define the appropriate response to the grace He had lavished on them. Total acceptance of the will of the divine Benefactor would be the correct and reasonable response.[77]

Second, love was a response in kind, a form of divine imitation.[78] The Lord had clearly demonstrated his affection for and faithfulness to Israel through their calling, deliverance, sustenance, and law (4:37; 7:13; 10:15). Moreover, he carefully planned their well-being, so that they would flourish in Canaan. He demonstrated benevolent intentionality toward Israel as their suzerain. He had saved them from bondage and did not subjugate them by brute force, unlike the nations that attacked one another for spoils and glory. Thus, Israel's duty was to mimic Yahweh's intentionality as stewards and image bearers, seeking his glory on earth and the best interests of their countrymen as a testimony to the nations (4:6).

---

75. With reference to the propaganda mechanisms and the mentality of empire of later imperial powers in the ninth to the sixth centuries BC, see Aster, "Transmission of Neo-Assyrian Claims," 1–44; Stuart, "David's Costly Flirtation with Empire," 17–53.

76. See Arnold, "The Love–Fear Antinomy," 551–69; Ackerman, "The Personal is Political," 437–58.

77. Block, "The Grace of Torah," 8.

78. O'Dowd, *Old Testament Wisdom Literature*, 45–46.

Anatomy of Love

The word "heart" (*leb*), as we have seen, denotes more than emotions and often refers to the mind.[79] Indeed, the heart functions, as it were, as an epistemic rudder for the soul. Carasik depicts the heart as the "organ of knowing and understanding."[80] It includes the mental capacity to receive, inventory, and evaluate data. When it functions well, the heart acquires critical understanding.[81] In epistemological terms, it "knows that" (i.e., facts about God and the world), "knows how" (learning in relationship), "knows why" (teleology and obligation), "knows who" (knowledge derived from and oriented to God), and "knows where" (knowledge situated by God through creation and covenant).[82] With reference to the *Shema* (in 6:4–5 and chapters 4–8 generally), "such a heart as this" discerns an essential ontological fact: there is only one God—Yahweh Elohim—and that thinking must be conditioned by covenantal love.

The term "soul" (*nepesh*) appears in the Old Testament with a range of meanings, depending on the context. As we saw earlier, *nepesh* includes the imagination and curiosity. In many settings, however, such as the *Shema*, it also refers to desire—physical, psychological, and spiritual. As such, the "soul" is associated with longing, motivation, and passion.[83] Psychologically, deepest motives (often hidden or unknown), real aspirations, and what one is willing to do (rightly and wrongly) arise from the "soul." For this reason, Paul Overland adds that "'to love God with the

---

79. Its provenance is difficult to capture in English, for as Waltke (*The Book of Proverbs*, 91) explains, "No other English word combines the complex interplay of intellect, sensibility, and will." In fact, there is no Hebrew term for "mind."

80. Carasik, *Theologies of the Mind*, 106.

81. Interestingly, Craigie comments that he rendered "with all your heart" (6:5) in "the traditional manner" and explains that his translation of 4:29 is closer to the original meaning, "seek him with all your mind" (*The Book of Deuteronomy*, 170, note 16 and 138).

82. Overland argues that Proverbs 3:1–12 draws upon the Shema of Deut 6:4–9. He writes, "The sage accompanied 'heart' in Proverbs 3 with expressions which clarify its connotation as intellect. Following the injunction 'Rely on the Lord with all your heart' the sage employed two phrases referring to intellect: 'Do not lean on your own perception' (*bina*) and 'In all your ways know (*yada*) him.' Consequently, it is best to understand 'Rely on the Lord with all your heart' as a command referring to intellect" ("Did the Sage Draw from the Shema?" 437).

83. Craigie (*The Book of Deuteronomy*, 138) also contrasted the "traditional" rendering of *nepesh* as "soul" with the original nuance as "desire."

soul' means to advance one's devotion to God beyond all longings of a mental or physical sort."[84]

"Strength" (*meod*) can be translated as "greatly," "very," or "exceedingly." But in this context, it conveys an economic nuance: stewardship of abundance, wealth, or resources. The Israelites were obligated to use all with which God had endowed them—material assets, economic prowess, physical capacity, social capital, personal gifting, and intellectual ability—for his honor and human well-being alone. Thus, loving God with all one's might meant that nothing could be withheld for egoistic or secular motives or rededicated to an illicit religious affiliation.

The threefold "all" (or "whole" *kol*) indicated that every aspect of life should be fully engaged in loving God with covenantal fidelity. To love God according to the *Shema* entailed a life dedicated to *divina imitatio*: imitating God's thoughts, motives, and beneficence in accord with creational and covenantal norms. Similarly, to love others required God-oriented thinking, desire, and conduct.

Scholars have noted, however, a phenomenological pattern associated with 6:4–5.[85] The process implies listening, learning, and application. A mind informed by revelation generated godly motivation and fostered stewardship that demonstrated love in action.[86] In other words, the *Shema* shows the centrality of the mind and how thinking covenantally impacts every area of life.[87] The mind, desire, and capacity—in that

---

84. Overland, "Did the Sage Draw from the Shema?" 429.

85. See McBride, "The Yoke of the Kingdom," 303–4; Block, "How Many Is God," 202–3.

86. By way of example, consider one of the last kings of Israel, Josiah (c. 640–609). He was the only ruler to receive God's approbation for fulfilling the demands of the Shema with the vocabulary of the Shema: "Before him there was no king like him, who turned to the Lord with all his heart and with all his soul and with all his might, according to all the Law of Moses, nor did any like him arise after him" (2 Kgs 23:25). From an early age Josiah demonstrated intellectual and motivational intentionality for the Lord (2 Chr 34:3). When the "Book of the Law" was rediscovered and Josiah heard the words of the Lord, he responded with heartfelt repentance (2 Kgs 22:11). He assembled the leaders to read the Law, and together they "renewed the covenant" (23:3). Josiah restored the Temple, reinstituted Passover, expelled corrupt officials, destroyed pagan artifacts, disrupted syncretistic practices, and provided generously from his own assets for public welfare (2 Chr 35:7).

87. McBride, Block, and Hoekema contrast popular anthropologies within evangelicalism derived from ancient Greek ideas and modern psychology. The net effect is often ignorance and anti-intellectuality. See McBride, "The Yoke of the Kingdom," 303–4; Block, "How Many Is God," 202–3; Hoekema, "The Whole Person," 203–26.

order—should be dedicated to the Lord. This principle can be illustrated by the following diagram:

mind/heart ⟹ motive/soul ⟹ capacity/might

In summary, in chapters 4–8 vassals of Yahweh's kingdom learned about their suzerain and what he expected from them intellectually and existentially. They discovered how to use their minds profitably as apprentice rulers, architects, economists, and philosophers in Israel. They learned what walking in his ways, keeping his statutes, and heeding his voice meant epistemologically. In these ways, they nurtured minds that served the one and only Lord with every motive and every resource provided to them.

CONCLUSION

At the beginning of this chapter, I quoted the medieval Christian philosopher Anselm. Below are three additional citations from Anselm that express the mindset God desired for his people in Deuteronomy 5:29, "Oh that they had such a heart as this always, to fear me and to keep all my commandments."

> What shall he do, O most exalted Lord? What shall Your servant do, anguished out of love for You and cast far away from Your face? . . . Indeed, I was made for seeing You; but not yet have I done that for which I was made. O the unhappy fate of man when he lost that for which he was made! O that hard and ominous fall![88]

> Teach me to seek You, and reveal Yourself to me as I seek; for unless You teach [me] I cannot seek You, and unless You reveal Yourself I cannot find You.[89]

> O Lord, I do not attempt to gain access to Your loftiness, because I do not at all consider my intellect to be equal to this [task]. But I yearn to understand some measure of Your truth, which my heart believes and loves. For I do not seek to understand in order to believe, but I believe in order to understand.[90]

---

88. Anselm, *Complete Philosophical and Theological Treatises*, 91.
89. Anselm, *Complete Philosophical and Theological Treatises*, 92.
90. Anselm, *Complete Philosophical and Theological Treatises*, 93.

The book of Deuteronomy teaches once again that repentance and the fear of God are the gateway to redemptive epistemology. Moses, Joshua, and Caleb knew that heeding or not heeding God's voice meant life or death, flourishing or privation, knowledge or folly. They understood that the source of everything that happened to them and all they aspired to was God. Indeed, he was the bond that held their world together and the presupposition of their worldview. For them, nothing was truly secular and no other ideology could be syncretized with the Lord's revelation. They acknowledged the covenantal imperative to listen diligently to his voice alone, since there was no justification for intellectual disloyalty.

Moses, Joshua, and Caleb recognized their cognitive situatedness as vassal-knowers. They possessed knowledge about God as Lord and acknowledged that all knowing was subject to God as Lord. They learned how and what to think because of finitude and fallenness, as well as creation and covenant. They became astute observers and interpreters of their environment. They were not naive about the spiritual and cultural antithesis that Canaan represented. They were, in fact, theologically sophisticated. They became "everyday theologians," for they realized that ignorance and anti-intellectualism were covenantally unacceptable and spiritually dangerous.[91]

Intellectually speaking, Israel possessed a North Star. They knew in which direction they should orient themselves ontologically. They possessed a Global Positioning System by means of the covenant, providing a path to their destination. They also possessed a gyroscope to maintain equilibrium amidst turbulence and uncertainty. The fear of the Lord balanced their minds amidst disorienting messages from the other nations. Most importantly, they perceived the intrinsic value of the epistemological map provided to guide them on their spiritual pilgrimage—Scripture. Yahweh Elohim told them, "You shall not add to the word that I command you, nor take from it, that you may keep the commandments of the Lord your God that I command you" (4:2).

---

91. Vanhoozer, *Everyday Theology*, 15–21.

10

A Learning Community

"Blessed is the man who walks not in the counsel of the wicked, nor stands in the way of sinners, nor sits in the seat of scoffers; but his delight is in the law of the Lord, and on his law he meditates day and night."

—Psalm 1:1–2

WE HAVE SEEN THROUGHOUT this book that the noetic effects of sin are pervasive and profound. But we are also learning that we should and can think as creatures made in God's image—by grace.

In the last chapter, we considered the mindset that God longs for in his people: "such a heart [mind] as this" (5:29). In this chapter, we examine the pedagogical infrastructure that produced godly fear and righteousness. To put it another way, the educational strategy depicted in Deuteronomy fosters the mentality expressed in Psalm 1: "His delight is in the law of the Lord, and on his law he meditates day and night."

This chapter also explores the potential for future understanding, especially after sin and repentance. In fact, the prospect of future knowledge is the purpose and plan of God. One day the impact of sin upon the mind and motivation will be reversed. Our brains, body, and soul will completely serve and honor the Lord, because knowing God is the *telos* of creation. Habakkuk 2:14 declares, "For the earth will be filled with the knowledge of the glory of the Lord as the waters cover the sea."

But first, this chapter deals with the specter of exilic epistemology in Deuteronomy. The second section of this chapter surveys the teaching, learning, and remembering functions in Israel. The third section summarizes the intellectual possibility of future knowledge and faith.

FOOLISH AND SENSELESS PEOPLE

Deuteronomy also depicts a mindset that does *not* listen to God's voice, obey his commands or fear the Lord. This is exilic epistemology: a way of thinking that does not fulfill the *Shema*. It does not serve God with the intellect, sanctified desire, or eager stewardship according to his royal norms.

This faulty outlook prevailed among the first generation that had fled Egypt by God's mighty hand. Due to unbelief, they did not follow his orders and enter the Promised Land (Deut 1:26). Even worse, they reasoned falsely ("murmured") about God's motives and declared audaciously, "Because the Lord *hated* us he has brought us out of the land of Egypt, to give us into the hand of the Amorites, to *destroy* us" (v. 27). God calls those who thought in this way "this evil generation" (1:35).

Similarly, at the end of the book the Lord predicted that the generations to come would embrace unsound reasoning, resulting in idolatry. He told Moses, "Behold, you are about to lie down with your fathers. Then this people will rise and whore after the foreign gods among them in the land that they are entering, and they will forsake me and break my covenant that I have made with them" (31:16). Yahweh described these future apostates with epistemological terminology: a "crooked and twisted generation" (32:5), "foolish and senseless people" (v. 6), and a "nation void of counsel" with "no understanding in them" (v. 28).

Thus, Deuteronomy provides a profile of those who did not possess "such a mind as this." To this end, three strands of data depict the rebel's mindset: vocabulary and idioms, erroneous reasoning, and the covenantal curse on unrighteous thought.

Vocabulary and Idioms

The book of Deuteronomy depicts many Israelites who "would not go up" (1:26), would "not believe" (9:23), and would "not obey the voice of the Lord" (8:20). They were "stubborn" (9:6), "murmured" (1:26, against the Lord) and acted "presumptuously" (1:43). They did not endure as followers but "turned aside" (9:12) from the commandments, left "the way" (5:33), and "abandoned the covenant" (29:25).

Furthermore, those who did not pay attention forgot God (4:23). They put the Lord to "the test" (6:16), did what is "right in [their] own eyes" (12:8), inquired about forbidden religions (12:30), harbored "unworthy thoughts" (15:9), and "presume[d] to speak a word in my name" (18:20). They applied their minds to nefarious ends, such as "doing what is evil" (4:25), "covet[ing]" (7:25), "pervert[ing] justice" (16:19), "showing partiality" (16:19), accepting a bribe that "blinds the eyes" (16:19), "act[ing] dishonestly" (25:16), and "mislead[ing]" (27:18). In addition, idioms of the heart indicate a skewed mentality: forgetting the lessons they learned and miracles they experienced by letting them "depart from [their] heart" (4:9), pride and a "heart lifted up" (17:20), and a "grudging" heart that does not share (15:10).

Non-listeners are attracted to idolatry (30:17). The Lord said about the people, "I know what they are inclined to do" (31:21). They would learn about and be enticed by other gods. Their misplaced curiosity would produce "eyes" that look "to heaven" in idolatry (4:19). Their hearts would be "deceived" and "turn away" to foreign deities (11:16). Concretely, they would act "corruptly" by making a "carved image" (4:16), "plant a tree as an Asherah" (16:21), "set up a pillar" (16:22), and "practice divination" (18:10).

Twisted Reasoning

Exilic epistemology is also characterized by reasoning untethered to God's revelation and decontextualized from creation and covenant. It is unrestrained and delusional. The following instances of self- and groupthink typify minds that do not fear God or heed his instructions. They do not interpret reality with a self-awareness conditioned by finitude and fallenness.

As we saw, the first generation assumed incorrectly that Yahweh "hated" them and desired to "destroy" the Israelites. They reasoned in the same way as Pharaoh, whose myopic mindset and twisted worldview caused him to see Yahweh as an enemy. Many Hebrews who escaped Egypt geographically were still enslaved by Egypt's mentality and hostility to the Lord. Despite Moses' counterargument about the Lord's miraculous care for them in the exodus (1:29, 33), they maintained their stubborn and ungodly outlook.

Similarly, four occurrences in Deuteronomy of the idiom "in the heart" express faulty but unspoken thinking. Carasik explains that the expression "is found extensively in contexts that indicate disregard or defiance of God."[1] In 8:17, the Lord warned the people about self-delusionary thinking linked to prosperity. He said, "Beware lest you say in your heart, 'My power and the might of my hand have gotten me this wealth.'" He also warned them against the error of self-congratulatory military prowess or moral virtue: "Do not say in your heart, after the Lord your God has thrust them out before you, 'It is because of my righteousness that the Lord has brought me in to possess this land'" (9:4). He forewarned them about "an unworthy thought in your heart" that would foster stinginess and reason, "'The seventh year, the year of release is near,' and your eye look grudgingly on your poor brother, and you give him nothing" (15:9). And most seriously, he urged utmost vigilance about detecting those "whose heart is turning" to idolatry, for they were a "root bearing poisonous and bitter fruit" in the community. Such people were self-delusional and deceived others. The deluded man "blesses himself in his heart, saying, 'I shall be safe, though I walk in the stubbornness of my heart'" (29:18-19).

Indeed, an undisciplined and impulsive imagination not hemmed in by the covenant leads to disaster. In 12:30, the Lord told the Israelites, "Do not inquire about their gods, saying, 'How did these nations serve their gods?—that I also may do the same.'" Similarly, in chapter 13 he demanded that they not even consider "a prophet or a dreamer of dreams" who entices them by saying, "Let us go after other gods," even if their proclamation is accompanied by a supernatural "sign or a wonder" (vv. 1-2).

A Covenantal Curse on Unrighteous Thought

Because of their chronic and systemic refusal to acknowledge God's voice through Moses, Israel suffered dystopian consequences. Deuteronomy 28:16-68 delineates in great detail the full dimensions of the judgment that will cause the nation's demise. Particularly telling, however, are the epistemological implications expressed in verses 28 and 29a: "The Lord

1. Carasik, *Theologies of the Mind*, 116, 118.

will strike you with madness and blindness and confusion of mind, and you shall grope at noonday, as the blind grope in darkness."

The verb "strike" (*nakah*) appears often in the Old Testament in scenes of divine warfare where "the Lord" is the subject. The terms "madness" (*shiggaon*) and "blindness" (*ivvaron*) appear rarely in the Old Testament. "Confusion" (*timmahon*) occurs only twice. Because of the rarity of each term, it is difficult to discern their significance in Deuteronomy. However, all three words appear in Zechariah 12:4, and their use in that setting provides an indication of their significance in Deuteronomy. Zechariah 12:4 describes a scene of judgment against Israel's enemy and states, "On that day, declares the Lord, I will strike (*nakah*) every horse with panic (*timmahon*) and its rider with madness (*shiggaon*) . . . when I strike every horse of the peoples with blindness (*ivvaron*)."

The vocabulary indicates divinely initiated dysfunction and cognitive breakdown due to aggression against Israel. The animals were not able to receive or interpret sensory data correctly. The riders could not control the horses due to bewilderment and panic. The result was disorientation, inability to function properly, and ensuing disaster. Obviously, those who cannot see are most vulnerable at a moment of danger and chaos.[2]

The phenomenological impact of "confusion," "madness," and "blindness" is portrayed in Deuteronomy and Zechariah as groping in darkness. Groping entails epistemological uncertainty and psychological distress. In other passages, to "grope" (*mashash*) depicts Isaac's hapless investigation of Jacob's forearms to determine his true identity (Gen 27:22) and Egypt's state of disorientation in the darkness imposed by Yahweh (Exod 10:21). In Job 5:14, groping is linked to the failure of those who concoct unrighteous schemes. In Job 12:25, it is associated with listless wandering and the stupor of drunkenness.

Extrapolating back from Zechariah to Deuteronomy, the mind under judgment is depicted as a battlefield. Not listening to God through Moses (and, by extension, through Torah) would produce a negative impact. Israel would experience stupor, disorientation, and dysfunctionality because they did not acknowledge God's transcendent wisdom and

---

2. "Blindness" is linked to a state of culpable ignorance of God and his ways in Isaiah. The "blind" (*ivver*) are "prisoners who sit in darkness" (Isa 42:7) and "without knowledge" (56:10). They "sees many things, but does not observe them; his ears are open, but he does not hear" (42:20). They "grope" and appear as "dead men" (59:10). Zephaniah declares that the blind "have sinned against the Lord" (1:17).

authority. In essence, the mind ceased to function properly with reference to God and revelation. We learned in chapter 7 that this is punitive epistemology.

Knowing God and his law was the key to understanding everything, so minimizing his teaching by forgetting or syncretism inevitably produced error and folly. In Deuteronomy 28:28–29a, God promised to impose noetic dysfunction as punishment for covenantal disobedience. As a result, Israel would not and could not wisely fulfill their vice-regency. In fact, they suffered reversal in all its social, spiritual, ethical, and intellectual aspects.

LEARNING TOGETHER

Deuteronomy describes God's solutions to two problems that Israel confronted as they renewed the covenant in Moab. The short-term issue concerned Moses' imminent death. How would the nation hear from the Lord going forward? Who would lead them in battle? God's answer was threefold: a written text, prophecy, and new leadership for the upcoming conquest (Joshua).

The long-term problem concerned the nation's viability through future generations. First, there were negative conditions to avoid so that they could survive as the Lord's people. A prominent danger was arrogance and its impact, expressed by the conditional term "lest." For instance, they should always listen to the Lord's instructions lest they suffer defeat (1:42). They should guard their minds with care, lest they deceive themselves with misplaced confidence (8:17) or incite the "anger of the Lord" due to misdirected worship (6:15; see also 4:16; 7:25; 11:16; 29:18). Similarly, forgetfulness was an ever-present challenge. They might "forget the covenant" with their ancestors (4:31), "forget" what their "eyes have seen" in the exodus (4:9), or even overlook the Lord himself "by not keeping his commandments" (8:11).

Second, there were positive conditions to maintain in order to flourish in the Promised Land. They should "choose life" (*chay*) so that they would flourish. If so, God would "take delight in prospering" them (30:9) because of their covenantal fidelity. Life was also associated with a successful conquest of the Promised Land ("possession," 4:1), population growth ("multiply," 8:1), prolongation in Canaan ("live long in the land," 11:9), peace and security ("rest from all your enemies," 12:10), and divine blessing (30:16). Through obedience, things would "go well" (*yatab*) for the nation and their offspring ("children," 4:40).[3] Likewise, God's abundant goodness (*tob*) would prevail in the "good land," and so would abundant "prosperity" from their divine benefactor.[4]

Third, societal infrastructure must be established to practice righteousness in accordance with the law. Economic, legal, and social norms were stipulated. Rules for the conquest of Canaan and relations with the peoples of the land were laid down. Institutions such as the priest, king, and prophet, as well as public rituals, were codified in the covenant, especially in chapters 12–27. An educational system was established to teach Israel's special identity and mission to future generations.

The long-term sustainability of the nation, therefore, centered on three essential conditions—the acquisition of knowledge, cultivation of a proper disposition toward the Lord, and the development of individual and communal disciplines. Israel was expected to maintain an exclusive relationship with their suzerain according to his covenant. They must develop a ready disposition to learn and obey "the words of this law in a book" (31:24). They must actualize Israel's history of redemption personally and corporately. And they must develop discernment to navigate the cultural milieu of the ancient Near East.

Teaching

The transition from oral to written revelation occurred in two basic stages.[5] First, God spoke and then wrote the Ten Commandments (5:22). Likewise, Moses first taught and then wrote God's law (Torah). The term "book" (*seper*) is associated directly with Moses' ministry in 31:24: "Moses had finished writing the words of this law in a book (*seper*) to the very end." Moses' teaching is also called "the book of this law" (28:61) and "curses of the covenant written in this Book of the Law" (29:21). Especially noteworthy is 31:26 since it affirms the canonical status of the prophet's words from the beginning: "Take this Book of the Law and put it by the side of the ark of the covenant of the Lord your God, that it

---

3. Occurrences of *yatab* include 5:16, 29; 6:3; 8:16; 12:25; 22:7; 30:5.

4. Occurrences of *tob* include 1:25; 3:25 (twice); 4:21–22; 6:10; 8:7; 9:6; 10:13; 11:17; 23:6; 26:11; 28:11–12; 30:9 (twice).

5. Block provides the details of the process in "Recovering the Voice of Moses," 385–408.

may be there for a witness against you." Furthermore, the use of written Scripture was enjoined as a reminder on the "doorposts" of homes and at city "gates" (6:20; 11:18–21), on memorial stones (27:1–8), and for a future king's personal reading (17:18–20).

The Torah, broadly speaking, comprised the "covenant" (27 times), "commandments" (32), "statutes" (29), "word(s)" (41), "rules" (19), "law" (22), and "testimonies" (3).[6] Teaching (*lamad*) the Torah was of paramount importance for Israel's intellectual, ethical, and religious well-being.[7] Carasik says, "The idea that the laws must be the basic content of the mind, to be maintained through the ages by transmission from one generation to the next, is fundamental to Deuteronomy."[8] Moses taught as a divine commission (4:1, 5, 14; 5:31; 6:1). Parents were commanded to teach their children (4:10; 11:19; 31:12). Priests supervised the education of kings (17:18), addressed the people (20:2), decided legal disputes (19:17), and cared for the Book of the Law (31:9). The origin, content, mediation, and application of God's instruction are summarized below. (The number of occurrences of each term is indicated in parenthesis. God refers to his instruction by the pronoun "my," and third-person references are "his" and "of the Lord.")

Divine Origin	Content	Moses' Mediation	Israel's Application
"My"	covenant (2), words (2), teaching (2), commandments (2), speech (1)	explain (1), command (32)	learn (7), teach (4)
"His"	"covenant (3), words (1), voice (8), statutes (9), commandments (13), ways (5), rules (2), testimonies (6)	teach (5), speak (5), write (6)	write (5), read (2), remember (13)
"Of the Lord"	commandments (7), word (2), justice (1), statutes (1), command (2), covenant (4), voice (9)	recite (1), command (1)	not forget (2)

6. Three related terms are "judgment" (1), "discipline" (2), and "work" (1).

7. *Lamad* is translated as both "teach" (in 4:1, 5, 10, 14: 5:31; 6:1; 11:19; 20:18; 31:19, 22) and "learn" (in 4:10; 5:1; 14:23; 17:19; 31:12–13).

8. Carasik, *Theologies of the Mind*, 187.

Finally, the acquisition of knowledge was often expressed with idioms of the heart (mind). Mental focus was expressed by the phrase "with all of your heart" (4:29; 6:5; 10:12; 11:13; 13:3; 26:16; 30:2, 6, 10). Keeping the law at the forefront of one's consciousness was conveyed by the expressions "lay it to your heart" (4:39), "on your heart" (6:6), "know then in your heart" (8:5), and "circumcise therefore the foreskin of your heart" (10:16). Similarly, Israel was urged to "seek the Lord" with "all your heart" (4:29) and "turn to the Lord" with "all your heart" (30:10).

Learning

The principal intent of Moses' instruction was that the generations to come would "learn to fear the Lord" (4:10; 5:29; 6:1–2; 14:23; 17:19; 31:12, 13). A godly outlook entailed a reverent posture before "his glory and greatness" (5:24) and a ready disposition to learn from him. Yahweh told Moses, "Gather the people to me, that I may let them hear my words, so that they may learn to fear me all the days that they live on the earth, and that they may teach their children so" (4:10). Godly reverence could be learned and was crucial to their survival.

To fear God was an acknowledgment that Yahweh Elohim was the ultimate and exclusive point of reference for all knowledge and every deed. Gerhard Von Rad associated Hebrew epistemology with the fear of the Lord:

> Israel attributes to the fear of God, to belief in God, a highly important function in respect of human knowledge . . . that effective knowledge of God is the only thing that puts a man into a right relationship with the objects of his perception, that it enables him to ask questions more pertinently, to take stock of relationships more effectively and generally to have a better awareness of circumstances.[9]

From a positive point of view, godly fear presumed theological understanding provided through written revelation. The six passages that demand instruction concerning the fear of the Lord presuppose a transcendent thinker who communicated with Israelites created in his image. In 4:10, the Lord gathered his people to hear "my words." In 5:29 and 6:1, he taught the "commandment" through Moses. In 14:23, the

---

9. See Von Rad, *Wisdom in Ancient Israel*, 67–69.

Lord revealed "his name." And in 17:19 and 31:12, he communicated the "words of this law."

From a negative point of view, Deuteronomy echoes Proverbs 3:7, "Be not wise in your own eyes; fear the Lord, and turn away from evil." Negative epistemic injunctions include "do not inquire about their gods" (Deut 12:30), "[do] not listen to the words of that prophet" who leads people astray (13:3), and "[do] not learn to follow the abominable practices of those nations" (18:9).[10] In addition (as noted earlier), the idiom "in your heart (mind)" coupled with a thinker who does not fear God denoted erroneous reasoning (8:17; 9:4; 15:9).

Fearing God also involved an elenctic dimension. Spiritual and ideological discernment was essential, especially amidst the alluring religious bazaar in the ancient Near East.[11] The expression "fear of the Lord" presupposed a polemical stance vis-à-vis Canaanite spirituality.

They could, for instance, embrace a functional pluralism whereby the Lord assumed his place within the pantheon of the Canaanite El, "the father of the gods." Or they could adopt an adversarial henotheism that boasted of Yahweh's reign, though limited to his people and their land alone. Both options, however, diminished God's supremacy as revealed in his covenant and creation. Both alternatives employed an unwarranted extrapolation from plurality to ontological perspectivalism. And either preference presumed an autonomous Israelite who determined what was cosmologically valid or chose whatever persuasion was preferable—with the assumption of impunity for doing so. All such endeavors were prohibited by the First Commandment and the fear of the Lord.

Finally, to fear God presumed an epistemological pedagogy, in particular among parents and royalty. The first citation below appears before and after the *Shema* (6:4–5) and concerns the instruction of children. The second provides guidelines for future kings. Consider first what both classes have in common (in italics).

> Now this is the commandment—the statutes and the rules—
> that the Lord your God commanded me to teach you, that you

---

10. Other negative demands with epistemic import include "You shall not be partial in judgment" (1:17), "not add to the word that I command you, nor take from it" (4:2), "not forget how you provoked the Lord your God to wrath" (9:7), and "not turn aside from the verdict that they declare to you" (17:11).

11. See Walton, *Ancient Near Eastern Thought*; Finegan, "Canaanite Religion" in *Myth and Mystery*, 119–54; Block, "Other Religions in Old Testament Theology" and "No Other Gods" in *The Gospel According to Moses*, 200–71.

may do them in the land to which you are going over, to possess it, *that you may fear the Lord your God*, you and your son and your son's son, by keeping all his statutes and his commandments.... And these words that I command you today shall be on your heart. You shall teach them diligently to your children, and shall talk of them when you sit in your house, and when you walk by the way, and when you lie down, and when you rise. You shall bind them as a sign on your hand, and they shall be as frontlets between your eyes. You shall write them on the doorposts of your house and on your gates. (6:1–2, 6–9)

And when he sits on the throne of his kingdom, he shall write for himself in a book a copy of this law, approved by the Levitical priests. And it shall be with him, and he shall read in it all the days of his life, *that he may learn to fear the Lord his God* by keeping all the words of this law and these statutes, and doing them, that his heart may not be lifted up above his brothers, and that he may not turn aside from the commandment, either to the right hand or to the left, so that he may continue long in his kingdom, he and his children, in Israel. (17:18–20)

God's intention was that both parties might learn to fear the Lord as their anchor in life and their basis for long-term viability. The Lord wanted them to perform his commandments and promised that if they did so, they would thrive in the land.[12] He also intended that future generations might also learn to fear God by learning his law and practicing it.[13]

Moreover, both parents and royalty were called to intellectual intentionality. Moses told the former in verse 6, "Let these things that I command you today be on your mind."[14] They were commanded to "teach diligently" (v. 7) by discussing the law and its implications at all times and with applications in every sphere of life, and even to reproduce divine script for personal use (v. 9). Likewise, the king was required to "write for himself in a book a copy of this law" (v. 18) under the tutelage of the

---

12. Craigie (*The Book of Deuteronomy*, 170) comments, "The commandments, which provided the framework... were to be 'upon the heart'—that is, the people were to think on them and meditate about them, so that obedience would not be a matter of formal legalism, but a response based upon understanding."

13. A focus on future generations appears often in Deuteronomy: "children" (4:9–10; 11:19; 29:29; 31:12–13; 32:46) and "sons" (6:2, 20, 21).

14. The use of "mind" is how Carasik renders "heart" in the ESV. He suggests the same cognitive nuance appears in 4:39, 8:5, 11:18, and 30:1. See Carasik, *Theologies of the Mind*, 211 and note 110.

priests. It was to be readily accessible and contemplated "all the days of his life" (v. 19).

Second, consider what instruction is particular to each group. Parents were commanded to "teach diligently" (*shanan*).[15] This verb appears nine times in the Old Testament. Three times the term refers to sharpening or sharp objects, such as "your arrows are sharp" (Ps 45:5; Isa 5:28) and "I [the Lord] sharpen my flashing sword" in judgment (Deut 32:41). Six times, however, *shanan* assumes a metaphorical nuance, representing words that are "sharpened" and that "sharpen" the mind.[16] And in one passage, the term applies to the forceful use of words for the formation of the intellect: "You shall teach them diligently (*shanan*) to your children" (Deut 6:7). The immediate context indicates mental sharpening through repetition and practiced reasoning.[17]

Clearly, Deuteronomic pedagogy was more than mere repetition or rote memorization.[18] Knowing what and how to think was imperative. Parents, together with the supportive community, taught young people a hermeneutic of reality based upon their ontological assumptions. To accomplish this, the words of revelation were taught incisively to the youth so that they learned how to infer, deduce, and discern. They practiced how to reason from and with Scripture (intertextuality). Indeed, just as

---

15. There is debate about the meaning of this verb. Does it mean "to sharpen/whet" or "to repeat"? Craigie (*The Book of Deuteronomy*, 170, note 17) argues that the "meaning of the verb has been clarified by Ugaritic" in favor of "repeat." The NSRV and CEB render it as "recite," the NABRE as "keep repeating." Other versions lean towards "sharpen" in a metaphorical sense: "teach diligently" in the ESV, EHV, and NSAB or "impress on" in the NIV. In this verse, *shanan* is in the Piel, indicating intensification provided by the parent, who is teaching. Whetting objects, such as weapons, requires repetition.

16. Four times they are weaponized as "tongues like swords (*shanan*)" (Ps 45:4) or "those who whet (*shanan*) their tongues like swords, who aim bitter words like arrows" (Ps 64:3; see also 140:3 and Prov 25:18). Once, the term applies to negative self-talk: "when my soul was embittered, when I was pricked (*shanan*) in heart" (Ps 73:21).

17. Regarding the enigmatic verse 8 ("You shall bind them as a sign on your hand, and they shall be as frontlets between your eyes"), the injunction implies intellectual and ethical intentionality. Craigie (*The Book of Deuteronomy*, 171) writes, "Whether taken literally or metaphorically, the signs described in vv. 8–9 indicate that the individual (v. 8), his home, and his community (v. 9) were to be distinguished in their character by obedience to the commandments as a response of love for God." See also Block, *Deuteronomy*, 184–85; Overland, "Did the Sage Draw from the Shema?" 427–28, 436–37.

18. See Isbell, "Deuteronomy's Definition of Jewish Learning."

the words of the Lord cut deeply, so young people acquired intellectual skills to sharply perceive Israel's place in Canaan.

Deuteronomy's holistic teaching about fearing God was also apparent in its many didactic modalities and methods. In addition to verbal repetition and observation, youth learned, for example, from questions and answers (4:32–40), negative examples (1:19–37, 41–46; 3:21–26; 9:7–9, 13–14; 11:5–6), and positive examples (2:1–3:20; 5:23–29; 11:2–4). They discovered hypothetical scenarios (foils) to avoid (7:10–12, 17; 8:10–14, 17–18; 9:4–6; 12:30). They learned about prayer and intercession from Moses (9:18–19, 25–29; 10:10–11). They actualized Israel's story by private and public confession (6:20–25; 26:5–10, 13–15). Through public ritual they witnessed and re-enacted aspects of their covenantal relation with Yahweh (16:1–17; 27:14–26). And they heard the law recited on a periodic basis through public reading (31:10–13) and even in song (32:1–43). As Brent A. Strawn says, "All of space and time is to be marked by Deuteronomy and its 'words.'"[19]

Regarding the king, the law of God also "cut" deeply and "sharpened" the mind incisively.[20] In whatever area of consideration, the law clarified, distinguished, and set priorities. Learning to fear the Lord by diligently listening to his word developed in the king a penetrating outlook vis-à-vis himself, Israel, and the surrounding nations.[21] Johnson explains, "The Torah of YHWH is to act as guiding instruction, leading Israel toward a way of being in the world that fosters discernment."[22]

Let us now read a second passage about the king:

> When you come to the land that the Lord your God is giving you, and you possess it and dwell in it and then say, "I will set a king over me, like all the nations that are around me," you may indeed set a king over you whom the Lord your God will choose. One from among your brothers you shall set as king over you. You may not put a foreigner over you, who is not your brother. Only he must not acquire many horses for himself or cause the people to return to Egypt in order to acquire many horses, since the Lord has said to you, "You shall never return that way again."

---

19. Strawn, *The Old Testament Is Dying*, 198.

20. Though the term *shanan* ("teach diligently") does not appear in the law concerning a future king, surely the concept is present.

21. See Block, "The Burden of Leadership," 259–78; Goswell, "The Shape of Kingship in Deut 17," 169–81; Dutcher-Walls, "The Circumscription of the King," 601–16.

22. Johnson, *Knowledge by Ritual*, 164.

And he shall not acquire many wives for himself, lest his heart turn away, nor shall he acquire for himself excessive silver and gold. (17:14–17)

Note the presumption of fallenness and finitude in this passage. (The king's heart tends to "turn away" in self-pleasure (v. 17), be "lifted up" in pride (v. 20), and "turn aside" in apostasy (v. 20). He is highly susceptible to acquisitiveness and to illegitimately claiming "for himself" (three times) the trappings of power: wealth, women, and status (vv. 16–17). He is prone to forget his election by God (v. 15) and suffer from self-exaltation over fellow Israelites ("brothers," vv. 15, 20). He might even contemplate a "return to Egypt" for security reasons and thus lead the people back to slavery (v. 16). Most of all, he clearly lacks knowledge and piety, since he must "learn" reverence and needs continuous reinforcement (v. 19). A "copy of this law" (v. 18) must be "with him" for study "all the days of his life" (v. 19).

Moreover, the vassal king under Yahweh must not accumulate "horses," which enabled chariot warfare (v. 16). He must not accumulate "wives" (or harems), since they were a means of diplomacy and brought harmful religious influence (v. 17a). He must not seek "excessive" wealth, commonly received through taxation, servitude, and pillage (v. 17b).[23] Undoubtedly, the regulation concerning the king in Deuteronomy stands in contrast with the prevailing religious-political norms of the ancient Near East. Gregory Grossman writes, "The role of the Israelite king is circumscribed in ways that exemplify the teaching of Deuteronomy."[24] For this reason, copying the Torah under priestly supervision signified the

---

23. Hazony (*The Philosophy of Hebrew Scripture*, 153) summarizes the pitfalls of seeking a king "like all the nations that are around me" (v. 14) with respect to both Canaanite city-states and later imperial empires: "For the warning against horses is obviously aimed against maintaining very large standing armies of the kind needed for waging constant warfare. The warning against multiple wives is, similarly, aimed at too great an interest in foreign alliances, of which the accumulating of high-born foreign wives was an important instrument; as well as preventing the kingdom from being drawn into endless intrigues whose source is the ruler's sexual predations and the disputed lines of succession that result. And the warning against the hoarding of gold was aimed against a regime of heavy taxation, impressments, and conquests, such as would be necessary to pay for many horses and many wives at the people's expense. If we are to state this simply, the Law of the King was laid down to prohibit just the way of life that was characteristic of the great imperial states of the Bible."

24. Grossman, "The Shape of Kingship in Deut 17," 172.

king's submission to the covenant.[25] It also signified a mind disciplined by revelation.

Verses 19 and 20 provide four reasons (personal and corporate) for doing so: "that he may learn to fear the Lord his God," "that his heart may not be lifted up above his brothers," "that he may not turn aside from the commandment," and "so that he may continue long in his kingdom, he and his children, in Israel." Block calls the pious king an "exemplary Israelite" and the "embodiment of covenant fidelity," who learned to fear the Lord and was worthy of imitation.[26] Ideally, by learning to fear God, therefore, the king developed discernment in the midst of competing religiosities and political systems. He distinguished between good and evil practices and ideas. And he developed a vigilant mindset that knew where to preserve limits and where to extend boundaries. In short, he gained wisdom (Prov 1:7).

Remembering

Remembrance was enjoined as a sacred duty and intellectual imperative. The verb "remember" (*zakar*) appears with reference to redemptive history, especially the events of the exodus. Moses wrote, "You shall remember that you were a slave in the land of Egypt, and the Lord your God brought you out from there with a mighty hand and an outstretched arm" (5:15; see also 7:18; 15:15; 16:3, 12; 24:9, 18, 22). Likewise, Israel was to remember always the obedience and disobedience of their wilderness experience (8:2; 9:7; 25:17).

Remembering also situated Israel within its patriarchal history as an interpretive framework. The divine suzerain was now fulfilling the covenant made with the patriarchs, "See, I have set the land before you. Go in and take possession of the land that the Lord swore to your fathers, to Abraham, to Isaac, and to Jacob, to give to them and to their offspring after them" (1:8). References to "your/our/their fathers" are abundant in Deuteronomy (forty-seven times). The names Abraham, Isaac, and Jacob are mentioned five times, land twenty-five times, and "promise" five times. Terminology associated with Abraham's pact occurs thirty-two

---

25. See Block, "The Burden of Leadership," 272.

26. Block, "The Burden of Leadership," 276. Similarly, Grossman ("The Shape of Kingship in Deut 17," 173–74) describes the pious king as a "model Israelite" and "archetypical reader."

times ("covenant," "sworn," "oath," "love," "steadfast love," "confirm"). The language of grace and election ("give," "chose") appears twenty times.

In fact, remembrance placed the Promised Land within a cosmic story. On one hand, the "new garden" (Canaan) was depicted in terms of God's primeval garden, Eden. Canaan was a land of blessing (1:11; 7:13), where God "will not leave you or destroy you" (4:31), will "show you mercy and have compassion on you" (13:17), and most significantly will "establish you today as his people" and "be your God" (29:13). In the new Eden, Israel would thrive, for it was a "good land" (1:35) of "milk and honey" (6:3; 11:9; 26:15; 27:3; 31:20), where they would multiply (1:11; 8:1; 10:22; 11:21; 13:17; 30:5) and enjoy abundant prosperity (8:18; 28:11; 30:5, 9). The lexical and thematic connections between Genesis 1–2 and the Promised Land are clear enough that William J. Dumbrell comments, "One can hardly escape the impression that what is being depicted through such reference is Eden recaptured, paradise restored."[27]

On the other hand, Deuteronomy portrays the first generation's failure to enter the Promised Land as a recapitulation of Adam's sin in Genesis 3.[28] Their unbelief echoed Adam and Eve's refusal to acknowledge God's voice. Moses depicted the failure of the first generation as a foil to underscore what the second generation certainly must avoid. As they renewed the covenant and were about to enter the land, he told them urgently, in effect, "Do not repeat the same disastrous mistake as your fathers, who chose death and evil. Instead, embrace life and good. Listen to the Lord. Trust him."

Moses recounted the fateful moment when the nation refused to enter the Promised Land in Deuteronomy 1:19–40 and previously in Numbers 13–14. The account in Deuteronomy is shorter but adds several important details. It also presupposes that its listeners already knew the story in Numbers. The following summary depicts the pertinent aspects of both accounts.[29]

Moses told them, "You have come to the hill country of the Amorites, which the Lord our God is giving us. See, the Lord your God has set the land before you. Go up, take possession, as the Lord, the God of your

---

27. Dumbrell, *Covenant and Creation*, 120.

28. Johnson outlines connections between Genesis 1–3 and Deuteronomy 1, 4, and 28–30 in *Epistemology and Biblical Theology*, 88–94.

29. See Condie, "Narrative Features of Numbers 13–14," 123–37; Miller, "The Wilderness Journey in Deuteronomy," 50–68; Alster, "Narrative Surprise in Biblical Parallels," 475–80.

fathers, has told you. Do not fear or be dismayed" (Deut 1:20–21; Num 13:2–3). Moses sent a team of twelve to reconnoiter the place and people. He told them what to look for and how to evaluate what they saw. He said, "See what the land is, and whether the people who dwell in it are strong or weak, whether they are few or many, and whether the land that they dwell in is good or bad, and whether the cities that they dwell in are camps or strongholds, and whether the land is rich or poor, and whether there are trees in it or not" (Num 13:18–20). From a tactical perspective, they observed that the residents were indeed "strong" and "many," and that their towns were fortified. On the other hand, they saw that the land was "good," "rich," and verdant.

Their initial and partial report was positive, for they testified that Canaan "flows with milk and honey" (Num 13:27) and that "It is a good land that the Lord is giving us" (Deut 1:25).[30] No doubt, Moses expected a realistic but positive reckoning, based on what Yahweh had done for them in Egypt (Exod 3:8, 17; 14:13–14, 19). No doubt, he expected that they would reason from their awareness that "The Lord has promised good to Israel" (Num 10:29). Certainly, he hoped that the people would concur with Caleb's positive recommendation, "Let us go up at once and occupy it, for we are well able to overcome it" (Num 13:30).

But instead, a dispute broke out. Ten spies interpreted the data differently from Caleb and Joshua. They countered, "We are *not* able to go up against the people, for they are stronger than we are" (Num 13:31b), and they added this embellishment: "We seemed to ourselves like grasshoppers, and so we seemed to them" (v. 33b). Their "bad report" (Num 13:32) made the people's "heart melt" (Deut 1:28). That night they lamented their pitiful fate and "wept" with dread regarding the future (Num 14:1). They "grumbled" (or "murmured," Deut 1:27) against their leaders. Moreover, they imputed a malevolent motive to the Lord, reasoning, "Because the Lord hated us he has brought us out of the land of Egypt, to give us into the hand of the Amorites, to destroy us" (Deut 1:27). As a result, they conceived an alternative plan. They planned to kill their current leadership (Num 14:10) and choose someone else (v. 4).

---

30. The idiom "milk and honey" appears numerous times, which indicates its significance (Exod 3:8, 17; 13:5; 33:3; Lev 20:24; Num 13:27; 14:8; 16:13–14; Deut 6:3; 11:9; 26:9, 15; 27:3; 31:20; Josh 5:6; Jer 11:5; 32:22; Ezek 20:6, 15). For a social-economic analysis of the term, see Levine, "The Land of Milk and Honey," 43–57. For a possible elenctic purpose contra Baal, see Stern, "The Origin and Significance of 'The Land Flowing with Milk and Honey,'" 554–57.

Moreover, they foolishly determined that it would be better "to go back to Egypt" (v. 4).

Caleb pleaded with them and highlighted the very positive nature of the land and the very vulnerable state of its inhabitants: "Only do not rebel against the Lord. And do not fear the people of the land, for they are bread for us. Their protection is removed from them, and the Lord is with us; do not fear them" (Num 14:9). Moses added, "Do not be in dread or afraid of them. The Lord your God who goes before you will himself fight for you, just as he did for you in Egypt before your eyes, and in the wilderness, where you have seen how the Lord your God carried you, as a man carries his son, all the way that you went until you came to this place'" (Deut 1:29-31).

Obviously, the Lord was not pleased with their negative perspective and characterized them as a "wicked congregation" (14:27) who "gathered together against me" (v. 35). He asked, "How long will this people despise me? And how long will they not believe in me, in spite of all the signs that I have done among them?" (v. 11). Moses added this indictment: "You . . . rebelled against the command of the Lord your God" (Deut 1:26).

The word "despise" (*naats*) functioned as the covenantal opposite of love, representing total disregard and unfaithfulness.[31] Deuteronomy 31:20 associates the term with idolatry: "For when I have brought them into the land flowing with milk and honey . . . they will turn to other gods and serve them, and despise (*naats*) me and break my covenant." The expression "not believe in me" in Numbers 14:11 indicates a lack of trust. Such incredulity was also cited in Deuteronomy 1:32 and 9:23 as a reason for exclusion from the conquest of Canaan. Indeed, when the rebels insinuated that the Lord had ill motives, they questioned his character, as if he were unfaithful to the covenant he himself had initiated. Implicitly, they likened him to the petty and fickle gods of the land, who were inherently unreliable. They reasoned with an exilic mindset.

Caleb and Joshua, however, were paradigmatic exceptions. God said, "But my servant Caleb, because he has a different spirit and has followed me fully, I will bring into the land" (Num 14:24). Keith Condie comments:

> Caleb and Joshua are the foils to the Israelites in this story . . . . They see matters from the divine perspective and that

---

31. See Sakenfeld, "The Problem of Divine Forgiveness," 321-22.

orientation provides a framework for interpreting experience. They are not ignorant or naive. They perceive the same threats and obstacles as the majority of the spies, but they trust the Lord God who is with them and who will give them the land (13:30; 14.8).[32]

Moreover, Moses' use of the expression "knowledge of good and evil" explicitly connected the unbelief of the first generation with the sin of Adam and Eve.[33] The Lord told the unbelievers, "And as for your little ones, who you said would become a prey, and your children, who today have no knowledge of good or evil, they shall go in there. And to them I will give it, and they shall possess it." Moses wanted the second generation to avoid the mistake of Adam and their fathers' generation—thinking as if God's promises were not determinative. They could still listen to God's voice. They had not yet committed the same blunder concerning the knowledge of good and evil. For this reason, Moses told them:

> See, I have set before you today life and good, death and evil. If you obey the commandments of the Lord your God that I command you today, by loving the Lord your God, by walking in his ways, and by keeping his commandments and his statutes and his rules, then you shall live and multiply, and the Lord your God will bless you in the land that you are entering to take possession of it. But if your heart turns away, and you will not hear, but are drawn away to worship other gods and serve them, I declare to you today, that you shall surely perish. You shall not live long in the land that you are going over the Jordan to enter and possess. (Deut 30:15–18)

Johnson comments, "As with the story in Genesis 2–3, the garden imagery used throughout Deuteronomy highlights either faithfulness in knowing YHWH or faithlessness in erroneous knowledge."[34] Like Adam, the first generation evaluated their observations of the Promised Land without regard to covenant and seemingly without context. They did not remember as instructed. They determined what they knew and what they should do without regard to ontology or sacred history. They interpreted

---

32. Condie, "Narrative Features of Numbers 13–14," 136.

33. Johnson (*Epistemology and Biblical Theology*, 90) points out that the five occurrences of this idiom all have epistemological significance. Interestingly, several instances of the expression "good or bad" indicate an intellectual nuance as well (Lev 27:12, 14, 33; Num 13:19; 24:13; Jer 42:6).

34. Johnson, *Epistemology and Biblical Theology*, 90.

the facts as if they themselves were free of bias. Clearly, however, their sinful prejudice affected their reasoning. Their minds were not oriented to God's priorities and promises. Ironically, whereas Adam was expelled from the primeval garden, the first generation after the exodus was excluded from the new Eden.

THE POSSIBILITY OF FUTURE KNOWLEDGE

Shortly before Moses died, the Lord told him, "Behold, you are about to lie down with your fathers. Then this people will rise and whore after the foreign gods among them in the land that they are entering, and they will forsake me and break my covenant that I have made with them.... For I know what they are inclined to do even today, before I have brought them into the land that I swore to give" (31:16, 21b). Moses knew that Israel would soon embrace an exilic outlook and experience exile in other lands.[35] He knew that Yahweh would "scatter" them among the nations for disobedience (4:27; 29:28; 30:1). How, then, might Israel return to a redemptive epistemological outlook?

Turning

Deuteronomy 4:25-31 depicts the judgment that would befall Israel for its idolatry. Verses 29-31 anticipate a return and restoration from exile under certain circumstances. The important condition is italicized:

(25) When you father children and children's children, and have grown old in the land, if you act corruptly by making a carved image in the form of anything, and by doing what is evil in the sight of the Lord your God, so as to provoke him to anger....

(27) The Lord will scatter you among the peoples, and you will be left few in number among the nations where the Lord will drive you ....

(29) But from there you will seek the Lord your God and you will find him, *if you search after him with all your heart and with all your soul.*

---

35. Regarding the setting see Markl, "No Future without Moses," 711-28; O'Dowd, *The Wisdom of Torah*, 91-106.

(30) When you are in tribulation, and all these things come upon you in the latter days, you will *return* to the Lord your God and *obey his voice.*

(31) For the Lord your God is a merciful God. He will not leave you or destroy you or forget the covenant with your fathers that he swore to them.

Moses understood that the purpose of exile was not merely punitive but also didactic, due to God's covenantal loyalty (v. 31). Turning to God would produce healing and insight after exile. If they reconsidered their suffering in relation to their covenantal violation (idolatry, v. 28) and turned to the Lord in repentance ("return," v. 30), then he would, in effect, "return" to them (v. 31). The condition was total and exclusive focus upon Yahweh, described with language from the *Shema* (6:5, "with all your heart"). If they relearned to fear the Lord and reaffirmed their epistemological and ontological orientation, they would be healed.

Similarly, Deuteronomy 30:1–10 describes a twofold turning—divine and human—and links the acquisition of knowledge, listening to the Lord, and obeying his statutes. In fact, "turn" (*shub*) appears seven times.

(1) And when all these things come upon you, the blessing and the curse, which I have set before you, and you *call them to mind* (*shub*) among all the nations where the Lord your God has driven you,

(2) and return (*shub*) to the Lord your God, you and your children, and obey his voice in all that I command you today, with *all your heart and with all your soul,*

(3) then the Lord your God will restore (*shub*) your fortunes and have mercy on you, and he will gather you again (*shub*) from all the peoples where the Lord your God has scattered you . . . .

(6) And the Lord your God will circumcise your heart and the heart of your offspring, so that you will love the Lord your God with *all your heart and with all your soul,* that you may live . . . .

(8) And you shall again (*shub*) obey the voice of the Lord and keep all his commandments that I command you today.

(9) The Lord your God will make you abundantly prosperous in all the work of your hand, in the fruit of your womb and in the fruit of your cattle and in the fruit of your ground. For the Lord will

again (*shub*) take delight in prospering you, as he took delight in your fathers,

(10) when you obey the voice of the Lord your God, to keep his commandments and his statutes that are written in this Book of the Law, when you turn (*shub*) to the Lord your God with *all your heart and with all your soul*.

The seven "turns" and the two subjects may be summarized in this way:

Verse 1	Israel	call them to mind (the blessing and the curse)
Verse 2	Israel	return (to the Lord)
Verse 3	Yahweh	restore (your fortunes)
Verse 3	Yahweh	gather again (from exile)
Verse 8	Israel	again obey (the voice of the Lord)
Verse 9	Yahweh	again take delight (in prospering you)
Verse 10	Israel	turn (to the Lord)

For some, the exile would provoke reflection and remembrance, leading to considered change.[36] Verse 1 foresees that the exiles would "call to mind" the stipulations of the covenant (blessing and curse). This expression derives from *shub* plus "heart," signifying "turn to the mind," "take them to heart," or simply "remember." Craigie renders the phrase as "return to your senses."[37] The phrases "obey his voice/the Lord/the voice of the Lord your God" (30:2, 8, 10) are stock expressions of redemptive epistemology, particularly in Deuteronomy. As we know, the verb *shama* plus *qol* means to listen to, obey or hear the voice (of the Lord). Likewise, the phrase "with all your heart and all your soul" (vv. 2, 6, 10) echoes the covenantal credo in the *Shema* (6:5). Importantly, listening to God's voice was now focused on what was "written in this Book" (v. 10).

Indeed, the Lord often turned toward Israel in response to repentance. Zechariah 1:3-4 declares, for instance, "Thus declares the Lord of hosts: 'Return (*shub*) to me, says the Lord of hosts, and I will return

---

36. A similar mental transformation occurred when King Nebuchadnezzar's "reason returned" after a period of ostracism (Dan 4:36), when the psalmist "discerned" the fate of the wicked (73:17), and when the prodigal son "came to himself" during a time of privation (Luke 15:17).

37. Craigie, *The Book of Deuteronomy*, 361.

(*shub*) to you.'" Similarly, Leviticus 26:40–42 describes a fourfold turning (Israel from God, God from Israel, Israel to God, God to Israel):

> But if they confess their iniquity and the iniquity of their fathers in their treachery that they committed against me and also in walking contrary to me [Israel from God], so that I walked contrary to them and brought them into the land of their enemies [God from Israel]—if then their uncircumcised heart is humbled and they make amends for their iniquity [Israel to God], then I will remember my covenant with Jacob, and I will remember my covenant with Isaac and my covenant with Abraham, and I will remember the land [God to Israel].

The language of repentance, therefore, presumes obligation and epistemic humility. As John Calvin wrote, "Humility is the beginning of true intelligence."[38] Repentance also assumes capacity. Israelites could know the truth and could respond accordingly, and some of them did. Moses, Joshua, and Caleb evidenced a repentant orientation and feared the Lord. They viewed the world with an "above the sun" perspective and turned from homocentric reasoning. For these reasons, they qualified for God's honor roll as exemplary thinkers in the Old Testament. Their disposition, perception, and conduct, like Isaiah's, demonstrated redemptive epistemology. In the next four chapters, we will see other God-fearing thinkers and covenant keepers who would also "return to the Lord their God and obey his voice."

This Great Nation

God's grand epistemic design for ancient Israel is expressed in Deuteronomy 4:5–8. This passage describes a potential twofold knowledge acquisition in the future: if Israel fulfilled the covenant, they would acquire wisdom *and* the watching world would gain a powerful testimony. Israel's intellectual motivations and methods would model for the watching world how to love God with the mind and how to construct society. In this passage, a key expression (repeated three times) is italicized:

> (5) See, I have taught you statutes and rules, as the Lord my God commanded me, that you should do them in the land that you are entering to take possession of it.

---

38. Calvin, *Commentaries on Ezekiel 1–12*, 43.

(6) Keep them and do them, for that will be your wisdom and your understanding in the sight of the peoples, who, when they hear all these statutes, will say, "Surely this *great nation* is a wise and understanding people."

(7) For what *great nation* is there that has a god so near to it as the Lord our God is to us, whenever we call upon him?

(8) And what *great nation* is there, that has statutes and rules so righteous as all this law that I set before you today?

Several inferences arise from this passage. First, the name Yahweh Elohim presumes a particular ontology (v. 5). God is transcendent and immanent. He created the world and rules over every aspect of the earth. He brought Israel into existence and providentially governs human history in accordance with his purpose. The intimacy of serving this God appears in the rhetorical question in verse 7.

Second, the relation between Yahweh Elohim and Israel was theocratic, that is, covenantal. Designated spokesmen such as Moses ("I" and "me," v. 5) "set before" the people God's instructions (v. 8). Moses declared "rules and statutes" (v. 5) codified as "law" (v. 8). Third, God's commands obligated the people, for they must "do" (v. 5) and "keep" his statutes (v. 6). Fourth, compliance produced righteousness (v. 8). Fifth, obedience conveyed epistemological significance (v. 6). Sixth, Israel's testimony was missional and would fulfill God's promises to Abraham. The expression "great nation" recalls God's promise in Genesis 12:2, "And I will make you a great nation," and that through Abraham's progeny "all the nations of the earth be blessed" (22:18). The passage thus indicates that Abraham's global mission was enabled through the Mosaic covenant. The redemptive-historical progression may be depicted in the following manner:

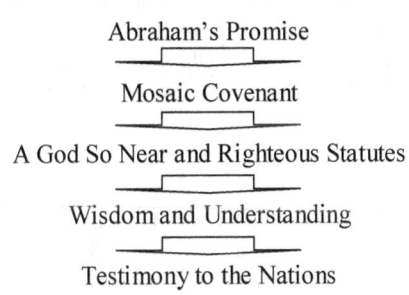

Indeed, the Old Testament infers that a longing for paradise (return to Eden or thirst for utopia) was hard-wired, as it were, in the human soul. In the ancient Near East, Israel's mission to model social righteousness would function through example or attraction. Their very unique society rooted in their religion would serve as an edenic model to the nations.[39] Their unique covenant with the true God would provoke admiration and longing among non-Hebrews, who were created in the image of God but who suffered under dystopian regimes. Christopher J. H. Wright explains:

> Theologically, the purpose of Israel's existence was to be a vehicle both for God's revelation and for the blessing of humanity. They were not only the bearers of redemption, but were to be a model of what a redeemed community should look like, living in obedience to God's will. Their social structure, aspirations, principles and policies, so organically related to their covenantal faith in the Lord, were also part of the content of that revelation, part of the pattern of redemption .... They, the medium, were themselves part of the message.[40]

In this passage, therefore, practicing the law leads to wisdom. In time, this understanding produces prosperity, which in turn arouses admiration and curiosity among those who observe.[41]

Prophetic Knowledge

In addition to an authoritative, written text composed of Moses' teaching, the Lord established an administrative infrastructure in Israel: judges (16:18–20, 17:8–13), kings (17:14–20), priests (18:1–8), and prophets

---

39. Imagine what might have transpired in the ancient Near East if Israel had fulfilled this mission. The distinct wisdom and understanding inherent in the Lord's revelation and the fear of God it engendered might have mitigated geopolitical tensions among ancient, competing empires. Old Testament "righteousness, justice, and equity" (Prov 1:3) might have impacted civilizations in the political, economic, religious, and legal realms. Most likely, Israel would have enjoyed long-term security and prosperity.

40. Wright, *Old Testament Ethics*, 62.

41. A modern analogy might be the Marvel film *The Black Panther*, in which an often disregarded race produced a utopia. Their nation had been hidden from public view, but it was a highly advanced civilization that emerged in full maturity as the envy of the world. By example, Wakanda would bring peace, prosperity, and advanced technology for the good of mankind.

(18:9-22). This last group was critically important, for the prophets conveyed further revelation. Their role is described in 18:14-18 (important themes are in italics):

(14) For these nations, which you are about to dispossess, listen to fortune-tellers and to diviners. But as for you, the Lord your God has *not allowed* you to do this.

(15) The Lord your God will *raise up* for you a prophet *like me* from among you, *from your brothers—it is to him you shall listen*—

(16) just as you desired of the Lord your God at Horeb on the day of the assembly, when you said, "Let me not hear again the voice of the Lord my God or see this great fire any more, lest I die."

(17) And the Lord said to me, "They are right in what they have spoken.

(18) I will raise up for them a prophet like you from among their brothers. And I will *put my words in his mouth*, and he shall speak to them all that I command him."

Whom Israel listened to and how were of paramount importance. The expressions highlighted above presuppose a plurality of voices and methods of ascertaining God's will. They also presume a necessary differentiation between speakers who beckoned for their attention. They assume that the religious marketplace in Canaan was fraught with danger (v. 14). They presume contrasting ontologies, cosmologies, and epistemologies that the people would have to navigate under the aegis of Moses' teaching.

In fact, Israel had to make a choice. They could listen to and imitate "these nations" (v. 14), or they could heed God's voice (vv. 15-18) and receive his instructions as mediated through prophets like Moses.[42] Spokesmen would be "raised up" by God from "your brothers" (members of the covenant community) and communicate "my words." The preferred choice was clear (v. 14b): "it is to him [the prophet of God] you shall listen" (v. 15b). Moses was the archetypical prophet, and his teaching was the plumb line for all further revelation (34:10). O'Dowd explains:

> While Moses represents the supreme prophet and Israel's fundamental connection to Yahweh, his "words" and the "words of this torah" will require further supplementation in the land;

---

42. See Block, *Deuteronomy*, 431-39; Tucker, "Deuteronomy 18:15-22," 292-97.

what is lacking will be added by Yahweh through his choice of a prophet. Yet, it is Israel who must use Moses' present "words" in Deuteronomy as the standard to measure and confirm the nature of future "words."[43]

The evaluation of prophetic declarations, therefore, presupposed a theological corpus well understood by a knowledge class (priests, scribes, etc.), as well as biblical literacy among the people. Tucker comments, "Those who would decide whether a prophet's words were true or false—and that includes all the people of God—must become theologians."[44] In the short term, Israel learned to interpret potential canon (prophecies and teaching) by existing canon (the Decalogue), that is, by intertextual reasoning. In the long term, Scripture emerged as the judge and foundation of all knowing.

Circumcision

In Deuteronomy 10:16, the Israelites were commanded to circumcise (*mul*) their hearts (minds). The indicative reality that justified circumcision was expressed in verses 14–15. The imperatives that resulted appear in verses 12–13 and 16b. The meaning of heart circumcision can be gleaned from the context, specifically the expressions in apposition to verse 16a (in italics):

(12) And now, Israel, what does the Lord your God require of you, but to fear the Lord your God, to walk in all his ways, to love him, to serve the Lord your God with all your heart and with all your soul,

(13) and to keep the commandments and statutes of the Lord, which I am commanding you today for your good?

(14) Behold, to the Lord your God belong heaven and the heaven of heavens, the earth with all that is in it.

(15) Yet the Lord set his heart in love on your fathers and chose their offspring after them, you above all peoples, as you are this day.

(16) Circumcise therefore the foreskin of your heart, and *be no longer stubborn*.

---

43. O'Dowd, *The Wisdom of Torah*, 68.
44. Tucker, "Deuteronomy 18:15–22," 296.

Verses 14–15 provide two essential affirmations. Verse 14 states an ontological reality, whereas verse 15 expresses a covenantal commitment on God's part toward Israel. Verse 16 is the ensuing imperative: "Circumcise therefore the foreskin of your heart." As physical circumcision was a visible sign of covenantal commitment, circumcision of the heart indicated a subjective sanctification of one's mental powers to the Lord, as expressed in verses 12–13 (positively) and 16 (negatively).[45] In other words, just as circumcision was a physical sign setting apart God's people, circumcision of the heart indicates an epistemological orientation that distinguishes his people from the other nations.

Further, this passage presumes Israel's cognitive ability but moral inability (or unwillingness). Their cognitive apparatus existed, but it was often utilized improperly or misdirected to illegitimate ends. O'Dowd expresses this idea: "The fault is not with the torah or its standards, but must lie within Israel's own nature. Yahweh and his torah are near, but Israel will not have them."[46]

Thus, given Israel's chronic and systemic failure to love God with all their heart/mind, soul, and might, Yahweh promised to fundamentally reorient their minds and motives for the better in the future. On the cusp of the conquest, Moses told them, "And the Lord your God will circumcise your heart and the heart of your offspring, so that you will love the Lord your God with all your heart and with all your soul, that you may live" (30:6). In other words, because of his commitment to the nation and their dispositional weakness, the Lord would one day impress his law on the hard drive of their minds. By grace alone, he would undermine their innate stubbornness and endow them with the moral capacity to listen to his voice and think his thoughts.

---

45. Ezekiel 18:31 is similar: "Cast away from you all the transgressions that you have committed, and make yourselves a new heart and a new spirit! Why will you die, O house of Israel?" Compare Ezekiel 36:25–27: "I will sprinkle clean water on you, and you shall be clean from all your uncleannesses, and from all your idols I will cleanse you. And I will give you a new heart, and a new spirit I will put within you. And I will remove the heart of stone from your flesh and give you a heart of flesh. And I will put my Spirit within you, and cause you to walk in my statutes and be careful to obey my rules." See also Jeremiah 24:7; 32:39–40.

46. O'Dowd, *The Wisdom of Torah*, 99.

Eyes to See

The book of Deuteronomy highlights the acquisition of knowledge and the consequences of flawed thinking. It reveals to whom Israel ought to listen so as to interpret what they witnessed during the exodus and how to navigate the treacherous milieu in Canaan. In particular, Deuteronomy associates knowing with sight and listening, as well as with divine enablement. Let us consider, as the final passage in our tour of Deuteronomy, 29:2b–4:

(2b)   You have seen all that the Lord did before your eyes in the land of Egypt, to Pharaoh and to all his servants and to all his land,

(3)   the great trials that your eyes saw, the signs, and those great wonders.

(4)   But to this day the Lord has not given you a heart to understand or eyes to see or ears to hear.

The phrase "heart to understand" means an "understanding mind."[47] As we have learned, the heart is the faculty that receives and processes the data of sight and sound. It is the "organ of knowing and understanding" and the location of "mental verbalization."[48] The heart retains information and evaluates it. It acts upon the world and is acted upon. All the verbs of cognition, such as pondering, categorizing, comparing, analyzing, and evaluating, are activities of the heart. It is fully engaged with its surroundings.[49]

Furthermore, observation and experience provide the data for knowledge. The verb "see" and the noun "eyes," as well as the idioms "in the eyes of" and "in the sight of," express this dynamic.[50] However,

---

47. "Heart" appears also in the EHV and NKJV, whereas "mind" occurs in the NIV and NRSV, as well as Block (*Deuteronomy*, 691) and Craigie (*Deuteronomy*, 354).

48. Carasik, *Theologies of the Mind*, 105, 106.

49. The prepositions associated with "heart" in Deuteronomy bear this out: "from" (4:9), "with" (4:29; 6:5; 10:12; 11:13; 13:3; 26:16; 30:2, 6, 10), "on" (6:6), "in" (7:17; 8:2, 5, 17; 9:4; 11:18; 15:9; 18:21; 30:14), "of" (9:5; 28:47; 29:19), and "to" (4:39; 10:16; 43:46).

50. For example, the Hebrews saw "the great and terrifying wilderness" (1:19), "how the Lord carried you as a man carries a son" (1:31), "his great fire" at Horeb (4:36), and "the discipline of the Lord" (11:2). They observed the "detestable things" associated with idolatry in Canaan (29:17). They also saw with their own eyes "all that the Lord has done to these two kings" (Og and Sihon) (3:21), "all that he did in the land of Egypt" during the Exodus (29:2), and all that he did in the wilderness, for "you

these observations were not raw data. They were pre-interpreted by Yahweh and conveyed through Moses. For this reason, the Israelites were admonished to reinterpret all that they witnessed and experienced with the same criteria provided to Moses. Nothing was left to their independent judgment or so-called objective evaluation. There were no brute theophanies. As Johnson writes, "Brute seeing is not believing as there is no self-interpreted seeing in these texts."[51] And so they needed to learn how to see and listen under authority.

On the other hand, their evaluation of all they experienced and everything that Moses told them introduced an epistemological conflict. Israel evaluated the information with sinful bias. John Wick Bowman summarizes this idea: "The trouble with man is, not that he cannot hear and see, but that he will not. Sin has stopped his ears and blinded his eyes. The ears are still present and the eyes are present—man is whole and intact. Only, since the incursion of sin into his experience, man chooses to listen other voices than God's."[52] Thus, the Israelites were not dispassionate observers, but instead were deeply tainted by their own exilic epistemology, as well as biblical ignorance and religious syncretism. They were not inclined to view the mighty deeds of the Lord with true understanding, faith, or hope.[53]

For this reason, Johnson writes, "Israel has not known *because* she has not seen what YHWH was showing her *because* she was not listening to the voice of the prophet."[54] By means of hearing (revelation in all forms), Israel acquired the criteria to understand truly and respond wisely. The orientation of the mind toward or away from the Lord disposed them to pay attention. And a listening mind that heeded Yahweh's instruction interpreted what was seen and experienced, evaluating it by God's criteria and responding with God's standards.

Furthermore, the expressions "eyes to see" and "ears to hear" indicate more than simply the mind's capacity for sensory perception. Rather, seeing and hearing also signify discernment or wisdom. A "heart

---

have lacked nothing" (2:7b).

51. Johnson, *Biblical Knowing*, 78.

52. Cited in Johnson, *Epistemology and Biblical Theology*, 99.

53. Moses described them as an "evil generation" (1:35) and "stubborn people" (9:6). They were "right in [their] own eyes" (12:8) and "children in whom is no faithfulness" (32:20). They were quickly "drawn away" to other gods to "bow down and serve them" (4:19).

54. Johnson, *Epistemology and Biblical Theology*, 101 (emphasis in original).

to understand" perceives the big picture and how the parts relate to the whole. It understands how to interpret the events of the exodus and wilderness journey. The mind that understands knows how to evaluate Canaan.

In the short term ("now," "today"), Moses' prognosis for Israel was indeed grim. He predicted that the nation would not see correctly or listen carefully to God's voice. They would not learn to fear the Lord or discern reality according to the worldview communicated through Moses. Instead, the nation would yield to idolatry and embrace flawed knowledge to their harm. In the long term, Deuteronomy 29:4 suggests positive expectancy. The expression "to this day," however, presumes possible future moral enablement to heed God's word. Likewise, the promise of restoration in "the latter days" (4:30) and "circumcision" (30:6) indicate future knowledge rooted in the fear of God.

CONCLUSION

Deuteronomy provides a path to redemptive epistemology. It begins with neither a positive nor negative assessment of one's mental posture, but a radically realistic analysis. It implies a deeper biblical literacy and the capacity to reason intertextually. This should produce intellectual piety, situational discernment, and strategic implementation.[55]

This pedagogical process is nurtured by hope and expectancy. The Lord promises to renew people's minds and instruct prospective thinkers with truth, when they seek him with all their heart, soul, and might.

Similarly, Psalm 19:7–11 provides a vision for those who learn the fear of the Lord and recapitulates the epistemological posture described in Deuteronomy:

> The law of the Lord is perfect, reviving the soul;
> the testimony of the Lord is sure, making wise the simple;
> the precepts of the Lord are right, rejoicing the heart;
> the commandment of the Lord is pure, enlightening the eyes;
> the fear of the Lord is clean, enduring forever;
> the rules of the Lord are true, and righteous altogether.
> More to be desired are they than gold, even much fine gold;
> sweeter also than honey and drippings of the honeycomb.
> Moreover, by them is your servant warned; in keeping them there is great reward.

---

55. See Strawn, *The Old Testament Is Dying*, 194–211.

Psalm 19:12–14 concludes, in response to these exhortations, with a suitably humble prayer of repentance seeking to be guided on the path of knowledge:

> Who can discern his errors? Declare me innocent from hidden faults.
> Keep back your servant also from presumptuous sins; let them not have dominion over me!
> Then I shall be blameless, and innocent of great transgression.
> Let the words of my mouth and the meditation of my heart be acceptable in your sight,
> O Lord, my rock and my redeemer.

11

My Servant Job

"The goal of Job's quest toward understanding is also the ultimate goal of human existence—to see God (42:5)."

—LELAND RYKEN, *WORDS OF DELIGHT*

READING THE BOOK OF JOB through the prism of redemptive epistemology reminds me of Charles Dickens's depiction of nineteenth-century London and Paris: "It was the best of times, it was the worst of times, it was the age of wisdom, it was the age of foolishness, it was the epoch of belief, it was the epoch of incredulity, it was the season of light, it was the season of darkness, it was the spring of hope, it was the winter of despair."[1] Job modeled each of these characteristics intellectually. He was the best in every way as a righteous, prosperous sage, but under duress he also typified mankind's erroneous thinking about God.[2]

Metaphorically, the book depicts reality like a Russian doll. The outside doll provides the exterior packaging for a drama occurring within. Job's story occurs within a sequence of interlocking realities: the heavenly court, original readers, Job himself (his mental, emotional, and physical state), his friends, and the community. We can also say that Job's knowledge was situated within a cosmic learning community under the

---

1. Dickens, *A Tale of Two Cities*, 10.

2. Concerning Job's provenance, historicity, date, and genre, as well as the structure, argumentation, "the satan," and the book's message, see Longman, *The Book of Job*, 23–74; Walton, "Book of Job 1," 333–46; Hartley, *The Book of Job*, 3–35.

tutelage of the transcendent pedagogue. Learning about each perspective helps us to understand the drama as it unfolds:

God	knows everything
Accuser	knows more than the original readers
Original readers	know more than Job[3]
Job	knows more than his wife and friends
Friends	know more than the community
Community	knows even less
Current readers	know the least but learn the most

The book of Job concerns wisdom. Would Job correctly assess what happened to him and respond properly? Or would he incorrectly evaluate his experience and generalize falsely on that basis concerning creation and the Creator? The accuser ("the satan")[4] believed that he would miss the point entirely and curse God for his misfortune. Even the original readers, who knew what had transpired in heaven, were left in suspense as they awaited the resolution of the dilemma and the Lord's evaluation of Job's plight.

The book of Job is a real-world test of redemptive epistemology under extreme pressure. In this sense, the book provides a perennial philosophy about how to think in a milieu east of Eden typified by noetic corruption, inherited wisdom, enigma, and suffering. Indeed, what happened to Job happens to all of us, to some degree. We all suffer loss and encounter paradoxes in this life. We all experience the "dark night of the soul." For the descendants of Adam, reality sometimes appears as "a riddle wrapped in a mystery inside an enigma."[5] Certainly, this is how Job experienced the world during his period of affliction.

In this chapter, I begin with the outermost doll—the divine court. In the next two sections, I illustrate how the author foreshadowed coming themes and important developments in the story. The next three sections describe the book's focus on the mind and some of the assumptions

---

3. Concerning the role of the original readers, see Wilson, "Preknowledge, Anticipation, and the Poetics of Job," 243–56; Fox, "Job the Pious," 351–66.

4. Hartley (*The Book of Job*, 71) explains this term: "Here the Hebrew word *hassatan* has the article, so it functions as a title rather than as a personal name. The Hebrew root *stn* means 'to oppose at law.'"

5. The expression is attributed to Winston Churchill concerning Russia's agenda on the eve of World War II.

that Job and his friends embraced. The following chapter analyzes the dramatic interchange recounted in Job 38–42, as the protagonist directly encounters God.

THE PROLOGUE

The first verse of Job 1 reveals four traits that distinguished Job before his trial: "blameless and upright, one who feared God and turned away from evil." He was "blameless" (*tam*), as were Noah, Abraham, and David.[6] Elsewhere, "blameless" (*tamim*) refers to sincerity and is coupled with "faithfulness" (Josh 24:14). It is associated with the terms "walk" and "way" as a lifestyle that pleases the Lord (Pss 84:11; 119:1; Prov 2:7; 10:9; 19:1; 28:6). It is rendered as "integrity" that flows from a "heart" (mind) that serves God (Gen 20:5, 6; 1 Kgs 9:4).

"Upright" (*yashar*) indicates "faithful adherence to God's statutes and an honest, compassionate manner in relating to others."[7] Indeed, by his own testimony Job was righteous in his relationships according to the law. His sexual ethic was impeccable (31:1, 9). He was truthful in speech (vv. 5, 33) and generous with the needy ("widow," "poor," "fatherless," "stranger") under the law (vv. 16–21, 31–32). He dealt fairly with his servants (vv. 13, 39). He avoided greed (vv. 24–25) and vengeance (vv. 29–30). He sacrificed weekly for his children (1:5). And he forsook idolatry (vv. 26–27). He was faithful in all his obligations, recognizing that to do otherwise "would have been false to God above" (v. 28). Job realized, as well, that God assessed all his "ways and number[ed] all [his] steps" (v. 4).

In all these ways, Job showed that he "feared God" and "turned away from evil." God affirms this designation twice in the prologue (1:8; 2:3), and six times in the book he calls Job his "servant" (1:8; 2:3; 40:7; 42:8 three times). Indisputably, Job listened to God and obeyed his commandments (6:10b; 23:11–12). He enjoyed the legitimate benefits of obedience promised in Deuteronomy (28:1–14) and the prosperity associated with wisdom (Prov 3:2; Pss 1:1; 22:29; 106:5).

Moreover, despite his great losses described in chapters 1–2, Job affirmed his faith in God. He declared his dependence: "Naked I came

---

6. The adjective *tamim* is used of Noah (Gen 6:9), Abraham (Gen 17:1), and David (2 Sam 22:24).

7. Hartley, *The Book of Job*, 67.

from my mother's womb, and naked shall I return. The Lord gave, and the Lord has taken away; blessed be the name of the Lord" (1:21-22). He confessed God's sovereignty: "Shall we receive good from God, and shall we not receive evil?" As a result, the narrator affirmed after the second wave of loss, "In all this Job did not sin with his lips" (2:10b).

However, as films often foreshadow what is coming, the narrator foreshadowed Job's titanic struggle to interpret his suffering correctly. After the first onslaught, he wrote, "In all this Job did not sin or charge God with wrong" (1:22). This statement presumes an important question as the dialogue begins: Will Job persevere in this pious mindset, or will he charge God with injustice? This implied inquiry provides the dramatic tension that drives the story forward.

As in the movie *Matrix*, where two coterminous dimensions of reality interact in unseen ways, the debate about Job occurred both on earth and in heaven. Unbeknownst to Job and his interlocutors, "the satan" (1:6; 2:1) suggested that Job's piety was merely instrumental, and that he served the Lord only for the resulting benefits (1:9). The accuser told Yahweh that Job would surely "curse you to your face" (1:11; 2:5) if he suffered severe loss. The ensuing dialogue concerns the veracity of the accuser's assessment of Job's character: will he really curse God?

As the prologue shows, Job did not deserve physical, emotional, economic, or social deprivation. Indeed, he experienced an existential and theoretical anomaly, for what happened to him contradicted accepted wisdom. But his greatest loss was the absence of God's voice, for God was silent until the very end. Lacking this orientation, Job experienced a loss of meaning and intellectual anomie. The debate with his friends focused on key questions. Who is interpreting the enigma of his experience correctly? Who is suffering a wisdom deficit? How can we make meaning of Job's experience?

ANTICIPATION

The writer of the book of Job provided contemporaneous readers with guidance to help them interpret the story.[8] In the prologue, they received privileged information, an "above-the-sun" perspective, and discovered

---

8. See Habel, "Plot Anticipation," in the *Book of Job*, 28-29, 31-32; Wilson, "Preknowledge, Anticipation, and the Poetics of Job," 243-56; Miller, "The Vision of Eliphaz," 98-112.

the all-important back story about Job.⁹ As the dialogue began in chapter 4, they already knew that Job had been blessed because of his righteousness and that he did not merit suffering. They also knew how Job's trial came about. They were not hemmed in by an "under-the-sun" outlook, unlike the participants in the unfolding drama.

The original readers heard in advance the accuser's cynical allegation against God. By testing Job, he desired to expose a cosmic charade. In the accuser's view, mankind served God for the benefits alone and God solicited adoration by pandering to them. Justice was a farce, a convenient pretense. Religion was nothing more than an enormous feedback loop. For the accuser, Job was merely the ideal test case, since he was supposedly the most righteous person and the most blessed by God on earth.

The readers also knew that Job and his friends lacked wisdom. None of them knew how to interpret what had happened, because they had not heard what occurred in God's council. Without a doubt, the readers were also inclined to wonder about God's justice and the apparently unfair testing of Job, given the divine affirmation of his innocence. Perhaps they came to realize early on that the friends' remedy for Job's loss verified the accuser's insinuation. They also viewed Job's piety in an instrumental manner.

Thus, the first readers followed the story on two levels—on earth and in heaven—anticipating the resolution of the interlocking trials, or the plot within a plot. They learned that Job presumed erroneously that he was on trial, whereas actually God was the presumed defendant, according to the accuser's point of view. On the other hand, they lacked complete understanding as well. They did not know how to reconcile the story in heaven or on earth. For this reason, the author foreshadowed in the dialogue how the tension would be resolved. Three themes appear as the drama unfolds: knowledge, wisdom, and reversal.

Knowledge

The writer of Job provided two examples of knowledge gained by revelation: the vision of Eliphaz (4:12–21; 15:14–16)¹⁰ and the theophany that

---

9. Fox ("God's Answer and Job's Response," 2) comments, "The book of Job is not for Job; it is for its readers. Readers, who observe Job's world from above, and who, unlike Job, have read the Prologue, are allowed a privileged, superior perspective and are even given insight into the mind of God."

10. Eliphaz also cited, as sources of knowledge: natural revelation (5:10) and

appeared to Job (38:1–41; 42:7–8).[11] Both speakers (the spirit cited by Eliphaz and Yahweh) presumed supernatural veracity as the voice of God. Both purported to illuminate Job's plight. For the reader, Eliphaz's vision revealed the need for supplemental heavenly insight and special divine sanction to buttress his case against Job.[12] After Job's self-annihilating curse in chapter 3, Eliphaz describes the vision in 4:12–16:

(12) Now a word was brought to me stealthily; my ear received the whisper of it.

(13) Amid thoughts from visions of the night, when deep sleep falls on men,

(14) dread came upon me, and trembling, which made all my bones shake.

(15) A spirit glided past my face; the hair of my flesh stood up.

(16) It stood still, but I could not discern its appearance. A form was before my eyes; there was silence, then I heard a voice.

Eliphaz's vision probably aroused suspicions in the original readers due to the unusual nature of the insight. The phrase "deep sleep" (*tardemah*, v. 13) appears seven times in the Old Testament (Gen 2:21; 15:12; 1 Sam 26:12; Job 4:13; 33:15; Prov 19:15; Isa 29:10). Six refer to a God-induced state of altered perception, for both positive and negative purposes. Isaiah 29:10, for instance, stresses epistemological themes and the "motif of divinely imposed delusion."[13] Similarly, the "spirit" (*ruach*) that spoke to Eliphaz appears to be an idiomatic reference to the "spirit of falsehood."[14] Esther J. Hamori analyzes eight appearances of the term, which are translated as a "evil spirit" (Judg 9:23), "harmful spirit" (1 Sam 16:14–23; 18:10–12; 19:9), "lying spirit" (1 Kgs 22:22–23), "spirit of confusion" (Isa 19:14), "spirit" (Job 4:15), and "spirit of whoredom" (idolatry, Hos 5:4). Several commonalities occur in these passages: the spirits are

---

observation of human sinfulness (4:6; 5:3).

11. Two other friends alluded to supernatural insight. Zophar said that "out of my understanding a spirit (*ruach*) answers me" (20:3b), and Elihu testified, "It is the spirit (*ruach*) in man, the breath of the Almighty, that makes him understand" (32:8).

12. Hamori, "The Spirit of Falsehood," 15–30; Harding, "The Spirit of Deception," 154–65.

13. Hayes, "A Spirit of Deep Sleep," 51; see also Hamori, "The Spirit of Falsehood," 24.

14. Hamori, "The Spirit of Falsehood," 24.

associated with deception, they are sent by God, and they influence those already committed to a wrong point of view.[15] Hamori concludes, "The spirit is sent to people who have already chosen falsehood."[16]

The mode of revelation also likely raised suspicions for the readers, especially in hindsight. James E. Miller provides these contrasts between the spirit's vision and God's theophany later in Job:

Vision	Theophany
at night	during the day
in deep sleep	awake and conscious
private	public
listens only	listens and responds
speaks about the human race	speaks to Job particularly
an angel	God
no relation with Eliphaz	deep relation with Job[17]

Similarly, the message of the vision (4:17–19) was problematic:

(17) Can mortal man be in the right before God? Can a man be pure before his Maker?

(18) Even in his servants he puts no trust, and his angels he charges with error;

(19) how much more those who dwell in houses of clay, whose foundation is in the dust, who are crushed like the moth.

According to the vision, no created being is righteous—neither humans nor angels.[18] To Eliphaz, this message was a gift from heaven, providing divine sanction for his point of view. James E. Harding summarizes the reasoning: "Since it is in human nature to sin, everyone, Job included, must expect to receive at least a little temporary punishment."[19] Job suffered because, like everyone, he sinned. Eliphaz embraced the vision wholeheartedly and based his accusation against Job upon it. He adamantly reaffirmed the message in his second discourse (15:14–16). Bildad restated it (25:4) and Job referred to it (9:2).

15. Hamori, "The Spirit of Falsehood," 28.
16. Hamori, "The Spirit of Falsehood," 26.
17. Miller, "The Vision of Eliphaz," 102–7.
18. Whitekettle, "When More Leads to Less," 445–48.
19. Harding, "The Spirit of Deception," 154.

Nevertheless, the readers had cause to doubt the veracity of the visitation. In addition to its mode and message, it frankly contradicted what God had declared about Job's character in the prologue. It simply reaffirmed what Eliphaz already believed, which was quite incorrect from God's point of view, as all would eventually discover (42:7).[20]

But the vision serves a rhetorical purpose as preparation for further revelation.[21] The readers now knew that Eliphaz relied upon revelatory knowledge to validate his indictment of Job, but that his account was inadequate. In fact, the vision raised more questions than it answered. Perhaps the readers wondered if a competing revelation in support of Job would be presented next. John E. Hartley notes that Job lacked "the full picture that is necessary to understand how a particular occurrence fits within God's comprehensive plan."[22] Because of that unmet need, Eliphaz's vision foreshadowed the upcoming theophany of Yahweh to Job (chapters 38–41). That revelation would provide what he needed to understand the broader context for his suffering.

Wisdom

Zophar declared that God possessed wisdom that Job desperately needed. He posed several questions designed to provoke in Job a deep sense of inadequacy: "Can you find out the deep things of God? Can you find out the limit of the Almighty? It is higher than heaven—what can you do? Deeper than Sheol—what can you know?" (11:7–8). According to Zophar, wisdom presupposed a great gulf between the Creator and mankind in terms of knowledge and power. In this way, Zophar's questions anticipated God's later theophanic inquiry of Job and Job's response.

Zophar also suggested that a direct encounter with God would resolve Job's erroneous complaint: "For you say, 'My doctrine is pure, and I am clean in God's eyes.' But oh, that God would speak and open his lips to you, and that he would tell you the secrets of wisdom! For he is manifold in understanding" (11:4–6a). Again, Zophar's counsel foreshadowed the Lord's appearance.

---

20. Harding ("The Spirit of Deception," 154–59) points out that the Hebrew in 4:12–17 is ambiguous and invites differing interpretations. Concerning the phrase "right before God," see also Whitekettle, "When More Leads to Less," 445–48.

21. Miller, "The Vision of Eliphaz," 8–11.

22. Hartley, *The Book of Job*, 197.

Further, Job's meditation on wisdom in chapter 28 anticipated his upcoming encounter with God. The poem contrasts two searches for great treasures. Verses 1–6 and 9–11 describe the acquisition of precious metals:

(1) Surely there is a mine for silver, and a place for gold that they refine.

(2) Iron is taken out of the earth, and copper is smelted from the ore.

(3) Man puts an end to darkness and searches out to the farthest limit the ore in gloom and deep darkness.

(4) He opens shafts in a valley away from where anyone lives; they are forgotten by travelers; they hang in the air, far away from mankind; they swing to and fro.

(5) As for the earth, out of it comes bread, but underneath it is turned up as by fire.

(6) Its stones are the place of sapphires, and it has dust of gold . . . .

(9) Man puts his hand to the flinty rock and overturns mountains by the roots.

(10) He cuts out channels in the rocks, and his eye sees every precious thing.

(11) He dams up the streams so that they do not trickle, and the thing that is hidden he brings out to light.

In the ancient Near East, silver, gold, iron, and gems were obtained by strenuous effort and ingenuity.[23] Such precious objects were acquired through trade, conquest, and exploration and extracted at great risk for the slaves and prisoners who provided the labor.[24] These very costly natural resources undergirded the economic and religious power of the royal class and state. The poem compares this craving for worldly wealth and power with the search for God's wisdom. Clearly, both require great exertion. But one is subject to human power and understanding; the other is not. One is determined by sin and corruption; the other is not. One is

---

23. Regarding ancient mining methods and Job 28:1–11, see Van Wolde, "Ancient Wisdoms, Present Insights," 55–74.

24. Concerning heroic royal exploration and adventure, see Jones, "Job 28 and Modern Theory of Knowledge," 487–89.

focused on earthly gain, whereas the other aims for heavenly insight. The two quests, therefore, presume differing locations ("place," v. 12), means of acquisition ("path" or "way," v. 23), and kinds of knowledge:

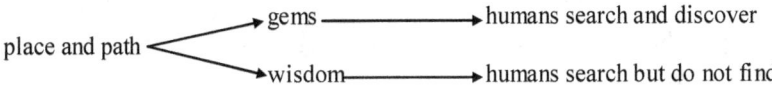

According to Job's meditation, humans do not accurately appraise wisdom's worth (v. 13a; see also vv. 15–19), nor do they discern its location (v. 13b; see also vv. 14, 21–22). For this reason, Job asked, "But where shall wisdom be found? And where is the place of understanding?" (v. 12) and "From where, then, does wisdom come? And where is the place of understanding?" (v. 20). Even though the location of wisdom is "hidden" and "concealed" from "the eyes of all living" creatures (v. 21), God knows its place and "understands the way to it" (v. 23). The distinction between divine and human knowledge is displayed in this way:

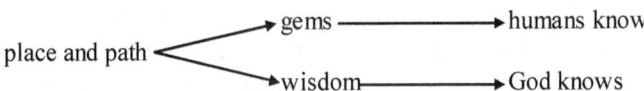

Job provides the reason for God's superior knowledge in 28:24, indicated by the preposition "for" (*ki*): "For he looks to the ends of the earth and sees everything under the heavens." Tremper Longman comments, "The poet explains why God alone would have this knowledge. After all, though the birds have a high vantage point from which to look at the world (v. 7), they do not compare to God, who 'looks to the ends of the earth.' He sees everything under heaven (v. 24)."[25] God observes all things spatially (horizontal and vertical, height and depth) and temporally (past, present, and future).

But wisdom is not, first and foremost, associated with a place but with a time: primordial time and the act of creation. Ryan O'Dowd explains the broader context: "Job provides a test of wisdom in the throes of life and, in its own way, serves to affirm the reliability of the created order."[26] Job wrote about God's deeds in creation (28:25–27):

25. Longman, *The Book of Job*, 331.
26. O'Dowd, *The Wisdom of Torah*, 153.

(25) When he gave to the wind its weight and apportioned the waters by measure,

(26) when he made a decree for the rain and a way for the lightning of the thunder,

(27) then he saw it and declared it; he established it, and searched it out.

These verses reveal God as the divine architect depicted in Genesis 1–2. The Creator designed, arranged, and constructed his terrestrial palace. He set limits for nature and made his world intelligible.[27] Scott C. Jones explains, "In vv. 25–27, God takes on the role of a royal builder, whose building project is not only guided by a set plan, but also offers the occasion for further revelation."[28]

Yet wisdom is not static or passive, akin to primordial time, but an active and ever-present person. The divine ruler, builder, benefactor, and philosopher is the embodiment of wisdom. For this reason, Job needed God, the source of wisdom, to make sense of his predicament. But he also needed God to show him the path. Echoing Proverbs 3:7, Job declared in 28:28, "And he said to man, 'Behold, the fear of the Lord, that is wisdom, and to turn away from evil is understanding.'" Thus, Job *already* knew (or presupposed) the way to wisdom. He realized that a dependent, expectant, and submissive intellectual posture ("fear of the Lord") coupled with social righteousness ("turn away from evil") led to wisdom. In effect, then, Job looked back (without knowing) to the Creator's depiction of his piety in the prologue (1:1; 2:3) and anticipated his response when God spoke again (42:2–6).

In summary, Hartley explains how chapter 28 anticipated the theophany and prepared the readers for the pending resolution:

> This hymn authenticates Job's turning away from his comforters to petition God directly. It is telling him that he will receive genuine insight into his suffering when God himself speaks to him. Thus this hymn prepares Job for Yahweh's appearing. More specifically, it indicates the approach that Yahweh will take in his discourses. He will address Job's lament by recounting the wise

---

27. Similar themes appear in 9:7–10; 12:7–10; and 26:7–14.

28. Jones, "Job 28 and Modern Theory of Knowledge," 494. Similarly, Longman (*The Book of Job,* 331) suggests, "As creator, he understands how it works, which is the essence of wisdom. Thus he is able to describe precisely where one may find wisdom, and he is willing to reveal it to humanity."

and marvelous way he has created the world. Thereby he will demonstrate that Job's suffering does not discount the truth that he rules the world wisely and justly.[29]

Reversal

The readers saw that Job enjoyed edenic prosperity but suffered an expulsion from his proverbial garden. He was cast out, as it were, from all that was pleasant and secure. He transitioned from blessing to privation, order to chaos, life to death, light to darkness, belonging to isolation, and prominence to outcast status. The readers also realized that Job could not feign repentance to secure his restoration. They saw that appeasement affirmed the accuser's proposition and was unworthy of the Lord.

Perhaps they also recognized in Job a recapitulation of Adam. Samuel A. Meier outlines the resonances between Genesis 1–3 and Job 1–2.[30] Like Adam, Job was depicted as an entirely unique human being: "There is none like him on the earth" (1:8a; 2:3a). His life was idyllic, evidenced by abundant prosperity, vibrant family life, and dominion over his assets (1:2–3).[31] Like Adam, Job was devout, "a blameless and upright man, who fears God and turns away from evil" (1:8b; 2:3b). He was "so meticulously pious that he imitated God's activity in the creation week (Gen 2:2–3)," as he sacrificed on behalf of his children every week (Job 1:5).[32] Indeed, Job's "idyllic festivity" and prosperity echoed Adam's pre-fall existence.[33]

However, the readers undoubtedly observed that Job experienced a "de-creation" as Adam. Meier says that Job's demise is "described in terms deliberately reminiscent of the Genesis traditions."[34] His blessings listed in 1:2–3 are recounted in reverse in verses 14–19. The "great wind" (*ruach gedolah*, 1:19) that turned order to chaos for Job resonated with God's creative "wind" (*ruach*, Gen 1:2) that turned chaos to order in creation.[35] Like Adam, Job depicted his unwanted status before God as nakedness (Job 1:21; Gen 3:10). He suffered powerlessness and futility.

---

29. Hartley, *The Book of Job*, 384.
30. Meier, "Job 1–21: A Reflection of Genesis 1–3," 183–93.
31. Meier, "Job 1–21: A Reflection of Genesis 1–3," 186.
32. Meier, "Job 1–21: A Reflection of Genesis 1–3," 187.
33. Meier, "Job 1–21: A Reflection of Genesis 1–3," 187.
34. Meier, "Job 1–21: A Reflection of Genesis 1–3," 188.
35. Meier, "Job 1–21: A Reflection of Genesis 1–3," 188.

He endured the antithesis of his former life in every sense: economic and social impoverishment, spiritual exile, erroneous thinking, and identity confusion.

Two insufficient interpretive options are offered to explain Job's change of fortune. On one hand, the friends offered false hope. Repeatedly, they argued that re-reversal would come about through repentance from Job's presumed unrighteousness. Elihu declared about sinners, "If they listen and serve him, they complete their days in prosperity, and their years in pleasantness" (36:11; see also 33:24–26). Job, by implication, no longer prospered because he did not listen to or serve God. He was a sinner.[36]

On the other hand, Job embraced false pessimism. First, he expressed a fatalistic outlook that presumed the impossibility of re-reversal. After his great loss, he resigned himself to God's inscrutable sovereignty (1:21b; 2:10b).[37] For Job, reversal ran in only one direction—from blessing to curse. This attitude appears again in Job's negative depiction of reversal in 12:13–25.[38] Job believed that Israel's God gave but also took away, inexplicably and viciously. He wrote in a manner that appeared autobiographical:

> If he tears down, none can rebuild; if he shuts a man in, none can open. (12:14)

> He deprives of speech those who are trusted and takes away the discernment of the elders. (12:20)

> They grope in the dark without light, and he makes them stagger like a drunken man. (12:26)[39]

Second, Job explicitly lamented his change of fortune in chapter 3. He implored God to implement reversal to the bitter end—death and oblivion. He wanted God to rewrite history by means of self-obliteration. He mused about reversing his life's trajectory: his mother's infertility (v.

---

36. Eliphaz argued similarly (5:17–26; 22:21–30), as did Bildad (8:5–7, 20–22).

37. Job's affirmation is similar to Qohelet's skeptical comment, "As he came from his mother's womb he shall go again, naked as he came, and shall take nothing for his toil that he may carry away in his hand" (Eccl 5:15).

38. See Longman, *The Book of Job*, 202–4.

39. Hartley suggests, "The author is deeply indebted to Israel's hymnic tradition for this long piece. Psalm 107:40 is echoed in vv. 21a and 24b." (*The Book of Job*, 212, Note 17). The psalm in its entirety associates reversal *and* re-reversal with God's covenantal love and wisdom.

10), negation of his day of birth (vv. 3, 5), or emerging stillborn (vv. 11, 16).[40] But he also extrapolated from his personal experience and postulated that his suffering typified all creation (vv. 20–23). Craig G. Bartholomew and Ryan O'Dowd explain, "Essentially, his accusation is that something is wrong with the way God has made the world or perhaps that God has failed to uphold its order against the forces of chaos."[41] Seemingly, Job decided autonomously that a cosmos ruled by a capricious, remote, and incomprehensible deity was not worthy of existence. For this reason, he vividly envisioned the undoing of creation using imagery and idioms reminiscent of Genesis 1–2.[42]

Conceivably, then, the original readers wondered how might Job be restored, given his negative outlook. Or would Job remain a tragic enigma, doomed to loss and grief for the remainder of his life?

ABOUT THINKING

The intellectual character of the book of Job is self-evident. Hartley observed, "By vigorously lamenting his bitter feelings, he comes to grip with his anguish and channels his mind to seek some solution to his predicament."[43] Clearly, the book invites its readers to think deeply along with Job. In fact, the text contains a plethora of terms associated with knowledge.[44] The common verb "know" (*yada*) occurs over sixty times.

---

40. Smick ("Another Look at the Mythological Elements," 215) comments, "Job's error, for which he can scarcely be excused, was in damning the day of his birth, questioning the sovereign purpose of God."

41. Bartholomew and O'Dowd, *Old Testament Wisdom Literature*, 136.

42. For the parallels between Genesis 1–2 and Job 3, see Bartholomew and O'Dowd, *Old Testament Wisdom Literature*, 135–36; Hartley, *The Book of Job*, 102; Habel, *The Book of Job*, 104.

43. Hartley, *The Book of Job*, 48. Bartholomew and Ryan O'Dowd (*Old Testament Wisdom Literature*, 154) comment, "Job has long been recognized as a book about the limits of human knowledge. Knowledge, in fact, permeates every turn and fold of the narrative, starting with the scene at the divine courts."

44. By my count, there are more than forty terms, excluding words describing verbal thought such as "word" and "say." All the numbers in this section do not include the divine speeches (chapters 38–41). Regarding the quantity of Job's words and their use to convey ideas, Pelham ("Job's Crisis of Language," 333–34) notes, "Words are all Job has in the most literal sense possible. . . . The book of Job consists almost entirely of its characters' speech, and no character is as wordy as Job. When his friends speak a chapter, he generally answers with two chapters of his own, sometimes even three. Even God's words, though grand in scope, come nowhere near to approaching Job's

The vocabulary of the mind in the book of Job is diverse and broad, including these terms:

> know, knowledge, understand, understanding, wisdom, wise, think, thoughts, discern, discernment, believe, schemes, foolish, fool, folly, perceive, falsely, false, falsehood, counsel, counselor, searches, search out, test, reprove, reproof, deceive, deceitfully, deceit, empty talk, vain, instruct, instruction, teach, teacher, pay attention, remember, stupid,[45] windy knowledge/words[46]

Additionally, specialized vocabulary occurs in connection with at least three themes. First, terms associated with legal disputation appear: contend, case, argue (a case), argument, answer, prove, acquit, plead, arbiter, brought a complaint, plead the case, and show (partiality).[47] Second, there are many idiomatic expressions with "heart" (*leb*, twenty-nine times). In particular, "heart" is translated with reference to thinking as "wise" (2:4) and "understanding" (9:4; 17:4).

Third, several terms linked to wisdom occur: knowledge (*daat*, eleven times), understanding (*bin/binah*, twenty-three), counsel (*estah*, nine), purpose (*mezumah*, two), and wisdom (*chokmah*, eighteen).[48] These terms often function together as well.[49] In addition, expressions denoting the fear of God occur thirteen times. In particular, "wisdom" and "understanding" are coupled with the "fear of the Lord" in Job's discourse about wisdom (28:12, 20, 23, 28).

---

for sheer bulk."

45. The term appears twice: "stupid" (*nabub*) meaning "empty-headed" or "hollowed out" (11:12) or "stupid" (*tamah*) alluding to the lack of intelligence of farm animals (18:3).

46. Eliphaz accused Job of spouting "windy knowledge" (15:2) and Job retorted that his speech was "windy words" (16:3). The expressions resemble the modern idiom "full of hot air," meaning that one's thoughts and words signify nothing of value or utility and are not worth considering.

47. Commentators debate whether the book should be understood as a courtroom drama. Habel (*The Book of Job*, 54–57) argues that litigation plays a major role, as does Magdalene, "Who is Job's Redeemer?" 292–316. Longman (*The Book of Job*, 36–37) disagrees and disputes litigation as a controlling metaphor. Walton summarizes the arguments for and against Job's case ("Book of Job 1," 340–42).

48. Hartley (*The Book of Job*, 11) provides a list of phrases and metaphors that Job and Proverbs share.

49. *Chokmah* appears with *bin* (nine times), *bin* with *daat* (ten times), and *etsah* one time each with *bin* and *chokmah*, with *daat* and *chokmah*, and with *daat* plus *bin*.

Furthermore, the use of questions underscores the deliberative nature of Job's debate with his friends and with God. Interrogatives begin with "can" (thirty times), "do" (thirty-one), "what" (two), "when" (sixteen), "is there" (seven), "should" (four), and "how long" (four). Job also posed many "why" questions specifically addressed to God:

> Why did I not die at birth, come out from the womb and expire? (3:11)
>
> Why have you made me your mark? Why have I become a burden to you? (7:20)
>
> Why do you hide your face and count me as your enemy? (13:24)
>
> Why do the wicked live, reach old age, and grow mighty in power? (21:7)

In these ways, the dialogue contains argumentation between Job, God, and his friends (chapters 4–37). Each critiqued the vapid reasoning of the other, given their assumptions. The friends perceived intellectual snobbery in Job and asked, "Why are we counted as cattle? Why are we stupid in your sight?" (18:3). They polemicized against Job vigorously: "You are doing away with the fear of God and hindering meditation before God. For your iniquity teaches your mouth, and you choose the tongue of the crafty. Your own mouth condemns you, and not I; your own lips testify against you" (15:4–6). But Job's retorts were just as severe: "As for you, you whitewash with lies; worthless physicians are you all. Oh that you would keep silent, and it would be your wisdom!" (13:4–5).

DISSONANCE

The book of Job can be read as an abstract theological or philosophical debate—and it often is. However, Job is depicted as an embodied thinker who experienced cognitive and existential dissonance.[50] Before his affliction, he enjoyed blessing, consistent with traditional Hebrew teaching. His life made sense. He flourished. After his affliction, he suffered a reversal of fortune that was disorienting and enigmatic. His world was

---

50. Pelham ("Job's Crisis of Language," 351) describes the confusion as "God-as-God-ought-to-be-and-is" versus "God-as-God-ought-not-to-be-but-is" or "God-as-God-ought-to-be-but-is-not."

turned upside down.[51] Clearly, his search for understanding was not a mere intellectual exercise. He was situated in suffering and perplexity.[52]

The accuser remarked in the prologue, "Have you not put a hedge around him and his house and all that he has, on every side?" (1:10a). The word "hedge" (*suk*) implies an enclosure or existential-intellectual context. The insinuation was that God protected Job within a box, so to speak, that shielded him from reality and his own worst tendencies. The only other Old Testament occurrence of the term makes this clear: "Therefore I will hedge up (*suk*) her way with thorns, and I will build a wall against her, so that she cannot find her paths" (Hos 2:6). Due to idolatry, God hemmed in Israel to deprivation ("thorns") and disorientation ("paths"). They were no longer free to pursue their ill-chosen agenda and alternative reality. Similarly, during his test, Job was boxed in a second time by God—but into an entirely different context. Job pondered his predicament in parallel rhetorical questions:

> Why is light given to him who is in misery, and life to the bitter in soul? (3:20)
>
> Why is light given to a man whose way is hidden, whom God has hedged in? (3:23)

Indeed, God hemmed Job in, but the new milieu was entirely different from anything he had known. In this new setting, the words "bitter" and "bitterness" appear eight times to describe Job's dismal outlook. These terms are coupled with "anguish of my spirit" (7:11), "never having tasted prosperity" (21:25), and "groaning" (23:2). Job testified that God was, in fact, the agent of his desolation: "As God lives, who has taken away my right, and the Almighty, who has made my soul bitter" (27:2; see also 9:18). The term "way" (*derek*) refers to lifestyle and purpose. Norman C. Habel describes how a "hidden" path is a "misery of meaninglessness" and explains: "The crisis of Job is not only the problem of unjustified suffering but also the meaning in life when there is no future, no justice, no relief, and no purpose he can discern."[53] Job saw that "God himself has

---

51. Van Leeuwen, "Proverbs 30:21–23 and the Biblical World Turned Upside Down," 599–610.

52. Pelham ("Job's Crisis of Language," 349) adds this observation: "Adrift in an ocean of uncertainty, this is his one certainty—God is silent." See also Dell, "What Was Job's Malady?" 61–77.

53. Habel, *The Book of Job*, 34.

obscured that 'way' and created chaos."⁵⁴ Job declared, "He has walled up my way, so that I cannot pass, and he has set darkness upon my paths" (19:8). In other words, God withdrew his patronage, protection, and purpose, and as a result life no longer made sense.

In the former milieu depicted in the prologue, God spoke and Job heard and obeyed. But in the new context, God was enigmatically silent and remote. Job lamented the change: "Behold, he passes by me, and I see him not; he moves on, but I do not perceive him" (9:11). Job asked, "Why do you hide your face?" (13:24a; see also 23:3-9). He said, "I cry out, 'Violence!' but I am not answered; I call for help, but there is no justice" (19:7; see also 30:24, 28). In fact, Job ended his plea to God with an expression of plaintive longing: "Oh, that I had one to hear me! (Here is my signature! Let the Almighty answer me!)" (31:35). In this unwanted setting, Job professed profound doubt that God would even listen (19:16).

In the new context, therefore, the greatest dissonance Job experienced was with God himself. Indeed, from Job's point of view he became God's avowed "enemy" (13:24; 33:10), for God had "torn me in his wrath and hated me" (16:9). When Job referred to God in the third person ("he," "God," "Almighty"), the harshest expressions appeared. He testified that God "crushes me" (9:17), "gives me up to the ungodly" (16:11), "broke me apart" (v. 12a), "set me up as his target" (v. 12b), has "worn me out" (16:7a), "made me a byword of the peoples" (17:6), "stripped me from my glory" (19:9), "made my heart faint" (23:16), and "cast me into the mire" (30:19). Job also addressed God directly: "You scare me with dreams and terrify me with visions" (7:14); you "made me your mark" (v. 20b); and "I became a burden to you" (v. 20c). He also said to God, "[You] contend against me" (10:2b), "favor the designs of the wicked" (v. 3), "know that I am not guilty" (v. 7), "write bitter things against me" (13:26), "persecute me" (30:21b), and "will bring me to death" (v. 23a). In fact, Job frequently asserted that God was unjust and unkind. God "oppressed" (10:3) and "destroyed" him (v. 8). Like a venomous spider, he "closed his net about me" (19:6b).⁵⁵ God was hostile and "counts me as his adversary" (19:11b).

---

54. Habel, *The Book of Job*, 112.

55. Hartley (*The Book of Job*, 284) suggests a hunting image: "The truth is that God has been the aggressive hunter who has thrown his net around his prey so that there is no possibility for him to get away." Habel (*The Book of Job*, 289, 300), on the other hand, renders the text as a scene of battle: "He has thrown up his siege works against me." Habel comments, "Job is under siege with no opportunity of vindication, no right to a civil trial."

Indeed, he was "cruel" and "persecuted" his servant (30:21). For all these reasons, Job stated three times, "I loathe my life" (7:16; 9:21; 10:1).

The dissonance was also felt intellectually. Job pointed often to the apparently unfair and illogical administration of justice in the world—not only in his personal experience but also among the wicked: "The earth is given into the hand of the wicked" (9:24; see also 12:6; 21:7–17; 24:1–23). Job extrapolated from his individual experience of futility, turmoil, and transience to general truths about humanity. He postulated that his misfortune was paradigmatic of the human condition and insinuated that mankind would fare better if God simply left them alone:

> Man who is born of a woman is few of days and full of trouble. He comes out like a flower and withers; he flees like a shadow and continues not. And do you open your eyes on such a one and bring me into judgment with you? . . . Since his days are determined, and the number of his months is with you, and you have appointed his limits that he cannot pass, look away from him and leave him alone, that he may enjoy, like a hired hand, his day. (14:1–3, 5–6; see also Ps 39:13)

Indeed, the dissonance was so acute that Job determined that God's absence was actually preferable. For this reason, he prayed four times, "Leave me alone" (7:16, 19; 10:20; 14:6). He thought that a terrible, paradoxical existence without God was better than a horrible, enigmatic existence with him. Job implored of the divine inquisitor, "Are not my days few? Then cease, and leave me alone, that I may find a little cheer" (10:20). Eric Ortlund suggests, "If Job cannot live under God's favor, he implies that he does not see any point to his existence at all, blessed or otherwise."[56]

Still, Job was of two minds. The dissonance manifested psychologically in his deepest longings and fears. Before loss overwhelmed him, he had anticipated its possibility: "For the thing that I fear comes upon me, and what I dread befalls me" (3:25).[57] He often expressed utmost pessimism: "My eye will never again see good" (7:7b). But he also professed hope: "I know that my Redeemer lives, and at the last he will stand upon the earth" (19:25). Expressions of strong desire with the interjection "Oh"

---

56. Ortlund, "How Did Job Speak Rightly about God?" 354.

57. Ortlund, "How Did Job Speak Rightly about God?" 354. See also Habel's translation in *The Book of Job*, 99–100.

also reveal both positive and negative aspirations.[58] There is great pathos: "Oh that I might have my request, and that God would fulfill my hope, that it would please God to crush me, that he would let loose his hand and cut me off!" (6:8–9). But also, Job confessed a longing for divine nearness: "Oh, that I were as in the months of old, as in the days when God watched over me, when his lamp shone upon my head, and by his light I walked through darkness... when the friendship of God was upon my tent, when the Almighty was yet with me" (29:2–5a).

Similar disorientation is evident in Job's prayers. Based on his experience, God appeared duplicitous, since he gave and took away unjustly; or perhaps even worse, God operated a cosmic bait-and-switch scheme (10:8–9). Job audaciously challenged God in this way:

> Do not condemn me; let me know why you contend against me. Does it seem good to you to oppress, to despise the work of your hands and favor the designs of the wicked? Have you eyes of flesh? Do you see as man sees? Are your days as the days of man, or your years as a man's years, that you seek out my iniquity and search for my sin, although you know that I am not guilty, and there is none to deliver out of your hand? (10:2b–7)

But he also prayed with earnest piety:

> Only grant me two things, then I will not hide myself from your face: withdraw your hand far from me, and let not dread of you terrify me. Then call, and I will answer; or let me speak, and you reply to me. How many are my iniquities and my sins? Make me know my transgression and my sin. (13:20–23)

Thus, because of the great dissonance that he experienced, Job complained *to* God and affirmed truths *about* God. He did not forsake his faith. He did not embrace another worldview. Rather, his descent into cynicism and confusion occurred with reference to the God of the Bible. That above-the-sun orientation would save him, though clearly Job did not think so at the time.

THE GREAT DEBATE

If the book of Job consisted of only the prologue (chapters 1–2), with the account of Job's righteousness, his great loss, and his confessions of faith,

---

58. They are found in 6:2, 8; 13:5; 14:13; 19:23, 24; 23:3; 29:2; and 31:35.

then it could have closed logically with his restoration in the epilogue (42:7–17). In that case, the question of the accuser—"Does Job fear God for nothing?"—would have been answered in the negative. Job did not serve God for the benefits. His faith was not instrumental. He did not attempt to appease God. Likewise, the assertion posed by the narrator—"Job did not sin by charging God with wrongdoing"—would have been confirmed. End of story.

But the narrative was not that simple. Ostensibly, a significant transition occurred in Job's mind during the seven days of silence as he tried to interpret his dramatic reversal (2:11–13).[59] Perhaps the severity and duration of his affliction overwhelmed him. Maybe the divergence between his expectations of God and his experience with God unnerved him. By way of illustration, let us engage in another creative thought experiment about what Job thought while he grieved alone.

> My God, why is this happening to me? I did everything you told me. I was not corrupt in any matter or with anyone. I did not turn aside to other gods. I did exactly as you taught me. I wanted to be acceptable in your eyes. And you confirmed my uprightness, because you blessed me more than anyone else. You made me an example for others to follow. But why have you taken it all away? Have I sinned against you? Why have I become as the wicked in your eyes? Please show me my fault.
>
> I have lost everything dear to me: my children, my home, my prosperity, my status in the community, my health. Even my wife disowned me. She told me to curse you and die. I am now a misfit, the embodiment of curse. But most of all, I have lost you—yes, *you*! Why are you silent? Why do you not listen to me, as I listened to you? Why do you not intervene?
>
> My God, this is so painful! I worried about disaster and now it has happened. I feel so ill. I hurt everywhere. I have no strength. Nothing appeals to me. I feel so alone. And it makes *no* sense. I do not know why this is happening. I do not know how I erred. I do not know why you ignore me. I do not know how to pray anymore. Nothing works. I am so confused, so unhappy, so

---

59. Pelham ("Job's Crisis of Language," 337) suggests this possibility: "Yet, the fact remains that the gulf between Job's words of chs. 1 and 2 and those of ch. 3 demands an explanation.... We must look to the seven days of silence to explain the shift in Job's attitude. I do think Job's silence is a response to his growing recognition of the seriousness of his situation." Longman (*The Book of Job*, 98) adds about chapter 3, "He is just giving vent to his intensely felt inner feelings and thoughts. His three friends overhear, of course, and it is the attitude that is expressed by this speech that leads them to challenge Job."

disappointed. My hope is almost gone and I see little chance of escape. I cannot endure much longer in this state. My God, why is this happening to me? What does it mean?

Seemingly, Job verbalized with his friends what he felt and pondered after the week of hushed commiseration (chapter 3). Clearly, an evolution occurred in his mental and emotional posture during this time. In the prologue he assumed a submissive attitude (chapters 1-2), during the dialogue he manifested a vigorous polemical stance (chapters 4-37), and in the epilogue he once again demonstrated a reverent compliance (chapters 38-42). The text suggests two motivations for this transformation after the seven days of mourning: psychological and intellectual.

Job's distressed psychological outlook impacted his evaluation of the dilemma.[60] In the prologue he expressed trepidation about calamity. For this reason, he preemptively sacrificed on behalf of his children (1:5). After their death and further disaster, he remarked, "For the thing that I fear comes upon me" (3:25a; see also 9:28; 30:26). Apparently, he harbored disquietude about God prior to his loss.[61] Indeed, Job evidenced a dichotomy between trust and dread throughout the dialogue. In chapter 23, for instance, he declared with hope that "an upright man could argue with him, and I would be acquitted forever by my judge" (v. 7) and "when he has tried me, I shall come out as gold" (v. 10b). But he also testified, "What he desires, that he does" (v. 13b) and "He will complete what he appoints for me" (v. 14a). For these reasons, Job confessed, "Therefore I am terrified at his presence" (v. 15a). Job was clearly disoriented by the dissonance he experienced.

Furthermore, Job greatly lamented the reversal brought about in his life and expressed deep nostalgia for the past. He wrote, "I was at ease, and he broke me apart; he seized me by the neck and dashed me to pieces" (16:12). Referring to his former life, Job commented, "Then I thought, 'I shall die in my nest, and I shall multiply my days as the sand'" (29:18). He expressed a profound sense of loss: "My days are past; my

---

60. He described his emotional ordeal as "sighing" and "groaning" (3:24), "misery" (7:3), "anguish" (v. 11), "darkness" (10:21), "pain" (16:6), "weeping" (v. 16), "pouring out tears to God" (v. 20b), "spirit broken" (17:1a), "heart faints" (19:27), "impatient" (21:4), and "soul poured out" (30:16).

61. Or was Job's sense of dread prescient? Hartley (*The Book of Job*, 100) suggests that this was so: "This statement reveals that before his trial Job had dreaded that some ill might befall his household.... He had also feared that some tragedy might end his prosperity." See also Bartholomew and O'Dowd, *Old Testament Wisdom Literature*, 137.

plans are broken off, the desires of my heart" (17:11; see also 29:1–18). In the end, Job's emotional state was shattered. He wished that he had not been born (3:3) and that God might put an end to him (6:9; 9:25; 17:1). He believed that he would never again see good (7:7), and as a result his hope was destroyed (14:19b; 17:15).

Conceptually, Job and his friends were boxed in by several public and private affirmations. Positively, they presupposed Old Testament ontology and anthropology.[62] But negatively, they inaccurately embraced the retribution principle as a representation of God's moral administration of the world.[63] Longman explains: "If you sin, then you suffer; so if you suffer, then you are a sinner." But the opposite was also valid: "If you are righteous (godly, wise), then you are blessed; so if you are blessed, then you are righteous (godly, wise)."[64] Conceptually, the principle presumed a rigid interpretation of Deuteronomy 28 and its rationale for blessing and woe. Nevertheless, the theory provided an explanation for injustice in the world that was simple and predictable. Moral law was akin to the laws of nature: God established physical laws to rule over the environment and also decreed the law of retribution to rule among mankind.

Both Job and his friends presumed this truism. For the friends, it explained Job's predicament. They knew the reason for his affliction: he suffered because he sinned. He was no longer righteous. It also provided the remedy: Job needed only to repent and thereby secure his restoration (4:6–11; 5:17–26; 8:5–7). As John H. Walton notes, they reasoned with the mindset of the ancient Near East: for Job to reestablish his former state, he must somehow "appease a deity who was angry for unknown reasons."[65] This, of course, was also the accuser's rationale: religion was useful. Job used piety for instrumental motives.

---

62. Regarding God: omnipotent (5:9; 9:5, 19; 23:13; 25:2), omniscient (5:13–14; 11:7–9), wise (9:4; 12:13; 21:22; 28:23), Creator (9:7–9; 10:8–9; 12:10; 26:7–13; 28:25–27; 31:15), providence (14:5), righteous (4:17), judge (8:20–22; 19:29), not a man (9:32), no one holds God to account (9:33), reproves humans (5:17–18; 22:21–30). Regarding human beings: finite (4:18–21; 10:5; 14:1–2), dependent (31:2); fallen (22:5–9; 13:15–16; 25:4–6), prone to idolatry (12:6; 31:24–27), lack wisdom and understanding (12:2, 24; 13:5, 7; 16:3), contentious (13:2, 4; 19:2–3; 21:3; 30:1, 9–16), treacherous (6:15; 16:20; 19:14, 19, 22), wicked (21:7–15; 24:1–7). Concerning the book's thematic connections with Genesis, see O'Dowd, "A Chord of Three Strands," 75–79.

63. For an explanation of the retribution principle in its ancient Near East context and in the Old Testament, see Walton, "Retribution," 647–55.

64. Longman, *The Book of Job*, 56.

65. Walton, "Retribution," 650.

But for Job, the retribution principle inferred something insidious about God. Job was absolutely convinced that *he* had not violated the principle. He had not sinned and did not deserve to suffer. He declared repeatedly in one form or another, "Till I die I will not put away my integrity from me. I hold fast my righteousness and will not let it go; my heart does not reproach me for any of my days" (27:5b-6; see also 9:20, 23; 10:7a; 16:17; 29:14). Thus, he wondered instead about God's justice, because God caused unmerited affliction with little hope of restoration (5:8; 8:5-6, 20-21; 11:14-20; 22:21-30). And worst of all, God was absent from the debate.

For his friends, however, a denial of the postulate was blasphemous, since it impugned God's character. On this basis, they concluded that Job had erred and deserved affliction, despite his avowals of innocence. But Job could not reconcile his atypical experience with the principle.[66] Nor could he interpret the reverse fact that the wicked (who according to the axiom merited judgment) often prospered with impunity (9:24; 10:3; 16:11; 21:7). In reality, the retribution principle was a conceptual straitjacket for both Job and his friends.[67] They could not imagine both God's justice and Job's innocence in the midst of his suffering. The friends preserved God's integrity but maligned Job's character; Job retained his innocence but maligned God's justice. They both attempted to reason from below, so to speak, using the retribution principle as their guide.

Nevertheless, even as Job slipped further into hopelessness and cynicism, he tried to make sense of his circumstances. He embraced four key assumptions. First, he affirmed one indisputable fact—his innocence—and reasoned from there. God's moral government, on the other hand, was at best irregular and seemingly incoherent. The normal modes of communication—prayer and lament—had broken down. And wisdom in the form of his friends' counsel fell short of illuminating his unusual dilemma. Second, he perceived his hardship as divine evaluation. God the "watcher of mankind" (7:20; 10:14) was "testing" (7:18) or "trying" (23:10) him in a very aggressive manner.[68] God was "seeking out" and "searching for" sin in his life (10:6). From Job's point of view, God was obsessively hounding him for no good reason. Third, Job believed

---

66. Jackson ("Who Is This Who Darkens Counsel?" 157) suggests, "Job is searching for an understanding whereby both God and Job are vindicated as righteous (ch. 27)."

67. Fox ("Job the Pious," 359) comments that Job was "handicapped by constricted vision, flawed assumptions, and unwarranted inferences."

68. God "sees" and evaluates mankind's steps (7:8, 17-20; 10:14; 13:27; 14:3).

incorrectly that he was unjustly implicated in a lawsuit (*rib*) initiated by God against him (10:2).[69] Fourth—albeit implicitly—the narrative presumes a residual hopefulness. Indeed, Job prayed throughout his ordeal and searched for a way back to God. If he had been truly devoid of faith or resigned to nihilism, suicide or fatalism might have seemed reasonable.

Thus, Job implemented two strategies to compel God's attention and his communication once again. First, he audaciously countersued God and sought redress concerning his integrity. Gerhard von Rad commented about this tactic, "He goes to the limits of piety and blasphemy in order to force this God, whom he nevertheless continues to regard as his God, out of his ambiguity."[70] Job issued a formal legal challenge: "Who is there who will contend (*rib*) with me?" (13:19a). He declared with greatest urgency, "As for me, is my complaint against man? Why should I not be impatient?" (21:4).[71] As the presumed defendant, Job sought to know the charges against him: "Let me know why you contend (*rib*) against me" (10:2b; see also 13:23) and "Oh, that I had the indictment written by my adversary!" (31:35b). But he also pondered the insurmountable challenges of deposing almighty God (9:2–3, 14–16). He prepared and practiced his defense (10:1; 13:18; 31:1–34, 38–40). He intended to justify his "ways" (way of life or social righteousness) to God in the most direct manner conceivable: "to his face" (13:15b).[72]

Second, Job authored an oath of innocence (31:1–40). He argued on the basis of the retribution principle: "Is not calamity for the unrighteous, and disaster for the workers of iniquity? Does not he see my ways and number all my steps?" (vv. 3–4). According to Abigail Pelham, Job reasoned in this way: "I call upon him to punish me if I am guilty of any offense, or, by not punishing me, to proclaim my innocence."[73] His oath comprised a series of positive affirmations regarding his rectitude under

---

69. *Rib* appears as "contend" (9:3; 10:2; 13:19; 23:6; 33:13; 40:2), "plead the case" (13:8), and "brought a complaint" (31:13).

70. Von Rad, *Wisdom in Israel*, 220.

71. Walton ("Job 1," 340) explains that the lawsuit was in reality brought by the accuser (and Job) against God, though Job lacked this "above the sun" knowledge or "below the sun" self-awareness.

72. Habel (*The Book of Job*, 230) explains Job's audacity: "In coming before the very presence of God Job is faced with the task of achieving the impossible, since traditionally no person can see God's face and live (Exod 33:20)."

73. Pelham, "Job's Crisis of Language," 351.

the law.[74] He also expressed sixteen self-imprecatory propositions: "if I have done this . . . then bring that to pass, for I deserve punishment."[75] In addition, he articulated two petitions for a positive evaluation of his righteousness or a written indictment of any wrongdoing:

> Let me be weighed in a just balance, and let God know my integrity! (31:6)

> Here is my signature! Let the Almighty answer me! Oh, that I had the indictment written by my adversary! (v. 35)

In this way, Job sought the rhetorical initiative and attempted to turn the tables on God, as it were. In effect, he queried, "Why am I denied favor when I have performed righteousness?" He sought to box God in and compel him to speak or act. Walton summarizes the rationale:

> The climax of Job's discourses is found in Job 31 as he attempts to turn God's silence, which has been serving as evidence of his guilt, to his advantage. By pronouncing his extended oath of innocence, he has challenged God in such a way that silence would vindicate him. After all, if he has sworn falsely, it is God's obligation to strike him down. If God does not do so, that lack of response stands as Job's exoneration.[76]

In essence, Job challenged God to defend himself. He wanted to understand why wickedness was rewarded when it deserved the opposite (10:3). Job insinuated that righteousness and wickedness co-exist in God's world in a very precarious and unreasonable manner. In effect, therefore, Job called upon God to provide an apologetic (or theodicy) for himself and his enigmatic moral rule.

CONCLUSION

The book of Job shows that our epistemological context is very complex. We often imagine ourselves as self-directed and self-sufficient thinkers,

---

74. He spoke about lust (31:1-4), deceit (vv. 5-6), greed (vv. 7-8), sexuality (vv. 9-12), fair dealing for servants (vv. 13-15), care for the poor (vv. 16-20), social justice (vv. 21-23), money and power (vv. 24-25), and idolatry (vv. 26-28).

75. Illicit actions and intentions ("if"): 31:5, 7, 9, 13, 16, 19, 20, 21, 24, 25, 26, 29, 31, 33, 38, 39. "Then" statements: 31:8, 10, 22. Self-exculpatory insertions include: verses 11-12, 14-15, 18, 23, 28, 30, 35-37.

76. Walton, "Job 1," 338. The implicit assumption is that Job is innocent (and therefore confident of acquittal) or harbors an unhealthy death wish.

but Job shared his mental universe with others. Visible and invisible, mortal and supernatural minds inhabit the same space, as it were. All that Job sought to understand was first thought by God. Job's plight was deliberated in the divine council. In particular, "the satan" emerged as a contrarian theorist with an adversarial motive.[77] The accuser's impact was not limited to heaven, however, for a "spirit" influenced Job's friends on earth.[78] Clearly, the devil and his minions do not play fair and are loose with the truth.

Job's interpretive criterion was inherited. He, his friends, and his community shared a mistaken concept of divine justice. That model provided the lens through which they evaluated Job's experience and directed their expectations in life. The retribution principle presupposed a skewed ontology and instrumental relationship with God derived from the surrounding cultures. Job and his community were informed by religious assumptions that were inherently syncretistic and rooted in idolatry. Similarly, today we often deliberate using plausibility structures, biases, and paradigms as if they were worldview-neutral or truly objective. We sometimes do not subject ideas to thorough biblical critique. Perhaps, like Job, we evaluate experience with inherited but flawed wisdom.[79]

Worldview matters for epistemology. Job learned that ontology determined knowledge. He discovered that the gods of appeasement were not like the Lord of the Bible. Job learned that his experience was meaningful, but only within the biblical worldview, in particular a biblical understanding of creation. During his affliction, however, his outlook resembled that of Asaph, who also faulted divine justice: "Thus my heart was grieved, And I was vexed in my mind. I was so foolish and ignorant; I was like a beast before You" (73:21–22, NKJV). But as we will see in the next chapter, the Lord addressed Job personally and pedagogically. He discovered his role within God's much bigger drama. He was able to see the world with new priorities. Like Habakkuk, he could then testify from a higher and broader perspective:

77. Notably, "the satan" possessed enormous powers in Job, with God's permission: authority to appear before the heavenly council and challenge Yahweh, freedom to travel throughout the earth, the ability to incite humans to attack and kill, the ability to cause deadly atmospheric conditions, and the capacity to afflict people with illness (1:13–19; 2:7–8).

78. This episode underscores the necessity of extreme caution regarding private, supernatural knowledge.

79. The Bible's teaching about unbelief is critically important and points to the relevance of elenctics, apologetics, and worldview critique.

Though the fig tree should not blossom, nor fruit be on the vines, the produce of the olive fail and the fields yield no food, the flock be cut off from the fold and there be no herd in the stalls, yet I will rejoice in the Lord; I will take joy in the God of my salvation. God, the Lord, is my strength; he makes my feet like the deer's; he makes me tread on my high places (3:17–19).

12

Out of the Whirlwind

"You have heard of the steadfastness of Job, and you have seen the purpose of the Lord, how the Lord is compassionate and merciful."

—JAMES 5:11

WE DO NOT KNOW exactly when the dialogue between Job and his interlocutors ended. In all likelihood, the mudslinging had exhausted itself—emotionally and intellectually. A cessation of hostilities was inevitable. Job was firm in his position and his friends were too foolish to know better. Probably, Elihu was droning on (chapters 32–37), pontificating to no one except himself, when the theophany burst upon them.

No one expected Yahweh's advent, except perhaps as a destructive climax to Job's folly. Clearly, Job was not expecting him, for he maintained little hope of adjudication (9:16). In fact, Elihu opined that God does not make court appearances, especially with unrighteous persons like Job who impudently indict the divinity. He confidently declared, "It is not for man to set a time to come before God in judgment" (34:23).[1]

The climactic encounter between God and Job is the focus of this chapter. The first section examines the interaction between the divine judge and his would-be plaintiff (38:1). I then turn to God's introductory query in 38:2, "Who is this who darkens knowledge by words without knowledge?" The third section explores the significance of Yahweh's

---

1. This is Hartley's rendition (*The Book of Job*, 455). Habel's is similar: "It is not for a mortal to set a time to come before El in litigation" (*The Book of Job*, 527).

query in 40:2, "Shall a faultfinder contend with the Almighty?" The fourth section, "Catch-22," concerns Job's faulty legal reasoning (40:8-9). I then deal with Job's intellectual myopia (41:10-11) and finally with Job's repentance as an intellectual reversal (42:1-8).

THEOPHANY

Yahweh appeared unexpectedly and dramatically: "Then the Lord answered Job out of the whirlwind" (38:1). The word "then" indicates an interruption, if not a rupture. The name Yahweh specifies the divine being with whom Job contested so vigorously. The moniker identifies Yahweh as the covenant-making deity of Israel. David testified to his uniqueness and supremacy: "There is no one like you, and there is no God but you" (1 Sam 7:22, NIV; see also Exod 3:7-8a; Deut 6:4-5).

The verb "answered" highlights several important points in this context. Job lamented the absence of God's voice and longed to receive vindication. Above all, he wanted God to make sense of his experience. For this reason, he mourned the loss of God's "friendship" (*sud*, 29:4b). In the past, God was "an intimate in his tent" who provided wise and trusted counsel.[2] Until he spoke again, Job's communication with him was functionally one-way, a monologue. By means of the theophany, however, the Lord addressed Job in all his particularity. Presumably, the others were present, and later they too heard from Yahweh directly (42:7). But the Lord spoke first to Job "face to face," as an intimate. In this way, he elevated Job's status publicly and likened him to the ancient fathers with whom God spoke directly (Noah, Abraham, Moses, David, and the prophets).

The Lord answered Job "out of the whirlwind" (*caar*, also translated as "tempest" or "storm"). About thirteen times in the Old Testament, storms (*saar*) occurred that expressed wrath, and nine times they were linked with revelation, miracle, or providence.[3] Job depicted his suffer-

---

2. This is Hartley's translation of *sud* (*The Book of Job*, 387). Elsewhere in Job, the word is translated as "counsel of God" (15:8) and "intimate friends" (19:19). In the Old Testament, the term appears as "sweet counsel together (Ps 55:14), "council of holy ones" (89:7), "company of the upright" (111:1), and "revealing his secret to his servants" (Amos 3:7).

3. *Saar* as judgment appears in Pss 55:8; 83:15; Isa 29:6; 40:24; 41:16; Jer 23:19 (twice); 25:32; 30:23; Ezek 13:11, 13; Jonah 1:12; Zech 9:14. It appears as revelation in 2 Kgs 2:1, 11; Job 38:1; 40:6; Pss 107:25, 29; 148:8; Ezek 1:4; Jonah 1:4. Storms also functioned as theophanies in Exod 19:19-20; Judg 5:5-6; Ps 18:8-16.

ing as a tempest from God in the midst of judgment (9:17). Likewise, he lamented God's silence in the "storm" (*shava*): "I cry to you for help and you do not answer me; I stand, and you only look at me .... You lift me up on the wind; you make me ride on it, and you toss me about in the roar of the storm" (30:22). Presumably, when the Lord finally appeared in the whirlwind, Job felt dread, not relief. He expected terror and death (6:8–10; 13:15–16; 19:25–27).

After surviving the initial blast, Job must have wondered what kind of storm this was: negative and characterized by wrath leading to destruction, or positive and dedicated to reproof? Zophar had predicted that the Lord's coming would be vindictive (21:19–20). Or was Yahweh's objective pedagogical, as suggested by Eliphaz: "Behold, blessed is the one whom God reproves; therefore despise not the discipline of the Almighty" (5:17)? Obviously, at that moment of shock and awe Job did not know that the encounter would lead to repentance and restoration. As T. C. Ham suggests, "Despite Job's expressed desire that God would simply crush him (6:8–9), God does nothing of the sort. God speaks, meeting Job's other expressed desire (13:3; 23:4)."[4]

WHO IS THIS?

The Lord's first utterance (38:2), then, was not merely sarcastic or dismissive. Rather, he expressed a negative diagnosis of Job's outlook. Yahweh asked, "Who is this that darkens counsel by words without knowledge?" The phrase "who is this" was rhetorical, acknowledging Job as the would-be litigant against and presumptive pedagogue for the Lord.[5]

The term "counsel" (*etsah*) refers to deliberation focused on planning, purpose, and power.[6] In fact, *etsah* is a word associated with wisdom. In Proverbs Lady Wisdom says, "I have counsel (*etsah*) and sound wisdom; I have insight .... By me kings reign, and rulers decree what is just" (Prov 8:14–15). God declares that his plan entails the power to carry it out: "I am God, and there is no other; I am God, and there is none like me, declaring the end from the beginning and from ancient times things

---

4. Ham, "The Gentle Voice of God in Job 38," 534.

5. Ham, "The Gentle Voice of God in Job 38," 532–34. It also echoes Job's query in 13:19, "Who is there who will contend with me?"

6. Fox, "Words for Wisdom," 160–61.

not yet done, saying, 'My counsel (*etsah*) shall stand, and I will accomplish all my purpose'" (Isa 46:9b–10; see also Ps 33:10–11).

In a moment of lucidity, Job esteemed God's counsel: "With God are wisdom and might; he has counsel (*etsah*) and understanding" (12:13).[7] But conceptually, Job also questioned God's design of and plan for the cosmos. And existentially, he told God four times, "Leave me alone." In this sense, Job's best plan resembled the wicked person's counsel. He foisted upon reality an image of a remote deity with a flawed design in a futile attempt to survive apart from God.

The word "knowledge" (*daat*) is also a term associated with wisdom. *Daat* is linked to the fear of the Lord (Isa 11:2), the call of Lady Wisdom (Prov 1:22), and the wisdom of creation (3:19–20). Job asked at one point, "Will any teach God knowledge (*daat*), seeing that he judges those who are on high?" (21:22). Together, the terms "knowledge" and "counsel" constitute the path of wisdom taught in Proverbs: "Have I not written for you thirty sayings of counsel (*etsah*) and knowledge (*daat*)?" (22:20–21a). The words "counsel" and "knowledge" are paired four times in the Old Testament (Job 38:2; 42:3; Prov 22:20; Isa 11:2).

These two terms, however, are modified by two negative characteristics: "darkens" (counsel) and "without" (knowledge). The verb "darkens" (*chashak*) in this context indicates obfuscation and misinterpretation. The phrase "without knowledge" means "without the proper context" and is therefore conceptually parallel with "darkens counsel."

Elihu anticipated this epistemological assessment three times in the final discourse. He commented, "Job speaks without knowledge; his words are without insight" (34:35). He added, "Job opens his mouth in empty talk; he multiplies words without knowledge" (35:16). In other words, Job did not know what he was talking about. He expressed "windy knowledge" regarding the Lord.

Thus, Yahweh's indictment that Job "darkens counsel by words without knowledge" indicated that Job had responded to his affliction with an improper interpretive framework. His worldview was, in fact, reductionistic insofar as all things cohered in the retribution principle and egoistic insofar as his personal situation was functionally the center of reality. As a result, he misrepresented God's governance (9:22). He misjudged his motive and character. He embraced erroneous conclusions that obscured the truth. In this way, he discredited and undermined God's design

---

7. The context, however, betrays Job's negative assessment of God's "counsel" as mainly destructive (12:14–25).

("counsel") in creation by questioning his moral government. Job lacked understanding and wisdom, but more than anything else, he lacked the intellectual humility befitting a creature.

Job 38:3 shows that an intellectual reorientation was absolutely necessary: "Dress for action like a man; I will question you, and you make it known to me." Job, the presumptive teacher of God, would now instruct the Creator—if he could. Longman explains that Yahweh's questions about the order of nature in chapters 38–39 were designed to restore Job's epistemic humility, as well as his transcendent reference point:

> God then decides to demonstrate clearly that Job is accurately described as ignorant: God commands Job to prepare for a test, a series of questions that he must answer. It will soon become clear that Job cannot answer these questions; indeed, no human could ever answer these questions. Of course, that is the point. God is in the process of showing Job who is God and who is a creature.[8]

THE FAULTFINDER

Yahweh's second utterance diagnosed Job's epistemological outlook with even greater clarity and also reversed the charges on Job. "Shall a faultfinder contend with the Almighty? He who argues with God, let him answer it" (40:2). Translations of this verse vary, but the logic is clear: "But you have argued that I am wrong. Now you must answer me" (CEV).[9] From chapter 3 to chapter 31, Job was the protagonist and God the presumed antagonist of the drama. Job the hero was unjustly charged by the divine antihero. Two obstacles, however, could not be overcome by Job's oratory: God's silence and Job's dreadful affliction. For this reason, he enacted a lawsuit and oath to compel God to speak—but on Job's terms. His rationale was homocentric. He wanted God to validate his innocence and unmerited suffering under the retribution principle.

Three verbs ("contend," "argues," and "answer") and one noun ("faultfinder," *yissor*) determine the message of 40:2. The noun is especially critical. It is most likely derived from the verb *yasar*, meaning to

---

8. Longman, *The Book of Job*, 427.

9. Renderings depend on how to translate key terms, such as *yissor* ("faultfinder," a *hapax legomenon* noun), and whether to accent the litigious nuance of the vocabulary, such as *rib* ("contend," "make charges," "argue").

reprove, rebuke, chastise, instruct, warn, or discipline. In nearly every instance where the verb appears, these characteristics occur: (1) a superior confronts or challenges an inferior; (2) the relationship presumes accountability and obligation; (3) an evaluation occurs according to a standard; (4) the superior knows what is best for or exercises judgment against the inferior. About twenty-five times, the subject of the verb is the Lord, for he is the faultfinder of human beings.

In this case, however, the roles are reversed. Job functioned as the one who determined fault—in God. He assessed God's governance based upon his individual experience and observation. He reasoned from below with under-the-sun criteria. He believed that he possessed the big picture when he had only a snapshot. He demanded an intervention, if not an explanation. He was, in fact, epistemologically narcissistic.

Job reasoned in a univocal manner. He extrapolated erroneously from his microcosmic perspective to a macrocosmic dimension. He tried to box God into an unyielding formula of blessing and retribution. He presupposed norms to which the Lord was equally accountable. Thus, he overstepped the limits of the Creator–creature distinction. He did not reckon rightly with either his finitude or fallenness. Worst of all, he tacitly assumed an ontological assent, using God's norms against him and putting God on trial. Thus, 40:2 may be summarized in a manner that shows the reversal of litigious roles:

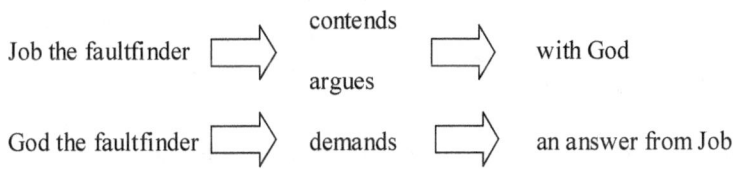

Further, the verb "argues" (*yakach*) appears fifty-nine times in the Old Testament in disputatious settings and often shares the characteristics associated with *yasar* above.[10] *Yakach* occurs in Job as "reprove" (5:17; 6:25, 26; 22:4), "reproof" (6:25), "rebuke" (13:10 twice; 33:19), and "refute" (32:12), but also as "arbiter" (9:33), "argue" (13:15; 15:3; 16:21; 23:7; 40:2), and "argument" (19:5). Noteworthy is Job 23:4–7: "I would lay my case before him and fill my mouth with arguments. I would know what

---

10. The term appears in ethical contexts, translated as "reprove," "rebuke," and "discipline," and in litigious contexts, rendered as "reason frankly," "arbiter," "argue," "argument," "refute," "decide disputes," "contend," and "judge."

he would answer me and understand what he would say to me.... There an upright man could argue (*yakach*) with him, and I would be acquitted forever by my judge." As we saw earlier, Job posed an argument to God concerning the prosperity of the wicked: "Does it seem good to you to oppress, to despise the work of your hands and favor the designs of the wicked?" (10:3).

"Answer" (*anah*) in this context indicated a summons from God, but also a very critical recognition of Job. Before the theophany, a great deal of verbiage passed between Job and his interlocutors, but there was very little real communication. Likewise, Job complained that God would not answer. Not being heard by both humans and God indicated his profound loss of status.[11] In the past, Job called out to God and he answered (12:4) as a friend (29:4). Before his servants responded with respect (19:16), his words influenced others (4:3–4), and his speech conveyed import in the community (29:7; 31:21). Now he was invisible, functionally irrelevant. His friends did not take him seriously and neither did his wife. Worst of all, the Lord appeared remote and uncaring. But all this changed radically when the Lord "answered" Job from the whirlwind (38:1; 40:6).

The verb *rib* ("contends" in 40:2) conveys legal significance and appears twelve times in Job, such as "contend" (9:3; 10:2; 13:19; 23:6; 33:13; 40:2), "pleadings" (13:6), "plead the case" (13:8), "cause" (29:16), and "complaint" (31:13).[12] Armed with his skewed evaluation of reality, Job litigated against the Lord. But as we will see, Yahweh was not impressed.

CATCH-22

Yahweh's third utterance (40:8) posed two questions that further undermined Job's position and turned the tables on Job. First, he confronted Job's titanic mental hubris: "Will you even put me in the wrong?"[13] The adverb "even" (*aph*) seems to indicate incredulity. Perhaps we can imagine what the Lord meant: "Really? How could you imagine such an idea? You know better. You are way out of line and gravely mistaken." The notion

---

11. See Pelham, "Job's Crisis of Language," 333–54.
12. "Accuser" is Longman's translation (*The Book of Job*, 362). Hartley's is "opponent at law" (*The Book of Job*, 424). Habel's is "adversary at law" (*The Book of Job*, 425). As Habel notes, there are several litigious terms in the book of Job.
13. The KJV says, "Will you also disannul my judgment?" as if to say "on top of everything else." The NKJV inserts "indeed" and the NASB "really." Interestingly, the serpent also said to Eve with feigned incredulity: "Did God actually (*aph*) say . . . ?"

that Job could justifiably charge God with wrongdoing was implausible. The possibility that Job would indict God was inconceivable, based on the narrator's testimony (1:22).

The second question exposed the zero-sum logic of Job's argument: "Will you condemn me that you may be in the right?" (40:8). Walton explains the apparently no-win situation that Job attempted to foist upon the Lord. There was a way that Job could win the case against God: "if God admits, on the basis of the retribution principle system, that he acted unjustly and, in effect, apologizes."[14] Walton adds, however:

> In this way, Job wins (the retribution principle stands and Job's righteousness is affirmed), but he wins at a terrible cost: God loses not only the case but also his dignity. He is no longer a God worth serving.[15]

In verse 8, therefore, the Lord deconstructed Job's presuppositions. Both questions revealed egregious errors in Job's thinking. For Job to condemn God presupposed various functional equivalencies such as ontological similarity and equal or better moral status. Job also presumed intelligence and wisdom commensurate with divinity.[16] Such blunders resembled the epistemic autonomy of Adam and his aspiration to become like God. At his worst, Job expressed the mindset of exilic epistemology.

In the following verses (40:9-14), however, the Lord resituated the debate from the theoretical to the tangible, from reasoning alone to the demonstration of power. In this manner, he deepened and broadened his critique of Job's position. In effect, Yahweh declared to Job, "You presumed to think like God, so let us see you act like him as well." In other words, using a modern idiom, he insisted that Job "put up or shut up":

(9) Have you an arm like God, and can you thunder with a voice like his?

(10) Adorn yourself with majesty and dignity; clothe yourself with glory and splendor.

(11) Pour out the overflowings of your anger, and look on everyone who is proud and abase him.

---

14. Walton, "Job 1," 341.
15. Walton, "Job 1," 341.
16. Of course, Yahweh's questions in chapters 38-41 disabused him of these assumptions.

(12) Look on everyone who is proud and bring him low and tread down the wicked where they stand.

(13) Hide them all in the dust together; bind their faces in the world below.

(14) Then will I also acknowledge to you that your own right hand can save you.

The Lord demanded that Job function "like God" as a divine warrior and transcendent faultfinder (v. 9). The nouns in verses 10-13 represent dominion and grandeur ("arm," "voice," "anger," "majesty"). Similarly, the verbs "adorn" and "clothe" imply royalty and vestments that display authority. The other verbs show power in action with reference to judgment ("pour out," "bring low," "tread down," "hide," "bind").[17] The verb "look" underscores the capacity to observe and evaluate human conduct.

Verses 9-14 functioned, therefore, as both a thought experiment and object lesson that generated two important insights. First, the Lord pressed Job to imagine a consistent application of the retribution principle on Job's terms. Habel explains: "If Job, like Elihu and the friends, still believes that God should rule the world by administering according to a rigid law of moral retribution which necessitates the immediate punishment of the wicked . . . then Job had better demonstrate how it should be done."[18] The problem for Job, however, was that he was not God and therefore incapable of following through. If he were capable of doing God's work, then verse 14 stated the logical consequence: "Then will I also acknowledge to you that your own right hand can save you." Indeed, Job could not "tread down the wicked," nor could he "save" himself. Only Yahweh could do so. The obvious implication was that Job should "acknowledge" the Lord who *can* "save."

Second, Yahweh situated his moral governance within a much broader human context. Verses 11-13 refer to mankind in general as God's concern ("everyone," "the wicked," "them all," "their faces"). In this way Yahweh recontextualized Job's particular case within a worldwide

---

17. God's "arm/hand" and "voice" represent his capacity to intervene in time and space (Exod 6:6; 15:6; Deut 4:34; 5:15; Pss 44:3; 89:13). Rule is displayed though "majesty and dignity" and "glory and splendor" (Pss 96:6; 104:1; 111:3). The "proud" experience God's judgment (Isa 2:11-22; 13:11). "Bring low" means to abase and discredit (Ps 18:27; Isa 2:12). "Hide them in the dust" and "bind their faces" refer metaphorically to reversal and death (Pss 7:5; 22:15; Mic 7:17).

18. Habel, *The Book of Job*, 564.

setting. Habel summarizes the rationale: "Yahweh moves the focus from Job's concern for personal vindication before the court to the wider question of his own responsibility for cosmic governance and control."[19] This theme is especially clear in the subsequent depiction of Behemoth (40:15-24) and Leviathan (41:1-34).

In the ancient Near East, Behemoth and Leviathan represented the unruly forces of chaos and destruction.[20] Job alluded to this tradition by associating Leviathan with "those who curse the day" of his birth (3:8) and by comparing God's "guard over" him with his guard over a primordial "sea monster" (7:12). However, the two beasts in the book of Job are more than metaphorical or mythical depictions of disorder; they likely represent supernatural forces antithetical to God and hostile toward Job.[21] In fact, the diabolical realm played a disruptive role in Job's search for wisdom. As we saw, the accuser promoted a divergent view of reality in God's council. His test of Job was a pretext that threatened to undermine God's glory (1:9-11; 2:4-5). Likewise, Eliphaz received dubious counsel from a "spirit" (4:12-16), as did Zophar (20:3b) and Elihu (32:8).

For this reason, third, Yahweh asked Job to consider the administration of good and evil within a supernatural setting. Ortlund writes, "Yahweh broadens Job's horizon to show him the fearsome power that has attacked him."[22] Job learned, though, that these powers were well beyond his control or understanding. He discovered that he was infinitely unqualified to serve as a divine warrior (v. 8).[23] On the other hand, Yahweh showed Job that even the most powerful spiritual foes were subject to him and did not usurp his dominion (41:5).

Finally, the readers also observed the critical role that the supernatural played in Job's dilemma. They saw how the accuser sought to undermine Job, but God reined him in. They witnessed the reliance of Job's fellow disputants on illicit supernatural authority. Similarly, they

---

19. Habel, *The Book of Job*, 562.

20. Mabie, "Chaos and Death," 41-54.

21. See López, "The Meaning of 'Behemoth' and 'Leviathan' in Job," 401-24; Ortlund, "The Identity of Leviathan," 17-30; Smick, "Semeiological Interpretation," 135-49; Smick, "Another Look at the Mythological Elements," 213-28.

22. Ortlund, "The Identity of Leviathan," 28.

23. Bartholomew and O'Dowd (*Old Testament Wisdom Literature*, 95) comment, "There continues to be chaos in the world, albeit always under divine superintendence. Justice thus has a dynamic character to it and must constantly be reestablished by means of victory over evil. This is God's work, but Job is hardly up to the task."

discovered with Job that the forces of chaos do operate in the world, though God in every way hems them in.[24] Ortlund explains, "Yahweh's manner of governing the world is to allow these chaotic and sinister elements to exist—but this does not count as mismanagement of creation."[25] Most importantly, with Job they learned that the world is very complex and not subject to formulaic pronouncements, such as the principle of retribution.[26]

UNDER THE WHOLE HEAVEN

The Lord's fourth statement (41:10b–11) imposed the *coup de grace* on Job's epistemological myopia. The immediate context includes verses 9–10a:

(9) Behold, the hope of a man is false; he is laid low even at the sight of him.

(10) No one is so fierce that he dares to stir him up. Who then is he who can stand before me?

(11) Who has first given to me, that I should repay him? Whatever is under the whole heaven is mine.

Verse 9 looks back on the fearsome depiction of Leviathan in verses 1–8 and states the obvious: no human can subdue the monster in any way. Verse 8b says, in fact, that if one tries, "you will not do it again!" Indeed, to provoke his wrath ("to stir him up") is sheer folly. Terror and avoidance at all costs represent the only rational response to Leviathan.

However, there is a parallel between Job's relationships with Leviathan and with the Lord (41:10b–11).[27] Just as Job cannot control Le-

---

24. Habel (*The Book of Job*, 66) comments, "The universe is a paradoxical world where the regular and the unexpected, the good and the bad, the successful and the sufferer coexist."

25. Ortlund, "The Identity of Leviathan," 24.

26. Yahweh re-taught them, as Jesus later re-instructed Israel, when tradition usurped the Scriptures, "You have heard that it was said . . . . But I say to you" (Matt 5:27–28).

27. The Hebrew in this passage is difficult, but I concur with the ESV, NSAB, NIV, NKJV, and others that the references are to Yahweh ("before me") and not Leviathan ("before it"). The comparison between Leviathan and Yahweh is implied by "then" in verse 10 and the vocabulary as it appears in Job and the Old Testament. See also Hartley, *The Book of Job*, 527 note 6, 531–32.

viathan, even more can he not control Yahweh, for whom the beast is a harmless pet (v. 5). Just as Job should not aggravate the monster, even more should he not incite the Lord ("stir him up"). Just as Job cannot "stand before" Leviathan with a demand or accusation, so he should not confront Yahweh as if he were an equal. Furthermore, just as Job cannot obligate Leviathan, neither can he oblige Yahweh that he might "repay" him in any way. All such aspirations are illusionary. In reality, Job stands in an exceedingly weak position relative to both supernatural powers.

Verse 11 shows also that Job was embedded within a web of meaning imposed by the Creator: "Whatever is under the whole heaven is mine." "Whatever is" includes absolutely everything under the sun. The word "mine" indicates that Job was situated in a milieu that belongs to, finds its source in, and exists by virtue of the transcendent ruler, architect, economist, and philosopher.[28] This meant that Yahweh was the single actuality that accounted for Job's existence. He was the bond that held Job's world together. Moreover, the Creator–creature distinction obligated Job in every way. In particular, his mind belonged to the Lord. What he conceived, how, and why were subject to God's rule. The moral standards and social righteousness by which he lived derived from divine law. Even his erstwhile friends, his Eve-like wife, and his affliction belonged to God. Every created fact presupposed the Creator because "whatever is under the whole heaven" belongs to the Lord.

Given this ontological reality, Job's contrarian epistemology was truly not viable. He could not really reason in a transcendent or original way. He was not actually the source of or standard for any intellectual construct. He was not in any way self-attesting or intellectually autonomous. He could not think in a univocal manner, though he aspired to do so. He could not presume an independent and transcendent moral norm to which he and the Lord were equally accountable in a court of law. His would-be epistemic autonomy was a non-starter.

Still, the Lord did not hand the epistemological sinner over to his folly (Ps 81:11–12). Rather, Yahweh mercifully restored Job's mental balance. God's multitudinous questions in chapters 38–41 and his dramatic appearance enabled Job to distinguish between reality and his own twisted outlook. Job did not obtain what he sought in his particular case. He did not discover what caused his suffering. But he gained wisdom and

---

28. God counts as his own ("mine"), for instance, "all the firstborn of Israel" (Exod 13:2), "all the earth" (19:5), "the land" (Lev 25:23), "every beast of the forest" (Ps 50:10), and "all souls" (Ezek 18:4).

heard God's voice again, "face to face." He perceived the broader context of God's governance in the cosmos. He learned to fear the Lord more profoundly.

DUST AND ASHES

The Lord's last statement was addressed to the three friends, but he also spoke about Job (42:7–8). The key terms are italicized:

(7) After the Lord had spoken these words to Job, the Lord said to Eliphaz the Temanite: "My anger burns against you and against your two friends, *for* you have not *spoken* of me *what is right*, as my servant Job has.

(8) Now therefore take seven bulls and seven rams and go to my servant Job and offer up a burnt offering for yourselves. And my servant Job shall pray for you, *for* I will accept his prayer not to deal with you according to your *folly*. For you have not *spoken* of me *what is right*, as my servant Job has."

The ancient readers undoubtedly understood why the Lord condemned the three friends. The conjunctions "for" (*ki*) in verses 7 and 8 indicate the reason for God's anger and why Job's intercession on their behalf was needed. The word "folly" (*nebalah*) refers in the Old Testament to the most egregious public offenses and is translated as "outrageous thing" or "vile thing." Folly refers to sexual crimes[29] and coveting objects dedicated to the Lord (Josh 7:15). Folly also encompassed intellectual error such as the discourse of fools (Isa 32:6) and the false prophecies of those who "have spoken in my name lying words" (Jer 29:23).

Eliphaz, Bildad, and Zophar were associated with this reprehensible cabal due to their "lying words" about God and dishonorable conduct toward Job (vv. 7–8). Their unwavering advocacy of the retribution principle made them allies with the accuser and Job's wife. They thought in a univocal and instrumental manner about God, as if he were manageable and subject to appeasement. In fact, their reasoning echoed pagan spirituality. Their unrelenting critique and character assassination added to Job's suffering. Worse, they never offered intercessory prayer on his behalf or spoke with endearment about God. Thus, God's affirmation of Job

---

29. Incest (Gen 34:7), prostitution (Deut 22:21), homosexual group rape (Judg 20:6), and the rape of a sister (2 Sam 13:12).

was explained—at least in part—by way of contrast. The friends spoke folly about God whereas Job expressed wisdom—that is, "what is right."

Perhaps Yahweh's validation of Job's discourse engendered cognitive dissonance for the original readers (like many readers today), given the nefarious accusations that he hurled at the Lord.[30] Yoram Hazony explains, however, that the verb "speak" (*dabar*, vv. 7–8) has a multivalent meaning.[31] The term refers to both verbal utterance and "silent speech" (thoughts or understanding). Words are realities known to God as articulated or unexpressed conceptions among human beings. Hazony comments, "The biblical *dabar*, which is an understanding or an object as understood, is one and the same whether it is before the mind, or given expression in words."[32] For example, Moses told the Israelites, "Be careful not to harbor this wicked thought (*dabar*)" (Deut 15:9a; see also 30:14; Josh 14:7).[33] As to the truth or falsity of a *dabar*, Hazony adds, "This will depend on whether the *dabar*, or thing, in question can be counted on to be what it ought to be through time and circumstance."[34] In other words, true words are reliable throughout time.

Yahweh testified that Job's words regarding him (spoken and unspoken) were accurate. He discerned truthfulness in Job's speech. He affirmed his communication as valid "through the time and circumstance" of enigmatic suffering.[35] Moreover, Job's communication in words, understanding, and action presupposed God's reliability. With this broad purview, then, three sections of the book provide evidences of Yahweh's positive evaluation of Job: the prologue (chapters 1 and 2), the dialogue

---

30. Ortlund ("How Did Job Speak Rightly about God?" 350) vividly summarizes Job's allegations: "Extrapolating outward from his tragedy as narrated in chs. 1–2, Job names God an amoral tyrant who destroys everyone regardless of moral character (9:22), who laughs at good people when they suffer disaster (v. 23), and deliberately frustrates the execution of justice in the world (v. 24; see further 12:13–25). In Job's horrifying new vision of the universe, God is a moral monster, and his creation a kind of inner-city ghetto, filled with the unanswered screams of the innocent (21:7–34)."

31. Hazony, *The Philosophy of Hebrew Scripture*, 193–218.

32. Hazony, *The Philosophy of Hebrew Scripture*, 213.

33. Jesus taught similarly when he declared, "But I say to you that everyone who looks at a woman with lustful intent has already committed adultery with her in his heart" (Matt 5:28).

34. Hazony, *The Philosophy of Hebrew Scripture*, 211.

35. Krüger, however, explained an important caveat. Job "does not revoke *everything* he has said, and in 42:7 God in turn obviously does not approve *everything* Job has said about him." Kruger, "Did Job Repent?" 227 (emphasis in original).

(chapters 3–31), and especially Job's twofold response to the Lord in the theophany (chapters 40 and 42).

In the prologue, Yahweh announced that Job feared God. Job expressed reverence, despite his great loss, and the narrator testified to his piety. Similarly, during the contentious dialogue (and notwithstanding his unorthodox utterances), Job demonstrated godly fear. As we have seen, he endured affliction and perplexity *coram Deo* (with reference to God and under his authority). He prayed often and spoke constantly about God. He lamented the loss of God's presence and friendship, and he longed to hear God's voice. He realized that only a direct encounter with the Lord would resolve his dilemma. Moreover, Job demonstrated that the accuser's words were false. As Ortland says, "But even as he curses, Job's theology is good in the sense that Job rightly values God and God's favor more highly than any earthly blessing."[36] Despite all that transpired, Job's spiritual North Star remained true: he feared God and the others did not.

In addition, while debating with his would-be friends, Job steadfastly maintained his innocence, though he did not know God's prior declaration and could not discern the meaning of his predicament. He declared correctly that God had permitted his suffering and demise. He also knew that he could not declare vindication autonomously or with certainty without additional revelation (14:13–17; 19:23–24; 23:15; 31:35).[37] He acknowledged, if only rarely, his epistemic finitude and fallenness by asking, "How many are my iniquities and my sins? Make me know my transgression and my sin" (13:23). In this manner also, Job spoke "what is right."

Job's two comments in response to the theophany demonstrated that he eventually understood the Lord's message (40:3–5 and 42:1–6). When Job challenged God by oath in his closing discourse (chapter 31), he envisioned acquittal followed by a kind of victory lap (vv. 35–37).[38] He then boasted audaciously, "I would give him an account of all my steps; like a prince I would approach him" (v. 37). With this in mind, the

---

36. Ortlund, "How Did Job Speak Rightly about God?" 355.

37. Ortlund makes this point in "How Did Job Speak Rightly about God?" 356–57.

38. Job claimed that he would carry his written indictment from the Lord: "Surely I would carry it on my shoulder; I would bind it on me as a crown." Longman (*The Book of Job*, 365) comments, "He even imagines wearing it proudly like a crown. He is so sure of his innocence that he imagines his approach to God not cringing like a supplicant or a criminal, but rather boldly like a prince."

Lord's first statement to Job was blunt: "Who is this that obscures my plans with words without knowledge? Brace yourself like a man; I will question you, and you shall answer me" (38:2–3). Henry Rowold explains what followed in chapters 38 and 39 as the Lord systematically undercut Job's vaunted self-image and confronted his skewed intellectual outlook:

> By form, the questions are even more pointed, for they address Job not as inquiring student but as one who sets himself up as rival, both in his perspective of Yahweh's ways and in his affirmation of a righteousness greater than Yahweh's. Each repetition of the question "who" hammers home the confrontational message. At this level, then, the Yahweh-speech functions as Yahweh's self-asseveration of creative lordship and as a denial of Job's stance as princely rival who can stand before Yahweh on his own terms and righteousness.[39]

Thus, after round one of the Lord's withering didactic assault, Job ceded a defeat of sorts and commented in 40:4–5:

(4) Behold, I am of small account; what shall I answer you? I lay my hand on my mouth.

(5) I have spoken once, and I will not answer; twice, but I will proceed no further.

Job recognized that the Lord had taken control of the rhetorical initiative. He said of himself, "I am of small account" (40:4a). The term "small account" derives from a word signifying diminishment (*qaloti*). Job acknowledged his unjustified and overweening self-confidence compared to Yahweh. He coupled his words with a gesture of shame by covering his mouth (v. 4b).[40] In this case, it is not clear whether Job reverently honored God through confession and sign or just sullenly acknowledged his superior. In the best-case scenario, Job followed the counsel of Proverbs as the beginning of repentance: "If you have been foolish, exalting yourself, or if you have been devising evil, put your hand on your mouth" (Prov 30:32).[41]

---

39. Rowold, "Yahweh's Challenge to Rival," 210.

40. Earlier, Job urged his tormentors to cover their mouths so that they would stop talking and leave him alone (21:5). He also described how community leaders formerly covered their mouths and "refrained from talking" in his presence as act of deference (29:9).

41. Aimers ("Theodicy in an Ironical Sense," 368–70) argues that the dialogue presents Job as a "composite portrait of a particular type of fool." He adds, "In this

After another round of blistering inquiry in chapters 40–41, Job's second speech indicated a radical change of perspective (42:1–6). At that point, he completed his epistemic journey and received the Lord's approbation for speaking "what is right" (v. 7).[42]

(1) Then Job answered the Lord and said:

(2) "I know that you can do all things, and that no purpose of yours can be thwarted.

(3) 'Who is this that hides counsel without knowledge?' Therefore I have uttered what I did not understand, things too wonderful for me, which I did not know.

(4) 'Hear, and I will speak; I will question you, and you make it known to me.'

(5) I had heard of you by the hearing of the ear, but now my eye sees you;

(6) therefore I despise myself, and repent in dust and ashes."

Let us make several initial observations before considering each verse individually. First, verses 2–5 provide a rationale for the conclusion stated in verse 6, indicated by "therefore." Second, Job cited Yahweh's previous words in verses 3a and 4 to undergird his reasoning. This demonstrates that he paid attention and took the Lord's assessment to heart. Third, knowledge vocabulary predominates: "know" (twice), "hides," "purpose," "counsel," "knowledge," "things too wonderful for me," "speak," "understand," "question," "make known," "hearing," and "see." Fourth, a change occurred in Job's thinking, as indicated by "therefore" (logical) and "now" (temporal). Fifth, Job overcame a lack of knowledge and wisdom deficit. Sixth, based upon the knowledge acquired from God, Job repented.

---

final stage, the ultimate fool blames all for their self-inflicted demise, most notably the deity, so as to absolve themselves of sin (Prov. 19:3). This most certainly resonates with the character of Job, who would not only blaspheme God but go so far as to sue God in court for injustice, a prerogative normally reserved for God against other deities (Ps. 82)."

42. This passage is exceedingly complex due to its syntax and vocabulary. I follow in particular the exegesis of Van Wolde in "Job 42:1–6: The Reversal of Job," 223–50 and Fox, "God's Answer and Job's Response," 1–23.

Verse 2

This verse functions as the topic sentence for the paragraph. But it implies an important question: What did Job learn that he did not already know about God's power?[43] What *new* understanding produced a positive orientation to the Lord and an act of repentance? The answer is that Job developed a deeper appraisal of divine sovereignty and the Creator-creature distinction intellectually.

Before his affliction, Job viewed God's rule as delimited by the retribution principle. Nothing, he believed, could thwart the implementation of blessing or woe according to proper or improper conduct. Accordingly, Job did not believe that God allowed the innocent to suffer or caused the wicked to prosper. After disaster struck, however, he reckoned with the radical implications of his reversal and his world fell apart. The concept of deity that he had inherited failed. The ontology presupposed by the retribution principle could not explain the chaos that enveloped him. During his affliction, Job perceived divine power in a very adversarial manner.

The theophany situated Job anew, however, and renovated his view of God's governance. Unquestionably, the Lord's tone was firm and his rhetoric strident, for Job had erroneously positioned himself as both victim and faultfinder. As a result, Yahweh gave Job a crash course in biblical ontology. For instance, in verse 2 the word "purpose" (*mezummah*) refers to the private thoughts and secret intentions of the Lord.[44] Clearly, his ruminations were not accessible to Job, nor could he discern or prevent ("thwart") their implementation. Furthermore, Job discovered that the retribution principle could not hem God in. God allowed Job to suffer and no indictment or oath could force his hand or disclosure.[45] On the

---

43. See 9:5–10; 12:14–25; 27:13–23.

44. This term was an unusual choice, for it usually depicts the evil "schemes" or "plots" of humans. "Purpose" (*mezummah*) appears in a verse we read earlier: "If you have been foolish, exalting yourself, or if you have been devising (*mezummah*) evil, put your hand on your mouth" (Prov 30:32). "Purpose" and "thwart" (*batsar*) occur together in Genesis 11:6: "And the Lord said, 'Behold, they are one people, and they have all one language, and this is only the beginning of what they will do. And nothing that they propose (*mezummah*) to do will now be impossible (*batsar*) for them.'"

45. Longman (*The Book of Job*, 449) makes this point in connection with Genesis 11:6: "In language surprisingly similar to Gen. 11:6 ("nothing that they propose to do will now be impossible for them," NRSV), Job acknowledges—in a way that the actions of the tower builders attempted to deny—that only God controls events. God can do anything he plans, including allowing an innocent person like Job to suffer."

other hand, Job learned that Yahweh's power was exceedingly great in the natural and supernatural domains. As a result, Job turned from a cynical evaluation of God's power (10:13) to a new estimation of the Creator's immense wisdom and beneficence at work in the world.

Thus, the theophany re-educated God's disaffected student. The Lord appeared, but contrary to all expectations, he did not destroy Job. He did not intensify Job's suffering or make him a cosmic object lesson in stupidity. Rather, God simply showed up and spoke, as Job desperately wanted. Under the Lord's tutelage, he acquired a new appraisal of all that had occurred in his suffering. He realized how reductionistic and univocal his reasoning was. And because God drew near as Creator and Lord, Job gained wisdom. By way of summary, the two learning environments are depicted below:

During the Affliction	During the Theophany
God's silence	God's voice
God's absence	God's presence
bitterness	friendship
pride	humility
myopic view	broader view
self-orientation	God-centered
reductionistic reasoning	holistic reasoning
way to wisdom blocked	way to wisdom opened

Verse 3a

This verse quotes the Lord's first statement to Job in 38:2, but with two differences (in italics):

> Who is this that *darkens* counsel by *words without knowledge*? (38:2)

> Who is this that *hides* counsel *without knowledge*? (42:3a)

The verb "darkens," as noted above, means to obfuscate and distort. With that interpretive grid, Job misinterpreted his affliction and God's purpose. Similarly, the verb "hides" (*alam*) means to conceal from others, God, and oneself.[46] It often entails a negative motivation to disregard or

---

46. The noun (*taalumah*) appears three times, as "thing that is hidden" (Job 28:11)

deny. In some cases, the term indicates willful blindness (self-deception) and is expressed as "blind my eyes" (1 Sam 12:3; see also Prov 28:27). Both terms share a minimization of Yahweh's "counsel" through discounting and obscuring the truth. In addition, the phrase "without knowledge" in 42:3a might be a deliberate intensification of the phrase "words without knowledge" in 38:2. In other words, the totality of Job's thinking was skewed due to obfuscation and denial of God's counsel. William Morrow writes, "It is possible to understand the divine address as an indictment of Job's challenge of God (42:3a, 4), the refutation of a false theology or world view (42:5), or a revelation of the reality of divine power (42:2, 5)."[47]

Most importantly, by citing Yahweh's first utterance Job acknowledged his negative epistemological diagnosis. Explicitly, the Lord declared that Job's malady was not simply human ignorance but culpable unknowing, distortion, and denial of what he already knew. Clearly, Job darkened and hid *something*. He failed to acknowledge God's "counsel," that is, his plan and purpose. Certainly, Job thought about the meaning of the world, but he thought wrongly in both content and method. In other words, Job's failure was rooted not merely in finitude or fallibility but also in fallenness. His problem was not only ignorance but also autonomy. Implicitly, Job sinned by substituting his own ideas about divine justice and God as codified in the retribution principle.[48] That doctrine presumed a deity who was manageable and a world that was predictable. It was also an interpretive lens by which everyone was assigned to well-defined categories of blessing or suffering based on their behavior.[49] Based on that understanding of God and his creation, Job launched his lawsuit and oath. Fortunately for Job, the Lord did not respond in kind.

---

or "secrets" (Job 11:6; Ps 44:21).

47. Morrow, "Consolation, Rejection, and Repentance," 224.

48. Job's twisted epistemology resonates with Jeremiah's depiction of idolatry (2:11–13) and Paul's description of unbelief (Rom 1:18–23). Kuyper ("Repentance of Job," 94) writes, "Job now discerns his folly in employing words or arguments within a moralistic, reward–retribution framework. These words he now rejects as worthless and repents of his folly in using them: 'therefore I reject (my words), and I repent in dust and ashes.'"

49. Admittedly, not just Job but his friends and presumably the community embraced the same notions.

Verse 3b

In verse 3b, Job reached a preliminary conclusion as indicated by the adverb "therefore." With the rediscovery of his intellectual finitude and fallenness, he recognized the vast chasm between the Lord's knowledge and his own. With homocentric reasoning, he had elevated himself as the point of reference rather than Yahweh. He had played God epistemologically. Interestingly, the phrase "things too wonderful for me" appears also in Psalm 131:1 with reference to the mind: "O Lord, my heart is not lifted up; my eyes are not raised too high; I do not occupy myself with things too great and *too marvelous* for me. But I have calmed and quieted my soul, like a weaned child with its mother; like a weaned child is my soul within me."[50] The psalmist acknowledged God's epistemic supremacy, unlike Job until this point.

Verse 4

This verse contains the second citation of Yahweh. The first part of the verse ("hear and I will speak") alludes to all that God declared in chapters 38–41. The second part of the verse ("I will question you and you make it known to me") is a quotation from 38:3b. From a negative point of view, the verse exudes irony. Job, the man of many queries, heard instead from Yahweh: "I will question *you*" and "hear and *I* will speak." The Lord turned the rhetorical tables on Job with a tsunami of unanswerable questions. Moreover, the verb "make known" (*yada*, Hiphil) refers to God's mode of self-revelation: "It is God who causes, or is asked to cause, someone to know."[51] Job, the pseudo-divinity, could not answer God's questions, nor was he self-revelatory.

From a positive perspective, Ellen van Wolde points out that Job transferred the point of reference (right of predication) to the Lord, since Yahweh is quoted as speaking in the first person.[52] She writes about Job, "Here he actually sees through the eyes of Yahweh." She adds, "The game

---

50. Both Job 42:3 and Psalm 131 use the verb *pala*, referring to God's surpassing and awesome wonders. The verbal construction "things too wonderful," also found in Job 42:3, appears thirteen times in the Old Testament. In Job 42 and Psalm 131, God's surpassing wisdom and understanding are contrasted with mere human counsel and knowledge.

51. Carasik, *Theologies of the Mind*, 25.

52. Van Wolde, "Job 42:1–6: The Reversal of Job," 233.

of reversion, of who knows and who does not know, of who asks and who makes known, of who must listen, has apparently been played long before. It is this game that Job is referring back to. In this sense verse 4 superbly summarizes this game in YHWH's speech(es)."[53]

Verse 5

Here Job exclaims, "I had heard of you by the hearing of the ear, but now my eye sees you." The words "now" and "sees" refer to Yahweh's appearance in the whirlwind—without an intermediary. Job experienced his heart's deepest desire to encounter God (along with the great benefit of living to tell about it). He said, "And after my skin has been thus destroyed, yet in my flesh I shall see God, whom I shall see for myself, and my eyes shall behold, and not another. My heart faints within me!" (19:26–27). The phrase "heard of you by the hearing of the ear" likely looks back to hearing God's voice when "the friendship of God was upon my tent" (29:4b). Two other possibilities include listening to God's voice in the public recitation of Scripture or attending to the Lord's long discourse in chapters 38–41.

The language of seeing and hearing also links verse 5 with chapter 28 and the quest for wisdom. As noted previously, Job 28 contrasts the search for precious metals with the search for wisdom. The terminology of seeking and seeing, finding and hearing pervades the passage. The miner sought a "place for gold" (v. 2b) and "searches out to the farthest limit" (v. 3a). The "path" to riches "no bird of prey knows," for the "eye has not seen it" (v. 7). Seekers "overturn mountains" (v. 9b) and "cut out channels" (v. 10a) to "see every precious thing" (v. 10b). They look for the treasure "that is hidden" to "bring out to the light" (v. 11b).

Like gems, wisdom cannot be easily detected: "The deep says, 'It is not in me.' And the sea says, 'It is not with me'" (28:14). Wisdom, Job said, was "hidden from the eyes of all living" (v. 21a), and even death admitted meekly, "We have heard a rumor of it with our ears" (v. 22). Job inquired,

---

53. Van Wolde, "Job 42:1–6: The Reversal of Job," 241. Similarly, Habel (*The Book of Job*, 581) comments, "By citing these quotations from Yahweh's speeches, Job is making it quite explicit that he is responding formally to the challenge of Yahweh as his adversary. Job's response (v. 3b–c) is a public confession that he is 'indeed' the one who obscured Yahweh's cosmic design with ignorant accusations and that he did not possess the wisdom or 'discernment' (*bina*, 38:4b) which Yahweh challenged him to display."

therefore, "Where shall wisdom be found?" (v. 12a). He answered that God alone "understands the way to it, and he knows its place" (v. 23). Fortunately, Job "heard" about wisdom and also discovered where to find it. However, only with God as his guide and source did he gain the necessary insight. God's appearance in the whirlwind was the culmination of his quest for wisdom.

Furthermore, verse 5 links Job with Isaiah and redemptive epistemology, though some of the resonances are implicit. As we saw in chapter eight, Isaiah 6:9–10 depicted an intellectual process: input (revelation) was received though sensory perception that the mind evaluated. Assuming repentance, Job's eyes saw God's deeds and experienced his presence, and the ears heard his voice. Then, the intellect interpreted the information according to biblical criteria. The process yielded deeper understanding of the Creator, his world, and the self. It also produced zeal to serve on God's terms and for his glory. Like Isaiah, Job encountered God through theophany. Isaiah confessed his sin and Job acknowledged his folly. Like Isaiah, Job became disposed to listen and obey. In the end, both were given a heart to understand and further opportunity to serve the Lord. Like Isaiah, Job was also an archetypical God-knower east of Eden.

Verse 6

Finally, verse 6 is the crux of Job's reasoning in verses 1–5, if not the entire book: "Therefore I despise myself, and repent in dust and ashes."[54] In this verse his intellectual quandary was resolved, not in terms of comprehension but in orientation. He rediscovered his epistemological point of reference. He turned from autonomy and criticism to re-embrace the content and method of thinking befitting a creature. He acknowledged his fallibility and foolishness. He recognized the low estate into which he had fallen. Of course, he learned from the theophany, but much more

---

54. The debate regarding this verse is intense and divisive due to the ambiguity of the text and the presuppositions informing the exegesis and hermeneutics. Divergent perspectives exist concerning the verbs "despise" (*maas*) and "repent" (*naham*), the preposition "in" (*al*), and the idiom "dust and ashes" (*apar waeper*). I follow the translations of the ESV, NIV, NIVUK, NASB, NKJV, and NRSV. In addition to Van Wolde and Fox, I rely upon Longman, *The Book of Job*, 448–50; Krüger, "Did Job Repent?"; Morrow, "Consolation, Rejection, and Repentance"; Kuyper, "Repentance of Job"; Brueggemann, "From Dust to Kingship," 1–18; and Muenchow, "Dust and Dirt in Job 42:6," 597–611.

importantly he understood how the facts cohered and were situated by God within creation.[55]

His quest for wisdom was fruitful, for Job retraced the path of Proverbs: "Be not wise in your own eyes; fear the Lord, and turn away from evil" (Prov 3:7). In fact, Job himself foreshadowed this trajectory at the end of his ode to wisdom: "Behold, the fear of the Lord, that is wisdom, and to turn away from evil is understanding" (28:28). Job rejected his former self-referential orientation and turned from "evil" modes of thought. He rejected pseudo-wisdom incompatible with fearing God. Indeed, the Lord, knowing his servant so deeply, anticipated the drama's resolution, for he saw that Job's godly fear would eventually guide him home. Like Pilgrim in John Bunyan's story, Job passed through the "slough of despond." He experienced profoundly "many fears, and doubts, and discouraging apprehensions."[56] In the end, though, Job rightly appraised his error ("I despise myself") and repented of folly.[57]

This interpretation of verse 6 presupposes the argument advanced throughout this chapter. Several assumptions are vital. First, his friends anticipated his repentance, though they were woefully mistaken about his sin. Job did not change his mind about his innocence or seek to appease the Lord. If he had, the accuser's allegation about the instrumental nature of Job's faith would have been valid. Second, Job did not repent of any sin prior to his ordeal, for the Lord declared him righteous. So if he did repent, then it must have been for offenses committed during his affliction. If not, then the book of Job is merely a tragic moral drama with little or no redemptive impact.

Indeed, Job's sins were intellectual. His error was not merely a cognitive mistake derived from finitude that required additional education.

---

55. According to Krüger ("Did Job Repent?" 227), Job learned that God is "not Job's persecutor," is "not engaged in a permanent fight against chaotic forces," "does not punish [humans] in a petty-minded way," "cannot be summoned to court," and "does not declare guilty the innocent." O'Dowd ("A Chord of Three Strands," 77) adds, "Job interprets his suffering in the context of his cosmological understanding of the whole, which—in this case, has proven insufficient. What he seeks is a new account of creation."

56. Bunyan, *The Pilgrim's Progress*, 46.

57. Even if on interpretive grounds the term "repent" is not warranted, certainly the concept is present and presupposed by the narrative. Van Wolde ("Job 42:1–6: The Reversal of Job," 250) comments, "Summarizing one could state that Job 42:1–6 portrays the reversal that takes place inside Job . . . . Because Job's view changes, there can also be a reversal of his attitude: Job turns away from what is past and turns round towards the future."

Neither did he commit a slight intellectual peccadillo that required only admonition. Rather, Job's noetic offense was a type of intellectual crime that necessitated repentance, forgiveness, and reorientation.

In this way, Job was both a model and an antitype. At his worst, he exhibited grievous features of exilic epistemology. However, at his best he was an embodiment of redemptive epistemology in the Old Testament. His deepest motives derived from godly fear, even under extreme duress. He suffered, prayed, spoke, and contemplated with reference to God. As O'Dowd says, "Job provides a test of wisdom in the throes of life."[58]

CONCLUSION

The book of Job shows that noetic depravity is quite real and very complicated. Job's bodily and emotional affliction impacted how he processed information. He was situated socially, and the disapproval of the community caused disorientation. Because he was a sinner, his intellectual orientation was homocentric. He reasoned in a univocal manner, as if the quality and quantity of his understanding were equal to God's. His theorizing was reductionistic, as he extrapolated from his particular perspective to reality in general. And when his scheme failed to produce coherence or blessing, he blamed God. Like all of us, Job was influenced by an under-the-sun perspective and earth-bound criteria. Like us, he used his fallen and finite mind to impose order on chaos, bring clarity to mystery, and subdue every power that threatened his edenic lifestyle.

Moreover, like Job, we need wisdom to navigate life. As he discovered, contrary to his hopes and expectations, the real world is convoluted and Kafkaesque. Often, the wise path or the best perspective is not easy to discern. Even the distinction between good and evil is sometimes not simple to demarcate. Job desperately needed to know what truly mattered in his situation and what concretely to do about it. He sought a cosmic GPS so that he could reorient himself to the painful reality that assaulted him. He needed to discover Ariadne's proverbial thread out of the enigmatic suffering that engulfed him. What he desperately needed—and graciously received— was an accurate perception of reality.

Yahweh in his infinite wisdom and power knew that greater good would accrue to Job and his nation through his unjust affliction. Because of Job's example, they could learn and perhaps adjust their erroneous

---

58. O'Dowd, *The Wisdom of Torah*, 153.

concept of retribution and blessing, as well as their instrumental view of God. Even more crucially, they could repent. Perhaps even Job confessed afterwards with the psalmist, "It is good for me that I was afflicted, that I might learn your statutes" (Ps 119:71).

God's wisdom is even more evident, however, in the fact that thousands of years later we are still reading the book of Job. We continue to seek wisdom about suffering, justice, and knowledge. We continue to bring our questions to and are questioned by the book. We still seek to understand God better, especially in the midst of our own Job-like suffering. In this sense, the wisdom of Job is perennial.

Finally, the book of Job foreshadowed the New Testament in at least three ways. First and foremost, Job foreshadowed Jesus Christ, who was the one and only innocent sufferer but also God's wisdom incarnate. Job asked, "But where shall wisdom be found?" (28:12); the ultimate answer is Jesus Christ. The Lord Jesus demonstrated how to love God with his mind. He feared God and turned away from evil.

Second, the New Testament sheds much more light on our epistemic adversary, "the satan," as well as his tactics. Jesus testified, "He was a murderer from the beginning, and does not stand in the truth, because there is no truth in him. When he lies, he speaks out of his own character, for he is a liar and the father of lies" (John 8:44).[59] Second Corinthians 4:4 explains the devil's epistemological strategy: "The god of this age has blinded the minds of unbelievers, so that they cannot see the light of the gospel of the glory of Christ, who is the image of God."

Third, Ephesians 2:1–3 reveals an intellectual context that echoes Job:

> And you were dead in the trespasses and sins in which you once walked, following the course of this world, following the prince of the power of the air, the spirit that is now at work in the sons of disobedience—among whom we all once lived in the passions of our flesh, carrying out the desires of the body and the mind, and were by nature children of wrath, like the rest of mankind.

Paul taught that Satan is directly involved in human history and culture as the "prince of the power of the air." He operates in two interconnected domains: the sinful individual ("trespasses and sins in which you once walked") and skewed worldviews (the "course of this world").

---

59. Other characterizations include "accuser" (Rev 12:10) and "tempter" (Matt 4:5).

The "world" embodies the fallen anti-biblical belief systems (religions and ideologies) that distort reality and misrepresent the Lord. Similarly, Job struggled as an individual, within a community and its ideological commitments, and also against spiritual opponents.

Most likely, we will never reach the pinnacle of rectitude that Job possessed. Nor will we likely suffer so intensely. However, we are likely to replicate many of his intellectual errors. In this sense, we are *all* Job. We all suffer and try to make sense of life, often incorrectly. We are, as he was, a confusing mix of good and bad, wise and foolish, humble and proud. Yet Job found the way out of the labyrinth of exilic epistemology—repentance rooted in the fear of the Lord. He demonstrated how to love God with the mind in the real world of sin and enigma. Job was an Old Testament epistemic hero.

13

The One Who Knows

"Immortal, invisible, God only wise, in light inaccessible hid from our eyes, most blessed, most glorious, the Ancient of Days, almighty, victorious, thy great name we praise."

—Walter Chalmers Smith,
"Immortal, Invisible, God Only Wise"

We have seen that the mind plays a crucial role in Old Testament spirituality. How, what, and why Israel thought and whom they listened to affected every aspect of life and society. At their best, their intellectual motivations and methods modeled for the watching world how to love God with the mind and how to construct society.

But as we know, Israel did not obey the covenant and did not fulfill its commission. In the chaos that ensued, divergent voices proclaimed contradictory guidance from God in the face of judgment, as the books of Jeremiah and Daniel indicate. How would they discern God's voice in the cacophony of impending exile?

As the people contemplated the existential and epistemological implications of deportation, they undoubtedly wondered how God's promises and even God himself were to be understood in captivity. What was their spiritual identity without its supporting political infrastructure and geographical identity? How could they maintain their economic well-being and cultural identity in Babylonian servitude? How could they love God with the mind in a foreign theocracy?

This chapter outlines the possibility of knowledge in the midst of disorientation. Israel's dilemma provides epistemological insights that are relevant even for our age. The first section examines Jeremiah's letter to the captives in chapter 29; section two concerns the testimony about exile in Psalm 137.

JEREMIAH'S LETTER TO THE EXILES

As we learned in chapter 7, God situated Israel within a highly problematic geopolitical and religious context. The nation was located in the land of Canaan, coveted property at the crossroads of warring imperialistic theocracies.[1] Israel and Judah suffered periods of vassalage coupled with shifting fealty and rebellion against their overlords. But the nation also languished under ineffective political leadership. Jeremiah witnessed the demise of Judah's last rulers—Josiah, Jehoahaz, Jehoiakim, Jehoiachin, and Zedekiah. Systemic vice and apostasy arose among the populace, as well as skepticism and obduracy to God's word (Jer 2). Droughts and the threat of famine unsettled the people (3:3; 5:24–25; 14:1–6). Various prophetic spokesmen denigrated Jeremiah (chapters 26–29), proposing alternative interpretations of God's purpose in the face of impending doom. In the midst of multidimensional chaos, the people desperately needed answers: Who knows the truth? Who discerns reality and understands what to do? Jeremiah's letter to the exiles in chapter 29 was situated in this tumultuous setting.

The natural response to the threat of destruction at the hands of Nebuchadnezzar was to fight or flee—and many Israelites did one or the other. But Jeremiah's counsel challenged accepted wisdom. First, contrary to expectations, he said they should submit to their Babylonian overlords and that Judah would not suffer death or raw chattel servitude. Rather, they would survive and even thrive in exile. They would enjoy a measure of cultural and economic autonomy. Second, he declared that they could preserve their distinct ethnic identity and maintain covenantal disciplines. Third, the exile was Yahweh's purpose and provision for the holy remnant. Indeed, his mighty hand would intervene on their behalf for good. Nevertheless, following the prophet's counsel required enormous courage, wisdom, and faith.

---

1. For two brief historical summaries, see Lundbom, "Builders of Ancient Babylon," 154–66; Kelle, "Israelite History," 408–13.

The letter to the exiles begins with the salutation in 29:4: "Thus says the Lord of hosts, the God of Israel, to all the exiles whom I have sent into exile from Jerusalem to Babylon." The opening expression "Thus says" appears 150 times in Jeremiah.[2] It was spoken with obvious transcendent and covenantal authority. The designation "the Lord of hosts, the God of Israel" appears thirty-three times in Jeremiah;[3] the phrase "Lord of hosts" occurs an additional thirty-seven times.[4] In Jeremiah, this title is associated with themes drawn from creation, covenant, and wisdom. For instance, the Lord of hosts is the Creator of the world (10:12) and the Creator of Israel (v. 16). The Lord of hosts evaluates the thoughts and motives of human beings: "O Lord of hosts, who judges righteously, who tests the heart and the mind" (11:20a). He is sovereign and his providence governs the earth: "It is I who by my great power and my outstretched arm have made the earth . . . and I give it to whomever it seems right to me. Now I have given all these lands into the hand of Nebuchadnezzar, the king of Babylon, my servant" (27:5–6). And regarding his long-term relationship with Israel, the Lord of hosts declared, "And it shall come to pass that as I have watched over them to pluck up and break down, to overthrow, destroy, and bring harm, so I will watch over them to build and to plant, declares the Lord" (31:28).

Furthermore, the term "hosts" (*tsaba*) in Jeremiah is often associated with Yahweh's covenantal lawsuit against his obdurate and idolatrous people (at least forty-three times).[5] In fact, this litigious emphasis appears at the beginning of the book. After Jeremiah catalogues their covenantal violations in 2:5–8, verse 9 (NIV) declares, "'Therefore I bring charges (*rib*) against you again,' declares the Lord. 'And I will bring charges (*rib*) against your children's children.'"[6]

---

2. The vast majority appear with the first person "I," and three others occur with the first person "me."

3. The two phrases appear together only four times outside Jeremiah (1 Chr 17:24; Isa 21:10; 37:16; Zeph 2:9).

4. Similar designations are "Lord God of hosts" (twenty-one times) and "God of hosts" (ten times).

5. *Tsaba* appears at least twenty-one times in contexts of judgment against other nations. In these settings, military terminology often appears. The remaining occurrences of the term are mixed: return and restoration, and doxology. Quine ("The Host of Heaven and the Divine Army," 741–55) argues that the phrase "Lord of hosts" does not usually refer to divine warfare.

6. The verb "bring changes" (*rib*, "contend" in the ESV) means to indict under covenantal law. The term occurs seven times in Jeremiah. In 2:29, the Lord expressed

In the book of Jeremiah, therefore, the phrase "Lord of hosts" coupled with the designation "God of Israel" provided a theological orientation for both Israel and Babylon.[7] The destruction of the nation and the exile of the righteous remnant came to pass by Yahweh Elohim's decree. He prosecuted disobedient Israel, using the Babylonian empire as his chosen instrument. Seven times the phrase "is his name" precedes or follows the idiom "Lord of hosts" to express this point polemically.[8] Indeed, even though the causal chain of exile runs through Babylon and Nebuchadnezzar, God alone "sent" the captives there (vv. 4, 7). It was critical that the exiles understood and acknowledged these facts.

Concerning the exiles sent to Babylon,[9] Angelika Berlejung explains that a clear picture of the captives' sojourn is difficult to ascertain. She comments:

> It is striking that the Hebrew Bible gives no continuous account of the exilic period. All that is narrated is how the forced Babylonian exile and the voluntary Egyptian diaspora came about (2 Kgs 24–25; Jer 39–43; 2 Chr 36) . . . . According to the biblical presentation, the "history," which had come to a standstill in the Babylonian period, resumed only in 539 BC with the books of Ezra and Nehemiah.[10]

There were three deportations (597, 587, and 582 BC). The Hebrews were mostly settled in semi-autonomous ethnic enclaves alongside irrigation canals. The prophet Ezekiel mentions Tel-Abib by the Chebar canal (Ezek 3:15). The scribe Ezra lists Tel-Melach, Tel-Harsha, Kerub-Addon,

---

amazement that Israel brought charges against himself. In 12:1, Jeremiah pleaded (*rib*) with God, "Why does the way of the wicked prosper?" In 50:34 and 51:36, God declared that he will "plead" (*rib*) Israel's case against Babylon and then execute "vengeance" on their behalf.

7. The letter was sent, as well, to the emperor as official correspondence: "The letter was sent by the hand of Elasah the son of Shaphan and Gemariah the son of Hilkiah, whom Zedekiah king of Judah sent to Babylon to Nebuchadnezzar king of Babylon" (29:3).

8. See 10:16; 31:35; 46:18; 48:15; 50:34; 51:19, 57.

9. By and large, Jeremiah reverses the usual meaning of the term "remnant." The holy remnant is called the "captives" or "exiles" (*galah*, eighteen times) who been "taken captive" (*shabah*, six times) to Babylon. Except for three positive occurrences of *galah* concerning a future ingathering of the righteous remnant (23:3; 31:7; 50:20), the negative expression "the remnant (*sheerith*) of Judah" refers to those who did not heed Jeremiah's call to submit to Babylonian exile (twelve times). See Rom-Shiloni, "Group Identities in Jeremiah," 11–46; Morgan, "Remnant," 658–64.

10. Berlejung, "New Life, New Skills and New Friends," 12.

Immer (2:59), and Casiphia (8:17). Residents were organized by family lineage, according to upon Ezra 2 and Nehemiah 7:5–72.[11] They were ruled by elders (Jer 29:1; Ezek 8:1; 14:1; 20:1), priests (Ezra 1:5), and prophets (Ezek 1:1). During the exile, many Hebrews preserved their former religious identities. Ezra mentioned "the priests, the Levites, some of the people, the singers, the gatekeepers, and the temple servants" (2:70). Some Jews gained prominence in captivity, such as Nehemiah (1:11b), Daniel (1:1–7; 2:47–49), and his three friends (1:3–6; 3:12). Especially in the first displacement, the Babylonians set aside the nation's elite and skilled persons for special service and additional training (2 Kgs 24:14–16; Jer 24:1; 29:2; Dan 1:3, 17). This group also received royal patronage (Dan 1:5). Clearly, some deportees prospered greatly in exile, based upon the donations made for the restoration of the temple after the return to the land (Ezra 2:68–69; 8:24–30; Neh 7:70–71; Zech 6:10–12).

From ancient Babylonian records, we learn that Jeremiah's counsel was well-founded. Babylon settled ethnic minorities in separate communities and permitted their self-organization. In addition to the settlement named by Ezekiel, other Hebrew enclaves were called "Judah City" (*Āl-Yāh(ūdu)*) and the "City of Judeans" (*Āl-Yāhūdaya*). In addition, many Israelite villages were named after their founders. Berlejung summarizes the research from the cuneiform sources regarding the deportees' labor:

> They were farmers with a dependent juridical status (*šušanu*). They had to cultivate the crown land that had been assigned to them, but which they did not possess. They irrigated, plowed and farmed this land, lived on it and paid taxes. Leases and sub-leases of the land were possible. In addition to delivering taxes, they were obliged to serve the king each year for a limited time—usually two months—in military service or compulsory labor (e.g., for building projects).[12]

The imperial authorities provided the necessary elements to survive: seed, water, and a plot of land. But they also valued entrepreneurialism, since it suited their economic agenda. Those with special skills, such as language ability (Aramaic and Babylonian) or valuable trades, advanced quickly. And though the exiles were totally dependent upon their captors for their economic well-being and personal security, Rainer Albertz

---

11. Berlejung, "New Life, New Skills and New Friends," 12.

12. Berlejung, "New Life, New Skills and New Friends," 23. Lundbom ("Builders of Ancient Babylon," 160–62) describes Nebuchadnezzar's grandiose building projects and his need for workers.

concludes, "All in all, the exiles appear to have been treated leniently" and "There is no evidence of oppression on ethnic or religious grounds."[13]

Second, consider the Lord's instructions in verses 5–6 explaining what they must do in Babylon. The key verbs are in italics.

(5) *Build* houses and live in them; *plant* gardens and eat their produce.

(6) Take wives and have sons and daughters; take wives for your sons, and give your daughters in marriage, that they may bear sons and daughters; *multiply* there, and do not *decrease*.

Nine imperatives structure these two verses: "build" (*banah*), "live (in)" (*yashab*), "plant" (*nata*), "eat" (*akal*), "take" (*laqach*, twice), "have" and "bear" (*yalad*), and "multiply" (*rabah*). The imperatives are causally linked to the indicative statement in verse 4, since God "sent" them ("caused to be taken captive," *galah*) to Babylon. Their present location was not due to unfortunate happenstance. Rather, they were brought there by God's express purpose. They were, in fact, on mission.

Three of the four italicized terms in verses 5–6 indicate a positive nuance and one conveys a negative significance. The positive words are explained by their use in Jeremiah and in the Old Testament. They can also be contrasted with antonyms that appear elsewhere in Jeremiah:

Positive	Negative
build	break down, destroy, overthrow
plant	pluck up
multiply	decrease

Evidence in the book suggests that Jeremiah (the writer of the letter) and the readers in exile were highly literate. They knew Old Testament history, its worldview, and the covenant. They discerned in the imperatives ("build," "plant," "multiply") allusions to creation, Canaan, and covenant. From Genesis, they knew that God "built" (*banah*) Eve. They recognized that building and planting were normal activities of creatures made in God's image and commissioned as stewards. As we saw in our study of Genesis 1–11 in chapters 1–3, humans construct and build as apprentice architects. For instance, Enoch, Nimrod, and the Babelites

---

13. Albertz, *Israel in Exile*, 99, 101.

"built" cities (4:17; 10:11; 11:4). Jeremiah and his readers knew, as well, that God "planted" (*nata*) a garden from which "every tree that is pleasant to the sight and good for food" flourished (Gen 2:8-9). In fact, they viewed Canaan in arboreal and paradisiacal terms akin to Eden.[14] Günther Wittenberg summarizes the surprising vision the letter depicts in light of building and planting in Babylon: "The house is the dwelling of the family, the place for rest, work and play, the field the foundation for its existence. Vineyards, too, are part of the new existence. The planting of vineyards assumes symbolic significance for a full and satisfying life. Working on the fields and in the vineyards will not be in vain, but will be crowned by success."[15]

But they were also aware that living in the land was conditional. They understood Moses' warning, "Take care lest you forget the Lord your God by not keeping his commandments and his rules and his statutes . . . lest, when you have eaten and are full and have built (*banah*) good houses and live in them, and when your herds and flocks multiply (*rabah*) . . . [and] all that you have is multiplied, then your heart be lifted up, and you forget the Lord your God" (Deut 8:11-13). They knew, as well, the futile consequences of covenantal violation: "You shall build (*banah*) a house, but you shall not dwell in it. You shall plant (*nata*) a vineyard, but you shall not enjoy its fruit" (28:30).[16]

In fact, in Jeremiah, the word pair "build" and "plant" appears often (1:10; 24:6; 31:4-5, 28; 35:7; 42:10; 45:4). Adele Berlin shows further that the trio "build," "plant," and "marry" alludes to Deuteronomy 20:5-7 concerning exemptions from military service: "Is there any man who has built (*banah*) a new house and has not dedicated it? Let him go back to his house. . . . And is there any man who has planted (*nata*) a vineyard and has not enjoyed its fruit? . . . And is there any man who has betrothed a wife and has not taken (*laqach*) her? Let him go back to his house."[17]

---

14. The Promised Land is described as a "garden of Eden" (Ezek 36:35; Joel 2:3), "garden of the Lord" (Gen 13:10; Isa 51:3), and "garden of his delight" (Isa 5:7; see also Jer 31:12). It was a land of "milk and honey" (Exod 3:9), a place of peace and plenty where everyone could "eat and be satisfied" (Deut 8:10, 12; 11:15; 14:29; 29:12; Ps 104:28; Isa 66:11-13). It was also a land of prosperity where all enjoyed the bounty of God and "lived in safety, each man under his own vine and fig tree" (1 Kgs 4:25).

15. Wittenburg, "To Build and to Plant," 63.

16. Elsewhere in the Old Testament, the pair appears in Josh 24:13; Deut 28:30; Ezek 28:26; 36:36; Amos 5:11; Zeph 1:13.

17. Berlin, "Jeremiah 29:5-7: A Deuteronomic Allusion," 4-5. She suggests that Isaiah 65:21-23 and Psalm 107:36-38 also express the same thematic trio: build, plant,

Clearly, the intertextual images of building and dwelling, planting and eating, marriage and children conveyed meanings linked to creation, covenant, and Canaan.

Likewise, the verb "multiply" (*rabah*) conveys rich inner-biblical resonances. Within Jeremiah, the word appears three other times with a post-exilic and eschatological significance. God promises to multiply his people: "Then I will gather the remnant of my flock out of all the countries where I have driven them, and I will bring them back to their fold, and they shall be fruitful and multiply" (23:3; see also 30:19 and 33:22). Indeed, the command to multiply was given to Adam and Eve (Gen 1:22, 28) and to Noah (9:1). When God initiated the covenant with Abraham, he promised to "multiply [him] greatly" (17:2; see also Exod 32:13; Lev 26:9). But again, their multiplication was dependent upon covenantal obedience. Moses told them at the end of his life:

> If you obey the commandments of the Lord your God that I command you today, by loving the Lord your God, by walking in his ways, and by keeping his commandments and his statutes and his rules, then you shall live and multiply, and the Lord your God will bless you in the land that you are entering to take possession of it. But if your heart turns away, and you will not hear, but are drawn away to worship other gods and serve them, I declare to you today, that you shall surely perish" (Deut 30:16–18a).

Perishing is a nuance associated with the antonyms listed above ("pluck up," "break down," "destroy," "overthrow," "decrease"). Three times the positive and negative terms occur in tandem. In Jeremiah's call, the Lord told him, "See, I have set you this day over nations and over kingdoms, to pluck up and to break down, to destroy and to overthrow, to build and to plant" (1:10; see also 18:7–10; 30:19). The verb "pluck up" is an agricultural metaphor referring to Israel as God's special "vine." Psalm 80:8 says, "You brought a vine out of Egypt; you drove out the nations and planted it." The Lord told the tribe of Judah, "I planted you a choice vine, wholly of pure seed. How then have you turned degenerate and become a wild vine?" (Jer 2:21; see also 5:10; 6:9; 8:13). The other three verbs in the group indicate dismantling and annihilation, especially places of idol worship and apostate peoples.[18]

---

marry.

18. In Jeremiah, the image of tearing down (*nathats*) occurs in 1:10; 18:7; 31:28; 33:4; 39:8; 52:14; the image of destruction (*abad*) appears in 1:10; 6:21; 10:15; 15:7;

Indeed, the specter of perishing as a nation covenanted to Yahweh Elohim, whether due to judgment or loss of identity because of assimilation, was the ultimate disaster. For this reason, the Lord commanded the exiles in Jeremiah 29:6b, "Multiply there, and do not decrease (*maat*)." Even though they had been sent into exile, they had work to do. They had a calling. Their corporate responsibility was self-preservation, minimally speaking. Maximally, the vocabulary indicated that they were still subject to Adam's commission and the patriarchal promises—even in captivity.

Later in the letter, God revealed his long-term intention, covenantal affection, and commitment to them: "When seventy years are completed for Babylon, I will visit you, and I will fulfill to you my promise and bring you back to this place. For I know the plans I have for you, declares the Lord, plans for welfare and not for evil, to give you a future and a hope" (29:10–11). He emphatically foretold restoration and multiplication after the exile: "Behold, I will restore the fortunes of the tents of Jacob and have compassion on his dwellings; the city shall be rebuilt on its mound, and the palace shall stand where it used to be. Out of them shall come songs of thanksgiving, and the voices of those who celebrate. I will multiply them, and they shall not be few; I will make them honored, and they shall not be small" (30:18–19). But, in the meantime, they must continue to reproduce and cultivate their spiritual identity within their families.[19]

Third, 29:7 commands the exiles to behave in an entirely unexpected and implausible manner: "But seek the welfare of the city where I have sent you into exile, and pray to the Lord on its behalf, for in its welfare you will find your welfare." On one hand, this demand was pragmatic—an ancient form of realpolitik—due to their state of economic dependency and military powerlessness. As John Hill suggests, "A prosperous and secure Babylon would offer the exiles a better life there than would a Babylon which was torn by strife or under threat."[20] On the other hand, the command was pedagogical, teaching the captives how to think about their captivity and how to pray in light of what God had promised them.

The imperative "seek" (*darash*) presumes deliberation and intentionality about personal and corporate ends, good or bad. Subjectively, it implies a disposition or an attitude for or against something or someone. Objectively, it entails facilitation and purposeful action. The noun "peace"

18:7; 23:1; 27:10, 15; 40:15; 48:36; 49:7,); and "overthrow" (*haras*) occurs in 1:10; 24:6; 31:28; 45:4; 50:15.

19. Concerning the family, see Albertz, "More or Less than a Myth," 30.
20. Hill, *Friend or Foe?* 152.

(shalom) indicates well-being and wholeness, as well as the concrete conditions for safety and prosperity. Throughout the Old Testament, shalom often means security (Lev 26:6–10; 2 Kgs 20:19; Ps 122:6–7) and success (Deut 23:6; Ezra 9:12; Zech 8:12). But it is also associated with subjective themes like truth and faithfulness (Esther 9:30; Zech 8:16, 19) or righteousness (Ps 85:10; Isa 32:17; 60:17).

The idiom "seek the peace" appears four times in the Old Testament (Deut 23:6; Jer 29:7; 38:4; Ezra 9:12). Deuteronomy and Ezra associate peace with prosperity. Jeremiah 38:4 contrasts peace with harm and loss of motivation. In Jeremiah 29, the exiles were commanded to pursue and pray for the well-being, prosperity, and security of *Babylon*—in effect, to intercede for the Babylonians. Hill explains the irony: "Prayer for the welfare of Jerusalem is turned into praying for the welfare of the city which is Jerusalem's conqueror.... The place now in which YHWH is to be found is not in the Jerusalem temple, but in the city of the conqueror, an alien and unclean place."[21] To add insult to injury, Jeremiah was told *not* to intercede on behalf of Jerusalem (7:16; 11:14; 14:11). Formerly, he most likely echoed Psalm 122:6–9: "Pray for the peace of Jerusalem! 'May they be secure who love you! Peace be within your walls and security within your towers!' For my brothers and companions' sake I will say, 'Peace be within you!' For the sake of the house of the Lord our God, I will seek your good." Now, they were to seek the welfare of Babylon and pray to the Lord for its sake.

Fourth, verses 8–9 confront the chaotic epistemological context in Jerusalem:

(8) For thus says the Lord of hosts, the God of Israel: Do not let your prophets and your diviners who are among you deceive you, and do not listen to the dreams that they dream,

(9) for it is a lie that they are prophesying to you in my name; I did not send them, declares the Lord.

The would-be prophets ("who are among you") presented a clear and present epistemic danger to the exiles ("deceive you"). They were unauthorized spokesmen ("I did not send them"). Their message was false ("a lie") and so were their methods ("dreams" and "diviners"). They misrepresented themselves as Yahweh's messengers ("prophesying to you in my name"). The two conjunctions "for" (*ki*) coordinate and contrast

---

21. Hill, *Constructing Exile*, 151.

the Lord's imperatival logic of verses 5–7 with the prophet's contrarian reasoning in verses 8–9.

The false prophets "went after things that do not profit" (2:8b). The word "profit" (*yaal*) occurs seven times in Jeremiah, including three times referring to idolatry (2:8, 11; 16:19) and three times to the emptiness of the impostors' ideas (7:8; 23:32 twice). As expected, God assessed their mindset and discourse harshly: "The prophets will become wind; the word is not in them" (5:13a). J. A. Thompson explains, "They will be shown to be windbags who have no substance to their words."[22] In reality, their true inspiration arose from "the deceit of their own minds" (14:14; see also 23:16, 26). And they also plagiarized each other: "Therefore, behold, I am against the prophets, declares the Lord, who steal my words from one another" (23:30). Thompson remarks, "The false prophets were so devoid of personal inspiration, not having received a word personally from Yahweh, that they could only repeat what they heard others say."[23] Obviously, they were not learning from the Lord, for they "did not pay attention to my words" (29:19; see also 18:18).

Furthermore, the false prophets were characterized by ethical deviation: "adultery" (23:14), "ungodliness" (v. 15), and greed (6:13). Indeed, both they and the people had "become like Sodom and Gomorrah" (23:14). They "walk[ed] in lies" (23:14) and their speech was exemplified by "deceit" (*sheqer*).[24] They "prophes[ied] falsely" (5:31; 23:26) and offered "lies" and "lying visions" (14:14; 23:25, 26, 32). They were religious syncretists who "prophesied by Baal" (2:8; 23:13) and used "divination" (14:14). For this reason, the Lord told the nation, "Do not listen to your prophets, your diviners, your dreamers, your fortune-tellers, or your sorcerers" (27:9).[25]

---

22. Thompson, *The Book of Jeremiah*, 244 note 11. In 23:32, unprofitability is coupled with a rare term translated as "recklessness" (*pachazuth*, from the word *pachaz* found in Judg 9:4 and Zeph 3:4). In the three passages, the terms are rendered as "worthless [or fickle] and reckless." But the KJV renders the terms as "lies, and by their lightness" (Jer 23:32), "vain and light" (Judg 9:4), and "light and treacherous" (Zeph 3:4). Perhaps the notion of "lightness" captures an important nuance about the prophets' words that "profit" little. They were lightweights intellectually and, as a result, their declarations and deeds were both reckless and harmful.

23. Thompson, *The Book of Jeremiah*, 502.

24. The contrasts between truth and falsehood, trust and deception are major themes in Jeremiah. See Osuji, "True and False Prophecy," 437–52.

25. Jeremiah relies on Deuteronomic guidance about spiritual discernment; for example, "There shall not be found among you anyone who . . . practices divination or

Indeed, the false prophets operated within a toxic feedback loop. They told the nation what it wanted to hear and already believed. The Lord told them, however, "An appalling and horrible thing has happened in the land: the prophets prophesy falsely, and the priests rule at their direction; my people love to have it so, but what will you do when the end comes?" (5:30–31). Their misplaced triumphalism was highly intoxicating, deceptive, and destructive.

The people preferred what Anthony Osuji calls a "counter view of reality," that is, the "official view, voiced by the Jerusalem establishment and sustained on the lips of the 'false prophets.'"[26] They asserted the inviolability of Jerusalem as God's holy city and affirmed hypnotically, "This is the temple of the Lord, the temple of the Lord, the temple of the Lord" (7:4). Their prophets, therefore, announced that they would escape judgment: "You shall not see the sword, nor shall you have famine, but I will give you assured peace in this place" (14:13; see also 37:19); "You shall not serve the king of Babylon" (27:14). They directly contradicted Jeremiah, rejecting the counsel in his letter and denying his claim that "Your exile will be long; build houses and live in them, and plant gardens and ear their produce" (29:28). Sadly, their skewed message bore fruit, for they "have made this people trust in a lie" (28:15; see also 29:31)[27] and "led my people Israel astray" (23:13; see also v. 32 and 50:6). For all these reasons, God declared that the prophets' discourse was "deceptive words" (7:4), "filling you with vain hopes" (23:16).

For those who sat on the epistemological fence, however, the challenge was how to distinguish who discerned reality and understood what to do. The quarrel between Hananiah and Jeremiah illustrates this struggle. As Osuji says, "The confrontation of Jeremiah and Hananiah in a single combat, at the centre of the block [chapters 26–29], therefore poses directly the question of the discernment of the true and of the false prophet."[28] Edwin Searcy describes the scene vividly: "Jeremiah enters the epistemological courtroom, stands in the witness box, and gives daring testimony. He offers no half-truths, no spin-doctoring, no soft soap.

---

tells fortunes or interprets omens, or a sorcerer or a charmer or a medium or a necromancer or one who inquires of the dead . . . for these nations, which you are about to dispossess, listen to fortune-tellers and to diviners. But as for you, the Lord your God has not allowed you to do this" (Deut 18:10–14).

26. Osuji, "True and False Prophecy," 439.

27. "Trust" (*batach*) is in the Hiphil indicating causation, "to make to trust."

28. Osuji, "True and False Prophecy," 441.

Jeremiah names suspects, exposes lies, neutralizes counter-testimony, competes with adversaries, and calls for a hearing."[29]

Four forms of evaluation were available. First, listeners could evaluate by means of ethical criteria, including the negative behavior of the false prophets. Second, they could assess the differing means of spiritual discernment. The pseudo-prophets used illicit methods to determine God's will, whereas Jeremiah did not.[30]

Third, they could compare results. To this end, the Lord instructed Jeremiah to construct and wear a symbolic yoke to demonstrate the upcoming conquest of Nebuchadnezzar and their servitude in Babylon (27:2–15).[31] Hananiah countered with this oration and enactment in chapter 28:

(2) "Thus says the Lord of hosts, the God of Israel: I have broken the yoke of the king of Babylon.

(3) Within two years I will bring back to this place all the vessels of the Lord's house, which Nebuchadnezzar king of Babylon took away from this place and carried to Babylon . . . .

(10) Then the prophet Hananiah took the yoke-bars from the neck of Jeremiah the prophet and broke them.

(11) And Hananiah spoke in the presence of all the people, saying, "Thus says the Lord: Even so will I break the yoke of Nebuchadnezzar king of Babylon from the neck of all the nations within two years."

Jeremiah replied to Hananiah using the criteria for verifying prophetic speech in Deuteronomy 18: "When a prophet speaks in the name of the Lord, if the word does not come to pass or come true, that is a word that the Lord has not spoken; the prophet has spoken it presumptuously. You need not be afraid of him" (v. 22). In other words, if what Hananiah predicted (peace for Jerusalem) or Jeremiah prophesied (judgment and exile) came to pass, that indicated true prophecy. In 29:6–9, Jeremiah told all those who heard the interchange:

---

29. Searcy, "A People, a Name, a Praise, and a Glory," 333.

30. References to banned methodologies include 14:14; 23:16, 25–28; 27:9; and 29:8.

31. For the symbolic meaning of the yoke in the ancient Neat East, see Silver, "Performing Domination/Theorizing Power," 186–216.

(6) Amen! May the Lord do so; may the Lord make the words that you have prophesied come true, and bring back to this place from Babylon the vessels of the house of the Lord, and all the exiles.

(7) Yet hear now this word that I speak in your hearing and in the hearing of all the people.

(8) The prophets who preceded you and me from ancient times prophesied war, famine, and pestilence against many countries and great kingdoms.

(9) As for the prophet who prophesies peace, when the word of that prophet comes to pass, then it will be known that the Lord has truly sent the prophet."

Jeremiah also confronted Hananiah: "Listen, Hananiah, the Lord has not sent you, and you have made this people trust in a lie. Therefore thus says the Lord: 'Behold, I will remove you from the face of the earth. This year you shall die, because you have uttered rebellion against the Lord.'" The narrator reports, "In that same year, in the seventh month, the prophet Hananiah died" (28:15-17). In this instance and in this manner, Jeremiah was authenticated as the real prophet with the true message for the people in their moment of acute existential and intellectual crisis.[32]

Fourth, hearers could assess the differing forms of argumentation employed by Hananiah and Jeremiah, specifically their diverging starting points. On one hand, Dalit Rom-Shiloni points out that Hananiah used common rhetorical devices in his prophetic utterance. For instance, he expressed a typical prophetic introduction: "Thus says the Lord of Hosts, the God of Israel" (28:2a). He repeated the main ideas in verse 2b and 4b: "I have broken the yoke of the king of Babylon." He also repeated the promise of early return of the vessels (v. 3) and the exiles (v. 4). Thus, as Rom-Shiloni comments, "Hananiah's listeners could easily recognize stylistic and thematic markers in this prophecy, which were typical devices of the prophetic proclamations of his colleague, the prophet Jeremiah."[33] In addition, the symbolic breaking of Jeremiah's yoke echoed divine warrior themes expressed in Isaiah 9:4 and 10:27 and in Nahum 1:13.

---

32. See Rom-Shiloni, "Prophets in Jeremiah in Struggle for Leadership," 355–63 about the conflict between the two prophets. See also Yates, "The Prophet Jeremiah as Theological Symbol," 1–21.

33. Rom-Shiloni, "Prophets in Jeremiah in Struggle for Leadership," 355.

Jeremiah, however, reasoned differently and did not rely upon divinatory methodology. Rather, he drew from a deep intertextual corpus that presumed profound biblical–theological literacy.[34] He evaluated his nation's plight on the basis of the broader Deuteronomic tradition in which Yahweh as divine warrior prosecuted his covenant against obdurate Israel. Rom-Shiloni summarizes the distinctions in both content and method between the pseudo-spokesmen and the true prophet:

> The practical ways to achieve the goal of speaking in the name of God . . . [were] to phrase the prophetic words with echoes and allusions to pentateuchal materials, literary and mostly legal traditions and phraseology taken from different covenant traditions. Hence, while the peace prophets relied on visions, dreams, thoughts of their own hearts, etc., the prophet Jeremiah considered pentateuchal materials to supply greater legitimacy and authority for himself and his messages.[35]

She adds this important observation: "This clear intellectual and rhetorical choice constitutes a significant transformation in prophecy from the intuitive prophecy that is based on different divinatory devices such as visions and dreams to a prophecy that is based on oral/written traditions."[36] The false prophets argued on the basis of private revelation for Israel's abiding sovereignty and sustainability, despite the obvious threats. Their minds were skewed by triumphalism and establishment ideology. In contrast, Jeremiah reasoned from Scripture. He thoroughly understood Israel's redemptive–historical trajectory anchored in the ancient promises and covenant. He could reason on behalf of his nation like the sons of Issachar, "who had understanding of the times, to know what Israel ought to do" (1 Chr 12:32).

In the midst of chaos, therefore, those who listened received answers as to who really knew what to do. Jeremiah 29:4–9 and his disputes with the phony prophets and their fake news show clearly that God alone

---

34. Scholars have noted for some time the many pentateuchal allusions in Jeremiah, especially to Deuteronomy. See Weinfeld, "Jeremiah and the Spiritual Metamorphosis of Israel," 1–41; Leuchter, "The Exegesis of Jeremiah," 72–76; Hill, *Constructing Exile*, 38–58; Yates, "Intertexuality and the Portrayal of Jeremiah," 286–303; Rom-Shiloni, "How Can You Say, 'I Am Not Defiled . . . '?" 757–75; Rom-Shiloni, "Facing Destruction and Exile," 189–205; Rom-Shiloni, "On the Day I Took Them Out of the Land of Egypt," 621–47; and Rom-Shiloni, "Prophets in Jeremiah in Struggle for Leadership," 369–70.

35. Rom-Shiloni, "Prophets in Jeremiah in Struggle for Leadership," 369.

36. Rom-Shiloni, "Prophets in Jeremiah in Struggle for Leadership," 369.

knows and he reveals his message to Jeremiah only.[37] With respect to the exile, God told the captives, "I know the plans I have for you" (v. 11). But from the perspective of ontology and omniscience, he identified himself as "the one who knows" (v. 23).[38]

Finally, Psalm 107 looks back on the exile as an object lesson in understanding and wisdom. Verses 1–3 announce a call to worship: "Oh give thanks to the Lord, for he is good, for his steadfast love endures forever! Let the redeemed of the Lord say so, whom he has redeemed from trouble and gathered in from the lands, from the east and from the west, from the north and from the south." At the end of the psalm, verses 33–42 provide a meditation on God's power of reversal, with obvious reference to Israel's captivity and the destruction of their captors. The following terminology from Psalm 107 echoes the imperatives of Jeremiah 29:5–6 (build, plant, marry):

> He turns rivers into a desert, springs of water into thirsty ground, a fruitful land into a salty waste, because of the evil of its inhabitants. He turns a desert into pools of water, a parched land into springs of water. And there he lets the hungry dwell, and they establish a city to live in; they sow fields and plant vineyards and get a fruitful yield. By his blessing they multiply greatly, and he does not let their livestock diminish. When they are diminished and brought low through oppression, evil, and sorrow, he pours contempt on princes and makes them wander in trackless wastes; but he raises up the needy out of affliction and makes their families like flocks. The upright see it and are glad, and all wickedness shuts its mouth.

Significantly, verse 43 casts the theological lesson in terms of God's covenantal faithfulness and wisdom: "Whoever is wise, let him attend to these things; let them consider the steadfast love of the Lord." Although the exile made little theological sense at the time, the people learned to yield their understanding to the Lord as an existential and epistemic necessity. They learned to listen to and learn from God. In this way, they rediscovered that the fear of the Lord was the beginning of wisdom.

---

37. As we learned in chapter 7, epistemic themes appear prominently in Jeremiah.
38. The words "know" and "knowledge" occur over seventy times in Jeremiah.

PSALM 137

This psalm, though largely negative in perspective, provides several insights about the experience of some individuals brought to Babylon in the first deportation. Here are verses 1–6:

(1) By the waters of Babylon, there we sat down and wept, when we remembered Zion.

(2) On the willows there we hung up our lyres.

(3) For there our captors required of us songs, and our tormentors, mirth, saying, "Sing us one of the songs of Zion!"

(4) How shall we sing the Lord's song in a foreign land?

(5) If I forget you, O Jerusalem, let my right hand forget its skill!

(6) Let my tongue stick to the roof of my mouth, if I do not remember you, if I do not set Jerusalem above my highest joy!

These exiles enjoyed time for leisure, cultural expression (singing and communal lament), freedom of assembly, and personal security. In this case, they were likely former temple musicians who were able to bring their instruments.[39] John C. Ahn notes a cruel paradox, however: "Ironically, those who were formerly in political, social, and religious control of Judah, that is, the royal officials and the members of the temple, were now reduced to corvée. In this reversal of power, the once high and mighty were stripped of status and forced to labor for Babylonian economic gain."[40] In verse 1, "waters" probably refers to irrigation canals beside which the exiles dwelt in ethnic settlements and that they were obligated to maintain.[41] Two antagonists are identified in verse 3: "captors" (Babylonians) and "tormentors" (likely other captive ethnicities living nearby). The setting depicted in this psalm presumes a pluralistic setting: proximity to and friction with persons of other cultures, religions, and ethnic identities.[42] Apparently, the Jews were sometimes mocked for their predicament.

---

39. Ahn argues that the speaker was a probably a right-handed musician and a Levite. See "Psalm 137: Complex Communal Laments," 284.

40. Ahn, "Psalm 137: Complex Communal Laments," 278.

41. Ahn, "Psalm 137: Complex Communal Laments," 277.

42. Jeremiah's letter and Psalm 137 presume acute challenges that the exiles faced. Ahn ("Exile," 201) lists ten: "(1) tensions between local and central politics; (2) clashes between cultural/traditional values and new ones; (3) struggles of socioeconomic

Psalm 137 presumes an important theological question: What does Babylon have to do with Jerusalem? Jeremiah responded as if to say, "Very much!" whereas those who lamented their loss concluded, "Very little!" The terminology of the psalm indicates this bifurcated outlook. These explicit and implicit contrasts appear:

Babylon	Jerusalem
weeping	joy
foreign land	Zion/Jerusalem
silence ("hung up our lyres")	singing
lesser joys (Babylon)	highest joy (Jerusalem)
forget	remember
captors/tormentors	we/our/us

In their misery and disorientation, some of the earliest deportees struggled to internalize Jeremiah's positive perspective of the exile. They could not imagine serving God apart from the enabling infrastructure of the Israelite state (monarchy, temple, land).[43] Perhaps they did not listen attentively to the Lord or suffered from double-mindedness: "For they have not listened to my words," declares the Lord, "words that I sent to them again and again by my servants the prophets. And you exiles have not listened either" (Jer 29:19, NIV). Perhaps they idolized the temple and Zion ideology—"the pride of your power, the delight of your eyes, and the yearning of your soul" (Ezek 24:21). As Heath A. Thomas suggests, they did not discern this critical lesson: "Holy sites do not enable Yahweh's presence among his people, but holy people do (Jer 7:3–11; 26:1–6)."[44]

---

classes; (4) challenges of preserving one's first language (Hebrew) in the immediacy of one's family and community while dealing with the language or languages of the dominant culture (e.g., Aramaic for speaking and Akkadian/Sumerian for reading or writing); (5) restrictions of food or diet; (6) issues of gender and marriage (e.g., at what generational point does intermarriage become a realistic possibility); (7) problems of raising children and grandchildren in bifurcated or dual culture; (8) questions of partial or full acculturation or assimilation; (9) struggles to maintain religious practices, including those for the sake of social identity; (10) defining the concept of home (is it Babylon or Judah/Yehud?"

43. Seemingly, they possessed little room for the concepts of common grace or common good in their thinking.

44. Thomas, "Zion," 910.

On the other hand, the polemical exchange between the would-be singers of the songs of Zion and their abusers implies Psalm 79's elenctic emphasis and urgent plea, "Why should the nations say, 'Where is their God?'" (v. 10; see also 115:2). Or perhaps the mockery functioned as a fitting rejoinder to Hebrew arrogance: "All who pass along the way clap their hands at you; they hiss and wag their heads at the daughter of Jerusalem: 'Is this the city that was called the perfection of beauty, the joy of all the earth?'" (Lam 2:15). Their captors called them an "outcast," adding, "It is Zion, for whom no one cares!" (Jer 30:17b).

The tormentor's cynicism implied a critique of Israel's God. His character and veracity were challenged. Was he merely an impoverished national deity in the face of Babylon's awesome Marduk? Did he abandon his people or break his promises due to lack of covenantal fidelity? Such reasoning would imply, of course, that the Lord was not omniscient or omnipotent, since he failed to anticipate the threatening tectonic political movements of the ancient Near East and could not defend his people.

The psalm also presupposes a decision. Verses 5–6 contain three conditional clauses with the word "if" (*im*):

> If I forget you, O Jerusalem
> If I do not remember you
> If I do not set Jerusalem above my highest joy

The explicit options are to forget or remember Jerusalem. Forgetting means a repudiation of the covenant and calling. The implicit option is to embrace Babylon in religious and cultural assimilation. The verbs "remember" and "set" are correlative. The latter term indicates a single-minded preference for Zion.[45] "Remember" presumes a motivation to distinguish between foreign and Hebrew priorities and to maintain them at all costs, as indicated by the writer's self-deprecation in verses 5–6. Furthermore, as we saw in chapter 9 of this book, "remember" (*zakar*, vv. 1, 6) presupposes a pedagogical infrastructure. On one hand, it refers to self-defining ontological and historical, as well as ethical, concepts and practices that define Israel in distinction to other peoples. On the other hand, remembrance presumes an educational infrastructure designed to

---

45. VanGemeren explains the literal meaning: "If I do not consider [lit., 'bring up'] Jerusalem my highest joy [lit., 'on the head of my joy']" (*The Expositor's Bible Commentary*, 829, note 6). The verb is used similarly in Ezekiel 14:7 to indicate a negative preference: "set up idols in their hearts and put a wicked stumbling block before their faces" (NIV).

prevent forgetfulness (apostasy). Israel's intellectual intentionality was expressed through study, recitation, ritual, and celebration in the family and community. However, setting Jerusalem as the "highest joy" also presumes a hierarchy of preferences, allowing lesser and permissible pleasures available in Babylon. Their challenge was to know where to draw the lines. What was allowed and what was forbidden in their new and alien milieu?

CONCLUSION

The dejected singers in Psalm 137 provide a discordant path to follow in the midst of disorientation. The musicians could not imagine blessing and service apart from their former temple setting and their customary lifestyle in Canaan. Their mental state resembles a scene in book 7 of *The Chronicles of Narnia*.[46] A group of exceedingly closed-minded dwarfs stubbornly refused to perceive or partake of the blessings set before them. They preferred what they had previously, even though that was no longer available to them. They willingly deceived themselves, embracing a false perception of reality. They did not proceed into the land of prosperity prepared for them by Aslan.

Psalm 137 raises important questions about knowledge and power, especially in adversarial and intellectually diverse contexts. The musicians had unwillingly transitioned from a monocultural to a pluralistic setting. They lost social, religious, and economic capital. In a very real sense, they were impoverished and suffered spiritual nakedness. Their manner of thinking was adversely impacted. They did not discern how their view of reality or themselves was conditioned by power and its loss. As a result, they did not perceive their opportunity or responsibility. They did not seek the common good for the glory of God, as Jeremiah counseled. They did not declare God's name as exiles in their elenctic context.

This kind of thinking and behavior resembles that of many North American evangelicals. The United States has been associated closely with the Promised Land of ancient Israel. North Americans, it is often thought, constitute a special community akin to the covenanted peoples of the Old and New Testaments. Now that evangelicals have most likely lost the culture war, the ensuing disorientation feels like internal exile. Many, it seems, refuse to embrace the opportunities and responsibilities

---

46. Lewis, *The Last Battle*, 171–86.

inherent in the new setting. Inordinate longing for the cultural domination of the past and related forms of thinking, however, is neither spiritually healthy nor intellectually pious.

The book of Jeremiah and Psalm 137 reveal the need for redemptive epistemology in our time. Christians today must discern contrary views of reality and the entrapment of toxic feedback loops. They must carefully distinguish between true and false messages. The prophet Jeremiah demonstrated the manifold benefits of biblical–theological literacy and fluency. With such knowledge and skills, believers develop discernment and discover what must be done in the midst of unwanted change.

The lessons of Jeremiah 29 and Psalm 137 are still intensely relevant. We will learn more about opportunity and responsibility in the final chapter. Daniel modeled a mindset rooted in the fear of God and wisdom, discerning both the common good and the challenges of the Babylonian milieu.

14

God Gave Learning and Skill

"Behold, I am sending you out as sheep in the midst of wolves, so be wise as serpents and innocent as doves."

—Matthew 10:16

The book of Daniel offers a very different response to Jeremiah's letter from Psalm 137. Whereas the psalm depicts hopelessness and defeat, Daniel and his three companions display cautious optimism and vigilant discernment. While the temple musicians felt utter disorientation, the four youths relied upon Hebrew wisdom and prophetic revelation to interpret themselves and their new environment. They knew who they were, where they came from, why they were in Babylon, and where the future would lead them.[1]

The book of Daniel also describes a much more challenging encounter with Babylonian culture than Psalm 137. The characters portrayed in the psalm were situated at a distance culturally, whereas Daniel and his three friends were "high-profile deportees,"[2] enlisted as future administrative servants and counselors to the king. Their great test was setting boundaries and avoiding corruption while deeply embedded in the royal court. In this context, they operated within a perverse intellectual

---

1. Jeffrey Foster contributed helpful insights for this paragraph.
2. Berlejung, "New Life, New Skills and New Friends," 13.

environment and subject to court intrigue—a milieu designed to promote ethical and ideological capitulation.[3]

In the book of Daniel, the theme of knowledge is central and a knowledge deficit drives the plot forward. The Babylonians believed that they possessed true wisdom. But over and over again, Daniel triumphs over the best and brightest Chaldean. In this chapter, we learn why and how this discrepancy occurs. The first three sections concern the relationship between power and knowledge. The fourth section focuses on Daniel's intellectual preparation for exile. The last section analyzes his critique of Babylonian wisdom and knowledge.

THE QUESTION OF POWER

The book begins with these two verses:

(1) In the third year of the reign of Jehoiakim king of Judah, Nebuchadnezzar king of Babylon came to Jerusalem and besieged it.

(2) And the Lord gave Jehoiakim king of Judah into his hand, with some of the vessels of the house of God. And he brought them to the land of Shinar, to the house of his god, and placed the vessels in the treasury of his god.

Babylon invaded and conquered Judah and deported the elite and skilled classes. The Babylonians also carried away implements associated with worship in the temple. They appeared to control Judah's destiny.

The idiomatic expression "gave into his hand" appears often in the Old Testament. (The hand represents agency and power.) Twenty-two times it occurs in Israel's favor: nineteen times to express divinely enabled defeat of their enemies and three times with reference to blessings accorded to the nation.[4] Nineteen times, however, God gave Israel "into the hands" of its enemies as punishment for sin.[5] In each occurrence (for

---

3. The three friends were tossed into a fiery furnace because of anti-Jewish sentiment among the advisors to the king (3:8–12), and the lion's den episode arose because of jealousy of Daniel (6:4–5).

4. Defeat of enemies: Deut 2:36; 3:3; Josh 10:30, 32; 11:8; 24:8, 11; Judg 1:4; 3:10; 6:9; 11:21, 32; 12:3; 1 Sam 24:10; 26:23; 2 Sam 21:9; 2 Chr 16:8; Neh 9:24; Jer 44:30; blessing: Josh 21:44; 24:8; 2 Kgs 13:5.

5. See Judg 2:14; 6:1; 13:1; 2 Kgs 13:3; 17:20; 2 Chr 13:16; 28:5, 9; 36:17; Ezra 5:12; Neh 9:27, 30; Ps 106:41; Isa 47:6; Lam 1:14; Ezek 39:23.

or against Israel), the agent was the God of Israel.[6] The verb "gave" (*natan*) demonstrated the true source of power and sovereignty over human history (v. 2). Daniel announced this truth to the king in the interpretation of his second dream: "The Most High rules the kingdom of men and gives it to whom he will and sets over it the lowliest of men" (4:17b).[7] Likewise, Jeremiah designated Nebuchadnezzar as God's "servant" and prophesied that Judah would endure seventy-five years under his yoke (25:9–11; see also 27:5–7).

Verses 1–2 also provide clues about Judah's negative—but realistic—assessment of Babylon's grandeur. The association of Babylon with the "land of Shinar" is an allusion to Genesis 11:1–9 and the Tower of Babel. As we saw in chapter 3, the tower episode was the primeval apex of collective, noetic sinfulness and apostate human prowess. Babel was the paradigmatic nexus of religion, culture, and politics for nefarious ends. It was a manifestation of mankind's cultural mandate (Gen 1:26) gone deeply awry. Similarly, Babylon was intimately associated with apostate religion and titanic ambitions. It was considered the greatest city of the ancient Near East in its day, in fact, the center of the world.

Like all imperialisms of the ancient Near East, Babylon imbibed the mentality of empire, as we learned in chapter 4. Some kings, such as Nebuchadnezzar, were selected by the gods to represent divinity on earth and establish an empire. Imperialism presumed the conquest of other religions and the assimilation of deported peoples into the empire's worldview. Conquerors confiscated religious emblems of vanquished peoples and carried them off "to the treasury of [their] god" (v. 2). Similarly, Babylon demonstrated the supremacy of its patron deity Marduk over Yahweh by plundering the temple's artifacts.[8]

Indeed, Babylon intimidated by its pomp and immensity. Jack R. Lundbom provides details about the city and its king. He writes, "Excavations have shown that outer and inner walls were each six or seven meters thick.... The two walls with rubble in between thus formed an elevated

---

6. In addition, the term "Lord" appears twenty-four times in Daniel: fourteen times for "Yahweh" and ten times for "*adonai*" (especially in chapter 9 where Daniel prays for the end of exile). Longman (*Daniel*, 46) explains that *adonai* indicates "God's ownership, his control."

7. In fact, Daniel announced the same truth four times in chapter 4 (vv. 17, 25, 26, 32).

8. 1 Samuel 4–5 describes what happened when the Philistines captured the ark of the covenant and placed it in the temple of their god Dagon.

roadway seventeen to twenty-two meters wide." Inside the city, "Temples, gates, and other buildings . . . were adorned with gold, bronze, and other precious metals."[9]

During his forty-three-year reign, Nebuchadnezzar expressed and expanded the city's prestige and his own. This included "rebuilding the main river wall and wharf," "building, rebuilding, and widening more than twenty canals," "rebuilding and embellishing more than twenty-four city streets," "rebuilding the stepped pyramid temple, the ziggurat," and "continuing work on a temple to Marduk." His construction projects demonstrated the opulence of Babylon, including "temples and chapels, some decorated with geometric designs or overlaid with gold." As for the king's palace, "its upper walls were decorated all around with blue-glazed enameled bricks, and doors of cedar, ebony, or other fine wood were encased in bronze or inlaid with silver, gold, and ivory. Rooms were roofed with huge cedar beams from Lebanon or select pine and cypress logs, and some were covered in gold." Finally, Lundbom noted with reference to the Hebrews and other captive peoples, "Nebuchadnezzar's military campaigns contributed to the effort, as he brought home considerable booty and many prisoners of war to do the work."[10] For no small reason, then, the king boasted, "Is not this great Babylon, which I have built by my mighty power as a royal residence and for the glory of my majesty?" (Dan 4:29–31).

Nebuchadnezzar ruled in unheard-of glory and triumph. He credited his success to Marduk: "Without you, my lord, what exists? . . . You begot me and entrusted me with the rule over all peoples . . . . Make the fear of your godhead be in my heart. Prolong the days of the one who pleases you, for you truly are my life."[11] He believed that Babylon was the center of civilization and saw himself as its steward. He said about himself, "The palace, the seat of my royal authority, a place of union of mighty peoples, abode of joy and happiness, the place where proud ones are compelled to submit, I rebuilt upon the bosom of the wide world . . . . My royal decisions, my imperial commands, I caused to go forth from it."[12] Paul Ferguson comments, "Nebuchadnezzar stood on his palace roof, which had been made of cedar from the forests of Lebanon. Stacked

---

9. Lundbom, "Builders of Ancient Babylon," 157.
10. Lundbom, "Builders of Ancient Babylon," 161.
11. Cited by Ferguson, "Nebuchadnezzar, Gilgamesh, and the 'Babylonian Job,'" 331.
12. Cited by Ferguson, "Nebuchadnezzar, Gilgamesh, and the 'Babylonian Job,'" 324.

all around were over fifteen million bricks, each containing his name and royal titles."[13] He adds, however:

> He had forgotten that all the bricks were made of mud. He had also forgotten the affirmation made at his accession that all he possessed came from one deity. He had not remembered that his father had represented himself on a monument as the "son of nobody," helpless without his god. He had failed to notice two streets below him called "Bow Down, Proud One" and "May the Arrogant Not Flourish." He did not even recall that one of the names of his palace was "The Place Where Proud Ones Are Compelled to Submit."[14]

Indeed, Babylon's pomposity did not escape the prophets' notice. Isaiah referred to Babylonia as "the glory of kingdoms" (13:19), "leaders of the earth," and "kings of the nations" (14:9). He mentioned their "towers" and "pleasant places" (13:22), as well as their "pomp" and "sound of harps" (14:11). Similarly, Jeremiah noted their "treasures" (50:37), "mighty voice" (51:55), and "broad wall" (v. 58). He called them the "praise of the whole earth" (v. 51). Ezekiel affirmed Nebuchadnezzar's military power: "king of Babylon, king of kings, with horses and chariots, and with horsemen and a host of many soldiers" (26:7). Daniel said to him, "Your greatness has grown and reaches to heaven, and your dominion to the ends of the earth" (4:22). For this reason, the king inspired great fear: "All peoples, nations, and languages trembled and feared before him. Whom he would, he killed, and whom he would, he kept alive; whom he would, he raised up, and whom he would, he humbled" (5:19).

THE QUESTION OF KNOWLEDGE

We now continue on to 1:3–7:

(3) Then the king commanded Ashpenaz, his chief eunuch, to bring some of the people of Israel, both of the royal family and of the nobility,

(4) youths without blemish, of good appearance and skillful in all wisdom, endowed with knowledge, understanding learning, and

---

13. Cited by Ferguson, "Nebuchadnezzar, Gilgamesh, and the 'Babylonian Job,'" 321.
14. Cited by Ferguson, "Nebuchadnezzar, Gilgamesh, and the 'Babylonian Job,'" 321.

competent to stand in the king's palace, and to teach them the literature and language of the Chaldeans.

(5) The king assigned them a daily portion of the food that the king ate, and of the wine that he drank. They were to be educated for three years, and at the end of that time they were to stand before the king.

(6) Among these were Daniel, Hananiah, Mishael, and Azariah of the tribe of Judah.

(7) And the chief of the eunuchs gave them names: Daniel he called Belteshazzar, Hananiah he called Shadrach, Mishael he called Meshach, and Azariah he called Abednego.

From the king's perspective, a great knowledge gap existed between the Hebrews and the Babylonians (v. 4). Nebuchadnezzar believed that Babylonia possessed far deeper understanding than Israel, that Babylon was a more enlightened and just city than Jerusalem,[15] and that his gods expressed reality more clearly than Yahweh. Carol A. Newsom writes, "This differential access to knowledge is often crucial to the tension that fuels the plot."[16] As king and vice-regent of Marduk, therefore, Nebuchadnezzar possessed superior insight and knew what the Jews must learn in order to function properly in the royal court.[17] For this reason, he delegated to Ashpenaz the education of his Hebrew protégés, since even the very best of Israel required retraining by indoctrination and enculturation (v. 3). They must be taught to think and behave like Babylonians.

Verses 4, 5 and 7 stipulate four aspects of their educational program. First, they learned the language of Babylonia: Akkadian and writing in cuneiform. In verse 4, the language is called "Chaldean," a term associated with the practice of mantic wisdom and divination. Initially,

---

15. See Coxon, "Nebuchadnezzar's Hermeneutical Dilemma," 87-97.

16. Newsom, *Daniel*, 41.

17. Presumably, Nebuchadnezzar knew that children of the elite in whatever nation he conquered were likely to be highly educated and prepared to "stand before" royalty as counselors, diplomats, and administrators. According to Newsom (*Daniel*, 42), deportees were "incorporated into positions within Mesopotamian court households," and commonly "aristocratic youths were to be given an education that included basic literary and memorization of a standard set of classic texts." Examples in the Israelite monarchy of those (young and old) who "stand before" the king appear in 1 Kgs 12:6, 8; 2 Chr 10:6, 8.

they focused on writing and grammar through copying word lists and excerpts of traditional literature.

Then, Daniel and his friends learned the *sefer* ("book") of Babylon, the written wisdom traditions (v. 4). They copied parts of Babylonian sagas, such as *Enuma Elish* and the *Epic of Gilgamesh*, as well as documents associated with divination. Alan Lenzi explains the didactic purpose of the curriculum: "As many students would spend their scribal careers in service to the major institutions (i.e., the palace and temples), the compositions that were used in their education also internalized royal ideology as well as a knowledge of the gods and the created order."[18] Cultural literacy, therefore, enabled conceptual fluency—the ability to reason from ontological and epistemological presuppositions embedded in the Babylonian worldview.[19]

This knowledge and skill equipped them to counsel the king among the "wise men of Babylon" (2:18), those commissioned to discern divine communication.[20] Verse 4 indicates an assembly of international specialists (together called "Chaldeans" in 2:2). Among these were "magicians" (practitioners of divination and interpretation of omens from Egypt), "enchanters" (astrologers and exorcists), and "sorcerers" (those who conjure up spirits).[21] As Newsom notes, "The picture is thus that of a king who can command the whole spectrum of mantic experts from all of the national and ethnic traditions of the empire."[22] Seemingly, the king of Babylon had the best and brightest of the whole empire at his disposal. He harnessed total power and knowledge—at least he thought so.

---

18. Lenzi, *An Introduction to Akkadian Literature,* locations 998–1000. See also Stökl, "'A Youth without Blemish,'" 223–52.

19. See Strawn, *The Old Testament Is Dying,* 6–13.

20. Newsom (*Daniel,* 45) provides an ancient depiction of the wise man's function: "For being assigned to the service of the gods, they spend their entire life in study, their greatest renown being in the field of astrology. But they occupy themselves largely with soothsaying as well, making predictions about future events, and in some cases by purifications, in others by sacrifices, and in others by some other charms they attempt to effect the averting of evil things and the fulfillment of the good. They are also skilled in soothsaying by the flight of birds, and they give out interpretations of both dreams and portents."

21. Lenzi ("Secrecy, Textual Legitimation, and Intercultural Polemics," 337) provides a list of "the traditional Mesopotamian scholarly crafts": exorcism (*āsipūtu*), medicine (*asûtu*), divination (*barûtu*), ritual lamentation (*kalûtu*), and astrology (*tuppsarrūtu*).

22. Newsom, *Daniel,* 68.

The third aspect of the reidentification and socialization of the Hebrews was renaming. As we learned in chapter 1, designating a name defined identity, foretold purpose, and established a covenantal relationship. In effect, the king delegated to Ashpenaz authority to form a new covenant with the four Hebrews by realigning their religious identity and associating them with a different deity. Renaming also implied that their divine patron Yahweh Elohim was incorporated into the pantheon of Babylon. Newsom summarizes the sociological significance: "It is simultaneously an honor conferred by the king to mark the recipient's new status and a sign of the expectation of loyalty to the king who bestows the name."[23] These implications appear in their old and new names:

Hebrew	Babylonian
Daniel ("God is my judge")	Belteshazzar ("may [a god] protect his life" or "may the Lady [a goddess] protect the king"; "He who was named Belteshazzar after the name of my god," (4:8)
Azariah ("Yah is my help")	Abednego ("servant of [the god] Nebo")
Hananiah ("Yah has been gracious")	Shadrach ("shining" or "brilliant")
Mishael ("Who is what God is?")	Meshack (a version of the Persian god Mithra)[24]

The fourth feature of their education was socialization into the lifestyle and expectations of the court. On one hand, this included an examination by Nebuchadnezzar himself 1:18, 20). On the other hand, they were sustained during the acclimation process by the king's beneficence ("daily portion," v. 5). The term "portion" (*patbag*) occurs only in Daniel (1:5, 8, 13, 15, 16; 11:26), and twice it appears with the expression "wine that he drank" (1:5, 8).[25] In every case, the owner of the food and wine was the king. In the Old Testament, to eat at the king's table implied covenantal loyalty and dependence (1 Sam 20:30–34; 2 Sam 9:9–13; 19:27–29). Similarly, the reinstatement of the exiled Jewish king Jehoiachin to the Babylonian's king's table and his regular stipend implies this same significance (2 Kgs 25:27–30). Also, the sixth use of *patbag* in

---

23. Newsom, *Daniel*, 47.
24. Compiled from Newsom, *Daniel*, 46 and Longman, *Daniel*, 50–51.
25. See Seufert, "Refusing the King's Portion," 644–60.

Dan 11:26 indicates that loyalty was assumed among those who "eat his [the king's] food."

DANIEL'S DECISION

Verse 8, however, inserts tension into the narrative: "But Daniel resolved that he would not defile himself with the king's food, or with the wine that he drank. Therefore he asked the chief of the eunuchs to allow him not to defile himself." Two issues arise—religious identity and the acquisition of wisdom—and both were resolved by God's empowerment. In this verse, the adversative conjunction "but" and the verb "resolved" indicate conflict. The word "resolved" derives from the idiom "set (*sum*) the heart (*leb*)." Approximately nineteen times, the phrase appears with an intellectual significance—for instance, "pay attention" (Exod 9:21), "set your mind on" (1 Sam 9:20), "consider" (Job 2:3), and "mark well" (Ezek 44:5). To "set the heart" indicates cognition: assessment, evaluation, and intentionality. In this case, Daniel discerned a problem, analyzed his options, and implemented a plan.

Thus, Daniel determined that a boundary had been reached regarding food and defilement that would violate his religious identity. Longman explains the context:

> Up to this point, Daniel and his three friends have provided no recorded resistance to their assimilation into Babylonian culture and society. They have received new names, submitted to a foreign educational curriculum, and perhaps even had their gender erased.... What does Daniel hope to accomplish by his determined stand?[26]

A partial answer, as we saw, concerns the question of loyalty to and dependence upon a foreign ruler and the gods he represented.[27] Perhaps Daniel rejected the king's provision to affirm his covenantal loyalty and

---

26. Longman, *Daniel*, 51–52. The reference to gender probably originates with a prophecy in Isaiah: "Then Isaiah said to Hezekiah, "Hear the word of the Lord of hosts: Behold, the days are coming, when all that is in your house, and that which your fathers have stored up till this day, shall be carried to Babylon. Nothing shall be left, says the Lord. And some of your own sons, who will come from you, whom you will father, shall be taken away, and they shall be eunuchs in the palace of the king of Babylon" (39:5–7).

27. See Seufert, "Refusing the King's Portion," 644–48, for a survey of likely interpretations.

dependence on Yahweh Elohim. Longman suggests, however, another rationale that answers the question: Who is the ultimate source of the four Hebrews' success?

> Daniel and his three friends are in a process of education and preparation for service. Their minds as well as their bodies are being fed by the Babylonian court. If they prosper, then to whom should they attribute their development and success? . . . Their robust appearance, usually attained by a rich fare of meats and wine, is miraculously achieved through a diet of vegetables. Only God could have done it.[28]

On one hand, verses 9–16 explain that God "gave" Daniel and his friends a threefold provision to remedy their dilemma concerning the "daily portion." In verses 9 and 14, he provided social capital: "favor and compassion" with the imperial authorities who supervised them.[29] Implicitly, he gave Daniel tact and wisdom for a "test" that validated their vegetarian diet (vv. 12, 14).[30] And God granted physical potency: "And at the end of ten days their appearance seemed better, and they were fatter than all the youths who had been eating the king's choice food" (v. 15).[31]

On the other hand, the issue of wisdom (language acquisition, cultural understanding, and religion, as well as the behavioral expectations in the royal court) appears in verses 17–20. Significantly, God "gave" them an understanding of *Babylonian* wisdom surpassing even that of the native scholars who advised the king. In effect, he enabled them to beat the Chaldeans at their own game. Verses 17–20 explain the cognitive resources God provided Daniel and his companions, as well as the result:

(17) As for these four youths, God gave them learning and skill in all literature and wisdom, and Daniel had understanding in all visions and dreams.

---

28. Longman, *Daniel*, 53.

29. Regarding Daniel's communicative skills, 2:14 says, "Then Daniel replied with prudence and discretion to Arioch, the captain of the king's guard, who had gone out to kill the wise men of Babylon."

30. By faith, Daniel took the initiative without knowing with certainty that the proposal would succeed (see also 2:16).

31. Seufert ("Refusing the King's Portion," 648–59) argues that Daniel's decision not to partake of the king's food is best explained intertextually, referencing allusions found elsewhere in the Old Testament. He reasoned from Israel's experience with manna during the exodus, as depicted in Exodus 15–16.

(18) At the end of the time, when the king had commanded that they should be brought in, the chief of the eunuchs brought them in before Nebuchadnezzar.

(19) And the king spoke with them, and among all of them none was found like Daniel, Hananiah, Mishael, and Azariah. Therefore they stood before the king.

(20) And in every matter of wisdom and understanding about which the king inquired of them, he found them ten times better than all the magicians and enchanters that were in all his kingdom.

DANIEL'S INTELLECTUAL PROFILE

Clearly, God enabled Daniel to prosper within his alien environment. This raises a question about his intellectual preparation for exile. To put it another way, the word "resolved" (v. 8) presumes interpretive criteria and evaluation. What norms and priorities did Daniel presuppose to navigate the Babylonian labyrinth? What did he know theologically that enabled him to excel in his roles as sage and prophet? Fortunately, the book of Daniel provides several explicit and implicit indications of his epistemic profile.

The narrator described Daniel as a member of Israelite nobility (1:3), underscoring the likelihood of theological and practical education as future servants of the court. The narrator described Daniel's intellectual posture with vocabulary derived from the wisdom genre: "gifted in all wisdom, possessing knowledge and quick to understand" (v. 4, NKJV) and "knowledge and skill in all literature and wisdom" (v. 17, NKJV). As we learned in chapter 6, these terms also appear in Proverbs: "gifted" (*sakal*), "wisdom" (*chokmah*), "knowledge" (*daat*), and "understand" (*bin*). The words "quick" (v. 4) and "knowledge" (v. 17) are translated from *madah*, a term that appears only six times in the Old Testament. Significantly, it occurs three times in 2 Chronicles in Solomon's prayer for wisdom to govern Israel (1:10, 11, 12). The image conveyed by this vocabulary is that Daniel possessed the "beginning of wisdom" because he feared the Lord (Prov 1:7a). Or from the viewpoint of the angel Gabriel, Daniel listened to God's voice, for he "set [his] heart to understand and humbled [him]self before [his] God" (10:12).

Furthermore, as we noted, Daniel's Hebrew name was theophoric, identifying him with biblical ontology. God testified that Daniel was "greatly loved" (9:23; 10:11), righteous (Ezek 14:14, 20), and wise (28:3). The Babylonians stated that he was "faithful, and no error or fault was found in him" (Dan 6:4). Nebuchadnezzar declared about Daniel's friends—and, by implication Daniel—that they "trusted in him [God], and set aside the king's command, and yielded up their bodies rather than serve and worship any god except their own God" (3:28). King Darius announced that Daniel served God "continually" (6:20) and that all people should "fear before the God of Daniel," which was what Daniel modeled. The narrator said that Daniel prayed three times daily toward Jerusalem (6:10). Daniel stated that he was "blameless" before God (6:22).

The narrator asserted that Daniel was "ten times better than all the magicians and enchanters" of Babylon (1:20). He interpreted enigmatic dreams (chapter 2; 4:19–27) and prophetic handwriting (chapter 5). He was made chief of the wise men (2:48). The queen mother testified that Daniel possessed "understanding and wisdom" and that he had "an excellent spirit, knowledge, and understanding" (5:12). Daniel continuously sought understanding from God (7:16, 19; 8:15; 12:8) and often received instruction (8:19; 9:22–23, 25; 10:1, 14, 21; 11:2). For all these reasons, the angel included him among the "wise" who are "refined, purified, and made white, until the time of the end" (11:33; see also 12:3, 10).

Furthermore, Daniel's prayer in chapter 9 provides critical insights about his thinking while in captivity.[32] His narrow aim concerned "the number of years that . . . must pass before the end of the desolations of Jerusalem" (v. 2). His broader focus was "gaining insight by [God's] truth" (v. 13b). Regarding the former, he learned from reading Jeremiah that the time of restoration and return had come, and he prayed accordingly. Regarding the latter, he sought to understand God's providence and Israel's future. Yoram Hazony explains that "truth" (*emet*) in the Old Testament refers to what or who can be relied upon, as well as facts that reflect reality and correspond to expectations, "despite the hardships thrown up by changing circumstance."[33] In this case, Daniel pursued sure knowledge about Israel's plight according to the Lord's perspective, presupposing his covenantal faithfulness even in the midst of judgment. In contrast to Qohelet (chapter 5), Daniel sought an "above the sun" perspective.

---

32. For details, see Newsom, *Daniel*, 286–309; Longman, *Daniel*, 218–43.
33. Hazony, *The Philosophy of Hebrew Scripture*, 200.

He wanted to discern reality from the Lord's point of view and in terms of covenant. Having this outlook and knowing God's diagnosis, Daniel implemented the God-given prescription: penitential prayer (vv. 4b–19).

His petition shows that he knew the theological foundation of intercession. He grasped the epistemic role of repentance ("turning"), as we saw in chapter 11. Deuteronomy, for instance, foretold exile for covenantal disobedience (4:27). However, Daniel knew that restoration was possible, if "from there . . . you search after him with all your heart and with all your soul" (v. 29, echoing the language of the *Shema*; see also Deut 30:1–10; Lev 26:40–42). For this reason, also, Solomon modeled how to intercede for the people while in captivity:

> If they sin against you—for there is no one who does not sin—and you are angry with them and give them to an enemy, so that they are carried away captive to the land of the enemy, far off or near, yet if they turn their heart in the land to which they have been carried captive, and repent and plead with you in the land of their captors, saying, "We have sinned and have acted perversely and wickedly," if they repent with all their heart and with all their soul in the land of their enemies, who carried them captive, and pray to you toward their land, which you gave to their fathers, the city that you have chosen, and the house that I have built for your name, then hear in heaven your dwelling place their prayer and their plea, and maintain their cause. (1 Kgs 8:46–49)

Thus, Daniel formulated his prayer upon covenant theology and the example of Solomon, as well as the teaching of Jeremiah (29:10–14). This is why he prayed with the "windows in his upper chamber open toward Jerusalem" (Dan 6:10). Post-exilic leaders, such as Ezra (9:6–15) and Nehemiah (1:5–11; 9:6–37), also expressed penitential prayers based on this precedent.

Daniel sought understanding in the written revelation of Israel. He mentioned, for example, "the books" (*separim*) and the "word of the Lord to Jeremiah" (9:2). He also referenced the "curse and the oath" that are "written in the law of Moses" (vv. 11, 13). The term "books" may refer to the letters of Jeremiah or multiple scrolls of his book. On the other hand, there is ample evidence of Pentateuchal allusions in Daniel's prayer and intertextual reasoning.[34] For instance, terms such as "sinned," "acted wickedly," "turned aside," "rebelled," "not listened to," "curse," "poured out,"

---

34. See Stead, "Intertextuality and Innerbiblical Interpretation," 355–64.

and "desolation" reflect covenantal theology expressed in Leviticus and Deuteronomy, as well as 1 Kings, 2 Chronicles, and the Psalms.[35] Daniel used Deuteronomic vocabulary, such as "commandments," "rules," and "law" (vv. 4, 5, 11), including the covenantal name Yahweh (vv. 8, 10, 14). In addition, his reference to the Exodus (v. 15) compared Israel's deliverance from Egyptian slavery with the Judeans' liberation from Babylonian servitude.

Furthermore, Daniel very likely knew various references in the Deuteronomic history and prophets that foreshadowed the Babylonian exile. Jeremiah 25:9–14 called Nebuchadnezzar "my servant" raised up against Israel and prophesied seventy years of servitude. Isaiah 39:6 foretold the spoliation of the temple and forced servitude of aristocratic men as eunuchs (see also 2 Kgs 20:16–19; Jer 27:20–22). Similarly, Daniel likely read the forty-nine references to the Chaldeans in Isaiah and Jeremiah. He was probably aware of the idol polemic in those two books ("gods" are mentioned forty-two times) and the denunciations of Bel (Marduk).[36] He likely knew about Babylon's inevitable destruction as well (Jer 27:6–7; 29:10).

The reason why he sought the Lord was twofold. Daniel identified himself with the people's sin. The multiple self-imprecatory references in his prayer associated Daniel with the nation's corporate failures—"we," "us," and "our." He experienced the pathos of Israel's "open shame" (Dan 9:8; see also v. 16) and Jerusalem's "desolations" (v. 18). Moreover, the captives had not met the critical condition for restoration: "As it is written in the Law of Moses, all this calamity has come upon us; yet we have not entreated the favor of the Lord our God [Yahweh Elohim], turning from our iniquities and gaining insight by your truth" (v. 13).

How he prayed, therefore, reveals a mind attuned to the Lord. Daniel "turned his face" heavenward (9:3), indicating mental focus, dependence, and hopeful expectancy.[37] He applied his intellectual capacity to the study of Scripture (v. 2). He expressed his new understanding by seeking, pleading, praying, and confessing (v. 4). He aligned his mental state with external action, "fasting with sackcloth and ashes" (v. 3). He also reasoned with God, arguing that the exodus from Egypt paralleled the restoration of the exiles to the land (v. 15). He appealed to God's

---

35. See Newsom, *Daniel*, 293–98.

36. See Hill, *Constructing Exile*, 38–57.

37. Jeremiah described the opposite sentiment in rebellious Israel: "They have turned to me their back and not their face" (32:33).

character—his "righteousness" (v. 7) and "mercy and forgiveness" (v. 9). He formulated his plea in terms of Yahweh's covenantal faithfulness: "For we do not present our pleas before you because of our righteousness, but because of your great mercy" (v. 18). And he urged God to intervene for his own self-interest: "O, Lord, hear; O Lord, forgive. O Lord, pay attention and act. Do not delay, for your own sake, O my God, because your city and your people are called by your name" (v. 19).

Clearly, Daniel was biblically literate. He knew the facts of Israel's history. He knew the travails and blessings of the nation. He knew the heroes and villains. He understood his people's covenants and calling, as well as their corruption and failures. But he was also biblically fluent.[38] He reasoned from the Scriptures as "a way of constructing and understanding the world."[39] He interpreted his environment with revelational criteria. He discerned how to navigate the Chaldean labyrinth. Therefore, he was willing to risk everything—personal power and status, even his life—for the truth revealed in God's word. He could not be bought with all the pomp, power, and prestige of Babylon.

Daniel was well prepared intellectually for exile. (He was certainly *not* anti-intellectual.) He was not ignorant and naive, a *tabula rasa* ready to be written upon by the Babylonians. His interpretive criteria and norms were derived from Hebrew ontology, epistemology, and sacred history. His worldview was grounded in creation and covenant. He acknowledged God as the transcendent ruler, creative architect, just economist, and wise philosopher, as we learned in chapter 1. He experienced sin and folly intellectually, but also grace and redemption. He demonstrated the fear of God with a willing mind and humble outlook. Undoubtedly, Daniel knew how to love God with the mind.

Thus, there was indeed a great knowledge gap in the book of Daniel, but it belonged to Nebuchadnezzar and the Babylonians. Like Babel before them, Babylonia erroneously claimed sovereignty for themselves and their gods. What escaped the king and his people was a fundamental lesson expressed four times in relation to the king's second dream: "The Most High rules the kingdom of men and gives it to whom he will" (4:17; 25, 26, 32). When Nebuchadnezzar finally understood, the resolution of

---

38. Durgin defines literacy and fluency in "Are You Bible-Literate?"
39. Strawn, *The Old Testament Is Dying*, 9.

the plot was achieved, for at that point "all of the characters share the same understanding of reality," as Newsom noted.[40]

DANIEL'S CRITIQUE OF BABYLONIAN KNOWLEDGE

The book of Daniel expresses two powerful epistemological critiques of Babylonian knowledge. The first asks who is really transcendent—Marduk or Yahweh Elohim—or which divine being possesses correct understanding. This is similar to the challenge that Pharaoh posed to Moses: "Who is the Lord, that I should obey his voice and let Israel go?" (Exod 5:2). It is also akin to the challenge of the Assyrian commander representing the god Asshur: "Has any of the gods of the nations delivered his land out of the hand of the king of Assyria?" (Isa 36:18). From this perspective, the entire book of Daniel presents a series of contests to determine real transcendence, sovereignty, and knowledge.[41]

In chapter 1, the Lord showed his superiority over Marduk through Daniel's improbable diet and endowed the four Hebrews with superior understanding. In chapter 3, the Lord overcame Nebuchadnezzar regarding the power of life and death in the fiery furnace. In chapter 4, Daniel interpreted the king's upsetting dream, representing Yahweh. He declared that Nebuchadnezzar would suffer delirium until he discerned that "heaven rules" (v. 26). Furthermore, he told the king that he should "break off [his] sins by practicing righteousness, and [his] iniquities by showing mercy to the oppressed" (v. 27). In chapter 5, the Lord demonstrated that he controlled the life of Belshazzar individually and Babylon corporately. With an Old Testament elenctic critique, Daniel denounced the "gods of silver and gold, of bronze, iron, wood, and stone, which do not see or hear or know" (5:23a). In chapter 6, the Lord overcame the king's absolutism and the threat of death in the lion's den. Chapters 7–12 showed that God alone knows, reveals, and controls all knowledge and implements his plan throughout human history.

In chapter 2, Daniel's polemic undermined the content and the source of Chaldean wisdom. In Babylon, the scribal profession—court scholars and divination specialists—was the revered custodians of revelatory secrets. They believed that their scribal arts and understanding

---

40. Newsom, *Daniel*, 41.

41. This battle resembles the confrontation between Elijah and the prophets of Baal in 1 Kgs 18:20–40.

descended from the god of wisdom, Ea. According to Benjamin R. Foster, they thought that "Mesopotamian civilization was the achievement of literate men and that the continuity of civilization depended on their cultivation of letters." Foster adds that "civilization began with a book, and ... Nabu, the patron of Babylonian scribal art, gained such an exalted place in the scholarly view of the pantheon."[42] It is no doubt significant—and ironic in terms of chapter 2—that Nebuchadnezzar means "O Nabu, guard my firstborn."

Lenzi shows that the concept of secrecy and the term "secret" loomed large in the documentary corpus of "traditional Mesopotamian scholarly crafts" (exorcism, medicine, divination, ritual lamentation, astrology). He explains, "Scribal scholars indicated this status by explicitly using the words 'secret' or 'secret of the gods' (with variants) in their descriptions of the textual corpora and by attempting to restrict access to the learned material by means of written statements on the tablets that bore the texts."[43] They often included warning labels, such as "Secret of the great gods. The expert [literally, 'one who knows'] may show an(other) expert. A non-expert may not see [i.e., read] it. A restriction of the great gods."[44] Lenzi concludes, "By their own witness, the Mesopotamian scholars were *the* experts in secret matters pertaining to the proper interaction of humans and deities, and they were the custodians of written texts that claimed to be the 'secret of the gods.'"[45] Undoubtedly, then, scholarly pride was closely associated with esoteric prestige and political power.

However, Nebuchadnezzar clashed with his wise men concerning how to interpret his unsettling dream. Dreams were first disclosed and then subjected to hermeneutical analysis by well-trained experts. The king, however, suspected their political motivation and feared manipulation of the data. Thus, he demanded that they first somehow discern his dream and only then interpret it so as to verify its transcendent origin and their reliability as spiritual guides (2:8–9).

Dreams were sometimes omens, veiled messages from the gods. An evil dream warned of calamity, but that fate was avoidable if the suitable ritual was enacted. The phrase "till the times change" indicated the king's concern, for the expression implied the demise of rulers and dominions.

---

42. Foster, "Wisdom and the Gods in Ancient Mesopotamia," 348.

43. Lenzi, "Secrecy, Textual Legitimation, and Intercultural Polemics," 337.

44. Lenzi, "Secrecy, Textual Legitimation, and Intercultural Polemics," 339.

45. Lenzi, "Secrecy, Textual Legitimation, and Intercultural Polemics," 339 (emphasis in original).

Daniel verified this significance and remarked in his prayer, "Blessed be the name of God forever and ever . . . . He changes times and seasons; he removes kings and sets up kings" (2:20b–21a). Nebuchadnezzar suspected that the sages would minimize the dream's import, so that he would not respond properly with the correct remedy.[46] They would thereby facilitate the end of his reign and hasten his death.

Verses 10–11 (NKJV) highlight the sages' intellectual and existential dilemma:

(10) The Chaldeans answered the king and said, "There is not a man on earth who can tell the king's matter; therefore no king, lord, or ruler has ever asked such things of any magician, astrologer, or Chaldean.

(11) It is a difficult thing that the king requests, and there is no other who can tell it to the king except the gods, whose dwelling is not with flesh."

The words "matter," "things," and "thing" are translated from *millah*, a term found only in Daniel. The word refers to human communication, an issue or problem, or divine revelation. Five times the Chaldeans used it to refer to the king's unreasonable demand that they disclose both the dream and its interpretation (2:10 twice, 11, 15, 17). Daniel used it once to describe their untenable dilemma (v. 13). A rough synonym for this term in chapter 2 is "mystery" (*raz*, "secret").[47] Six times it appears with "reveal" and God as the agent (2:19, 28, 29, 30, 47 twice). The "matter" that troubled the king and challenged the scribes was a divine "secret" ("mystery" in the ESV), normally the competency of scribal interpretation alone.

In view of the king's requirement and threat, the wise men explicitly acknowledged their intellectual limitation and implicitly acknowledged the weakness of Chaldean mantic wisdom.[48] The pantheon had not spoken about this interpretive impasse to the assembled experts. In fact, on Old Testament assumptions they could not. And to the great astonishment

---

46. See Newsom, *Daniel*, 69–70; Lenzi, "Secrecy, Textual Legitimation, and Intercultural Polemics," 330–48.

47. *Raz* appears nine times and only in Daniel: 2:18, 19, 27, 28, 29, 30, 47 twice; 4:9.

48. The upstart Daniel's promotion (2:48b), coupled with the scribes' very public rebuke, was the likely antecedent of later antagonism against the "Jews" (3:8) and Daniel (6:4).

of the king's sages, the secret actually came from Yahweh Elohim and could be interpreted by his spokesman only.

In verse 27, Daniel affirmed the wise men's negative analysis and said, "No wise men, enchanters, magicians, or astrologers can show to the king the mystery that the king has asked." However, he affirmed that "there is a God in heaven who reveals mysteries ("secrets," *raz*, v. 28). Daniel also disclosed his epistemological method. In contrast to the scribes and their ancient divinatory arts, he commented, "But as for me, this mystery has been revealed to me, not because of any wisdom that I have more than all the living" (v. 30). Moreover, when the king's threat was made known, Daniel requested from Nebuchadnezzar time to "seek mercy from the God of heaven concerning this mystery" (v. 18). After he understood the dream (v. 19), he honored the source of all power and knowledge:

(20) "Blessed be the name of God forever and ever, to whom belong wisdom and might.

(21) He changes times and seasons; he removes kings and sets up kings; he gives wisdom to the wise and knowledge to those who have understanding;

(22) he reveals deep and hidden things; he knows what is in the darkness, and the light dwells with him.

(23) To you, O God of my fathers, I give thanks and praise, for you have given me wisdom and might, and have now made known to me what we asked of you, for you have made known to us the king's matter."

Michael Segal summarizes the epistemic significance of chapter 2 and anticipates Daniel's second critique in chapter 5:

> This contrast [between Daniel and wise men in chapters 2 and 5] is intended to demonstrate the superiority of divinely inspired knowledge over and above the extensive educational training of Mesopotamian scribes and scholars in Antiquity . . . . These two court tales therefore make a fundamental epistemological claim regarding the ultimate source of knowledge, championing the divine bestowal of wisdom upon those who are faithful, and simultaneously undermining the validity and stature of

the Mesopotamian mantic training and techniques, and their practitioners.[49]

Daniel's second assessment of Babylonian epistemology asks this question: what are the necessary preconditions for all thinking and religion? Chapter 5:18–23 includes a critique of Belshazzar's mental outlook:

(18) O king, the Most High God gave Nebuchadnezzar your father kingship and greatness and glory and majesty.

(19) And because of the greatness that he gave him, all peoples, nations, and languages trembled and feared before him....

(20) But when his heart was lifted up and his spirit was hardened so that he dealt proudly, he was brought down from his kingly throne, and his glory was taken from him.

(21) He was driven from among the children of mankind, and his mind was made like that of a beast ... until he knew that the Most High God rules the kingdom of mankind and sets over it whom he will.

(22) And you his son, Belshazzar, have not humbled your heart, though you knew all this,

(23) but you have lifted up yourself against the Lord of heaven. And the vessels of his house have been brought in before you, and you and your lords, your wives, and your concubines have drunk wine from them. And you have praised the gods of silver and gold, of bronze, iron, wood, and stone, which do not see or hear or know, but the God in whose hand is your breath, and whose are all your ways, you have not honored.

In chapter 5, God is designated in four ways: "God" (four times), "Lord of heaven" (once), "Most High God" (twice), and "he" (once).[50] God has total power and sovereignty over rulers and peoples. He is the source of "kingship, greatness, glory, and majesty" (v. 18). He teaches rulers to assess themselves in light of reality. Nebuchadnezzar, for instance, "was brought down from his kingly throne, and his glory was taken

---

49. Segal, "Rereading the Writing on the Wall," 174.

50. Newsom (*Daniel*, 112) points out that the expression "Most High God" was commonly used during the Hellenistic period and that "it is characteristically used by pagans (e.g., Melchizedek in Gen 14:19; Balaam in Num 24:16; the king of Assyria in Isa 14:14; Cyrus in 1 Esd 2:3; the pagan slave girl in Acts 16:17."

from him. He was driven from among the children of mankind, and his mind was made like that of a beast . . . until he knew that the Most High God rules the kingdom of mankind and sets over it whom he will" (vv. 20b–21). Furthermore, God enables human life, providing "breath," and enabling human agency, though he governs "all your ways" (v. 23). He communicates ("writing was inscribed," v. 24), evaluates ("weighed in the balance and found wanting"), and determines the future ("numbered your days," v. 26, and "your kingdom is divided and given to the Medes and Persians," v. 28).

In contrast with his father, however, Belshazzar thought too highly of himself and his self-assessment did not accord with reality. Verse 23 uses the idiom "lift up" (*rum*, promote or exalt) about Belshazzar self-referentially.[51] He did not "humble" his heart, even though he knew about his father's painful lesson under Yahweh's tutelage (v. 22). Rather, he exalted himself "against the Lord of heaven" and did "not honor" God as he ought to (v. 23). Later in the book, the angel informed Daniel of a future king who would imitate Belshazzar's blasphemous folly: "The king shall do as he wills. He shall exalt (*rum*) himself and magnify himself above every god, and shall speak astonishing things against the God of gods" (11:36a). In chapter 5, though, the concrete expression of his antipathy to God was the misuse of the temple vessels for carnal purposes in devotion to false gods. Belshazzar suppressed the truth he knew about the ruler of all things (5:22) and exchanged that truth for falsehood—the worship of idols that enabled his prestige and power (v. 23).

In 5:23, Daniel outlined in summary fashion what might be called a transcendental critique. He described the necessary preconditions for human existence that Belshazzar presupposed but refused to acknowledge.[52] He "used" God but failed to honor God as the divine king, builder,

---

51. A positive use of *rum* ("lift up") is found in the king's confession in chapter 4: "For his dominion is an everlasting dominion, and his kingdom endures from generation to generation; all the inhabitants of the earth are accounted as nothing, and he does according to his will among the host of heaven and among the inhabitants of the earth; and none can stay his hand or say to him, 'What have you done?' . . . Now I, Nebuchadnezzar, praise and extol (*rum*) and honor the King of heaven, for all his works are right and his ways are just; and those who walk in pride he is able to humble" (4:34b–35, 37). Negative examples of the idiom are found in Deut 8:14; 17:20; Isa 2:11, 17; 10:12; 37:23; Jer 48:29; and Hos 13:6.

52. Ramm argued similarly. In 1958, he described argumentation based on "the futility of the opposite" in "The Apologetics of the Old Testament," 15–20.

benefactor, and thinker.⁵³ The king operated as though he was self-sustaining, self-directing, and self-evaluating.

Verse 23b declares, "The God in whose hand is your breath, and whose are all your ways, you have not honored." The phrase "in whose hand" indicates control, source and benefaction—all derived from Yahweh Elohim. "Breath" (from *neshamah*) is shorthand for life itself. At creation, God "breathed into [Adam's] nostrils the breath (*neshamah*) of life" (Gen 2:7; see also Job 27:3). God created the infrastructure of the natural world. He made oxygen (*neshamah*) to breathe and lungs to inhale with.

Furthermore, God's breath embodied human beings so that they could exercise stewardship. As Job said, "But it is the spirit in man, the breath (*neshamah*) of the Almighty, that makes him understand" (32:8). "Ways" (from *orach*) means physical movement, but also human agency. In this way, Daniel reminded Belshazzar that God created the preconditions for Belshazzar's life and reign—even his rebellion and disrespect. His father came to understand this, but Belshazzar refused to honor God as God (Rom 1:21).⁵⁴ He relied upon God's goodness in order to sin. He misused God-given resources to blaspheme and consume wastefully. He presupposed and depended upon the real God but denied that truth in favor of idols.

"Honor" (*hadar*) and its related terms are often translated in the Old Testament with words such as "splendid," "glorious," "majesty," "power," "honor," "dignity," and "glory." In this context, Belshazzar should have blessed God by humbling himself intellectually (v. 22) and acknowledging God's supremacy (v. 21). The tribute that God expected was probably akin to the praise that Nebuchadnezzar expressed after he had been humbled in chapter 4:

(2) It has seemed good to me to show the signs and wonders that the Most High God has done for me.

(3) How great are his signs, how mighty his wonders! His kingdom is an everlasting kingdom, and his dominion endures from generation to generation....

---

53. Johnson (*The First Step in Missions Training*, 38–40) shows that Paul argues in a similar fashion in Romans 2:4, "Or do you presume on the riches of his kindness and forbearance and patience, not knowing that God's kindness is meant to lead you to repentance?"

54. See my dissertation, "The Supremacy of God in Apologetics," 13–61.

(34) At the end of the days I, Nebuchadnezzar, lifted my eyes to heaven, and my reason returned to me, and I blessed the Most High, and praised and honored (*hadar*) him who lives forever, for his dominion is an everlasting dominion, and his kingdom endures from generation to generation;

(35) all the inhabitants of the earth are accounted as nothing, and he does according to his will among the host of heaven and among the inhabitants of the earth; and none can stay his hand or say to him, "What have you done?" . . .

(37) Now I, Nebuchadnezzar, praise and extol and honor (*hadar*) the King of heaven, for all his works are right and his ways are just; and those who walk in pride he is able to humble.

CONCLUSION

The main personalities in this chapter—Nebuchadnezzar, Belshazzar, and Daniel—represent three epistemological outlooks.[55] Babylon's king demonstrated Adam's mandate gone awry. Nebuchadnezzar was Babel personified and in all its would-be grandeur—the epitome of collective noetic sinfulness. His empire existed for the benefit of the elite, legitimized by myth, and was parasitic on its populace and neighbors. Like all the imperialisms of the ancient Near East, it suffered from a center-of-the-universe fixation that imposed "civilization" upon others.[56] And like some modern "captains" of power—in knowledge, economics, technology, religion, popular culture, and politics—Nebuchadnezzar became self-obsessive, abusive, and myopic. He had to learn—quite unwillingly—that God is transcendent and all-powerful. The God of the Bible possesses all wisdom and reveals secrets to mankind.

The example of Nebuchadnezzar and Babylon teaches, as well, that believers today should be wary of skewed incarnations of the cultural mandate. Whenever a neo-Babelite battle cry is heard: "Let us build ourselves a city . . . that we can make a name for ourselves" or whenever would-be Pharaohs and Nebuchadnezzars proudly exclaim "Who is the Lord?" the church should be on guard. Believers today need just as

---

55. Jeffrey Foster contributed insights to this paragraph.

56. For further reflection on these issues, see my article, "Economics and the 'Present Evil Age,'" 354–63.

much—if not more—discernment as the believers in the days of Jeremiah and Daniel.[57]

Belshazzar was a paradigmatic fool. Flushed with power and self-absorption, he was a hedonist and cynic. He was not a true disbeliever in Yahweh Elohim, as became more than evident when God actually spoke to him. He enjoyed God's goodness but mocked his supremacy. In Pauline terms, Belshazzar presumed on "the riches of his kindness and forbearance," but did not acknowledge that "God's kindness is meant to lead [him] to repentance" (Rom 2:4). In this sense, Belshazzar is everyman. Apart from the grace of God, human beings are foolish. We undeservingly presuppose God's benefits. We express folly by depending on our own power and wealth, conditioned by our intellectual hubris and moral perversity.

Daniel was a paragon of redemptive epistemology. He modeled intellectual piety and wisdom in a perverse and hostile environment. He learned to fear the Lord and recognized the epistemic significance of repentance. He was intellectually curious and brought his brain to God. He remembered his Hebrew upbringing and did not forget the Creator–creature distinction. He was biblically literate and reasoned intertextually. He knew how to extrapolate from Scripture to applications in his present milieu. He navigated the turbulent waters of ancient Babylonian theocracy. Daniel discerned where to set boundaries and to avoid religious syncretism. He behaved wisely in the short term because he embraced a long-term vision. He was a strategic thinker and became a positive influence for the common good and the glory of God. And, as we saw, Daniel could not be co-opted by the Babylonian juggernaut. Instead, he functioned as God's prophet, sage, and ambassador in his flawed and twisted context. He practiced a holistic spirituality and loved God with his mind.

Furthermore, Daniel reasoned in a transcendental manner. He reckoned with the epistemic implications of the biblical view of God. As Cornelius Van Til wrote, "There can be no more fundamental question in epistemology than the question whether or not facts can be known without reference to God.... [A Christian's] fundamental and determining fact is the fact of God's existence. That is his final conclusion. But that must also be his starting point."[58] This kind of thinking accords well with Deuteronomy 8:3, "Man lives by every word that comes from the mouth

---

57. This paragraph is adapted from my article "Economics and the Present Evil Age," 7.

58. Van Til, *A Survey of Christian Epistemology*, 4–5.

of the Lord," and Psalm 36:9, "For with you is the fountain of life; in your light do we see light."

Because God is supreme, Daniel was not at the epistemological mercy of the Babylonian worldview. When they were tolerant, he retained his distinctive beliefs without duress. But when their imperialism extended to ontology, he was pressured to deny his faith or suffer the consequences, which he did. In the eyes of his captors, Daniel's exclusivist religion was at best irrelevant and untenable, at worst obscurant and toxic. From their perspective, the conquest of Jerusalem demonstrated Marduk's supremacy over Yahweh.

As it was for Daniel, the ontology and epistemology of the Bible are essential for us as well. Otherwise, we must salvage some kind of intellectual justification in this pluralistic milieu under a benign or hostile relativism. For most secularists and quasi-polytheists today, Christianity is merely one variety of generic religion. Devotees approach the sacred realm as a sort of experiential or intellectual smorgasbord. Beliefs are mixed and matched according to fad, fashion, and psychic need. Tolerance and relativism are foundational epistemic assumptions. Cynics charge that Christianity is merely another, particularly noxious "weed" in the "garden of god."[59] In this unfriendly context, most Christians lack a rationale for divine lordship in knowledge. Often, they are not "prepared to make a defense" (1 Pet 3:15–16) against or to meaningfully critique prevailing epistemological pluralism or skepticism.

Would Daniel have survived and prospered as a Hebrew in his setting had he embraced ontological pluralism? Probably not. Would he have thrived as God's prophet and wise man if he had affirmed epistemological relativism? Surely not. What Daniel did—and what we must do also—is to love God with our mind and learn to reason from the reality of God's existence as Creator and Lord. We must think presuppositionally in accordance with the biblical worldview (creation, fall, redemption, and restoration).

A focus of the Old Testament (and certainly the book of Daniel) concerns the eschatological diffusion of the knowledge of God among all peoples and in all places. Earlier in this chapter, I cited Carol A. Newsom's comment regarding the book of Daniel: "The resolution of the plot will be effected when access to crucial knowledge is equalized and the reader and all of the characters share the same understanding of reality." In fact,

---

59. This paragraph was adapted from my article "Apologia," 19–20.

this dynamic applies to the entire Old Testament (and the New Testament as well). In other words, when mankind finally acknowledges that "from him and through him and to him are all things" (Rom 11:36; see also Acts 17:28a), God's pedagogical agenda will be fulfilled.

The last four chapters of this book have profiled three epistemic models or exemplars—real-world thinkers who discerned the way out of the epistemological labyrinth. On one hand, Job demonstrated heinous aspects of noetic corruption. But on the other hand, his deepest motives arose from godly fear under extreme duress. He suffered, prayed, spoke, and thought with reference to God. He modeled redemptive epistemology. He demonstrated how to love God with the mind, despite sin and enigma. Jeremiah proclaimed truth within a chaotic and hostile intellectual environment. He suffered for declaring God's will about the exile, because Israel refused to accept reality. Similarly, Daniel struggled with religious syncretism in the context of exile and judgment. He modeled mental piety and wisdom as the way to honor God and serve nonbelievers in a hostile environment.

Job, Jeremiah, and Daniel struggled with paradox and folly. Each of them evidenced biblical knowledge and reasoning in their agonizing contexts. They were avid learners and sought discernment from God with all their strength. They benefited from an educational system that instilled the fear of the Lord as the prerequisite of knowledge. Thus, they were not totally bewildered, for they possessed "understanding of the times, to know what Israel ought to do" (1 Chron 12:32). Indeed, Job, Jeremiah, and Daniel perceived reality as covenantal servants and responded appropriately in ways that God affirmed in Deuteronomy 5:29: "Oh that they had such a heart [mind] as this always, to fear me and to keep all my commandments."

We should learn from Job, Jeremiah, and Daniel as we confront modern forms of enigma, sin, and suffering. We must love God with our minds in our time as God's apprentice rulers, architects, economists, and philosophers in this "present evil age" (Gal 4:1).

Postscript: *Community Gardens*

WE BEGAN THIS BOOK with a thought experiment—a negative and foreboding tale. As we close, let us consider another imaginary story—a positive and foretelling vision.

Imagine that the biblical worldview is like fertile soil. Plant a person or idea in this rich loam and a beautiful and fruitful yield results. Picture, further, how many more plants would grow in an entire garden.

Imagine that a garden is a learning community (formal and informal) created to grow Christian minds (lay and academic) for the glory of God and the blessing of mankind. Envision, also, the impact of countless community gardens over the course of time. The long-term impact of learning God's word profoundly and reasoning from its assumptions would be extensive in the church and the world. Consider these possibilities.

REPENTANCE

Aspiring thinkers bring their brains to God and turn back to the Bible as an act of worship. They evaluate whom they listen to and where they learn. They turn away from negative speakers and false messages. They discern our intellectual context (Eph 2:1–3). They distinguish between the trivial and the momentous. They reinvest their intellectual capacity in the true, good, and beautiful. They develop intellectual virtues—such as curiosity, discipline, creativity, and humility—in accord with the Scriptures.

LEARNING

Apprentice thinkers acknowledge with their whole mind, soul, and strength this essential truth: "Man does not live by bread alone, but man lives by every word that comes from the mouth of the Lord" (Deut 8:3). They build an educational infrastructure that fosters the fear of God as the foundation of knowledge. They learn the history, people, themes, and vision of the Bible. They study the cultures of the ancient Near East and Palestine. They practice intertextual reasoning and learn to think like the biblical authors. They listen to the global Christian community and learn from the theological tradition of the church.

SERVICE

Those who acquire wisdom serve their regional cultures, teach in their local churches, and mentor future leaders. Some are like Joseph and Daniel, serving with distinction in the world for the glory of God. Others function as ambassadors in the public square, like Dorothy Sayers and C. S. Lewis. Still others serve evangelistically, such as Francis Schaeffer and Timothy Keller. All seek existential and spiritual welfare within their particular setting.

STEWARDSHIP

Maturing thinkers honor God, recognizing that they are apprentice leaders, builders, benefactors, and thinkers. They evaluate the world with biblical assumptions. They affirm what is positive and promote the common good. They also critique and challenge what is false and evil. They demonstrate the gospel in ways that are intellectually plausible and existentially credible, "always being prepared to make a defense to anyone who asks" (1 Pet 3:15). Maturing thinkers support emerging scholars and entrepreneurs invest generously in educational endeavors of all kinds.

Imagine the positive impact of community gardens—nurturing Christian minds for the long term to the glory of God and the blessing of mankind.

Bibliography

Ackerman, Susan. "The Personal Is Political: Covenantal and Affectionate Love (*'āhēb*, *'ahăbâ*) in the Hebrew Bible." *Vetus Testamentum* 52.4 (2002) 437–58.
Ahn, John J. "Exile." In *Dictionary of the Old Testament: Prophets*, edited by Mark J. Boda and J. Gordon McConville, 196–204. Downers Grove: IVP Academic, 2012.
———. "Psalm 137: Complex Communal Laments." *Journal of Biblical Literature* 127.2 (2008) 267–89.
Aimers, Geoff John. "Theodicy in an Ironical Sense: The Joban Wager and the Portrait of Folly." *Journal for the Study of the Old Testament* 43 (2019) 359–70.
Aitkin, K. T. "Hearing and Seeing: Metamorphoses of a Motif in Isaiah 1–39." In *Among the Prophets: Language, Image and Structure in the Prophetic Writings*, edited by Phillip R. Davies et al., 13–23. Journal for the Society of the Old Testament Supplement 144. Sheffield: Sheffield Academic, 1993.
Albertz, Rainer. *Israel in Exile: The History and Literature of the Sixth Century BCE*. Society of Biblical Literature Studies in Biblical Literature 3. Atlanta: Society of Biblical Literature, 2003.
———. "More or Less Than a Myth: Reality and Significance of Exile for the Political, Social, and Religious History of Judah." In *By the Irrigation Canals of Babylon: Approaches to the Study of the Exile*, Library of Hebrew Bible/Old Testament Studies 526, edited by John J. Ahn and Jill Middlemas, 20–33. New York: Bloomsbury T. & T. Clark, 2012.
Alexander, Desmond T. *From Eden to the New Jerusalem: An Introduction to Biblical Theology*. Grand Rapids: Kregel Academic, 2008.
Alster, Baruch. "Narrative Surprise in Biblical Parallels." *Biblical Interpretation* 14.5 (2006) 456–85.
Anselm. *Complete Philosophical and Theological Treatises of Anselm of Canterbury*. Translated by Jasper Hopkins and Herbert Richardson. Minneapolis: Arthur J. Banning, 2000.
Antic, Radiša. "Cain, Abel, Seth, and the Meaning of Human Life as Portrayed in the Books of Genesis and Ecclesiastes." *Andrews University Seminary Studies* 44.2 (2006) 203–11.
Arnold, Bill T. "The Love-Fear Antinomy in Deuteronomy 1–11." *Vetus Testamentum* 61 (2011) 551–69.
Aster, Shawn Zelig. "Transmission of Neo-Assyrian Claims of Empire to Judah in the Late Eighth Century BCE." *Hebrew Union College Annual* 78 (2007) 1–44.

Augustine. *City of God*. Translated by Gerald G. Walsh et al., New York: Doubleday, 1958.

———. *Confessions*. Translated by Rex Warner. New York: Signet Classic, 2001.

Bahnsen, Greg L. *Van Til's Apologetic: Readings and Analysis*. Phillipsburg, NJ: Presbyterian and Reformed, 1998.

Baines, John. "Ancient Egyptian Kingship: Official Forms, Rhetoric, Context." In *King, Messiah in Israel and the Ancient Near East*, edited by John Day, 16–53. New York: Bloomsbury T. & T. Clark, 1998.

Barker, Paul A. *The Triumph of Grace in Deuteronomy: Faithless Israel, Faithful Yahweh in Deuteronomy*. Eugene: Wipf & Stock, 2006.

Bartholomew, Craig C., and Ryan O'Dowd. *Old Testament Wisdom Literature: A Theological Introduction*. Downers Grove: IVP Academic, 2018.

Bavinck, Herman. *The Doctrine of God*. Carlisle, PA: Banner of Truth, 1979.

Bavinck, J. H. *An Introduction to the Science of Mission*. Phillipsburg, NJ: Presbyterian and Reformed, 1960.

Beale, G. K. "An Exegetical and Theological Consideration of the Hardening of Pharaoh's Heart in Exodus 4–14 and Romans 9." *Trinity Journal* 5.2 (1984) 129–54.

———. *A New Testament Biblical Theology: The Unfolding of the Old Testament in the New*. Grand Rapids: Baker Academic, 2011.

———. *We Become What We Worship: A Biblical Theology of Idolatry*. Downers Grove: IVP Academic, 2008.

Becker, Ernest. *The Denial of Death*. New York: The Free Press, 1973.

———. *Escape from Evil*. New York: The Free Press, 1975.

Ben-Meir, Samuel. "Nabal, the Villain." *Jewish Bible Quarterly* 22 (1994) 249–51.

Bennett, Robert A. "Wisdom Motifs in Psalm 14 = 53: *nābāl* and (*'ēṣāh*." *Bulletin of the American Schools of Oriental Research* 220 (1975) 15–21.

Berlejung, Angelika. "New Life, New Skills, and New Friends in Exile: The Loss and Rise of Capitals of the Judeans in Babylonia." In *Alphabets, Texts, and Artifacts in the Ancient Near East: Studies Presented to Benjamin Sass*, edited by Israel Finkelstein et al., 1–46. Paris: Van Dieren, 2017.

Berlin, Adele. "Jeremiah 29:5–7: A Deuteronomic Allusion." *Hebrew Annual Review* 8 (1984) 3–11.

Berlyn, Patricia. "The Pharaohs Who Knew Moses." *Jewish Bible Quarterly* 39.1 (2011) 3–14.

Berman, Joshua. "What Does the Ox Know in Isa 1:3a?" *Vetus Testamentum* 64 (2014) 382–88.

Biddle, Mark E. *Missing the Mark: Sin and Its Consequences in Biblical Theology*. Nashville: Abingdon, 2005.

Blackburn, W. Ross. *The God Who Makes Himself Known: The Missionary Heart of the Book of Exodus*. Downers Grove: InterVarsity, 2012.

Blenkinsopp, Joseph. "The Cosmological and Protological Language of Deutero-Isaiah." *Catholic Biblical Quarterly* 73 (2011) 93–110.

———. "The Social Context of the 'Outsider Woman' in Proverbs 1–9." *Biblica* 72 (1991) 457–73.

Block, Daniel I. "The Burden of Leadership: The Mosaic Paradigm of Kingship (Deut. 17:14–20)." *Bibliotheca Sacra* 162 (2005) 259–78.

———. *Deuteronomy*. Grand Rapids: Zondervan, 2012.

———. *The Gospel According to Moses. Theological and Ethical Reflections on the Book of Deuteronomy.* Eugene: Cascade, 2012.

———. "The Grace of Torah: The Mosaic Prescription for Life (Deut. 4:1–8; 6:20–25)." *Bibliotheca Sacra* 162 (2005) 3–22.

———. "'How Many Is God': An Investigation into the Meaning of Deuteronomy 6:4–5." *Journal of the Evangelical Theological Society* 47.2 (2004) 193–212.

———. "'A Place for My Name': Horeb and Zion in the Mosaic Vision for Hebrew Worship." *Journal of the Evangelical Theological Society* 58.2 (2015) 221–47.

———. "The Privilege of Calling: The Mosaic Paradigm for Missions (Deut. 26:18–19). *Bibliotheca Sacra* 162 (2005) 387–405.

———. "Recovering the Voice of Moses: The Genesis of Deuteronomy." *Journal of the Evangelical Theological Society* 44.3 (2001) 385–408.

———. *The Triumph of Grace Literary and Theological Studies in Deuteronomy and Deuteronomic Themes.* Eugene: Cascade, 2017.

———. "'What Do These Stones Mean?' The Riddle of Deuteronomy 27." *Journal of the Evangelical Theological Society* 56 (2013) 17–41.

Boda, Mark J. "Walking in the Light of Yahweh: Zion and the Empires in the Book of Isaiah." In *Empire in the New Testament*, edited by Stanley E. Porter and Cynthia Long Westfall, 54–89. Eugene: Pickwick, 2011.

Borowski, Oded. "Hezekiah's Reforms and the Revolt Against Assyria." *Biblical Archaeologist* 58 (1995) 148–55.

Boyle, Marjorie O'Rourke. "The Law of the Heart: The Death of a Fool." *Journal of Biblical Literature* 120.3 (2001) 401–27.

Bricker, Daniel P. "Innocent Suffering in Egypt." *Trinity Bulletin* 52.1 (2001) 83–100.

———. "The Doctrine of the 'Two Ways' in Proverbs." *Journal of the Evangelical Theological Society* (1995) 501–17.

Brooks, David L. "The Complementary Relationship between Proverbs and Moses' Law." *Criswell Theological Review* 5 (2007) 3–32.

Bruckner, James K. "Boundary and Freedom: Blessings in the Garden of Eden." *Covenant Quarterly* 57.1 (1999) 15–35.

Brueggemann, Walter. "From Dust to Kingship." *Zeitschrift für die alttestamentliche Wissenschaft* 84.1 (1972) 1–18.

———. *Genesis.* Atlanta: John Knox, 1982.

———. *Peace.* St. Louis: Chalice, 2001.

Bullock, C. Hassell. "Ethics." In *Dictionary of the Old Testament: Wisdom, Poetry & Writings,* edited by Tremper Longman III and Peter Enns, 193–200. Downers Grove: IVP Academic, 2008.

Bunyan, John. *Pilgrim's Progress in Today's English.* Chicago: Moody, 1971.

Burnett, Joel S. "Changing God: An Exposition of Jeremiah 2." *Review and Expositor* 101 (2004) 289–99.

Byron, John. "Living in the Shadow of Cain: Echoes of a Developing Tradition in James 5:1–6." *Novum Testamentum* 48 (2006) 261–74.

Callender, Dexter E. *Adam in Myth and History: Ancient Israelite Perspectives on the Primal Human.* Winona Lake, IN: Eisenbrauns, 2000.

Calvin, John. *Institutes of Christian Religion*, vol. 1, edited by John T. McNeill. Philadelphia: Westminster, 1960.

———. *John Calvin's Bible Commentaries on Ezekiel 1–12*. Translated by Thomas Meyers and John King. Altenmünster, Germany: Jazzybee Verlag Jürgen Beck, 2017.

Carasik, Michael. "Qohelet's Twists and Turns." *Journal for the Society of the Old Testament* 28.2 (2003) 192–209.

———. *Theologies of the Mind in Biblical Israel*. New York: Peter Lang, 2006.

Chan, Michael. "Rhetorical Reversal and Usurpation: Isaiah 10:5–34 and the Use of Neo-Assyrian Royal Idiom in the Construction of an Anti-Assyrian Theology." *Journal of Biblical Literature* 128 (2009) 717–33.

Chisholm, Robert B. "'For This Reason': Etiology and Its Implications for the Historicity of Adam." *Criswell Theological Review* 10.2 (2013) 27–51.

Clifford, Richard J. "Another Look at Qoheleth 7:23–29." *Biblica* 100.1 (2019) 50–59.

Clines, D. J. A. "The Tree of Knowledge and the Law of Yahweh (Psalm 19)." *Vetus Testamentum* 24 (1974) 8–14.

Collet, Don. "Van Til and Transcendental Argument Revisited." In *Speaking the Truth in Love: The Theology of John M. Frame*, edited by John H. Hughes, 460–88. Phillipsburg, NJ: Presbyterian and Reformed, 2009.

Collins, John. "What Happened to Adam and Eve? A Literary–Theological Approach to Genesis 3." *Presbyterion* 27.1 (2001) 12–44.

Condie, Keith. "Narrative Features of Numbers 13–14 and Their Significance for the Meaning of the Book of Numbers." *Reformed Theological Review* 60.3 (2001) 123–37.

Cook, Gregory D. "Of Gods and Kings: Asshur Imagery in Naham." *Bulletin for Biblical Research* 29 (2019) 19–31.

Cox, Dorian Coover. "The Hardening of Pharaoh's Heart in Its Literary and Cultural Contexts." *Bibliotheca Sacra* 163.651 (2006) 292–311.

Coxhead, Steven R. "Deuteronomy 30:11–14 as a Prophecy of the New Covenant in Christ." *Westminster Theological Journal* 68 (2006) 305–20.

Coxon, Peter. "Nebuchadnezzar's Hermeneutical Dilemma." *Journal for the Study of the Old Testament* 66 (1995) 87–97.

Craig, Kenneth M. "Misspeaking in Eden: Fielding Questions in the Garden (Genesis 2:16–13)." *Perspectives in Religious Studies* 27.3 (2000) 235–47.

———. "Questions outside Eden (Genesis 4:1–16): Yahweh, Cain, and Their Rhetorical Interchange." *Journal for the Study of the Old Testament* 86 (1999) 107–28.

Craig, William Lane. "In Intellectual Neutral." In *Passionate Conviction: Contemporary Discourses on Christian Apologetics*, edited by Paul Copan et al., 2–16. Nashville: Broadman and Holman, 2007.

Craigie, Peter C. *The Book of Deuteronomy*. Grand Rapids: Eerdmans, 1976.

———. *Psalms 1–50*. Waco, TX: Word, 1983.

Crenshaw, James L. *Ecclesiastes*. Philadelphia: Westminster, 1987.

———. "Qohelet's Understanding of Intellectual Inquiry." In *Qohelet in the Context of Wisdom*, edited by A. Schoors, 205–24. Leuven, Belgium: Leuven University, 1998.

Christianson, Eric S. "Qoheleth and the/His Self among the Deconstructed." In *Qohelet in the Context of Wisdom*, edited by A. Schoors, 17–39. Leuven, Belgium: Leuven University, 1998.

Currid, John D. *Against the Gods: The Polemical Theology of the Old Testament*. Wheaton: Crossway, 2013.

Custance, Arthur C. "Who Taught Adam to Speak?" *Bulletin for Christian Scholarship Koers* 59.10 (1994) 303–18.
De Jong, Stephen. "God in the Book of Qohelet: A Reappraisal of Qohelet's Place in Old Testament Theology." *Vetus Testamentum* 47.2 (1997) 154–67.
Dekker, John. "Characterization in the Hebrew Bible: Nabal as a Test Case." *Bulletin for Biblical Research* 26 (2016) 311–24.
Dell, Katherine J. "What Was Job's Malady?" *Journal for the Study of the Old Testament* 141.1 (2016) 61–77.
Dembski, William A. "How to Debate an Atheist—If You Must." *Southwestern Journal of Theology* 54 (2011) 55–70.
Derouchie, Jason S. "The Blessing-Commission, the Promised Offspring, and the Toledot Structure of Genesis." *Journal of the Evangelical Theological Society* 56.2 (2013) 219–47.
Dickens, Charles. *A Tale of Two Cities*. Vancouver: Engage, 2019.
Dillard, Raymond B., and Tremper Longman III. *An Introduction to the Old Testament*. Grand Rapids: Zondervan, 1994.
Dor-Shav, Ethan. "Ecclesiastes, Fleeting and Timeless, Part 1." *Jewish Bible Quarterly* 36.4 (2008) 211–224.
———. "Ecclesiastes, Fleeting and Timeless, Part 2." *Jewish Bible Quarterly* 37.1 (2009) 17–23.
Dumbrell, William J. *Covenant and Creation: A Theology of the Old Testament Covenants*. Grand Rapids: Baker 1984.
———. "Genesis 2:1–17: A Foreshadowing of the New Creation." In *Biblical Theology: Retrospect and Prospect*, 53–65. Downers Grove: InterVarsity, 2002.
———. *The Search for Order: Biblical Eschatology in Focus*. Eugene: Wipf and Stock, 1994.
Durgin, Celina. "Are You Bible-Literate? How about Bible Fluent? These Terms Explained" (2021). https://hebraicthought.org/bible-literacy-fluency-explainer/.
Durham, John I. *Exodus*. Waco, TX: Word, 1987.
Dutcher-Walls, Patricia. "The Circumscription of the King: Deuteronomy 17:16–17 and Its Ancient Social Context." *Journal of Biblical Literature* 121.4 (2002) 601–16.
Eaton, Michael E. *Ecclesiastes: An Introduction and Commentary*. Downers Grove: InterVarsity, 1983.
Edwards, Jonathan. "Dissertation Concerning the End for Which God Created the World." In *The Works of Jonathan Edwards*, vol. 1, 94–121. Carlisle, PA: Banner of Truth, 1990.
Eliade, Mircea. *A History of Religious Ideas: From the Stone Age to the Eleusinian Mysteries*. Chicago: University of Chicago, 1978.
Ellul, Jacques. *Reason for Being: A Meditation on Ecclesiastes*. Grand Rapids: Eerdmans, 1990.
Enns, Peter. "Ecclesiastes 1." In *Dictionary of the Old Testament: Wisdom, Poetry and Writings*, edited by Tremper Longman III and Peter Enns, 121–32. Downers Grove: IVP Academic, 2008.
Eslinger, Lyle M. "The Enigmatic Plurals Like 'One of Us' (Genesis 1:26, 3:22, and 11:7) in Hyperchronic Perspective." *Vetus Testamentum* 56.2 (2006) 171–84.
Evans, Craig A. *To See and Not Perceive: Isaiah 6:9–10 in Early Jewish and Christian Interpretation*. Sheffield: Sheffield Academic, 1989.

Ferguson, Paul. "Nebuchadnezzar, Gilgamesh, and the 'Babylonian Job.'" *Journal of the Evangelical Theological Society* 37.3 (1994) 321–31.

Finegan, Jack. *Myth and Mystery: An Introduction to the Pagan Religions of the Biblical World*. Grand Rapids: Baker, 1989.

Foster, Benjamin R. "Wisdom and the Gods in Ancient Mesopotamia." *Orientalia* 43.3–4 (1974) 344–54.

Fox, Michael V. *Ecclesiastes*. Philadelphia: The Jewish Publication Society, 2004.

———. "God's Answer and Job's Response." *Biblica* 94.1 (2013) 1–23.

———. "The Inner Structure of Qohelet's Thought." In *Qohelet in the Context of Wisdom*, edited by A. Schoors, 225–38. Leuven, Belgium: Leuven University, 1998.

———. "Job the Pious." *Zeitschrift für die alttestamentliche Wissenschaft* 117.3 (2005) 351–66.

———. "Qohelet's Epistemology." *Hebrew Union College Annual* 58 (1987) 137–55.

———. *A Time to Tear Down and a Time to Build Up: A Rereading of Ecclesiastes*. Grand Rapids: Eerdmans, 1999.

———. "Words for Wisdom." *Zeitschrift für Althebraistik* 6 (1993) 149–69.

Frame, John M. *Doctrine of the Christian Life: A Theology of Lordship*. Phillipsburg, NJ: Presbyterian and Reformed, 2008.

———. *Doctrine of the Knowledge of God*. Phillipsburg, NJ: Presbyterian and Reformed, 1987.

———. *A History of Western Philosophy and Theology*. Phillipsburg, NJ: Presbyterian and Reformed, 2015.

———. *Systematic Theology: An Introduction to Christian Belief*. Phillipsburg, NJ: Presbyterian and Reformed, 2013.

Gault, Brian P. "A Reexamination of 'Eternity' in Ecclesiastes 3:11." *Bibliotheca Sacra* 165 (2008) 39–57.

Gericke, Jaco W. "Axiological Assumptions in Qohelet: A Historical–Philosophical Clarification." *Verbum et Ecclesia* 33 (2012) 1–6.

———. "A Comprehensive Philosophical Approach to Qohelet's Epistemology." HTS Teologiese Studies/Theological Studies 71.1, Article 2868. http://dx.doi.org/10.4102/ hts.v71i1.2868.

———. "Qohelet's Concept of Deity: A Comparative–Philosophical Perspective." *Verbum et Ecclesia* 34.1, Article 743.

Gilbert, Pierre. "Human Free Will and Divine Determinism: Pharaoh, a Case Study." *Direction* 30.1 (2001) 76–87.

Gordis, Daniel. "The Tower of Babel and the Birth of Nationhood." *Azure* 40 (2010), section IV.

Goswell, Gregory. "The Shape of Kingship in Deut 17: A Messianic Pentateuch?" *Trinity Journal* 78 (2017) 169–81.

Gould, Paul M. *The Outrageous Idea of a Missional Professor*. Eugene: Wipf and Stock, 2014.

Guinness, Os. *Fit Bodies, Fat Minds: Why Evangelicals Don't Think and What to Do About It*. Grand Rapids: Baker, 1994.

Habel, Norman C. *Book of Job*. Philadelphia: Westminster, 1985.

Hábl, Jan. *Lessons in Humanity From the Work and Life of Jan Amos Comenius*. Bonn: Verlag für Kultur und Wissenschaft, 2011.

Hafemann, Scott. "'Noah, the Preacher of (God's) Righteousness': The Argument from Scripture in 2 Peter 2:5 and 9." *Catholic Biblical Quarterly* 76 (2014) 306–20.

Ham, T. C. "The Gentle Voice of God in Job 38." *Journal of Biblical Literature* 132.3 (2013) 527–41.
Hamori, Esther J. "The Spirit of Falsehood." *Catholic Biblical Quarterly* 72 (2010) 15–30.
Harding, James E. "The Spirit of Deception in Job 4:15? Interpretive Indeterminacy and Eliphaz's Vision." *Biblical Interpretation* 13.2 (2005) 154–65.
Hartley, John A. *The Book of Job*. Grand Rapids: Eerdmans, 1988.
Hassler, Mark A. "Isaiah 14 and Habakkuk 2: Two Taunt Songs against the Same Tyrant?" *Master's Seminary Journal* 26 (2015) 221–29.
Hayes, Katherine M. "'A Spirit of Deep Sleep': Divinely Induced Delusion and Wisdom in Isaiah 1–39." *Catholic Biblical Quarterly* 74 (2012) 39–54.
Hazony, Yorum. *The Philosophy of Hebrew Scripture*. Cambridge: Cambridge University, 2012.
Hess, Richard. "The Roles of the Woman and the Man in Genesis 3." *Themelios* 18 (1993) 15–19.
Hill, John. *Constructing Exile: The Emergence of a Biblical Paradigm*. Eugene: Cascade Books, 2020.
———. *Friend or Foe? The Figure of Babylon in the Book of Jeremiah (MT)*. Biblical Interpretation Series 40. Leiden: Brill, 1999.
Hoekema, Anthony. *Created in God's Image*. Grand Rapids: Eerdmans, 1986.
Hoffmeier, James K. "The Arm of God versus the Arm of Pharaoh in the Exodus Narratives." *Biblica* 67.3 (1986) 378–87.
Hom, Mary Katherine. "'. . . A Mighty Hunter before YHWH': Genesis 10:9 and the Moral-Theological Evaluation of Nimrod." *Vetus Testamentum* 60 (2010) 63–68.
Horton, Michael S. *Covenant and Eschatology: The Divine Drama*. Louisville: Westminster John Knox, 2002.
———. "Meeting a Stranger: A Covenantal Epistemology." *Westminster Theological Journal* 66 (2004) 337–55.
Howell, Adam J. "Deuteronomy 30:14 as an Explanation for Israel's Sporadic Obedience." https://www.academia.edu/16503953/Deuteronomy_30_14_as_an_Explanation_for_Israels_Sporadic_Obedience.
Huffmon, Herbert B. "The Treaty Background of the Hebrew Yāda'." *Bulletin of the American Schools of Oriental Research* 181 (1966) 31–37.
Hurowitz, Victor A. "Paradise Regained: Proverbs 3:13–20 Reconsidered." In *Sefer Moshe: The Moshe Weinfeld Jubilee Volume: Studies in the Bible and the Ancient Near East, Qumran, and Post-Biblical Judaism*, edited by Chaim Cohen et al., 49–62. Winona Lake, IN: Eisenbrauns, 2004.
Irwin, Brian P. "Yahweh's Suspension of Free Will in the Old Testament." *Tyndale Bulletin* 54.2 (2003) 55–62.
Isbell, Charles. "Deuteronomy's Definition of Jewish Learning." *Jewish Bible Quarterly* 31 (2003) 109–16.
Jackson, David R. "'Who Is This Who Darkens Counsel?' The Use of Rhetorical Irony in God's Charges against Job." *Westminster Theological Journal* 72 (2010) 153–67.
Jacobs, Alan. *Original Sin: A Cultural History*. New York: HarperOne, 2009.
Janzen, J. Gerald. "On the Most Important Word in the Shema (Deuteronomy 6:4–5)." *Vetus Testamentum* 37.3 (1987) 280–300.
———. "Qohelet on Life 'Under the Sun.'" *Catholic Biblical Quarterly* 70 (2008) 465–83.

Johnson, Dru. *Biblical Knowing: A Scriptural Epistemology of Error*. Eugene: Cascade, 2013.

———. *Epistemology and Biblical Theology: From the Pentateuch to Mark's Gospel*. New York: Routledge, 2018.

———. *Knowledge by Ritual: A Biblical Prolegomenon to Sacramental Theology*. Winona Lake, IN: Eisenbrauns, 2016.

Johnson, Michael. "The Seeds of Epistemology and Ontology in Genesis 1." *Proceedings* 18 (1998) 1–10.

Johnson, Thomas K. *The First Step in Missions Training: How our Neighbors Are Wrestling with God's General Revelation*. Bonn: Culture and Science Publications, 2014.

Jones, Scott C. "Job 28 and Modern Theory of Knowledge." *Theology Today* 69.4 (2013) 486–96.

———. "The Values and Limits of Qohelet's Sub-Celestial Economy." *Vetus Testamentum* 64 (2014) 21–33.

Kamano, Naoto. "Character and Cosmology: Rhetoric of Qol 1:3–3:9." In *Qohelet in the Context of Wisdom*, edited by A. Schoors, 413–24. Leuven, Belgium: Leuven University, 1998.

Keefer, Arthur. "A Shift in Perspective: The Intended Audience and a Coherent Reading of Proverbs 1:1–7." *Journal of Biblical Literature* 136 (2017) 103–16.

Kelle, Brad E. "Israelite History." In *Dictionary of the Old Testament: Prophets*, edited by Mark J. Boda and J. Gordon McConville, 397–422. Downers Grove: IVP Academic, 2012.

Kline, Meredith G. *Kingdom Prologue: Genesis Foundations for a Covenantal Worldview*. Overland Park: Two Age, 2000.

Klingbeil, Gerald A. "Ecclesiastes 2: Ancient Near Eastern Background." In *Dictionary of the Old Testament: Wisdom, Poetry and Writings*, edited by Tremper Longman III and Peter Enns, 132–40. Downers Grove: IVP Academic, 2008.

Komenský, Jan Amos. *The Great Didactic*. Translated by M. W. Keatinge. Reprint, London: Forgotten Books, 2012.

Kraut, Judah. "Deciphering the Shema: Staircase Parallelism and the Syntax of Deuteronomy 6:4." *Vetus Testamentum* 61 (2011) 582–602.

Krüger, Paul A. "A World Turned on Its Head in Ancient Near Eastern Prophetic Literature: A Powerful Strategy to Depict Chaotic Scenarios." *Vetus Testamentum* 62 (2012) 58–76.

Krüger, Thomas. "Did Job Repent?" In *Das Buck Hiob und seine Interpretationen: Beitrdge zum Hiob-Symposium auf dem Monte Verita vom 14–19, 2005*, edited by Thomas Krüger et al., 217–29. ATANT 88. Zurich: Theologischer Verlag Zürich, (2007).

Kraus, Hans-Joachim. *Psalms 1–59*. Minneapolis: Augsburg, 1988.

Kuyper, Lester J. "Repentance of Job." *Vetus Testamentum* 9.1 (1959) 91–94.

Lalleman, Hetty. "Jeremiah, Judgment and Creation." *Tyndale Bulletin* 60 (2009) 15–24.

Leder, Arie C. "Hearing Exodus 7:8–13 to Preach the Gospel: The Ancient Adversary in Today's World." *Calvin Theological Journal* 43.1 (2008) 93–110.

Lenzi, Alan. *An Introduction to Akkadian Literature: Contexts and Content*. University Park: Penn State University, 2019.

———. "Secrecy, Textual Legitimation, and Intercultural Polemics in the Book of Daniel." *Catholic Biblical Quarterly* 71 (2009) 330–48.

Lessing, R. Reed. "Yahweh versus Marduk: Creation Theology in Isaiah 40–55." *Concordia Journal* (2010) 234–43.
Leuchter, Mark. "The Exegesis of Jeremiah in and Beyond Ezra 9–10." *Vetus Testamentum* 65 (2015) 62–80.
Levine, Etan. "The Land of Milk and Honey." *Journal for the Society of the Old Testament* 87 (2000) 43–57.
Levin, Yigal. "Nimrod the Mighty, King of Kish, King of Sumer and Akkad." *Vetus Testamentum* 52.3 (2002) 350–66.
Lewis, C. S. *The Last Battle*. New York: HarperTrophy, 1989.
Lewis, Theodore J. "Divine Fire in Deuteronomy 33:2." *Journal of Biblical Literature* 132.4 (2013) 791–803.
Limburg, James. "Root *rîb* and the Prophetic Lawsuit Speeches." *Journal of Biblical Literature* 88 (1969) 291–304.
Lints, Richard. *Identity and Idolatry: The Image of God and Its Inversion*. Downers Grove: InterVarsity, 2015.
Longman III, Tremper. *The Book of Ecclesiastes*. Grand Rapids: Eerdmans, 1998.
———. *The Book of Job*. Grand Rapids: Baker Academic, 2012.
———. *Daniel*. Grand Rapids: Zondervan, 1999.
———. *Proverbs*. Grand Rapids: Baker Academic, 2006.
López, René A. "The Meaning of 'Behemoth' and 'Leviathan' in Job." *Bibliotheca Sacra* 173 (2016) 401–24.
Lowery, Richard H. *Sabbath and Jubilee*. St. Louis: Chalice, 2000.
Lundbom, Jack R. "Builders of Ancient Babylon: Nabopolassar and Nebuchadnezzar II." *Interpretation* 71.2 (2017) 154–66.
Mabie, Frederick J. "Chaos and Death." In *Dictionary of the Old Testament: Wisdom, Poetry and Writings*, edited by Tremper Longman III and Peter Enns, 41–54. Downers Grove: IVP Academic, 2008.
Markl, Dominik. "No Future without Moses: The Disastrous End of 2 Kings 22–25 and the Chance of the Moab Covenant (Deuteronomy 29–30)." *Journal of Biblical Literature* 133.4 (2014) 711–28.
MacDonald, D. B. "Old Testament Notes." *Journal of Biblical Literature* 18.1/2 (1899) 212–15.
Machinist, Peter. "Assyria and Its Image in the First Isaiah." *Journal of the American Oriental Society* 103 (1983) 719–37.
———. "Fate, *miqreh*, and Reason: Some Reflections on Qohelet and Biblical Thought." In *Solving Riddles and Untying Knots*, edited by Ziony Zevit et al., 159–75. Winona Lake, IN: Eisenbrauns, 1995.
Magdalene, F. Rachel. "Who is Job's Redeemer? Job 19:25 in Light of Neo-Babylonian Law." *Journal for Ancient Near Eastern and Biblical Law* 10 (2004) 292–316.
McAffee, Matthew. "The Heart of Pharaoh in Exodus 4–15." *Bulletin for Biblical Research* 20.3 (2010) 331–53.
McBride, S. Dean. "The Yoke of the Kingdom: An Exposition of Deuteronomy 6:4–5." *Interpretation* 27 (1973) 273–306.
McConville, J. G. "Jeremiah." In *Theological Interpretation of the Old Testament*, edited by Kevin J. Vanhoozer, 211–20. Grand Rapids: Baker Academic, 2008.
McDonald, Nathan. "The Literary Criticism and Rhetorical Logic of Deut 1–4." *Vetus Testamentum* 56.2 (2006) 203–24.

McLaughlin, John L. "Their Hearts Were Hardened: The Use of Isaiah 6:9–10." *Biblica* 75 (1994) 1–25.

Meek, Russell L. "Fear God and Enjoy His Gifts." *Criswell Theological Review* 14.1 (2016) 23–34.

———. "The Meaning of הבל in Qohelet: An Intertextual Suggestion." In *The Words of the Wise Are like Goads: Engaging Qohelet in the 21st Century*, edited by Mark J. Boda et al., 241–56. Winona Lake, IN: Eisenbrauns, 2013.

Meeks, M. Douglas. *God the Economist: The Doctrine of God and Political Economy*. Minneapolis: Fortress, 1989.

Meier, Samuel A. "Job 1–21: A Reflection of Genesis 1–3." *Vetus Testamentum* 39.2 (1989) 183–93.

Middleton, J. Richard. *The Liberating Image: The Imago Dei in Genesis* 1. Grand Rapids: Brazos, 2005.

Miller, Daniel R. "Objectives and Consequences of the Neo-Assyrian Imperial Exercise." *Religion and Theology* 16 (2009) 124–49.

Miller, James E. "The Vision of Eliphaz as Foreshadowing in the Book of Job." *Proceedings* 9 (1989) 98–112.

Miller, Patrick D. *Deuteronomy: A Bible Commentary for Teaching and Preaching*. Philadelphia: Westminster John Knox, 1990.

———. "The Most Important Word: The Yoke of the Kingdom." *Iliff Review* 41 (1984) 17–29.

———. "The Wilderness Journey in Deuteronomy: Style, Structure, and Theology in Deuteronomy 1–3." *Covenant Quarterly* 55.2 (1997) 50–68.

Moberly, R. L. W. "Did the Interpreters Get It Right? Genesis 2–3 Reconsidered." *Journal of Theological Studies* 59.1 (2008) 22–40.

Mohler, Albert. "The Scandal of Biblical Illiteracy: It's Our Problem." https://albertmohler.com/2016/01/20/the-scandal-of-biblical-illiteracy-its-our-problem-4.

Morgan, David M. "Remnant." In *Dictionary of the Old Testament: Prophets*, edited by Mark J. Boda and J. Gordon McConville, 658–64. Downers Grove: IVP Academic, 2012.

Molière. *The Learned Women: Les Femmes Savantes*. London: Stage Door, 2018.

Morrow, William. "Consolation, Rejection, and Repentance in Job 42:6." *Journal of Biblical Literature* 105.2 (1986) 211–25.

Motyer, J. Alec. *The Prophecy of Isaiah: An Introduction and Commentary*. Downers Grove: InterVarsity, 1993.

Muenchow, Charles. "Dust and Dirt in Job 42:6." *Journal of Biblical Literature* 108.4 (1989) 597–611.

Murphy, Daniel. *Comenius: A Critical Reassessment of His Life and Work*. Portland: Irish Academic, 1995.

Newsom, Carol A. *Daniel: A Commentary*. Louisville: Westminster John Knox, 2014.

Neyrey, Jerome H. "God, Benefactor and Patron: The Major Cultural Model for Interpreting the Deity in Greco-Roman Antiquity." *Journal for the Study of the New Testament* 21A (2005) 465–92.

Niehaus, Jeffrey J. "Covenant: An Idea in the Mind of God." *Journal of the Evangelical Theological Society* 52.2 (2009) 225–46.

Nienhuis, David R. "The Problem of Evangelical Biblical Illiteracy" (2010). https://modernreformation.org/resource-library/articles/the-problem-of-evangelical-biblical-illiteracy/.Noegel, Scott B. "Moses and Magic: Notes on the Book of Exodus." *Journal of the Ancient Near Eastern Society* 24.1 (1996) 45-59.

Noll, Mark A. *Jesus Christ and the Life of the Mind*. Grand Rapids: Eerdmans, 2011.

———. *The Scandal of the Evangelical Mind*. Grand Rapids: Eerdmans, 1994.

O'Dowd, Ryan. "A Chord of Three Strands," Epistemology in Job, Proverbs and Ecclesiastes." In *The Bible and Epistemology: Biblical Soundings on the Knowledge of God*, edited by Mary Healy and Robin Parry, 65-87. Colorado Springs: Paternoster, 2007.

———. "Frame Narrative." In *Dictionary of the Old Testament: Wisdom, Poetry and Writings*, edited by Tremper Longman III and Peter Enns, 241-45. Downers Grove: IVP Academic, 2008.

———. *The Wisdom of Torah: Epistemology in Deuteronomy and the Wisdom Literature*. Göttingen, Germany: Vandenhoeck & Ruprecht, 2009.

Ortlund, Eric. "Deconstruction in Qohelet: A Response to Mark Sneed." *Journal for the Study of the Old Testament* 40.2 (2015) 239-56.

———. "The Gospel in the Book of Ecclesiastes." *Journal of the Evangelical Theological Society* 56.4 (2013) 697-706.

———. "How Did Job Speak Rightly about God?" *Themelios* 43.3 (2018) 350-58.

———. "The Identity of Leviathan and the Meaning of the Book of Job." *Trinity Journal* 34 (2013) 17-30.

———. "Laboring in Hopeless Hope: Encouragement for Christians from Ecclesiastes." *Themelios* 39.2 (2014) 281-89.

Osuji, Anthony. "True and False Prophecy in Jer 26-29 (MT): Thematic and Lexical Landmarks." *Ephemerides Theologicae Lovanienses* 82.4 (2006) 437-52.

Oswalt, John N. *Isaiah*. Grand Rapids: Zondervan, 2003.

Overland, Paul. "Did the Sage Draw from the Shema? A Study of Proverbs 3:1-12." *Catholic Biblical Quarterly* 62 (2000) 424-40.

Parker, Judith Faith. "'Blaming Eve Alone': Translation, Omission, and Implications of המע in Genesis 3:6b." *Journal of Biblical Literature* 142.4 (2013) 729-47.

Patrick, Dale. "Is the Truth of the First Commandment Known by Reason?" *Catholic Biblical Quarterly* 56 (1994) 423-41.

Pelham, Abigail. "Job's Crisis of Language: Power and Powerlessness in Job's Oaths." *Journal for the Study of the Old Testament* 36.3 (2012) 333-54.

Pemberton, Glenn D. "It's a Fool's Life: The Deformation of Character in Proverbs." *Restoration Quarterly* 50 (2008) 213-24.

———. "The Rhetoric of the Father in Proverbs 1-9." *Journal for the Study of the Old Testament* 30 (2005) 63-82.

Petrovich, Douglas. "Identifying Nimrod of Genesis 10 with Sargon of Akkad by Exegetical and Archeological Means." *Journal of the Evangelical Theological Society* 56.2 (2013) 273-305.

Phillips, Anthony. "The Attitude of Torah to Wealth." In *Essays on Biblical Law*, 148-63. London: Sheffield Academic, 2002.

Phillips, Elaine A. "Serpent Intertexts: Tantalizing Twists in the Tales." *Bulletin for Biblical Research* 10.2 (2000) 233-45.

Pinker, Aron. "Ecclesiastes Part II: Themes." *Jewish Bible Quarterly* 41.3 (2013) 163-70.

Piper, John. *Think: The Life of the Mind and the Love of God*. Wheaton: Crossway, 2010.

Plantinga Jr., Cornelius. *Not the Way It's Supposed to Be: A Breviary of Sin*. Grand Rapids: Eerdmans, 1995.

Poythress, Vern. S. *Redeeming Science: A God-Centered Approach*. Wheaton: Crossway, 2006.

Provan, Iain W. "To Highlight All Our Idols: Worshipping God in Nietzsche's World." *Ex Auditu* 15 (2000) 19–38.

Quine, Cat. "The Host of Heaven and the Divine Army: A Reassessment." *Journal of Biblical Literature* 138.4 (2019) 741–55.

Quoist, Michel. *Prayers*, Translated by Agnes M. Forsyth and Anne Marie de Commaille. New York: Sheed and Ward, 1963.

Ramm, Bernard L. "The Apologetics of the Old Testament: The Basis of a Biblical and Christian Apologetic." *Bulletin of the Evangelical Theological Society* 1.4 (1958) 15–20.

Reichenbach, Bruce R. "Genesis 1 as a Theological–Political Narrative of Kingdom Establishment." *Bulletin for Biblical Research* 13 (2003) 47–69.

———. "Cutting the Gift That Ties: Genesis 2–3." *Brethren Life and Thought* 31.2 (1986) 111–20.

Robinson, Geoffrey D. "The Motif of Deafness and Blindness in Isaiah 6:9–10: A Contextual, Literary, and Theological Analysis." *Bulletin for Biblical Research* 8 (1998) 167–86.

Rom-Shiloni, Dalit. "Facing Destruction and Exile: Inner-Biblical Exegesis in Jeremiah and Ezekiel." *Zeitschrift für die alttestamentliche Wissenschaft* 117 (2005) 189–205.

———. "Group Identities in Jeremiah: Is It the Persian Period Conflict?" In *A Palimpsest: Rhetoric, Ideology, Stylistics, and Language Relating to Persian Israel*, edited by Ehud Ben Zvi et al., 11–46. Piscataway, NJ: Gorgias, 2009.

———. "How Can You Say, 'I Am Not Defiled . . .'? (Jeremiah 2:20–25): Allusions to Priestly Legal Traditions in the Poetry of Jeremiah." *Journal of Biblical Literature* 133.4 (2014) 757–75.

———. "'On the Day I Took Them out of the Land of Egypt': A Non-Deuteronomic Phrase within Jeremiah's Conception of Covenant." *Vetus Testamentum* 65 (2015) 621–47.

———. "Prophets in Jeremiah in Struggle for Leadership, or Rather for Prophetic Authority." *Biblica* 99.3 (2018) 355–63.

Rowold, Henry. "Yahweh's Challenge to Rival: The Form and Function of the Yahweh-Speech in Job 38–39." *Catholic Biblical Quarterly* 47 (1985) 199–211.

Ryken, Leland. "Ecclesiastes." In *A Complete Literary Guide to the Bible*, edited by Leland Ryken et al., 268–80. Grand Rapids: Zondervan, 1993.

———. *Words of Delight: A Literary Introduction to the Bible*. Grand Rapids: Baker, 1992.

Sakenfeld, Katharine D. "The Problem of Forgiveness in Numbers 14." *Catholic Biblical Quarterly* 37.3 (1975) 317–30.

Schoors, A. "Words Typical of Qohelet." In *Qohelet in the Context of Wisdom*, edited by A. Schoors, 17–39. Leuven, Belgium: Leuven University, 1998.

Searcy, Edwin. "'A People, a Name, a Praise, and a Glory': False and True Faith in Jeremiah." *Word and World* 22.4 (2002) 333–39.

Segal, Michael. "Rereading the Writing on the Wall (Daniel 5)." *Zeitschrift für die alttestamentliche Wissenschaf* 125.1 (2013) 161–76.

Seow, C. L. *Ecclesiastes, A New Translation and Commentary*. New York: Doubleday, 1997.

———. "Qohelet's Eschatological Poem." *Journal of Biblical Literature* 118.2 (1999) 209–34.
Seufert, Matthew. "The Presence of Genesis in Ecclesiastes." *Westminster Theological Journal* 78 (2016) 75–92.
———. "Reading Isaiah 40:1–11 in Light of Isaiah 36–37." *Journal of the Evangelical Theological Society* 58 (2015) 269–81.
Seufert, Michael. "Refusing the King's Portion: A Reexamination of Daniel's Dietary Reaction in Daniel 1." *Journal for the Study of the Old Testament* 43.4 (2019) 644–60.
Silver, Edward. "Performing Domination/Theorizing Power: Israelite Prophecy as a Political Discourse beyond the Conflict Model." *Journal of Ancient Near Eastern Religions* 14 (2014) 186–216.
Silverman, David P. "Divinity and Deities in Ancient Egypt." In *Religion in Ancient Egypt: Gods, Myth, and Personal Practice*, edited by Byron E. Shafer, 7–87. Ithaca: Cornell University, 1991.
Sivan, Gabriel A. "The Siege of Jerusalem: Part I: Assyria the World Power." *Jewish Bible Quarterly* 43.2 (2015) 83–93.
Skillen, James W. "The Seven Days of Creation." *Calvin Theological Journal* 46 (2011) 111–39.
Smick, Elmer B. "Another Look at the Mythological Elements in the Book of Job." *Westminster Theological Journal* 40.2 (1978) 213–28.
———. "Semeiological Interpretation of the Book of Job." *Westminster Theological Journal* 48 (1986) 135–49.
Smith, Duane E. "The Divining Snake: Reading Genesis 3 in the Context of Mesopotamian Ophiomancy." *Journal of Biblical Literature* 134.1 (2015) 3–49.
Smith, Richard L. "Apologia." *The Outlook* 48.8 (1998) 19–24.
——— "Economics and the 'Present Evil Age.'" *Evangelical Review of Theology* 42.4 (2018) 354–63.
———. "The Root of Religiosity, Explicit and Implicit: According to the Apostle Paul in Romans 1" (2008). https://www.academia.edu/45080360/The_root_of_religiosity_explicit_and_ implicit_according_to_the_apostle_Paul_in_Romans_1.
———. "The Supremacy of God in Apologetics: Romans 1:19–21 and the Transcendental Method of Cornelius Van Til." Ph.D. diss., Westminster Theological Seminary, 1996.
Spero, Shubert. "He That Formed the Eye Shall He Not See?" *Jewish Bible Quarterly* 45 (2017) 51–55.
———. "Pharaoh's Three Offers, Moses' Rejection, and the Three Issues They Foreshadowed." *Jewish Bible Quarterly* 38.2 (2010) 93–96.
Staples, W. E. "'Profit' in Ecclesiastes." *Journal of Near Eastern Studies* 4.2 (1945) 87–96.
Stead, Michael R. "Intertextuality and Innerbiblical Interpretation." In *Dictionary of the Old Testament: Prophets*, edited by Mark J. Boda and J. Gordon McConville, 355–64. Downers Grove: IVP Academic, 2012.
Steel, Walter R. "Enjoying the Righteousness of Faith in Ecclesiastes." *Catholic Theological Quarterly* 74 (2010) 225–42.
Stefanovic, Zdravko. "The Great Reversal: Thematic Links between Genesis 2 and 3." *Andrews University Seminary Studies* 32 (1994) 47–56.

Steinmann, Andrew E., and Michael Eschelbach. "Walk This Way: A Theme from Proverbs Reflected and Expanded in Paul's Letters." *Concordia Theological Quarterly* 70 (2006) 43–62.

Stern, Philip D. "The Origin and Significance of 'The Land Flowing with Milk and Honey.'" *Vetus Testamentum* 42.4 (1992) 554–57.

Stökl, Jonathan. "'A Youth without Blemish, Handsome, Proficient in All Wisdom, Knowledgeable and Intelligent': Ezekiel's Access to Babylonian Culture." In *Exile and Return: The Babylonian Context*, edited by Jonathan Stökl and Caroline Waerzeggers, 223–52. Boston: De Gruyter, 2015.

Strawn, Brent A. *The Old Testament Is Dying: A Diagnosis and Recommended Treatment*. Grand Rapids: Baker Academic, 2017.

Stuart, Douglas K. "The Old Testament Context of David's Costly Flirtation with Empire-Building." In *Empire in the New Testament*, edited by Stanley E. Porter and Cynthia Long Westfall, 21–30. Eugene: Pickwick, 2011.

Swenson, Kristen M. "Care and Keeping East of Eden: Gen 4:1–16 in Light of Gen 2–3." *Interpretation* 60.4 (2006) 373–84.

Taylor, John E. P. "Moses and Old Covenant Obedience." *Churchman* 131 (2017) 343–59.

Thomas, Heath A. "Zion." In *Dictionary of the Old Testament: Prophets*, edited by Mark J. Boda and J. Gordon McConville, 907–14. Downers Grove: IVP Academic, 2012

Thomson, J. A. *The Book of Jeremiah*. Grand Rapids: Eerdmans, 1980.

Toews, Brian G. "The Story of Abel: The Narrative Substructure of Ecclesiastes." Paper presented in the November, 2007 meeting of the Evangelical Theological Society, San Diego.

Tucker, Gene M. "Deuteronomy 18:15–22." *Interpretation* 41.3 (1987) 292–97.

Van der Wal, A. J. O. "Qohelet 12:1a: A Relatively Unique Statement in Israel's Wisdom Tradition." In *Qohelet in the Context of Wisdom*, edited by A. Schoors, 413–18. Leuven, Belgium: Leuven University, 1998.

Vandici, Gratian. "Reading the Rules of Knowledge in the Story of the Fall: Calvin and Reformed Epistemology on the Noetic Effects of Original Sin." *Journal of Theological Interpretation* 10.1 (2016) 173–91.

VanDrunen, David. "Israel's Recapitalization of Adam's Probation under the Law of Moses." *Westminster Theological Journal* 73 (2011) 303–24.

VanGemeren, Willem A. *The Expositor's Bible Commentary: Psalms, Proverbs, Ecclesiastes, Song of Songs*. Grand Rapids: Zondervan, 1991.

Vanhoozer, Kevin, edited by *Everyday Theology: How to Read Cultural Texts and Interpret Trends*. Grand Rapids: Baker Academic, 2007.

Van Leeuwen, Raymond C. "Cosmos, Temple, House: Building and Wisdom in Ancient Mesopotamia." In *From the Foundations to the Crenellations: Essays on Temple Building in the Ancient Near East and Hebrew Bible*, edited by Mark J. Boda and Jamie Novotny, 399–422. Münster: Ugarit-Verlag, 2010.

———. "Creation and Contingency in Qohelet" (2021). https://www.academia.edu/42088970/Creation_and_Contingency_in_Qohelet.

———. "Liminality and Worldview in Proverbs 1–9." *Semeia* 50 (1990) 111–44.

———. "Proverbs." In *A Complete Literary Guide to the Bible*, edited by Leland Ryken and Tremper Longman III, 257–67. Grand Rapids: Zondervan, 1993.

———. "Proverbs." In *Theological Interpretation of the Old Testament*, edited by Kevin J. Vanhoozer, 171–78. Grand Rapids: Baker Academic, 2008.

———. "Proverbs 30:21–23 and the Biblical World Turned Upside Down." *Journal of Biblical Literature* 105.4 (1986) 599–610.

———. "Theology: Creation, Wisdom, and Covenant" (2010). https://www.academia.edu/42088970/Creation_and_Contingency_in_Qohelet.

———. "What Comes out of God's Mouth: The Theological Wordplay in Deuteronomy 8." *Catholic Biblical Quarterly* 47 (1985) 55–57.

Van Til, Cornelius. *The Defense of the Faith*. Phillipsburg, NJ: Presbyterian and Reformed, 1967.

———. *The Intellectual Challenge of the Gospel*. Phillipsburg, NJ: Presbyterian and Reformed, 1980.

———. *Introduction to Systematic Theology*. Phillipsburg, NJ: Presbyterian and Reformed, 1974.

———. *A Survey of Christian Epistemology*. Phillipsburg, NJ: Presbyterian and Reformed, 1969.

Van Wolde, Ellen J. "Ancient Wisdoms, Present Insights: Job 28:1–13 and some Archaeological Data." *Svensk exegetiskårsbok* 71 (2006) 55–74.

———. "Job 42:1–6: The Reversal of Job." In *The Book of Job*, edited by W. A. M. Beuken, 223–50. Leuven, Belgium: Leuven University, 1994.

Verheij, Arian. "Paradise Retried: On Qohelet 2.4–6." *Journal for the Study of the Old Testament* 50 (1991) 113–15.

Von Rad, Gerhard. *Wisdom in Israel*. London: SCM, 1978.

Vos, Geerhardus. *Biblical Theology: Old and New Testaments*. Grand Rapids: Eerdmans, 1948.

Waltke, Bruce. *The Book of Proverbs, Chapters 1–15*. Grand Rapids: Eerdmans, 2004.

———. "Righteousness in Proverbs." *Westminster Theological Journal* 70 (2008) 225–37.

Walton, John H. *Ancient Near Eastern Thought and the Old Testament: Introducing the Conceptual World of the Hebrew Bible*. Grand Rapids: Baker Academic, 2013.

———. "Book of Job 1." In *Dictionary of the Old Testament: Wisdom, Poetry and Writings*, edited by Tremper Longman III and Peter Enns, 333–46. Downers Grove: IVP Academic, 2008.

———. "Retribution." In *Dictionary of the Old Testament: Wisdom, Poetry and Writings*, edited by Tremper Longman III and Peter Enns, 647–54. Downers Grove: IVP Academic, 2008.

Wardlaw Jr., Terrance R. "The Significance of Creation in the Book of Isaiah." *Journal of the Evangelical Theological Society* 59 (2016) 449–71.

Watts, James W. "Rhetorical Strategy in the Composition of the Pentateuch." *Journal of the Society of the Old Testament* 68 (1995) 3–22.

Weinfeld, Moshe. "Jeremiah and the Spiritual Metamorphosis of Israel." *Zeitschrift für die alttestamentliche Wissenschaf* 88 (1976) 1–41.

Wenham, Gordon. *Genesis 1–15*. Grand Rapids: Zondervan, 2014.

Wessels, William J. "The Social Implications of Knowing Yahweh: A Study of Jeremiah 9:22–23." *Verbum et Ecclesia* 30.2 (2009) 77–83.

Westminster Shorter Catechism. Carlisle, PA: Banner of Truth, 1998.

Westphal, Merold. "Taking St. Paul Seriously: Sin as an Epistemological Category." In *Christian Philosophy*, edited by Thomas P. Flint, 200–226. Notre Dame: University of Notre Dame, 1990,

Whitekettle, Richard. "When More Leads to Less: Overstatement, *Incrementum*, and the Question in Job 4:17a." *Journal of Biblical Literature* 129.3 (2010) 445–48.

Whybray, R. N. "The Immorality of God: Reflections on Some Passages in Genesis, Job, and Numbers." *Journal for the Society of the Old Testament* 72 (1996) 89–120.

Wilson, Gerald. "Preknowledge, Anticipation, and the Poetics of Job." *Journal for the Study of the Old Testament* 30.2 (2005) 243–56.

Wilson, Lindsey. "Job." In *Theological Interpretation of the Old Testament*, 148–54. Grand Rapids: Baker Academic, 2008.

Wilson, Robert R. "The Hardening of Pharaoh's Heart." *Catholic Biblical Quarterly* 40 (1979) 18–36.

Wittenberg, Günther. "'To Build and to Plant' (Jer 1:10): The Message of Jeremiah as a Source of Hope for the Exilic Community and Its Relevance for Community Building in South Africa." *Journal of Theology for Southern Africa* 112 (2002) 57–67.

Wolterstorff, Nicholas. *Until Justice and Peace Embrace*. Grand Rapids: Eerdmans, 1983.

Wright, Christopher J. H. *Old Testament Ethics for the People of God*. Downers Grove: InterVarsity, 2004.

Yates, Gary E. "Intertextuality and the Portrayal of Jeremiah the Prophet." *Bibliotheca Sacra* 170 (2013) 286–303.

———. "The Prophet Jeremiah as Theological Symbol in the Book of Jeremiah." LBTS Liberty Baptist Theological Seminary Faculty Publications and Presentations 372 (2010) 1–21.

Yee, Gale A. "'I Have Perfumed My Bed with Myrrh': The Foreign Woman ('*iššâ zârâ*) in Proverbs 1–9." *Journal for the Study of the Old Testament* 43 (1989) 53–68.

Younger, K. Lawson. "The Deportations of the Israelites." *Journal of Biblical Literature* 117 (1998) 201–27.

Zvi, Ehud Ben. "Who Wrote the Speech of Rabshakeh and When?" *Journal of Biblical Literature* 109 (1990) 79–92.

Scripture Index

GENESIS

1:18–23	33
1:26	38
1:27	38
1:28–30	29
2:5	38
2:15	38
2:16–17	27
3:1–5	50
3:6–7	55
3:8–13, 17	58
4:4–5, 8	63–64
6:5	89, 102, 147n72, 209, 210n23
6:5–13	209
11:1–9	66–67
26:3–5	213

EXODUS

7:1–2, 8–12	78–79
35:34	229
36:2	229

LEVITICUS

26:40–42	280, 378

DEUTERONOMY

4:1	224
4:5–6	145
4:5–8	280–81
4:9, 15–16, 19, 23	244
4:25–31	277–78
4:35, 39	228n21, 233, 237, 239, 249
4:35–40	237–38
5:1	224
5:22–31	230–31
5:29	144n62, 230, 232, 234, 243, 256, 258, 266, 391
6:1–2, 6–9	267–68
6:4	252
6:4–5	21, 224, 225, 248, 249, 250n61, 254, 255, 267, 319
8:1–3	240
8:3	193n1, 241, 389, 394
8:11–14, 17	247–48
9:1–3	224
10:12–16	284
17:14–17	270–71
17:18–20	168
18:14–18	283
20:3–4	224
26:17–19	222
27:9–10	224
28:28–29	164, 173, 175, 201, 261–63
29:2–4	286
30:1–10	278–79
30:11–14	226
30:14	229
30:15–18	276
30:16–18	352

1 SAMUEL

25	148–150

1 KINGS

8:46–49	378

1 CHRONICLES

12:32	xxvi, 114, 139, 359, 391

2 CHRONICLES

9:23	229

JOB

3:11	305
3:20	306
3:23	306
4:12–16	295
4:17–19	296
7:20	305
10:2–7	309
12:14	302
12:20	302
12:26	302
13:20–23	309
13:24	305
14:1–3, 5–6	308
21:7	305
28:1–11	298
28:25–27	299–300
31:6	315
31:35	315
38:2	336
40:4–5	333
40:9–13	325–26
41:1–6	334
41:10–11	328
42:3	336
42:7–8	330

PSALMS

1:1	258, 292
1:4–6	xxiii
10:2–7, 9, 11	189–90
12:2–4	125
14	184–90
19:7–11	288
19:12–14	289
20:9–10	125–26
23	10
26:2	215n38, 216
36:2	125
36:9	193n1, 390
73:11	189
81:11–12	116, 164, 190, 201, 329
84:8–13	191
90:12–17	115–16
94	202–07
94:7	189
104:10–30	13
107:33–43	360
115:4–8	17
131:1–2	42, 117, 229n25, 216, 338
137	361–64
139:23	116, 216

PROVERBS

1:1	88
1:1–6	131
1:7	43, 88, 124, 127, 138, 141n55, 142, 145, 164, 272
1:23	152
1:24–25, 29–32	152
3:13–18	134–35
4:10–19	128–29
8:32–35	152
9:1–6	126
9:13–18	126–27
22:17–21	139

ECCLESIASTES

1:4–7	100–101
2:17–20	98
3:10–11	107
3:11	24, 91, 95n14, 106, 108
7:29	72, 102, 117
10:8–9, 11	103

ISAIAH

1:2–3	162
5:18–19	173
6:1–12	169
6:9–10	166, 167n46, 171, 172n56, 173, 180, 192, 197, 199, 201, 220n1, 340
29:15–16	175
36:4–6	156
36:16–17	159
36:18–20	159
42:17–20	171–72
44:19–20	197

JEREMIAH

4:22–26	181
5:12	189
5:21–25	180
9:23–24	182
17:9	182–83
28:2–3, 10–11	357
29:5–6	350
29:6–9	358
29:8–9	354

DANIEL

1:1–2	367
1:3–7	370–71
1:17–20	375–76
2:10–11	383
2:20–23	384
4:2–3, 34–37	387–88
5:18–23	385
5:23	9, 190, 193n1

HABAKKUK

3:17–19	317

ZEPHANIAH

1:12	189

MATTHEW

10:16	118
13:15	166n41

MARK

4:12	166n41

LUKE

2:46, 52	25n10
3:38	39n39
8:10	166n41
11:52	146
15:17	279n36

JOHN

3:12	66
8:44	343

9:10	54
12:28–31	21
12:40	166n41
16:8	246n56

ACTS

9:10	60
16:17	385n50
17:28	193n1, 391
28:27	166n41

ROMANS

1:21	63, 119, 387
1:18–25	70n59, 337n48
1:24, 26, 28	83n37
1:28	83n37, 197
2:4	9, 143n58, 190, 193n1, 287n53, 389
3:10	184n83
4:16	213
8:28	15
11:33–34	28n12
11:36	36n30, 391
12:1	42

2 CORINTHIANS

4:14	15
6:10	57

EPHESIANS

2:1–3	343

HEBREWS

11:4	104n44
11:10	214

1 PETER

3:15–16	390, 394

2 PETER

1:4	15
2:5	212

1 JOHN

2:16   123
3:12   66

Author Index

Anselm, 42, 137, 219, 256
Augustine, 1, 16
Bartholomew, Craig C., 243n57, 303, 311n61, 327n23
Beale, G. K., 8n23, 17n46, 28n14, 44, 49, 83n33, 171, 172
Berlejung, Angelika, 348, 349, 366n2
Block, Daniel I., 141n55, 222, 230, 232, 251, 252, 253, 272
Calvin, John, 23, 24n8, 28, 190, 214, 217, 280,
Carasik, Michael, 110, 113, 130, 138, 146, 153, 168, 226, 229, 254, 261, 265
Crenshaw, James L., 105, 106, 107
Edwards, Jonathan, 14
Fox, Michael V., 93, 98, 105, 111, 112, 114, 117, 139, 140
Frame, John M., xxi, 18, 20, 38, 40, 43n49, 205, 210, 214, 223
Gericke, Jaco W., 103n38, 111, 112
Hartley, John A., 291n4, 297, 300, 303
Hazony, Yorum, 69, 212, 271n23, 331, 377
Hill, John, 353, 354
Johnson, Dru, 33, 34, 35, 50, 56, 57, 60, 62, 87, 88, 141, 193, 194, 236, 270, 276, 287
Kline, Meredith G., 4, 46n8, 61, 213n35
Komenský, Jan Amos, 22, 23n7, 32, 47
Kraut, Judah, 250–251

Lenzi, Alan, 372, 382
Longman III, Tremper, 96, 108, 123, 134, 136, 140, 146n66, 166, 299, 312, 322, 374, 375
Middleton, J. Richard, 5, 7, 40, 70, 157
Newsom, Carole A. 371, 372, 373, 381, 390
Motyer, J. Alec, 165, 197
O'Dowd, Ryan, 92, 106, 110, 111, 134, 142, 210, 245, 246n57, 283, 285, 299, 303, 342
Ortlund, Eric A., 106, 108, 113, 115, 308, 327, 328, 331n30
Oswalt, John N., 160, 174
Pelham, Abigail, 303n44, 310n59, 314
Pemberton, Glenn D., 127, 146, 147
Poythress, Vern S., 13, 30
Rom-Shiloni, Dalit, 358, 359
Seufert, Matthew, 100, 102, 103, 104, 105
Smith, Richard L., 62n40, 389n57, 390n59
Strawn, Brent A., xx, 270
Van Til, Cornelius, 18, 22, 32, 41n44, 42, 48n13, 118, 230n27, 389
Van Leeuwen, Raymond C., 11, 12, 38, 101, 123, 124, 131, 133, 241
Von Rad, Gerhard, 142, 266
Waltke, Bruce K., 132, 244
Walton, John H., 75, 312, 315, 325
Wright, Christopher J. H., 31, 37, 282

Subject Index

above-the-sun outlook, 293, 309
Adam,
    as apprentice, 20, 24, 30, 50, 71, 145, 175, 256, 350, 391, 394
    as vice-regent, xxiii, 15, 20, 35, 39, 40, 42, 44, 50, 67, 143, 157, 193, 217
brute facts, 21, 42n45, 88, 287
covenant, xxv, xxvi, 17, 18, 19, 20, 22, 23, 28, 30, 37n35, 38, 41, 42, 43, 44, 45, 49, 51, 53, 61n36, 63, 67, 84, 87, 90, 114, 117, 118, 124, 127, 148, 153, 175, 176, 182, 196, 200, 205, 220–26, 228, 232, 242, 246, 257, 260–61, 264, 272, 279, 280, 319, 347, 350, 373, 378, 380
Creator-creature distinction, 28, 53, 62, 67, 69, 107, 142, 144, 165, 175, 217, 323, 329, 335
Eden, the garden of, 1, 8, 9, 11, 12, 14, 15, 21, 23, 25, 29, 31, 35, 40, 44, 46, 58, 60, 66, 69, 72, 103, 116, 134, 214, 242, 282
Empire, and imperialism, 39, 68, 69, 72, 76, 80, 87, 90, 154–156, 160, 163, 170, 176, 348, 368, 372, 388, 390
fear of the Lord, xxiv, 127, 131, 140, 142, 151, 176, 207, 234, 235, 257, 266, 267, 288, 344, 360, 391
finitude, and fallenness, 21, 27n12, 48n13, 102, 115, 118, 136n40, 193, 200, 201, 214, 238, 257, 260, 271, 323, 332, 337, 338, 341
God,
    as king, 1, 8, 17, 135, 145, 300, 329, 380
    as architect, 1, 5, 8, 16, 20, 24, 49, 136, 137, 300, 329, 380
    as economist, 1, 10, 16, 17, 20, 21, 24, 49, 52, 135, 137, 145, 264, 300, 329, 380, 387
    as philosopher, 1, 12, 13, 16, 17, 20, 21, 41, 48n13, 49, 50, 135, 137, 145, 193, 214, 266, 300, 329, 380, 387
heart, and mind, 94, 116, 146, 167, 181, 191, 197, 210, 228, 233, 254, 260, 261, 266, 285, 286, 374
hebel, 104, 105, 113, 115, 117, 120, 177, 204
imago Dei, 17, 24, 25, 30, 34, 37, 38, 40, 53, 61, 63, 72, 107, 117, 118, 146, 150, 160, 205, 282, 343
imago Satanas, 53, 54, 66
intertextual reasoning, 100, 102, 103, 269, 284, 288, 352, 359, 378, 389, 394
neutrality, epistemic, 42, 88, 123, 316, 389
noetic depravity, 70n59, 73, 102, 109, 120, 146, 154, 164, 173, 177, 192, 193, 201, 207, 226, 258, 263, 291, 342, 368, 388, 391
objective stance, 42, 123, 287, 316, 342
Satan, devil, xv, xviii, xix, 46, 50, 54, 55n23, 71, 73, 118, 316, 343
Shema, 134, 219, 220, 248, 254, 255, 259, 267, 278, 279, 378
transcendental, 193n1, 239, 386, 389
under-the-sun outlook, 108, 294, 323
worldview, xx, xxi, xxii, xxiii, 14, 31n20, 53, 54, 61, 66, 69, 70, 72,

74, 79, 80, 83, 88, 89, 92, 100,
105, 106, 113, 117, 118, 120, 121,
122, 123, 133, 142, 151, 156, 157,
190, 217, 244, 246, 247, 257, 260,
288, 309, 316, 321, 343, 350, 368,
372, 380, 390, 393